A Brief Guide to Beliefs

A Brief Note on the Author

Linda Edwards studied theology at Regent's Park College, Oxford University, and has wide experience in teaching religious education (consisting of up to six world faiths) in state schools in Britain for a number of years. In 1986, she became Lecturer in Religious Education at King's College, London, where she trained student teachers of religious education for the challenging task of teaching the subject in state secondary (high) schools in multicultural urban situations. Her work at King's also involved developing and teaching a MA course in the subject and supervising postgraduate research. Since 1998 she has worked freelance as an Adlerian counselor, writer, and part-time lecturer in theology and religious studies at Trinity College, Carmarthen, Wales.

Linda Edwards (née Smith) is also the author of several well-known textbooks for schools and colleges, including *Luke: A Gospel for Today* (Lion Publishing, 1989), and the coauthor of *A Beginner's Guide to Ideas* (1991)—an introduction to Western philosophy, past and present, which has been translated into many different languages. An extended edition (1999) was published by Zondervan in the United States under the title of *A Brief Guide to Ideas*.

A BRIEF GUIDE TO BELIEFS

Ideas, Theologies, Mysteries, and Movements

Linda Edwards

Westminster John Knox Press
LOUISVILLE • LONDON

Book design by Sharon Adams
Cover design by designpointinc.com

First edition
Published by Westminster John Knox Press
Louisville, Kentucky

This book is printed on acid-free paper that meets the American National Standards Institute Z39.48 standard.

PRINTED IN THE UNITED STATES OF AMERICA

02 03 04 05 06 07 08 09 10 — 10 9 8 7 6 5 4 3 2

Library of Congress Cataloging-in-Publication Data

Edwards, Linda, 1951–
A brief guide to beliefs : ideas, theologies, mysteries, and movements / Linda Edwards.—1st ed.
p. cm.
Includes bibliographical references and index.
ISBN 0-664-22259-5 (alk. paper)
1.Religions. I. Title.

BL80.2.E34 2001
291—dc21 2001017793

To the memory of Professor David Flusser,
1917–2000

David Flusser was Professor Emeritus at the Hebrew University, where he taught Judaism in the Second Temple Period and Early Christianity. In 1980 he was awarded the Israel Prize in literature. I and many other students will never forget his compelling portrait of Jesus painted on the canvas of Jewish thought and life in the first century.

As an older man he once upset a student by putting forward views that in his earlier writings he had repudiated. The young man pointed out the contradiction. In reply Professor Flusser replied in good humor, “Am I not also permitted to learn?”

Contents

List of Figures

Acknowledgments

So many people have aided the publication of *A Brief Guide to Beliefs*. My grateful thanks to all who have generously given their time to help—on the telephone, in person or via the Internet—in the research and editing of this book. Particular thanks to those who have provided books and booklets, and especially to the Rev. Dr. David Pusey.

Special thanks to Myra Newall for reading the first draft, despite the vicissitudes of life, and to Dr. Wendy Dossett of the University of Wales, Lampeter, for agreeing to peruse the sections on Eastern religions.

Thanks also to Peter Manning, King Henry VIII School, Coventry, for once again lending me his philosophical mind.

Finally and most importantly, thanks to Phil for his unquenchable optimism, and his generosity of spirit in all weather.

Chronology of Faiths and Movements

1500 B.C.E.	Hinduism (No specific founder)
1300 B.C.E.	Judaism—Moses
600 B.C.E.	Jainism—Mahavira
560 B.C.E.	Buddhism—Gautama Buddha
550 B.C.E.	Taoism—Lao Tzu
500 B.C.E.	Confucianism—K'ung Fu'tzu (Confucius)
500 B.C.E.	Zoroastrianism—Zoroaster (Zarathustra)
500 B.C.E.	Shintoism
350 B.C.E.	Therevada Buddhism
30 C.E.	Christianity—Jesus Christ
50	Gnosticism
50	Mahayana Buddhism
400s	Svetambaras
451	Coptic Orthodox Church
500s	Digambaras
500s	Shaivites
500s	Zen (Ch'an) Buddhism—Bodhidharma
610	Islam—Mohammad
650	Shi'ite Muslims—'Ali
700s	Sufism
700s	Vedanta—Shankara
900s	Vaishnava Vedanta
933	Russian Orthodox Church—Vladimir
936	Parsis
1000s	Druze
1054	The Great Schism (Major Eastern and Western branches of Christianity formally split, resulting in separate Catholic Church and Orthodox Church.)
1100s	Freemasonry
1100s	Veerashaivas (Lingayats)—Basavanna
1260	Nichiren Shoshu Buddhism—Nichiren Daishonin
1391	Tibetan Buddhism—dge-'Dun-grub-pa (First Dalai Lama)
1500	Sikhism—Guru Nanak
1517	Lutheranism—Martin Luther
1521	Anabaptists
1536	Mennonites—Menno Simons
1541	Calvinism—John Calvin
1560	Presbyterianism
1563	Anglicanism (Thirty–nine Articles)
1580	Congregationalism
1600	Unitarianism
1600s	Sthanakavasis—Lavaji, Dharmasimha
1612	Baptists
1614	Rosicrucianism
1654	Society of Friends (Quakers)—George Fox
1693	Amish—Jacob Amann

Chronology of Faiths and Movements *(Continued)*

1700s	Wahhabis—Abd al–Wahhab
1722	Moravian Church—Nikolaus von Zinzendorf
1760	Swedenborgianism—Emanuel Swedenborg
1774	Shakers—Ann Lee
1784	Methodism—John Wesley
1789	Episcopal Church of America
1830	Church of Jesus Christ of Latter–day Saints (Mormons)—Joseph Smith
1830	Plymouth Brethren—J.N. Darby
1832	Disciples of Christ (Campbellites)—Alexander Campbell, Barton Stone
1838	Tenrikyo—Nakayama Miki
1840s	Reform Judaism
1844	Bahā'ī—Bahā' u'llāh (Abul Baha)
1845	Southern Baptist Convention
1848	Christadelphianism—John Thomas
1848	Spiritualism—Kate and Margaret Fox
1859	Konko Kyo—Kawate Bunjiro
1860	Ch'ondogyo—Ch'oe Che–u
1863	Seventh-day Adventists—Ellen Harmon White
1870	Native American Church
1875	Theosophical Society—H.P. Blavatsky, Henry Olcott
1875	Church of Christ, Scientist (Christian Science)—Mary Baker Eddy
1878	Salvation Army—William Booth
1886	Jehovah's Witnesses—Charles Taze Russell
1889	Ahmadis—Mirza Ghulam Ahmad
1889	Old Catholics
1890s	African Independent Churches (various)
1900	Rosicrucian Fellowship—Max Heindel
1906	Pentecostalism—William J. Seymour
1913	Anthroposophical Society—Rudolf Steiner
1914	Assemblies of God
1920	Church of the Lord (Aladura)
1921	Kimbanguist Church—Simon Kimbangu
1922	Institute for the Harmonious Development of Man—Georgei Gurdjieff
1923	Arcane School—Alice Bailey
1923	International Church of the Foursquare Gospel—Aimee Semple McPherson
1924	Emin—Raymond Armin
1924	Meher Baba—Meher Baba
1925	Reiyukai—Kubo Kakutaro, Kotani Kimi
1925	United Church of Canada
1926	Cao Dai—Ngo Van Chieu
1927	Mind Science—Ernest Holmes
1928	Opus Dei—Josemaria Escriva de Balaguer
1930	Black Muslims (Nation of Islam)—Wallace D. Fard
1930	Rastafarianism—Marcus Garvey
1930	Seicho No le—Taniguchi Masaharu
1930	Soka Gakkai—Tsunesaburo Makiguchi, Josei Toda

Chronology of Faiths and Movements *(Continued)*

1930s Subud—Muhammad Subuh Sumohadiwidjojo
1933 Worldwide Church of God—Herbert W. Armstrong
1935 Sekai Kyuseikyo—Okada Mokichi
1935 Self-Realization Fellowship—Paramahansa Yogananda
1937 Brahma Kumaris World Spiritual University—Dada Lekh Raj
1938 Rissho–Koseikai—Naganuma Myoko, Niwano Nikkyo
1939 Sathya Sai Baba
1944 Silva Mind Control—Jose Silva
1945 Tensho Kotai Jingukyo—Kitamura Sayo
1946 P. L. Kyodan—Miki Tokuchika
1953 Way International—Victor P. Wierwille
1954 Aetherius Society (UFO's)—George King
1954 Church of Scientology—L. Ron Hubbard
1954 Unification Church (Moonies)—Sun Myung Moon
1955 Ananda Marga—Shrii Shrii Anandamurti
1955 Urantia Book—Bill Sadler
1957 United Church of Christ (USA)
1958 Institute of Divine Metaphysical Research—Henry Kinley
1958 Transcendental Meditation– Maharishi Mahesh Yogi
1959 Branch Davidians—Benjamin Roden
1960s Jesus Movement
1964 Sri Chinmoy—Sri Chinmoy Kumar Ghose
1965 Assembly of Yahweh—Jacob Meyer
1965 Eckankar—John Paul Twitchell
1965 ISKCON (International Society for Krishna Consciousness)
1966 Church of Satan—Anton LaVey
1966 Osho International—Bhagwan Shree Rajneesh
1968 The Family (Children of God)—David Berg
1969 Jesus Fellowship—Noel Stanton
1970 Elan Vital (Divine Light Mission)—Guru Maharaj Ji
1970 Findhorn Community—Peter and Eileen Caddy, David Spangler
1970 Sahaja Yoga—Mataji Nirmala Devi
1972 United Reformed Church (UK)
1974 Assemblies of Yahweh—Sam Suratt
1974 Church Universal and Triumphant—Elizabeth Clare Prophet
1974 Raelians—Claude Vorilhon
1975 Siddha Yoga—Muktananda Paramahamsa
1979 Church of Christ International—Kip McKean
1980 House of Yahweh (Abilene)—Jacob Hawkins
1980 Tara Center—Benjamen Crème
1988 Falun Gong—Li Hongzhi

Notes

1. Some dates in this chronology are approximate.
2. Some religious bodies are not listed here, either because they are very small or because it was not possible to determine the year in which they began.

Introduction

Some people are convinced that they have the truth and are anxious to ensure others also have it. These are fundamentalists.

Some people spend their lives in distractions and activity and are indifferent to the truth.

Some people deny there is any truth and devote their life to this denial.

Others construct their own truths or at least come to understand the forces that have constructed the truths by which they live.

A few, however, seek the Truth and knowing they will never find it in its entirety, stake their lives on trying to live it.

Peter Vardy, *What Is Truth?*

The Uses of the Book

A Brief Guide to Beliefs is both a reference book and a guide. To use the book as a reference book, you can read each self-contained unit of material to access a brief resumé of some of the key people, beliefs, and practices of a faith or movement. To use the book as a guide, you are invited to read the first six chapters, which, as explained below, will give you some philosophical and religious resources to keep in mind when engaging with various Western beliefs, and also to take forward into your reading of the rest of the book.

The Purpose of the Book

The purpose of *A Brief Guide to Beliefs* is to introduce the reader to the world of religion in a way that invites him or her to engage personally both with the issues and with the fundamental questions with which religion deals. The book is for the general reader or the Christian seminary student who wants to know more about the important key beliefs that underpin the practices and lifestyles of people in the major world religions, philosophies, and alternative religious and self-improvement movements that abound at the start of the third millennium of the Common Era.

I also write as a Christian who is committed in this book to an educational approach, wishing to inform Christians of the different faiths' histories and backgrounds, knowledge of which is often lacking.

The Scope of the Book

A Brief Guide to Beliefs does not aspire to being a full or complete history of each tradition, or a detailed analysis of scholarly disagreement on the various points of doctrinal departure that exist within religious faiths. Excellent histories and encyclopedias of religion are available for such detail. Within each faith or religious movement numerous subdivisions exist, increasingly so in a world marked more and more by the polarities of fundamentalism and liberalism. Some of these major divisions, e.g., Sunni and Shiʿa in Islam, are mentioned, but unfortunately space is not available to include all the variations of, say, Buddhism or Seventh-day Adventism. Generally speaking, as an introductory guide this book assumes the stance of a thoughtful orthodox member of a faith or movement.

The task of selecting material has been a challenging one, for the number of alternative spiritualities has escalated and multiplied at an unprecedented rate in the last few decades. Although no book of this sort can ever be complete, some of the entries are inevitably less detailed than others, while other groups, e.g., Subud and Echankar, regrettably do not appear in the text. Altogether about sixty different religions or spiritual movements are included, which are often representative of the many more in the United States and Britain, and quite a few of which are variants of older traditions.

The Approach Taken

Most chapters have a short introduction that discusses the issues surrounding the subject studied. I am aware that some movements or religions represented in this book would object to being included with all the others with whom they fundamentally disagree. This tension can occur within the different factions of a religion as well as between different religions. Any group which believes that it possesses the final truth about ultimate reality, God, or the universe necessarily feels that the rest of the world is deluded or amiss in its understanding. Conversely, others who refute the belief that ultimate truth can ever be known in an exclusive way see themselves as one path amongst many that are all equally valid in the world today. Both of these persuasions are included in this text, along with others.

The Issue of Truth

Intellectual integrity is crucial if one is committed to searching for truth and for taking seriously the question of how we may make the most of our lives given what we come to believe about the nature of our existence. The search process includes aspects of openness, reflection, and doubt. The approach in this book to issues of truth is to affirm human freedom of thought by trying to let each movement speak for itself, albeit briefly, through its sacred writings, source material, and the teachings of its founders and followers. I have also used other academic material where it helps to shed light on the beliefs and practices of new religious movements. This approach should not be perceived to deny issues such as historical accuracy, financial corruption, indoctrination, or sexual exploitation. Where well-documented accusations or sustained objections exist, they are referred to briefly, often with references for those readers who wish to follow up the line of inquiry.

Orthodoxy and Heresy

Questions about orthodoxy and heresy are crucial for many people who are observant members of a religion. For example, no self-respecting evangelical Christian or Muslim would say that a pagan or Satanist was "saved" or right with God. Such questions are mainly not addressed in the book, but not through any lack of personal concern. My aim has not been to promote my own views with readers but rather to give a taste of the different religious and spiritual worlds followed by thousands and millions of ordinary, intelligent people around the world. This aim is not aided by being adversely critical of others. Nevertheless, whereas I have tried to be as objective as I can, like everyone, my own religious background may sometimes color the approach taken.

Distinguishing Myth from History

The question of myth versus history crops up often when religious founders claim that certain stories are historically accurate. Incessant questioning of these truth claims would detract from the major task of this book, which is informational. I have tried to avoid a cynical approach—using language like "supposedly this happened," which is insulting to sincere believers. But if, on occasion, your sense of reason or credulity is severely overstretched, I may well share at least some of the same problem.

The Structure of the Book

While deciding on the possible structure of this book, I realized I would have liked to have covered a detailed historical background of each of the major world faiths, then looked at the mainstream form(s) of that religion in the world today and followed with some of the alternative expressions/movements that flow from it. However, such an enterprise would have made the book far too long. Because the book is initially to be published in the United States and Great Britain, where Christianity predominates, I have used Christianity to provide a model of this desired method. For that reason, the sections on Christianity are generally longer than others. I hope that some readers would be inspired to carry their own research further and apply the broad methodology to faiths other than Christianity.

The book begins (chapters 1–5) with a guide to key philosophical ideas and issues (e.g., postmodern theory, science, and religion) that permeate popular views about religion and morality, due to the influential role that the Judeo-Christian tradition has played in framing Western thought over two thousand years.

Chapter 6 attempts to provide the reader with a simple conceptual framework for studying religious beliefs. In the mid-1970s, Professor Ninian Smart of Lancaster University encouraged the phenomenological approach to religious studies, citing various "dimensions" of faith, for example, the ritual, the ethical, etc. I have employed a broad phenomenological approach in which I have aimed at empathetic (not sympathetic) understanding with the focus on what people believe. In taking this approach, the focus falls on eight aspects of religion:

1. God—What is the nature of ultimate reality?
2. Salvation—What does it mean to be a human being and how is life best lived?
3. Death and Afterlife—What happens after this life?
4. Moral Action—How do people act in this life and apply the values of their beliefs?
5. Prayer/Worship—In what ways can people articulate and offer their devotion to God/ultimate reality?
6. Gender and Religion—How have patriarchal systems of belief influenced the status and role of women?
7. Mysticism—How much is religious tradition open to exploring and giving expression to the further domains of religious experience?
8. Scriptures/Festivals—How are sources of revelation and faith protected and affirmed through texts and communal practice?

In chapter 6 the eight different aspects are explored conceptually with reference to one or more different religions. These categories then provide a stylized structure for chapter 7 and the study of twelve world faiths.

Chapter 7 discusses twelve classical world religions that have been chosen according to the list of religions described and which are most frequently cited in surveys and studied in courses on world religions (some of them are reviewed more for historical than contemporary reasons):

1. Hinduism
2. Buddhism

3. Sikhism
4. Judaism
5. Christianity
6. Islam
7. Shinto
8. Confucianism
9. Taoism
10. Zoroastrianism
11. Jainism
12. Babi/Baha'i

This world religions listing is derived from the statistics data in the Adherents.com database. Researchers who collected and organized the database consulted with university professors of comparative religions and scholars from various religions. The Adherents.com collection of religious adherent statistics now has over thirty-four thousand statistic citations covering some three thousand different faith groups in all parts of the world. Even so, the data is not complete, but Adherents.com provides the largest pool—by far—of data available on the Internet.

Chapter 8 follows with a selection of alternative religious movements flowing out of a number of mainstream world religions and which have been popularized both in the East and the West or which are indigenous to Native American and African culture.

Chapter 9 focuses on Christian beliefs and movements both past and present. It provides a brief, roughly chronological guide to Christian church history throughout the ages, introducing you to some of the martyrs, defenders, scholars, evangelists, designated heretics, councils, and creeds of two thousand years of faith. This brief history gives readers a linear guide to the most serious splits and schisms—e.g., Eastern/Western Christianity, Roman Catholic/Protestant—as well as a background to the major beliefs and historic heresies of the early Christian era, often revived and repackaged in the following centuries and termed "cults" or "sects" by mainstream believers. The purpose of chapter 9 is to offer a context for understanding alternative Christian movements in the next chapter.

Chapter 10 looks at a selection of popular, new, and alternative Christian movements, all of which claim a Christian heritage but which are often misunderstood, not recognized, and often considered highly controversial in mainstream Christian denominations. My aim is not to critique these movements, but I have in some sections compared different versions of Christian faith with mainstream views. I have taken this approach in the interests of clarity and in recognition that this book will be read in different ways. Some readers will turn to, say, the section on Christadelphianism, without any reference to the other sections of the book. To read about Christadelphianism without a general theological knowledge of mainstream Christian faith, Christadelphian beliefs may be unwittingly misunderstood. I have also offered comparisons of how the same religious language can mean very different things to different denominations.

Chapter 11 surveys beliefs on the practice of magic, occult, esoteric, and pagan thought. For readers who have been brought up in traditional Christian, Muslim, Jewish, or other mainstream religious backgrounds, material on subjects such as Satanism and the occult may be considered offensive or even blasphemous. I intend no disrespect or offense, but the world of the occult is a spiritual reality for many people. I have tried to present the elements covered in a clear and objective way.

Sometimes placing a religion in a certain category is difficult because of the eclectic and diverse elements in it. For example, Theosophy contains both Christian and Eastern elements blended with its own esoteric beliefs; therefore, Theosophy is placed under the section on esoteric movements.

In Chapter 12, I briefly visit three approaches to the belief in human potential: psychology, humanism, and Scientology. Once again selection has been a very difficult task, and some notable groups such as Freemasonry, Brahma Kumaris, or Konko Kyo have not been included. This exclusion in no way implies their insignificance but rather the difficult realities involved in any task of selection.

Notes of Caution

Name Changes. A number of new religious movements (NRMs) have changed their names. Where this has happened I have used the most recent version and put the original or older name in parentheses, e.g., The Family (Children of God).

Religious Language. Religious language like "God" or "salvation" derives from Judaism and Christianity and would not necessarily be recognized or given the same meaning within other world religions. These terms cannot be used definitively as the structure for others' thinking. Therefore, to avoid inaccurate harmonization where the term does not apply or is inappropriate in some way, the differences are covered by making them part of the discussion and drawing your attention to the inevitable elasticity of the categories and language being used.

Conclusion

An understanding of religious beliefs and concepts is not likely to be reached by taking extreme views. Two ways of taking an extreme approach are by being dogmatic and close-minded so that you only study what you consider to be the truth or by being so casual in your methods that you blur, reinterpret, or ignore the genuine details, difficulties, and differences that exist both within different groups within a faith or between world faiths.

Similarly, anyone who genuinely wishes to understand religion will almost certainly be ill-served if they abandon either their rational faculties or their religious experience, although the uncomfortable coexistence of the two has been the misfortune of many theologians who think critically and thoughtfully about their faith and also believe in miracles!

An educational approach takes place on the middle ground where open dialogue and investigation can uncover and explore both the agreements and disagreements among the religions, without the prerequisite to abandon what you think or know to be true. This middle way aims at deepening the commitment and understanding of religious groups in their own traditions and also enabling them to acquire an openness and readiness to learn about the religious world of others in the diverse spiritual world in which we all live.

Chapter 1
Postmodernism and the Challenge to Religion

Is it not necessary to draw a line between those who believe that we can continue to situate our present discontinuities within the historical and transcendental tradition of the nineteenth century and those who are making a great effort to liberate themselves, once and for all, from this conceptual framework?

Michel Foucault

What's going on just now? What's happening to us? What is this world, this period, this precise moment in which we are living?

Michel Foucault

Imagine you are shopping at the mall. At first you are not aware of it, but you gradually perceive that something is amiss. You suddenly realize what has happened. The buildings in the mall are all suspended in midair! The foundations have mysteriously disappeared. *Where have they gone? Who did this thing?* You arrive at your office and stand outside. *Surely it's not safe enough to enter, is it?*

This imaginary episode reflects the cultural transformation that many people in today's world find themselves experiencing. In the recent past, people in the West lived in what has been a modern age, where the foundations were solid and where the basis for their trust in society and the future rested on reliable beliefs and assumptions such as God, science, and dependable institutions and governments. Even empires were built on such figurative structures. But in the twenty-first century, the influence of such certainties has been and continues to be eroded. Of course, institutions and governments still exist, but we can no longer rely on one best way or one best belief or one best anything. We now live in what has been called a postmodern world. Western society is in the process of deconstructing all of the modern world's foundations. The world as we know it has changed beyond recognition since the turn of the twentieth century.

Rapid Change and Multiple Choice

Two factors that characterize the technological society of the twenty-first century are the multiple number of choices available and the rapid change that exists at every level.

Peter Berger (1979) noted that the vast multiplication of choice affects not only the way we live but our very consciousness and the way we perceive reality. Berger and others point out that as consumer choices expand—what to do or buy or watch on TV—a corresponding desire for choice emerges when it comes to religion. The rise in New Age religions and new religious movements (NRMs) indicates that the interest and need people have for some kind of spiritual expression has not declined; instead, in Western culture, religion increasingly is becoming a question of preference and choice rather than adherence to divine revelation or traditional belief or upbringing. Cultural background and place of birth were once major influences on a person's beliefs, but these factors are less important in an increasingly mobile world.

This chapter will look at

- The rise of postmodern culture through world events, globalization, and secularization
- The prevailing ideas and beliefs in today's postmodern world
- A brief introduction to the ideas of three postmodern philosophers: Jacques Lacan, Michel Foucault, and Jacques Derrida
- Fundamentalism as one of the responses to the lack of certainty

Modernity and the Grand Narratives

"Modernity" is the period that started well before World War Two and ended well after it. This period saw

- A sharp rise in scientific theory and influence
- The inauguration of the social state
- An increase in secular views that prevailed over religious belief

Freudian and Marxist outlooks dominated thought about how human beings functioned and how they should live in society. Modernism was intellectually dependent on what philosophers call reason (the human faculty of thinking using evidence, as contrasted with thinking that relies on revelation, emotion, or feeling) and rationalism (the belief in the possibility to obtain by reason alone a knowledge of the nature of what exists). These approaches to thought were allied to what postmodern theorist Jean-Francois Lyotard has called the "grand narratives," which are the overarching belief systems that functioned as absolute and authoritative. Lyotard claims that these grand narratives have now collapsed and that people living in the technological countries of the West are now living in postmodernity, i.e., the time after modernity.

Characteristics of Postmodernity

Generally, sociologists distinguish between the terms "postmodernism" and "postmodernity." *Postmodernism* is often used to describe a number of cultural features, such as the increased significance of computers and Internet information. *Postmodernity* refers to structural change—for example, globalization. Postmodernism defines itself over and against modernism. The former term has been widely used since the 1970s to denote a form of cultural change that marks a sharp break with the modern era.

The literature on postmodernity is vast and shows much disagreement over what being "postmodern" actually involves. Postmodernism is a multilayered concept that encompasses a wide range of developments in thought, art, and society that have radical implications for our culture and the way we think about reality and religion. Nevertheless, postmodernity can be traced from about 1980 to the present day. The concept is characterized by its rejection of the modernist ideals of rationality and individualism. Instead, postmodernism embraces a variety of new worldviews such as feminism, multiculturalism, and environmentalism. The tendency is to be anticapitalist, contemptuous of traditional morality, and committed to a notion of political correctness.

Globalization

Other developments have coincided with the collapse of the grand narrative. The communications technologies of computers and satellite television give anyone with access to such technology access to the lifestyles, beliefs, and products of the whole world. This process can be referred to as "globalization." In a globalized world, geographical distances are less important and the amount of information available seems infinite.

Jean Baudrillard has commented on the barrage of information that we consume. According to Baudrillard (1983), we are what we consume—that is, our own identities are created, formed, and changed through our acts of consumption.

One consequence of globalization for religions is that they become like other commodities: they compete in the marketplace to be consumed. Ze'ev W. Falk summarizes the postmodern situation:

> For Western society, postmodernism is the result of extreme individualism and multi-cultural society, leading to the collapse

> of the consensus of modernity. This absence of consensus has led in art and in religion to subjectivism, in philosophy to nominalism, and in politics to pluralism and anarchism—or by way of dialectics—to authoritarianism and totalitarianism. Other results of extreme individualism and scepticism are drugs, violence, terrorism and pollution. (Ze'ev W. Falk, 1994)

At one time, world religions used to be categorized as Western and non-Western, which usually meant that European and North American Christian (Western) religions were given priority. This way of thinking is now less and less relevant in countries like Britain, where there has been rapid social change in the last fifty years. The integration of what were once thought of as Eastern religions—Sikhism, Hinduism, Buddhism, and Islam—are now part of everyday life in major cities. There is now a plurality of beliefs and worldviews in both Britain and the United States.

A Summary of Prevailing Postmodern Ideas

In a postmodern world, a number of tendencies have surfaced. People are more likely to harbor beliefs such as the following:

- Objectivity and logic are not to be trusted. What we say is judged on how well it fits the situation rather than its logical consistency.
- Specialist teachers and their ability to show us the true meaning of concepts should not be trusted.
- There is no ultimate truth, only lots of truths, all relative in their own context.
- Tradition is irrelevant, and the judgment of historical analysis made by historians is placed in a particular cultural context and time. How can history be reliable when it excludes huge areas of human experience, such as women's history?
- Writers are unaware of the true meaning of their words.
- Readers read something and understand it from the perspective of their already existing point of view or world of meaning, regardless of what the writer intended. This subjectivity also occurs because texts are constantly in a state of flux. Although printed text is static, its meaning is constantly open to being interpreted in different ways by an individual rather than some external objective criteria that might come from the external world. (Jacques Derrida explored this concept, as we'll see later in this chapter.)
- The academic world is no longer a seat of power and privilege. A subject like theology is seen as a way to create a class of privileged professionals who rule over the Church.

The Secularization of Religion

Sociologists of religion refer to the process of secularization, which has influenced the way in which religion is seen in the Western world. Peter Berger (1979) sees secularization as "The process through which sectors of society and culture have been freed from the decisive influence of religious ideas and institutions."

Harry Blamires as early as 1963 was making poignant comment on the way the Christian Church has been mentally secularized in the United Kingdom: "In the UK today everywhere one meets examples of the abdication of the Church's intellectual authority which lies at the back of the modern Christian's easy descent into mental secularism." In his analysis, he cites areas and situations that show how the Christian Church is secularized:

- Churches that do not exist to give Christian teaching and doctrine but only to provide opportunities for communal worship.
- Except over a very narrow field of thinking, chiefly touching questions of strictly personal conduct, Christians in the modern world accept, for the purpose of mental activity, a frame of reference constructed by the secular mind.

Blamires says Christians have abdicated from the field of social discussion or discourse and that the real critics of popular culture are either humanists or mystics. For example, streams of talk go on everywhere—with friends, in newspapers, on TV documentaries, TV soaps, at the hairdressers, and in offices where issues such as unemployment, "downsizing," the monopoly of large businesses, inflation, and many others all arise in conversation. These streams compose a living field of discourse. Like all discourse, beliefs are at the heart of the discussion. Blamires argues that most contemporary talk is done using secular tools, e.g., humanist tools like the affirmation of human dignity and integrity and the protest movements. The Christian basis for such thought about the dignity of humanity is rarely affirmed. Blamires's charge is that the twentieth-century literature of protest has been written by those who are gifted and sensitive and outraged by the indignities heaped upon the human spirit, yet who offer no reference to God. He cites Franz Kafka, D. H. Lawrence, Henry Miller, and Samuel Beckett.

The Philosophical Roots of Postmodernism

The philosophical roots of postmodernism can be traced to the French academy of the 1970s whose thinkers are now called deconstructionists. They believed that the essence of any literary form (any "text"), is to be found in the reader, not in the author. To try to know what an author meant by what is written is therefore futile. What a person knows is what *he or she interprets from the text;* that interpretation which becomes the true meaning. Three postmodern philosophers who have contributed much to challenge the prevailing way people in the West think and live are Jacques Lacan, Michel Foucault, and Jacques Derrida.

Jacques Lacan's Challenge to Human Autonomy and Reason

Postmodern theory reflects the view that there has been an irretrievable loss of trust in "modern" culture, which saw the concept of human beings as autonomous individuals. This view of human nature came from the philosopher René Descartes (1596–1650) and has been challenged by Paris-born Jacques Lacan (1901–1981). Lacan played a very important role in developments within Freudian psychoanalytical theory and was influenced in his thinking by structuralism.

Structuralism is a philosophy about how language works. The father of structuralist thought was Ferdinand de Saussure (1857–1913), who viewed language as a social construct upon which each different community places its own assumptions and meaning. Structuralists also argued that to understand each individual term, one must consider how it differs from other terms. The idea of difference conferring meaning upon language is a key concept in much postmodern writing.

Lacan took the structuralist view of language and linked it to his way of thinking about the human subject. The result was a devastating challenge for all areas of thought. In Lacan's view, the signifier is always separated from the thing signified and therefore exists in language apart from it. *As a result, no words are ever able to connect or correspond absolutely with the physical world. The result is that signs, symbols, and images of all kinds become understood in a symbolic and metaphorical way, and self-identity can never be stable or fully known.*

With his approach, Lacan has challenged not only rationalism but the whole basis of scientific enterprise, which rests on the belief that words have an ability to provide a clear representation of an objective reality. People become detached from the objective world of reality because they understand reality only through the linguistic community to which they belong.

Michel Foucault: Reality Is Relativized

Michel Foucault (1926–1984) was a French philosopher who attempted to show that the basic ideas that people normally understand to be permanent truths about human nature and society change with time. Foucault put forward new concepts that challenged people's assumptions about prisons, the police, insurance, mental health care, rights for homosexuals, and welfare. His ideas challenged those of Marx and Freud. During the 1970s and 1980s his international reputation grew as he lectured internationally.

German philosophers Frederick Nietzsche and Martin Heidegger were both major influences on Foucault's thought. Nietzsche had argued that human behavior is motivated by a drive for power and that traditional values had lost their influence over society. Heidegger had argued against "our current technological understanding of being." Foucault's thought explored the shifting patterns of power within a society and the ways in which power relates to the self. He looked into how, at different times in history, changing rules could govern which claims could be seriously considered as true or false. Foucault also concentrated on how particular organizations or bodies of knowledge—such as the scientific community—hold power over people, and he argued that such groupings still fail to escape the problems of subjectivism and relativism.

In his major work, later published in an abridged version in English under the title of *Madness and Civilization*, Foucault was concerned with madness and reason as they related to the institutions of psychiatry. Foucault employs the term "discursive practice" which refers to the rule-governed set of statements that each human community at given points in time uses to ground its beliefs on what is considered to be "knowledge." As he studied how ideas change in relation to the culture within which they exist, Foucault doubted whether there was any possibility of any thought being true or truer than any other outside of a particular discursive practice. Taken to a conclusion, no criteria can discern truth from falsehood, outside of a particular community's discursive practices. Any attempt to maintain universal standards of logic and rationality is, therefore, invalid.

Jacques Derrida and the Deconstruction of Reality

Born in El-Biar, Algeria, Jacques Derrida taught at the Sorbonne in Paris. Since the early 1970s, he has divided much of his time between Paris and the United States, where he has taught at such universities as Johns Hopkins, Yale, and the University of California at Irvine.

Derrida's work also focuses on language. His view is that the traditional way of reading makes a number of false assumptions about the nature of texts. The traditional belief is that language is capable of expressing ideas without changing them, but Derrida's deconstructive style of reading rejects these assumptions and challenges the idea that a text has an unchanging, unified meaning.

Deconstruction shows the multiple layers of meaning at work in language. By deconstructing the works of previous scholars, Derrida attempts to show that language is constantly shifting. He set forth his theories in *Writing and Difference* (1967) and *Of Grammatology* (1967), basing his ideas on a broad reading of the Western philosophical traditions. He focuses on language and sets out to subvert narrative assumptions about the text of language by challenging the idea that text has an unchanging unified meaning.

Derrida says that philosophy must be redefined and let go of its desire to discover the truth about things. Rather philosophy must think of itself as a literary genre that attempts to examine the practice of how different genres think of themselves and interrelate with others.

Derrida's ideas have been instrumental in forming a new school of criticism known as "deconstruction," because he has sought to deconstruct the way people in Western culture rely on rational thinking. Although his thought is seen as destructive of philosophy, deconstruction may be seen as drawing attention to the inevitable tensions between the ideals of clarity and coherence that imbue philosophy and the inescapable shortcomings that attend its production and presentation.

Religion and Postmodernism

Postmodernism has had a variety of influences on religion, including the following:

- *A move towards Eastern Spirituality.* Postmodern Christianity has seen an opening up to Asian religion, as in the writings of theologians Thomas Merton and Paul Tillich. A similar movement towards Eastern spirituality occurs in Judaism in the writing of Zalman Schecher-Shalomi and others.
- *Hybridity*. Sociologists have documented a vast increase in new religious movements (NRMs) and New Age movements (NAMs). These movements are often hybrids, containing a mixture of several different traditions. The Unification Church, for example, is a combination of Hinduism, Buddhism, and Christianity. NAMs often contain mixtures of Christianity and esoteric religions or paganism.
- *Radical theology*. This development involves a radical questioning of key beliefs in the faith. Paul Van Buren argued for a secular interpretation of Jesus and the New Testament. In Judaism, Mordecai Kaplan and Harold S. Kushner cite the impossibility of divine miracles given the extent of individual human suffering. Richard Rubenstein takes this concept further when he argues that given the Holocaust there is no God of history. Less radical thinkers who wrestle with these same issues accept that the traditional concept of God—omniscient, omnipotent, and omnibenevolent—has become questionable in the light of the Holocaust.
- *Spirituality.* New Age beliefs are concerned with spiritual issues in the wide context of everyday life: employment, health, diet, interior design, the environment, etc. For example, the idea that the environment is an organism that we can harm—the concept of Gaia—turns the idea of environmentalism into something very much resembling a religious movement.
- *The rise of religious mass media*. The mass media play a very important role in the transmission of religion in the United States. One well-known example is Pat Robertson's Christian Broadcasting Network (CBN), which uses satellite and cable technology to broadcast into American homes twenty-four hours a day. At the time of this writing, religious broadcasters are far more influential in the United States than

in Great Britain. Generally, the message of televangelists is conservative and includes elements of what sociologists call fundamentalism.

Fundamentalism as the Flip Side of Postmodernity

As we have seen in this chapter, one of the major creeds of postmodernism is the process of deconstructing the thoughts and experiences that people have of reality. People who are critical of postmodern Western culture say that it is driven by a consumerist ideology which seeks immediate self-fulfillment and which generates a sea of chaos as more brand names, diverse products, and endless novelty and trivia jostle for recognition and consumption. Within this context many people are uncertain about how to decide what is worth pursuing and why it should be pursued. At the same time, many people are turning to fundamentalism. Although this movement predates modern culture, fundamentalism is attracting many people who are searching for intellectual security and certainty.

Fundamentalism has been identified by sociologists in both the religious and secular realms; even some uncompromising assertions made by feminists have been labeled "fundamentalist." Fundamentalism may be viewed as a tendency or habit of mind whereby a person tells himself or herself a story that is designed to encompass the truth about the whole of reality, a totally closed worldview that is not open to any real dialogue. Doctrines or beliefs are held to be true in a rigidly defined way, and truth is seen as being certain and identifiable with its own interpretation.

Fundamentalism is most clearly identified in the way it attacks liberal thinking. The movement commonly perceives of itself as being in a Holy War or battle for the truth. Fundamentalism is now understood as a worldwide phenomena. Postmodernity, although marked by increasing pluralism, is increasingly providing two basic and competing ideologies as two sides of the same coin:

1. On one side is an inability or reticence to commit to or believe in anything for any length of time: a belief that reality is always in flux.
2. On the other side is an overriding belief in the unquestionable truth of one specific worldview: fundamentalism.

The recent rise in fundamentalism is probably a response to postmodernity/late modernity with its radical doubt and philosophical insecurity.

These polarized worldviews serve as examples of the sort of tensions that the world will increasingly face in the future. Yet they are not the only responses to set the agenda. Lesslie Newbigin (1986) has pointed out that liberalism, at its best, carries an open mind and humility in which it can learn. Conservatism, at its best, carries a moral courage and perseverance that fails to give up on the truth. The question arises whether these two approaches can work together. Gary Dorrien, in his book *The Remaking of Evangelical Theology* (1998), would argue that the boundaries are no longer so well defined and that

> Today younger thinkers who do not share the defining generational experiences of the Evangelical establishment are testing the borders of possible rethinking. The conservative evangelical dream of a re-Christianized America is alien to them, as is the conservative evangelical fear that airtight epistemological certainty must be secured at all costs. The theorists of new-model evangelicalism do not expect to find objective intellectual certainty or to create a new evangelical Christendom. Many of them are open to postmodern theory, not merely because it is intellectually fashionable but because they share much of the sensibility and experience behind it.

Finally, a thought to ponder: Much postmodern thought, with its own certainties and its forceful rejection of all fixed worldviews, manifests the fundamentalist habit of mind in a very secular way in its certainty that the truth cannot be known. The paradox is not hard to detect. *How can a belief in no absolute truths be so absolutely certain of anything?*

Summary

The very foundations of thought itself were questioned during the last quarter of the twentieth century. A central question for the present day is, "What does it mean 'to know'?" How do we know that our ideas about how things are describe truly and accurately the way reality is? We arrive at such conceptions through our own minds and senses.

In the Christian West a movement has taken place away from traditional religion, which was once seen as true and absolute in the sense that its beliefs were timeless and eternally true. The rise in New Age religions and new religious movements indicates that the interest and need for a meaningful spirituality has not declined, but that, in Western culture, religion increasingly becomes a question of preference and choice rather than adherence to divine revelation or traditional belief.

Chapter 2
Philosophy and Religion: The Existence of God

"If God did not exist, it would be necessary to invent Him."
Voltaire (1768)

"Let us weigh the gain and the loss, in wagering that God is. Consider these alternatives: if you win, you win all; if you lose, you lose nothing. Do not hesitate, then, to wager that He is."
Pascal, *Pensees* (1670)

People through the ages have tried to make sense of the meaning of life so that they can understand their purpose in this world and their place in the cosmos. Sexuality, love, trauma, loss, creativity, art, and extreme beauty can all evoke responses from which a religious interpretation of life begins. In modern Europe and America, the philosophy of religion has been defined in different ways, but such studies include a number of questions, such as:

> What kind of experience might be interpreted as an "experience of God"?
>
> Does God exist?
>
> Can belief in God be justified rationally?
>
> Do miracles happen?

The issue of religious language is also important in philosophy. A Buddhist or a Hindu may have similar spiritual experiences without using the language of

Some Important Figures in the God Debate	
427–348 B.C.E.	Plato: God is the Ultimate Form
384–322 B.C.E.	Aristotle: God is the Unmoved Mover
1033–1109	Anselm: formulated the Ontological Argument
c.1225–1274	Thomas Aquinas: the "five ways"
1596–1650	René Descartes: idea of perfection
1632–1677	Benedict Spinoza: restated Ontological Argument
1703–1791	John Wesley: need for experience of God
1711–1776	David Hume: criticized Anselm and Aquinas
1724–1804	Immanuel Kant: cause and effect restricted to sense experience
1743–1805	William Paley: argument from design
1768–1834	Friedrich Schleiermacher: moved from philosophy to experience
1804–1872	Ludwig Feuerbach: God is psychological projection
1809–1882	Charles Darwin: Does evolution preclude creator?
1818–1883	Karl Marx: Religion is opium of the people
1856–1939	Sigmund Freud: God is our own "superego"
1872–1970	Bertrand Russell: heroic atheism
1878–1965	Martin Buber: relationship with God underlies all others
1886–1965	Paul Tillich: God is "ground of our being"

"God" to explain them. Very few people come to a religious faith in God just because they have rational reasons, but believers everywhere claim that their religion makes rational sense about life as it is. Philosophy examines this claim: that faith in God is rational.

Philosophy of Religion and the Existence of God

The philosophy of religion is for the most part a Western pursuit that has involved an interaction between Christian beliefs and Western secular philosophy. The three traditional ways in which to pursue the argument for the existence of God are as follows:

1. The *a priori approach*, which argues that the concept of God is of a being so perfect that his nonexistence is inconceivable.
2. The *a posteriori approach*, which takes evidence from the world of the observable empirical universe and then insists that God is necessary to explain certain features of the cosmos.

3. The *existential approach*, which believes that direct experience of God can be the way of personal revelation. This approach is not really an argument in the normal sense of the word, because one does not usually argue for something that can be directly experienced.

This chapter explores

- The major classical theories or arguments that have been offered for the existence of God
- The view that religious experience proves the existence of God
- Modern contributions to the debate about God's existence
- Arguments against the existence of God

A Priori Arguments: Understanding the Nature of God

Anselm and the Ontological Argument

Anselm (1033–1109) was born at Aosta, Piedmont, in what is today Italy. He entered the Benedictine monastery of Bec in Normandy as a novice when he was twenty-six years old. He was Archbishop of Canterbury from 1093 to 1109, and his theology was developed in the monastery during a time of turbulent politics. Anselm was the first great theologian of medieval times and the founder of Scholasticism. The centuries after Roman rule had crumbled in Britain are known as the Dark Ages, and monasteries had become the places of learning and culture. Many people had come to believe that Christianity could only be understood by faith, but Anselm's argument goes beyond faith and searches for rational grounds through which that faith may be articulated.

The ontological argument for God's existence comes from the meaning of the word "God." Anselm begins with a definition of *God* as that than which nothing greater can be conceived. Anselm would say that even atheists who possess no belief in God have a concept or definition of God, even if in order to dismiss his existence. So, in Anselm's view, God has to exist within reality because that which exists in reality is greater than that which exists entirely in the mind. Imagine being left one million dollars by your aunt. The thought is wonderful, but you would be ecstatic to actually have the money in your savings account.

The next part of Anselm's argument is to prove that God's existence is "necessary." For Anselm, God must be defined in such a way that it is impossible to think of God as not existing. Anselm believed that God's existence was more than just a figment of our own thinking. Anselm thought it obvious that anyone who possesses the idea of God as the most perfect conceivable being must realize he actually exists. He believed that you can think that something exists because it cannot be thought *not* to exist. Since God is infinitely perfect and not limited by time or space, he is "that than which nothing greater can be conceived." Such an approach to thinking about God led Anselm to affirm faith as seeking understanding. This stance is well summarized when he states in his *Proslogion*,

> I am not seeking to understand in order to believe, but I believe in order to understand. For this too I believe; that unless I believe, I shall not understand.

The ontological argument has had a long and volatile history, appealing to some of the finest minds in Western history: mathematicians like Descartes, Spinoza, and Leibniz. Two modern versions of the ontological argument are found in the work of Norman Malcolm (1911–1990) and Alvin Plantinga (b. 1932). Even so, ontology fails to persuade many people, who share the same suspicion as Kant that "the unconditioned necessity of a judgment does not form the absolute necessity of a thing." Anselm, however, believed in revealed truth from God (for example, the meaning of incarnation, that Jesus is both God and human), but that reason must be applied to faith so that "reason seeks to understand what faith believes."

Criticisms, Comments, and Defenses of Anselm's Argument

Anselm's argument has met objections from various thinkers such as Immanuel Kant, Gottlob Frege, and Bertrand Russell. One critic likened readers meeting Anselm's argument to "when they see a conjurer extract a rabbit from an apparently empty hat. They cannot explain how the rabbit got there, but they are pretty certain that the conjurer introduced it somehow." Anselm's proof rests on pure thought and not on experience. The proof is *a priori*; no previous knowledge of the world is required to understand it.

- Gaulino of Marmoutier, in his essay *On Behalf of the Fool*, said Anselm's logic was at fault in that you can think of the most perfect island but it need not exist.
- Descartes, in his book *Meditations*, said that the ontological argument claims that existence is one of the defining predicates of God. Just as a triangle is not a triangle if it does not have three sides, so God, if he does not exist, is not God.

A Posteriori Argument: What Can Be Seen in the World and the Universe

The Cosmological Argument

St. Thomas Aquinas (1225–1274) was a saint, a mystic, a theologian, and a metaphysician. Born near Naples and the son of the Count of Aquina, he went to school under the Benedictines at the famous monastery of Monte Cassino and then attended the University of Naples, where in 1244 he became a Dominican, one of a new order of poor monks. His family was outraged and kidnapped him, but Thomas stood firm and held true to his convictions. In his massive work the *Summa Theologica,* Thomas Aquinas claimed to prove the existence of God by saying that the world could not be as it is if not for the existence of the ultimate reality—that which we call God. Of his many arguments, two stand out.

The "First Cause" Theory

Everything that happens has a cause, according to Aquinas, and this cause in turn has a cause, and so on in a series. A starting point, itself independent of other causes, must exist. This point is God.

Everything in the world is contingent—that is, the existence of every thing depends upon prior activities. For example, this page of writing is dependent on trees, paper, and manufacturers. Something must have existed that did not depend on anything else for its existence. This start of the whole of existence is God.

The Five Ways

Aquinas set out five ways or "proofs" of God. The first three form his cosmological argument for God's existence:

1. *Change or motion.* Everything in the world is in a process of change or motion, and this motion must have been activated by something else, and something else before that. Yet change cannot go back into infinity. Aquinas affirmed the idea of the Unmoved Mover (following the philosopher Aristotle). For Aquinas, the Prime Mover was God.
2. *Cause and effect.* Aquinas said in his *Summa Theologica,* "Now if you eliminate a cause you also eliminate its effects, so that you cannot have a last cause, nor an intermediate one, unless you have a first." One is therefore forced to suppose a first cause, which is God.
3. *Contingency.* Aquinas claimed that if everything in the world could or could not exist, then there must have been a time when nothing existed. For Aquinas, as with Anselm, objects in the world have contingent existence (they can or cannot exist) but only God has necessary existence (God must exist).
4. *Goodness and perfection.* In the fourth proof, these qualities in their truest form reside in God.
5. *Order and goals in nature.* Aquinas wrote that everything in nature is directed to its goal by someone with intelligence and understanding, whom we call "God."

David Hume's Critique of Aquinas

David Hume (1711–1776) attacked Aquinas's notion that cause and effect must come ultimately from a first cause that could be called God. He argued that cause and effect in the world require no explanation, because it is either an arbitrary fact of experience or a function of the human mind as it interprets experience. Hume questioned why God had to be the first cause; why not another first cause?

Immanuel Kant and the Moral Argument

Kant (1724–1804) believed that the principle of cause and effect held true for the world of sense experience but only in that domain. As God exists beyond the world of sense experience, then a leap from reasoning about this world to reasoning about God is impossible. All reasoning about God is doomed to fail because such reasoning is beyond human capacity. Kant rejected not only the ontological argument but the teleological and cosmological arguments as well, based on his theory that reason is too limited to know anything beyond human experience. However, he did argue that religion could be established as presupposed by the workings of morality in the human mind ("practical reason"). God's existence is a necessary presupposition of any moral judgments that are objective, that go beyond mere relativistic moral preferences. Such judgments require standards external to any human mind; that is, they presume God's mind.

The Teleological Argument

The world we live in seems to be designed. The earth is just the right size, its rotation is within certain limits, its tilt must be correct to cause the seasons. The human biological structure is very fragile. A little too much heat or cold and we die. We need light, but not too much ultraviolet. We need heat, but not too much infrared.

Given these conditions, every thinker is faced with a choice. Either the universe was designed, or all these features developed by chance.

The from-design argument is popular and was clearly expressed by William Paley (1743–1803) in *Natural Theology*. Paley argues that the universe is like a complex mechanism. A carefully constructed watch presupposes a watchmaker. In *Dialogues Concerning Natural Religion*, David Hume made three criticisms of the argument from design:

1. The universe is not particularly like a vast machine. It could equally be seen to be a great inert animal or vegetable.
2. Even if there is a designer, it may not be God.
3. Although the universe appears to be designed, it may not be. We have no other universes to offer for comparison.

The Cumulative Argument for the Existence of God: Theism

This modern attempt to affirm the existence of God builds on the teleological argument coming from the work of F. R. Tennant in *Philosophical Theology* and R. G. Swinburne in *The Existence of God.* The argument states that when we take stock of the whole range of data—nature, creation, and human moral, cognitive, and aesthetic experience—God's existence becomes more probable than not. Such an affirmation of theism, however, remains open to criticism that it simply messes about with the statistics by construing the data through the already present eye of faith. This statement bequeaths the problem that underlies all philosophical discourse: How can we employ any common scales of rationality to weigh the evidence?

Other Types of Theology and Belief

Natural Theology: Premodern Concepts

The biblical doctrine of creation gives rise to the notion of a natural knowledge of God. If God created the world, we can reasonably expect that the created natural order would show his workmanship. Christian theology through the centuries has developed its thinking along this path.

- St Augustine of Hippo in his *De Trinitate* (*On the Trinity*) argues that the height of God's creation is humankind and therefore human nature. He further argues that the height of human nature is human reasoning. Therefore God ("vestiges of the Trinity") can be found in the human processes of reasoning.
- A number of theologians have developed natural theologies based on the sense of beauty that arises from contemplating the world. One very moving exploration of this theme comes from American theologian Jonathan Edwards. In his *Personal Narrative*, he wrote of his "sheer beholding of God's beauty":

  > As I was walking there and looking up into the sky and clouds, there came into my mind so sweet a sense of the glorious majesty and grace of God, that I know not how to express.I seemed to see them both in a sweet conjunction. . . . It was a sweet and gentle, and holy majesty; and also a majestic meekness.

- A group of thinkers sometimes called "fideists" believe that religious knowledge cannot be based in any way on reason, but only on faith. On this view, the power of human reason cannot stretch as far as reasoning about God.

- Pantheists believe that the universe is God and God is the universe; therefore no distinction exists between God and creation. God is everywhere and in everything and is everything. The most famous proponent of pantheism is Benedict Spinoza (1632–1677).
- Deists claim that God created the world and set it in motion, but God is now removed from the world and plays no active part in it. Deists do not believe in prayer nor any kind of personal relationship with God. Their philosophy grew out of the scientific advances of the seventeenth century and sought to account for the universe as self-contained and mechanical, like a clock. God was imagined as a watchmaker, but one who had long since retired.

Science and Religion: The Modern Debate

Today the debate regarding the existence of God has shifted. In Aquinas's day, his proofs were seen as scientific and theological at the same time. Now a visible gap separates the language of theology and science. (See our discussion in chapter 4.) Most theologians would doubt whether a scientific demonstration of God's existence could be given. They would say that Aquinas already had a prior faith as a basis to his reasoning. In contrast, many modern theologians such as Paul Tillich have come to question what the terms of "God" and "existence" mean.

Tillich (1886–1965) was a very influential thinker who redefined the meaning and focus of the word "God." One of his central arguments rests on the following view: as God cannot be said to exist in the way anything else in the world exists, then God cannot really be said to exist at all. For Tillich the picture of God in the Bible is one of ultimate human experience. Accordingly, he rejected the belief in a personal God. Instead he referred to God as the spirit within ourselves that provides our ultimate sense of significance and value and which forms the ground of our being. Tillich's theology is highly existential—that is, concerned with the subjective self. Scholars have debated whether Tillich's reworking of theological language—his redefining of "God"—carries within it an inherent pantheism, or whether its focus on the individual marks an inroad of secularism into Christian theology.

The Argument from Religious Experience

Other thinkers turn to religious experience as a proof of God's existence. The argument from religious experience states very simply that God exists because people have experiences of God and can express them.

American philosopher William James (1842–1910) wrote a classic work on *The Varieties of Religious Experience* (1902). In 1908 he stated that

> I think it may be asserted that there are religious experiences of a specific nature. . . . I think that they point with reasonable probability to the continuity of our consciousness with a

> wider, spiritual environment from which the ordinary prudential man is shut off.

Mystical experience has a place within many religious traditions, although it often lingers on the fringes of orthodoxy and is even sometimes regarded as heretical or deviant. Islam has Sufis, Judaism has the Kabbalah, and early Christian writers such as the Desert Fathers gave some of the first Christian mystical descriptions. Mystical experiences often involve a spiritual or holy presence, a sense of "oneness" with the universe and God, and an inner assurance. Philosopher Blaise Pascal (1623–1662) had a mystical experience that he wrote down on a piece of paper, which was found sewn into his clothing after his death:

> From about half past ten in the evening to about half an hour after midnight.
> Fire.
> God of Abraham, God of Isaac, God of Jacob.
> Not the God of philosophers and scholars.
> Absolute Certainty: Beyond reason. Joy. Peace.
> Forgetfulness of the world and everything but God.
> The world has not known thee, but I have known thee.
> Joy! Joy! Joy! Tears of joy!

Friedrich Schleiermacher (1768–1834) and Martin Buber (1878–1965) were two philosophers of religious experience. They both turned to the dimension of religious experiences as a starting point for talking about religion. Schleiermacher lived during a period when Christian faith was under attack from rational skeptics. At the same time, romanticism (a movement that put emphasis on feeling and subjective experience) was strong in European thinking. Schleiermacher removed the study of religion from its grounding in theology, ethics, and rational knowledge, instead claiming that religion was rooted in feeling and experience. According to this view, the essence of religion did not lie in knowing or doing, but in "the consciousness of being absolutely dependent on (and in relation to) God." Here the Bible is not treated as a revelation from God or as a record of events in history, but rather as a record of religious experience. In his thinking, Schleiermacher divorces religion from reason and faith from history. He put religion beyond the attack of rationalists. In an increasingly scientific world, such an approach to thinking about God became very influential because it provided a way of holding on to Christian faith without having to choose between God or science.

Martin Buber, a Vienna-born Jewish philosopher and theologian, was concerned with holding on to the idea of God while avoiding the tendency in natural theology to treat God as a thing or an abstract object to be debated. Within a Judeo-Christian framework, God is perceived as a personal creator being, never to be conceived or thought of as a thing. In his most famous work, *I and Thou* (1923), Buber rejects the "I-it" encounter engendered by natural theology and argues for an I-Thou relationship with God, showing a mutual exchange that treats neither party as an object.

Buber's idea of God is that the I-Thou relationship with God underlies all others. The whole of existence stands in a relationship with God, which leads people into a special religious experience of the world. He wrote:

> For those who enter into the absolute relationship, nothing particular retains any importance—neither things nor beings, neither earth nor heaven—but everything is included in the relationship. For entering into the pure relationship does not involve ignoring everything but seeing everything in the You, not renouncing the world but placing it upon its proper ground.

Agnosticism

Although many thinkers believe that the existence of God can be established by way of rational or natural evidence, revelation or experience, a different conclusion is that of the agnostic, who maintains that insufficient rational evidence can establish either the existence of God or nonexistence of a supreme being. Therefore agnostics declare that they do not know, which is the literal meaning of agnostic. An agnostic will withhold opinion until such a time as more decisive evidence is available to support one side or the other.

Arguments Against the Existence of God

Some thinkers say that no satisfactory rational evidence can prove God's existence. We now look briefly at three of the arguments against the existence of God.

The Sociological Challenge

Emile Durkheim (1858–1917) wrote *The Elementary Forms of the Religious Life,* in which he set out his sociological theory of religion. His main thesis was that God, or the gods whom people worship, are imaginary beings unconsciously fabricated by society for the purpose of controlling the thoughts and behavior of its citizens. Because we are social beings who need support from others during difficult times, we draw strength from being part of a group. So, the argument goes, just as God demands the sacred obedience of his laws from all believers, society also demands loyalty and obedience to its customs and laws, which are as sovereign as God's commandments.

In effect, Durkheim maintains that what humankind has done is to transform the natural requirements of society into a personified shape known as "God." One criticism of this view is that the theory fails to account for the universal nature of religion, which is concerned equally for all humanity, not just one particular society. Critics also claim that Durkheim does not explain the far-reaching claims of morality, which travel far beyond the everyday requirements of society.

Others point out that his theory fails to explain the power of conscience, which has often detached the individual from the laws of society, e.g., Martin Luther, Gandhi.

God as Psychological Projection

Ludwig Andreas Feuerbach (1804–1872) was one of the most talked-about philosophers in Europe in the 1840s. He had enormous influence on Marx and Freud. In 1830 Feuerbach published anonymously his *Thoughts on Death and Immortality*, in which he denied the existence of an immortal soul. This publication finished his career as an academic. In 1841 he published his enormously successful *The Essence of Christianity.* In 1842 Feuerbach transferred from studying theology at Heidelberg University to studying philosophy in Berlin under Hegel. Feuerbach was a humanist in that he believed humankind was the basis and starting point of all philosophical discourse. Religion was a fundamental expression of a person's deepest feelings. He said that "religion is the dream of the human mind." His focus was on anthropology, for finding out about God meant that you would find out about human beings. Christians have traditionally believed in the incarnation of Christ—that is, God becoming human. But for Feuerbach the human is in fact God, and Man has created God in his own image. Accordingly, the logical extension is that

> There is no supernatural; only the natural world exists.
>
> Religion is sociological, cultural, and psychological.

Feuerbach was not speaking about individual humans, but of Humankind as a whole. He believed that with social progress all religion would finally disappear. Feuerbach also pointed out that religion alienates people from their own nature. What is good in human beings is ascribed to God, and people are emptied of their own good qualities. This stance is psychologically harmful, as on this basis people cannot possibly know themselves as long as they deny the best part of themselves and say it comes from God. Feuerbach's whole approach is well summed up in this quotation from his *Essence of Christianity* (1841):

> The historical progress of religion consists therefore in this: That what an earlier religion took to be objective, it later took to be subjective; what formerly was taken to be God, and worshipped as such, is now recognized to be something human. What was earlier religion is later taken to be idolatry; humans are seen to have adored their own nature.

As a psychological explanation for belief in God, Feuerbach's writing is very convincing. "What man wishes to be, he makes his God." However, religion has not disappeared with social progress, as he predicted. Feuerbach's method does not necessarily lead to atheism. He was already an atheist before he ever started writing. The theologian Karl Barth summed up his own criticisms of Feuerbach in saying:

> Feuerbach discussed Man in general, and in attributing to him divinity had, in fact, not said anything about Man as he is in reality.

Feuerbach may be right in saying that many aspects of God are simply inventions of man, but does being able to talk about God in a human way mean that God is necessarily no more than a human product? Is atheism, then, Feuerbach's own personal projection?

Summary: The Question of Validity

How valid are all these proofs? People like Hume say that we should just suspend judgment and remain skeptics. Others like Pascal and Kant reject the traditional proofs and instead put forward practical grounds or reasons for accepting God's existence. Pascal's famous wager is an appeal to pragmatism; in view of the eternal consequences, betting on the existence of God makes sense.

The debate about the existence and nonexistence of God continues through the present day. Much contemporary philosophy of religion focuses on questions surrounding the use of language when referring to God. Following Hume, philosophers such as A. J. Ayer and A. G. N. Flew have argued that talk about God is as cognitively meaningless as mere gibberish, since it is incapable of empirical verifiability or falsifiability. A conclusive proof is not available for the existence of God; neither is there conclusive proof of God's nonexistence. The question of God's existence remains open.

Chapter 3
Ethics and Religion: The Meaning of Morality

Every person who reflects upon situations or troubles in his or her daily life is a philosopher of ethics to some extent. The difference between the thoughts of a lay person and the reflections of a professional philosopher is often one of generalization. You might be trying to solve a particular problem due to your circumstances, whereas the philosopher tries to generalize and ask the big questions: What is the goal for which all human beings should strive? Is it happiness, pursuit of pleasure, or doing one's duty? This kind of abstract thinking is called "ethical theory," and both the world of philosophy/metaphysics and the world's religions have much to say about the human concern for what is right and wrong or good and evil.

In ethical theory, the two approaches are subjective and objective. A subjective approach either expresses human feelings and intuitions about what is right or a personal prescribed course of action. An objective approach recognizes that features of the natural world and of human beings make a particular action right or wrong. Subjective approaches produce criteria for moral action that are personal and individual, and objective approaches produce criteria that can be universally applied. Generally speaking, the world's religions accept the objective approach, relying on divine revelation, natural law, sacred texts, and religious teaching to form the theoretical basis for moral actions. Unit 6:4 offers an introduction to the world's religions and moral action.

In this chapter we look at the world of Western philosophy through a brief tour of six ethical theories: absolutism (Plato), virtue ethics (Aristotle), natural law (St. Thomas Aquinas), deontology (Immanuel Kant), utilitarianism (John Stuart Mill), and contractarianism (John Rawls). All these theories deal with questions such as, "How ought people behave?" and "What is the good life for humankind?" We then look at a number of ethical theories both ancient and modern.

For example, one philosophical theory is hedonism, an ancient classical theory which argues that the good life is ultimately one of pleasure. Many theoreticians have found this theory plausible, but when studied carefully certain defects appear; for example, what about harmful pleasures (e.g., hard drugs like heroin) that give momentary intense pleasure but may lead to a life of suffering and misery? Living a good life cannot be identical with a life of pleasure when those pleasures are bad. So if pleasure is not the basis of the good life, then what is? Philosophers study ethics partly to form satisfactory answers to such questions.

A Brief Survey of Ethical Theories

Skeptical Theories

Skeptical theories seriously doubt or limit moral institutions. Among these theories are philosophies that can be considered amoral or that embrace moral relativism.

The *amoral approach* holds that "Morality is just a way people try to control one another or themselves." *Moral relativists* maintain the absence of universally binding moral standards or absolutes. In contrast to other forms of relativism, moral relativism is the view that moral standards are grounded in social custom. Arguments for moral relativism are based on two main beliefs:

1. A belief in de facto values—our moral thinking should be based on how people actually behave (de facto) and not on an ideal standard of how people should behave (ideal values).
2. A belief in cultural variation—that our moral values vary from culture to culture.

Nonskeptical Theories

The more traditional approaches from Western philosophy can be grouped as nonskeptical theories. Among these, classical theories tend to search for "the Good Life." Examples of nonskeptical theories follow.

Divine command/ontological theories (Plato, Calvin, C. S. Lewis) hold that the right thing to do is what God commands (or in Plato, according to the ideal forms) as revealed in conscience, natural law, and the scriptures. This view can be both rigid or flexible depending on how the scriptures are read.

For *virtue theories* (Aristotle, Aquinas), the good life is a life of virtue: courage, love, honor, etc. A more modern expression of this approach is found in self-actualization theory (Maslow), in the realization of one's actual potentials. Virtue ethics today is particularly associated with Alasdair MacIntyre and his recent work *After Virtue: A Study in Moral Theory.*

Natural law theories (Lao Tse, the Stoics) maintain that the good life exists only if people live according to nature and its laws.

Consequential theories focus on the consequences of an action or a policy. Examples of consequential theores are

- Utilitarianism (Jeremy Bentham, John Stuart Mill): What is right consists in what leads to the greatest good or happiness for the greatest number of people.
- Ethical egoism (social Darwinism): What is right is what each person perceives to be in his or her rational self-interest.
- Social contract theory (Hobbes, Locke, Rawls): What is right requires social rules that benefit the greatest number in society.

Deontological theories (Kant) are primarily concerned not with the consequences but with the internal form or character of actions. Right actions consist of doing one's duty or protecting human rights, regardless of consequences that may happen.

Plato: Absolutism

Personal character:	What kind of life should I live?
Ethical principle:	To conform to the Forms (The Ideals that constitute ultimate reality).
Basis of value:	The Form of Goodness (an absolute, unchanging, objective, ideal reality).
Ethical methodology:	To think out the nature of an unchanging ideal. Use of analogies.
Practical example:	Lying is wrong because it does not conform to the Form of Truth.

Plato (b. 428/427 B.C.E.) held the fundamental belief that evil is due to a lack of knowledge; if people could find out what is right ("the good"), they would not act badly. To find the good, however, people must first acquire certain levels of knowledge through the study of various disciplines such as philosophy or mathematics. Plato did not think that knowledge was a prerequisite to living a good life, but he did think that people who acquire such knowledge would lead a good life. Plato also thought that there is basically only one good life for all to lead, which is not to be understood by human inclination or opinion. Goodness exists independently of human beings and their experience (absolutism) and can be discovered if people are properly trained. The ethical theory of Plato has especially influenced Christianity, Judaism, and Islam. Criticisms of Plato's thinking are well documented. For example, critics charge that moral knowledge is not analogous to scientific or mathematical knowledge, and Plato's error was to imagine it was.

Aristotle: Virtue Ethics

Personal character:	What kind of person should I be?
Ethical principle:	Develop the soul in accordance with virtue and rationality.
Basis of value:	Human well-being is achieved through understanding and following God's final purpose.
Ethical methodology:	Understand what is "good" and achieve a balance between the extremes of excess and deficiency.
Practical example:	Lying is wrong as it is outside of the mean between the defect of understatement and the excess of boastfulness. Lying is therefore not virtuous.

Aristotle's most influential thinking on ethics and his related ideas on political theory are to be found in his *Nicomachean Ethics* and *Politics*. Although Aristotle (384–322 B.C.E.) was a great metaphysician, his ethical theory took a scientific/empirical approach. He therefore concentrated on examining the behavior and talk of everyday people, which led him to the conclusion that for most people the goal of life was happiness. He accepted the idea that all things by nature seek their own good, and that everyone would therefore agree that human beings' final good is happiness. What Aristotle meant by happiness has preoccupied philosophers for centuries. His famous definition is that happiness "is an activity of the soul in accord with perfect virtue." On examination of his writings one explanation (not the only one) is that Aristotle conceived of happiness as an activity rather than a goal. Generally people think that happiness is something to be arrived at in life, that by behaving in certain ways happiness will be ours.

This approach is wrong: Happiness is behaving with moral virtue, human habits or dispositions to choose to act as would a virtuous person. While we all possess natural capacities for virtue or for evil, the good traits must become habits through discipline and practice. In other words we all become virtuous by doing virtuous things, at first through early training but later through choice. Aristotle wrote:

> Arguments and teaching surely do not influence everyone, but the soul of the student needs to have been prepared by habits

> for enjoying and hating finely, like ground that is to nourish seed. For someone whose life follows his feelings would not even listen to an argument turning him away, or comprehend it; and in that state how could he be persuaded to change? And in general feelings seem to yield to force, not to argument. . . . (*Aristotle*, Nichomachean Ethics, *Book X, section 9*)

Aristotle went on to specify what kinds of actions lead to happiness:

- He introduced the mathematical idea of the mean. Action is a response to desire, and an individual may respond to desire either in an excessive way or a deficient way. The virtuous person follows a middle path or mean between these two.
- The mean is not an equal distance between two extremes but in morals the mean is relative to us, to our individual status or our given situation.

Aristotle's thinking is far more diverse than this short discussion allows. Although we do not have the space to discuss it in this book, his influence has been considerable on world religions.

St. Thomas Aquinas: Natural Law

Personal character:	What kind of person should I be?
Ethical principle:	Promote good and avoid evil. Family, knowledge, and ordered society are good.
Basis of value:	Human nature and the universe as created and determined by God.
Ethical methodology:	Examine human inclinations. Reason and think about the nature of law.
Practical example:	Lying is wrong because of the natural human inclination to reject ignorance and avoid giving offense to others; lying is therefore harmful in an ordered society.

Natural law is based on the belief that an intelligible and consistent order exists independent of either human opinion or human invention and that this order is a source for keeping moral commands and conduct. Natural law is prominent in Eastern religions—in the understanding of the Tao, for example. In the West, the first major expansion of the view came from St. Thomas Aquinas in the thirteenth century. Natural law is based on the ideas of Aristotle and has become central to Roman Catholic moral thinking. According to Aquinas, the eternal law of God is received by humans partly though the old law of the Ten Commandments (see the Bible, Exodus 20) and the new law of Christ's teaching in the Gospels, and also partly through what is open to our own human discernment in natural law.

In the context of the laws of nature, natural law is the basis of all science and the outworking of observing what happens in nature. Traditionally the natural law theory of ethics relies on the religious concept of a God who creates the universe with a purpose and end in mind. Humans are therefore expected to understand what that end is and act in accordance with it, if they are to do right.

Immanuel Kant: Deontology

Personal character:	What should I do?
Ethical principle:	The categorical imperative: act only upon the principle that you would be willing to have everyone act upon. People are to be treated as ends in themselves and not as a means to an end.
Basis of value:	The ultimate fairness of the universe. Rationality involves a reverence for reason and human autonomy.
Ethical methodology:	The human experience of moral obligation, the categorical imperative, and being consistent.
Practical example:	Lying is wrong because the idea of everyone doing it is inconsistent, therefore impossible, and hence cannot be willed.

The overwhelming consensus amongst philosophical thinkers is that Immanuel Kant (1724–1804) was a man with true greatness of mind. A. M. Quinton said of him that "he came as near as anyone ever has to combining in himself the speculative originality of Plato with the encyclopedic thoroughness of Aristotle."

Kantian ethics starts with the concept of freedom. His famous phrase "ought implies can" assumes that people ought to seek the higher good where virtue and happiness coincide. He also argued that the moral law requires that people be rewarded proportionately according to their measure of virtue. This outcome, of course, is not always seen in everyday life since the nonvirtuous person is often happier or more successful than the virtuous. Therefore, argues Kant, another existence must come after death in which the virtuous are rewarded. From this belief comes the conclusion that God and an eternal life exist.

The main focus of Kant's ethics is to answer the question of difference: In what sense is a moral action different from a nonmoral action? Kant answered this question by distinguishing two kinds of action:

- Acts done from "inclination"
- Acts done from a "sense of duty"

Acting out of inclination is to act out of preference. *I could watch a movie tonight or go see a friend. It is up to me to do what I am inclined to do.* But if I have promised to help my mother, then I ought to fulfill my obligation. "Inclination" is different that obligation. Obligation is what I ought to do despite my inclination.

Kant rejected moral theories that proposed acting on inclination alone. He believed that a moral act has to be the act of a free agent and that morality is closely allied to doing one's duty and obligation. Human beings ought therefore to strive to develop "good wills" so that they act in accordance with the dictates of reason. The rational person is free to choose.

Critics of Kant immediately launch an objection to his views: How can a person determine duty in different situations? Kant's phrase "the categorical imperative" is an attempt at an answer. He wrote,

> There is therefore but one categorical imperative, namely this: act only on that maxim whereby thou canst at the same time will that it should become a universal law. (*Groundwork of the Metaphysic of Morals,* 1785.)

Kant means that each action done should be considered in the light of what would happen if everybody did what you were doing. We should therefore treat people as ends in themselves because that is how we see ourselves. To treat someone only as a means of achieving what we want is to disregard his or her humanity and to show disrepect for his or her status as a rational human being.

Kant's moral thinking opposed utilitarianism (see next section). He believed that morality is found in the motive of the act. People who just do good through fear of reprisal or punishment are not moral. Acts are moral only if the person involved understands the duty to do the right thing.

John Stuart Mill: Utilitarianism

Personal character:	What should I do?
Ethical principle:	Maximize benefits over harms for the greatest number of people involved.
Basis of value:	Human happiness as conceived by the persons involved in the decision.
Ethical method:	Moral action based on a rational decision of what is the greatest good for the greatest number.
Practical example:	Lying is wrong, if and when it fails to maximize benefits over harms for the greatest number affected.

Utilitarianism has had a long and tenacious existence as a moral theory. In Britain and America many philosophers still accept it. John Stuart Mill (1806–1873) was the most eminent of a group of nineteenth-century British philosophers who developed the moral theory of utilitarianism. His starting point was the work of

Jeremy Bentham (1758–1832), a radical reformer who first expounded the idea of "the greatest happiness of the greatest number" as a moral principle. This concept was known as the principle of utility. Mill's most important works are *On Liberty* (1859), which is a strong defense of liberty for the individual; *A System of Logic* (1843), an empiricist approach to philosophical problems; *Dissertations and Discussions* (1859–75); and *Utilitarianism* (1863). Towards the end of his life he wrote *The Subjection of Women* (1869), which was a powerful case for equality between the sexes.

The utilitarian view is that actions are judged by their consequences and the amount of pleasure that everybody obtains from those consequences. The aim of utilitarianism is for the greatest happiness of the greatest number. In *Utilitarianism* he stated, "The creed of utility holds that actions are right in proportion as they tend to promote happiness, wrong as they tend to promote the reverse of happiness." In the last chapter of *Utilitarianism* Mill addresses people who object to his view that happiness is the highest moral value. The objection, stated briefly, is that happiness cannot be the ultimate value because in so many of life's situations, justice is put above happiness. In response, Mill put forward an impressive number of arguments designed to illustrate that although justice is highly important in the hierarchy of human values, justice does not rule the happiness principle but serves it. In the last analysis, Mill did not succeed in overcoming the objection.

Act Utilitarianism and Rule Utilitarianism

More recently, utilitarianism has been subdivided into act utilitarianism/situation ethics and rule utilitarianism. Act utilitarianism puts forward the view that each individual action taken should be assessed on the results that are produced from it. What is right is whatever leads to the greatest good or happiness for the greatest number in each case. So, for example, if you offer your time to help a charity, you must try and estimate how much happiness is accrued from that action on that occasion. Rule utilitarianism, as put forth by Peter Singer, does not concern itself with individual acts but with the usefulness of a rule for action itself. The right action is that which, as a rule, leads to the greatest good or happiness for the greatest number. For example, "Everyone should help with charity work." The idea here is to do what is best for the greatest number, even if on one particular occasion less happiness may result. Act utilitarianism asks, "What will be the result of my action in this situation?" Rule utilitarianism asks, "What if everyone did that, what would be the result?"

Social Contract Theory

Some philosophers (Hobbes, Locke, Rousseau, Paine, J. S. Mill, and Rawls) have put forward ethical theories based on a social contract. In such a contract, people agree to abide by certain rules; people limit what they are able to do in the interests of benefiting society and allowing everyone some measure of freedom and security. In social contract theory, the rights of an individual and the needs of society are balanced.

John Rawls: Contractarianism (a form of social contract theory)

Focal point:	Institutions—what social arrangements should be adopted?
Ethical principle:	Just arrangements are fair. First, individuals have equal rights to maximum compatible liberty. Individual rights imply social responsibilities that limit the expression of human freedom and action for the sake of the wider interests of the community. Second, economic inequalities are only allowed if they benefit the least advantaged.
Basis of value:	Human well-being as determined by rational self-interest.
Methodology:	Considered judgments and reflection. Reasoning about hypothetical and actual cases.
Practical example:	Lying cannot be a justified part of social behavior because of its incompatibility with similar liberty being granted to all.

Updating the Past: Modern Moral Theories

If we read Plato's *Republic* or Aristotle's *Ethics*, we would embrace the idea that despite the various preferences of individuals a rational basis for the idea of goodness and justice ultimately exists that arises from the nature of human life itself or the needs of a society to organize itself in an effective and harmonious way. Since about the time of Kant, moral theory has tended to draw away from looking heavenward to God as the giver of natural law. The quest is now on looking for the moral law within. Clues to God's existence and the way life should be lived are often sought within the realm of human experience, including emotional, psychological, aesthetic, and spiritual experience.

Ethics in the twentieth century has mostly centered around the meaning of moral statements and whether it is possible to discern if they are true or false. Among the primary approaches in twentieth-century ethics are

- *Intuitionism.* Key thinker: G. E. Moore, *Principia Ethica* (1903). "One knows instinctively when something is right."
- *Emotivism.* Key thinkers: A. J. Ayer, *Language, Truth and Logic* (1936); C. L. Stevenson, *Ethics and Language* (1947). With emotivism, people

use moral statements not to discern what is true or false but to express personal feelings about an issue (e.g., the statement, "Abortion is bad," is equivalent to "I disapprove of abortion") and influence the feelings of other people. To say that something is "good" means that a person should approve of it. To say that something is wrong is really another way of saying that you do not approve of it.

- *Prescriptivism.* Key thinker: M. Hare, *The Language of Morals* (1952). The view that the primary function of moral judgment is to prescribe a course of action.

Hedonism, Cynicism, and Stoicism

Hedonism

Epicurus (341–270 B.C.E.) held a view, sometimes called "Hedonism," which is the belief that pleasure is the sole good.

"Pleasure is 'the alpha and omega of the blessed life. . . . The first and native good.'" (Diogenes Laertius 10.128, 129) The ethical theory of Epicurus revolves around advice given for living in moderation but pleasurably and without suffering from any of the effects of pleasure. For the Epicurean the supreme pleasure is *ataraxia*, which is the calm serenity when the soul is at peace, "By pleasure we mean the absence of pain in the body and trouble in the mind." (Diogenes Laertius 10.131) The idea of pleasure could involve physical and sensual pleasure in the ancient Greek world; the Epicureans were famous for their disciplined lifestyles.

Cynicism

Cynicism is a doctrine with an antisocial focus; it is one of the forerunners of asceticism. The theory revolves around a negative view of civilization. The outworkings of civilized society—e.g., private property, religion, marriage, possessions, etc.—are worthless and artificial.

For the cynic, the only thing that matters is virtue, and virtue is an action, not a theory. If salvation and truth are to be found, society needs to be rejected in favor of a return to the simple life, free of refinements. Happiness cannot be found in material things that betray you in the end. "May the sons of your enemies live in luxury," said Diogenes. (Diogenes Laertius 6.8)

Early cynics such as Diogenes and Antiochenes lived in very frugal conditions Diogenes even attempted to eat his food raw.

The cynics were notorious in their day, for they did the most private things in full public view, with the belief that if it was right to do something, it could be done anywhere. (Diogenes Laertius 6.69) Their beliefs renounced both the ancient gods and the belief in pleasure. Pleasure is the enemy of life and toil (*ponos*) is the supreme good. Love, therefore, is also an enemy, for it makes a person the slave of their desires and passions. Cynicism has played a great role in influencing the monastic way of life and also pietistic religions.

Stoicism

Stoicism flourished, like cynicism, during the time of the collapse of the Greek city-states and the Alexandrian Empire. Stoics shared with cynics the desire to transcend external influences. They believed that good or evil depends on the individual, but the Stoics also believed in the predestined, preconceived plan of God for the world: "God is near you, with you, within you. I say it, Lucilius, a holy spirit sits within us, spectator of our evil and our good, our guardian." (Seneca, Letters 41.12)

Everything that happens in life happens by the will of God. The question arises as to how ethics can be discussed at all in such a system. If everything is decreed by God, how do human beings come into the equation at all? The stoic answer is that the all-important thing in human behavior is to choose to willingly accept the will of God. The power we have is one of assent. We can either assent to the will of God or we can struggle against it. Assenting to the will of God is freedom, but the person who struggles to change things is not free. By practicing indifference to events, you put yourself in the right frame of mind because outside events cannot then influence your fundamental character. The aim is to free yourself from desires and passions. The supreme good is the use of the will to accept what God (or nature) has decreed; the supreme evil, therefore, is emotion. Emotion is like a disease; there is a need for cleansing so that a person can endure the greatest pain and tragedy and still say that each circumstance is the will of God.

Baruch Spinoza

Spinoza (1632–1677) was a Jewish philosopher who was excommunicated from the Jewish community in 1656. He was reported as denying the law of Moses and the immortality of the soul. His major work, *Ethics* (1677), was published after his death. Spinoza's ethical theories could be characterized as predeterministic and relativistic. According to Spinoza, "All things which come to pass, come to pass according to the eternal order and fixed laws of nature." (*Ethics*) Spinoza was a relativist in that he believed that nothing is good or bad in itself, but only in relation to other people, circumstances, or things.

Given these two aspects of his thinking, Spinoza said that the good life exists when a person possesses a certain attitude to the world, which consists of a rational part (recognizing that all events are determined) and an emotional part (accepting that alll things are determined). He used the idea of eternity to give a context to the challenges of life. All events are part of a larger world: eternity, the natural pattern of things. To adjust your thinking to this view is to be liberated from the slavery of emotion, and hence to live the good life.

Many philosophers have pointed to the complexity of Spinoza's philosophy; his *Ethics* is a difficult text. This brief summary is only an introduction to his frame of thinking. Criticism of Spinoza bears similarity to the criticisms leveled against stoicism. Neither philosophy deals with the conflict between determinism and free will. If things are determined in nature, then we are effectively powerless to alter our attitudes, which are part of nature.

Summary

The classical (metaphysical) ethical theories suggest that if a person develops the right character or attitude, then proper actions will naturally follow. Ethical theorists are not so much concerned with specific actions but more with what tends to make someone the right kind of person. This branch of philosophers looks at actions in the light of what will help us to develop character, i.e., which actions help develop character and right attitude? How can I live the good life according to how things are meant to be (God's word or Nature)? Ethical theorists have been accused of vagueness compared to contemporary approaches.

Consequential theories stress the importance of considering the implications of one's actions. No one can be sure if an action is right until they see how others (or with egoism, oneself) will be affected. Utilitarianism has been popular with many governments and policy makers because it addresses the need to work for everyone's welfare. Yet this approach has been accused of overlooking the rights of minorities.

Deontological theories stress the importance of maintaining rights and fairness. They uphold the idea of strong limits, principles, and absolutes that need to be maintained, or society might be tempted to justify evil for the sake of expediency. Deonotologists are often criticized on grounds of inflexibility.

A Modern Ethical Debate: Alasdair MacIntyre

Morality, according to twentieth-century moral philosopher Alasdair MacIntyre, is not what it used to be. In the Aristotelian tradition of ancient Greece and medieval Europe, morality enabled the transformation from untutored human nature (as it happened to be) to human nature that could be realized if it understood its *telos* (fundamental goal). Eventually, he argues, belief in Aristotelian teleology declined, leaving the idea of imperfect human nature in conflict with the perfectionist aims of morality. This conflict doomed any attempt to justify the claims of morality, whether based on emotion (e.g., Hume) or on reason (Kant).

MacIntyre concludes that, as a result, ethical discourse and moral practice in the contemporary world are hollow; although the language and appearance of morality remains, the substance is no longer there. As a result of the Enlightenment's failed attempt to justify morality on its own terms, MacIntyre argues that we are left with nothing more than shards of a once complete and coherent moral tradition. The current state of morality, in MacIntyre's view, is a form of emotivism. In this view, moral thought and action are not a matter of facts, but of taste: expressions of a person's own preferences and emotions. To say that something is wrong, therefore, is really just another way of indicating disapproval.

Chapter 4
Science and Religion

We have seen that in past centuries, scientific and religious questions were often confused. On the one hand, literalists treated the Bible as a textbook in science. On the other, well-meaning scientists and theologians invoked the "God of the gaps" to explain the scientifically unknown, while naturalists and modernists tried to base theology on the findings of science. It is not surprising that twentieth-century thinkers wanted to preserve the integrity of both science and religion, and took great pains to put up No Trespassing *signs between them.*

Ian Barbour, *Science and Religion*

In the past, religion and science were in much closer agreement with each other than they are today. Until about the sixteenth century, philosophers and theologians were the scientists of their age.

- Nicolaus Copernicus (1473–1543 C.E.) was an astonomer. He was engaged by the Church to formulate an accurate calendar. His research led him to solve the laws of motion of the Sun and the Moon. The most significant feature of Copernicus's mathematical observations was his conclusion that the Sun was at the center of the universe and that the universe was heliocentric; that is, the Earth went around the Sun, as did the other planets, and only the Moon revolved around the Earth.
- Johannes Kepler (1571–1630 C.E.) discovered the three laws of planetary motion. Based on Kepler's work, Isaac Newton went on to discover the universal laws of gravity. Kepler held Christian beliefs that persuaded him that he would find order in the universe, as it was evidence of God's design.

- Galilei Galileo (1564–1642 C.E.) was the first astronomer to make systematic observation of the universe through a telescope. His investigations led to the realization that we did not live in a closed, Earth-centered universe but in the cosmic sphere of space. In his *Dialogue Concerning the Two Chief World Systems* (1632), he proved that the movement of the planets was natural and not the result of a prime mover. Yet this proof did not lead him to abandon his Christian faith; instead he said that the Bible must be metaphorical. Even after his discoveries, Galileo accepted that studying the universe equated with discovering more about God.
- Isaac Newton (1642–1727 C.E.) discovered the universal law of gravity, which states that the force of attraction between any two masses anywhere in the universe is proportional to the product of the two masses divided by the distance between them. Newton adopted a Christian worldview, believing that because human beings were made in the image of God, they had knowledge about God's creation. However, many of his successors abandoned their religious beliefs. Scientific discovery began to view the universe as governed by a set of unbreakable natural laws that could be found and understood by the process of scientific inquiry. Mathematics and experiments rather than philosophy became the arbitrators of truth. Religion and science began to separate. Many people with a scientific worldview now envisaged a universe that was like a machine with all the parts working together, in contrast to the former view that the world was a creation of God. Religion had become the "God of the Gaps," explaining features that science still did not understand. Scientists no longer needed to refer to God for their explanation of how the physical world operated.

Although the huge range of material on scientific understandings of the world cannot be included in a book of this nature, this chapter addresses some of the questions that science poses to religion. The chapter includes

- A summary of Charles Darwin's theory of natural selection
- A review of the creation-and-evolution debate
- A look back at science and religion in the twentieth century

Charles Darwin: The Challenge to the Teleological Argument for the Existence of God

In the early nineteenth century, the popular author William Paley argued that the magnificence of nature itself demonstrated the existence of an intelligent and benign creator. Paley wrote:

> Were there no example in the world, of contrivance, except that of the eye, it would be alone sufficient to support the conclusion which we draw from it, as to the necessity of an intelligent Creator. (William Paley, *Natural Theology: or Evidences of the Existence and Attributes of the Deity, Collected from the Appearances of Nature,* 1802; 19th ed., London: 1819).

In the West, the famous confrontation between science and religion in the middle and later nineteenth century has been associated with the publication of Charles Darwin's *On the Origin of Species by Means of Natural Selection* (1859). In this book he offered an agnostic model to account for the variety of species to be found in nature. But his later book, *The Descent of Man* (1871), evoked serious doubts about traditional Christian beliefs, such as the reality of the soul and origins of human conscience. Here Darwin (1809–1882) accounted for all human characteristics through the theory of natural selection from other life forms, reaching the conclusion that human beings descended from the apes. Darwin—who at one time had hoped to become a clergyman and who certainly did not see his theory as undermining belief in God—admitted that "many and grave objections" could be leveled against his "theory of descent with modification through natural selection." These objections included a famous quote from British Prime Minister Benjamin Disreali:

> What is the question now placed before society with a glib assurance the most astounding? The question is this: Is man an ape or an angel? I, my Lord, I am on the side of the angels.

Yet almost immediately Darwin's theory attracted support as Paley's had done, but with the added advantages of being able to account for apparently superfluous variations and also addressing the moral problem of suffering in the world without having to refer to a divine creator. Natural selection did not remove the element of design from the world, but gave a purely natural explanation of how it had come about—an explanation that appeared to make God redundant in the process.

The Evolution versus Creation Debate

Darwin's theory of evolution was seen to undermine the biblical account of creation for various reasons:

1. His theory showed how living things could develop in stages, concluding that such development could result from chance. This theory indicated that different forms of life were not finalized at the time of creation and therefore might not be the work of a designer.

2. The theory of evolution also indicated that life forms changed in accordance with their environment rather than the environment being created for the benefit of life forms, as is set out in the biblical account of creation in Genesis.
3. The "survival of the fittest" concept was not in keeping with natural theology's idea of a benevolent creator.

Darwin's attack was on the Christian belief that human beings were unique and made in God's image and also the belief that human beings have a spiritual soul that distinguishes them from the animals. Most recent evolutionary theories are in some way based on Darwin's theories. Although evolutionary theory is largely accepted in the scientific community, debate continues about the nature of life and its implications for religious belief.

Creationists maintain that the universe and everything in it were created directly by God and did not result from a long evolutionary process. Although many Christians and people of other faiths are still vigorous in their rejection of the theory of evolution, creationism is still a minority view. In today's world most of the scientific community and many Christians accept some form of evolutionary theory.

Creationists oppose the various theories of evolution for a number of reasons:

1. The records and findings of fossils show gaps; the evidence for evolutionary theory, therefore, is still incomplete.
2. An organism cannot be advanced into a higher life form by natural selection.
3. Scientists have never found the hypothetical link that must have occurred between apes and humans.

The Modern Sociobiological Debate

Since Jacques Monod's publication of *Chance and Necessity* (1970), a lively modern debate has ensued about the origins and evolution of the universe and the issue of random change and its implications. Monod argued for creative developments being possible through random chance. A more recent challenge to the teleological argument for God's existence comes from sociobiologists like Richard Dawkins. In *The Blind Watchmaker* (1986), he shows that random changes may lead to a multiple variety of apparently designed forms. His more recent book, *Climbing Mount Improbable* (1996), considers the improbability that atoms and molecules that are scattered (at the foot of the mountain) could ever assemble together and form complex entities like an eye (which represents the peak of this mountain of ascending complexity). He argues that the process of natural selection means that advantageous gene mutations are preserved and disadvantageous ones are rejected, thus providing a gradual path up the back of the mountain.

Following this process, complex forms will inevitably arise that are very well adapted to their environments. Dawkins employs computer simulations to show that with only a few variables, a wide range of complex shapes can emerge.

In contrast to Dawkins, John Polkinghorne (*Science and Creation* [1988]) argues that the probability of any single individual thing happening is so remote that the idea of the universe being controlled by blind chance is too improbable. He therefore puts forward the view that an overall intelligence accounts for it.

The Modern Debate between Science and Religion

Today, the debate regarding the existence of God has shifted. In Aquinas's day, his proofs were seen as scientific and theological at the same time. Now a visible gap exists between the languages of theology and science. As Barbour observes,

> For many centuries in the West, the Christian story of creation and salvation provided a cosmic setting in which individual life had significance. It allowed people to come to terms with guilt, finitude and death. It provided a total way of life, and it encouraged personal transformation and reorientation. Since the Enlightenment, the Christian story has had diminishing effectiveness for many people, partly because it has seemed inconsistent with the understanding of the world in modern science. Similar changes have been occurring in other cultures. (Ian Barbour, *Religion in an Age of Science*)

In the West, the ongoing relationship between science and religion has been variously described:

- The *conflict model*, in which science and religion diverge, can be seen in nineteenth-century books such as J. W. Draper's *History of the Conflict Between Religion and Science* (1874) and more recently in R. Dawkins *The Selfish Gene* (1989) and *Viruses of the Mind* (1992).
- The *convergence/assimilation* model takes an opposite view: the insights of religion are understood to express essentially the same truths as those claimed in modern science. Examples of this approach can be seen in F. Capra's *The Tao of Physics* (1979) and R. H. Jones's *Science and Mysticism: A Comparative Study of Western Natural Science, Theravada Buddhism and Advaita Vendanta* (1986).

Between these two extremes lie a number of ways of evaluating the relationship between science and religion. Even outside of these extremes resides a view that science and religion are such different enterprises that no valid connection can be made between them.

The conflict view continues to be popular in the West and among world religions which hold that the truth about creation is revealed in sacred texts, which conflict with scientific claims. However, one might argue equally that religion has inspired and provided resources for science, as has occurred in Islam (see S. H. Nasr, *Islamic Science: An Illustrated Study* [1976]). Furthermore, many of the greatest scientists in history believed in God: Newton, Boyle, Pasteur, Kepler, Copernicus, and Galileo, to name but a few. Today, John Polkinghorne affirms:

> I have spent most of my working life as a theoretical physicist and all of my consciously remembered life as part of the worshipping and believing community of the Church, so that I am someone who wants to take absolutely seriously the possibility of religious belief in a scientific age. (John Polkinghorne, "Religion in an Age of Science," McNair Lecture at the University of North Carolina, Chapel Hill, North Carolina, March 23, 1993.)

The Methods of Science and Religion

Today, a scientist and a religious believer who believe the same thing do so on different grounds. For the most part, science and religion rely on different methods. Science now works through the method of rational empiricism—that is, the rational examination of evidence. This approach can include a variety of methods:

- Observing and collecting data
- Forming a hypothesis based on the data
- Testing the hypothesis with experiments
- Induction, or working out a theory to account for the results of an experiment
- Checking out results by making predictions based on them
- Verifying the theory: testing it out by devising further experiments

Having undertaken these steps, you may think you have a virtual certainty about the knowledge gained by scientific method. Far from it. Philosopher David Hume (1711–1776) reasoned that however many examples of something you test, the possibility always exists that the next test you perform will prove you wrong. A careful scientist can form a well-argued hypothesis based on tested data, but the hypothesis can never be proved absolutely. Moreover, trust in empirical evidence rests largely on the view that the information that scientists collect is free from bias and personal interpretation.

During the twentieth century, however, the view that scientific data is neutral and uninterpreted was challenged by modern philosophers of science, including Karl Popper (*The Logic of Scientific Discovers* [1934], English translation [1959]), who argued very persuasively that all observation and data is interpreted, right from the start of the process. Some observers who take this view would argue that science in both its use of language and in its experience and methodology is a creative activity, a method that has much in common with the pursuit of religious inquiry.

Science and Religion in the Twentieth Century: Albert Einstein and the New Physics

Albert Einstein (1879–1955 C.E.) was born in the German city of Ulm, but grew up in Munich. He showed no real genius as a child. In 1901 he gave up his German citizenship and became a Swiss citizen. Einstein at first failed the entrance exam to study electrical engineering at Zurich Polytechnic, but he gained a place there a year later. After graduation, he failed to land an academic job and worked as a clerk in the Berne patent office.

Einstein rejected the notion of a personal God at an early age. He also rejected any fundamentalist reading of the Bible. If he embraced any philosophy it was the pantheism of Benedict Spinoza. Nonetheless, Einstein did have a religious reverence in the face of the universe.

Between 1904 and 1917 Einstein remade the world in his head. But to understand the importance of Einstein's work, we must first drop back a few years.

Physics before Einstein

Isaac Newton (1642–1727) had in 1686 given a mathematical expression for the force of gravity so that at last the movements of the heavens could be calculated. His mechanics had a deep significance. Once the present state and the forces operating in the universe were worked out, calculations about the future became possible. In theory, the entire future of the universe could be determined. Einstein inherited Newton's work on gravity and also the work of James Clerk Maxwell (1831–1879), whose theory (1873) concluded that light is an electromagnetic phenomenon. Maxwell's work was crucial to the understanding of electricity and magnetism. But Einstein also inherited a problem. Newton's theory showed that travel at the speed of light was possible, while Maxwell's work showed that this was impossible. Einstein then asked the crucial and original question: What happens if you move at the speed of light? The answer he posed was to revolutionize physics forever.

Einstein's Theory of Relativity

Until the twentieth century, scientists generally accepted that time and space were separate. But then Einstein developed his special theory of relativity (1905) dealing with high-speed motion, which led to his general theory of relativity (1915) addressing gravity. Einstein proved that time, space, energy, and mass are related to one another. Moreover, time and space are not fixed: Time depends on where a body is and how fast it is moving. He was able to demonstrate that a moving object increasingly slows down as it approaches the speed of light. The implications of this theory were mind-blowing at the time. For example, a person able to drive a car somewhere close to the speed of light might perceive events as happening in the present, whereas for another person traveling at a much slower rate, the events were long gone and in the past. Yet everything is actually happening at the same time. On the basis of Einstein's discovery of the theory of relativity, past, present, and future are indistinguishable.

Einstein's work showed that the observer was part of the process and that theories are "free creations of the human mind." For example,

- If you stand still on a beach, the waves move past you.
- If you are in a boat and move with the waves, you see no movement of the waves, just a straight line.

Both of these are perceptions and both are true, and Einstein showed that reality is like this. We may think we are standing still at a fixed point, but in fact we are moving. Einstein proved that time and space are not fixed and that absolute space and absolute time are no longer feasible; the theory of relativity has replaced them.

Einstein's general theory of relativity replaced the Newtonian theory of gravity. He showed that the universe contains a finite amount of energy. If you burn something or blow something up, the amount of energy in the universe does not increase; objects just change from one state to another. The energy in the universe always remains the same. Einstein's famous equation $E = mc^2$ states that energy resides in mass, in objects, and that energy is therefore matter and matter is energy. This theory sums up all action and creation in the universe and accounts for how stars continue to burn, how gravity bends light, how space is curved, and how the universe is expanding.

Einstein's work was astonishing, not least of all because of the beauty and spareness of his calculations. He worked without footnotes, he was ignorant to a large extent of the work of other scientists, but with an apparently effortless simplicity he worked out equations that, as he said, brought humankind "closer to the secrets of the Old One," by which he meant God.

Quantum Theory

Quantum theory was first put forward by the German physicist Max Planck (1858–1947) in 1900. Planck's work severed all connections with previous physics, which relied on the understanding of Newtonian physics that bodies obey fixed laws. The assumption of pre-quantum physics was that matter is solid and predictable and that in time it was possible to predict the behavior of matter in every situation. This certainty was lost with the arrival of quantum theory. If the theory of relativity deals with matter on a large scale, quantum theory does the same on a small scale, at levels lower than an atom. Werner Heisenberg (1901–1976) demonstrated that the smallest component parts of matter are subject to unpredictable fluctuations that appear to be spontaneous events. Heisenberg concluded that this effect is more than mere laboratory phenomenon. Matter itself is fundamentally uncertain, and any notion of absolutes must be abandoned.

Einstein argued against quantum theory, although his own work prepared the way for advances in it. He wrote to Max Born,

> Quantum mechanics is certainly imposing. But an inner voice tells me it is not yet the real thing. The theory says a lot, but does not really bring us any closer to the secret of the "Old One." I, at any rate, am convinced that he is not playing dice.

Summary: Einstein, God, the Universe, and Everything

Einstein's theories and the development of quantum theory have brought humanity face-to-face with the modern understanding of the universe. Einstein's physics also has implications for an understanding of God. In approaching the universe, many Christian believers acknowledge that their understanding of God must be cosmic as well as personal. John Polkinghorne is one such believer.

Polkinghorne is a British scientist who for twenty-five years was professor of mathematical physics at Cambridge. He distinguished himself in the field of elementary particle physics and in 1974 became a Fellow of the Royal Society. Five years later, Polkinghorne gave up a lucrative teaching appointment and again became a student, applying himself to the study of theology. He has published several books and articles in the fields of science and theology and has emerged as one of the world's leading thinkers attempting to correlate the labyrinth of quantum physics with the mysteries of the Christian faith.

Like theologian Thomas F. Torrance, Polkinghorne speaks about the extraordinary revolution presently taking place in human understanding, the shift from a Newtonian to an Einsteinian cosmology, and the second revolution embodied in the discovery of quantum theory. He also points to a third change in the picture that we hold of the physical world:

> A third change in our picture of the physical world is in terms of everyday physical processes—the so-called chaos theory has told us that intrinsic unpredictability, non-mechanical behavior is characteristic, not just of quantum theory in the subatomic roots of the world, but also of its everyday process. There are clouds as well as clocks around in the physical universe, and that means that the behavior of these systems relies in a sort of oxymoronic combination of order and disorder—"on the edge of chaos," as people sometimes say—halfway between a totally rigid world that would be sterile because nothing really would change in it, and a totally random world which would be sterile because it would be completely haphazard. In between, in the balanced interplay between a degree of order and a degree of openness, is the fruitfulness of this universe. (John Polkinghorne, interview with Lyndon F. Harris, General Theological Seminary, New York City, spring 1997.)

Summary

The universe is now a different place from the one scientists, philosophers, and theologians of previous generations had thought they knew. Space, time, energy, and matter are all interconnected. But while relativity theory and quantum theory work in their respective spheres, they do not fit together. The task facing modern physics is to develop a complete unified theory that will link these two perceptions.

As both a scientist and a theologian John Polkinghorne says,

> I'm a very passionate believer in the unity of knowledge. . . . Somewhere they've all got to fit together. I want to put them together in a way that respects the different characters of each level that I experience, as well as the fact that the experience is of one reality. I want a consonant relationship, for example, between science and theology. Science cannot tell theology how to construct a doctrine of creation, but you can't construct a doctrine of creation without taking account of the age of the universe and the evolutionary character of cosmic history. I also think we need to maintain distinctions—the doctrine of creation is different from a scientific cosmology, and we should resist the temptation, which sometimes scientists give in to, to try to assimilate the concepts of theology to the concepts of science. There is a distinction that needs to be maintained.

Chapter 5
The Problem of Evil and Suffering

Our greatest evils grow from ourselves.
Jean Jacques Rousseau, *Emile* (1762)

God seeks comrades and claims love, the Devil seeks slaves and claims obedience.
Rabindranath Tagore, *Fireflies* (1928)

Philosophers, theologians, poets, and writers all speak of evil in different ways. Philosopher Immanuel Kant thought that the only evil thing was the evil human will. Frederic Nietzsche said that a pure act of will, exercising real freedom, takes one "beyond good and evil." But for ordinary people the issue is more practical. The world has seen a history of human suffering, pain, and sickness. Today the senseless murder of individuals, the devastation of war, and the abuse of children often cause law-abiding people to feel that evil is triumphant. In the chaos and suffering of life the big questions are often asked: "Why is this happening to me/them/the world?" "How can there be a good God when all this happens?" "Who is responsible for this?" "What can I do about this?"

This chapter looks briefly at

- Satan: evil personified and belief in the devil in the Western world
- Evil as the perversion of good
- The problem of evil: How do Christian and non-Christian thinkers try to reconcile evil and suffering in the world with God's power and goodness?

- Does God intervene in evil: the issue of miracles
- Theodicies and process theology
- Eschatological solutions to evil

Satan: Evil Personified

Islam, Judaism, and Christianity all speak of Satan, who is variously the enemy of God, the representative of the forces of evil, and the tempter. In Islam the Qur'an names the devil as Iblis, derived from the Arabic *balasa,* "he despaired" (of the mercy of God). He is also called al-Shaitan, that is, Satan, the enemy of God. He was an angel created from fire and therefore thought himself superior to that which was created from earth. When the angels bowed down before Adam at his creation, Iblis rebelled, thinking himself greater. To this day he tempts human beings, yet the Qur'an is clear that Satan's power is limited over human beings.

> When you recite the Qur'an, seek refuge in God from accursed Satan: no power has he over those who believe and put their trust in the Lord. He has power only over those who befriend him and those who serve other gods beside God. (*The Koran,* Penguin Books, 1993)

Islam also has a belief that everyone has a personal angel who encourages him or her to good actions and a personal shaitan, who urges them to do evil.

Judaism

In Judaism the development of the idea of Satan appears mainly in the later books of the Bible, as in the prologue to Job where "The Satan" is a heavenly figure in the court of God who is given the task of testing God's servants. He is also identified with the serpent in the Garden of Eden who tempted Eve to eat of the forbidden fruit. In 1 Chronicles 21:1, King David decided to number the people of Israel by census. This action is attributed to Satan. In Jewish scripture, however, evil spirits are mentioned more than Satan. Evil spirits spread sickness (Psalm 91:6), they are responsible for insanity (1 Samuel 16:15), and their main task is to deceive the people of God (1 Kings 22). Even though Jewish scripture attributes such activity to evil spirits in the world, dualism is avoided. God is in control of the earth, and therefore even evil spirits must be from God. In the Apocrypha, Satan represents the forces of evil. The rabbis taught that he was responsible for all the sins recorded in the Bible and, according to one interpretation, the shofar is blown on Rosh Hashanah in order to confuse him.

Christianity

The description of the devil in the New Testament is a developed one. Theologians think that the literature written between the testaments—such as the Apocrypha, which was influenced by Persian Zoroastrianism—influenced later Jewish demonology. In the New Testament the picture of the Devil that emerges is an evil, malevolent figure who is the chief of evil spirits. He not only tempts the believer but he is the "god of this world," the "prince of the power of the air." In the Gospels the devil is seen in the following examples:

> The temptations of Jesus in the wilderness (Luke 4:1–13; Mark 1:12–13)
>
> The lives of the demoniacs whom Jesus cured by casting out demons (Luke 8:27–35; 11:14; 4:33–35; 9:38–43)
>
> The theology of John's Gospel, in which appears a kingdom of darkness, ultimately overcome by Jesus but an ongoing opponent against the kingdom of light.
>
> The letters of Paul where he presents the world being under the power of "principalities and powers," "thrones and dominions" in the spiritual world.
>
> In the letters of John the devil is the reason Christ appeared, "The reason the Son of God appeared was to destroy the devil's work." (1 John 3:8)
>
> The proclamation of the New Testament is that all powers are subject to Christ (1 Cor. 15:20–8; Eph. 1:18–23)

Belief in the Devil in the Modern Western World

Despite these strong appeals to a belief in the personal existence of the devil, many Christians and others today deny or doubt its existence. Rudolf Bultmann (1884–1976) believed devils and demons were part of the mythological worldview of New Testament times. His view was that Christians need to reject these beliefs in order to discover an authentic faith for today. A psychological perspective (from Freud) includes the view that the devil is a projection of human fears and insecurity. Some people think that modern science has dispelled belief in the devil because many of the phenomena once attributed to demon possession are now explainable in terms of medical science. Other modern Christian writers, such as Walter Wink (*Naming the Powers* [1984]), think that as heirs of the philosophical Enlightenment (and therefore a modern scientific worldview) we are not able to accept even the possibility that evil could be personified. Nonetheless, many Christians who believe in the devil and demonic powers or possession—particularly in the charismatic and fundamentalist wings of the church—denounce what they believe is occult activity, e.g., Harry Potter books, Ouija boards, seances. Great interest still persists today in the supernatural at every level.

Evil as the Perversion of Good

Certain Christian theologians reflect on the belief that since all created things are intrinsically good, then evil is not an existent being or substance. St. Gregory of Nyssa said that, "Sin does not exist in nature apart from free will; it is not a substance in its own right." A modern examination of this view comes from Bishop Kallistos Ware (1979), "Evil is always parasitic. It is the twisting and misappropriation of what is in itself good. Evil resides not in the thing itself but in our attitude towards the thing—that is to say, in our will." One criticism of this view is that saying "evil is nothing," underestimates evil's influence. But Bishop Ware claims that by saying evil is the perversion of good, and therefore in the final analysis an illusion and unreality, is not to deny its powerful hold over us. He writes, "For there is no greater force within creation than the free will of beings endowed with self-consciousness and spiritual intellect; and so the misuse of this free will can have altogether terrifying consequences."

In Eastern religions, the distinctions between good and evil are relative rather than absolute. Hindus do believe in demons who, like human beings, belong to the four different castes. The celestial demons are Vedic families of antigods [the *daityas,* or sons of Diti, and the *danavas*, sons of Danu—especially Vritra, the enemy of Indra (the supreme God of the Indo Aryans)]. Below this level are earthly demons who are anti-Brahman and who reflect human behavior. They steal or defile believers who make sacrifices. The most famous of these demons is Ravana, the enemy of Rama and *pishachas* (flesh eaters). But evil itself is not ultimate. Radhakrishnan reflects:

> Evil, error and ugliness are not ultimate. Evil has reference to the distance which good has to traverse. Ugliness is half-way to beauty. Error is a stage on the road to truth. They have all to be outgrown. No view is so utterly erroneous, no man is so absolutely evil as to deserve complete castigation. . . . In a continuously evolving universe evil and error are inevitable, though they are gradually diminishing. (Radhakrishnan, *The Hindu View of Life,* 1960)

In Buddhism the root cause of "evils" are greed, hatred, and ignorance. These approaches to life lead to more suffering, while what is rooted in generosity, compassion, and wisdom leads to Nirvana.

> All that we are is the result of what we have thought: it is founded on our thoughts, it is made up of our thoughts. If a man speaks or acts with an evil thought, pain follows him, as the wheel follows the foot of the ox that draws the wagon.
>
> All that we are is the result of what we have thought. . . . If a man speaks or acts with a pure thought, happiness follows him, like a shadow that never leaves him. (Dhammapada, *The Twin Verses*, v. 1, 2, trans. Irving Babbit, 1965)

The Problem of Evil

The Greek philosopher Epicurus voiced the question that if God is both almighty and absolutely good, why is there evil in the world? Throughout history this question has been repeatedly posed by people with this view of God, sometimes in response to the teleological argument for the existence of God (see chapter 2) and sometimes to launch an attack on classical theism itself. Classical theists acknowledge the existence of one God only, who is the all-powerful, all-knowing, all-good creator of the universe. If God has these characteristics, how then can evil happen?

One way to reconcile this concept of the divine with the evils that occur in this world is to portray God as lacking complete or absolute power or knowledge. The skeptics' charge against God is that either he cannot prevent pain and evil, in which case he cannot be called all-powerful; or he will not prevent evil, in which case in what sense can he be a just, holy, good God? In addition, if he can and he will prevent pain and evil, then why is there all the wickedness and suffering in the world as we know it?

David Hume (see chapter 2) set out this dilemma in his *Dialogues Concerning Natural Religion*. He looked at the qualities of omnipotence (all-powerful), omnibenevolence (all-goodness), and evil, and he concluded that only two of these can coexist. Therefore:

> God is not omnipotent, or
>
> God is not omnibenevolent, or
>
> Evil does not exist.

Hume concluded that since the effects of evil are felt all too often in the world, its existence cannot be dismissed; evil, therefore, exists. Because evil exists, then either God must be impotent (powerless) or malicious (nonbenevolent). Either way, according to Hume, the God of classical theism cannot be believed.

But not all people who accept Hume's analysis agree with his conclusion. Some argue that God's goodness is different than the human understanding of goodness, and that God's idea of good allows him to tolerate what we think of as evil as a temporary part of his plan for the world. In this view, believing in an all-loving, all powerful God and also believing that evil exists are not logically contradictory.

Does God Intervene to Prevent Evil? The Issue of Miracles

For some believers, God is willing to act in miraculous ways to prevent some instances of evil and suffering. Belief in miracles has persisted within the world's religions and elsewhere, even if people debate over what a miracle actually is.

A miracle can be seen as an event within human experience in which the observed operations of nature appear to be overruled or suspended; such events are usually ascribed to the intervention of divine power. Miracles have been understood in different ways:

- *Miracles don't exist.* Unexplained happenings can be explained by scientific rationality.
- *Miracles are coincidences.* Two "natural" events collide and seem to hold religious significance for the person involved.
- *Miracles are a logical impossibility.* David Hume argues that miracles are a logical impossibility both humanly and scientifically speaking:

> A miracle is a violation of the laws of nature; and as firm and unalterable experience has established these laws, the proof against a miracle from the very nature of the fact, is as entire as any argument from experience can possibly be imagined.

People believe in miracles because they want to. Hume also wrote,

> It forms a strong presumption against all supernatural and miraculous relations that they are observed chiefly to abound among ignorant and barbarous nations.

In other words, belief in miracles results from ignorance about how the world actually works.

- *Miracles cannot exist because God would not work them selectively*, e.g., a deliverance and healing from cancer but no deliverance for the Jews at Auschwitz.
- *Miracles exist but need to be defined carefully.*

Theologian Paul Tillich (1886–1965) defined miracles in this way:

> A genuine miracle is first of all an event which is astonishing, unusual, shaking, without contradicting the rational structure of reality. In the second place it is an event which points to the mystery of being, expressing its relation to us in a definite way.

In his book *Philosophy of Religion* (1983), John Hick writes,

> If a miracle is defined as a breach of natural law, one can declare a priori that there are no miracles. It does not follow, however, that there are no miracles in the religious sense of the term. For the principle that nothing happens in conflict with natural law does not entail that there are no unusual and striking events evoking and mediating a vivid awareness of God.

In Hick's view, however it is defined, a miracle is a marvelous event that is unexpected and causes wonder.

Miracles and World Faiths

Miracles in the Hebrew and Christian Bibles were recorded to provoke wonder at God's power and goodness. For Judaism, the exodus from Egypt and the division of the waters of the Red Sea became the symbols of all God's deliverances in history, the theme of much Jewish literature, and the hope of the Jewish future. The Talmud understands miracles as part of creation from the very beginning, though they are not viewed as evidence of religious truth claims. Everyday living was just as much of a miracle as anything else, even if people are often unaware of such things. The New Testament records Jesus performing miracles on some thirty-five occasions (see p. 197), and his miraculous resurrection from the dead is central to the Christian faith.

In other religions, miracles also confirm the validity of a revelation or a prophet or holy person. In Islam, the term used for miracle (although not from the Qur'an itself) is *mu'jiza,* something that could not normally be achieved. Isa (Jesus) raising the dead, Moses parting the waters of the Red Sea, and Muhammad (who could not write) receiving the Qur'an are all examples of this. The Qur'an speaks of natural phenomena and extraordinary happenings as "signs of Allah," which are seen as proofs of divine power and authority.

In Eastern religions, as in other traditions, miracles tend to surround the births of holy people. The yogis, the holy men who have attained the supreme goal and who are seen as living manifestations of the divine (*avatara*), also have Siddhi powers which include leaving the body and reentering it at will, becoming invisible, or even reducing the body to dust or to the size of a huge mountain.

Many people claim to have witnessed or experienced what they would call miracles. To some extent, everyone interprets such accounts according to their previous understanding of the world and reality.

- *Psychologically*, miracles have been seen as primarily human projection. We have no miracles in our own lives, so we fantasize of them elsewhere.
- *Scientifically and rationally,* futile attempts have been made to set religion against science and to use reason in a tit-for-tat fashion, but a miracle is by definition a very different state of affairs that points beyond what is normally, rationally understood as reality.

Rational arguments can be seen in Hume's critique of the miraculous, which has enjoyed widespread acceptance in an age dominated by naturalism. Many Christians have been reluctant to place much importance on miracles, some even explaining them away or seeing them as symbolic. Other Christian thinkers join C. S. Lewis, who in *Miracles: A Preliminary Study* (1963) has argued that an open mind must accept the possibility of divine "interferences" in the ordinary course of nature.

Theodicies

A theodicy is an attempt to defend the goodness and omnipotence of God in spite of the existence of evil. Theodicies take a number of different forms.

God Allows the Existence of Evil and Suffering

One form of theodicy argues that God allows the existence of evil and suffering. St. Augustine (354–430 C.E.) traced evil back to human free will, and Irenaeus (c. 130–202 C.E.) removed the logical problem of evil by accepting that God's world was not perfect and that evil has an important part to play in God's plan for humanity. The book of Job in the Bible is one of the earliest theodicies to teach that suffering is an inevitable part of human existence. One such explanation is that suffering is a punishment for sin, but Job reproached God for giving him undeserved suffering. An affliction of this kind can only be justified either by believing in reward and punishment in the afterlife or by seeing suffering as a purifying factor in the life of a godly person. Both views of suffering can be found in Judaism, and this area of reflection is crucial to faith when seen in the light of the Holocaust.

The Free-Will Defense

The free-will defense approach to theodicy holds that the human abuse of freedom is a primary cause of evil and suffering. Theological belief centers on God's purpose in creation: to have free agents who could enter into personal relations with himself. Free will was therefore essential in order to choose and respond to either good or evil. The alternative would be a robotic human race with no choice and therefore no potential to real love and relationship. In this view, human freedom is a price worth paying because of either its intrinsic good or because its good outcomes outweigh its bad ones. This theodicy, though, finds it hard to account for evil in the natural world, such as the floods, tornadoes, and earthquakes that result in many deaths each year.

Evil in the Natural World

Some ecologists formulating a theodicy see humanity's exploitation of the earth—e.g., the erosion of the ozone layer or the disappearance of valuable rainforests—as a reason for natural evil. Natural consequences and disasters resulting from such moves are the result of human evil in the form of greed and ambition. Some Christian theologians still see natural evil either as the result of the Fall (Adam and Eve's rebellion against God and its consequences) or as a condition permitted in order to build character and worthwhile attributes such as perseverance or human charity. John Hick takes this view of evil in his book *Evil and the God of Love*:

> Pain and suffering are a necessary feature of a world that is to be the scene of a process of soul-making; and . . . even the haphazard and unjust distribution and the often destructive and dysteleological effects of suffering have a positive significance in that they call forth human sympathy and self-sacrifice, and create a human situation within which the right must be done for its own sake rather than for a reward. (John Hick, *Evil and the God of Love,* 1968)

Process Theology

A modern Christian approach to the problem of evil lies in process theology. Process theology emerged after the First World War in the work of A. N. Whitehead (1861–1947) and Charles Hartshorne (1897–2000) and has been influential especially in the United States. One of the central beliefs of process theology is that the "I" in me is not a fixed entity passing unaffected through time. Rather "I" am a result of all the changes and experiences I have had. In other words the I that makes me is, in fact, a process. The same is true of God. Everything is thus "in God," but God is more than the sum of the parts (panentheism).

Process theology goes back to Greek ideas of permanence, which influenced Christian thought. Christianity in this view presents God as unchanging and remote. Process theologians claim instead that God is actually part of the process of evolution and change. He is therefore actively involved in the world and affected by events in the world. He can even change his mind. Process theologians also claim that God travels with his creation in time. The future is the future of God, not only for humanity. The whole of the cosmic process is God, and God works alongside the created order like the great companion, the fellow-sufferer who understands. Hartshorne opposed the classical doctrine of God's omnipotence, which put forward the belief that all events, as they occur, are determined by God. The process view avoids depicting God as directly responsible for all sin and evil. In contrast, Hartshorne said that within the limits set by God, humans determine the details of what happens.

In brief, the process view is that God is not an all-powerful creator responsible for everything. God is not omnipotent and he did not create the universe. Rather, God is a unique part of the universe who can influence the structure of things or change details according to present possibilities. God is not using controlling power in the universe, but instead is also subject to the limitations that are imposed on the universe.

The process approach to theodicy is that evil in the world is the measure to which God's will has been opposed. God always offers the best possibility to each situation in life as it occurs, but the created order is free not to conform to the divine plan. An important part of process theodicy is the belief that God suffers when evil is done. This outlook raises the issue of God's responsibility for evil in the sense that he must bear some responsibility for it as he initiated the process of evolution in the knowledge that he would be unable to control it. Process theodicy is called upon to give an explanation of why God took such a risk. Process thinkers reply that the universe in its process has produced more quality and good to outweigh evil, and this outcome justifies God's initiative.

Eschatological Solutions to Evil

Many religious people believe that the only solution to the problem of evil would be an eschatological (end times) one. Evil's rightful remedy is in the future, at the end of time. This view can have a dramatic impact on how people live their lives now. For example, consider the behavior of cults that think the last times have come, President Reagan thinking nuclear war would be ushering in the War of Armageddon to end the present order of things, or people disengaging with trying to change society because they look to a cosmic solution. Albert Camus (1913–1960) realized that belief in a just God gives people the assurance that evil will ultimately be defeated. However, belief in God was no option for Camus. The problem he faced was much more complex, because there is no certainty that justice will ever be done:

> The certainty of the existence of a God who would give meaning to life has a far greater attraction than the knowledge that without him one could do evil without being punished. The choice between these alternatives would not be difficult. But there is no choice, and that is where the bitterness begins. Confronted with this evil, confronted with death, man from the very depths of his soul cries out for justice. (Albert Camus, "The Myth of the Sisyphus," in Martin Esslin, *The Theatre of the Absurd,* Penguin, 1968)

Good and Evil: Matters of Time and Perception?

In world religions, the concept of evil tends to be linked to a concept of time itself. For example, religions with a linear view of time (Christianity, Islam, and Judaism) see evil as a force to be defeated both during this lifetime and at the Last Day or the Apocalypse at the end of time. Some people cannot imagine the existence of goodness without its complement of evil.

Other people argue that although many opposites (e.g., front and back, light and dark) are complementary, good and evil are not complementary. Goodness does not need evil in order to define itself. Goodness is defined with varying degrees of itself (i.e., some things are good, other things are better, and still other things are the best).

Monism is the belief that the universe is a single, harmonious unity that is, in essence, good. On the concept of evil, monism argues that evil is not a reality; if everything is good, evil must be just an illusion in the human mind. So if we could see the whole picture of reality we would recognize evil for the good that it is. One of the objections to monism is the lack of explanation as to why we suffer, and often so cruelly.

Religions such as Hinduism or Buddhism with a cyclical view of time tend to see evil as an inevitable feature on the way and as something to be encountered at the end of each cycle.

Chapter 6
Aspects of Religion

A religion is a unified system of beliefs and practices relative to sacred things, that is to say, things set apart and forbidden—beliefs and practices which unite into one single moral community called a Church, all those who adhere to them.

Emile Durkheim

What Is Religion?

Religion is a complex phenomenon that often defies definition or summary. The question arises: What is the best way to study it?

Emile Durkheim saw religion as being the social side of life in symbolic form, so that the social experience individual people gain from the practice of religion results in something greater than themselves. Others would see religion defined in terms of the transcendent or the search for truth, or even the realization of illusion.

Various disciplines examine a religion to find out its basic patterns or structures.

- *Psychology* views religious experience and feelings and to some degree the myths and symbols that express experience.
- *Sociology and social anthropology* look at the institutions of religious tradition and their relationship to beliefs and values.
- *Literary studies* explore the meanings of myths and other dimensions of faith.

- *Philosophy* has in general studied accounts of the nature of religion and of religious concepts, but disengaging philosophical inquiry from the concerns raised by normative theology is sometimes difficult.

The above disciplines are supplemented by history, archaeology, and other disciplines, each with their own methods of inquiry and discovery.

For readers without a specialist background in religion, the task of studying religion can be quite daunting. The introduction in this chapter gives a brief outline of four well-used approaches for studying religion and then sets out the method this book uses to guide you through a review of twelve different world religions existent today.

Four Approaches to the Study of Religion

Sometimes how we study is just as important and engaging as why or what we study. In the broadest terms, four approaches have been used in the scholarly study of religion: the historical, the confessional, the phenomenological, and the behavioral or social-scientific.

The Historical Comparative Approach

By studying the history of religions, scholars attempt to delineate facts without judging them from a particular standpoint. This method "aims to be as objective as possible about the nature and power of a religion; it is not concerned with whether a particular faith is true." (Ninian Smart, "Comparative-Historical Method," in Mircea Elaide, ed., *The Encyclopedia of Religion,* New York: Macmillan, 1987). Whether objectivity is possible in such an exercise is, of course, debatable. The same principle of objectivity is true for the comparative study of religion, though this approach sometimes is seen to cover the theology of other religions, such as the Christian appraisal of Jewish or Buddhist history. The historical-comparative approach deals with texts—doctrinal, devotional, or ritual texts that stem from the religious community, or secular documents such as statistics through which the historian attempts to reconstruct the religious life of different religious traditions and identify historical connections and differences. The inevitable problem arises as to whether or not one belief or practice rooted in an organic system can rightly be compared to a similar element in another organic system. Every religion possesses unique elements, and interreligious comparisons may obscure or hide these unique aspects. However, scholars generally agree that valid comparisons are possible, although not easy to make. People who take this approach often see the very uniqueness of a religion through comparison, which includes contrast. Setting religions side by side is known as the comparative study of religion.

The Confessional Approach

A confessional approach assumes the truth or value of one religious tradition and may or may not go on to evaluate other religions in the light of its own beliefs. People who take this approach are often concerned about the effect of studying religion objectively. They fear that such study can lead to a secular indifference to the study of all religion. By studying religions from a faith perspective, similarities between faiths may well be affirmed, but the confessional approach is not afraid to confront differences. For example, Jews disagree with Christians over the status of Jesus, which is perceived as a difference about truth. However, advocates of the confessional approach must be wary of misrepresenting another faith by judging that tradition against the standards of its own.

Phenomenological

The phenomenological study of religion often commences with a historical approach but then directs its attention to discovering the nature of religion—that is, the essential characteristics that underpin its historical manifestations. Three important works in the phenomenological study of religion are:

- Gerardus van der Leeuw's *Religion in Essence and Manifestation: A Study in Phenomenology* (1933; Eng. trans., 1938).
- E. J. Brill's *Method and Theory in the Study of Religion*, ed. Russell McCutcheon (North American Association for the Study of Religion [NASSR]).
- *A Guide to the Study of Religion*, eds. Willi Braun and Russell T. McCutcheon (London: Cassell Academic Press, 2000), which contains substantial articles on method and theory-related issues in the study of religion, many of them by leading scholars in the field.

Social and Psychological Approaches

Psychology, sociology, and especially anthropology have contributed greatly to understanding religious phenomena. In the psychology of religion, the two most important figures remain William James and Sigmund Freud. James's *Varieties of Religious Experience* (1902) established a set of topics and approaches to those topics that set the overall tone for a great deal of the later work in the field. While James dealt primarily with conscious expressions of religious experience, Freud and the subsequent psychoanalytic tradition aimed at fitting the various forms of religious experience into the framework of a general theory of the unconscious. C. G. Jung in particular has been influential among interpreters of religion, as the best developed alternative to Freud himself.

One problem usually associated with the psychological approach is the difficulty of moving from the individual's experience to the structure and experience of the religious community. The sociological and anthropological traditions have confronted this problem since the last third of the nineteenth century. William Robertson Smith, Emile Durkheim, and Max Weber were the leading figures in creating a sociological tradition in the analysis of religion.

The Approach of *A Brief Guide to Beliefs*

This book attempts to set out its information about the world's major religions in an objective and empathic way.

A measure of *objectivity* is essential in order to present accurately religious beliefs and practices, but objectivity can have its problems. One problem with attempting to write "objectively" about faiths is that such an approach can be cold and factual, when in reality so many members of the world's faiths are vibrant, committed, and engaged in their faith.

Another problem is that when different traditions are laid out with detachment—without any attempt to evaluate their practices or truth claims—the implicit message to the reader can be one of confusion. Why should anyone believe this religion rather than another one? Objective approaches can also present their own views of truth, which presuppose that the Western, liberal, scientific view of life is generally true and beneficial and where tolerance is perceived as an important social good.

Anyone who comes to study religion does it from a personal perspective; this author is no exception. However, a personal perspective does not necessarily result—one hopes—in distortions or misrepresentions. On the contrary, an *empathic* approach recognizes the need to be aware of one's own beliefs while attempting to understand another person's tradition. A degree of understanding faiths other than one's own is essential if people want to comprehend both their own and others' religious/nonreligious cultures in a world that is becoming more international and multicultural through globalization (see chapter 1). Objections to an empathic approach include the view that clear and informed knowledge of other faiths produces challenges to personal worldviews and causes people to doubt or modify their faith. Gaining knowledge of other faiths may, on the other hand, also lead people to affirm their own faith, with an even greater level of intellectual strength.

In addition to its attempts to be objective and empathic, *A Brief Guide to Beliefs* approaches its subject eclectically and conceptually.

An Eclectic Approach: Grasping the Character of Different Religions

The approach taken in this book is an eclectic one, making use of a number of approaches as appropriate for each case. A single methodology used to the exclusion of all others would only serve to increase the danger of misunderstanding and bias. The study of religion is much more than learning "facts" about individual religious traditions, so I have integrated a number of theories arising from those discussed above in order to get a flavor of or grasp the character of the world's religions. Quotes and excerpts from writers who belong to the different faith traditions appear throughout.

A Conceptual Map: Understanding Religious Beliefs

The next part of chapter 6 introduces you to eight aspects of religion, to give you an overview of some important beliefs and concepts that are not always obvious in books about world faiths. For example, in the study of a sacred text, various beliefs about divine revelation, origins, and what can be regarded as sacred are variously understood and sometimes disputed not only in Eastern and Western traditions but also within the different believers of one world faith. Being aware of, say, the nature of mysticism or the different concepts of God that exist in the world can equip a student or a general reader with a basic conceptual map that can support a further study of a specific faith.

With this book you can take a number of approaches. You can

- Read thematically in chapter 6 on a religious aspect such as God or prayer to get a grasp of the breadth of the subject across some of the world's faiths
- Study a specific faith, for example, Hinduism in chapter 7, where you find the faith explained in terms of the eight aspects of religion that have been chosen for study
- Cross-reference chapters 6 and 7 to consolidate your understanding of the scope of the subject

The eight aspects of religion we now introduce also appear where appropriate in the study of alternative faiths and movements in the rest of the book, although less systematically. Bearing in mind the perils of general characterizations, the eight aspects of faith covered in this book are

God/The Holy

Salvation (Beliefs)

Death and the Afterlife

Moral Action/Ethical Codes

Prayer and Meditation/Human Response

Gender and Religion

Mysticism/Religious Experience

Scriptures and Sacred Text

Though these eight aspects are not necessary or sufficient conditions if taken separately, they may jointly be understood as symptomatic of religions. The intention is not to impose them on faiths or produce misleading similarities, but to use them as guideposts to organize material so that general readers can follow some broad conceptual system to aid their study. Where the language used—e.g., "God" or "Salvation"—is inappropriate for a faith, I have tried to make the language and terminology part of the discussion as a way to explain the differences.

UNIT 6:1 GOD AND RELIGIOUS LANGUAGE

When we read a book, talk to believers, or listen to television we often hear the word "God" used. We could be tempted to think we know what the word means, but in today's pluralistic, postmodern world (see chapter 1) the word can connote a wide variety of beliefs and meanings.

Religions express their outlook on the holy or the sacred in the form of a sense of supreme value and ultimate reality. The holy can be variously understood as a personal God, as a realm of gods and spirits, as an impersonal reality, or as a cosmic power, to name but a few options. Some religions frequently claim to have their origin in revelations—distinctive experiences of the holy coming into human life and experience. Revelations can take the form of visions (Moses in the desert), inner voices (Muhammad outside Mecca), or events (the death and resurrection of Jesus Christ).

In this unit we give a few examples (by no means exhaustive) of the different beliefs in God and ultimate reality among the world's faiths. The unit also examines briefly the problem of talking about God, i.e., the philosophy of religious language. As you will see, ideas of God vary widely from religion to religion and from culture to culture.

Concepts of God

Many Gods: Polytheism

The worship of many gods, known as *polytheism*, characterized the religions of most of the ancient world. (Polytheism is not to be confused with *pantheism* [the belief in an impersonal God identical with the universe], although the two beliefs are sometimes found in the same religious tradition.) Ancient Egyptians, Babylonians, and Assyrians worshiped a plurality of deities, as did the ancient Greeks, Romans, and Norse. Polytheism also characterizes many present-day religions, including Shintoism, and also many contemporary African tribal religions.

According to Ninian Smart (1989), polytheistic deities are formed around a number of aspects of life, which include natural forces and objects, such as fertility and atmospheric conditions; vegetation, such as trees, sacred herbs, and vineyards; animal and human forms, such as cattle and animal-human hybrids; and even assorted functions, such as love, agriculture, healing, and war.

God as Creator

One approach to God portrays the deity as a creator. Various accounts of the creation of the world come from religious faiths. Creation out of nothing (*ex nihilo*) affirms the distinction between creator and creation. For example, in the biblical account offered in Genesis

> In the beginning when God created the heavens and the earth, the earth was a formless void and darkness covered the face of the deep, while a wind from God swept over the face of the waters. Then God said, "Let there be light"; and there was light. And God saw that the light was good; and God separated the light from the darkness. God called the light Day, and the darkness he called Night. And there was evening and there was morning, the first day. (Judaism and Christianity. Bible, Gen. 1:1–5)

Another view of God and creation portrays creation as an *emanation* of the absolute. This approach suggests that the creation of the world can be regarded as an overflowing of the creative energy of the creator. On this basis, a natural or organic connection exists between the creator (e.g., God) and the creation, which nevertheless remains distinct and transcendent—a view termed *panentheism*.

Buddhists and Jains deny a creator God because the gods that do exist for these religions are subject to rebirth and therefore incapable of creating the world. The Hindu, Native American, and Zoroastrian faiths focus on creation by the agency of one or several deities.

God/Ultimate Reality as a Mystery

In the monotheistic religions of Judaism, Christianity, and Islam, God is beyond any human concept: *"My thoughts are not your thoughts, nor are your ways my ways"* (Isa. 55:8). To cast God in a graven image or to make an idol is to reduce God, who is seen as infinite (unmeasurable), to being finite (measurable). Buddhism, Hinduism, Jainism, and Taoism affirm the ineffability of the ultimate reality in their belief that no words can properly convey its nature. The ultimate reality is beyond all duality and all attempts to think of it as a "thing" separate from other things. Its nature is emptiness, but using the word "emptiness" to describe God can cause misunderstanding. In the Eastern religions the term indicates a cognitive statement about reality. Buddhist scholar Edward Conze writes,

> Emptiness is not a theory, but a ladder that reaches out into the infinite. A ladder is not there to be discussed, but to be

> climbed. . . . It is a practical concept, and it embodies an aspiration, not a view. Its only use is to help us to get rid of this world and of the ignorance which binds us to it. It has not only one meaning, but several, which can unfold themselves on the successive stages of the actual process of transcending the world through wisdom. (Edward Conze, *Selected Sayings from the Perfection of Wisdom,* 1978)

Such concepts are not easy to understand. If you find them difficult, take heart in the fact that many scholars and devotees of the faiths do, too!

God as Personal

A belief in which God is seen as personal holds that God possesses attributes such as being good, loving, or compassionate. Here the scriptures of different faiths describe God's gracious provision to human beings, manifested in his help and love for the poor and downtrodden.

> The LORD is gracious and merciful,
> slow to anger and abounding in steadfast love.
> The LORD is good to all,
> and his compassion is over all that he has made.
> Judaism and Christianity. Bible, Psalm 145:8–9

> The Lord and Cherisher of the Worlds—
> Who created me, and it is He who guides me;
> Who gives me food and drink,
> And when I am ill, it is He who cures me;
> Who will cause me to die, and then to live again;
> And Who, I hope, will forgive me my faults on the Day of Judgment.
> Islam. Qur'an 26:77–82

In the Bible, God is portrayed as a real person who gives himself in reciprocal relationship to human beings as a genuine transcendent "Thou" or "Other" (the view of John Hick, who borrowed the term from Martin Buber).

- God as personal is presupposed in Genesis, where God is described as walking and speaking, working and resting.
- God also reveals himself in personal terms: "I AM WHO I AM" (Ex. 3:14).
- In the New Testament, Jesus addresses God personally as his Father (John 14:1–21f). Jesus speaks of God as the source and sustainer of his creatures who personally cares for them (Matt. 5:45; 6:26–32) and the one to whom people can turn.
- The Semitic biblical concept of the personhood of God is different from all abstract philosophical ideas of God as an impersonal first cause or prime mover deduced by reason, as well as different from all pantheis-

tic concepts of God and the world as essentially the same. In the Semitic biblical tradition, God is first and foremost a personal being who is creative and active. He reveals himself by names, especially the great personal name Yahweh (cf. Ex. 3:13–15; 6:3; Isa. 42:8).

- God's personality is seen in the fact that while he is the creator and preserver of all nature, he is encountered in the scriptures not primarily as the God of nature, as in pagan religions, but rather as the God of history, controlling and directing human events.
- The personal nature of God can be seen in the Jewish belief in the covenant, through which the Jews believe they were chosen to fulfill a unique destiny in the unfolding of God's salvation.

The personhood of God has, however, been called into question on the basis of our use of the word "person" when it applies to human beings, because when we use the word "personal" in this way it means to be an individual among individuals, which cannot be said of God. Christian theologians (e.g., Karl Barth) caution against an erroneous anthropomorphizing (making God out to be like humans), noting that we should only apply the term "personal" to God as an analogy and not literally.

Ultimate Reality as Impersonal

The ultimate reality is described in impersonal terms by some world faiths such as Taoism. Here, the impersonal Tao is the reality behind all existence and Tao is the only world, as there is no supernatural world. Tao is also the driving force that makes nature work, bringing sense and order to life and preventing chaos. Like Brahman (Hinduism), Tao is the ultimate source of everything, but wheras Brahman is eternal and timeless, the Tao is forever changing.

Brahman is the word used for ultimate reality or the absolute. It has no form or gender and may be addressed as He, She, or It. Hindus say:

> What is but one the wise call by many names. (Rig Veda 10)

False Gods: The Concept of Idolatry

The prohibition against idolatry is expressed in different ways among the world's faiths:

Islam

Chapter 112 of the Qur'an, known as Surah Al-Ilkhlas or Purity (of Faith), is considered the essence of the unity or the motto of monotheism. It reads:

> In the name of God (Allah), the One God, The Eternal,
> Absolute; He who has not begotten, nor has been begotten,
> and equal to Him is not anyone. (112:1–4)

Judaism

Biblical Judaism is opposed to idolatry. The Ten Commandments in Exodus 20 prohibited the Israelites to make graven images. Yet despite this prohibition, the ancient Israelites were involved in Baal worship, which led to condemnation by the prophets (e.g., 1 Kings 18).

Hinduism

Hindus are frequently accused by other faiths of worshiping idols because of the many images and deities that surround their worship of God. Yet Hinduism also condemns idolatry, for no words or images can contain God.

> Eye cannot see him, nor words reveal him;
> by the senses, austerity, or works he is not known.
> When the mind is cleansed by the grace of wisdom,
> he is seen by contemplation—the One without parts.
>
> Mundaka Upanishad 3.1.8

Describing God: Transcendence and Immanence

This unit has discussed God from different points of view. Some faiths believe that God is above and beyond human experience. Others suggest that God can be experienced here and now in the world.

To describe God as *immanent* is to say that he/she/it is involved in the world and not separate from it. Many types of prayer assume this view. For example, when believers pray for God's help in their situation or ask for justice to be delivered, they are assuming that God can be involved in everyday life.

To describe God as *transcendent* is to say that he/she/it is outside and beyond the material universe. In other words, God is not limited by the world in terms of time or space or by way of what God can do. A clear expression of this transcendence of all being and all thought is found in Mahayana Buddhism, which describes the ultimate principle in negative assertions and names it a Nothingness or Voidness. Religion of this kind may regard the Western notion of God, with its belief in personal being, as an inappropriate and even insulting way of regarding their own ultimate principle.

Some religions see God as both transcendent and immanent. For example, Christians believe in the Trinity of God. Traditional Christian belief is that God came into the world in time and history through the person of God the Son (Jesus of Nazareth), and was therefore immanent. But God the Father was and is still separate from the material world (transcendent). The Holy Spirit unites the two concepts of immanence and transcendence. As the third person of the Trinity, the Holy Spirit is coeternal—that is, he has always existed with the Father and the Son, yet he is in the world today doing the work of God. An excerpt from the Lenten Triodion of the Russian Orthodox Church reflects on Eastern Christian belief and worship of the Trinity:

Come all peoples, and let us worship the one
Godhead in three persons,
The Son in the Father with the Holy Spirit.
For the Father gave birth outside time to the Son,
Coeternal and enthroned with him;
And the Holy Spirit is glorified in the Father
together with the Son:
One power, one essence, One Godhead . . .
Holy Trinity, glory to thee.

God and the World Are Essentially the Same

In *pantheism* God and the world are essentially the same. Pantheistic religions believe that the divine is immanent; all reality is part of the being of God, but God is not depleted or exhausted by the world. *Panentheism* is the belief that God and the world are essentially identical; here the divine is totally immanent, so that all reality is viewed as part of the being of God.

- In modern philosophy, twentieth-century expressions of panentheism are found in the process theology of Alfred North Whitehead and Charles Hartshorne (see chapter 5).
- In Hinduism, the Upanishads speak of the concept of Brahman, which reflects a number of theistic, pantheistic, and panentheistic views.
- In Islam, pantheistic views interacted with monotheism and played an important role in developing the Sufism of al-Bistami, al-Hallaj, and others.
- In Judaism, pantheistic beliefs are central to the medieval Kabbalah and Hasidim.
- Christian mysticism was influenced by the pantheism of the neo-Platonist world, which is seen in the writings of St. Augustine of Hippo and 'pseudo-Dionysius,' the Areopagite. In the sixteenth century, the Protestant mystic Jakob Boehme wrote, "God is in heaven and Heaven is in man."

Critical Realism: Describing God Approximately

Religions speak about God as personal because it makes the God concept less theoretical and more accessible and approachable. Theologians who are known as *critical realists* are more cautious about the validity of talking in personal terms about God. They accept that anything which is said is provisional and approximate—in other words, far short and even wrong about God. In contrast are those religions that have confidence that God has overcome the problem of being known by revealing his word and his will to them. But even so, this revelation is transmitted through words that are not identical with the matter that they set out to convey.

To say that God is *impersonal* is to say that God has no human characteristics. The question then arises: How can human beings know him or conceive of him at all? Is God a spirit or a force? Do we know if our language is even capable of expressing the reality and truth about God?

Apophatic Theology: What God Is Not

All theistic religions have proponents who believe that God cannot be described in language, since God is far apart from human apprehension and cannot be defined by human categories in time and space (and is therefore transcendent). This view has led to apophatic theology, which recognizes that the only confidence we can have when we speak of God is to say what God is not (*via negativa*). This approach occurs often when we qualify the claims we make about God. But if God is the creator of all that is, a reasonable argument could be made that some relationship is present between his nature and all that he has created. The use of analogy is important here. But to qualify everything said about God—e.g., "God is a Father, but not exactly as we understand and experience fathers"—is to qualify God (metaphorically) out of all existence. This kind of process led philosopher Anthony Flew to proclaim the death of God by a thousand qualifications.

Religious Language

Religious language about God is rich, colorful, and expressive, yet it is capable of expressing both truth and falsity. Theologians are aware of the ways in which people are able to project onto God their own ideas and thoughts. Two people can be using the same words in a conversation yet mean something entirely different, especially when talking about God. Take a statement like "God exists":

1. In the philosophy of religion, a realist is someone who believes that a statement is true if it corresponds to a reality that is independent of language, culture, and society.
2. Realists believe that the language we use reaches out to a reality that is external to this world.
3. A statement is true if it successfully corresponds to some reality. If it does not, then a statement is untrue.
4. The realist says that the statement, "God exists," is true because it refers to—i.e., it corresponds to—the God who created and sustains the universe. This is called the *correspondence theory of truth.*

The antirealist will claim that the statement "God exists" is true because the statement coheres or fits in with other statements made by religious believers. This is called a *coherence view of truth.* Peter Vardy, in his book *The Puzzle of God* (1990), expands on the antirealist position:

> Take the case of morality. If you are a Roman Catholic, then the statement, "artificial Birth Control is wrong" will be true for you. (You may not, of course, choose to obey this moral rule, but it is nevertheless a rule which forms part of the Catholic way of life.) . . . If you are a Hindu, it is true that you must respect cows. If you are a Muslim, then it is true that you have an obligation to pray facing towards Mecca. . . . What makes these statements true is that they are part of or fit in with a particular form of life. Within the Catholic, Hindu or Islamic worlds, within their different forms of life, these statements are true. On this basis there can be different truths in different communities. Truth is not absolute, it is relative. Truth in one culture may be different from truth in another.

The difference between the realist and the antirealist can be seen more clearly when it comes to ethical issues and morality. For example, the following statements can be seen in different lights by both types of persons:

1. Homosexuality is wrong.
2. It is never right to steal.
3. Murder is always wrong.

The realist will say that these statements are either true or false. Their truth or falsity has nothing to do with the society that they inhabit. A realist will probably claim that, apart from any form of human society, there is a transcendental value—e.g., God's laws—which lays down moral statements. If human moral statements correspond accurately to the transcendental model, then they are true; if not, they are false. Antirealists would disagree and claim that there is no absolute morality; moral demands that may be valid and right in one society are not so in another one.

How Reliable Is Language about God?

Religious language is used to communicate ideas about God, faith, belief, and practice. The question of the reliability of human language when used to refer to things beyond human experience has brought forth a number of answers.

1. *Language is equivocal.* Equivocal language is language that is unclear or ambiguous. Human language cannot refer to the infinite (for example, God) because people's talk about this sort of subject gives rise to different interpretations and understandings of the words used. This is the view of some Christian mystics (e.g., St. John of the Cross) and is representative of the *via negativa.*

2. *Language is univocal.* Univocal language is straightforward and clear—(e.g., "Jupiter and Mars are planets"). From the univocal view, religious language presents no problem. Words that refer to God and to humanity have exactly the same meaning.

3. *Language is analogical.* There is an analogy between what a word means when it applies to humanity and when it applies to God. This use of language assumes a "proper proportionality" in language describing God's attributes and activities and human attributes and activities.

4. *Metaphysical language is meaningless.* Only propositions (e.g., the proposition of God) that can be empirically verified have meaning. Logical positivists such as A. J. Ayer and Rudolf Carnap insisted that there were only two ways to prove or verify language: through logical reasoning and by some form of sense experience or experiment. The logical positivist argues that it is pointless to talk about God or ethics because propositions such as these could not be verified using the senses. Second, knowing the conditions under which such abstract propositions could be proved true or false is impossible, therefore, talk about God must be meaningless, for how can you ever test it with your mind or your experience?

5. *Religious language is moral discourse.* Language about God is really language about how people should behave towards each other. (R. B. Braithwaite, Immanuel Kant, and Albrecht Ritschl)

6. *All "language games" exist within particular "forms of life."* Wittgenstein argues that speaking a language is a kind of activity. As such, "meaning" is best understood as "use." (Wittgenstein said, "Words do not have meaning; they have usage.") Thus speaking about God is as valid as any other activity.

7. *Religious language is metaphorical and symbolic.* A symbol is something that stands or is used in place of something else. A metaphor is a figure of speech where a word or a phrase is used to describe something different from the idea or object with which it is most often associated. Some thinkers believe that religious language contains helpful metaphors and symbols about God, but there is no way to substantiate them ontologically. Paul Tillich does not believe that we can talk about God as a "being" the same way we are "beings." Rather, for Tillich, God is the "ground of being."

(For a thorough treatment and investigation of the philosophical problems surrounding the nature and use of religious language, see Dan R. Stiver, *The Philosophy of Religious Language: Sign, Symbol, and Story* [Oxford: Blackwell Publishers, 1996].)

Summary

The debates about the nature of God, whether the divine can be known and on what basis, and how we should speak of God are still with us even in the present day. The conceptual approach to religion and religious language is not agreed on by all. Danish philosopher and theologian Søren Kierkegaard urges religion to be lived and experienced: "As you have lived, so have you believed." Our lives and the things we do may well be more important than the theoretical details of our propositional beliefs.

UNIT 6:2 SALVATION

Anyone that is fallen into the grip of lust, wrath, or attachment, Attached to stingy greed, Guilty of the four cardinal sins and evils, And demonic sins like murder; Who never has attended to scriptures, holy music, or sacred verse—By contemplation of the Supreme Being, With a moment's remembrance of God shall he be saved.

Sikhism. Adi Granth, Sri Raga, M. 5

'I testify that Thou art the Lord of all creation, and the Educator of all beings, visible and invisible. I bear witness that Thy power hath encompassed the entire universe, and that the hosts of the earth can never dismay Thee, nor can the dominion of all peoples and nations deter Thee from executing Thy purpose. I confess that Thou hast no desire except the regeneration of the whole world, and the establishment of the unity of its peoples, and the salvation of all them that dwell therein.

Baha'i Faith. *Gleanings from the Writings of Baha'u'llah*

The expectation of divine forgiveness and pardon is universal, reaching to believers in all the world's religions. An essential prerequisite for this view of salvation is the forgiveness of sins. Prayers, sacred texts, and teachings of the gurus or religious leaders all speak in different ways about being defiled by sin:

- Texts about being unworthy to enter the presence of God
- Passages about being corrupted by evil deeds and so unable to realize one's true inner nature
- God's forgiving nature and God's ever-present desire to forgive
- The idea of atonement—that sin must be taken away, either by a savior, a priest, or through the believer's own penance and devotion

Salvation is also the belief that human beings need safety and deliverance. Also, salvation is linked to the wish to be ultimately safe in this life and the next. For example, in certain forms of Hinduism and Buddhism, salvation is understood as liberation from the inevitable pain of existence in time by means of religious disciplines that ultimately achieve a state of being that is not determined by time-bound perceptions and forms of thought. Ideas of salvation may or may not be linked to the figure of a savior or redeemer or correlated with a concept of God. Yet all religions attract people who have a sense of insecurity when it comes to their human destiny, but the predicament and the way to overcome this insecurity are understood differently.

This unit introduces the reader to various beliefs:

- Universalism: the belief that everyone will be saved
- Islamic belief in hell and the day of judgment
- Escape from the endless cycle of death and rebirth in Hinduism
- Buddhism: the noble path to Nirvana
- Judaism: a messianic deliverance
- The Christian belief in the atonement of Christ for the sins of the world

Universalism: Salvation for All or Hell for Some?

Universalism (in contrast to particularism) is the belief that a religion is true for the whole of humanity—for example, the belief that salvation may come to all people through one central point. Questions arise out of the belief in universal salvation. When salvation is available to every soul who has lived regardless of one's actions, it is at odds with beliefs about hell and the last judgment. Universalists do not think this way. In Christianity, universalists like Origen believed that all beings will in the end be saved and that a loving God cannot impose eternal punishment in hell. Yet if God is a God of justice, why do the wicked receive salvation? The view of St. Thomas Aquinas and many others is that God will punish the wicked. Aquinas affirms the idea of hell, where one of the joys of the redeemed will be to look on the punishments of the wicked.

Islam: Belief in the Day of Judgment

> Say, "O my Servants who have transgressed against their souls! Despair not of the mercy of God: for God forgives all sins: for He is Oft-forgiving, Most Merciful." (Islam. Qur'an 39.53)

Muslims believe that the whole of creation, including the world itself, will one day be destroyed by God and then rebuilt in a very different form. This day is *qiyamah* or the day of judgment (*yawmuddin*). A Muslim constantly invokes the mercy of God: "in the name of God, merciful, compassionate." No one knows the exact timing of this last day, not even the prophet Muhammad, but on that last day every human being will account for what he or she has done and eternal existence will be determined on that basis. A record of each Muslim's deeds is kept by the angels and is to be handed over at the last day. "Every man's actions have we hung around his neck, and on the last day shall be laid before him a wide open book." (Qur'an, 17.13)

In the Qur'an, salvation depends on a person's actions and also their attitudes in living out their life in accordance with the Qur'an. The most common word for "salvation" is *najah* and it is used only once in the Qur'an: "O my people how is it that I invite you to salvation, but you invite me to the fire?" (40.44). A sinful man or woman, however, who has repentance—*tauba*—can be turned toward the virtue of salvation.

Muslims recognize that individuals have different degrees of insight into the truth. Each person is judged according to his or her situation, and people who live according to the truth to the best of their abilities will achieve heaven. Infidels, people who hear the truth of Islam and reject it, are given no mercy.

Hinduism: Escape from the Endless Cycle of Birth, Death, and Rebirth

> All evil effects of deeds are destroyed, when He who is both personal and impersonal is realized. (Hinduism. Mundaka Upanishad 2.2.9)

In many religions of the East, the unitive state is the final goal of salvation. This state may reflect the union of the worshiper with God/absolute reality and a union with all existence, where the boundaries between subject and object, the knower and the thing known, are dissolved. For example,

> Meditate upon him and transcend physical consciousness. Thus will you reach union with the Lord of the universe. Thus will you become identified with him who is One without a second. In him all your desires will find fulfillment.
>
> The truth is that you are always united with the Lord. But you must know this. (Hinduism. Svetasvatara Upanishad 1.11–12)

This kind of mystical union is less common in the monotheistic faiths of Judaism, Christianity, and Islam, which in their mainstay expression all emphasize an absolute distinction between the infinite God and even the most revered prophet.

The Concept of Hell

Buddhism, Hinduism, and Jainism regard all states of hell as punishments for a limited period of time, only so that evil karma might be burned up and the soul have a future opportunity to find the Way. Christian and Islamic theologians dispute the question of hell, each within their own faith, some believing in eternal hell, and others looking to universal salvation.

In Hinduism the notion of salvation is expressed in terms of release or escape. The *mukta* is one who gained release from ignorance (*avidya*) and therefore also from *samsara* (rebirth). This release can be accomplished through one's own efforts or with help from a savior, especially from an *avatara* of Vishnu or Krishna.

Here Agni, the deity embodied in the fire, symbolically burns away sin and mental pollution through the fire ritual.

> Shining brightly, Agni, drive away
> our sin, and shine wealth on us.
> Shining bright, drive away our sin.
>
> For good fields, for good homes, for wealth,
> we made our offerings to Thee.
> Shining bright, drive away our sin. . . .
>
> So that Agni's conquering beams
> may spread out on every side,
> Shining bright, drive away our sin.
>
> Thy face is turned on every side,
> Thou pervadest everywhere.
> Shining bright, drive away our sin.
>
> Hinduism. Rig Veda 1.97.1–6

The release for some Hindus can mean an eternal resting place in the arms of a loving, personal God, but it most commonly means the dissolving of all personality into the abyss of Brahman.

> As rivers flow into the sea and in so doing lose name and form, so even the wise man, freed from name and form, attains the Supreme Being, the Self-luminous, the Infinite. He who knows Brahman becomes Brahman. (Mundaka Upanishad 3.2.8–9)

Hindus can reach salvation by one of four *yogas*:

> *Jnana yoga* is the way of knowledge. The mind uses philosophy to comprehend the unreal nature of the universe.
>
> *Bhakti yoga* is the way of love and devotion, including ecstatic worship of divine deities.
>
> *Karma yoga* is the way of action. Here salvation is sought after by one's good actions, which are done without thought of reward or gain.
>
> *Raja yoga* is called "the royal road" and is usually the way of the wandering monks who give themselves wholly to meditative yoga.

For the vast majority of Hindus the first three yogas are valid.

Most Hindus believe that they have a number of incarnations ahead of them in the future before they can attain final salvation.

Buddhism: The Noble Path to Nirvana

Mahayana Buddhism (in contrast to Theravada Buddhism) started by considering the idea of a monk striving for his own salvation and concluding that this approach was not sufficient for the vast majority of other people. Mahayana Buddhism believes in figures akin to saviors (*bodhisattvas*) who have reached the point of nirvana, but who choose to not enter it until the rest of humanity has been brought along. Buddhists can appeal to the bodhisattvas, who give help and aid to attain salvation.

In Pure Land Buddhism, compassion reaches to the depths of hell. The grace of Buddha Amitayus, the Buddha of Infinite Life, or Buddha Amitabha (Japanese: Amida), the Buddha of Infinite Light (who are one and the same), is so great as to save even the worst sinner. In the Amitabha Buddha's original vow, he pledged to save all sentient beings who would repeat his name ten times:

> Let him utter the name, Buddha Amitayus. Let him do so serenely with his voice uninterrupted; let him be continually thinking of Buddha until he has completed ten times the thought, repeating, "Adoration to Buddha Amitayus." On the strength of [his merit of] uttering the Buddha's name he will, during every repetition, expiate the sins which involve him in births and deaths during eighty million kalpas. (Buddhism. Meditation on Buddha Amitayus 3.30)

In Buddhism, ignorance rather than sin prevents salvation. This ignorance can be seen in the illusory belief that the world as we know it and the self or soul truly exist. In Buddhist terms, the essential purpose of absolute truth is to liberate all sentient beings, and in popular Buddhism the bodhisattvas who attend the Buddha are revered in that they show gracious aspects of ultimate reality:

> Therefore, O Shariputra, it is because of his indifference to any kind of personal attainment that a bodhisattva, through having relied on the perfection of wisdom, dwells without thought-coverings. In the absence of thought-coverings he has not been made to tremble, he has overcome what can upset, and in the end he attains to nirvana. (Buddhism. Heart Sutra)

Every Buddhist seeks nirvana, which is a complex and sophisticated concept. Nirvana is the state of being where there is a ceasing of all attachment, including being involved in nirvana itself. Nirvana does not mean extinction or nihilism, and can be both positive (like something) and negative (unlike something).

As mentioned previously, the concepts just presented apply to Mahayara Buddhism. Theravada Buddhist teachings, on the other hand, emphasize the individual monk who uses self-control and meditation to work towards losing the illusion of the craving self.

Judaism: A Messianic Deliverance

Judaism is universalist in that it believes that the messianic redemption is for all humanity as is the absolute sovereignty of God. Judaism is also particularist because the survival of the Jewish people continues as a separate entity. In Judaism there is a call to moral behavior and attitudes through which one's eternal existence is decided. In early biblical Judaism there was hardly any idea of a personal life after death. Judgment was made on the people as a whole.

The Hebrew Bible gives voice to the belief in a time of future justice when the Lord will rule the earth. The prophet Isaiah spoke of "the Servant of the Lord" bringing justice (42:1–4):

> Here is my servant, whom I uphold.
> My chosen, in whom my soul delights;
> I have put my spirit upon him;
> he will bring forth justice to the nations. . . .
> He will faithfully bring forth justice.
> He will not grow faint or be crushed
> until he has established justice in the earth. . . .

In later Judaism there is a belief in the final eschatological judgment of God on the whole world. Jews still hope for the return of the Messiah, who will administer eternal judgment and reward to all. This hope is still largely a communal belief involving the whole of creation rather than the fate of the individual.

The Jewish Day of Atonement (Yom Kippur) is the most important day in the Jewish liturgical year. Here the individual who has sinned cleanses himself or herself by fearless self-examination and open confession. There is a resolve not to repeat the transgressions of the past year.

> Hide your face from my sins,
> and blot out all my iniquities.
> Create in me a clean heart, O God,
> and put a new and right spirit within me.
> Judaism. Bible, Psalms 51.9–10

The emphasis of Judaism concerning salvation and human destiny is that the proper concern for men and women is their moral life on earth and that final eternal judgments are God's concern.

> God is on the watch for the nations of the world to repent, so that He may bring them under His wings. (Judaism. Midrash, Numbers Rabbah 10.1)

> "As I live," says the Lord GOD, "I have no pleasure in the death of the wicked." (Judaism and Christianity. Bible, Ezekiel 33:11)

Judaism tends to be more optimistic about the human condition than Christianity. Judaism, for example, denies that the individual inherits a sinful nature. As Isidore Epstein says,

> Judaism rejects the idea of human proneness to sin. A natural tendency to evil would be a contradiction to the fundamental command of holiness, a contradiction to the holiness of God which man is called upon to reproduce in himself. . . . Sin lieth at the door, not within man himself, and is followed by "and thou shalt rule over him." (Isidore Epstein, *Judaism* [Epworth Press, 1939] cited in *The World's Religions* 1965).

The Christian Belief in the Atonement of Christ for the Sins of the World

In his lifetime Jesus preached, taught, and mediated reconciliation between people and God. The Christian belief in atonement (at-one-ment) of men and women to God is an attempt to answer the questions of what the death of Jesus adds to his life and teaching. Belief in Christ's atonement generally claims that the death of Jesus, which was a local and particular event in Jerusalem, does in fact have universal consequences for humankind. Five main theories about atonement fall into two groups: objective and subjective.

Objective theories stress that through Christ's death, God has done for humankind what we could not do for ourselves.

Christ's Death as a Substitute

Anselm argued that the death of Jesus (God-made-man) was a rational necessity if human rebellion in the form of sin is to be forgiven. Anselm's thinking is that sin is an infinite offense against God that therefore requires a correspondingly infinite satisfaction to be put right. Only God can do this. Christians with this theological starting point see Christ's death as a substitute for each individual who deserves the penalty from God.

Christ's Death as a Sacrifice

Christ's death is also seen as a sinless sacrificial offering taking away (expiating) the sins of the world. Although the word (Greek: *hilasmos* and its cognates) has been translated by some as "propitiation" and suggests an angry God in need of placating, the sacrificial view draws on and includes

- Old Testament theologies of the suffering servant (Isaiah 53:5: "wounded for our transgressions") and sacrifices (ritual slaughters of animals) made, which removed ritual and moral uncleanness (Leviticus 5), and
- the New Testament Letter to the Hebrews, which shows Christ's sacrificial offering as an effective and perfect sacrifice.

Later in Christian thought, Augustine said that Christ "was made a sacrifice for sin, offering himself as a whole burnt offering on the cross of his passion."

More recently, the use of sacrificial imagery in conceptualizing the atonement of Christ has declined. The secular use of the term "sacrifice" to refer to heroic actions of individuals in war or in danger has made many theologians hesitant to use biblical imagery. However, the Roman Catholic Church still continues to regard the Eucharist as a sacrifice and to see the spiritual value of its use.

Christ's Victory and Ransom Theories

The view of atonement called *Christus Victor* was very popular within the western Christian tradition until the Enlightenment. The medieval idea of the "harrowing of hell" saw Christ dying, descending into hell, and breaking down the gates in order to free the imprisoned souls. A modern representation of the view can be seen in C. S. Lewis's *The Lion, the Witch and the Wardrobe*. In the death of the good Lion-ruler Aslan, the forces of evil seem to have won a victory. But Aslan was not conquered; he surrendered himself to the wicked ones, allowing them power to do their worst and in so doing disarming them.

Subjective Theories

The salvation theology associated especially with Peter Abelard (1079–1142) includes traditional ideas about Christ's death as a sacrifice for human sin, but Abelard also stressed the subjective impact of the cross. Abelard sought to understand Christian doctrine in order to know what to believe. This approach reversed the method of Augustine and Anselm. Avelard thought theology had become a science instead of a meditation.

- On the issue of the atonement Abelard ridiculed the idea that the devil had any rights over humankind. He also disagreed with the view that the death of Jesus Christ was offered to Satan as a ransom for human beings, or that it was offered to God. Why should God need Jesus' death when God could simply forgive sin?
- Instead of these ways of interpretation Abelard saw the significance of the death of Jesus in the effect that it has on us. Jesus' love for us awakens our love for Jesus. He wrote:

> Now it seems to us that we have been justified by the blood of Christ and reconciled to God in this way: through this singular act of grace made known in us—in that his Son has taken our nature on himself, persevered in his nature, and taught us by both his word and his example, even unto death—he has more fully bound us to himself by love. As a result, our hearts should be set on fire by such a gift of divine grace, and true love should not hold back from suffering anything for his sake (*Expositio in Epistolam and Romans*, 2; in J. P. Migne, Patrologia Latina, 178–8 32C–D; 836A–B).

UNIT 6:3 DEATH AND THE AFTERLIFE

> *Death carries away the man who gathers flowers, whose mind is attached to sensuality, even as a great flood sweeps away a lumbering village.*
>
> Buddhism. Dhammapada 47

> *To fear death, my friends, is only to think ourselves wise, without being wise: for it is to think that we know what we do not know. For anything that men can tell, death may be the greatest good that can happen to them: but they fear it as if they knew quite well that it was the greatest of evils. And what is this but that shameful ignorance of thinking that we know what we do not know?*
>
> Socrates

On the subject of life after death, many questions arise both for the religious believer and the nonbeliever. Shall we have bodies or will we be bodiless souls? Will we be able to communicate with each other? Are we to be absorbed into the cosmos or the Godhead and become one with everything? If so, how will our lives have mattered or to what effect will they have been lived? Is there a day of reckoning and judgment when all our deeds will become known?

In a general sense, religions do not consider the belief in a future life merely as a comfort or as an antidepressant for pain in this life. Rather, the belief in a future life enhances the purpose and meaning of this life. How you live in this world influences and determines your ultimate destiny. Some religions teach that life in this world is the only chance to prepare for life in eternity, and that only in the next life will what has been sown through actions while on earth be completely reaped. In a similar vein, a person's character survives death: as a person was good or evil in this life, so he will continue to enjoy goodness or be pained by evil in the next. Therefore, many of the world's religions teach that the wise people keeps their eyes on the future by accumulating merit, repenting for misdeeds, and seeking to clear up all accounts before the day of death.

> This world is like a vestibule before the World to Come; prepare yourself in the vestibule that you may enter the hall. (Judaism. Mishnah, Abot 4.21)

> Men who have not led a religious life and have not laid up treasure in their youth perish like old herons in a lake without fish.
>
> Men who have not lived a religious life and have not laid up treasure in their youth lie like worn-out bows, sighing after the past. (Buddhism. Dhammapada 155–56)

This unit of material first discusses belief in the soul and how this affects the religious belief in the afterlife. Then follows a brief discussion of life after death as it is conceived in Islam, Judaism, Christianity, Hinduism, Buddhism, and Sikhism.

The Soul

Religious thinking about death and the afterlife involves the concept of what it is to be a human being. Many of the world's religions believe that to be human is to have a soul as well as a body. The idea of a soul is that it is an animating force that is part of the body in a human being but which separates from it at death (some religions believe it also separates when we dream). Other religious traditions see the soul as preexistent to any present human form (incarnation) we have but as immortal when detached from the body. Dualistic anthropology sees the soul as linked to the divine in a human being but as an opposing force to the body. In religious parlance, to "save someone's soul" is to save his or her unique quality as a person and an individual. The soul is therefore seen as a person's spiritual and moral personality, which often struggles with their self-centered "self." Believers who wish to reach God must conquer their "self."

- Western religions (Judaism, Christianity, Islam) believe that each person has one earthly lifetime in which to conquer self-orientation and to know or love or serve God in this world.
- Eastern religions such as Hinduism believe in several lives through reincarnation; these faiths maintain that it may not be possible to find God or be enlightened in yourself in such a short time.

Eastern and Western religions do not share the same concept of human nature, and therefore they disagree about how we will exist in the life hereafter. In Hinduism the aim is to release the soul (*atman* and/or *jiva*) from the "selfish" body so that they will never reunite. In this view physical bodily life drags the soul down, and we need to be set free from its effects. In Buddhism there is "no self" (*anatta*) because since there is no subsistent reality to be discovered in or underlying appearances, then it follows that no self or soul resides under the human appearance. For Buddhists, everything is subject to *dukkha* (transience and change and the suffering that comes from trying to find the nontransient within it).

All religions see this earthly life as a preparation for the next life.

Islam

> O people! Fear God, and whatever you do, do it anticipating death. Try to attain everlasting blessing in return for transitory and perishable wealth, power and pleasures of this world. . . .
>
> Beware that this world is not made for you to live forever, you will have to change it for hereafter. God, glory be to Him, has not created you without a purpose and has not left you without duties, obligations, and responsibilities. . . .
>
> You must remember to gather from this life such harvest as will be of use and help to you hereafter. (Islam [Shiite]. Nahjul Balagha, Khutba 67)

Muslims believe that life in this world is only transitory and that life in the hereafter is a real place. All creatures will be resurrected in body as well as spirit when Allah calls them. Between death and the day of God's judgment, every spirit passes through a stage of being. If souls remain committed and attached to this earthly world they go on to suffer, but pure souls enjoy bliss. The Hadith speak of a divine balance that weighs human actions, and the As-Sirat Bridge, over which every soul passes, is thinner than hair and sharper than the sword. Muslims believe in *Jannah* (paradise) and *Jahannam* (hell). Paradise is described in the Qur'an:

> A state banquet shall they have of fruits; and honoured shall they be in gardens of delight, upon couches face to face. A cup shall be born round among them from a fountain. (Surah 37:38)

Alternatively, hell is made up of suffering in terms of molten metals and boiling liquid. Only people in heaven will ever see Allah. But if someone prays for the dead, the dead person receives the beneficial effects of the prayer immediately.

Muslims also believe that when an individual is staying in heaven or hell, progress can be made in their relationship with God.

> Those who are wretched shall be in the Fire . . . [T]hey will dwell therein for all the time that the heavens and the earth endure, except as your Lord wills; for your Lord is the sure Accomplisher of what He plans. (Islam. Qur'an 11.106–07)

Based on this verse, some Muslim theologians have deduced that the penalties in hell are not eternal, for "the time that the heavens and the earth endure" has a limit; in the end the heavens and the earth are to be dissolved and renewed. Life after the resurrection is a journey to stay closer to God. After people have been purified through suffering, even hell itself will be purged.

Judaism

In Judaism, belief in life after death is not so defined as in Islam. Some Jews (but not all) believe the soul is immortal, but only undefined teaching is available about what life after death is like. In the past scholars spoke of a shadowy place called Sheol, where the ghosts of the dead went until they came to be resurrected. The Bible portrayed Sheol as under God's control and divided up into sections for the good and the bad (Isa. 14:9–10; Job 3:11–19). In the later apocryphal literature, the belief in the resurrection of the dead emerges. For this reason the Sadducees, relying on the absence of any specific teaching in the Torah, denied the resurrection. In the first century C.E. Philo taught that the individual soul was immortal. Since then rabbis and other thinkers have put forward many other views, and the Jewish tradition has come to believe that human life continues through death. Furthermore, a consummation of the purposes of God will come in the messianic age. Today, while Orthodox Jews still believe in a bodily resurrection, many Reformed Jews are more concerned with ongoing spiritual existence. Some Jews see "afterlife" as what you leave behind in the community.

Christianity

The Christian hope is that death is not to be feared because it is the gateway to eternal life. Believers who accept Christ's death as a sacrifice for the world trust that their own sins are pardoned and that a place is secured for them in heaven.

> For God so loved the world that he gave his only Son, so that everyone who believes in him may not perish but may have eternal life. (John 3:16)

In the New Testament, heaven is the place where all believers in Jesus Christ will reign with him in glory after the last judgment. The traditional Christian belief is that after the resurrection of the dead, bodies and souls will be reunited in heaven.

Jesus taught that it was important to control the desire for material wealth in this life:

> "Do not store up for yourselves treasures on earth, where moth and rust consume and where thieves break in and steal; but store up for yourselves treasures in heaven, where neither moth nor rust consumes and where thieves do not break in and steal. For where your treasure is, there your heart will be also." (Christianity. Bible, Matthew 6:19–21)

Christian beliefs about the afterlife were first formed in the context of the time of Jesus, the second temple period in Israel. Jesus' ministry and teaching fell into a time of vigorous Jewish debate about the likelihood and nature of the afterlife. Arguing against the Sadducees and closer to the Pharisees, Jesus affirmed belief in the afterlife.

Christian Belief in Judgment

Early Christianity believed that the Jewish Messiah had come in the form of Jesus. Jesus therefore became the agent of God's judgment. This will happen at his second coming (Acts 10:42, 2 Cor. 5:10) when the dead are resurrected. Judgment hinges on both belief in Jesus as Christ (messiah) and as the Son of the Father (John 5:22f). A person is also judged on whether they have shown a godly quality of love (*agape*) in their actions to others (Matt. 25:31–46). Traditionally a distinction is made between the final judgment of God on all people at the end of history as we know it (the day of judgment) and the "individual" judgment on each person when they die and the body separates from the soul.

Roman Catholic Christians (see also 9:11) teach that at death the soul enters either the beatific vision, purgatory, or hell.

In conclusion, Bishop Kallistos Ware of the Eastern Orthodox Tradition offers his readers the thought that judgment is going on all the time and that hell is the natural consequence of human choice.

> Judgement, as St. John's Gospel emphasizes, is going on all the time throughout our earthly existence. Whenever, consciously or unconsciously, we choose the good, we enter already by anticipation into eternal life; whenever we choose evil, we receive a foretaste of hell. The Last Judgement is best understood as the moment of truth when everything is brought to light, when all our acts of choice stand revealed to us in their full implications, when we realise with absolute clarity who we are and what has been the deep meaning and aim of our life. And so, following this final clarification, we shall enter—with soul and body reunited—into heaven or hell, into eternal life or eternal death.
>
> Christ is the judge; and yet, from another point of view, it is we who pronounce judgement upon ourselves. If anyone is in hell, it is not because God has imprisoned him there, but because that is where he himself has chosen to be. The lost in hell are self-condemned, self-enslaved; it has been rightly said that the doors of hell are locked on the inside. (Bishop Kallistos Ware, *The Orthodox Way*)

Hinduism

For the Hindu, death means the separation of the soul from the body. At death the soul flies like a bird either to the world of ancestors (*pitriloka*) or gods (*devaloka*), depending on the merit of the earthly ritual you have accomplished. In a wide variety of later Upanishadic teachings (900–200 B.C.E.), the idea of a universal soul as the source of everything including individual souls is promoted. Here, the soul (*atman* or *purusha*) is seen as having qualities in relation to God. The soul resides in the heart and is identical with the ultimate source of the creation, Brahman. Later Upanishad thinkers disagree on the soul's relationship to the body and its relationship with the absolute reality of God.

The Hindu belief in reincarnation has become popular even in the Western world. A person's soul (*jiva*) is sexless; the soul was never born and will never die because it migrates from one body to another. This transmigration process is called *Samsara*, which literally means "that which flows together." On this basis, life is always changing and in flux.

Atman (soul) starts from inanimate objects like stones and moves to plant life or animal life automatically until it reaches a human being. From that point, reincarnation begins, and the *jiva* is reborn in people on the principle of karma. According to the law of karma, every action has a consequence that will come to fruition in either this life or a future life. Good consequence comes for good actions or bad for bad actions. On this basis, a person's present situation is explained by reference to past actions.

> Giving no pain to any creature, a person should slowly accumulate spiritual merit for the sake of acquiring a companion in the next world. . . .
>
> For in the next world neither father, nor mother, nor wife, nor sons, nor relations stay to be his companions; spiritual merit alone remains with him. (Hinduism. Laws of Manu 4.238–39)

After the cycles of transmigration the soul finds its *atman* (real self), at which point it becomes part of the Godhead and achieves release (*moksha*) from the endless cycle of rebirth. Hindus vary about how they see this absorption into the Godhead. Some people believe that the soul is completely absorbed with no distinction; other adherents say that slight differences still remain so that an individual soul can be identified.

In Hinduism God does not judge you. You determine your own future because you are responsible for your own actions. However, Hinduism acknowledges that even a store of good merit through conscientious actions or karma is not enough to achieve the highest goal, which is to end the cycle of rebirth. Thus, Hindus need to engage in disciplines such as yoga, which require meditative actions and devotions and knowledge and grace to escape the process or result of karma.

The law of karma also marks the way to classify men and women into strict classes and castes. Brahmins are the highest caste and therefore have a better chance of finding their *atman* (real self), but lower castes can find it, too.

Sikhism

> O shrewd businessman, do only profitable business:
> Deal only in that commodity which shall accompany you after death.
>
> Sikhism. Adi Granth, Sri Raga, M.1, p. 22

In Sikhism, the Hindu ideas on reincarnation are not only seen in terma of karma. Sikhs believe that all are equal in the sight of God. The highest form of life is the human one, and human status is not attributed to being in any class or caste system. For those who hearken to the name of God, death holds no terrors: "Death vexes not in the least those that hearken to the name. They are beyond Death's reach" (*The Japji*, trans. by Trilve han Singh et al., 1960). Sikhs believe that a person will be reincarnated again and again until his or her soul is united with God. But whether a person is reborn again depends as much on God's grace as on past deeds.

Buddhism

Buddhism rejects the Hindu belief in the transmigration of souls. The teaching of the Buddha was that eternal souls do not exist. This belief is called *anatta*, and the idea is that a person does not have a part of him or herself that lasts separate from the body for eternity. Here there is no belief in a self or a soul, or even an "I."

Siddhartha Gautama (ca. 566–486 B.C.E) taught that the effects of a person's karma could be broken by giving up greed, hatred, and ignorance—that is, the desire to have things or indulge in selfish feelings. Our attitudes must be born again and again until they are "right," until the craving has stopped. Only then will there be nothing that can be born again. For Buddha, rebirth is the eternal transmission of energy that comes from our actions.

> Relatives and friends and well-wishers rejoice at the arrival of a man who had been long absent and has returned home safely from afar. Likewise, meritorious deeds will receive the good person upon his arrival in the next world, as relatives welcome a dear one on his return. (Buddhism. Dhammapada 219–20)

A person who is enlightened (who has achieved nirvana) is one who has blown out the fires of greed, hatred, and ignorance. Nirvana is a state of being where all greed, hatred, and ignorance—even attachment to nirvana itself—has ceased. This status does not indicate extinction or nihilism; it can be both positive (like something) and negative (unlike anything else). For Buddhists, nirvana may be achieved in this life or in many lives to come. Nirvana is the place of freedom and absolute truth, where we are freed from the illusions of our existence.

Mahayana Buddhists believe in figures akin to saviors (bodhisattvas) whose intention is to take all sentient beings with them to nirvana. Buddhists can appeal to bodhisattvas, who can give help and aid to attain enlightenment. This offer is illustrated by belief and devotion to Amitabha Buddha, who has vowed to save everyone who calls to him in faith. The Sukhavati (Pure Land of the Western Paradise) is a heaven in which even the birds sing the teachings of the Buddha.

Summary

Beliefs about the situation and condition that await human beings after death or at the end of time vary greatly between religions. But overall, the world faiths share a strong belief that our human actions in this lifetime profoundly affect our destiny after death and in the afterlife.

UNIT 6:4 MORAL ACTION

> *If, as is the case, we feel responsibility, are ashamed, are frightened at transgressing the voice of conscience, this implies there is One to whom we are responsible, before whom we are ashamed, whose claim upon us we fear. . . . If the cause of these emotions does not belong to this visible world, the Object to which (our) perception is directed must be Supernatural and Divine.*
>
> J. H. Newman, *A Grammar of Assent*

Everyone in life has to make moral choices or take moral action. Morality is about right and wrong, innocence and guilt, or what people mean about living good or bad lives. The news is full of the results that are incurred after moral choices have been made. Prominent politicians choose extramarital sexual liaisons, a woman denies her ex-husband access to the children, a thug robs and beats an old person. We may decide to lie to save face. The explanations given for such behaviors vary, but whoever we are we cannot escape from having to make moral decisions and moral choices.

For the observant religious believer, religion and morality are closely linked or even inextricably linked. The relationship between religion and morality is expressed in different ways:

- Through the moral requirements of religious teachings and sacred texts
- Through the ideal characters of saints, gurus, and messengers of God
- Through the appeal to divine origins for moral codes and teachings
- Through beliefs in the reality of divine judgment or Karmic results of good and bad deeds
- Through providing a variety of ways to respond to the guilt people feel when they fail to aspire to moral thinking and action.

Virtually all of the world religious traditions embody specific codes of moral conduct. Ethical monotheism is the worship of one God where morality is based on experience and/or revelation, rather than derived at from philosophical explanation and argument. Not surprisingly, then, where a religion maintains a belief in the revealed word of God—e.g., the Qur'an or the Torah—claims abound to have the "absolute" truth that exists for all time.

Unlike the laws described by modern science, the unchanging divine law is innately moral and provides the basis for human ethics. For example, the Hindu concept of Dharma encompasses ethical, social, legal, and cosmological principles providing a basis for belief in an ordered universe and an ordered society. Religion tends to affirm that ethical values in human life are just as absolute as the fact that the Earth revolves about the Sun and that the way to salvation is found in following the divine laws and revealed teachings—e.g., the Torah (Judaism), the Reading (Islam), the Tao (Taoism), the eternal Dharma (Hinduism and Sikhism), the Dhamma of the Buddha, or the Word of God Incarnate revealed in the Gospels (Christianity).

Most religions, including Buddhism, Islam, and Christianity, teach a single standard of law applicable to all. Hinduism, however, teaches different Dharmas for people of varying social status (*varna*), stage of life (*ashrama*), and quality of inborn nature (*guna*), even though these differences should not obscure an underlying unity in the divine principle.

Even with these differences among faiths, an underlying common ground for the moral law—often referred to as natural law—transcends religion and social tradition. Generally speaking, religions have tended to believe in a naturally good way to live and to behave. In this book I use Western terminology—i.e., "moral action"—to describe the ethical dimensions of religious faiths. At the same time I acknowledge that it would be unjustified to use "morality" as an overarching descriptive term. I have thus made the conceptual differences part of the ongoing discussion in the book.

A central issue for all, but especially for believers in religions that claim to be based on God's revelation, is whether God has laid down unalterable rules or laws or whether human beings possess the innate autonomy to make their own moral decisions based on reasoning. If you decide on the latter—that it is valid to make your own moral decision outside of any moral code or teaching—then it seems that the moral decisions you have to face in your everyday life—e.g., to abort a child, to cheat the tax system, to commit adultery—are now all relative and dependent on the various situations that you as an individual have to face. On this basis, the consequences of the action determine which action is right or wrong, and you have entered the field of situation ethics (see chapter 3).

In this unit we explore the following ideas:

- Human nature and moral accountability
- The five precepts of Buddhism
- Hinduism: Dharma, karma, and the stages of life

- Islamic ethics: past and present
- Jesus' ethical teaching
- Approaches to Christian ethics today

World Religions and Moral Accountability

Virtually all the world's religions contain written codes of moral conduct or spiritual and moral teaching from their founders or leaders. World religions may see good living and moral accountablility in different ways, but generally speaking the faiths converge on what constitutes a good person and good actions. Views of this kind often depend on a person's anthropological beliefs, i.e., what they believe about human nature.

Some religions (Christianity, for example) believe that human beings are born with inborn defects of sin (original sin) or that they are born inclined to sin and always in the state of having to choose between good and evil. Buddhism, Hinduism, and Sikhism see human beings born with the accumulation or residue of their past behavior in previous lives (karma).

Religions affirm the belief that people are capable of (1) knowing the difference between good and evil and (2) acting on that knowledge. Religions also offer help to people in order to achieve these ends. In Christianity, God's grace is a concept of divine empowerment or aid to help with life's challenges. In Buddhism, help may come from saints, gurus, or the ancestors.

Buddhism

In Buddhism, "goodness" needs to be achieved before you can reach nirvana. The Buddha's teaching of the "middle way" to enlightenment embodies the idea of right conduct. For ordinary people this way is proclaimed in the Five Precepts, which are affirmations spoken by lay Buddhists each morning, and the Ten Precepts for members of monasteries. Buddhists are committed to these basic obligations.

The Five Precepts

1. Abstain from harming humans or animals
2. Abstain from taking what does not belong to you or has not been given to you
3. Refrain from improper sexual relations (monks are to abstain completely)
4. Refrain from false speech
5. Do not lose control of the mind through alcohol or drugs

Mahayana Buddhism has developed in so many different directions that citing them here is impossible. But at the heart of the good life for Buddhists of this tradition is the bodhisattva ideal, which shows that generous compassion and wisdom is at the center of right action to help lead all beings to Buddhahood. The wise person sees that all beings and all things are connected with one another. As a consequence, he or she acts spontaneously and compassionately to alleviate suffering in others and to help them to escape suffering completely in nirvana.

Hinduism

Hinduism contains many diverse styles of religious belief and practice that have evolved during the past three thousand years. A central belief is that the aim of life is to achieve *moksha* (liberation from the continuous cycle of rebirth), which has been described as a state of ultimate bliss, the absorption of the self into the absolute, or the joy of beholding the deity's presence. Liberation or release comes from seeing clearly, and good actions play one important part in the journey to liberation. According to the law of karma every deed, including moral deeds, binds each person to the empirical world (the earthly world of the senses) and determines one's moral status. The accumulation of good actions or bad actions in this life will cause an effect (karma) in subsequent lives until life is ordered towards liberation. When liberation is achieved, the soul does not return to earth but is absorbed into Brahman (God), the ultimate being. According to some Hindu philosophers a person has to become an ascetic (*sannyasin*) to achieve *moksha*.

Hindu ethics are grounded in the concept of Dharma, which refers to the natural order that makes the universe possible. Central to this concept is the duty of the Hindu in relation to the class/caste system. Even two thousand years ago the Gita dealt with the issue of performing caste duty, thus indicating that this system has its critics. A person's birth in a specific caste indicates the measure of moral progress accrued in previous lives. The Vedas speak of Brahman assigning separate duties to those who sprang forth from the first man's (Purusha's) head, arms, thighs, and feet. This teaching gave way to belief in four castes of people, and each Hindu must follow the duty (dharma) according to where he is placed by birth.

Hindus recognize four paths (*yogas*) that you can follow to obtain *moksha*. Hinduism divides life into four stages (*ashramas*). Not all Hindus follow all these stages today, but they are seen as the ideal way of life. Within these stages are the ritual obligations that provide the basis for Hindu life and morality.

1. The learning stage: the student or immature stage of life
2. The householder stage: earning a living, marrying, and having family
3. The retirement stage: beginning with the birth of the first grandchild, retiring from society, and traditionally becoming a forest dweller

4. Renunciation of the world: homelessness, wanderers, holy men, and women who break their ties with family and community in order to devote themselves to God.

Traditionally the proper ordering of things fell to the priests. The Vedas and the rituals associated with them were in time supplemented by shastras—manuals regulating conduct and ritual. One such is the Laws of Manu, which lay down dietary laws, essential rituals, and duties for each class, including laws, rituals, and duties for birth, death, and marriage.

Islam

In Western thinking, the study of ethics indicates the study of practical justification of the basis for one's actions. In Islam, there is no equivalent concept. Instead, several terms signify various disciplines developed during the classical period of Islamic civilization (ca. 750–1258). Three disciplines central to the study of ethics are signified by the terms *falsafa* (philosophy), *kalam* (dialectical theology), and *fiqh* (jurisprudence).

Falsafa and al-Farabi

The famous mystic philosopher al-Farabi (ca. 870–950) was Turkish. His philosophy contained elements of Aristotle, Plato, and Sufism. He wrote on a wide range of subjects, including mathematics, psychology, politics, and music. Al-Farabi's main work was *Attainment of Happiness,* where he defended the basis of divine revelation against free thinkers such as Al-Rawandi, who believed that the use of reason was sufficient in the search for truth and knowledge. Al-Farabi essentially put forward the idea that prophecy and philosophy are one, the difference being that the prophet perceives truth by inspiration, not the perspiration of being a philosopher. He also indicated that the prophet possesses the ability to make truth accessible to those who do not have the capacity for philosophical reflection, although the primary foundation for ethical judgments is philosophy, not the words of the prophet.

Kalam and Al-Ashari

The Muslim theologian Al-Ashari (873–935), who is often thought of as the founder of *kalam*, doubted the power of human reason to solve human dilemmas. For Al-Ashari and his followers, nothing happens apart from God's will. When people perform deeds, whether good or evil, they do so by the will of God. Moral judgment on these acts can only be judged by referring to the texts chosen by God, which are self-revealing.

Fiqh and Al-Shafii

Al-Shafii (d. 820) was the founder of the Shafi'ite school of Muslim law (*shari'a*). The *fiqh* scholars, in their theory of *usul al fiqh* (the sources of comprehension), focused on a hierarchy of revealed texts (the primary text is the Qur'an, which is extended by the exemplary practice [*Sunna*] of the prophet) and to acceptable methods of reasoning, especially *qiyas* (analogy). Al-Shafi'i attempted to specify rules that would regulate the exercise of *qiyas*, which were then used to establish a middle way to approach moral issues that fell between conservative and more liberal innovative traditions.

Today, much of Sunni Islamic thought has come to regard practical judgment in matters of morality as a matter of obedience to God's commands shown by specific revealed texts that are interpreted by recognized scholars.

Islam does not share a belief in the caste or class system of human beings. Because God is One, the goal is to create one single community of equals throughout the world (*umma*).

Muslim ethics are based on the Qur'an. The Qur'an, however, does not cover the whole spectrum of human experience. Further moral teachings for Muslims are found in the Hadith, although this volume does not possess the same authority as sacred text.

The Shar'iah (The Clear Path) instructs Muslims on how to live their lives. It applies the Qur'an and the Sunnah (Muhammad's recommendations in the Hadith) to the daily life of the believer. The Shar'iah has five types of obligation (Fard) to be followed. The first four of these are *Halal* (permitted) and the fifth is *Haram* (forbidden). Among the obligations are the Five Pillars of Islam (see unit 7:6), which lay down clear practices and the duty of Muslims throughout the world.

Faith in God as the Basis for All Morality

The first pillar is the *Shahada* (declaration of truth) and is the most important: "There is no god but Allah and Muhammad is His Prophet." This belief in God is the basis for all goodness. The Muslim should be conscious of God and fearful of God. The Qur'an says that the faithful are those "who believe, their hearts being at rest in God's remembrance" (13:28).

Moral Virtues

A number of important moral virtues are described in Islamic texts. They include the following:

> *Truthfulness* is important in Islam (Qur'an 9:120).
>
> *Justice* and *Fairness* come before friends and family: "O believers, be you securers of justice, witnesses for God, even though it be against yourselves, or your parents and kinsmen" (Qur'an 4:133).

Mercy and *Compassion*: Because the Prophet Muhammed was merciful to the Quraysh unbelievers when he conquered Mecca, Muslims should follow his example.

Sufi Muslims

Muslims who are Sufis have sought to engage in close personal experience of God. Historically there have been clashes between this focus in Islam and the emphasis on Shar'iah law and practice. However, no fundamental reason is apparent for this opposition. With exceptions, Sufis have insisted on proper Islamic observance.

Jesus' Ethical Teaching

Christian ethics focus on Jesus' summary of the Jewish Law, which he gave in answer to a request common in his day. Jewish rabbis and teachers were often asked to give their choice of verse that summarized the Torah. Jesus' answer was based on the Jewish teaching of the day:

> 'You shall love the Lord your God with all your heart, and with all your soul, and with all your mind.' This is the greatest and first commandment. And a second is like it: 'You shall love your neighbor as yourself.' On these two commandments hang all the law and the prophets. (Matt. 22:37–40)

In the Sermon on the Mount, Jesus elaborated on what loving God and one's neighbor might mean. For example:

- Thought is as important as action. One leads to the other.

  "You have heard that it was said, 'You shall not commit adultery.' But I say to you that everyone who looks at a woman with lust has already committed adultery with her in his heart." (Matt. 5:27–28)

- Love has to extend to the unlovable.

  "You have heard that it was said, 'You shall love your neighbor and hate your enemy.' But I say to you, Love your enemies and pray for those who persecute you, so that you may be children of your Father in heaven; . . . For if you love those who love you, what reward do you have? Do not even the tax collectors do the same? And if you greet only your brothers and sisters, what more are you doing than others? Do not even the Gentiles do the same?"(Matt. 5:43–47)

- Love is the hallmark of the followers of Jesus.

  "I give you a new commandment, that you love one another. Just as I have loved you, you also should love one

> another. By this everyone will know that you are my disciples, if you have love for one another." (John 13:34–35)

Through his ministry of healing and forgiveness, Jesus claimed to be uniquely embodying the power of God. Claims such as these led to the Sadducees (the temple authorities) to feel threatened. In time, this impression led to Jesus' crucifixion.

Approaches to Christian Ethics Today

Jesus' ethical teaching is based on the principle of love. But each generation of Christians since his time have had to work out how that principle operates in specific life situations—e.g., divorce, politics, marriage, and euthanasia. To summarize, three major approaches have developed to ethics in a Christian context.

A Situational Approach

As we have noted (chapter 3) Christianity has traditionally been heavily influenced by natural law, which, Peter Vardy says, "denies the demands of love, but natural law has the great advantage that people can be told what to do—it brings us back to the Christianity of the Grand Inquisitor" (in Dostoevsky's *The Brothers Karamazov*; see the discussion in *The Puzzle of Evil*, Vardy [1992]). Bishop John Robinson, in his book *Honest to God* (1963), said that

> The moral precepts of Jesus are not intended to be understood legalistically, as prescribing what all Christians must do, whatever the circumstances, and pronouncing certain courses of action universally right and others universally wrong. They are not legislation laying down what love always demands of everyone: they are illustrations of what love may at any moment require of anyone.

- A Christian who adopts situation ethics would ask what is the best decision to be made in order to love and help the person/people in the situation.
- A Christian who followed natural law would ask what the law says and than follow its teachings.

The Infallible Approach

In the Roman Catholic Church, the pope can decide on matters of morals and faith. These rulings are infallible. The word "infallible" is a negative term, which means what it is not—the ruling does not include error—rather than a positive term, like inspiration, saying what it is. Encyclicals (such as *Humanae Vitae*) also carry enormous authority; many believers count them as infallible.

Ethics Involving the Bible and Conscience

Many Christians reject both the situational view of ethics (which also rejects the notion of conscience) and an infallible approach, but they turn to the Bible's teachings as their guide, especially the New Testament. Some division exists within the faith as to what extent scripture can be seen as nonnegotiable. Throughout history, Christians of all persuasions have believed in the power of human conscience to guide them in their behavior. Here, conscience is at the heart of what it means to be human and plays a central role in decision-making.

Summary

The human preoccupation with what is right and wrong is as strong as ever in today's world, especially in an era of rapid technological, social, and scientific advances. Hard moral choices and ethical judgments face the world in the light of progress: Are genetically modified crops justifiable? Should what is shown on television be controlled? Is human cloning a good or bad thing? The world's religions in their varied ways look to divine revelation, sacred texts and writings, the wisdom of the great teachers, the natural laws of the cosmos, and inner conscience or enlightened consciousness to help them make moral decisions. Large areas of moral agreement exist among the world faiths—e.g., on helping the poor, not murdering or stealing, and in sexual ethics—although differences remain in how these areas are defined.

UNIT 6:5 PRAYER AND MEDITATION

Set me free, I entreat thee from my heart;
If I do not pray to thee with my heart,
Thou hearest me not.
If I pray to thee with my heart,
Thou knowest it and art gracious unto me.
African Traditional Religion.
Boran Prayer (Kenya)

For the Great Spirit is everywhere; he hears whatever is in our minds and hearts, and it is not necessary to speak to him in a loud voice.
Native American Religion. Black Elk, Sioux Tradition

"And whenever you pray, do not be like the hypocrites; for they love to stand and pray in the synagogues and at the street corners, so that they may be seen by others. Truly I tell you, they have received their reward. But whenever you pray, go into your room and shut the door and pray to your Father who is in secret; and your Father who sees in secret will reward you.

"When you are praying, do not heap up empty phrases as the Gentiles do; for they think that they will be heard because of their

> *many words. Do not be like them, for your Father knows what you need before you ask him."*
>
> Christianity. Bible, Matt. 6:5–8

Prayer is an ancient human practice. To pray is to present your self and your soul to God, or to gods, in an attitude of trust and humility. Prayer can be done in many different ways: by way of petition (making requests), praise of God, adoration of God, thanksgiving, listening to God, or focusing on the divine presence (contemplation). Prayer can also be individual or corporate. Various religious traditions emphasize different prayer practices, including prayer clothing, ritual cleansing, religious artifacts, use of sacred text, mental discipline, or concentration.

Meditation is the complement to prayer. While prayer directs the heart to God or ultimate reality as a transcendent object, meditation cleanses the heart of all that obscures reality so that its ultimate point may be found within.

In this unit, we look briefly at the practices of meditation and prayer in world faiths.

Meditation

Meditation takes different forms and techniques. In some forms, the mental discipline of meditation alters consciousness. In Taoism meditation may be a form of psychic purification and spiritual integration of "returning to the root" or the Tao.

Hindu, Jain, Taoist, and Buddhist scriptures describe meditation as sitting in a quiet spot, restricting all sense stimuli, controlling the mind's wandering thoughts and feelings, and finally attaining a stillness that reveals the true self-nature within. This self-nature may be the original nothingness, or union with the creative spirit that flows through all things. In Confucian meditation, this tranquillity helps make the mind clear and receptive to the impartial evaluation of knowledge.

In Christianity, Judaism, and Islam, the practice of meditation came through the monastics long after the scriptures had been compiled. Examples for each religion are as follows:

- *Christianity*: *Spiritual Exercises* of St. Ignatius Loyola and *The Dark Night of the Soul* by St. John of the Cross set out meditations on events in Jesus' life and passion. The meditator identifies his or her own spiritual journey with theirs.
- *Islam*: Muslim Sufis often base their meditation on one or several of the Qur'an's Ninety-nine Most Beautiful Names of God.
- *Judaism*: Jewish mystics may meditate on a verse of Torah to uncover its hidden meaning.

Prayer

The world's religions affirm that prayer should be done constantly, sometimes involving lengthy vigils. Prayer should be honest, quiet, and sincere conversation from the heart. Genuine prayer is accompanied by deeds, and the prayer of the hypocrite is without effect. The most authentic prayers are for the welfare of others ahead of oneself. For the believer who calls, an answer is available:

> The LORD is near to all who call on him,
> to all who call on him in truth.
> Judaism and Christianity.
> Bible, Ps. 145:18

> If the poorest of mankind come here once for worship, I will surely grant their heart's desire. (Shinto. Oracle of Itsukushima in Aki)

Sikhism

In Sikhism the focus in prayer is calling God to mind. This activity is called *nam simaran* from which the believer accrues great benefit:

> What then are the benefits to be derived from remembrance of the divine Name? The benefits of the divine Name include a life of quiet contentment; God's permanent presence within one's heart; the joy of singing with his devout disciples; and freedom from the need to rely on one's own infirm understanding. Instead of relying on his own limited strength, (enlightened man) puts his trust in the grace of the Guru, renouncing all intellectual pride and overweening arrogance. Aided by the Guru he crushes his self-centred pride and lives thereafter a life of pious deeds, a life which reflects his total obedience to God. (Sahib Singh, Sri Guru Granth Sahib Darapan, Vol. 3 [Jalandhar, 1963])

Ardas or "Petition" is formal, three-part prayer that is recited at the conclusion of most Sikh rituals. The first section is an invocation extolling the ten Gurus, the second section remembers past trials and triumphs of the Panth (the whole community of Sikh followers), and the final section is the actual prayer of petition. Guru Nanak encouraged believers to petition God, "Whoever cries and begs at the door of God will be heard and blessed."

Buddhism

For those who follow a monotheistic faith such as Islam, Christianity, or Judaism the spiritual power for personal change in life comes from God through prayer. For Buddhists it comes through training the mind and recognizing one's true nature.

The Theravada Buddhist discipline of the Four Arousings of Mindfulness aims at achieving awareness of all movements, sensations, feelings, thoughts, and ideas as they come and go in the body and mind. The Buddha's teachings in the Satipatthana Sutta stress the importance of being mindful each moment of the ceaseless changing of the phenomena of body, senses, and the process of thought. Through this meditation, the practitioner realizes that everything in his or her body and all the workings of the mind are transitory and unreal, and thus also realizes the truth of Dependent Origination. Within Indian tradition both "mind" and "heart" are aspects of consciousness and can be used interchangeably, not separately as in Western thought.

A Mahayana Buddhist tends to concentrate in meditation on constructing a mental image: for example, an image of Buddha, a bodhisattva, or the Pure Land.

Hindu Mantras

For the Hindu, prayer is pervasive, flowing through life.

> Lord of creation! no one other than thee
> pervades all these that have come into being.
> May that be ours for which our prayers rise,
> may we be masters of many treasures!
> Hinduism. Rig Veda 10.121.10

In Bhakti Yoga (Path of Love Devotion), the emotions—not the mind—search for truth. Love is the emphasis; God is loving to his creation, so adherents should meditate on him and give to him fully:

> "Engage your mind always in thinking of Me, engage your body in My service; and surrender unto me. . . . Completely absorbed in Me, surely you will come to Me (for anyone devoting himself to Me). I am the swift deliverer from the ocean of birth and death. . . . Just fix your mind upon Me, the Supreme personality of Godhead . . . [T]hus you will live in me always." (Bhagavad Gita)

Hindu prayer also involves mantras. At dawn, midday, and sunset, devoted Hindus sit facing east. They meditate by touching the body at six different points to express the presence of God in their physical being. They recite the most sacred of all Vedic verses, the *Gayatri* mantra (Mother of the Vedas): "Aum, let us meditate upon the most excellent light of the radiating sun (*shavitri*): may he guide our minds." If the sacred sound OM (symbolizing the past, present, and future of the whole world) is toned correctly, the worshiper can feel his inner self withdraw from his body. His consciousness is pulled up to merge with the absolute origin of sound (*Sabdabrahman*).

Islam

Prayer in Islam is a more formal concept than in Hinduism. All prayer emanates from the *Shahada*, which is the witness that all Muslims bear to God in their hearts: *"I bear witness that there is no god but God, and Prophet Muhammad is his Messenger."* This "bearing witness" is not simply a matter of saying words. Bearing witness means being convinced deep within that God exists and putting your trust in him. It also involves belief in Muhammad as the prophet of Allah (God) so that you become a better Muslim by being like the prophet himself. The three main kinds of prayer in Islam are *salat, dhikr*, and *du'a*. In Islam, the English word "prayer" does not indicate all that is meant by the word salat.

Salat (prayer) is one of the five pillars of faith in Islam. The Friday congregational *salat* reinforces the worldwide community of Islam as worshipers face the holy Ka'ba in Mecca, where it is believed that heaven and earth touch. Salat cannot be performed if you are unclean and impure, so Muslims have to ritually cleanse themselves (*taharah*) before they can pray. Two forms of cleansing are *wudu* (ablution) and *ghusl* (bath). The Qur'an states that while prayer is the key to paradise, purification is the key to prayer.

> O believers, when you stand up to pray wash your faces, and your hands up to the elbows, and wipe your heads, and your feet up to the ankles. If you are defiled, purify yourselves; but if you are sick or on a journey, or if any of you comes from the privy, or have touched women, and you can find no water, then have recourse to wholesome dust and wipe your faces and hands with it. God does not desire to make any impediment for you; but He desires to purify you, and that He may complete His blessing upon you; haply you will be thankful. (Islam. Qur'an 5.6)

Muslims must perform *salat* five times a day, but not as an empty ritual. Intention (*niyyah*) is all important. External ritual washing (*wudu*) can be made invalid by deep sleep or by being unconscious or by natural discharges from the body. If this happens, a Muslim must repeat his or her *wudu*.

Dhikr is a Qur'anic word that calls the faithful into "remembrance of God." It is an act of devotion during and after obligatory prayer (*salat*). But in Islam some Muslim mystics called Sufis seek ongoing direct personal experience of God. In Sufism, *dhikr* is thought of as spiritual food or sustenance, is one of the core practices of the faith, and involves the use of Qur'anic words and verses to remember Allah. Each Sufi order is focused on a *dhikr* of its own, which is given by the founder of the order. Sufi worship involves speaking and chanting its own *dhikr*, and spiritual Sufi guides choose and teach a *dhikr* that is appropriate to the spiritual stage of the novices in the order. A *dhikr* is effective only when there is right concentration and intention involving the body, mind, and speech of a believer. When the believer is united wholly with the *dhikr* itself, then oneness of subject and object is achieved and the heart is purified to receive divinely given attributes. The great thirteenth-century mystic poet Jalal Ud-Din Rumi wrote:

> When you seek Him, look for Him in your looking. Closer to you than yourself to yourself.

Du'a prayer in Islam is when a person calls upon God or makes private requests in prayer. This is different from the formal *salat* prayer. It is not to be equated with spontaneous mental or said prayer as in other religious traditions. *Du'a* prayer involves the use of set texts and rules, which are to be kept by individuals or groups of believers making the *du'a*.

Jewish Prayer: A Sign of the Covenant

In Judaism daily prayers are said at home as well as in the synagogue and especially on the Sabbath. The beliefs surrounding prayer are often symbolized by religious clothing. It is traditional for practicing male Jews to put on a *kippah* or *yarmulke* (small round cap) to show reverence for God above everything else. The Jewish male also attaches *tefillin* or phylacteries to his forehead, to remind him to concentrate his thoughts on the service of God, and to his left arm (right arm, if left-handed) to remind him to subject the desires of his heart to God, therefore prompting him to take action about his faith. Phylacteries are small black leather cubes and contain squares of parchment on which is written the *Shema* ("Hear"), which speaks of God's covenant relationship with Israel (Deut. 6:4–9; 11:13–21; Ex. 13:1–10; Ex. 13:11–16).

> *Hear, O Israel: The Lord* is our God, the Lord alone. You shall love the Lord your God with all your heart, and with all your soul, and with all your might. Keep these words that I am commanding you today in your heart. Recite them to your children and talk about them when you are at home and when you are away, when you lie down, and when you rise. Bind them as a sign on your hand, fix them as an emblem on your forehead, and write them on the doorposts of your house and on your gates. (Deuteronomy 6:4–9)

Jews do not wear phylacteries on the Sabbath or on festival days, as these events themselves bear witness to God's covenant with Israel. When the strap of the *tefillin* is being strapped around the middle fingers of the left hand, a special prayer is said:

> I will betroth thee unto Me forever
> I will betroth thee unto Me in righteousness
> And in judgment and in loving kindness and in mercy. . . .
> And in faithfulness and thou shalt know the Lord.

Tefillin are sometimes spoken of as "bridal garments," for they reflect the devotion and the affection between Israel and God. Like a marriage, within such a relationship both parties have obligations. God commits himself to take care of his people, and Jews undertake to keep the obligations of the prayer in doing righteousness (*sedaqa*) and justice (*mispat*), loving kindness (*hesed*) and faithfulness (*emet*). These acts are to be shown not only to God but to fellow Jews as well, because God showed these qualities when he brought Israel out of bondage in the land of Egypt.

Mikveh

A *mikveh* is a Jewish bath used for ritual cleansing. Jews must perform ritual cleansing after menstruation or after contact with the dead, otherwise they are not "clean" to worship God. The laws of purity are ancient in Israel. At the time of Jesus, during the second temple period, the Jewish historian Flavius Josephus described the *mikveh* purification before entry to the Temple area. Archaeologists have found *mikvot* all over Israel, but especially at the southern excavations of the Temple area in Jerusalem.

Christian Prayer

In Christianity, prayer is expressed in a variety of forms.

The first form of Christian prayer is *speaking to God*. In the Lord's Prayer, Jesus taught his disciples to address God as "Our Father in Heaven." Here he used the Aramaic word *Abba*, which is the intimate word for "father." The prayer is said by Christians all over the world. The prayer moves from adoration of the Father to surrendering to his will on earth, to a request for basic sustenance, to a plea for forgiveness in the evil world we inhabit and a cry of help and deliverance from God.

The Lord's Prayer

> When you are praying, do not heap up empty phrases as the Gentiles do; for they think that they will be heard because of their many words. Do not be like them, for your Father knows what you need before you ask him.

Pray then in this way:

> Our Father who art in heaven,
> Hallowed be thy name.
> Thy kingdom come,
> Thy will be done
> On earth as it is in heaven.
> Give us this day our daily bread;
> And forgive us our debts,
> As we also have forgiven our debtors;
> And lead us not into temptation,
> But deliver us from evil.

For if you forgive others their trespasses, your heavenly Father will also forgive you; but if you do not forgive others, neither will your Father forgive your trespasses." (Matt. 6: 7–15)

The second form of Christian prayer is *listening to God* in the practice of meditation. It is about experience rather than theory, a way of being rather than merely a way of thinking. Indeed, meditation has been described as a way of life, a way of living from the deep center of one's being.

The focus of meditation in Christianity is Christocentric, i.e., centered on the prayer of Christ that is continuously poured forth by the Holy Spirit in the depth of each human being. Meditation is the way of "pure prayer," where Christians leave all thoughts, words, and images behind in order to set their minds on the kingdom of God. In so doing they leave their egotistical self behind to die and rise to their true self in Christ.

The inner journey is one of silence, stillness, and simplicity. Practiced meditators embrace poverty of spirit, a radical letting-go, as the primary beatitude of the kingdom. This approach has been taught by the early desert monks such as John Cassian and more recently by John Main. The believer takes a single sacred word or phrase (mantra) and faithfully repeats it during the period of meditation. John Main recommended the ancient Christian prayer "maranatha." In Aramaic, the language of Jesus, it means "Come Lord Jesus" and is repeated silently and inwardly as four equally stressed syllables. Whatever thought, image, or feeling comes is returned to the mantra.

In 1977 John Main and another Benedictine monk, Laurence Freeman, were invited by the Archbishop of Montreal to found a small meditation community of monks and lay people in that city. Since John Main's death in 1982, a worldwide community of Christian meditation has come into being.

The third form of Christian prayer is *contemplation*, which is the practice of concentrating on God's presence. Contemplation is different from meditation in that there is less human effort and more receptivity to direct divine grace. Contemplation is often associated with Christian mysticism. Thomas Merton (1915–1968) entered a Trappist monastery after a sudden conversion to Catholicism in 1941.

His vow of silence and solitude lasted for twenty-seven years, during which time he became famous through his authorship of several best-selling spiritual books. Merton taught that ultimate truth existed in realizing God through deep contemplation. He wrote: "I have only one desire, to disappear into God, to be submerged in his peace." Through contemplation and nonactivity, the barriers of set ritual and over-organized religion could be broken down and an authentic spirituality found.

A fourth form of Christian prayer is *prayer with and for others* (*intercession* and *petition*). This involves *thanksgiving* to God for blessings received, *penitent* prayer, which confesses sin and asks for forgiveness, and *petitionary* prayer in which the congregation or individuals within that congregation make specific requests of God. Lastly, *intercessory* prayer is prayer made on behalf of others. This type of prayer is seen in the teaching of Jesus, who encouraged his hearers to address God in their need:

> "Ask, and it will be given you; search, and you will find; knock, and the door will be opened for you. For everyone who asks receives, and everyone who searches finds, and for everyone who knocks, the door will be opened. Is there anyone among you who, if your child asks for bread, will give a stone? Or if the child asks for a fish, will give a snake? If you then, who are evil, know how to give good gifts to your children, how much more will your Father in heaven give good things to those who ask him!" (Matt. 7:7–11)

All Christian prayer, whether in the Eastern or Western traditions, finds its supreme expression in the Eucharist (also Mass, Lord's Supper, Holy Communion—see Unit 8:5), where the grateful Christian in humility remembers, encounters, and receives once again the one and only sacrifice of Christ for the forgiveness of sin.

Summary

Prayer is of central importance and takes very different forms in the world's religions. It can mean set prayer to God (or gods) through the use of written and liturgical forms or, as in Sikhism, the calling to mind of God. In other religions such as Shinto, prayer is closely associated with rites of purification and offerings to the deities.

Meditation in Western use tends to be discursive and therefore involves thinking or concentration, e.g., on aspects of scripture, to enable deeper understanding or deeper personal response to the faith. In Eastern religions—for example, Buddhism—meditation is the process of training, purifying, and developing the mind. For the Buddhist this process includes the cultivation of tranquillity as an important state of being, because uncontrolled emotions and instability or obsessive thought are believed to trap people in the endless and beginningless round of rebirths and redeaths (*samsara*):

Sitting cross-legged,
They should wish that all beings
Have firm and strong roots of goodness
And attain the state of immovability.

Cultivating concentration,
They should wish that all beings
Conquer their minds by concentration
Ultimately, with no remainder.

When practicing contemplation,
They should wish that all beings
See truth as it is
And be forever free of opposition and contention.
Buddhism. Garland Sutra 11

Christian contemplation is a form of prayer that transcends the mind (nondiscursive) and has less to do with personal human effort but more to do with God's activity through divine grace. The focus here is on knowing God through a sense of presence or union with the divine. Many "mystics" of other traditions would identify with the same or similar aspirations.

UNIT 6:6 GENDER AND RELIGION

So God created humankind in his image,
in the image of God he created them;
male and female he created them.
Judaism and Christianity.
Bible, Genesis 1:27

Throughout most of Jewish history the synagogue has primarily been the domain of men. It has also been a very important communal institution. Was the synagogue so important because it was the domain of men, or was it the domain of men because it was so important? Perhaps the question becomes more relevant if we ask it another way. If women become leaders in the synagogue, will the synagogue become less important?

Laura Geller, "Reaction to a Woman Rabbi", in
On Being a Jewish Feminist: A Reader, ed. Susannah Heschel.
New York: Schocken Books, 1983

The equality of all—whether rich or poor, male or female, of any race, class, or caste—is taught in the scriptures of all faiths, even though the traditions of many different cultures discriminate between people on the basis of caste, or class, race, or sex. On occasion this kind of discrimination is fueled by interpretations of passages from sacred texts.

In the monotheistic faiths of Judaism, Christianity, and Islam, the equality of all people is supported by the traditional teaching that God is the parent of the human race and that the whole of humanity is descended from Adam and Eve, our original ancestors. In Buddhism, Jainism, Hinduism, and Confucianism, the notion of equality resides in the fact that enlightenment, unity with the absolute, or the realization of goodness is available to all universally.

Religious beliefs about the status and nature of male and female are very much at the forefront of discussion within modern society. At one level, the feminine is often celebrated in world religions as the source of life and creative fertility. The feminist critique of religion has focused on the subjection of women by the hierarchical systems of major religious traditions. This study has brought increased attention to exploring the interaction of gender and religion. Various writers, theologians, religious leaders, feminists, and psychologists have noted the key beliefs and attitudes which support the view that religions treat women as inferior to men. These beliefs and attitudes include the following:

- The belief that God is male, through the use of religious language that is masculine.
- The belief that something innate in women warrants their subordination and that something innate in men legitimizes their superiority.
- The belief that sacred writings (edited and written by men) have been the only legitimate guide to how women are viewed.
- Fears and superstitions about female sexuality. In almost every society, menstruation and childbirth are universally regarded as polluting, leading to complex ritual systems that segregate men from women during collective worship and require women to withdraw from active participation.
- Religious sanctions on women as to how they dress, choose a career or husband, what freedoms they are permitted, what property they can own, etc. These sanctions are the direct result of male inferiority, which has to assert itself as superiority and domination.
- The conviction that women by their very nature have gifts in bearing and rearing children and nurture of family life. Men have different gifts and roles. (Parallel arguments to these were made in support of the slave trade.) These gifts do not vary on an individual basis.

These beliefs and others are reviewed in this unit's brief study of gender issues.

Hinduism

Scholars of Hinduism tend to study the position of women by citing three historical periods in history: From ancient times to about third century B.C.E., a middle period from third century B.C.E. to the nineteenth century (when there was little change) and modern times. The story of the middle period is one of suppression for women.

Hindu society focuses on the appropriate order of things. The traditional role of women can be found in the Laws of Manu (c. 300 C.E.), which state that a woman should never be independent. When she is a child she depends on her father, as a wife she depends on her husband, and when elderly she depends on her sons. Nothing must be done independently, even in her own house. Elsewhere in the Laws of Manu women receive great honor as faithful wives:

> Where women are honoured, there the gods are pleased; but where they are not honoured, no sacred rite yields reward. Where the female relations live in grief, the family soon perishes; but that family where they are not unhappy ever prospers. The houses on which female relations, not being duly honoured, pronounce a curse, perishes completely, as if destroyed by magic. (*The Laws of Manu*, Manu 3.56–58 trans. George Bühler [New York: Dover Publications, 1969].)

In India, goddesses are still the main focus of devotion for many Hindus. Here, goddesses are often portrayed as independent and powerful, even destructive, and only when they have the companionship of their consort (for example, Siva) do they become fruitful in their endeavors. Elsewhere in the Hindu scriptures the wife is to worship her husband as if he is a deity:

> Though he be destitute of virtue, or seeking pleasure elsewhere, or devoid of good qualities, yet a husband must be constantly worshipped as a god by a faithful wife. (*Laws of Manu* 5:150–155)

In Indian culture the caste system put forward a rigorous definition of a woman's role. The Dharmasatras teach that women are ritually impure and therefore a source of impurity that forbids them from (among other things) studying or reciting mantras. A woman should not approach the family shrine during menstruation or pregnancy and should avoid the kitchen and food preparation, which can be difficult in small family units.

From a study of modern press reports, some of the ongoing injustices to women that have historically existed within Hindu practice, such as female infanticide and bride burning, although not mainstream, still occur in some areas today. In Hinduism, female infanticide arose from the general Vedic attitude towards women. The large dowries prescribed by the Vedas (the body of sacred knowledge revered by Hindus) meant that a girl was seen as a burden. The woman who gave birth to a daughter was ashamed, and much stigma attached to a woman who only gave birth to daughters. Hence infanticide, the killing of baby daughters or female fetuses, arose as a way out of this stigma. A recent U.N.

report stated that discrimination against baby girls was still in existence, extending to the abortion of female fetuses. In 1921, there were more than 97 women for every 100 men in India. Seventy years later, the number is reported to have dropped to 92.7. (Sonali Verma, "Indian women still awaiting Independence," Reuters. 12 Aug. 1997, New Delhi.)

Other modern news reports have claimed the ongoing practice of bride-burning. This activity is related to dowry, when the bride's family cannot pay up to the amount demanded by the in-laws. Often the in-laws make demands in excess of those made at the time of marriage. When the deadline runs out, the bride is burned. The press reports an estimated five thousand women dying each year for not bringing in enough dowry, despite the practice of levying dowry being illegal. At least a dozen women die each day in "kitchen fires" that are often passed off as accidents, because their in-laws are not satisfied with their dowries. Only a few of the murderers are reportedly brought to justice. ("Kitchen fires Kill Indian Brides with Inadequate Dowry," July 23, 1997, UPI, New Delhi.)

Many Hindus and human rights groups condemn such practices and work tirelessly to try to bring change, but where social injustices against women are linked with a lack of education or sustained religious teaching and cultural tradition, change is difficult, because such oppression is ingrained in the mindset of so many people. There are also Hindus who strongly maintain that the Indian government has no right to interfere in religious matters.

Buddhism

Buddhism and Jainism were both protest movements against the Vedic Brahmanical system. Women in sixth-century India endured a hard existence. Although *Sati* (Hindu widow-burning) was opposed by these reformers, women were still considered as hurdles on the path to liberation. Initially, the Buddha was very strict in his insistence on asceticism. He left his home and wife to attain nirvana, and some commentators say that he considered women a hindrance to that goal:

> Buddha is said to have induced his disciples not to look at a woman or even talk to her. (Bhatt, N. N. *History of Indian Erotic Literature.* New Delhi: Munshiram Manoharlal Publishers Pvt. Ltd., 1975.)

Major changes in the status of women within Buddhism were not at first obvious. However, against this wide cultural background the Buddha was more positive in his attitudes towards women. According to legend, after conversing with his disciple Ananda he decided to ordain his stepmother and fifty other women.

Fundamental Buddhist doctrines include compassion, the unity of all things, and the emptying of the mind of attachments, which includes emptying notions of sexuality. All of these doctrines de-emphasize gender.

Padmasambhava, also known as the great Guru Rinpoche, is associated with the introduction of Buddhism to Tibet in the eighth century C.E. He spoke of the special talents women bring to the spiritual path, which may, in the end, give them a greater potential. But although Buddhism has had great female teachers of the past, such as Sukhasiddhi and Niguma in India and Yeshe Tsogyal, relatively few women have been recognized.

Different traditions of Buddhism have a bearing on this situation. Theravada Buddhism has tended to be dominated by monks where the segregation of males and females was strictly observed in the context of renunciation, and communities of nuns in Tibet and elsewhere were historically small. In the Theravada tradition there is also the question of the subservient status of ordained women to monks, an ongoing issue that has been resolved for the Western branches of Buddhism. Theravada Buddhism also strives to control emotions that produce suffering. The situation reflects differently in Vajrayana, the Diamond Way, which is the Tantric aspect of Mahayana Buddhism. The Diamond Way works with the totality of one's being, which includes both male and female principles. Holding negative views towards women, therefore, would block a male practitioner's own development and would be a transgression against the tantric vows. The Kagyu Mahamudra and the Nyingma traditions of Buddhism reflect the doc-trine that followers are already fundamentally enlightened; through transmission from an empowered teacher working directly, a person's energy, luminosity, and wisdom are reawakened so that the primordial state of illumination shines through. Disturbing emotions are experienced "as they are" and without transformation.

Accomplished female practitioners are sometimes called *dakinis*. Fully enlightened wisdom dakinis as well as worldly dakinis played an important part in the life of many of the great masters of the past. The following story comes from the life of the Mahasiddha Saraha and is an example of how a wife (whose name was not even given) gave wisdom to her husband.

> One day Saraha asked his wife for some radish curry. She prepared the dish, but in the meantime Saraha entered a deep meditation from which he did not emerge for twelve years. He then immediately asked for his radish curry. His wife was astonished, "You have been in meditation for twelve years; now it is summer and there are no radishes." Saraha then decided to go to the mountains for more meditation. "Physical isolation is not a real solitude," replied his wife. "The best kind of solitude is complete escape from the preconceptions and prejudices of an inflexible and narrow mind, and, moreover, from all labels and concepts. If you awaken from a twelve-year samadhi and are still clinging to your twelve-year-old curry,

> what is the point of going to the mountains?" Saraha listened to his wife and after some time attained the supreme realization of the Mahamudra. (*K. Dowman, Masters of Mahamudra* [State University of New York Press, 1985].)

In the Sacred Teaching of Vimalakirti, stories point to the Buddhist belief that sexual differentiation belongs only to the phenomenal sphere, which is transient and illusory. In reality, beyond all appearances, sexuality is transcended.

Islam: Women in the Qur'an and the Sunna

At its inception, Islam surfaced from a culture where women suffered cruel inferiority as the property of men. Female infanticide was practiced, and there were no rights of inheritance. Islam brought great advantages to women. In the Qur'an, women are not seen as the source of sin. Eve (Hawwa) is not named, the implication being that Adam and Eve were both at fault. In Islam, no difference exists between men and women as far as their relationship to Allah is concerned, as both are promised the same reward for good conduct and the same punishment for evil conduct.

The Qur'an emphasizes the essential unity of men and women in a simile: "They (your wives) are a garment to you and you are a garment for them" (2:187), and also in a *Hadith* that expresses the equality of all:

> For the white to lord it over the black, the Arab over the non-Arab, the rich over the poor, the strong over the weak or men over women is out of place and wrong. (Hadith of Ibn Majah)

Women have independence in that they can make any contract or bequest in their own name. A woman can inherit in her position as mother, wife, sister, and daughter (half the amount inherited by a son), and women can receive education.

Mothers command great respect in Islam. Abu Hurairah reported that a man came to the Messenger of Allah and asked, "O Messenger of Allah, who is the person who has the greatest right on me with regards to kindness and attention?"

He replied, "Your mother."

"Then who?"

He replied, "Your mother."

"Then who?"

He replied, "Your mother."

"Then who?" He replied, "Your father."

The father is only referred to after the mother.

Islam strongly affirms marriage, and the sexual bond of marriage is akin to worship and a foretaste of heaven. The faith urges believers to have children as early as possible in adult life. Very rarely is abstention from marriage acceptable. Islam does not practice monasticism.

Women in Islam Today

In recent years questions have been raised over the implementation of the Qur'an and *Hadith*. For example, the veil (*hijab*) and total covering (*chaddor*) is not a command or duty in the Qur'an, whereas modest dress is, for both men and women (24:31). The Qur'an sets out the rights of women but then follows such affirmation with the statement that men have *darajah* ("rank" or "status") over women (2:228). The passage comes in a section setting out issues of divorce and could be interpreted to relate only to the ways in which men and women initiate divorce. The sense of the verse, however, is often taken generally to refer to all men having status over all women. Another verse (4:34–38) says that men have authority over women because God has made one superior to the other. Then appears an instruction for disobedient women to be admonished, sent to separate beds, and beaten, but taken with the prophet Muhammad's teaching for husbands to treat their wives well this passage is not a license to beat women. In marriage the woman retains her own name, though the children of the marriage take the father's name.

Clear role differences exist between the genders in Islam. The home is the wife's responsibility, and relations between the family and the outside world are the husband's. Many Muslims explain that role differentiation does not imply inequality but simply acknowledges the different strengths of men and women. The Qur'an, however, states that the man is the head of the household: "Women have such honourable rights as obligations, but their men have a degree above them" (Qur'an 2:228).

Women and the Bible

Feminist writers such as Annie Laurie Gaylor have pointed to the negative emphasis in both the Hebrew and Christian Bibles regarding women. In her book *Woe to the Women: The Bible Tells Me So,* she claims that more than two hundred Bible verses specifically belittle and demean women. Her list also includes a number of verses in the New Testament, such as the teaching of Paul in 1 Corinthians 11:3–15, where a husband is promoted as head of his wife because only man was made in God's image:

> For if a woman will not veil herself, then she should cut off her hair; . . . [A] man ought not to have his head veiled, since

> he is the image and reflection of God; but woman is the reflection of man. Indeed, man was not made from woman, but woman from man.

Other verses include

- 1 Corinthians 14:34–35: Women keep in silence, learn only from husbands
- Ephesians 5:22–33 "Wives, be subject to your husbands. . . ."
- Colossians 3:18: More "Wives, be subject. . . ."
- 1 Timothy 2:11–14: Women learn in silence in all submissiveness; Eve was sinful, Adam blameless. Yet women will be saved through bearing children. . . .

Annie Laurie Gaylor asks the question: Why should women—and the men who honor women—respect and support religions that preach women's submission, that make women's subjugation a cornerstone of their theology? As an American she is also wary of the future. She writes:

> When attempts are made to base laws on the Bible, women must beware. The constitutional principle of separation between church and state is the only sure barrier standing between women and the Bible.

Christianity: Jesus and Women

In Jesus' time, women were legally minors, on a par with children, and could be divorced easily by their husbands. The Torah was not taught to girls, and no woman was allowed to pass through the Gentile porch of Herod's temple. Because Adam had been tempted by Eve, a man could not be alone with a woman unless she was his wife. He could not even look at a married woman or he would be ritually unclean.

Against this cultural background, Jesus' attitude and treatment of women is remarkable for its day.

- Although Jesus had twelve male disciples, women also traveled with him, and some were his closest associates (Luke 8:1–2).
- Jesus' one-to-one conversation with the Samaritan woman (John 4) at the well broke down religious laws concerning women and rigid social barriers regarding Gentiles.
- Jesus healed the woman with the issue of blood (Luke 8:43–48).

The medical condition of the woman in Luke would have excluded her from all religious ceremonies and from social contact. Anyone who touched her would have become unclean themselves. She was an outcast. Secretly, as the crowd pressed in upon Jesus, she reached out and touched the fringes of his garment. The fringes symbolized Jewish law, and that law said her action should have made Jesus unclean. Instead of Jesus becoming unclean, the woman herself became clean. Jesus healed her and commended her for her faith.

- The story of the woman caught in adultery and the story of Jesus' feet being anointed by the sinful woman (Luke 7:36–50) are both accounts where Jesus shows compassion and respect towards women.
- All four gospel accounts report that, at his resurrection, Jesus appeared first to the women, even though legally their word did not count in Jewish society.

Despite the radical and positive attitude of Jesus to the women of his day, Christianity has developed along patriarchal lines (see unit 7:5), seeing the value and status of women as inferior. Of course many Christians past and present (see also unit 7:5) would oppose such views. Still, Christianity has exhibited a long history of promoting the subordination of women to men.

UNIT 6:7 MYSTICISM

Without mysticism, man can achieve nothing great.
André Gide

During the twentieth century the classic work of American philosopher William James, *Varieties of Religious Experience* (1902), incited thought and research into mystical experience. He identified mystical experience as an extension of human consciousness that possesses four basic qualities:

- Ineffability (sublime)
- A noetic quality (insights into depths of truth via the intellect)
- Transiency (short-lived)
- Passivity (they or it comes to you)

Philosopher Henri Bergson considered intuition to be the highest state of human knowing and mysticism the perfection of intuition. In the modern world scientists investigate ways in which certain drugs seem to induce quasimystical states. Some scholars describe a common core for mystical experience, but these descriptions have been criticized on several grounds, including the semantic problem of how words can sufficiently describe and classify experience that transcends the normal realities of life experience in this physical world. Because mystical experience lies far beyond description, some people assume that various experiences of this kind must essentially be at the heart of all religion; that view however, remains an assumption that falls short of being effectively demonstrated.

Finnish historian of religions Ilkka Pyysiäinen has produced a provocative analysis of the problem (in relation to Buddhism). Pyysiäinen addresses a number of the philosophical questions that have bedeviled the study of mysticism in recent decades, e.g.:

- Is mystical experience incommunicable, either within or across cultures?
- Is mystical experience amenable to psychological description?
- What are the characteristics of a mystical state that set it apart from other extraordinary subjective religious experiences?
- Do pure consciousness events actually occur, and are they the same everywhere? (Ilkka Pyysiäinen, "Beyond Language and Reason: Mysticism in Indian Buddhism" [dissertation 1993] in "How Mystical is Buddhism?" by Roger B. Jackson, *Asian Philosophy* 6, no. 2 [July 1996].)

After examining the positions of such theorists as Gadamer, Heidegger, Wittgenstein, and Rorty, Pyysiäinen concludes that, either within or across cultures, mysticism, like experience in general, is communicable, though we must always remain aware of the complex nature of the relation between experience and expression, and of the special problems raised by the frequently alleged ineffability of mystical experience.

This unit now surveys different aspects of mystical experiences that people have expressed through the ages.

Important Aspects of Mysticism

Despite the searching questions posed above, a survey of mystic writers, thinkers, and sages through the ages suggests that aspects of mysticism are recognized, albeit in various ways, throughout the world.

Mystical Knowledge

Mystical knowledge does not focus on facts, beliefs, and doctrines but on the natural state of consciousness, experience, and a state of knowing. This type of knowledge does not depend on academic or scholarly qualifications but on personal knowledge and the experience of the nature of reality itself. The difference is akin to that between talking about someone whom you only know by name and meeting them for yourself. Mystics often allude to the futility of ordinary knowledge. Medieval mystic St. Catherine of Siena (1347–1380) recorded God speaking to her in a vision:

> You cannot imagine how great is people's foolishness. They have no sense or discernment, having lost it by hoping in themselves and putting their trust in their own knowledge. (*The Dialogue of the Seraphic Virgin*)

Oneness

Although mystics follow very different paths, there is a sense in which their destination is a common one, leading to the One Truth. Muslim mystic Jalal Ud-Din Rumi expresses this notion, "The lamps are many, but the light is One" Jan Van Ruysbroeck (1293–1381) also wrote, "We can speak no more of Father, Son and Holy Spirit or of any creature, but only of one Being, which is the very substance of the Divine Persons. There we all are before our creation . . . There the Godhead is, in simple essence, without activity; Eternal Rest, Unconditioned Dark, the Nameless being, the Superessence of all created things." (Jan Van Ruysbroeck, *The Seven Degrees of Love.*)

Communion with the Divine

Mystical experience includes a sense of direct, intimate union of the soul with God through contemplation, meditation, and love.

> The simple, absolute and immutable mysteries of the divine Truth are hidden in secret. For this darkness, though of deepest obscurity, is yet radiantly clear; and, though beyond touch and sight, it more than fills our unseeing minds with splendours of transcendent beauty. . . . And we behold that darkness beyond being, concealed under all natural light. (Dionysius the Areopagite)

Loss or Transcendence of the Self

One type of mystical experience is losing oneself in God and/or union and harmony with the transcendent order through ecstatic contemplation. Another experience is reliance on spiritual intuition or exalted and blissful feeling. As Meister Eckhart (1260–1329) said,

> Oh wonder of wonders! When I think of the union of the soul with God!
>
> The divine love-spring surges over the soul, sweeping her out of herself into the unnamed being of her original source. . . . In this exalted state she has lost her proper self and is flowing full-flood into the unity of the divine nature. . . . Henceforth I shall not speak about the soul, for she has lost her name in the oneness of the divine essence. There she is no more called soul: she is called infinite being. (Meister Eckhart, Tractate 11)

Initiation into the Mysteries

The world "mystic" comes from the Greek root word *mystes*, which means to close (the lips or eyes). The primary sense is something like one who has vowed to keep silence. A mystic can be someone initiated into the mysteries as the means of acquiring knowledge of mysteries inaccessible to intellectual apprehension.

Mystic Writings

Many mystics have written of their experiences, providing a rich source of knowledge. Poetic language is frequently the vehicle of expression. Light, fire, an interior journey, the dark night of the soul, a knowing that is an unknowing . . . these images and symbols are often used for communicating about the mystical experience.

Heresy, Radicals, and Nonconformity

There have been countless examples throughout the history of world religion of people who have departed from the prevailing religious beliefs and practices of their day. These people have been labeled as heretics or radicals, dissenters or nonconformists (see chapter 9), but they are not necessarily of the mystical tradition. They may disagree over doctrine or sacraments or whatever as a specific issue and still have their spiritual feet well earthed in the known realities of religion. But people who have preferred to place their ongoing trust in their own personal experience rather than external religious authority come closer to being mystics. More often than not such people are controversial in challenging the prevailing beliefs in their religious culture. Some have seen Jesus as a Jewish mystic (although according to many theologians the gospel accounts portray him as a observant Jew). Through his miracles and teaching he became a challenge to the spiritual leaders of his day. Christian mysticism flowered among the early Gnostics in the first century, and in sixth-century India the Buddha gained Enlightenment and was a challenge to the Hindu tradition of his day. Islamic mysticism flourished with the Sufis in the tenth, eleventh, and twelfth centuries.

None of these mystical traditions can be said to have the same experiences, but each of them can claim a rising above the limitations of this world to that other spiritual plane, to experience the revelation of God or the enlightenment of being, and to transcend what they see as dogmatic formalism in so much of what goes by the name of faith and religion.

The Use of the Word "Mysticism"

Evelyn Underhill claimed that the word "mysticism" was one of the most abused in the English language. She wrote

> It has been claimed as an excuse for every kind of occultism, for dilute transcendentalism, vapid symbolism, religious or aesthetic sentimentality, and bad metaphysics. On the other hand, it has been freely employed as a term of contempt by those who have criticised these things. It is much to be hoped that it may be restored sooner or later to its old meaning, as the science or art of the spiritual life. (Evelyn Underhill [1911])

When referring to mysticism in the review of world religions that follows (see chapter 7), Evelyn Underhill's broad definition of the term "mysticism" will be employed. It will be taken to broadly represent that *tendency of the human spirit toward complete harmony with the transcendent order; whatever be the theological formula under which that order is understood. . . . Whether that end be called the God of Christianity, the World-soul of Pantheism, the Absolute of Philosophy—so long as this is a genuine life process and not an intellectual speculation.*

UNIT 6:8 SCRIPTURE AND SACRED TEXT

> *Your word is a lamp to my feet*
> *and a light to my path*
> Psalm 119:105

> *Indeed, the word of God is living and active, sharper than any two-edged sword, piercing until it divides soul from spirit, joints from marrow; it is able to judge the thoughts and intentions of the heart.*
>
> Hebrews 4:12

When something is "revealed" it is unveiled. "Revealed" religions are those that were originally revealed or sent to humankind by God. Proponents of these religions claim that such truths would not otherwise be known, or at least not in the same way. In the context of religion, the source of these truths is usually God. A scripture can be regarded as a sacred text in which messengers of God have written down divinely revealed teaching. Sometimes the period of revelation is over hundreds or even thousands of years, as in the case of Hinduism and Judaism. The Sikh scriptures were revealed and collated in nearly two hundred years. The standard text of the Qur'an was completed during the Caliphate of Uthman, perhaps by 651 C.E., which is only forty years after Muhammad had received his first revelation. Although the New Testament books were written in a period of between forty and one hundred years, the Christian Bible includes the scriptures of Judaism as its Old Testament, so truly the Christian Bible took fifteen hundred years to produce. But in all these religions the view is that the text is sacred, of divine origin and inspiration. Most religions also have writing—for example, credal statements, liturgies, and teachings—that are respected but not seen as sacred because they are humanly inspired by spiritual men and women. A belief in God's revelation and the sacred nature of the written word unites religious thinkers of many persuasions. In this unit we briefly examine the nature and some of the beliefs that surround sacred texts in two of the world's religions: Hinduism and Judaism. Then we look at the issue of interpreting sacred text with reference to Christianity.

Sacred Text in World Faiths

Hinduism—The Content and Nature of Scripture: Shruti and Smrti

Hinduism is an ancient religious tradition that has produced many sacred works. The most ancient and authoritative are the revealed literature (*shruti*): the Vedas, which include the Samhitas, Brahmanas, Aranyakas, and Upanishads.

In Hinduism the sacred writings are divided into two groups, *shruti* (meaning "that which has been heard") and *smrti* (meaning "remembered"). The remembered texts are important because they are human recollections of God's message to the world.

The Vedas: *Shruti* Literature

The Vedas are *shruti* and are believed to have no human author. The Vedas have the authority of "being there" and in some sense are seen to be revealed, although the exact sense of this revelation is not agreed:

- In Purva-mimamsa, which is one of the six orthodox systems of Indian philosophy, the Vedas are eternal, without beginning or end.
- Other schools of thought see God as the source of the Vedas, though not as an author but as part of his creative function, so that as humanity begins to fall (as it systematically does) into chaos and disorder, God incarnates himself to restore the Vedic order. He does this at the start of each new cycle of time, and the Vedas are manifested exactly as they were in the previous cycle.
- In the philosophy of Vedanta, the Vedas, like everything else not real, are *maya* (illusion) but they point to the reality that is beyond themselves.

The concept of sound is also linked to how Hindus relate to their scriptures. Direct experience of God (Brahman) arises from meditating on texts in the Upanishads, as they are heard, not from silent meditation.

> The work which the sages saw in the sacred sayings
> Are manifestly spread forth in the triad of the Vedas.
> Follow them constantly, you lovers of truth!
> This is your path to the world of good deeds.
>
> Hinduism. Mundaka Upanishad 1.2.1

The ancient seers of early Hinduism would go off to live in the forests alone, where they would become so holy and advanced in consciousness that they could "hear" the truths of the cosmos. The Upanishads themselves originate from the Vedas. Of the four Vedas, the most important is the Rig (Royal) Veda, which is a collection of hymns in ten sections called the mandalas. The traditional view is that these hymns were composed by Aryans who came from the plains of Central Asia east of the Caspian Sea and who occupied northern India around 1750 B.C.E. Whether the Aryans (meaning "noble") of this time believed in one god or many is not clear, but some parts of the writings suggest belief in the One:

> For an awakened soul Indra, Varuna, Agni, Yama, Aditya Chandra—all these names represent only one basic power and spiritual reality. (Yajur-Veda [a collection of prayers and writings based on the Rig Veda])

Smrti Literature

Smrti literature, popular with most Hindus today, reveals the truths about the universe through symbolism, mythology, and stories in the history of religion. In modern times some of the writings have been made into TV serial episodes. *Smrti* literature includes:

- *The Mahabharata*—written in the ninth century B.C.E. in Sanskrit but refined and extended during the following seven hundred years—is the world's largest poem, containing two hundred thousand verses. It has been translated into most languages. The poem is about the War of the Bharatas (the old name for India). They were a royal family who were in dispute between themselves over who should rule. But the importance of the tale for believers in not in the historical and mythical details. The epic touches on every part of human life and experience: war, intrigue, politics, social issues, wisdom of the elders, and so forth. The *Mahabharata* has influenced storytellers all through the ages and even today inspires theatre and puppetry in the villages of India.
- *The Ramayana,* which contains twenty-four hundred Sanskrit couplets, is a moral tale of duty, devotion, and right relationships and centers around Prince Rama and his wife Sita, who are the ideal couple. The story is of the workings of karma, which destined Rama to be banished to the forests. Accompanied by his wife and brother, they lived a reclusive life and were befriended by the holy men who meditated in seclusion. Sita is abducted by the demon Ravana, and Rama pursues and rescues her, aided by the monkey-general Hanuman. They both return to the city of Ayodha, where they are received with great joy by the people.
- The *Bhagavad-gita* (Song of the Adorable One) is one part of the Mahabharata and is the most famous of Hindu scriptures, written in probably the second century B.C.E. The text is based around the story

of Arjuna, a skilled warrior who wins an archery contest. He is going into battle when he suddenly orders his charioteer to withdraw, because he sees he must fight members of his family, his trusted and great teachers, and many whom he loves dearly. But his charioteer argues with him and then teaches him. As the story proceeds, readers are aware that the charioteer is no ordinary person; he is Vishnu, manifested on earth in the form of Krishna. This is God, not the god of popular myth but the one Supreme God who has taken human appearance to show Arjuna the truth about the nature of the self, about the path to Brahman and about *dharma* and *moksha*. The spiritual focus of the *Bhagavad-gita* is the love that God asks of his followers. With love, any offering, whether it is dying in battle, or offering God the smallest of gifts, is acceptable. But without it, all worship is worthless. This call to Hindus is for personal religion and devotion (*bhakti*) the way that is seen as the highest. Selfless offerings of serving others and perseverance are also commended. Many modern Indians turn to the Gita for inspiration.
- *The Laws of Manu* were written at the time of the *Bhagavad-gita* and are a very different genre. They include rules governing most aspects of life, including the roles ascribed to the four castes that exist in Hinduism.
- *The Puranas* are tales about the gods of the Vedas but are taken from more recent collections of texts about a thousand years old.

In *Smrti* literature, people are brought close to God. Through the stories and the dramas, it is revealed what is required of human beings to be their very best. The *Ramayana* and the *Mahabharata* give a thorough understanding of the concept of dharma: "what is right." Rama and Sita are perfect examples of how a man and a woman should be, both in their own character and in their relationship with each other. The ultimate religious question of "What is right?" is learned through the actions and character of Rama, Sita, and Laksmana, not through the rational philosophical speculation of the West.

Judaism

In Judaism, the sacred scriptures are divided into three sections—Torah (first five books of Moses), *Nebi'im* (Prophets), and *Ketubim* (Writings)—and from the initials of these, TNK, the word Tanakh is derived. Its books were written over a period of some thirteen hundred years of Jewish history, from the time of Moses until several centuries before the common era. The meaning of "Torah" is "teaching."

Various beliefs surround Torah:

- Moses Maimonides wrote in his thirteen principles of the Jewish faith that Torah is immutable and that it was given wholly to Moses.
- Orthodox Judaism believes to this day in the divine origin of both the

written and oral Torah. Through the Torah, God is felt to speak directly to the Jewish people. For some Jews, God's words must be taken literally and obeyed totally; for others, God's words need to be interpreted by people so that they can understand God's message to humankind.

The Content of Jewish Scripture

The center of this scripture is the Torah, the Five Books of Moses. The sages of the Talmud identified the Torah as the instrument by which the world was created (Avot 3.14), and they warned that no Jew who denied that the Torah came from heaven had a place in the world to come (B. Sanh. 10.1). Orthodox believers still hold this view, and some believe that God continues to act and be revealed in the study of Torah, but Progressive Jews have a variety of different opinions.

The book of Genesis contains stories of creation, the Fall of Man, and the lives of the patriarchs: Noah, Abraham, Isaac, Jacob, and Joseph. Exodus, Leviticus, Numbers, and Deuteronomy recount the Jews' liberation from slavery in Egypt and the revelation of the Law to Moses on Mount Sinai.

The Prophets include the books of Joshua, Judges, Samuel, and Kings, recounting the history of Israel in the days when it was guided by its prophets. Isaiah, Jeremiah, Ezekiel, Amos, Hosea, Micah, Habakkuk, Jonah, Haggai, Zechariah, Malachi, etc., record the words of individual prophets.

The Writings are the book of Psalms, containing prayers and hymns; Proverbs, Ecclesiastes, and Job, containing wise sayings and meditations on the human condition; Lamentations, which laments the destruction of the Temple; Song of Songs, where love poetry is often seen as describing the mystical relationship between God and Israel or God and humankind; and Daniel, which contains heroic stories of faith in the midst of persecution.

Oral Torah

In addition to the Tanakh, a tradition of Oral Torah was passed down to the rabbis of the first several centuries of the common era. The Oral Torah has been codified in the *Talmud,* which is made up of the *Mishnah* and the *Gemara,* and is authoritative for the observant Jew. The *Talmud* and *Midrash* discuss codifications of law, but also contain reflections of universal spiritual and ethical wisdom, the most famous of which is a small tractate of the Mishnah called the Abot or Sayings of the Fathers.

The Statutory Prayers

Jewish tradition also hallows the books of statutory prayers. The mystical treatise called the *Zohar* and several other works together constitute the Kabbalah, or mystical tradition, which has canonical status for many Jews. A number of theological works, notably *The Guide for the Perplexed* by Moses Maimonides

(1135–1204) and *Shulhan Arukh* by Joseph Caro (sixteenth century) are also held in the highest regard.

The Shema

The Torah contains the Jewish affirmation of belief in one God, the Shema. For Jewish faith, the Shema is the revealed word of God. These verses from Deuteronomy 6:4–6 are the first words a Jewish child should learn and the very last words a Jew should try and say when he or she passes from this life to the next:

> Hear O Israel: The LORD is our God, the LORD alone. You shall love the LORD your God with all your heart, and with all your soul and all your might.

The same passage goes on to speak of the lasting significance of these words from God, so that they should continue for every generation.

> Keep these words that I am commanding you today in your heart. Recite them to your children and talk about them when you are at home and when you are away, when you lie down and when you rise. Bind them as a sign on your hand, fix them as an emblem on your forehead, and write them on the doorposts of your house and on your gates. (Deut. 6:7–9)

These words are still found in a small metal container called a *mezuzah* placed on the lintel of the outside door and of the inside rooms of a believing Jewish household. They are written by hand on parchment, using ink of a special formula and with a goose quill for a pen. If a scribe makes a mistake during the writing of the scroll, it can be erased. But if a mistake is made writing the name of God, it cannot be erased. That part of the scroll must be buried and rewritten. Old and worn Torah scrolls are also buried.

The Masoretes

The Masoretes wrote in the eighth, ninth, and tenth centuries. They were scholars in Babylon and (at that time) Palestine who gave themselves to writing biblical texts free from errors. As time went on, the text of Ben Asher won universal acceptance. A famous old copy dates from 1008, but this was written about eleven hundred years after the last book of the Jewish Bible, the book of Daniel. Therefore the issue of reliability is a crucial one for scholars. In 1947, the Dead Sea Scrolls were discovered in caves at Qumran. The scrolls were written versions of the Hebrew Bible from before the Jewish Revolt of 66 C.E. Every book with the exception of Esther was found. This discovery showed that the Masoretes had been remarkably accurate in preserving the text.

The importance of the Torah can be seen in the reverence shown to the Torah in synagogue worship.

- When not in use the Torah is kept in the Ark, a set cupboard in the wall of the synagogue that faces Jerusalem.
- During the service it is reverently taken out and carried in procession to the *bimah* (reading desk).
- Men reach forward as it passes and touch it with their prayer shawls, which they then raise to their lips.
- It is a great privilege to read the scroll or to be called up to carry it. A blessing accompanies such an act, "Blessed is he who has given the Torah."
- The Torah is often capped with a silver crown because it is called "The crown of life."
- The person who reads follows the words with a pointer, not touching in case the ink becomes smudged.
- Only someone who is specially trained can read the scroll, because although it is written in Hebrew, it has no punctuation and no vowels.

The significance of the Bible in Judaism can also be seen in the history of its transmission and the careful way in which the Oral Torah has been preserved. Rabbi Akiba declared it to have been, *"the precious instrument by which the world was created."*

Christianity: The Content and Nature of Scripture

Beliefs about the divine origin and revealed nature of sacred texts have been illustrated above through a brief examination of sacred writings in Hinduism and Judaism. However, in all religious traditions some people call for sacred texts to be interpreted. Using Christianity as a focus, we can see how different views about the nature of revelation and the role of human reason influence how a believer regards and understands the concept of revelation and the interpretation of sacred text.

The Christian Bible includes the Old and New Testaments. The Old Testament itself formed the scripture of Jesus and his followers, who were themselves Jews. The Old Testament is identical to the Jewish Bible, but its books appear in a different order. Christians tend to focus on prophetic books in the Old Testament, for they are understood to announce the advent of Jesus Christ.

The Deutero-Canonical Books

Roman Catholic and Orthodox Bibles include a number of additional books, called *deutero-canonical* books, in the Old Testament. The most notable are the wisdom books, Sirach and the Wisdom of Solomon, the stories of Tobit and Judith, and the history of the Maccabean revolt, containing stories of martyrdom in 1–4 Maccabees. These books were known well among Jews during the last two centuries before Christ and were included in the Septuagint, the Greek translation of the scriptures. The New Testament was written in Greek. The early Christians largely spoke Greek, and they used the Septuagint as their Old Testament. But the deutero-canonical books were not included in the canon of Hebrew scriptures as decided upon by the rabbis at Jamnia in 90 C.E.. In the sixteenth century, at the time of the Protestant Reformation, the Reformers returned to the Hebrew rabbinic text as their prototype and went on to omit the deutero-canonical books from their vernacular translations of the Bible, e.g., Luther's Bible and the English King James Version. The omitted books are known collectively to Protestants as the Apocrypha. The Roman Catholic Church reaffirmed their status as holy scripture at the Council of Trent (1545–1603), and they remain part of the Orthodox scriptures as well. Many modern translations of the Bible now include them.

The New Testament

The New Testament contains the four Gospels: Matthew, Mark, Luke, and John. The first three are called "Synoptic Gospels" and have much in common, recording the life and sayings of Jesus, his death, and his resurrection. The Gospel of John presents a life of Christ as seen as the mystical source of salvation.

Acts of the Apostles, written by Luke, is a history of the church from the first Pentecost and includes the evangelical missions of Peter, Paul, and the earliest Christians.

The epistles of Paul, Peter, James, John, and others discuss matters of doctrine, faith, and morals for the early Christian Church of the first century. Paul's writings include the epistle to the Romans, 1 and 2 Corinthians, Galatians, Philippians, 1 Thessalonians, and Philemon. Other letters attributed to Paul, and which certainly are indebted to his influence, include Ephesians, Colossians, 1 and 2 Timothy, Titus, and Hebrews.

The Book of Revelation is apocalyptic and shows a vision of the end of the world and the second coming of Christ.

The books of the New Testament were written within one hundred years of Jesus' death, but the final decision about which books would be included or excluded from the New Testament canon was not made until the fourth century.

The Concept of the Revelation

The Catechism of the Catholic Church (1994) on the Authority of Scripture says,

> In order to reveal himself to men, in the condescension of his goodness God speaks to them in human words: indeed, the words of God, expressed in the words of men, are in every way like human language, just as the Word of the eternal Father, when he took on himself the flesh of human weakness, became like men. Through all the words of Sacred Scripture, God speaks only one single Word, his one Utterance in whom he

> expresses himself completely. . . . In Sacred Scripture, the Church constantly finds her nourishment and her strength, for she welcomes it not as a human word, but as what it really is: the word of God. In the Sacred books, the Father who is in heaven comes lovingly to meet his children, and talks with them.

A strong reliance on God's revelation and human inability to discern can be seen in the writings of the Greek-speaking Jewish philosopher Philo of Alexandria (c. 30 B.C.E.–c. 45 C.E.), who argued that the authors of the scriptures were passive instruments for communicating God's will. The picture in the New Testament (2 Tim. 3:16–17) is the thought of scripture as breathed by God (*theopneustos*).

Scripture and the Reformation

At the time of the Reformation, John Calvin (1509–1564) defended the authority of scripture against two main groups:

1. The Catholic Church argued that scriptural authority rested on scripture being recognized as authoritative by the Church.
2. The radical evangelicals (for example, Anabaptists) believed that every individual had the right to ignore scripture altogether in favor of personal divine revelation given by the Spirit.

Calvin preached that the Spirit worked through scripture, not by bypassing it. Instead he said that the Spirit lent authority to scripture by inspiring it. Calvin thus put forward the reformed view that the Church need not lend authority to God's word for that word to be authoritative.

Calvin's position is an important one, for it shows that the reformers (see chapter 9) did not see inspiration as directly linked with a view of absolute historical inerrancy. In his doctrine of accommodation, Calvin—following Genesis 1—suggests that a series of ideas, such as the "days of creation" are ways of speaking, a form of divine "baby talk." The idea here is that God reveals himself to different communities in ways that are suited or tailored to those who are to receive his revelation.

Today, conservative and fundamentalist views on sacred text engage in talk of biblical infallibility or inerrancy, but this development within Protestantism can be traced to the United States in the middle of the nineteenth century.

How a Christian thinks about divine revelation is often related to his or her theology of the Fall. In other words, to what extent have human beings fallen away from God? Are they so sinful that they cannot discern God's revelation unless it is laid down for them in the sacred text? Do people submit to its every word or is there a point of contact for divine revelation within human nature?

The Barth-Brunner Debate about Human Nature and Divine Revelation

In the 1930s Emil Brunner (1889–1966), a Swiss theologian, published *Nature and Grace*. The essence of his thinking was that there is a ready-made point of contact for divine revelation within human nature. Despite the fact that human beings are sinful, the ability to discern God remains because they are made in the "image of God." Brunner argues that biblical teaching, such as the command to "repent of sin," makes little sense unless people already have some idea of what sin is. Revelation enhances what we already know (i.e., what sin means) and in so doing it builds upon existing human awareness.

Brunner's colleague and friend Karl Barth (1886–1968) was outraged at the suggestion, as he saw it, that God needed help to become known or that humanity cooperated with God in the act of revelation. For Barth, any point of contact in human nature was the result of divine revelation itself; it did not exist unaided within human nature.

Chapter 7
Twelve World Faiths

UNIT 7:1 HINDUISM

Arjuna saw all the universe
in its many ways and parts,
standing as one in the body
of the god of gods . . .
Then filled with amazement,
His hair bristling on his flesh,
Arjuna bowed his head to the god,
Joined his hands in homage, and spoke . . .
I see your boundless form
everywhere,
the countless arms,
bellies, mouths, and eyes;
Lord of All,
I see no end,
Or middle or beginning
To your totality.

The Eleventh Teaching (the Vision of Krishna's Totality, *Bhagavad-gita*)

Hinduism is one of the oldest of the world's religions; the earliest of its beliefs dating back to perhaps 3000 B.C.E., though the basics of Hindu belief and philosophy were shaped during the Vedic period (1500 B.C.E.–600 C.E.). The term "Hindu" actually refers to the people and culture in the Indus Valley, which borders on Pakistan and India, so "Hindu" is therefore a geographical term rather than a religious one. To do justice to its complexity and diversity, Hinduism is best understood as a group of interconnected traditions. People do not generally call themselves "Hindu," instead, they are devotees of Krishna, Shiva, or one of the other gods. Statistically, there are over 700 million Hindus, mainly in India and Nepal. Hinduism is referred to as Sanatana Dharma, the eternal faith, and is not strictly a religion. Hinduism is based on the practice of Dharma, the code of life. No founder is recognized, and anyone who practices Dharma can call himself or herself a Hindu.

God as Ultimate Reality

In the Upanishads, Brahman is the name given to the One Supreme Reality, God. "Brahman" is not to be confused with the words *Brahmin* (the priestly caste) or *Brahma* (the Hindu creator-god). Brahman is beyond all description, without attributes, unmanifest, eternal, all-knowing, all-pervading, and all-powerful. In time this ultimate reality began to be described in terms that were more understandable to ordinary worshipers, and the transcendent Brahman was described as having "qualities," because the whole world was filled with them. One such description was Brahman as the Supreme Soul (*Parama-atman*), which indicated a relationship between Brahman and the soul of an individual living being. For Hindus, every possible aspect of the created world has some divine spark in it. Hindus worship many aspects of the divine in creation, for example:

Indu, Chandra	the moon
Surya, Savita, Mitra	the sun
Dhruva	the pole star

In earliest forms of the religion of the people of India and in the later sacred texts of the Puranas, God is not only male but also female; that is, goddesses began to be worshiped in their own right, and not merely as consorts of the gods. The Mother Goddess in her different manifestations is called Shakti and is the female energy in creation. Shakti is worshiped as the supreme female aspect of Brahman.

Brahma

Brahma is the creator aspect of Brahman, worshiped at only two of India's temples and portrayed with four heads and four arms and holding a drinking vessel, a bow, a sceptre, and a book. His *vahana* (the bird or animal on which a Hindu, Jain, or Buddhist deity is conveyed) is a swan.

The two great theistic movements within Hinduism are Vaishnavism, the worship of Vishnu, and Shaivism, the worship of Shiva. Hindu belief, however, usually holds that the universe is populated by a multitude of gods. These gods share some features of the Godhead but are seen as behaving similar to humans and being related to each other as humans are. The *samkhya* system of Hinduism and Buddhism does not accept the existence of a divine being.

Vishnu

Vishnu is the preserver god and has appeared in nine forms (avatars: incarnations of God) and is expected to appear in a tenth one. The most popular of these avatars of Vishnu are Rama and Krishna. Vaishnavism involves bhakti yoga (see unit 6.2).

Satya Sai Baba is a living saint and Hindu guru who, as the incarnation of truth and righteousness, is equated by his devotees with Rama and Krishna, and also with Kalki, the final avatar of Vishnu. Sai Baba was born on November 23, 1926, and resides primarily at his Puttaparthi ashram. He is believed to be the anavatar (manifestation) of the famous 1920s figure of the same name. He is venerated by hundreds of millions in India and abroad who believe that he is god-man. Sai Baba is well-known for his miraculous powers.

Shiva

Shiva is the destroyer god who resides on battlefields and in places of cremation. He wears a garland of skulls. He has three eyes with which to see the past, present, and future and four hands—two hold the balance between construction and destruction, two offer salvation and protection to humankind. He dances on the back of the demon Ignorance, which has to be destroyed if souls are to be saved. Shiva's dance energizes the universe. Shaivism also includes devotion by bhakti yoga.

Other popular gods are relatives of a supreme god, such as Ganesha, the elephant-headed god, a son of Shiva and Parvati. Kali, or Durga, the consort of Shiva, is worshiped widely throughout India in the autumn. Hanuman, the monkey-faced god, is depicted in many shrines, and along with Lakshmi, Vishnu's wife, is among the most important deities associated with Vaishnavism. Some people claim that 330 million gods and goddesses are recognized by Hindus, but this number can be misleading. The gods and goddesses are worshiped as *Murtis* (statues), pictures, or symbols. These representations are so numerous and diverse that the Hindu concept of the divine appears to be polytheistic. For this reason, Hinduism has been seen by monotheistic religions—e.g., Christianity and Islam—as a pagan religion. However, beyond the deities exists the one ultimate reality of Brahman, who is mysterious, transpersonal, and without gender.

Evil

Hindus do not think about sinfulness, which is a Judeo-Christian concept; instead Hindus are conscious of the need to perform dharma (duty). According to the law of karma, every deed, including moral deeds, binds a person to the earthly world and determines moral status. Hindus believe in demons, and like human beings demons belong to different castes (see unit 6:2). The vices recognized in Hinduism include:

Lust (*kama*)

Greed (*krodha*)

Delusion (*moha*)

Pride (*mada*)

Malice (*matsarya*)

All these vices should be avoided in thought, word, and deed.

The Way of Release and Liberation (see unit 6:2)

The aim of life for a Hindu is to achieve "release" or liberation (*moksha*) of the spirit, soul, or atman from an apparently endless cycle of rebirths. There are different ways to liberation, including the way of the sannyasin, who withdrew from the world, but most Hindus perform karma marga, which includes deeds of selflessness and puja or bhakti marga, acts of caring devotion to God. In the final analysis, liberation is the way of seeing clearly. The Hindu problem is *maya*, which is the name for visible things that are falsely assumed to be real. What we think of as reality is really all illusion, because one day everything will pass away. Illusionary goals such as power, sexual satisfaction, greed, and possessions all deceive us into thinking life is so satisfying that we need look no further for fulfillment. Only Brahman is real. The concept of *maya* has many connotations, including ignorance of the ultimate reality, which produces the illusory world of form.

For many adherents, the purpose of Hinduism is summarized in the following prayer:

> Lead me from the unreal to the real; lead me from darkness to light; lead me from death to immortality. (Brhadaranyaka Upanishad 1, 3.27)

Death and the Afterlife: The Law of Karma

The Hindu aspires to good works involving different forms of yoga (disciplines) to move along the path of life. There are many forms of yoga, one of which is karma-yoga, the discipline of action. The Hindu belief in *samsara* (rebirth) means that the indestructible soul (*atman*) enters a new body when a person dies. The actions performed in each lifetime determine the subsequent lives of the soul.

This is the law of karma, the cosmic principle of cause and effect. For each good action a person does, he or she will effect good results, and for each bad action—bad results. Through subduing the material world or meditation that transcends it, the atman can be freed. This cycle of rebirth continues until the soul finally achieves release by being united with the ultimate being of Brahman.

Moral Action

Class and Castes

The Vedas teach that Brahman assigned different duties to those who burst forth from Purusha's (the first man's) head, arms, thighs, and feet. Every Hindu is born into a different local caste group and national varna (color) occupational class. Each must therefore perform the dharma (duty) of his or her position in that class. The four castes are

1. Brahmins, color white; the priestly class representing the brains from Purusha's head and made up of teachers, lecturers, researchers, doctors, etc.
2. Kshatriyas, color red; the warrior and ruler class, representing the brawn of Purusha's arms and made up of civil servants and local regional workers.
3. Vaishyas, color yellow; representing the stomach from Purusha's thighs and made up of the lower official classes, farmers, traders, etc.
4. Sudras, color black; from Purusha's feet and made up of those who do hard labor in the community.

In addition to the four castes there were (and still are, despite reforms) the "untouchables" who are outside of the Hindu varna structure and who are permanently polluted because of their birth and their occupation. They are outcasts who do the most menial work in society.

The great and influential leader Mahatma Gandhi (1869–1948) was born into the Vaishya caste and adopted a nonresistant form of protest based on *ahimsa*, nonviolence, which originally only applied to creatures. He did much to oppose the caste system. Gandhi searched for a dharma that would include and affirm the value of all. He encouraged his followers to do tasks, e.g., cleaning toilets, that represented work typically reserved for the untouchables. Another reformer of the caste system was Dr. Ambedkar (originally an untouchable himself and the man who drew up modern India's constitution), who outlawed caste and promoted the presence of untouchables in fields like education.

The Ashramas

The Ashramas are the four stages of life; each has specific duties and implies certain moral choices. The stages are Student, Householder, Retired, and Ascetic.

Although a Hindu man or woman may work hard or be ambitious, the aspirations they hold about the future could well be determined as much by their birth as the actual opportunities they are given in society.

Dharma

The concept of Dharma (duty) in Hindu ethics imposes duties on each person. Your particular Dharma depends on who you are and what stage of life you have reached. Ethical teaching is divided into:

- Specific dharma—duties to one's caste
- General dharma—duties to one's stage in life, e.g., being a father, mother.

Early Hindu literature identified three cardinal virtues:

Self-control (*dama*)

Charity (*datta*)

Compassion (*daya*)

Other important virtues include nonviolence (*ahimsa*), truthfulness (*satya*), non-stealing (*asteya*), purity (*shaucha*), detachment (*vairagya*), nonpossession (*aparigraha*), fortitude (*virya*), and fearlessness. Of all these virtues, nonviolence is seen as the most important. *Ahimsa* is not limited to refraining from killing, but it also promotes a positive approach to treat all life (not just human life) as sacred. Suicide is not considered wrong in Hindu society. Often it is perceived as a religious act, not as a means of escaping from suffering.

Moral Reformer: Ram Mohan Roy

Ram Mohan Roy (1772–1833) founded the Brahmo Samaj (Society of the One God) in 1828. He was of the Brahmin caste and had studied both Christianity and Islam. Roy saw the need to concentrate on the ethical side of Hinduism rather than the devotional. Founded in 1828 in Calcutta, the Brahmo Samaj (initially known as the "Brahmo Sabha") is a religious movement. At its center is the belief in one omnipresent and omniscient God. The movement initially evolved in India, where it differed from existing practice in its rejection of idol worship and the caste system.

Profoundly influenced by European liberalism, Ram Mohan Roy concluded that radical moral reform was necessary in the religion of Hinduism and in the social practices of Hindus. His services to the cause of abolishing *sati* are well-known. He was one of the first feminists in India, and his book *Brief Remarks Regarding Modern Encroachments on the Ancient Rights of Females* (1822) is a reasoned argument in favor of the equality of women. He also worked at translating parts of Hindu scripture into English. Roy died in Bristol, England. Although the move towards his ideals was not great, he raised important issues in the modernization of the religion.

Prayer and Worship

Prayer permeates the whole of Hindu life. Worship is characterized by its immense diversity. Whether at home or at the temple, worship is a daily event, obligatory (*nitya*) for a practicing Hindu. Worship starts at dawn. The priests greet the awakening of the deity (god), they wash him (or her) and provide clothing ready for the god to receive worshipers. Worship (*puja*) commences by evoking the presence of the deity in the home, temple (*mandir*), or shrine. Congregational acts of worship consist of three main parts.

- *Havan* (the offering of fire): the priest kindles a sacred fire with wood, camphor, and ghee (butter). The fire represents the mouth of the god who devours the offerings given to him.
- *Prayer for purity*: the priest ceremonially washes himself by touching each part of his body. The worshipers copy him. Candles are used to represent the worship of light. Incense and flowers represent the earth. A fan represents the air, water is in the shell, and a dot of red paste is placed on the foreheads of the statues of the gods. The Arti dish of candles is then passed over the worshipers' heads, enabling them to receive the blessing of the gods.
- *Prasad*: distribution of blessed food. This act shows the approval of the gods, who have allowed the worshipers to eat the leftover food. If they have faith, the food destroys sin and pain.

Love and devotion are the main characteristics of *puja*. Devotion can take the form of singing, dancing, or offerings to the god. Hindus relate to God and to its images in different ways; as a mother to a child, as a beloved to his/her lover, as friend to friend. Also, the devotion and care that are poured out to the deity enable worshipers to transcend their own mortality and egocentricity and thus provide access to the *atman* within.

Evoking the presence of God is also very important through the practice of saying mantras such as *aum*, making mandalas and yantra (sounds and diagrams), and worshiping in sacred places or rivers that are associated with manifestations of God.

Hinduism and Gender

Hindu women come from diverse cultural and social backgrounds, and their roles vary over time and in literary tradition. To do justice in the space of this book to the breadth of Hindu thought and practice on this issue is impossible, but some general points can be made.

Even though society at the time of the *Rig-Veda* was patriarchal, women were given significance both in the family and in society. In particular, women's intellectual and spiritual lives were recognized, evidenced by the fact that the sacred rite of initiation marking the commencement of Vedic study was open to both men and women, and public religious rituals were performed by both husbands and wives. In time the ritual and educational roles of women became marginalized, as in the Brahmana texts where sons came to be valued more highly and rituals were enacted to prevent the birth of daughters.

The Upanishads

The order *Rig-Veda* texts honor marriage and family, while the Upanishads elevate the ascetic life with its emphasis on meditation and knowledge. Although a minority of learned women appear in the Upanishads (200 B.C.E.), women ascetics are few. Unlike Buddhism where nuns have a place in the religious structure, Hinduism did not favor women taking on the monastic role. When the life of a man came to be divided into four stages, marriage was only important in the householder stage when the religious duties were shared with his wife. The desire for salvation (*moksha*) meant that he later turned to leave home, became a forest dweller, and meditated on other-worldly concerns. In the Hindu texts a woman could accompany her husband into this stage at his request, but even in the forest a wife's duty was to serve her husband and forego sexual relations. Whereas a man could seek salvation through the ascetic way of life, a woman's goals were seen in terms of both marriage and rebirth. In the Mahabharata (early period), the sage Dirghatamas taught that no woman should stay unmarried. A celibate woman named Kuni was told that she could not go to heaven unless she married; no personal qualities could enable going to heaven. She subsequently married the sage Shringavat and stayed with him for one night. In so doing, she fulfilled the requirement.

Ambivalent Attitudes towards Women

Scholars have held that Hindu myths and ideology portray an elevated view of women as both godlike and also as sexually dangerous and in need of male "taming." This outlook is apparent in Sanskrit mythology about goddesses and temple representations of goddesses (with the exception of Kali). Hindu ideology stresses that this female power must be under male control in order to be positive and beneficial, though without female power the gods are helpless. [See also Hawley and Wulff, eds. *The Divine Consort* (1986).]

In some traditions of Hinduism, sexual taboos define ritual impurity. Sexual intercourse and menstruation renders one impure; a menstruating woman is treated like an untouchable. Yet the tantric tradition in both Buddhism and Hinduism contrasts these negative attitudes. In one form of Tantrism a woman's menstrual blood is seen as so powerful that the ideal ritual sexual intercourse takes place during menstruation. Tantrism reversed mainstream views and taboos and ritualized them.

In the legal texts a wife is supposed to be totally submissive to her husband. She must treat her husband as a god. In the Laws of Manu women were both deified and demonized. Although these texts reflect the period of the day, they are understood more as a description of idealized society. Women are to be revered as mothers, but as sexual partners they are obstacles to the man's spiritual journey. (Note: Regarding these laws I have chosen not to avoid those controversial matters relating to the caste system. The degenerate caste system is probably the one feature of Hinduism that is repudiated by most modern Hindu reformers and scholars.) When the *bhakti* movement emerged in Hinduism (sixth and seventh centuries C.E.), the religious status of women improved, though not the social. The *bhakti* cults challenged the hierarchical caste structures and were open to all castes and to either sex.

Even today, a son is still preferred to a daughter, no doubt partly for economic reasons as daughters leave home to marry, while sons remain with their parents and provide security for them in old age.

In 1994 a further indication of the lower status of women was the restriction Parliament placed on the use of amniocentesis and ultrasound in determining the sex of a fetus. This restriction was necessary because of the alarming rate of abortion of female fetuses. Recent movements within Hinduism, however, such as the Brahmo Samaj, continue to alter this situation.

Sati and Hinduism

Sati is illegal; the last known case was reported in 1987. But anyone reading a history of Hinduism will encounter its place in Hindu practice. A Hindu widow "became *sati*" by being burned on her husband's funeral pyre. At the moment of her death, a woman who commits *sati* was believed to transfer to her husband her own power, her *shakti*. The act protects him from the effects of death and cancels out any bad karma that he might have earned in life. This concept is very powerful. A *sati*'s protection extends to her family and her own children in future generations, and even to the onlookers. The widow then joined the ranks of the "*sati* mothers" who are revered as intermediate between earthly humans and the gods.

Hindu Mysticism

> The Lord of Love is before and behind. He extends to the right and to the left. He extends above; he extends below. There is no one here but the Lord of Love. He alone is; in truth, he alone is. (Mundaka Upanishad Part 2, 2:12)

At the heart of Hinduism are two beliefs about inner and outer reality.

- The inner belief that we all possess a divine soul (*atman*), which is a person's essential essence.
- The outer belief is in Brahman, who is absolute reality or "Being."

Hindu mystics search inwardly for the immortal absolute *atman* hidden within the body, the realization of the reality that the self is God. This outlook is summed up by the phrase, "Atman is Brahman."

Hindu mysticism is concerned with the nature of reality, which is obscured by *maya,* the illusion of separateness that creates the world of appearances. The individual struggles to attain both a clear vision of reality and the transformation of consciousness that accompanies such vision:

> The Lord of Love is one. There is indeed no other. He is the inner ruler in all beings. He projects the cosmos from himself, maintains and withdraws it back into himself at the end of time. His eyes, mouths, arms, and feet are everywhere. Projecting the cosmos out of himself, he holds it together. He is the source of all the powers of life. He is the lord of all, the great seer who dwells forever in the cosmic womb. May he purify our consciousness! (Shvetashvatara Uparishad 3:2–4)

Advaita Vedanta

In the eighth century, the eminent Hindu philosopher Sankara (c. 788–820) established Advaita Vedanta (nondualist) thought. According to tradition his childhood achievements parallel that of many mystics. At the age of five he became a Brahmin priest, and legend holds that he knew all the Vedas by heart. By age eight he was an initiate in an ascetic order. As a young man he renounced the world and traveled extensively, showing memorable skill in his ability to teach and dispute. He went on to found a monastic order and a number of monasteries throughout India. Sankara believed that Brahman is the underlying reality in all that appears to be. The different objects that are perceived via the senses are not real. There is only Brahman, and the disciples who have trained themselves to see realize this. The goal of human wisdom is to realize that there is no duality or difference between the self and Brahman.

Yoga

Hindu mystics practice many different types of yoga to raise mystical experience and seek union with the oneness of God.

- *Hatha yoga* is used to locate and activate the energy body that surrounds the physical body. The energy body possesses seven psychic centers of energy called "chakras," all associated with different states of consciousness, each with a different color. Hatha yoga raises the dormant spiritual powers (*kundalini*) to life.

- *Kundalini yoga* consists mainly of different body postures and intricate and sustained control of the breath. The Kundalini Research Institute was formed in 1976 in Canada and claims that Kundalini can evoke outstanding creativity and mystical experience. This form of yoga is used by new religious movements and sects such as the Rajneesh movement.
- *Bhakti, Karma, and Jñana yoga.* The *Bhagavad-gita* speaks of three kinds of yoga: *Bhakti yoga* is the path of love and devotion (see more in next section); *karma yoga* refers to acting without attachment to the consequence or result; and *Jñana yoga* is the path of knowledge—seeing through the illusion of separateness and coming to knowledge of the oneness of God.

The Path of Loving Devotion

Bhakti is the belief in the possibility of a relationship with God based on love.

- *Ramanuja* (c. eleventh–twelfth centuries) was a notable Hindu theologian who sought to give the devotional path more of a philosophical foundation. He agreed with Sankara on the sole reality of Brahman without distinction, but he disagreed with him that nothing else is real and all else illusion or appearance (*maya*). Ramanuja believed that the world of matter and individual selves is real; however, they all depend on Brahman for their very existence. This view is often referred to as qualified nonduality. Unlike Sankara, Ramanuja believed that Brahman was not without characteristics, in that although God is far beyond description, his earthly manifestations (*avatara*, see glossary) in the world act as analogies for the divine character.
- Mystics may practice all three types of yoga but in following the path of *Bhakti yoga*, the disciple loses the separate self in devotion. One famous Bhakti saint was Caitanya (1486–1533), a devotee of Krishna. He was a scholar in his day but he experienced very powerfully a form of religious love that caused him to renounce his Brahmanic learning and embrace a life of asceticism. Caitanya was an ecstatic who celebrated his love for God in singing, dancing, and shouting. Recent expressions of his legacy can be seen in the Hare Krishna movement (see unit 8:2).

Mantras

Mantras are words or phrases that are chanted or repeated as part of the practice of *Bhakti yoga*. The mystic believes that a mantra has the power to raise and attune awareness, leading the mystic to transcend the mind and merge with the oneness of God. The most famous mantra is *Aum,* an ancient word for God. Hinduism maintains the belief in the power of words to invoke or realize the divine presence.

This awareness has to a large extent become dimmed in Western culture. But in various religious and magical traditions, including Hinduism, people who practice mantra believe that to do so with focused awareness is to bring to consciousness the object of their meaning.

Paramahansa Yogananda (1893–1952)

Paramahansa Yogananda was born Mukunda Lal Ghosh in Gorakhpur, India. He is recognized as an influential modern Hindu sage and mystic. When he was seventeen, Yogananda met and became a disciple of Swami Sri Yukteswar Giri. He graduated from Calcutta University in 1915, and became a monk in India's monastic Swami Order, at which time he received the name Yogananda (signifying bliss, *ananda*, through divine union, yoga). In 1917, Yogananda founded a boy's school, where he combined modern educational methods with *Kriya Yoga* training (based on practical efforts). Mahatma Gandhi visited the school and wrote: "This institution has deeply impressed my mind."

Yogananda wrote of the perils:

> Do not think that you can comprehend the Infinite Lord by reason. . . . Man's highest faculty is not reason but intuition: apprehension of knowledge derived immediately and spontaneously from the soul, not from the fallible agency of the senses or of reason.

In 1920, Yogananda was sent by his guru as an emissary to the West. That same year he founded the Self-Realization Fellowship. For the next several years, he lectured and taught on the East Coast, and afterwards he traveled and lectured widely.

Yogananda taught the underlying unity of the world's great religions and methods for attaining direct personal experience of God. He also introduced the ancient techniques of *Kriya Yoga.*

Yogananda's life story, *Autobiography of a Yogi*, was published in 1946 and expanded by him in subsequent editions.

On March 7, 1952, Paramahansa Yogananda entered *mahasamadhi*, a God-illumined master's conscious exit from the body at the time of physical death. On the twenty-fifth anniversary of his death, his contributions to the spiritual welfare of humanity were given formal recognition by the government of India in the issuing of a commemorative stamp.

Scriptures (see also unit 6:8)

Shruti Texts

Shruti texts are traditionally called shruti, or "hearing," because they are believed to be eternal and were "heard" by men directly from God.

The Vedas (1200–1000 B.C.E.): These are four separate compositions: *Rig-Veda*, the *Yajur-Veda*, the *Sama-Veda*, and the *Atharva Veda*. Each of the Vedas has four parts: the Aranyakas and the Upanishads.

The Samhitas: Many mantras from these texts are used in modern Hindu worship and ritual. The Gayatri verse from the *Rig-Veda* is widely recited in daily worship.

The Brahmanas (800–500 B.C.E.): These manuals of prayer and ritual are written in prose for the guidance of priests.

The Aranyakas (400–200 B.C.E.): These texts came from discussions in the forests about meditation and ritual.

The Upanishads (400–200 B.C.E): These contain mystical concepts of Hindu philosophy and were originally tutorials given by gurus to their pupils who sat at their feet to receive the teaching. They form the basis of Vedanta philosophy.

Smriti Texts

Smriti texts are the educational texts that were composed after the Veda, but which are thought to be essential to its study. They deal with a variety of subjects including literature, rituals, law, astronomy, phonetics, and systems of philosophy. *Smriti* literature also contains the texts on Hindu mythology, the Puranas, and the texts of various Hindu sects who worship Vishnu, Shiva, and the Mother Goddess. Most Hindus accept the *Smriti* texts as law as they do not conflict with the *Shruti* texts, which have supreme authority.

The Hindu epics, the Mahabharata and the Ramayana, are classed as *Smriti* texts. They include moral and religious writings from the "remembered" tradition.

The *Bhagavad-gita* is a *Smriti* text, but it is considered to be the word of God since Krishna is an incarnation of the God Vishnu.

Hindu Festivals

There are literally thousands of different celebrations within Indian culture. At many times, similar events will be observed differently from one town to another, and some festivals are only celebrated by certain people (often caste members) in certain areas at certain times. However, a few major celebrations based in Hindu belief can be found in large areas of India in one form or another. Certain festival days are celebrated throughout India on a day fixed according to the Hindu lunisolar calendar.

- Ramanavami (Lord Rama's birthday), March/April
- Rathayatra (Pilgrimage of the Chariot at Jagannath), June/July

  The town of Puri, on the Bay of Bengal, is especially dedicated to Krishna. Each summer, huge chariots are brought out from the temples and are led in a majestic procession to a temple outside of the town. In this way, Krishna (also known as Jagganath) makes the move from his winter home in town to his summer garden palace, the temple surrounded by fields. In the past, faithful believers used to throw themselves in the path of the wheels, believing that being crushed beneath them would guarantee passage to heaven.

- Jhulanayatra ("Swinging the Lord Krishna"), July/August
- Raksha Bandham ("Tying the Lucky Threads"), July/August
- Krishna Janamashtami (Birthday of Krishna), August
- Navaratri (Festival of Nine Lights), September/October
- Dashara (Festival of Warriors), September/October

  This ten-day period honors the Mother Goddess, culminating in Dashara, the tenth day, a day of processions and celebrations. This festival is extremely important in Bengal, where it is known as Durga Puja.
- Lakshmi-puja (worship of the goddess Lakshmi), September/October
- Diwali (or Dipavali, Festival of Lights), October/November
- Mahashivratri (Night Sacred to Shiva), January/February
- Makara Sankranti, January

  When the constellation Makara (the alligator) is at its high point, many Hindus try to make a pilgrimage to the Ganges River where they can perform ritual bathing in the holy water and gain a remission of sins.
- Holi (Festival of Fire), February/March

  Holi, a spring festival in February or March, is a day of great funmaking often involving temporary suspension of caste and social distinctions, and practical jokes.

Seven Sacred Cities

The seven sacred cities of Hinduism are the following: Varanasi (Benares), Hardwar, Ayodhya, Dwarka, Mathura, Kanchipuram (Conjeeveram), and Ujjain. Other important pilgrimage spots include Madurai, Gaya, Prayaga (Allahabad), Tirupati, and Puri.

UNIT 7:2 BUDDHISM

> *The Buddha was once asked, "What is the Self?" and refused for a long time to answer. Eventually he said that "man will find out only when he no longer identifies himself with his person, when he no longer resists the external world from within its fortifications, in fact, when he makes an end of his hostility and his plundering expeditions against life."*
>
> Alan Watts, *The Spirit of Zen*

The central message of Buddhism is very simple: Anyone who exists is suffering and needs to be freed from it.

Buddhism traces its origin to the person of Siddhartha Gautama (c. 563–486 B.C.E.), who is revered as the Buddha (the Awakened One) in Buddhist tradition. But a word of caution needs to be sounded about the use of the word "Buddhism" to apply to all Buddhists, for their beliefs and practices vary greatly. Furthermore, the story of the Buddha does not commence with the birth of Siddhartha, but, as we shall see, with the previous lives of the bodhisattva (future Buddha) whose actions of self-sacrifice and generosity prepared for his final birth as Siddhartha Gautama.

The Story of Siddhartha's Going Forth

The Buddha's story is legendary and important for Buddhists throughout the ages who have seen the account of his spiritual quest as an example to them. Siddhartha was born into a royal family in the region of the Himalayan foothills of Northern India, which is today Nepal. At the boy's birth it was astrologically predicted that if he remained with the world he would become a great conqueror, but if he forsook the world and its pleasures he would become a world renouncer. His father decided to steer his son in the direction of the world and so he provided everything imaginable: three palaces, forty thousand dancing girls, but with strict orders that he should not see suffering and death. Siddhartha grew up and married, but he became restless to know about the outside world. When he was thirty years old, he outwitted his father's guards and left the palace grounds with his charioteer. Then he saw the four sights that changed the whole course of his life. He saw a sick person, an old person, a corpse, and finally an ascetic holy man (*samana*) who was trying to move beyond suffering and death by renouncing the pleasures of ordinary existence.

Siddhartha left his wife and son and the life of opulence and set out to find the causes of suffering and how to cure them. This event is known as the Great Going Forth.

The Path of Self-Denial and the Great Awakening

For six years Siddhartha wandered from place to place to seek the wisdom of religious holy men and practiced strict self-denial that was designed to overcome the needs and desires of the body. He then fasted till he was near the point of starvation. Finally he concluded that such strictness was not the way. He took up a more balanced form of self-discipline called the Middle Path, which avoided the extremes of self-indulgence and self-denial. When he was thirty-five years old, he at last came to the town of Gaya and sat under the Banyan tree (which became known as the Bodhi tree after the Enlightenment) and made a vow to stay there until he had understood the mystery of suffering. After a series of temptations and an intense time of meditation, he broke through to the realization for which he had searched. This was the "Great Awakening" from the sleep of ignorance that enslaves people in suffering and death. After this, Siddhartha was called The Buddha, the Enlightened One.

Theravada and Mahayana Buddhism

The initial disagreement within Buddhism probably concerned the involvement of laypeople (those who were not monks). The Theravada group thought that the finest expression of Buddhism lay in the monastic life of monks, whereas the Mahayana group saw a much greater role for laypeople. Theravada (the way of the elders) teaches that the Buddha was a historical figure who reached Nirvana purely by his own efforts, and his followers should follow that example. For Theravada Buddhists, prayer to the Buddha makes no sense as he is dead and "gone" into Nirvana. He has left them what they need, the teaching and his example.

Mahayana Buddhism took a different view, claiming that escape from the wheel of existence was possible for all who put their trust in the eternal Buddha. This claim suggests that Buddha can be worshiped almost as a salvitic figure. The ideal of the Mahayana tradition is the bodhisattva. The term "bodhisattva" refers to someone who has perfected wisdom who did not cross into Nirvana but out of compassion vows to take all sentient beings to Nirvana with him/her. He/she shares the merit they have gained from their many lives of self-sacrifice with others to help them. Mahayanan Buddhists regard bodhisattvas as agents of compassion to whom they can pray.

Tantric Buddhism, which is sometimes separated from the Mahayana as a distinct "Thunderbolt Vehicle" (Vajrayana), became especially important in Tibet, where it developed somewhere around the fifth to seventh centuries C.E. Tantric Buddhists emphasized the different use of techniques to leave the cycle of birth and death. Tibetan Buddhists, like all other Buddhist schools of thought, see meditation as a major force in the quest for enlightenment, but they also believe that Enlightenment can be achieved through the power of ritual. Furthermore, in contrast to other schools that see the attainment of enlightenment taking several lifetimes, the Tibetan school says it can be achieved in one lifetime, if one is prepared to take risks. Enlightenment can come suddenly like a thunderbolt! Vajrayana represented the last phase of Buddhism in India, where the religion—partly by being reabsorbed into the Hindu tradition and partly by persecution by Muslim invaders—ceased to exist by the thirteenth century.

God

Neither Mahayana nor Theravada Buddhism holds a concept of an omnipotent creator, indescribable absolute or theistic God. Though there are gods, they are no more than fellow travelers in the cycles of lives that every individual goes through. Buddhists argue that the presence or knowledge of a God and afterlife does not matter, because neither helps in the quest to root out greed, hatred, and ignorance. The Buddha was more concerned with how people improve their lives rather than worrying about ultimate questions of existence. One analogy he used was that of a person who is shot with a poisoned arrow: What would be the use of refusing to remove the arrow until the person had discovered who had shot it, and why, from where, and what was the kind of poison used on the tip?

When reading accounts of the Buddha's life, one must feel the sheer magnitude of his personality and the effect it had on almost all who met him. When problems were placed before him, they were addressed dispassionately. He would reach the heart of the real issues by breaking down the problem into various components and then reassembing them in a logical, orderly way, showing the true nature of the problem. He was undoubtedly a great teacher of great insight and wisdom who compelled people to listen through his creative use of stories and images. He was also a man of unceasing compassion, which so impressed his biographers.

Buddha taught in the context of a Hindu cosmology that saw the self or soul (*atman*) reborn, moved by karma, towards release or salvation (*moksha*). (See 6:1.) However, he greatly modified Hindu beliefs by his insight into three universal truths:

1. All appearance is impermanent and transient (*anitya/anicca*).
2. Suffering arises when we seek something permanent or eternal to rely on (*dukkha*).
3. There is no essence, eternal soul, or self soul to go to heaven, only the dependent chain of cause and effect or energy putting different lives into existence.

The Buddha knew about indulgence from his upbringing in the palace and about extreme self-denial from his renunciation. By meditation he developed the middle way that leads to Enlightenment and Nirvana.

The Way of Enlightenment: The Four Noble Truths and the Eightfold Path

The teaching of the Buddha is captured in the Four Noble Truths and the Eightfold Path.

The Four Noble Truths are

1. *Dukkha.* All life is unsatisfactory in that we suffer not just physical pain, but the lack of harmony we find in life. Part of the Buddha's teaching is to alert people to the human situation of anxiety and unsatisfactoriness. He pointed to six moments in life when we all find ourselves dislocated:

- The trauma of birth
- Sickness
- Decrepitude: getting old and the fears that accompany it
- Fear of death
- Being yoked with your greatest dislikes (e.g., disease, personality defects)
- Being apart from what you love

2. *Samudaya.* The origin of *dukkha* is *tanha* (craving, desire, and greed). Our aversions to things in life—e.g., death—cause us to crave immortality. Our craving or greed for wealth can cause war and death. Craving means that you are ignorant about how you inflict *dukkha* on yourself.

3. *Norodha,* which means "to control." The cure for *dukkha* involves overcoming selfishness and release from craving, to cease (*nirodha*) wanting and desiring things. The Buddha used the metaphor of impure water to identify Five Mental Hindrances that would impede a cure for *dukkha*:

> Discolored water—Greed, e.g. food
>
> Boiling water—Hate
>
> Water choked with weeds—Sensual craving
>
> Storm waves—Restlessness and anxiety
>
> Muddied water—Indecision and fearful doubting

4. *Magga.* This is the Middle Way—that is, the Eightfold Path. One might start anywhere on the path and work on various areas at a time; one need not take only one step at a time.

The object of following the eightfold path is to depart from worldly thinking and action, which is unwholesome (*akusala*), and to travel the spiritual road to wholesome thinking and action (*kusala*). When this happens, craving will cease, and you will be free from the force (*karma*) that causes you to be reborn. The bliss of nirvana can be found in this life; you do not have to die to find it. The path involves "right" or "appropriate" elements.

1. *Right Concentration.* Developing penetrating insights. Meditation techniques were learned by the Buddha in the context of his times and overlap to some extent with those of Hindus.

2. *Right Views.* Recognizing the nature of suffering and the need for a path; having the conviction that the path is the way to travel.

3. *Right Attitude.* Being single-minded, applying yourself, having a heart to do the task ahead. Intention is central to Buddhism.

4. *Right Speech.* Speaking the truth. Deceit is foolish. It reduces your being because we deceive almost always to avoid revealing who we really are. Speaking with charity and compassion and avoiding gossip, slander, etc.

5. *Right Action.* Understanding the five precepts: not killing (including animals), not stealing, not lying, avoiding sexual misconduct, and avoiding drugs and drink, which cloud the mind.

6. *Right Livelihood.* Working in such a way as causes no harm. The Buddha considered some professions incompatible with spiritual goals, e.g., prostitution, slave trading, being a butcher or a soldier.

7. *Right Effort.* Maintaining your willpower. The Buddha said,

> Those who follow the Way, might well follow the example of an ox that marches through the deep mire carrying a heavy load. He is tired, but his steady gaze, looking forward, will never relax until he comes out of the mire. O monks, remember that passion and sin are more than the filthy mire, and that you can escape misery only by earnestly and steadily thinking of the Way. (Quoted in Pratt, *The Pilgrimage,* p. 40)

8. *Right Mindfulness.* Being aware or attentive and seeing things as they really are. Ignorance, not sin, is the problem. We need to be alert and exert control over our minds by training.

Death and Beyond

Rebirth happens because our craving and desire fuels us to be reborn again and again. The goal of life is nirvana, which means "to blow out" or "to extinguish." Here the image of fire is used to talk about ultimate things. These fires are not ritual fires which the Brahmins had to light, but the interior ethical fires of greed, hatred, and ignorance. The meaning of nirvana is that these fires have been extinguished.

The Buddhist idea of karma is different from Hinduism's. The Buddha rejected the Hindu belief in the transmigration of souls, because he taught that eternal souls did not exist. Instead, rebirth is the ongoing transmission of one's impulse or energy. It is the things we do and the cravings or desires we have that cause us to be born again and again.

Moral Action: The Five Precepts

Buddhists believe that all ethical actions (karma) have consequences, so that what you do today will affect the kind of person you become in the future. This is the law of natural consequences. The *Dhammapada* opens with the words, "What we are today comes from our thoughts of yesterday, and our present thoughts build our life of tomorrow; our life is the creation of the mind." If you are unwise you will stay trapped in a cycle of craving and unsatisfactoriness.

Guidelines for Buddhists in their moral actions come in the form of the Five

Precepts, which all committed Buddhists undertake to follow. These were mentioned earlier but bear repeating:

1. Not to destroy life (no human killing, no negative attitude to life)
2. Not taking what is not given (avoiding dishonesty)
3. Not indulging in harmful sexual activity
4. Not saying what is not true
5. Not taking things that cloud the mind (alcohol, drugs, etc.).

Meditation and Worship: The Sangha

The pattern of relationship between a Buddhist king and the monastic community (*sangha*) came about through the Emperor Asoka in the third century B.C.E. The relationship was symbiotic so that, in exchange for the loyalty and religious support of the *sangha*, the emperor became the patron of the Buddhist dharma.

Traditionally monks were beggars, and in Southeast Asian countries they still go on daily alms rounds. Buddhist monks have also traditionally been celibate. They depend on the lay community for food, financial support, and new recruits. Often children enter a monastery and their formative years are spent as novices: studying, learning, and doing chores. Then, following ordination, they take their vows and become full members of the community.

A typical day for a Buddhist monk includes ritual, devotions, meditation, study, teaching, and preaching.

- *Offerings*. A central concept behind the rites and festivals of Buddhist laity and monks is that of offering (*dana*). For the laity, this act includes the giving of food and new robes to the monks, as well as flower offerings, incense, and praise to the image of the Buddha, to stupas (temples or mounds), or bodhi trees, or, especially in Mahayanist countries, to bodhisattvas.
- *Puja*. *Puja* means "worship" or, more generally, "honor, respect," in Theravada Buddhism. The Buddha is not worshiped, but his teaching is honored at the shrines and temples. Buddhist temples vary very much in design from one country to another, but they are usually built to symbolize the Five Elements: Wisdom, Water, Fire, Air, and Earth. For many lay Buddhists, temple visits are frequent, as performing *puja* is a source of merit and of good karma, including offerings of flowers, candles, and incense. Gratitude for the dharma of the Buddha is shown by bowing, kneeling, and prostrating. An important focus of *puja* can be the Three Jewels or Refuges of Buddhism:

  I go to the Buddha for refuge

  I go to the Dharma for refuge

  I go to the Sangha for refuge

- *Meditation.* Through meditation Buddhists seek to transcend the restrictions of ordinary thought and the senses that so affect our minds and keep us from attaining quietness and tranquility. Buddhist monks have meditative practices that are highly developed and which help them on the path to enlightenment, but concentration and meditation are the last two components of the Noble Eightfold path for all Buddhists. Still, meditation is necessary to break passion and ignorance and to help the practitioner to nirvana.

Gender and Buddhism

The Buddha initially resisted the institution of nuns (*bhikkhunis*) for fear that they might bring distraction and moral impropriety. From the beginning, however, Buddhism has allowed women to be nuns, but with eight additional rules to those imposed on men.

Despite this unequal treatment, many women chose the monastic life and while still subservient, they were freed from wifely duties. Buddhist literature contains the Therigatha, which are verses of seventy-three senior *bhikkhunis*; the *Bhikkhuni-Samyutta*, which are more verses of ten women elders; and lastly the *Apadana,* biographies (in poetic form) of forty nuns who were living at the time of the Buddha. Both monks (*bhikkhus*) and nuns aspired to teach the Dhamma and attain Arahantship. Two famous *bhikkhunis* were *Dhammadinna* and *Bhadda Kappilani*, who both preached and expounded the Dhamma. In Tibet, the most important deity is Tara (Sanskrit = "star"), a female bodhisattva, who for many Tibetans has already become a Buddha. She was advised of the spiritual advantages of being reborn as a male, but she vowed to remain in female form.

With regard to the role of women in society, the Buddha upheld the traditional values of his time where wife and husband had mutual obligations, the woman's role being largely domestic. Although the Buddha taught that anyone who wished to could become enlightened, in Indian society there continued to be a strong dominant male influence limiting women and preventing equal status.

Today many Buddhist teachers and writers address women as equal with men. A recent message from the Dalai Lama to women worldwide spoke of equality.

> Mere tradition can never justify violations of human rights. Thus, discrimination against persons of a different race, against women, and against weaker sections of society may be traditional in some places, but because they are inconsistent with universally recognised human rights, these forms of behaviour should change. The universal principle of the equality of all human beings must take precedence.
>
> Whenever Buddhism has taken root in a new land there has always been a certain variation in the style in which it is observed. . . . Especially heartening is that Buddhist women

> are casting off traditional and outmoded restraints and dedicating themselves to implementing and promoting Buddhist practice.
>
> Peaceful living is about trusting those on whom we depend and caring for those who depend on us. Even if only a few individuals try to create mental peace and happiness within themselves and act responsibly and kind-heartedly towards others, they will have a positive influence in their community. As well as being equally capable, women have an equal responsibility to do this.
>
> Remembering the kind influence of my own mother, I pray that women working for inner peace and, through that, peace in the world, may be blessed with success. (Excerpts from a message sent by His Holiness the Dalai Lama to the fourth International Conference of Buddhist Women, held in Ladakh, August 1995. Reprinted from *Sakyadita*, the magazine of the International Association of Buddhist Women, Spring 1996.)

Mysticism

> Not thinking about anything is zen. Once you know this, walking, standing, sitting, or lying down, everything you do is zen. To know that the mind is empty is to see the buddha. . . . Using the mind to look for reality is delusion. Not using the mind to look for reality is awareness. Freeing oneself from words is liberation. (*Bodhidharma*)

According to accounts, Bodhidharma (fifth century C.E.) brought Zen Buddhism to China. Scholars have expressed doubt about the historicity of the accounts, yet we are told that he traveled to China by ship and arrived in Southern China around 475. After finding little success in his mission, he wandered to the north by crossing the Yangtze River on a reed. Legend has it that he entered motionless *zazen* meditation for nine years by facing a rock wall near to The Shaolin Temple (famous for kung fu).

Bodhidharma's teaching emphasized meditation and strict practice. The word for meditation is "Ch'an" in Chinese and "Zen" in Japanese; therefore this teaching became known as Ch'an Buddhism in China and Zen Buddhism in Japan. Ch'an first established itself in the line of those who taught the Lankavatara Sutra. Bodhidharma transmitted the patriarchship to Hui-k'o. Bodhidharma died in 528. Legend says that he cut off his eyelids to prevent himself from falling asleep while meditating. Tea-plants are said to have sprung up where his eyelids fell to the earth.

In *The Zen Teaching of Bodhidharma*, the author says:

A special transmission outside the scriptures;
No dependence on words and letters;
Direct pointing to the mind of man;
Seeing into one's nature and attaining Buddhahood.
Bodhidharma

Zen teaches that the written word can distract the unenlightened mind. Because enlightenment is beyond the limited ability of the human mind to conceptualize it, we must despair of language, reason, and logic, and use only intuition.

After the persecution of Buddhism in 845, Zen survived as the dominant Chinese sect.

The Soto Shu (Chinese: Ts'ao-Tung) and Rinzai Schools of Zen

Soto Zen was brought from China and introduced into Japan by Dogen (1200–1253) in the thirteenth century. Soto Zen lays stress on seated meditation without conscious striving for a goal (*zazen*). Zazen is at the heart of Soto Zen. Sitting is the sole practice. There is no focus on mantras, neither on the teachings of the Buddha. The Soto Zen Buddhist sits in simplicity on a chair or on the floor and faces a blank wall. Eyes are focused downwards and following the line of the nose to a point on the wall some short distance above the floor. Then when thoughts come into their mind they are just brushed away and not allowed to flourish or develop. This brings peace and tranquillity and allows the buddha-nature, which is below the normal layers of consciousness, to surface.

Zazen is a Japanese word with two characters: *za*, "to sit (cross-legged)," and *zen*, from the Sanskrit *dhyana,* meaning at once concentration and contemplation. Daily Zazen practice is indispensable to Zen as Zazen leads one beyond oneself as knower, to oneself as known. In Zazen, no reality exists outside what is here and now.

Zazen is both something one does—sitting cross-legged, with proper posture and correct breathing—and something one essentially is, both at the same time. To emphasize one of these aspects over and against the other is to miss the whole experience. In our everyday experience, we tend to separate being and doing, which inevitably leads to a state of self-alienation. Through the practice of Zazen, self and other are experienced as one (*samadhi*). The external spiritual search is over as the disciple goes within to reach spirit of the Buddha: his own Self-Nature.

Rinzai-shu Zen was founded by the Chinese master Lin-chi I-hsuan (d. 867) and is thought to have been brought to Japan by Yosai (1141–1215), but it rose to prominence through the work of Hakuin Ekaku (1685–1768). Rinzai-shu is known as a lively dynamic form of Zen focused on interactive exchanges between master and disciple, which eventually brings realization (*satori*). Modern Rinzai also emphasises the koan (paradoxical teaching transcending logical thought). These are mental stumbling blocks or riddles that the Zen disciple must solve to the satisfaction of his master. Rinzai Zen stresses intuitive knowledge, which is knowledge about the essence or the reality of things. This is not the same as knowing *about* things. To know at this level means breaking down the normal barriers of the mind and the logical processes of thought. Zen masters have been known to use a variety of methods to interrupt common patterns of thought; some masters even kept sticks at hand to give their students a quick reminder!

Koans

Zen Buddhists are often given koans to meditate upon. These are nonrational and paradoxical sayings given out by the master to test the enlightenment of students. The Zen teaching of sudden enlightenment (*satori*) goes back to Hui-neng, an illiterate master of the seventh century who understood enlightenment as the realization of one's own original nature (i.e., Buddha). Rational thought cannot solve a koan, for a koan is akin to the order of life itself, which also is not solved through logical thought. The answers to the deep questions of life come through insight. One of the most famous koans is: "What is the sound of one hand clapping?"

Zen Buddhism: Important Beliefs

The special contribution of Zen is the realization of the Buddha's enlightenment in one's own life, in one's own time.

> I have passed in ignorance through a cycle of many rebirths, seeking the builder of the house. Continuous rebirth is a painful thing. But now, housebuilder, I have found you out. You will not build me a house again. All your rafters are broken, your ridge-pole shattered. My mind is free from active thought, and has made an end of craving. (Dhammapada [153, 154])

- *The nonduality of all things.* Generally Zen Buddhism accepts the nonduality of everything so that all beings possess Buddhahood and they share equality.
- *The interconnectedness of the cosmos.* The cosmos itself is in everything and in every being.
- *The actualization of Boddhisattva.* An advanced aim of Zen is aim is to actualize Bodhisattva (enlightened being), which is the spirit of love and compassion for humanity. This actualization is developed through continual spiritual purification and self-discipline.

Zen Monasticism

The heart of Zen monasticism is the practice of meditation. Monastic life includes the strict discipline and training of Zen monks, daily physical regimes of work, ongoing challenge of koans, lengthy meditations, and intensive periods of practice (*sesshin*), all of which are necessary for the path of enlightenment.

However, in Zen teaching, enlightenment is thought of as being sudden. The disciple needs awakening, and the relationship between the Zen master and the disciple is crucial.

Zen and the Sutras

Different sects of Buddhism believe in the validity of certain Sutras, the written teachings of Buddha. Zen takes the Heart Sutra and the Lotus Sutra to be the greatest lessons of Buddha. The Heart Sutra's message that "form is emptiness, emptiness is form" has influenced Zen thought since its origins.

Criticisms of Zen Buddhism

Some Buddhists see Zen Buddhism as a short-cut attempt to true enlightenment. But the Zen tradition of Buddhism, with its emphasis on the here-and-now experience of life and the hope of realized enlightenment, has given hope to millions of Buddhists and non-Buddhists alike. Moreover, the Zen use of Haiku poetry evokes awe and wonder in the beauty of simplicity.

Haiku Poetry

Haiku is a traditional Japanese verse form, notable in its specific form, which is three lines totaling seventeen syllables, measuring 5-7-5. In Zen Buddhism the form assumed religious dimensions. A masterful Haiku involves keen observation and a web of associated ideas (*renso*) that evokes an active mind on the part of the listener. Haiku emerged through Basho (1644).

Traditionally a haiku gives a pair of contrasting images, one suggestive of time and place, the other a vivid but fleeting observation creating mood and emotion.

> Now the swinging bridge
> Is quieted with creepers
> Like our tendrilled life

Issa (1763–1827) was a Japanese haiku poet of the Edo period (1600–1868). His background was an unhappy one as his mother died when he was very young, and his father's second wife actively disliked him. So he left home at the age of thirteen for Edo (Tokyo), living in poverty for twenty years. Issa started to write haiku at about the age of twenty-five. Although he was named the beneficiary of his father's will, his stepmother and half brother successfully kept Issa from his property for thirteen years. He wrote:

My dear old village,
Every memory of home
pierces like a thorn

Tragedy followed him throughout his life. He married at the age of fifty-one, but his four children died in infancy, his wife died in childbirth and his house burned down.

Issa wrote personal poetry in the common language and avoided the dogmatism of certain Buddhist teaching. His poems show remarkable compassion. Following the death of one of his children, he wrote:

This world of dew
is only a world of dew -
and yet

Scriptures

Each of the three schools of Buddhism (Theravada, Mahayana, Vajrayana) has its scriptures:

- Mahayana Buddhism uses Theravada scriptures and adds to them many sutras.
- Vajrayana uses Mahayana scriptures and adds to them many tantric texts.

The contributions of each school are as follows:

Theravada Main Scriptures

- Tipitaka
- Popular: Dhammapada—Sayings of Buddha

Mahayana Main Scriptures

- Sutras (sacred texts)—2184 sacred writings.
- Popular: Lotus Sutra—A sermon by the Buddha on Bodhisattva, buddha-nature.
- Perfection of Wisdom Sutra (*Prajna-paramita*)—Describes emptiness and others.

- Popular: Heart Sutra—Describes nirvana, emptiness, and ultimate reality.
- "Land of Bliss" Sutra—Describes the pure land of Amitabha Buddha.

Vajrayana Main Scriptures

- Tantric texts and commentaries—Deal mainly with ultimate reality as singular unity, and the sexual union of world (male) and cosmos (female).
- Great Stages of Enlightenment—Deals with ethical behavior and control of mind.
- Tibetan Book of the Dead—Deals with stages of dying, death, and rebirth.

Introduction to Tipitaka

The Pali Canon, Tipitaka, is a collection of Pali language texts that form the doctrinal foundation of Theravada Buddhism and is the main body of scriptures for Buddhists. Tipitaka is translated as "three" (Ti) "baskets" (pitaka), in the Pali language. The three baskets are:

1. *Vinaya Pitaka*: Basket of (Monastic) Discipline—Rules of discipline for monks (*bhikkhus*) and nuns (*bhikkhunis*)
2. *Sutta Pitaka*: Basket of Discourses—Discourses of the Buddha
3. *Abhidhamma Pitaka*: Basket of Further Dhamma—Analytical Commentaries

Buddhist Festivals and Special Days

Many special or holy days occur throughout the Buddhist year. Many of these days celebrate the birthdays of Bodhisattvas in the Mahayana tradition or other significant dates in the Buddhist calendar. The most significant occasion happens every May on the night of the full moon, when Buddhists all over the world celebrate the birth, enlightenment, and death of the Buddha over twenty-five hundred years ago. It has come to be known as Buddha Day.

Some holy days are specific to a particular Buddhist tradition or ethnic group. Most Buddhists, with the exception of the Japanese, use the lunar calendar, and the dates of Buddhist festivals vary from country to country and between Buddhist traditions. Of the many Buddhist festivals, some of the more important ones are:

- *Buddhist New Year*. The Buddhist New Year depends on the country of origin or ethnic background of the people. For example, Chinese, Koreans, and Vietnamese celebrate in late January or early February. In Theravadin countries—Thailand, Burma, Sri Lanka, Cambodia, and Laos—the new year is celebrated for three days from the first full moon day in April. In Mahayana countries, the new year starts on the first full moon day in January.

- *Vesak or Visakah Puja* ("Buddha Day"). Traditionally, Buddha's birthday is known as *Vesak* or *Visakah Puja* (Buddha's Birthday Celebrations). Vesak is the major Buddhist festival of the year as it celebrates the birth, enlightenment, and death of the Buddha on the one day, the first full moon day in May, except in a leap year when the festival is held in June. This celebration is called *Vesak*, which is the name of the month in the Indian calendar. The festival includes colorful processions and the exchange of greeting cards. In many southeast Asian countries some Buddhists buy caged animals and set them free.

  Mahayana Buddhists have a similar festival. In some parts there are festivals for the dead where offerings are made to the dead and lit candles put in paper boats to guide their spirits.
- *Magha Puja Day* (Fourfold Assembly or "*Sangha* Day"). *Magha Puja* Day takes place on the full moon day of the third lunar month (March). The Buddha went to Rajagaha city where 1,250 Arhats (enlightened saints) who were the Buddha's disciples, with no prior appointment, returned from their wanderings to pay respect to the Buddha. The Buddha preached to them and announced that he would pass away in three months. The event is marked by lighting 1,250 candles.
- *Asalha Puja Day* ("Dhamma Day"). Asalha Puja means to pay homage to the Buddha on the full moon day of the eighth lunar month (approximately July). It commemorates the Buddha's first sermon on the Middle Way.

UNIT 7:3 SIKHISM

The Lord is the Truth Absolute,
True is His Name.
His language is love infinite;
His creatures ever cry to Him;
"Give us more, O Lord, give more"; The Bounteous One gives unwearyingly.

What should we offer
That we might see His Kingdom?
With what language
Might we His love attain?

In the ambrosial hours of fragrant dawn
Think upon and glorify
His Name and greatness.
Our own past actions
Have put this garment on us,

But salvation comes only through His Grace.

O Nanak, this alone need we know,
That God, being Truth, is the one Light of all.
The Japji, in *Selections from the Sacred Writings of the Sikhs*

Guru Nanak (1469–1539 C.E.) was the founder of Sikhism (means discipleship). He was born in Talwandi village, which is now called Nanakana, in Pakistan. At his birth a local midwife saw a bright halo surrounding his head, which led a local Hindu priest to say that a great man had just been born. As a young boy he was unable to concentrate at school because he was always thinking about God, so his father withdrew him from formal education and gave him a Brahmin tutor instead. But even in this situation he caused concern for he questioned the tutor on why he should be a Hindu at all—was it not good enough just to be a man?

Somewhere around 1500, Nanak mysteriously disappeared while bathing in a river. He reappeared four days later and said, "Since there is neither Hindu nor Muslim, whose path shall I follow? I will follow God's path. God is neither Hindu nor Muslim, and the path I follow is God's." Nanak explained that during these three days he had been taken to God's court, where he was offered a cup of nectar (*amrit* = Amritsar, the holy city of Sikhism) and the words were spoken to him:

> This is the cup of the adoration of God's name. Drink it. I am with you. I bless you and raise you up. Whoever remembers you will enjoy my favor, Go, rejoice in my name and teach others to do so also. Let this be your calling.

Thus began his thirty-year missionary journey, which included thousands of miles on foot. Sikhism arose in a Hindu culture (the Punjab) that was at the time under Muslim control. Nanak could see the value of both religions, and he sought to bring Hinduism and Islam together. To symbolize this union, he wore a yellow robe like the Hindu gurus and the turban and beads of a Muslim.

The theological beliefs of Sikhism, whether consciously or unconsciously, tend to reflect Nanak's desire for reconciliation between the two faiths. Today there are some 13 million Sikhs worldwide, most of them living in India. Their holy center is at the Golden Temple in Amritsar. Guru Nanak was the first of ten gurus, all men who had achieved *moksha* (spiritual release from rebirth). They are seen as perfect human beings who have been sent to earth to preach God's message.

The Ten Gurus

- *Guru Angad* (1504–1552). Sixty-two of his hymns are in the Adi Granth, and he promoted Sikh learning via the language of Punjabi.
- *Guru Amar Das* (1479–1574). He introduced the practice of eating *langar* (the gift of the sharing of food) to help Sikhs of different castes to

socialize together and with anyone else who came, thus expressing equality and commonality. Sikhism was expanding during his time and so he set up *manjis* (places for spiritual instruction) to cope with this expansion. He composed *Anand Sahib*, a hymn used on religious occasions.

- *Guru Ram Das* (Slave of God, 1534–1581). He was known as a humble, spiritual man committed to seeing the Sikh religion expand, and he therefore consolidated missionary work.
- *Guru Arjan* (1563–1601) became the fifth guru while still a teenager. He founded the Golden Temple at Amritsar. The temple has four doors open to all castes and classes and creeds. He selected a Muslim holy man to lay the foundation stone, but his life was ended as the first Sikh martyr because the Muslim Emperor Jahangir requested that praise of Muhammad be included in the *Guru Granth Sahib*, the sacred book. Guru Arjan refused the request and was tortured with boiling water and burning sand. During his time, the Sikhs began their struggle against Muslim rule.
- *Guru Har Gobind* (1595–1644). Under his leadership the Sikhs increased their military strength and expertise. His son wore two swords, the Meeri (Temporal) and the Peeri (Spiritual) swords.
- *Guru Har Rai* (1630–1664) retained a peaceful coexistence with the Muslim Empire. He kept a well-organized army ready for battle, and he also side-stepped and avoided the politics of the Muslim Mughal court.
- *Guru Har Krishan* (1656–1664) was called the child guru. He died of smallpox but is loved by Sikh children.
- *Guru Tegh Bahadur* (1621–1675) was beheaded by the fanatical Emperor Aurangzeb for refusing to become a Muslim. His name means "expert swordsman," but he actually focused on devotion rather than military action.
- *Guru Gobind Singh* (1666–1708) was the son of Tegh Bahadur. He recognized that if the Sikh religion was to survive in a hostile world, it needed strong leadership and organization. Gobind Singh called for those people who were prepared to give their lives unreservedly to the faith to step forward. To the "beloved five" who did, he gave a special initiation, thereby instituting the Khalsa. He started the Khalsa (pure order), which continues to this day, open to men and women who are prepared to fulfill its obligations. At the time of the first Khalsa the Guru extended his own name "Singh" (meaning lion) to all Sikh men, and to women he gave the name "Kaur," or princess. At its inception twenty thousand Sikhs were initiated into the Khalsa.

Though the Gurus were critical of miracles as the means of exploiting naïve and credulous people, miracles are attributed to their lives and actions.

The last guru is the Guru Granth Sahib, the holy book, and it is the perpetual Guru to this day. The tenth guru, Guru Gobind Singh, conferred Guruship on the Adi Granth, thus making it the Guru Granth Sahib.

Sikh History

Guru Gobind Singh involved his followers in an unsuccessful martial struggle against Mogul rule. After Gobind's assassination, the Sikhs were persecuted by the Muslim Mogul rulers until 1799 when Ranjit Singh (1780–1839) laid claim to a large part of northwest India. After Ranjit's death, his Sikh kingdom fragmented. The British moved into the Punjab, and the Sikh Wars followed (1845–46, 1848–49).

The Sikhs were defeated, and the British annexed the Punjab. Sikhism recovered in the twentieth century, when the Sikhs were given control of their holy places (*gurdwaras*). The Indian subcontinent was partitioned in 1947; the western Punjab became Pakistani territory, and the eastern Punjab part of India. The Sikhs suffered from ensuing communal rioting, especially in Pakistan's Punjab, and about 2.5 million Sikhs moved from Pakistan into India.

God

Sikhs affirm the ultimate supreme formless idea of God who is beyond human conception. Like Islam, Sikhism rejects the belief in *avatars* (divine manifestations), the caste system, and images to help worship. However, Sikhism accepts a belief in reincarnation, which is nearer to Hindu beliefs. Although Nanak became a guru, in Sikhism the only true guru is God; other gurus are those through whom God speaks. At the beginning of the sacred book, the *Guru Granth Sahib*, there is a sacred chant called the *Mool Mantra*, which states Sikh belief in God. Every Sikh is expected to recite it daily. The English translation is given below:

> There is only one God
> His Name is Truth
> He is the Creator
> He is without fear
> He is without hate
> He is beyond time (Immortal)
> He is beyond birth and death
> He is self-existent
> He is realized by the Guru's grace.

Beautiful poetry and simile are used to describe God's control of history and the importance of the name of God:

> By his writ some have pleasure, others pain
> By his grace some are saved,

Others doomed to die, relive and die again
Japji

As is the dream of night, so is this world.
As is the staff in the hand of a blind person,
So is, to us, the Name of God.
Salvation and the Goal of Human Life

Salvation

At the heart of the Sikh concept of salvation is union with God. This is realized through love, that is, through the person of God who dwells deep in the depths of their being. According to Guru Nanak, every person has power or merit; he or she is a part of the divine. Human beings are not weaklings, mere products of the chain reaction of karma. The Sikh is essentially a person of action, with a strong sense of self-reliance.

At the beginning of the *Japji*, which contains the *Mool Mantra*, Guru Nanak defines God and sums up his attributes. The goal of human life is for a union with the divine being, often called salvation or nirvana. This union is achieved through self-surrender and a submission to God's divine will (*hukam*).

How can a believer merge with divinity? Guru Nanak suggests that in the early hours of the morning the devotee should meditate on "His Name" and praise his greatness.

The first step is to listen for "The Name." By careful listening, the worshiper becomes free from sorrow and sin. The second step is true and firm belief in "The Name." People who have firm faith in "The Name" not only free themselves from the cycle of birth and death but also liberate others. In the world, some people do good, while others are busy in doing evil works. Action is followed by reaction. As a man sows, so shall he reap.

Just as dirty clothes are cleaned by soap, so is man's evil washed away by "The Name." God is vast. Not even holy ones can ever fathom his greatness. No one can visualize the infinite God. He alone knows himself. The conquest of one's ego under the control of the self is the only way to merge the individual soul into the universal soul.

The disciple has to follow a strict discipline—namely to control the mind and body—a fearless attitude, perseverance, and a constant remembrance of "The Name," in order to reach the goal. Salvation depends not upon caste or ritual or even self-denial, but upon the constant meditation on God's name and the immersion into his being:

Lord, mighty River, all knowing, all seeing,
And I like a little fish in your great waters,
How shall I sound your depths?
How shall I reach your shores?

> Wherever I go I see you only.
> And snatched out of your waters I die of separation.
> Adi Granth

True Sikh followers have radiant faces of divine light that bring peace and happiness to all whom they meet.

Asa di Var

After Japji each morning, a hymn of Guru Nanak—the Asa di Var—is repeated. It speaks of God's grace being essential to complete the task of moving to perfection and that one has to deserve such grace:

> God Himself shapes men as vessels, and brings them to perfection.
> In some is put the milk of loving and kindness, others ever are set on the fire of passion.
> Some lie down to sleep on cushions, others stand to watch over them.
> God regenerates those on whom He looks with grace.

The hurdles on the path to God—such as the ego, hypocrisy, evil thoughts, and immoral actions—are discussed and remedies are suggested.

Sikhism emphasizes *Bhakti Marg*, or the path of devotion. It also recognizes the limited value of *Gian Marg* (Path of Knowledge) and *Karam Marg* (Path of Action) and lays stress on the need for earning God's grace in order to reach the spiritual goal.

There is no tradition of renunciation, asceticism, or celibacy in Sikhism. Sikhs are family-oriented and they donate one-tenth of their income to charity.

Life after Death: Sikh Belief in Reincarnation

The Hindu view of reincarnation has been altered by the Sikh Gurus, who believed that everyone is equal before God and thus rejected the Hindu caste system. As in Hinduism, a person's soul passes through all the stages of existence, which is called *samsara*. This passage is called the evolution of the soul. In Sikhism, a person is not born basically evil but evil overshadows them. Your deeds follow your soul like a shadow. Good deeds and God's grace enable you to gain salvation. The practice of repentance, prayer, and love to all brings God's grace to you, which neutralizes your accrued karma from other lives.

> Karma determines the nature of our birth, but the door of salvation is found only through grace. (Adi Granth, 2)

Guru Nanak believed that only reincarnation could help explain the age-old question of why some people have lives of misery and others live in untold wealth and happiness. The Guru himself, however, never commented on whether people lived one life or many lives on earth.

Moral Action

Those Sikhs whose daily life is a constant remembrance (*simaran*) of God will express the will of God (*hukam*) in what they do. Self-centeredness (*haumai*) must yield to a Godward orientation. The *gurmukh* is one who resists lust, anger, greed, attachment to worldly things, and pride (*Ikam*, *krodh*, *lobh*, *moh*, and *ahankar*, respectively).

Guru Nanak did not divide the world into spiritual and secular; hence, for him, political and social orders are inseparable from the universal order, that is, the divine harmony in which everything takes its part, its dharma. He taught

> Lords of the ocean and kings with mountains of wealth
> Are not equal to an insect
> That never forgets God in its heart.
>
> Adi Granth, 5

Guru Nanak's teaching also included these statements:

- There is only one God; worship only him and no others.
- God alone can ascertain his own greatness.
- Men and women are equal before God.
- With God, there is no black and no white, no rich and no poor; rather your actions and intent define your religious status.
- Love everyone and work and pray for the human good.
- Show kind actions to animals.
- Be truthful.
- Show simplicity in your material needs, dress, food, etc.

Other prohibitions include idol worship and the caste structure (although in practice, Sikh society does have its divisions).

Sikhs may not cut their hair or drink alcohol, take drugs, gamble, steal, or commit adultery. There is no explicit teaching on homosexuality; the Sikh expectation is that every man and woman will marry and have children. Ethics and religion go together. Moral qualities and the practice of virtue in everyday life are necessary steps towards spiritual development. Qualities like honesty, compassion, patience, and humility can be built up only by effort and tenacity.

Above all the virtues, Sikhs must aspire to truthfulness in thought, word, and deed. "Truth is above everything, but higher still is truthful living" (Adi Granth, 62). The emphasis here is on self-control and a path between the extreme abstention of asceticism and self-indulgence that has disregard for consequences. Justice is crucial, and other people must never be exploited: "Depriving others of their due is (like) eating pork for a Muslim or beef for a Hindu" (Adi Granth, 141).

The Khalsa is the body of initiated Sikhs or it can also mean any true Sikh. All members of the Khalsa have to abstain from alcohol, meat, and tobacco, and they wear "the five Ks"—designated thus because in Punjabi all the items begin with the letter K. They are:

1. Uncut hair—together with the comb, uncut hair shields the skull and allied to the Yogic belief that uncut hair conserves energy and draws it upward. The hair is usually covered with a turban.
2. Comb—symbolizing good order and cleanliness
3. Steel bracelet—hands should be in God's service
4. Undershorts—always dressed for immediate action
5. Dagger—defense of the weak

Prayer and Worship

The holiest place for Sikhs is the Golden Temple at Amritsar (now in the Indian state of Punjab) founded by the fourth guru, Ram Das. The *gurdwara* is the place of communal worship, and in any *gurdwara* the prayer room is the most important because it houses the Guru Granth Sahib around which worship is conducted. The *takht* is the platform upon which the Guru Granth Sahib is placed. Cloths and cushions support the Book and protect it from dust. A chauri is a ceremonial whisk made of the tail hair of a white horse or yak embedded in a silver or wooden handle. When the Book is being read, either a reader or attendant waves a *chaur* over it. The focal point of the room is therefore where the enthroned Guru Granth Sahib sits, a symbol of royalty.

Corporate Sikh worship is called *diwan* and is not confined to particular days or times. Sikhs bathe before entering a *gurdwara*, and shoes are always removed as a mark of respect. Sikhs visit the *gurdwara* at any time or any day for worship. Worship does not begin at any time; people come and go at will.

Prayer is rooted in *nam simaran*, which is remembering. This activity is brought about through meditation, praise expressed through *kirtan* (devotional singing), and petition. All prayer begins and ends with *ardas*, which contain three main elements:

- Invocation of God
- A command to recall each of the ten Gurus, to meditate on the Guru Granth Sahib, and to recall the "forty saved ones" and other faithful Sikh martyrs who sacrificed their lives
- Petitioning of God to protect his khalsa; to keep them faithful and protect them so that they can be victorious; and to bestow gifts of discipleship, discipline, discernment, and faith, which is the greatest gift of all

Music and Worship

The *Anand Sahib*, or "The Song of Bliss," is the spiritual and musical masterpiece of Guru Amar Das. Its theme is of man's spiritual goal, namely the merger into the Divine Essence. Stanzas twenty-one to twenty-five speak about the God-oriented person, the *Sunmukh*, who is radically different from the egoistic, worldly person, the *Bemukh*. The fortieth and last stanza speaks of the benefits of *Anand*, which banishes all tension and sorrow. People who sing this stanza with devotion become purified and liberated.

Gender and Religion

In the Guru Granth Sahib, a recurring image occurs of the soul offering itself to God, as a chaste woman surrenders to her husband. This image reflects the traditional relationships within the community. Sikhs are expected to marry, and motherhood is honored.

Sikhs refer to the time of Guru Nanak when the tyranny of caste had left its mark on women. The practice of a widow burning herself on her husband's funeral pyre to become a *sati* was a Hindu custom rejected by the Gurus. Guru Nanak placed women on an equal footing with men:

> In a woman, man is conceived,
> From a woman he is born
> With a woman he is betrothed and married,
> With a woman he contracts friendship.
> If one dies another one is sought for,
> Man's destiny is linked to woman,
> Why denounce her, the one from whom even great people
> are born?
> From a woman, a woman is born,
> None may exist without a woman.
>
> Guru Granth Sahib, 473

Sikhism sought to give women equal status with men in a number of ways:

- The Sikh Gurus removed the false notion that women were inherently evil and unclean.
- Guru Nanak held the view that marriage was monogamous.
- Sikhism conferred religious rights on women. Some Hindu scriptures affirmed that they were unworthy of participation in religious worship. A woman was regarded as the incarnation of temptation. The Gurus exposed these views as false and began a program of human rights. Religious gatherings and *kirtan* (communal singing) were thrown open to women; they could participate fully in religious ceremonies and received the baptism (*Amrit*) on equal terms with men.
- Guru Amar Das trained missionaries to spread Sikhism throughout the country. Of the 146 missionaries Guru Amar Das trained and

sent out, fifty-two were women. At one time the country of Afghanistan and Kashmir were under the jurisdiction of women *masands* (priests). These women had complete jurisdiction in decision making, collection of revenues, and preaching to congregations. Guru HarGobind referred to woman as "the conscience of man." In religious gatherings, men and women sang and preached without any distinction.

- In contrast to Hindu thought, Guru Nanak taught a form of asceticism without renouncing family and becoming a hermit; instead, he emphasized purity while abiding in the world rather than escaping the world. He chose a family man as his successor, thus closing the door to asceticism. Guru Amar Das likewise taught:

  > By contemplating truth,
  > Light dawns,
  > Then amidst sensual pleasures one remains detached.
  > Such is the greatness of the true Guru
  > That living with his wife and children,
  > One obtains salvation.
  >
  > Guru Granth Sahib, 661

  The Gurus therefore established *grihasth* (the life of the householder or married person) as the ideal and normal way of life.

- Guru Amar Das condemned the practice of female infanticide and *sati.* He said that widows could remarry. Guru Tegh Bahadur blessed the women of Amritsar and said that by their devotion they had made themselves "acceptable to God." Women were not even to veil their faces.

Mata Gujri was an inspiring force behind her husband, Guru Tegh Bahadur, and her son, Guru Gobind Singh. After the martyrdom of Guru Tegh Bahadur, Mata Gujri guided and inspired Guru Gobind Singh. She was responsible for the training of the Sahibzadas (the four sons of Guru Gobind Singh) who gave up their lives for Sikhism at a young age. Guru Gobind Singh gave *amrit* (Sikh initiation) to men and women alike.

Sikh history also names many women who inspired men to heroic deeds. Mai Bhago was the brave woman who shamed the forty deserters to return to the battle of Muktsar. She led them into battle, where they achieved martyrdom and were blessed by Guru Gobind.

In the Indo-Pakistan conflict of 1971, Sikh women on the border formed the second line of defense and gave valuable assistance to the Sikh fighting forces. A Sikh woman is an individual in her own right; she is under no compulsion or expectation to take her husband's name.

However, despite the Gurus' teachings of full equality, Sikh women today do not share equal leadership roles with men. Contrary to Sikh teaching, in the past many baby girls were smothered at birth. Few women have been members or officiates of *gurdwara* management teams, and also few women sing hymns or read the Guru Granth Sahib. Modern Sikh writers (e.g., Kanwaljit Kaur-Singh in Holm and Bowker [1994]) draw attention to a number of contributory factors leading to women's inequality, including the unwillingness of Sikh males to surrender their dominant role. Another factor is the issue of Sikh history:

> Sikh history has been written by men only, who either chose to disregard women's contributions, or did not think their contributions worthy of note. Whatever the reason, women's contributions have been kept out of the record, and, as a result, Sikh women have not been able to transmit their achievements to later generations, which have therefore not had positive images to emulate. Sometimes (as in the case of Mata Gujri) the male historians have even attributed women's contributions to their male relatives.

Mysticism

Guru Nanak practiced a mysticism of love. He often described his relationship with God to be like that of a bride longing for her husband. Guru Nanak believed God to be present everywhere—that is, "as much in a worm as in an *elephant*." By means of God's grace, a believer can enter into a deep inner awareness of his or her own nature, becoming one with God, the *Satguru*.

Sikh Scriptures

The Adi Granth ("first book") was compiled by Guru Arjan in 1604 C.E. Any room in which the Adi Granth is kept is a *gurdwara*. The scriptures are treated with the same respect and devotion that would be shown to a human Guru. The Adi Granth has 1,430 pages and the language is varied. The basic language used is akin to modern Hindi or Punjabi and is the language of fifteenth- and sixteenth-century Hindu and Muslim mystics, indicating the Sikhs' willingness to draw on the wisdom of other faiths. Guru Nanak wrote over 900 hymns, and Guru Arjan includes 2,216 verses of his own, which are sung to music. All the other Gurus have made contributions, as have poets contemporary with the Gurus.

The contents are written in meter and, with the exception of the Japji, are to be sung. The religious writings address the concept of devotion to one God, the importance of the Guru, personal purification, the importance of karma, the need to reject idol worship, and the priesthood. The social and political writings focus on service to others, the breaking down of the caste system, the injustice of rulers and the need to oppose it, help to those who are oppressed, the *gurdwara* (temple), and free food (*langar*).

In 1708 Guru Gobind Singh declared that the Granth would succeed him as the Guru.

The Dasam Granth is a collection of religious, moral, and political poems by the tenth guru Guru Gobind Singh. He was a poet and he entertained poets at his court. The Dasam Granth is seldom read, although it is especially important to the Nihangs (the militant core of the Sikh Khalsa).

Festivals

Sikhs celebrate two different kinds of festivals. The first are fairs or meetings that reinterpret Hindu festivals, and the second are called *gurpurbs*, which commemorate the births and deaths of the ten gurus. Of the *gurpurbs*, the most notable is Guru Nanak's birthday celebration, which lasts three days and includes the procession where the Guru Granth is carried, followed by music, drama, and singing.

Hola Mohalla, the Sikh equivalent of Hindu Holi, was begun by Guru Gobind Singh and includes sporting events such as horseriding and athletics. He used it to encourage bravery and expertise.

Baisakhi falls on April 13 and is the New Year Festival. This holiday was begun by Guru Amar Das. During the previous forty-eight hours, the *Arkand Path* (continuous reading) of the Guru Granth will have been undertaken. Originally during this festival, novices could be initiated, believers could meet the Guru, and people of various social backgrounds could all meet up in brotherhood.

Diwali is the festival where Sikhs remember and celebrate the release of Guru Har Gobind from his arrest in 1620. Sikhs at that time prayed outside the prison until he was released, and so the festival celebrates good triumphing over evil. Har Gobind also arranged for the release of fifty-two Hindu Rajas.

UNIT 7:4 JUDAISM

> *So now, O Israel, what does the* Lord *your God require of you? Only to fear the* Lord *your God, to walk in all his ways, to love him, to serve the* Lord *your God with all your heart and with all your soul, and to keep the commandments of the* Lord *your God and his decrees that I am commanding you today, for your own well-being.*
>
> Deuteronomy 10:12–13

The major sources of information concerning the origins of Judaism and the Jewish people come from the books which they believe to be revealed and inspired by God, the Torah ("Law"—the first five books of the Bible), Nebi'im (Prophets) and Ketubim (Writings). These three divisions of the Hebrew Bible are known as the *Tanakh*. The Mishnah contains the interpretations of the Torah by the rabbis, which became known as the Oral Torah. Eventually the Mishnah needed new interpretation, leading to the Talmud, which is the debates and continued arguments of rabbis over the Jewish sacred texts.

At the heart of being Jewish is the sense of belonging to a people and a historical community. At the heart of the Jewish faith is the belief in the one God and the duty to love him. Rabbis (teachers) of the faith are relentless in their rejection of polytheism (many gods) and idolatry (the worship of anything less than God). God is clearly revealed in the life and history of God's people Israel, as it is shown in the Hebrew Bible.

Judaism as a religion is very diverse. There are major divisions: Orthodox and Neo-Orthodox, Hasidic, Reform, and Conservative, as well as Humanistic, Liberal, Sephardic (Mediterranean Jews), Ashkenazic (Jews from Central and Eastern Europe), Secular, and Reconstructionalist. Trying to put forward a view of normative Judaism meets with little success. However, the relationship between the people and the religion is a unique one.

Biblical history records Abraham as the first great father or patriarch of the faith. Abram was a farmer who lived in about 1800 B.C.E. (see his life history in Gen. 11:26–25:10). He lived in the city of Ur, which is today located near the Persian Gulf, then moved to Haran, which is where the moon god, *Sin*, was worshiped. For the Babylonian, Syrian, and Mediterranean people of that day, each major power of nature was a distinct deity. Beginning with Abraham, the Jews differed from their neighbors by focusing on God as the Lord of Nature. The basic contribution of Judaism to the religious thought of the Middle East was monotheism. In the story of Abraham, God is ultimately one and personal. In Haran, Abram heard God's promise to him of a divine covenant:

> *Now the LORD* said to Abram, "Go from your country and your kindred and your father's house to the land that I will show you. I will make of you a great nation, and I will bless you, and make your name great, so that you will be a blessing . . . and in you all the families of the earth shall be blessed." (Gen. 12:1–3)

With the promise of the covenant and promise of land and of many ancestors, Abram's name was changed to Abraham (father of multitudes), and at age seventy-five he left Haran and moved by stages into Canaan.

- Abraham was the first patriarch, his son Isaac the second, and Isaac's son Jacob the third.
- From Jacob's twelve sons came the twelve tribes who eventually conquered and settled in the land of Canaan. Different tribes or kinships had different histories. One of the most dramatic and memorable was enslavement in Egypt around the year 1300 B.C.E. and an escape under the leadership of Moses, which is now commemorated in the annual Passover festival of Judaism. Not only the people of Israel but also the land of Israel is at the heart of Judaism.
- Successive covenants were made between different tribes and between the people and God, for whom the consonants "JHWH" stand in the Hebrew text. How this name was originally pronounced is not known,

> and Orthodox Jews would not speak the name of God but say "Ha Shem," the Name.

Under the rule of King David (c. 1000 B.C.E.), Jerusalem was established as the religious center, and his son Solomon constructed the first temple, the center of religious ritual. But ritual and kingship were never self-sufficient: both were monitored by prophets who spoke directly from God.

The Babylonian exile (586 B.C.E.) brought certain changes in Jewish religious life. When deprived of land, temple, and priestly functions, Judaism adopted a nonsacrificial religion. Jews began to gather in homes to read the scripture and pray, heralding the earliest beginnings of the synagogue. Now "lip sacrifice" (prayer and penitence) rather than "blood sacrifice" (sheep and goats) were the focus for spiritual life.

Scribes became the priestly interpreters of the Torah. By the second century B.C.E., the Pharisees were teaching that oral law carried the same authority as the law of Moses.

- The destruction of Herod's temple in 70 C.E. meant the Jews were scattered abroad, and the priesthood waned. A Pharisee called Johanan ben Zakkai was permitted by the Romans to open an academy at Jabneh. He brought in rabbis as the keepers and legislators of Torah. By word of mouth, the rabbis passed their teachings from generation to generation until the oral law (Mishnah) was written down around 200 C.E.
- By 500 C.E. the Talmud was completed as was the Gemara, a rabbinical commentary on the Mishnah (the authoritative collection of oral laws containing all the decisions made in Jewish law dating from earliest times to the beginning of the third century C.E.) with references to more than two thousand scholar-teachers. There are two Talmuds: the Jerusalem (or Palestinian) and the Babylonian Talmud. The Talmud became the basic document of rabbinic Judaism, and still holds a major place in shaping Jewish thought.

Moses Maimonides

Moses Maimonides (1135–1204) was the foremost intellectual figure of medieval Judaism. He is famous for three works: his commentary on the Mishna, his code of Jewish law, and his "Guide of the Perplexed." He was born into an educated family, who left Spain for Morocco because of the persecution of the Jews of Cordoba by a fanatical Islamic sect. There Maimonides began to study medicine, but his family fled again due to persecution and moved to Palestine. They finally settled in the 1160s near Cairo in Egypt, where he eventually became the court physician for Sultan Saladin and his family. He was also a lecturer, a doctor with his own practice, and a leader of the Jewish community. His writings are vast. As a rationalist he believed that reason should guide all things, but only if the absolute beliefs and doctrines in the Bible were not sacrificed. In his *Guide for the*

Perplexed he promotes the need for a rational philosophy of Judaism. He believed that a godly spirituality could live alongside the rational mind. Maimonides opposed all aspects of religion that failed the test of reason. For example, he said of miracles, "A miracle cannot prove what is impossible; it is useful only to confirm what is possible." More conservative scholars dismissed views of this kind as conveying Hellenism rather than Judaism.

From the fall of the temple in 70 C.E. when the Jews were scattered abroad, they had no official homeland until 1948 when, in the aftermath of the Holocaust of World War Two, the United Nations adopted a resolution calling for the partition of Palestine into Jewish and Arab areas. On May 14, 1948, the State of Israel was proclaimed.

God

Covenant

Jews believe that they are bound to God by a covenant (*b'rit*). The Torah tells what this covenant involves and lays down the laws (*mitzvot*) about it. Although God has revealed himself through his covenant, Judaism was not given as a religion already formed to the Jewish people.

God and History

Slowly, over the centuries, Jewish faith in God emerged through the divine revelation of God's being and his active will revealed at various times in the nation's history. Even the prophets of Israel, some of whom had powerful mystical experiences, were rooted in the history and events of their times.

God is Not Identical with His Creation

Jewish belief in God is in one God, "the LORD alone" (Deut. 6:4). He is the creator of the universe who created human beings in his own image, but importantly, God is not identical with his creation.

Masculine Attributes

God is portrayed predominantly with masculine attributes in Judaism as Father, King, Shepherd, Husband, Judge, etc. Later Jewish thinkers such as Maimonides said that God had no attributes and that descriptions in the Bible are only human reflections of God's activities.

The Attributes of God

The God of Israel was formerly referred to as the "God of Abraham, Isaac, and Jacob." He is all powerful (Job 42:2), all knowing (Job 28:23), and omnipresent

(Ps. 139:7–12). God is also eternal and unchangeable. He has revealed himself through history and he is king of all the nations of the world. Even so, the Jews believe themselves to be chosen by God through his initiative in making a covenant with them and that they therefore are his witness to the world.

(For additional information on God, see also unit 6:1.)

Salvation

According to the teaching of Judaism, no set of beliefs exists upon the acceptance of which a Jew may find salvation. Judaism does, however, focus on the need to overcome sin and for a final messianic victory.

The Bible puts forth the belief that Israel has a part to play in bringing light and justice to the whole world. Jews interpret the servant as Israel, and they view the following passage as a statement of Israel's vocation to be a light to the world.

> Here is my servant, whom I uphold,
>   my chosen, in whom my soul delights;
> I have put my spirit upon him;
>   he will bring forth justice to the nations.
> He will not cry or lift up his voice,
>   or make it heard in the street;
> a bruised reed he will not break,
>   and a dimly burning wick he will not quench;
>   he will faithfully bring forth justice.
> He will not grow faint or be crushed
>   until he has established justice in the earth;
>   and the coastlands wait for his teaching.
>
> Isaiah 42:1–4

In the Hebrew Bible the term "messiah" often applies to priests or kings; no books reference an eschatological (last days or things) figure who will save Israel. During the second temple period, however, when Rome ruled Israel, native Jewish belief developed into a belief in a redemptive figure like King David, who had delivered Israel in days of old. Thus, the destruction of the second temple in 70 C.E. heightened Jewish messianic expectation.

In the Talmud some attention is given to the messianic age, which will include an end to Jewish exile and an in-gathering of dispersed Jewish people from all over the world to the land of Israel. By the Middle Ages, various beliefs and writings about the Messiah became formalized into a set doctrine. Jewish medieval mysticism tended to spiritualize the idea of the Messiah to say that he would end spiritual exile from God.

The history of Judaism is well stocked with messianic volunteers for the title of Messiah, and various movements have come and gone. In modern times the Nazi Holocaust and the subsequent creation of the State of Israel have meant that messianism has been reevaluated. Among the various secular and nonsecular responses, some Orthodox Jews see it as an ongoing live issue, with the return of Jews to Israel as the beginning of messianic redemption.

Death and the Afterlife

Judaism believes in the human soul and its immortality, but no real comment is available on what life after death entails. In the past there was talk of Sheol, which was a shadowy place under the ground where the ghosts of those long dead went while waiting for bodily resurrection. Sheol was divided up into different areas for good people and evil people (Isa. 14:9, Job 3:11–19). In the past, Jews spoke about heaven and hell but these terms were not clearly defined. Reform Jews are not expecting an individual messianic person to come, but strict Orthodox Jews believe in the coming of the Messiah and the setting up of his kingdom culminating in the day of judgment. On that day, everyone's body who has lived on earth will be resurrected and brought back to life to face God's judgment.

Unlike other religions like Buddhism, Hinduism, and Sikhism, Judaism is permeated with the idea that the soul and the body stay together at the ultimate end. Jews believe that you get the judgment that you deserve; if you have lived a good life, there is no need to fear.

> This world is like a vestibule before the World to Come; prepare yourself in the vestibule that you may enter the hall. (*Mishnah,* Abot 4.21)

The rewards of righteousness are for all people, Jewish or non-Jewish. Jewish people who hear of someone's death sometimes say, "Blessed be the true judge." Arrangements for death are made quickly, within twenty-four hours if at all possible, and everything is done simply in recognition that all are equal in death. Orthodox Jews prohibit cremation because it is wrong to deliberately destroy a body as it is made in God's image. The Jewish belief is that death is a doorway to the next life. There is no belief in reincarnation.

Moral Action

Judaism has put more stress upon the deed (*miswa*) than the creed (*'ani ma 'amin,* "I believe"). Yet from Talmudic times, as a way of life Judaism has been distinguished by giving special emphasis to certain beliefs and ethical values. In the Mishnah (Abot 1:2), one sees the broad philosophy that governed the minds of the early rabbis:

> By three things is the world sustained:
> by the law
> by the (temple) service
> and by deeds of loving kindness.

This basic teaching underpins the threefold function of the synagogue as a

- House of study (for learning of Torah)
- House of prayer (for worship of God)
- House of assembly (for the care of community needs)

Sources of Authority

Jewish ethics are derived from three basic sources of authority:

1. *The revelation of God in the Torah.* The word "Torah" is often transcribed as "Law," but its meaning is much wider. Torah gives the guidance and the means by which the broken relationship with God (see the story of Adam and Eve in Genesis) can be set right. Jewish anthropology sees humanity as being inclined in two ways: either with a good inclination or an evil inclination. Keeping the Torah and its commandments is the way Jews can agree to the guidance of God. This is not to accrue merit for its own sake, but to give knowledge of God to the whole world.

2. *The Talmud and Oral Law* (see also unit 6:8). A tradition of Oral Torah has been passed down from the rabbis of the first several centuries of the common era. It has been codified in the *Talmud*, which is constituted by the Mishnah and the Gemara, and which is authoritative for the observant Jew.

Because Torah cannot cover every human situation, the oral law (believed also to be given to Moses on Mt. Sinai) is another source of moral authority. The discussions of the rabbis throughout the ages brings the Torah to each generation as new challenges are met with the advance of progress. For example, when the electric light was invented, debate ensued among the rabbis as to whether or not turning it on during Shabbat would constitute lighting a fire, which is forbidden. Each rabbi who is asked to rule makes his own decision, and in this case the majority decided that turning on the electric light was like lighting a fire and therefore the halakah (the accepted consensus of the correct course of action) says it is forbidden.

3. *Halakah.* Judaism has a system of law, known as *halakah* (or "path") regulating civil and criminal justice, family relationships, personal ethics and manners, social responsibilities—such as help to the needy, education, and community institutions—as well as worship and other religious observances. There are always new areas where the *halakah* is being considered, and it is frequent for the level of debate and argument to be vigorous in the Jewish community as a variety of viable interpretations are always available. This active debate has resulted in Jews valuing the study of Torah, articulate dialogue, and freedom of thought, all in the context of actions that benefit the community.

Different groups within Judaism vary in the level of strict adherence they put into keeping the rules.

Only three moral absolutes are to be found in *Kiddush ha-Shem* (the sanctification of the divine name). God's name is sanctified by prayer, righteous conduct, and martyrdom, and providing an ethical example to non-Jews (Gentiles) is particularly important. The history of Jewish martyrs is well documented and is the result of a refusal to break the laws against idolatry, murder, and lack of chastity.

Kosher

In one sense, everything in Judaism is concerned with ethics and right moral action. All the ritual is intended to guide better behavior. The dietary laws illustrate the way that the religious, the ritual, and the ethical coincide in the faith. There are three main aspects to keeping kosher:

1. Only certain species are permitted for eating: cows, sheep, chicken, and fish; others are forbidden (pigs, shellfish).
2. The slaughter of animals must be done in a certain way to minimize pain. (The Torah includes a law against slaughtering a calf in the presence of its mother.)
3. There is no mixing of meat and dairy products at a meal.

Rabbi Harold Kushner comments on the spirit behind the dietary laws:

> God cares about the little things. It is not that there is anything intrinsically wrong with pork and right with chicken; instead dietary laws turn eating into a religious activity. The reason for observing the dietary laws is not hygiene nor legalism, but love of God. God has suggested that we try and tame our appetites for him in the most basic of activities. In learning how to deny ourselves small things we are trained to resist big things. Furthermore, we turn each meal into an opportunity to be reminded of the love of God and the covenant relationship between God and his people. (Harold Kushner, *To Life: A Celebration of Jewish Being and Thinking* [London: Little, Brown and Company, Ltd., 1993], 59–60.)

Prayer and Worship

Orthodox male Jews when they pray wear religious dress that has great symbolism. The *Tallit* is a prayer shawl that is wound around the worshiper while he is reciting prayer, to show that God's law and commandments are wrapped around him.

Tefillin are prayer phylacteries worn on the arm and head of a pray-er during *Shachrit*, the morning service. (Neither *tallit* or *tefillin* are worn on the Sabbath day.) There are two kinds of *tefillin*: *tefillin shel yad* (for the hand) and *tefillin shel rosh* (for the head). A special prayer is recited when donning the *tefillin*:

> I will betroth thee unto Me forever
> I will betroth thee unto Me in righteousness

> And in judgment and in loving kindness and in mercy. . . .
> And in faithfulness and thou shalt know the Lord.

This prayer speaks of the devotion and affection between Israel and her God. The binding of something on to a person is symbolic. It is not only a spiritual binding to the prayer, but also physical, which evokes spiritual power.

- On *waking in the morning* the prayer is

  > I give thanks to you, Ruler of life everlasting, Who, in mercy, has returned my soul to me. Our trust in You is great.

- At *the opening of Sabbath*, the prayer is

  > Blessed be He and blessed be His name. Blessed are You, O Lord our God, Ruler of the universe, Who has sanctified us with His commandments and commanded us to kindle the light of Sabbath.

- At *the end of the day*, The *Shema*, the Jewish statement of belief and the most central prayer in Jewish life, is recited:

  > Hear O Israel, the Lord our God, the Lord is One. And you shall love the Lord your God with all your heart, with all your soul, with all your might. And these words which I command you this day shall be on your heart. You shall teach them to your children, and you shall speak of them when you sit at home and when you go out on the road, when you lie down and when you rise up. And you shall bind them as a sign upon your arm and they shall be as frontlets between your eyes and you shall write them on the doorposts of your house and on your gates. (Deuteronomy 6:4–9. Prayers taken from Blu Greenberg, *How to Run a Traditional Jewish Household* [New York: Simon & Schuster, 1983].)

The *Shema* is also recited when a person dies. Rabbi Akiba (50–135 C.E.) was a Jewish scholar and martyr. When he was taken out to be killed by the Romans, they tore off his flesh with metal combs and flayed him alive. As this was happening, he recited the *Shema*. His disciples cried, "Even now?" He replied, "All my days I was troubled by the explanation 'with all your soul'—even if He takes it from you. Now this is in my power, should I not fulfill it?" Rabbi Akiba died as he recited the word "One." Jews, therefore, try to recite the *Shema* on their death.

The *Amidah*

The *Amidah* is a prayer containing eighteen benedictions. Nowadays, however, it has nineteen benedictions, as during the temple times a paragraph was added to curse those who informed on the Jews. Those informers would be unable to recite the paragraph because of their allegiance, and they would be recognized as informers.

As a person begins to pray, reciting the words, "O Lord, open my lips and let my mouth declare Your praise," the presence of God comes in.

The *Kaddish*

The *Kaddish* is the mourner's prayer, recited by the family of the departed one. It is said during *Shiva*, the seven days of mourning, and for the following three weeks (*Shloshim*). *Kaddish* is also recited once a year on the *Yartzeit*, the anniversary of the death. To recite the *Kaddish*, there must be a *minyan*, a group of ten men.

The *Mezuzah*

The *Mezuzah* is a scroll (in a box) that is affixed to every doorpost (except the bathroom) of most Jewish homes. The *Mezuzah* contains extracts from the Torah: Deuteronomy 6:4–9 (the *Shema*) and Deuteronomy 11:13–21.

Worship in the Synagogue

Jews worship in synagogues (meaning: "bringing together"). The Holy Ark is a cupboard that contains the Torah on a scroll. The Torah is handwritten in Hebrew. In front of the Ark is the *ner tamid* (the lamp of perpetual light, see Ex. 27:20–21), burning continuously to represent the continuity of Jewish tradition and of God's presence. In Orthodox synagogues, men and women separate for worship, services are in Hebrew, and singing is unaccompanied. Reform synagogues sometimes have family seating and there may be a sermon; some of the service is in Hebrew. In Liberal synagogues, men and women sit together and singing is sometimes accompanied; the service is not in Hebrew. The rabbi is an expert on the Jewish religious law. He is not a priest, but a teacher. In their Sabbath worship, Jews use prayer books (*siddur*), which set out the reading of psalms extolling God's deliverance to them from Egyptian slavery and other acts of God's mercy and loving-kindness. The climax of the service is the *Shema* ("hear"). The Sabbath *Amidah* (standing) prayer is one of praise, in contrast to the rest of the week when prayer recalls the Eighteen Blessings, e.g., good harvests, the rebuilding of Jerusalem. The whole of the Torah is read through in the yearly cycle of Sabbath services. The *Kaddish* prayer is also said:

> Magnified and sanctified be His great Name in the world which He has created according to His will. May he establish His kingdom during your life. . . .

The people respond with,

> Let His name be blessed for ever and for all eternity.

Gender and Religion

In the Mishnah and the Talmud, discussions about women are numerous and deal with the legal status of women in both the public and private aspects of life. They are mostly references to women in general terms, with the occasional affectionate or critical remark from one writer about his mother or other female relative! The Talmud says that husbands should regard wives as equal, to be honored and supported. The Talmud is concise: "If your wife is short, bend down to listen to her advice." However, while there is respect for women on the one hand, severe criticism of them occurs elsewhere in the Talmud. Much of the criticism of women derives from the second creation story in the book of Genesis, in which woman is made from the rib of man and she disobeys God by eating the fruit of the tree of the knowledge of Good and Evil. This story contrasts with the first creation narrative in Genesis 1, in which men and women are created equal. The rabbis' commentary on this includes the view that Adam had two wives, the first Eve, who they call Lilith, and the second Eve, who ate the fruit in Genesis 2. The commentary sees Lilith arguing with her husband that she is equal, but she uttered God's name and was therefore changed into demon form to haunt humanity; she caused the serpent to tempt the other Eve in the Garden of Eden. God punished her for this and made her subservient to men.

In the Hebrew Bible, men and women suffered the same fate for adultery or apostasy, but women were still seen as lesser in status. A woman had no right to divorce, and lineage was passed down through the patriarchal line in biblical times. However, there are also stories of influential matriarchs, e.g., Sarah, Rebekah, Leah, and Rachel. Deborah's leadership as a judge of Israel is also notable.

Modesty and Divorce

In the Mishnah, the rabbis speak of women as eavesdroppers, lazy, spiteful, thieves, and gluttons. Rabbinic thought also reflects a preoccupation with modesty. For example, for a woman to appear in public without a head covering was a legitimate cause for divorce, in the sense that it equated with unfaithfulness, which was the only other reason for divorce. Today a minority of very Orthodox Jewish women still cover their hair by using a wig.

Traditionally in Judaism, only men are allowed to initiate divorce. The Talmudic discussion on grounds for divorce concludes by suggesting that a man can divorce his wife on trivial grounds:

> The School of Shammai held that a man should not divorce his wife unless he has found her guilty of some sexual misconduct, while the School of Hillel says that he may divorce her even if she has merely spoiled his food. Rabbi Akiva—he may divorce her even if he simply finds another woman more beautiful than she. (Gittin 90a–b)

Subsequently, Rabbenu Gershom (eleventh century) introduced a medieval ban on a woman being divorced without her consent.

In the post biblical period, women were and some continue to be vulnerable if their husbands refuse to grant divorce. In the past, Jewish courts have gone to such lengths as imprisoning a husband in order to influence him into divorcing his wife, if the wife's request is a reasonable one. The *get* is the bill of divorce given by a man to his wife, which releases her from marriage and permits her to remarry. In Jewish religious law, even if a civil divorce is granted, without the *get*, a woman may not remarry but a man can. At the time of this writing, Judaism has already begun to redress this inequality. In New York State the civil courts make the provision of a religious divorce a necessary condition of receiving a civil divorce.

Gender Roles

In strict Orthodox Judaism, women and men have traditionally had clearly defined and very separate roles. Women are superior in the home, in teaching their children, and in preparing for Shabbat and other festivals. Men have total supremacy in the public domain, i.e., in religious life, in synagogues, and in courts.

Various prohibitions have contributed historically to the separation of men's prayer and women's prayer. For example, women were not allowed to be counted in a *minyan* (the quorum of ten men required for an act of public worship) and women were segregated from men in both the temple and in the synagogue.

Reform Judaism has accepted women rabbis and abolished partition. Progressive Judaism believes in the equality of men and women so that women can fully participate at every level of synagogue leadership and worship. Women have been ordained since 1972 in America and since 1975 in Great Britain. In 1994 the Chief Rabbi of the United Kingdom convened a commission that issued a progressive report on the status of women in Orthodox Judaism, calling for women to be able to participate in *Kaddish*, the end of segregation in the synagogue, and rights to file for divorce.

In America, Orthodox rabbis allow women to conduct their own services, which includes reading from the Torah, but they may not undertake those duties on behalf of men. In Great Britain, women are not allowed to conduct their own services on the premises of a synagogue, but only privately in a home.

Jewish Mysticism

> The rabbi of Kobryn taught:
> God says to man, as He said to Moses: "Put off thy shoes from thy feet"—put off the habitual which encloses your foot, and you will know that the place on which you are now standing is holy ground. For there is no rung of human life on which we

cannot find the holiness of God everywhere and at all times. (Martin Buber, *Tales of the Hasidim: Later Masters* [New York, Shocken Books, 1948], 17.)

The Jewish mystical school known as Kabbalah comes from the Hebrew root of - *Bet-Lamed*, meaning "to receive, to accept," usually translated as "tradition." In Hebrew, the word does not have any of the dark or sinister connotations that it does in English. Just as there is a written scripture—the "Revealed Torah (Law)" (the first five books of the Bible attributed to Moses)—so there is also an inner or "hidden" Torah, a "secret" (*sod*), which gives the inner meaning of the Torah. This work conceptualizes on theologies such as the nature of God, the nature of man, creation, and the origin of the cosmos. Since the twelfth century the Hidden Torah has been committed to writing, but until then it had supposedly been handed down by word of mouth. This body of work constitutes the Kabbalah, which is seen as the occult or mystical branch of the Jewish religion. Its followers often mark it as the inner counterpart to the outer or legalistic doctrine of the Torah or "Law."

The Hebrew Bible and Mysticism

Since the end of the Bible period, there has been a steady stream of esoteric Jewish tradition based on secret teachings, which include transcending the human realm of experience to unite with the divine realm. The Hebrew Bible does not speak of mysticism in the sense of esoteric secrecy or unity with divine reality, although throughout the Bible a sense of mystery surrounds the theophanies of God—for example, the Call of Moses at the Burning Bush (Ex. 3:2f)—and his appearances/presence on earth. The Torah contains many stories of visitations by angels, prophetic dreams, and visions, as well as a wealth of mystical phenomena. When Isaiah had his vision of God in the temple (Isa. 6:1f), he cried out in woe because he had gazed with his own impure eyes upon the glory of the Lord of Hosts, a sight that even the angels could not bear and thus shielded themselves with their wings.

Merkabah Mysticism

The earliest documents (c. 100–c. 1000 C.E.) associated with Kabbalah describe the attempts of Merkabah mystics to penetrate the seven halls (*Hekaloth*) of creation and reach the Merkabah (throne-chariot) of God. These mystics practiced fasting, chanting, prayer, and posture to attain trance states in which they struggled to advance past terrible seals and guards to reach an ecstatic state in which they "saw God." An early and highly influential work (*Sepher Yetzirah*) appears to have originated during the earlier part of this period. The earliest speculations of Merkabah were to do with prophetic visions of God in the heavenly realms and the angelic creatures surrounding him, developing in later thought into description of multilayered heavens (often seven) guarded by the angelic hosts and surrounded with lightning and flame. The highest heavenly realm has seven palaces, and the innermost realm houses the divine image or glory of God seated on the throne and surrounded by angelic praise. The Talmud contains vague hints of a mystical school of thought that was taught only to the most advanced students because of the dangers of being overzealous and because it was not committed to writing. Fragments of Merkabah traditions have been found in the Dead Sea Scrolls and in rabbinic *midrash*, and modern scholars look at the use of Merkabah theology in early Jewish-Christian gnosticism.

Mystical Ascent in Merkabah Mysticism

The debate continues as to when and how the theme of individual mystical ascent into the heavenly was introduced into these images. Many scholars see the third century as the most probable time, but ongoing dispute surrounds the question of whether ascent themes were a result of Gnostic influence in the Jewish faith or a genuine strand of religious thought and experience within rabbinic Judaism.

Hasidic Mysticism

Like many aspects of Jewish belief, the area of mysticism is wide open to personal interpretation. Some traditional Jews take mysticism very seriously. Mysticism is an integral part of Hasidic Judaism, for example, and passages from kabbalistic sources are routinely included in traditional prayer books. Other traditional Jews do not accept mysticism as a serious or valid aspect of their faith.

Kabbalah

"Kabbalah" is sometimes translated as "collected teachings." The word is spelled "cabala" in the Merriam-Webster dictionary. Waite and Mathers used "Kabbalah." Aleister Crowley used "qabalah," the correct transliteration of the Hebrew (QBL: Qoph Beth Lamed).

While rooted in Jewish mysticism, Kabbalah has absorbed elements of gnosticism, neo-Platonism, and Oriental thought. The *Zohar* (probably the central book of Kabbalah) was written by Moses de Leon in the thirteenth century.

Kabbalah is usually divided into four sections:

1. *Practical Kabbalah*, involving talismanic and ceremonial magic
2. *Literal Kabbalah*, involving the altering of words, consisting of *gematria*, *notariqon*, and *temurah*
3. Unwritten Kabbalah, containing knowledge transmitted orally and never committed to writing
4. Dogmatic Kabbalah, containing published doctrines and treatises of the Kabbalah

Four important texts constitute the bulk of the dogmatic Kaballah: the *Sepher ha-Zohar* (book of splendor), the *Sepher Sephiroth* (book of emanations), the *Sepher Yetzirah* (book of formation), and the *Esh Mezareph* (purifying fire).

Kabbalists claim to have been badly misunderstood, stemming largely from the fact that kabbalistic teachings have been seriously distorted by non-Jewish mystics and occultists. Others take kabbalistic symbolism out of context for use in tarot card readings and other forms of divination and magic that were never a part of the original Jewish teachings. Even so, the hidden, secretive part of Kabbalah, commonly known as "practical Kabbalah," involves use of hidden knowledge to affect the world in ways that could be described as magic. Among other sources, the Talmud ascribes supernatural activities to many great rabbis. For example, some rabbis pronounced a name of God and ascended into heaven to consult with God and the angels on issues of great public concern. However, this area of Kabbalah is the least known and practiced; all magical incidents and effects were instead understood to be achieved through the power of God, generally by calling upon the name of God. There have been claims that Jesus healed in a similar way and that he was associated with the Essenes, a sect involved in Jewish mysticism, although this view is not widely accepted by scholars.

The most important medieval magical text is the "Key of Solomon," and it contains elements of classic ritual magic: names of power, the magic circle, ritual implements, consecration, evocation of spirits, etc.

Ein Sof and the Ten *Sefirot*

Fundamental concepts of kabbalistic thought are the concepts of God as *Ein Sof*, the Ten *Sefirot*, and the kabbalistic tree of life. (Note at this point that any explanation that can be offered here is, at best, an oversimplification, and that the subject cries out for finer and more detailed research.)

- *The essence of God.* According to Kabbalah, the true transcendent essence of God cannot be described, except with reference to what it is not. The true essence of God is *Ein Sof* (without end), involving the idea of God's lack of boundaries in both time and space. In essence, even the *Ein Sof* is so transcendent that it cannot interact directly with the universe. Any interaction of *Ein Sof* comes through ten emanations known as the Ten *Sefirot*.
- *The Ten* Sefirot *correspond to qualities of God.* Together they form the world of divine light in the chain of being. They are, in descending order:

  Keter (the crown)

  Chokhmah (wisdom)

  Binah (intuition, understanding)

  Chesed (mercy) or *Gedulah* (greatness)

  Gevurah (strength)

  Tiferet (glory)

  Netzach (victory)

Hod (majesty)
Yesod (foundation)
Malkut (sovereignty)

- The middle five qualities are spoken of explicitly and in order in 1 Chronicles 29:11: "Yours, O LORD, are the greatness, the power, the glory, the victory, and the majesty."

- *The Tree of Life.* The *Sefirot* are commonly represented as a diagram known as the Tree of the *Sefirot* or the Kabbalistic Tree of Life, and great significance is given to the position of these various attributes and their interconnectedness. The Ten *Sefirot* include both masculine and feminine qualities, as Kabbalah pays attention to the feminine aspects of God. The *Sefirot* connect with everything in the universe, including humanity. The good and evil that we do resonates through the *Sefirot* and affects the whole universe, including God. The concept of *Sefirot* has been influenced by gnostic thought and attempts to explain the mystery of how a transcendent God can interact with the world.

By the early Middle Ages, further, more theosophical developments had taken place, chiefly a description of "processes" within God, and a highly esoteric view of creation as a process in which God manifests in a series of emanations. In thirteenth-century Provence and northern Spain, theosophic kabbalists introduced neo-Platonic images and language in their attempts to explain the process of the emanations of the *Sefirot* from the infinite. In so doing, they also practiced contemplative prayer to promote the intellectual ascent of the mystic soul to union with the divine. This involved ecstasy and visions, and the process of knowing divine powers included a state of illumination where the powers were visualized as lights or as letters of the divine names.

The Hasidic Ashkenaz

In the thirteenth century, the German Pietistic movement included the Haside Ashkenaz or German Pietists led by Judah ben Samuel (Regensburg) and his follower, Eleazar ben Judah of Worms, who taught that "Nothing is more beautiful than forgiveness." They kept the old merkabah texts but also brought in their own theosophy, combining the ancient teaching with the various philosophies of other Pietists and especially the neo-Platonism of Abraham ibn Ezra (c. 1092–1167). The heart of Pietist theosophy was the question of the nature of the divine glory (*kavod*). Through his glory, God, who is totally beyond human understanding, "is closer to all than the body is to the soul." (Eleazar ben Judah)

From this doctrinal focus came the esoteric tradition of the identification of the divine glory with the Tetragrammaton (the four letters of the Divine Name, JHVW or Jehovah/Yahweh) and the image of these letters as a human figure.

Prophetic Kabbalah

Prophetic or ecstatic Kabbalah emerged in the latter half of the thirteenth century. The Spanish mystic Abraham Abulafia (born c. 1240) was a highly educated man who had an intense mystical experience at the age of thirty-one. He believed that God cannot be conceptualized using everyday symbols, and he used the Hebrew alphabet in intense meditations lasting many hours to reach ecstatic states. These letter combinations were used as entry points to altered states of consciousness, but failure to carry through the processes correctly could have a drastic effect on the kabbalist, involving extreme and potentially harmful forms of ecstasy. Abulafia warned: *"Your whole body will be seized by an extremely strong trembling, so you will think that surely you are about to die, because your Soul, overjoyed with its knowledge, will leave your body."*

The kabbalistic document, the "*Sepher ha Zohar,*" was published by the Spanish Jew, Moses de Leon, in the latter half of the thirteenth century. The "*Zohar*" is a series of separate documents covering a wide range of subjects. It includes a verse-by-verse esoteric commentary on the Pentateuch, and advanced theosophical descriptions of processes within God. The "*Zohar*" has been widely read and highly influential within mainstream Judaism.

The Safed School of Mystics

The Safed school of mystics were led by Moses Cordovero (1522–1570) and Isaac Luria (1534–1572). Luria was a highly charismatic leader who exercised almost total control over the life of the school and is now regarded by many as a saint. Emphasis was placed on living in the world and bringing the consciousness of God into the world in a practical way.

Hasidism

> In all that is in the world dwell holy sparks, no thing is empty of them. In the actions of men also, indeed even in the sins that a man does, dwell holy sparks of the Glory of God. (*The Baal Shem Tov* [1700–1760])

Israel ben Eliezer, the Baal Shem Tov, or BeSHT ("Possessor of the Good Name" or "Master of the Divine Name") was born in the Ukraine and was the founder of the European Hasidic movement. He traveled as a teacher and healer through the communities of Eastern Europe, emphasizing joy in prayer and worship. His teachings came partly from the Kabbalah, but his main emphasis was on personal individual salvation through which the world would be redeemed. Faith, according to Baal Shem Tov, was the "adhesion of the soul to God." He also emphasized study of the Torah by contemplating the significance of each individual letter, which would make men wise and also radiate light and eternal life. His antinomian tendencies were generally acceptable to mainstream Judaism. He left no written works, but his followers have preserved many of his memorable sayings:

> "There is no room for God in one who is full of himself."
> "Pray continually for God's glory that it may be redeemed from its exile."

A follower of the Baal Shem Tov was Polish kabbalist Rabbi Schnuer Zalman (1747–1813), founder of the *Chabad* or Lubavitcher (after the town of Lubavitch) sect of Hasidism. The Lubavitchers are the largest surviving sect of Hasidism. Zalman's most important work was known as the *Tanya* ("that which has been revealed"). It contains religious kabbalistic, and psychological material.

Kabbalah in the Modern World

Jewish Kabbalah has vast and varied literature, much of which is almost entirely untranslated into English. It has been adopted by many Christian mystics and occultists through the centuries. Renaissance philosophers such as Pico della Mirandola were familiar with Kabbalah, and they mixed it with gnosticism, Pythagoreanism, neo-Platonism, and hermeticism in a heady theoretical cocktail that continued to intoxicate mystics down the centuries. It has exerted enormous influence and it would not be wildly inaccurate to say that, from the Renaissance onwards, European occultists and magicians of note had a working knowledge of Kabbalah. The most important "modern" influences are the French magician Eliphas Levi and the English "Order of the Golden Dawn." At least two members of the Golden Dawn (S. L. Mathers and A. E. Waite) were knowledgable kabbalists, and other members have popularized Kabbalah: Aleister Crowley, Israel Regardie, and Dion Fortune.

Festivals

The whole Jewish year is punctuated with special days, most of which center around the home.

Sabbath

The Jewish Sabbath lasts from sunset on Friday until sunset on Saturday. The word *sabbat* means "rest," and therefore no unnecessary work or activity is done. Jewish Sabbath is part of keeping the covenant (Ex. 31:16–17). Orthodox and Conservative Jews keep the Sabbath regulations strictly, whereas Reform Jews do not.

Rosh Hashanah: The New Year

Traditionally, the Jewish New Year begins in the autumn with the month of *Tishri*. Rosh Hashanah is now a two-day festival. The Jewish New Year is a time to ask for forgiveness, and to this end prayers of repentance are made. The ram's horn (*shofar*) is blown in the synagogues, calling people to return to God, change their behavior, and be forgiven. A meal follows in which bread and apples are dipped in honey to symbolize the hope for a sweet year ahead. It is also believed that on Rosh Hashanah, the heavenly Book of Life is opened and the good and evil deeds of each Jew are counted. On Jewish New Year cards, the Hebrew writing often appears, "May you be inscribed for a good year."

Yom Kippur

Yom Kippur, the Jewish Day of Atonement, is celebrated in early fall on *Tishri* 10 of the Jewish calendar, ten days after Rosh Hashanah, the New Year. Yom Kippur is marked by fasting, confession to God of sins committed during the last year, and prayers of forgiveness. Observance begins on Yom Kippur eve with the *kol nidre* service of repentance. Originally, Yom Kippur was the only day of the year when the high priest entered the inner sanctuary of the Temple (the Holy of Holies) to offer sacrifice. A goat—the so-called scapegoat, symbolically carrying the sins of the Jewish people—was then driven into the desert. Yom Kippur is the holiest day in the liturgical year. This is a day of fasting for all fit adults. At the synagogue, the rabbi and many others wear white to symbolize purity.

Sukkoth

Sukkoth is the harvest festival and is also known as "Tabernacles," which begins five days after Yom Kippur and lasts for seven days. Jews construct leafy booths (*Sukkoth*) in their gardens to commemorate the time when the people of Israel were instructed by God to build booths to live in when they were brought out of the land of Egypt (Lev. 23:42–43).

Hanukkah

Hanukkah begins about two months after Sukkoth on the twenty-fifth day of the month of *Kislev*. It lasts eight days and is a festival of light commemorating a miracle of God (c. 165 B.C.E.), when a son of the priest Mattathias, a man called Judah, was given the name Judas Maccabee (meaning "hammerer") because after three years of fighting he succeeded in defeating the Syrian Greek army. The rule of Antiochus IV over Israel had seized the Jewish temple and installed a statue of the Greek God Zeus, demanding the Jews cease Sabbath and worship idols instead. After his victory, Judas Maccabee cleansed and purified the temple of pagan worship. In the account of this story in the Talmud, they found a single jar of holy oil in the temple, just enough to keep the eternal light before the ark burning for one day, but miraculously it burned for eight days and nights. The special Hanukkiyah menorah has nine candles instead of eight. Over the years Hanukkah candles have become powerfully symbolic of religious freedom.

Other Jewish Festivals

Purim commemorates the story of Esther in the Bible. Passover (*Pesach*) remembers the deliverance of the Israelites from Egyptian slavery. *Shavuot* (Feast of Weeks) celebrates the giving of the Ten Commandments at Mt. Sinai.

UNIT 7:5 CHRISTIANITY

Above all the grace and the gifts that Christ gives to his beloved is that of overcoming self.

St. Francis of Assisi

A man who was completely innocent offered himself as a sacrifice for the good of others, including his enemies, and became the ransom of the world. It was a perfect act.

Mahatma Gandhi

Christianity has been (and is) the greatest single obstacle to the communication of the message of Jesus.

Prabhu Guptara

The origins of the Christian faith lie in the life and ministry of the historical figure of Jesus. Within Christian faith he has come to be known as Jesus Christ. Christ is a title designating Jesus as the Messiah (Hebrew = "anointed") of the Jewish people.

Jesus was a Jew, living in Palestine under Roman occupation during the reign of Emperor Augustus (27 B.C.E.–14 C.E.) and King Herod the Great (73–4 B.C.E.). According to one modern reckoning he was born in c. 6–4 B.C.E. Most of what we know of him comes from the Christian gospels, and there is also reference to him in writings of the first century.

Tacitus (*Annals* 15.44) records that the Christian movement began with Jesus, who was sentenced to death by Pontius Pilate. Suetonius (*Claudius* 25.4) refers to the expulsion of the Jews from Rome because of a riot instigated by one "Chrestus" in c. 48 C.E. Pliny the Younger (*Epistles* 10.96), in a letter to the Emperor Trajan, says that the early Christians sang a hymn to Christ as God.

Among the historical Jewish writings, the Jewish historian Flavius Josephus, The Talmud, and other later references to Jesus in rabbinic literature are mostly of anti-Christian sentiment. An early reference in the Babylonian Talmud says that Jeshu ha-Nocri was a false prophet who was hanged on the eve of the Passover for sorcery and false teaching. The evidence from the historian Josephus is problematical. He recounts (*Antiquities* 20.9.1) the martyrdom of James, "the brother of Jesus called the Christ," in 62 C.E. Another passage in the *Antiquities* (18.3.3) gives an extended account of Jesus and his career, but the positive attitude of the text to Jesus indicates that the original text of Josephus was amended by later Christian copyists.

Life of Jesus

According to the gospels, Jesus' family came from the Northern Palestinian town of Nazareth in Galilee. He was born in a stable in Bethlehem, because Mary and Joseph were there to enroll at Joseph's place of ancestry for a national census. The gospels of Matthew and Luke refer to angels, shepherds, and Eastern kings led by a star to his birth. The worldwide influence of one man who was born in an insignificant place, never traveled more than a hundred miles from his birthplace, owned little, attended no college, wrote no books, and was put to death at about age thirty-three, is a phenomenon in itself. Such was the influence of this Galilean (Northern) Jew that for centuries the Western calendar referred back to his birth in its dating, e.g., A.D. (*Anno Domini*, in the year of our Lord, B.C. = before Christ).

Jesus lived during the second temple period of Judaism. He lived and taught as a nonsectarian observant Jew keeping the Jewish law. For a detailed scholarly discussion, see David Flusser, *Jesus* (Jerusalem: Magnus Press, Hebrew University, 1997), chap. 4. He began his work of God when he was about thirty years old (Luke 3:23). He was baptized by John the Baptist in the river Jordan where the Spirit of God came upon him and the heavenly voice addressed him as "Son" (Matt. 3:17). Before his public ministry Jesus went into the desert to be alone with God, and there he was tempted in three different ways by the devil to build his own empire instead of God's (Luke 4:1–13). After overcoming these temptations, Jesus began his ministry in the synagogue of his hometown of Nazareth. He was called upon to read from the words of Isaiah the prophet referring to a promised servant of the Lord who would come to save Israel.

> *The Spirit of the* L*ORD* G*OD* is upon me,
> because the LORD has anointed me; he has sent me to
> bring good news to the oppressed,
> to bind up the broken hearted,
> to proclaim liberty to the captives,
> and release to the prisoners;
> to proclaim the year of the LORD's favor,
> and the day of vengeance of our God;
> to comfort all who mourn. . . .
>
> Isaiah 61: 1–2

Luke, writing about this incident, identifies Jesus with the expected servant of the Lord and also the long-awaited Jewish Messiah.

Jesus then added,

> "Today this scripture has been fulfilled in your hearing." (Luke 4:21)

Jesus as Son of God

Unlike Islam and Judaism, Christians believe that Jesus was unique in being both God and human and not just another prophet (John 14:9; 20:28; Mark

1:10–11). Jesus called twelve disciples to follow him during his short ministry. From the outset, those who heard and recorded Jesus' life and ministry believed that he was acting in the power of God and closely associated with God. This sentiment was expressed in the elevated titles and status given to Jesus as God's Son. The title of God's Son was no unusual thing for miracle workers of the day, but the Gospels go further when they depict Jesus as knowing his Father in heaven in a unique way:

> "I thank you, Father, Lord of heaven and earth, because you have hidden these things from the wise and the intelligent and have revealed them to infants; yes, Father, for such was your gracious will. All things have been handed over to me by my Father; and no one knows the Son except the Father, and no one knows the Father except the Son and anyone to whom the Son chooses to reveal him." (Matt. 11:25–27)

Elsewhere, John reports Jesus as saying, *"The Father and I are one"* (John 10:30) and again, *"Whoever has seen me has seen the Father"* (John 14:9).

Through such texts as these and the early Christian hymns and creedal statements incorporated by the apostle Paul in his letters to the Philippians (2:5–11) and Colossians (1:15–20), it is clear that affirmations of Jesus as the Messiah (Acts 2:14–42) were supplemented by the practice of giving worship to Jesus, as God incarnate, from the earliest days of the movement. That a group of Jewish monotheists should speak of Jesus in such terms signifies a shift in their conception of a messiah, who is not only from God, but who is also God here on earth. That they were able to make such a shift in thinking arises out of resurrection faith and, according to scholar Larry Hurtado (*One God, One Lord* [1988]), the increasing tendency within some of the Jewish literature of the intertestamental period to personify divine agency and attributes—albeit, unlike Jesus they did not receive worship. Thus, the early Christian community had come to conceive of Jesus as having a unique relationship to the God of traditional Jewish belief; indeed, everything was done in the name of Jesus (2 Cor. 12:19) and prayer is directed to Jesus. The implications of such belief and practice toward God were to take several hundred years to unpack (see chapter 9 on Christian history). Nevertheless, within his lifetime the popularity of Jesus among the ordinary people of his day, and the way in which the power of God was believed to be working through him—forgiving sins and healing sicknesses—inevitably threatened the Temple authorities (Sadducees) who had come to rely on the political status quo provided by the Romans, whose own authority would not brook any challenge from messianic expectations. These circumstances led to Jesus' death by Roman crucifixion (Mark 15/Luke 23/John 19/Matthew 27), and as affirmed by the New Testament, to his bodily resurrection from the dead (Mark 16/Matthew 28/Luke 24/John 20), his post-resurrection appearances and his eventual ascension to God (Acts 1). Early Christianity believed that Jesus was the promised Messiah of the

Jews and that his death was a perfect sacrifice for sin, representing a new covenant with Israel and the world. For the majority of Jews these claims were untenable, and as a result the two religions of Christianity and Judaism that exist today developed out of a common network of religious traditions, albeit in their separate ways. Still some Jewish people today see Jesus as the Messiah and some Christians seriously seek to explore Judaism and especially the Jewish background to life at the time of Jesus.

God

Belief in the Trinity (see units 9:2 and 9:3) is a predominantly Christian belief and understanding of the essence and nature of the Godhead. It is a concept of God that has been misinterpreted so that Christianity has been falsely accused of having three gods. Christians believe that there is one God who exists in three persons: Father, Son, and Holy Spirit. This belief is based on the understanding that a form of relationship exists between God and the created world which points back, and provides evidence for, a complex relationship within the Godhead.

The Christian belief in the Trinity means that God is not monistic or abstract; his inherent character is relational, as the Father, Son, and Spirit define their own existence through an ongoing communion with each other. Because God is by nature relational, he also relates to this world through his Son (Jesus) and through his Spirit (who guides, teaches, and empowers believers).

The Central Message of Jesus: The Kingdom of God

Although the concept of the kingdom of God (also referred to as the kingdom of Heaven) can be found in Judaism before the Christian writings, it either referred in a general sense to God's continuing rule over Israel or the world (e.g., Psalm 97) or a future end-of-time event (e.g., Daniel 2). However, in the parables of Jesus, the kingdom of God was at the core of his teaching. For about three years Jesus taught about the kingdom of God through his miracles (acts of power) and through his teaching (parables).

Miracles in the Gospels

In the synoptic Gospels (Matthew, Mark, and Luke) the Greek word used for "miracles" is *dunameis*, meaning "acts of power." John's Gospel uses the word *semeia* or "signs." Jesus' miracles in the Gospel accounts (Matthew, Mark, Luke, and John) number about thirty-five occasions. In them the rule or kingdom of God has come. Jesus looked for faith as the right response to his saving presence and deeds. Yet faith on the part of human participants is not a necessary condition of a miracle in the sense that God is unable to act without human faith.

These miracles fall generally into four different groups, and through them Christians see different facets of God.

Healing the sick. This act shows the love of God reaching out to people who were suffering, e.g., the woman with a hemorrhage in Luke 8:43–48.

Raising people from the dead, showing that the power of God was stronger than death, e.g., the widow's son at Nain (Luke 7:11–15).

Casting out demons from those who were possessed, indicating that the kingdom of God was stronger than the kingdom of Satan—and that Satan was being defeated (e.g., the man with demons at Gerasenes [Luke 8:27–35]).

Power over nature and the natural world, showing God's power at work in his world. God's acts are unexpected and seemingly impossible, but with God all things are possible (e.g., Jesus feeding the five thousand [in all four gospels]).

False Miracles

The gospels show that Jesus consistently refused to work wonders in order to guarantee his teaching and authenticity as the Son of God. In the Bible there is frequent reference to wonder working by those opposed to the purposes of God (Deut. 13:2–3 and Matt. 7:22, 24:2). Judaism and Christianity both share the view that any miracle worker who denies the Lord (Deut. 13:2–3) is to be rejected. Jesus himself stressed that his works were done in constant dependence on the Father (e.g. John 5:19). Traditional Christian faith sees the authoritative manner of Jesus' works of power as messianic. In the virgin birth, the resurrection, and the ascension is the testimony of what God did in Christ. Paul taught that in the resurrection, like no other miracle, rests the whole structure and hope of Christian faith (1 Cor. 15:7). The early Christians and apostles worked miracles that were seen as part of the proclamation of the kingdom of God, not an end in themselves.

The debate continues in Christian theology as to whether the function of miracles was of necessity only for the apostolic age and therefore not for today.

The Parables

Jesus was a Jewish theologian, and as such he was familiar with the rabbinic use of story to convey knowledge of the nature of God and the human predicament. About one third of Jesus' teaching was in parables (Greek = *parabole*; Hebrew = *mashal*), which are mostly found in the Gospels of Luke and Matthew. In the parable of the lost son, Jesus weaves a wonderful tale of the naked ambition of a young man, sibling rivalry, rejection of the family, riotous living, the dissatisfaction of self-indulgence, the hollow vacuum of being lost and downtrodden and alone, and the unconditional love of the father who rejoices that his son has returned. This parable is the longest one Jesus told, but in more than any other the Christian belief in the nature of God the Father is explored and communicated.

Where to Find Jesus' Miracles

	Matthew	Mark	Luke	John
Healing				
Man with a skin disease	8:2–3	1:40–42	5:12–13	
Roman officer's servant	8:5–13		7:1–10	
Peter's mother-in-law	8:14–15	1:30–31	4:38–39	
Two men from Gadara	8:28–34	5:1–15	8:27–35	
Paralyzed man	9:2–7	2:3–12	5:18–25	
Woman with a hemorrhage	9:20–22	5:25–29	8:43–48	
Two blind men	9:27–31			
Man dumb and possessed	9:32–33			
Man with a paralyzed hand	12:10–13	3:1–5	6:6–10	
Man blind, dumb and possessed	12:22		11:14	
Canaanite woman's daughter	15:21–28	7:24–30		
Boy with epilepsy	17:14–18	9:17–29	9:38–43	
Two blind men	20:29–34			
Bartimaeus; one blind man		10:46–52	18:35–43	
Deaf mute		7:31–37		
Man possessed		1:23–26	4:33–35	
Blind man at Bethsaida		18:22–26		
Crippled woman			13:11–13	
Man with swollen limbs			14:1–4	
Two men with a skin disease			17:11–19	
The High Priest's slave			22:50–51	
Official's son at Capernaum				4:46–54
Sick man, Pool of Bethzatha				5:1–9
Command over the forces of nature				
Calming of the storm	8:23–27	4:37–41	8:22–25	
Walking on the water	14:25	6:48–51		6:19–21
5,000 people fed	14:15–21	6:35–44	9:12–17	6:5–13
4,000 people fed	15:32–38	8:1–9		
Coin in the fish's mouth	17:24–27			
Fig-tree withered	21:18–22	11:12–14		
Catch of fish		20–25	5:1–11	
Water turned into wine				2:1–11
Another catch of fish				21:1–11
Bringing the dead back to life				
Jairus' (Matthew: a Jewish official's) daughter	9:18–19	5:22–24	8:41–42	
	9:23–25	5:38–42	8:49–56	
Widow's son at Nain			7:11–15	
Lazarus				11:1–44

Where to Find Jesus' Parables

	Matthew	Mark	Luke
Lamp under a bowl	5:14–15	4:21–22	8:16; 11:33
Houses on rock and on sand	7:24–27		6:47–49
New cloth on an old coat	9:16	2:21	5:36
New wine in used wineskins	9:17	2:22	5:37–38
Sower and soils	13:3–8	4:3–8	8:5–8
Mustard seed	13:31–32	4:30–32	13:18–19
Weeds	13:24–30		
Yeast	13:33		13:20–21
Hidden treasure	13:44		
The pearl	13:45–46		
The net	13:47–48		
Lost sheep	18:12–13		15:4–6
The unforgiving servant	18:23–24		
Workers in the vineyard	20:1–16		
Two sons	21:28–31		
Tenants	21:33–41	12:1–9	20:9–16
The wedding feast; a man without wedding clothes	22:2–14		
The lesson of the fig tree	24:32–33	13:28–29	21:29–32
Ten girls	25:1–13		
The silver coins (Matthew); gold coins (Luke)	25:14–30		19:12–27
Sheep and goats	25:31–36		
The growing seed		4:26–29	
The moneylender			7:41–43
Good Samaritan			10:30–37
Friend in need			11:5–8
Rich fool			12:16–21
Watchful servants			12:35–40
Faithful servant			12:42–48
Unfruitful fig tree			13:6–9
Best places at a wedding feast			14:7–14
The great feast and the reluctant guests			14:16–24
Counting the cost			14:28–33
Lost coin			15:8–10
The lost son			15:11–32
The shrewd manager			16:1–8
Rich man and Lazarus			16:19–31
The master and his servant			17:7–10
The widow and the judge			18:2–5
The Pharisee and the tax collector			18:10–14

The Parable of the Lost Son: Luke 15:11–32

Jesus also told them another story:

> Once a man had two sons. The younger son said to his father, "Give me my share of the property." So the father divided his property between his two sons. Not long after that, the younger son packed up everything he owned and left for a foreign country, where he wasted all his money in wild living. He had spent everything, when a bad famine spread through that whole land. Soon he had nothing to eat.
>
> He went to work for a man in that country, and the man sent him out to take care of his pigs. He would have been glad to eat what the pigs were eating, but no one gave him a thing.
>
> Finally, he came to his senses and said, "My father's workers have plenty to eat, and here I am, starving to death! I will go to my father and say to him, 'Father, I have sinned against God in heaven and against you. I am no longer good enough to be called your son. Treat me like one of your workers.' "
>
> The younger son got up and started back to his father. But when he was still a long way off, his father saw him and felt sorry for him. He ran to his son and hugged and kissed him.
>
> The son said, "Father, I have sinned against God in heaven and against you. I am no longer good enough to be called your son."
>
> But his father said to the servants, "Hurry and bring the best clothes and put them on him. Give him a ring for his finger and sandals for his feet. Get the best calf and prepare it, so we can eat and celebrate. This son of mine was dead, but has now come back to life. He was lost and has now been found." And they began to celebrate.
>
> The older son had been out in the field. But when he came near the house, he heard the music and dancing. So he called one of the servants over and asked, "What's going on here?"
>
> The servant answered, "Your brother has come home safe and sound, and your father ordered us to kill the best calf." The older brother got so angry that he would not even go into the house.
>
> His father came out and begged him to go in. But he said to his father, "For years I have worked for you like a slave and have always obeyed you. But you have never even given me a little goat, so that I could give a dinner for my friends. This other son of yours wasted your money on prostitutes. And now that he has come home, you ordered the best calf to be killed for a feast." His father replied, "My son, you are always with me, and everything I have is yours. But we should be glad and celebrate! Your brother was dead, but he is now alive. He was lost and has now been found." (CEV)

The Kingdom of God

Jesus' teaching about the kingdom of God included the following:

- The kingdom of God is not a place; it is the rule of God within people's hearts at the present time (Luke 17:20f).
- You must be born again of water (baptism) and the Spirit to enter the kingdom of God (John 3:1–8).
- The kingdom of God is both in present time and in the future when the final rule of God will come (Matt. 25:41, Matt. 13:36–43).
- The signs of the kingdom include the lame walking (Mark 2:3–12), the deaf hearing, the blind seeing (Mark 8:22–26; Mark 10:46–52), and the dumb speaking (Matt. 12:22), but the way is narrow (Luke 13:24). Money and status can be serious obstacles to God's rule or kingdom coming to a person.
- The kingdom of God is for the childlike. Trust and simplicity are paramount qualities (Luke 18:16–17).
- The kingdom of God is for the lost. Jesus was criticized in his day for eating with criminals, prostitutes, and the much-hated tax collectors (Luke 15:1–2).
- The kingdom defeats evil. Immediately after reading in the synagogue and his subsequent rejection at Nazareth Jesus went to Capernaum where he cast out a demon/unclean spirit from a man. In the teaching of Jesus the kingdom of God defeats the power of the devil.

Salvation

The Christian concept of salvation is multi-faceted. Jesus' teaching presupposed the reality of universal sin and human need originating in rebelliousness towards God (Matt. 11:20–24; 24:12). This rebelliousness brings a sickness of soul (Mark 2:17; Matt. 15:17–20), residing in the human personality and defiling it (Matt. 7:15–16; 12:35; cf. 5:21). Jesus therefore called everyone to repentance (Mark 1:15; Luke 5:32), to a change of mind and a style of life that enthrones God (Luke 8:1–3; 19:1–10). Jesus urged daily prayer for forgiveness; he himself offered forgiveness to others (Mark 2:5) and taught that humility and penitence were the only acceptable attitudes from which to approach God (Luke 18:9–14).

In the Gospel of John salvation is from death and judgment. John speaks in terms of eternal life abundant and experienced as love (John 3:5–16; 5:24; 12:25; 1 John 4:7–11; 5:11). In the book of Acts, Peter also called people to repentance (Acts 2:38), promising forgiveness and the Spirit to whoever called upon the Lord.

Paul recognized his own failure to attain legal righteousness because of the power of sin, which brought with it death. According to Paul, salvation is therefore made up of acquittal and deliverance. Despite the just condemnation of God, people can be acquitted on the grounds of Christ's expiation of sin by his sacrifice on the cross (Rom. 3:21–26).

People can be delivered by the indwelling power of the Spirit of the risen Christ—that is, the Holy Spirit in the life of the believer who accepts Christ's death on his or her behalf (Rom. 8:9–11). The Holy Spirit also unites the believer and Christ so closely that they "die" to sin and rise to new life (Rom. 6:1–4). According to Paul, the results are Christians free from the power of sin (Rom. 8:2), filled with an inner joy in the power of the Spirit who dwells within and an unassailable assurance of being a child of God (Romans 8). As time goes on, the Christian conforms more and more to be like Christ; death is no longer feared, and believers are prepared for life everlasting (Rom. 6:13, 22–23; 8:11).

Later Approaches to Salvation

The Eastern Church traced the effect of Adam's fall mainly in terms of human mortality, with salvation as especially the gift of eternal life through the risen Christ. The Western Church understood the effect of Adam's fall chiefly in terms of inherited guilt (Ambrose) and the corruption (Augustine) of humankind and salvation as especially the gift of grace through Christ's death. Divine grace alone could cancel guilt and deliver from corruption.

Anselm and Abelard saw the suffering and death of Jesus as satisfaction for sin, or as a redeeming example of love; Luther saw salvation in relation to men and women receiving faith; Calvin viewed salvation in relation to God's sovereign will.

Roman Catholic thought has focused on the objective aspects of salvation within a sacramental church, and Protestantism has focused on the subjective experience of salvation within the individual soul.

Death and the Afterlife

Jesus' teaching on death and the afterlife, though not detailed, gives firm hope to his followers:

- Whoever believes in him will never die (John 11:25–26).
- There is a place prepared by Jesus for those who follow him (John 14:1–4).
- Jesus will come back as king and judge the world. He will divide the righteous and the unrighteous, each of whom has chosen their eternal destiny (Matt. 25:31–46).
- The new bodies in the afterlife are different (Luke 20:34–36).

The writings of Paul include more reflection and speculation about life after death, including belief in the resurrection of the body (see 1 Cor. 15:20–26, 35–38, 42–44, 53–57; 1 Thess. 4:13–18).

Traditionally Christians have buried their dead, with a sprinkling of earth on the corpse, which is usually buried with feet toward the east, the direction from which the return of Christ on the day of resurrection was expected. The practice of cremation began to be adopted in the West in the nineteenth century, where it was at first opposed by most Christians who thought it to be incompatible with a belief in the resurrection of the body.

The Roman Catholic Church

Today, the Roman Catholic Church teaches that only people who had led a pure life will enter God's presence immediately. Others will have to go through a purification process called purgatory, where they will suffer by losing their vision of God. They will have no pleasures of this world to distract them, so it will be a time of preparation that increases their desire for God. People in purgatory are aided by masses said for them, the prayers of living friends and relatives, and the saints.

Protestant Churches

Most Protestant Christians would say that the opportunity to respond to God is limited to this life, and therefore no future "in-between" state exists when people can be prepared for heaven. More recently, some Protestant Christians have tended to see the body as mortal and the soul as immortal and everlasting.

The Eastern Orthodox Church

Eastern Orthodox teaching holds that our bodies will be restored to life again: "At the resurrection," declare *The Homilies of St. Macros*, "all the members of the body are raised: not a hair perishes."

Hell

Traditional Christian theology teaches that people who have not repented of their sins go to hell after this life, while those redeemed by faith in Christ's sacrifice for their sins go either to purgatory or directly to heaven. The belief in hell is shaped by New Testament verses such as Matthew 13:25, 41–42, 46, and the description of the "second death" in Revelation 21:8 where there are those who are cast into "a lake that burns with fire and sulfur." A modern conservative Christian position on the subject sees hell as a necessary consequence of human free will that chooses against God. One cannot contradict God's love or justice. Hell has also become an issue in modern Christianity: is hell an eternal condition or will Christ's atoning work eventually bring all to salvation? Some modern theologians reject the whole notion of everlasting punishment.

Moral Action

Christianity developed out of Judaism and therefore accepts the moral basis and the principles of the Jewish Torah, interpreted in the light of Jesus' life and teaching, as part of its own body of scripture.

Christian sources of morality vary between the different denominations but include

- The authority of the Christian Bible
- The authority of the Church and its teaching
- Human reason (see chapter 3 on Natural Law)
- Conscience
- The direct guidance and inspiration of the Holy Spirit

Christian ethics flow from Jesus' summary of the Jewish Law to love God with all your power and your neighbor as yourself. The "Golden Rule" taught by Jesus is to "Do to others as you would have them do to you" (Matt. 7:12; Luke 6:31).

The Sermon on the Mount (Matthew 5–7; Luke's Sermon on the Plain [Luke 6:20–49]) is a collection of sayings in which Jesus outlined attitudes and actions central to the Christian life. Jesus also urged his hearers to seek humility and to avoid hypocrisy and religious pride. The sermon also warns of the lure of wealth and the folly of judging other people when you can't even see your own faults. At the heart of the sermon is the call of God for his people to trust him. In a compelling manner Jesus calls his followers to a different value system, one based on simplicity and trust in God, not anxious craving:

> "Therefore I tell you, do not worry about your life, what you will eat or what you will drink, or about your body, what you will wear. Is not life more than food, and the body more than clothing? Look at the birds of the air; they neither sow nor reap nor gather into barns, and yet your heavenly Father feeds them. . . . And why do you worry about clothing? Consider the lilies of the field, how they grow; they neither toil nor spin, yet I tell you, even Solomon in all his glory was not clothed like one of these. But if God so clothes the grass of the field . . . will he not much more clothe you—you of little faith? . . . But strive first for the kingdom of God and his righteousness, and all these things will be given to you as well.
>
> "So do not worry about tomorrow, for tomorrow will bring worries of its own. Today's trouble is enough for today." (Matt. 6:25–34)

Prayer and Worship

Christian prayer takes many forms, including speaking to God (see the Lord's Prayer, unit 4:6), listening to God, contemplating God, praising God, and making petition to God for the needs of others.

The Eucharist, also called the Lord's Supper or Communion, is the central rite of Christian celebration. The Church of England, Episcopal, Roman Catholic, and Orthodox churches celebrate it weekly. Other Protestant denominations vary as to when they take communion. The bread and wine (or grape juice in some groups) are either consecrated by a priest and believers approach the altar to receive it, or in denominations believing in the priesthood of all believers and not just ordained priests, the bread and wine is offered and shared with the congregation. This rite is done at the order of Jesus, who said at the Last Supper, "Do this in remembrance of me." For the Catholic churches as well as some Protestant churches, the Eucharist is regarded as a sacrament that both symbolizes and effectively makes present the union of Christ with the worshiper.

The early Christians ate meals in remembrance and believed that Christ was present in the breaking of the bread. Early theologians and Roman Catholics accepted Christ's statements—"This is my body" and "This cup is the new covenant in my blood"—as the explanation of the transformation of the bread and wine into body and blood. This event is called *transubstantiation*. In the sixteenth century, Protestant reformers offered several different views, including the doctrine of consubstantiation, which maintains that the bread and wine are conjoined with the body and blood of Christ.

Gender

Jesus' interaction with women was conducted with an openness not in keeping with the norms of his day (see unit 6.6). The Acts of the Apostles confirm that women played an important part in the ministry of the early church. However, the letters of Paul reaffirm traditional Jewish attitudes leading to the continuing subordination of women to the authority of their husbands and to men in the Church (1 Cor. 14:34; Eph. 5:22f; Col. 3:18; 1 Tim. 2:11f). Yet, Paul also sees faith in Christ breaking down the traditional social barriers that are of the world. Here there is "no longer Jew or Greek . . . slave or free . . . male and female; for all of you are one in Christ Jesus" (Gal. 3:28).

Women and the Created Order

The story of the Creation and Fall in Genesis 1–3 seems to be the most influential text that has been reused over the centuries to effect an inferior status regarding women's place in the Christian religion, in society, and in the home. Genesis includes two different accounts of creation. Genesis 1:1–2:3 speaks of man and woman being created at the same time. They are the high point of creation and are both given dominion over all the other creatures. Here, the image of God is not restricted to the male.

> So God created humankind in his own image,
> in the image of God he created them;
> male and female he created them
> (Gen. 1:27)

The second account in Genesis 2:4–3:24 includes the story of the Fall where God sent Adam into a deep sleep and created woman out of Adam's rib, and they belonged together as "one flesh." In this account, the woman persuades Adam to disobey God's commandment to eat of the fruit of the tree of the knowledge of good and evil.

Historically, the second creation account has been used in two different ways by Christian writers and theologians through the centuries: (1) to justify the natural hierarchy of male superiority and (2) to emphasize the fundamental wickedness of women.

Christian writers, often following Paul, have used the creation narrative to justify a notion of authority, i.e., that there was a divine order given in nature:

> Indeed, man was not made from woman, but woman from man. Neither was man created for the sake of woman, but woman for the sake of man. (1 Cor. 11:8–9)

Many Christian writers have taught that women are responsible for leading men astray, the idea being that if in the creation account the woman had not tempted the man, he would not have sinned:

> For Adam was formed first, then Eve; and Adam was not deceived, but the woman was deceived and became a transgressor. (1 Tim. 2:13–14)

Later the prevalent view amongst many Christians was that the knowledge Eve gained from eating the fruit of the tree was carnal sexual knowledge, and Eve was therefore responsible for introducing Adam to sexuality. Women are therefore the tempters, and sex became seen as the greatest of all temptations. One classic example of this theological view comes from Tertullian, a Christian author living in North Africa at the turn of the third century, who said:

> And do you not know that you are an Eve? The sentence of God on your sex lives in this age; the guilt must live too. You are the devil's gateway; you are the unsealer of that tree; you are the first deserter of the divine law; you are she who persuaded him whom the devil was not valiant enough to attack. You destroyed so easily God's image, man. On account of what you deserve—that is, death—even the Son of God had to die. (De cultu feminarum 1.1.)

Augustine thought that while a woman's soul was as worthy as a man's, her body still posed a problem and made her subordinate. In order to pursue reason women had to overcome the fact of their gender.

Augustine also combined older, male-oriented translations of Genesis 1:27 with 1 Corinthians 11:7–16 to put forward his view that woman was not made in the image of God in the same way that a man was. Asking in what way should the apostle Paul's teaching be understood—i.e., that the man is the image of God (and therefore forbidden to cover his head) but the woman is not (and must therefore cover her head)—Augustine says:

> The woman together with her husband is the image of God, so that the whole substance is one image. But when she is assigned as a help-meet, a function that pertains to her alone, then she is not the image of God; but as far as the man is concerned, he is by himself alone the image of God, just as full and completely as when he and the woman are joined together in one.

Tertullian and Augustine are but two examples of early Christian writers, but they represent the prevalent attitude of educated men throughout a large period of Christian history up until the middle ages. However, notable women, such as Hildegard of Bingen and other educated women (Labalme, 1980), rose in prominence and eloquence in various cultures. But a combination of the traditional fear that Christian men held about female sexuality and women's skill as orators lead into the accusations of witchcraft which fuelled the inquisitions (see also unit 11:7).

The Reformation initially made matters worse for women by removing the religious orders in which they could find and exercise levels of autonomy. They were confined to children and kitchen (under the authority of their husbands). However, Luther's strong emphasis on the priesthood of all believers and the scripture for all and his call for education for all (1524) brought a measure of liberation in women exercising gifts and spiritualities in the church. He claimed that it was the legacy of "ungodly celibacy that aspersions are cast against the female sex" (Lectures on Genesis 2:8). Also the reformers introduced divorce and remarriage of the injured party in Geneva in 1561 and the right of a woman to divorce her husband for adultery.

John Wesley presented a positive view of women as equals. In 1739 he controversially appointed women as "class leaders" and Sarah Mallet as a preacher. Methodist Bible commentator Adam Clarke said in the next century that *"under the blessed spirit of Christianity, [women] have equal rights, equal privileges, and equal blessings."*

In 1865 William and Catherine Booth founded the Salvation Army on egalitarian lines. Such groups represent a trend that persisted against the tide of mainstream Christian thought and teaching and that has lasted until even the present time. In areas of the church, however, where beliefs about creation include either some sort of evolutionary process and not a literal historical truth, or a rethinking of the value of traditional theology, more Christians accept the principles of sexual equality, although such acceptance is by no means universally the case.

Women in the Christian Church today

The issue of the status and role of women has come to focus on the issue of the ordination of women. At the time of writing (in the year 2001), neither the

Roman Catholic Church nor the Eastern Orthodox Church ordain women. In 1994 Pope John Paul II discouraged all further future discussion on the issue. In 1995 his "Letter to all Women" apologized for the oppression that women had suffered at various points in history. Still, the document as a whole functioned with the common male strategy of approving of the gifts women possessed according to their natures, but at the same time restating that a woman's nature prevents her from undertaking certain roles including priesthood that are the domain of men only. Roman Catholicism opposes change because of their belief in unbroken tradition going back to the earliest Christian believers.

The Church of England (Anglican Church) has officially ordained women since the historic vote of the synod in 1992, although in some parts of the Anglican Church—e.g., in the United States, New Zealand, and Hong Kong—ordination of women has been possible for some time. Many nonconformist denominations—e.g., Baptists or Methodists—officially ordain women, yet factions within such traditions still oppose the movement. However, across all denominations the picture is growing more positive for women as Christian men and women realize that it is only a question of time before practices change on a more widespread basis.

Christian Mysticism

In the Christian tradition, mysticism is understood as the result of God's action in the life of a believer, the unmerited grace or gift that they receive from union with God. Christianity benefits from the many Christian mystics who have documented their experiences, including St. Francis of Assisi, St. Teresa of Avila, St. John of the Cross, and George Fox, who founded the Quaker movement.

The Desert Fathers were the earliest Christian monks of Egypt (third to fifth centuries). St. Pachomius living in the Egyptian desert is said to have experienced mystical visions of the invisible God during prayer.

In the Eastern Church, with the Cappadocian Fathers—especially Gregory of Nyssa—a more mystical approach to faith developed. Gregory said, "Every concept grasped by the mind becomes an obstacle in the quest to those who search."

Other leading monastics, such as John Cassian (c. 360–435), Augustine of Hippo, and the obscure figure known as Dionysius the Pseudo-Areopagite, created the foundations for later medieval mysticism. Dionysius spoke of the unknowability of God, the way to whom is described in his work, *The Mystical Theology*:

> Leave behind the senses and the operations of the intellect,
> that you may arise, through "unknowing," towards the union
> with Him who transcends all being and all knowledge.

The *Philokalia* is a collection of texts written by spiritual masters of the Orthodox Christian tradition between the fourth and fifteenth centuries. The

Philokalia has exercised an influence far greater than that of any book other than the Bible in the recent history of the Orthodox Church. It is a rich source for Orthodox believers of all persuasions but especially for the mystic. Here in rich and evocative language the *Philokalia* describes the mystery of light.

> The guarding of the intellect may appropriately be called light-producing, lightning-producing, light-giving and fire-bearing, for truly it surpasses endless virtues, bodily and other. Because of this, and because of the glorious light to which it gives birth, one must honour this virtue with worthy epithets. . . . [Those who have become contemplatives] bathe in a sea of pure and infinite light, touching it ineffably and living and dwelling in it. They have tasted that the Lord is good (cf. Ps. 34:8). . . . (*Philokalia* [Vol. 1], p. 192, text 171)

> The sun rising over the earth creates the daylight; and the venerable and holy name of the Lord Jesus, shining continually in the mind, gives birth to countless intellections radiant as the sun. (*Philokalia* [Vol. 1], p. 197, text 196)

"Contemplation" was the word used for centuries to describe the mystical experience of God. In its original form, this word (Greek = *theoria*) refers to absorption in the loving viewing of an object or truth. Only later in the medieval writings of those like Thomas Aquinas are there detailed descriptions of what the contemplative life entails.

In the fourteenth century the German Dominican, Master Eckhart, taught that the image of God in humans was the "ground" (*Grund*) of the soul or the "spark of divinity" in the human soul.

> To gauge the soul we must gauge it with God, for the Ground of God and the Ground of the Soul are one and the same.

This teaching on the spark of the soul achieving union with God sounded to many that the two were merged and thus brought opposition.

> For the soul is nearer to God than it is to the body which makes us human. It is more intimate with him than a drop of water put into a vat of wine, for that would still be water and wine; but here one is changed into the other so that no creature could ever again detect a difference between them. (Master Eckhart, *The Essential Writings*, trans. and ed. E. Colledge and B. McGinn [1981])

Master Eckhart's teaching was also centered on Jesus Christ. He insisted on the reality of God's gift to humanity of himself in his son. Such a gift that deifies humanity sounded like pantheism to the orthodox of his day.

The Discipline of Prayer

In the sixteenth century the emphasis on practical and methodical prayer brought about a spiritual renewal in the Ignatian (Ignatius Loyola) and Carmelite (Teresa of Avila, John of the Cross) schools.

The Ignatian way in prayer is based on *The Exercises* and aims to take religion from the head to the heart, moving towards absolute devotion of God:

> Take, Lord, and keep, all my freedom, my memory, my understanding, and all my will, whatever I have and possess, you gave them to me, and I will restore them to you. . . . Give me your love and your grace: that is enough for me.

St. Teresa of Avila wrote several works for the nuns in her order, speaking of the spiritual life as a journey towards union with God in the "spiritual marriage." "It is more necessary to love much than to think much; always do that which impels you most to love." (St. Teresa of Avila, *The Interior Castle*)

Julian of Norwich might well be called a mystic poet. She speaks with intimacy and knowledge about the Holy Trinity, which for centuries had only been described in creedal formulas:

> As verily as God is our Father, so verily God is our Mother; and that shewed He in all (her revelations) and especially in these sweet words where He saith: I it am. That is to say, I it am, the Might and the Goodness of the Fatherhood; I it am, the Wisdom of the Motherhood; I it am, the Light and the Grace that is all blessed Love: I it am, the Trinity; I it am, the Unity: I am the sovereign Goodness of all manner of things. I am that maketh thee to love: I am that maketh thee to long: I it am, the endless fulfilling of all true desires. (*Revelations of Divine Love*)

The Doctrine of the Fall

Christian mysticism draws upon the doctrine of human beings created in the image of God and on the doctrine of God becoming human in Christ (the incarnation). Christian mystics have understood mystical union as a restoration of the image and likeness of God that was distorted or lost at the original fall from innocence into sin and separation (Genesis 1 and 2). This image is distorted but not destroyed in humanity, and it remains as the foundation for the journey from separation to union with God.

Mysticism and the Bible

Some of the major biblical sources for Christian mysticism can be found in the following passages and texts:

- The incarnation doctrine (*Logos*) of John's Gospel
- The supernatural happenings and miracles surrounding Jesus' life and ministry that transcend human understanding

- Biblical imagery—e.g., vine and branches (John 15) or the Paraclete Passages in John 14f where the Holy Spirit is seen as a counselor, Spirit of truth, and Advocate.
- Mystical theology, which attempts to describe the experience of the believer. For example, Paul's rapture into the third heaven (2 Cor. 12:1–4) or the transfiguration of Jesus in the Synoptic Gospels.
- Theophany passages where God "appears," e.g., Moses' "vision" of God (Exod. 33:12–34:9) and the reflection of God's glory upon leaving Mount Sinai (Exod. 34:29–35; cf. 2 Cor. 3:7).
- Allegories that explain mysteries, as appear in the spiritual marriage of the Song of Solomon and the Old Testament wisdom literature.

Roman Catholicism

In Catholic circles mystical theology was almost submerged under a tide of enlightenment rationalism in the eighteenth century. Controversies surrounding the relation of mystical theology to "ordinary" prayer and the Christian striving for holiness or perfection then dominated the early decades of the twentieth century. In the twentieth century some Catholic theologians (e.g., L. Bouyer, A. Stolz), have worked to put mystical theology in a scriptural and liturgical context, with an emphasis on the participation of the believer in the mystery of God's reconciliation with his people in Christ, through the sacraments.

Protestantism

Mainstream Protestantism has largely mistrusted or been openly hostile toward a mystical dimension of the spiritual life, preferring to focus on the biblical text and preaching, with notable exceptions.

The seventeenth- and eighteenth-century Pietists (see unit 6:8) were thoroughly Protestant in their reliance on scripture, but the movement also focused on the whole person and the affective realms of emotions and lived experience. Aiden Wilson Tozer (1897–1963) was a mainstream, twentieth-century Protestant pastor. Although many Christians believe that once they have found God through Jesus Christ they no longer need to seek him, in his book, *The Pursuit of God*, Tozer disagrees. He says:

> I want deliberately to encourage this mighty longing after God. The lack of it has brought us to our present low estate. The stiff and wooden quality about our religious lives is a result of our lack of holy desire. Complacency is a deadly foe of all spiritual growth. Acute desire must be present or there will be no manifestation of Christ to His people. He waits to be wanted. Too bad that with many of us He waits so long, so very long, in vain.

On the pervasiveness of God, Tozer writes:

> So when we sing, "Draw me nearer, nearer, blessed Lord," we are not thinking of the nearness of place, but of the nearness of relationship. It is for increasing degrees of awareness that we pray, for a more perfect consciousness of the divine Presence. We need never shout across the spaces to an absent God. He is nearer than our own soul, closer than our most secret thoughts. (A. W. Tozer, *The Pursuit of God* [Wheaton, Ill.: Tyndale House, 1982].)

Christian mystics have often attempted to describe the direct experience they have had of God: a knowing or seeing so direct that it prompts a variety of language, metaphor, and imagery to portray what they have felt in their innermost being—union with the living God, Father, Son, and Holy Spirit. Even so, Christians have always been divided on the issue of mysticism. Some Christians simply reject it as an occult activity.

Scriptures

The Christian's holy book is the Christian Bible, to which there are two main parts: the Old Testament—which contains the books of the Jewish Pentateuch (these are the five books attributed to Moses—Genesis, Exodus, Leviticus, Numbers, and Deuteronomy), the Prophetic (Jewish prophets) books, Wisdom literature including the Psalms, and other collections of Jewish scripture—and the New Testament—which contains the four Gospels (Matthew, Mark, Luke, and John), the Acts of the Apostles, and various writings of Paul and early Christians. These books are important to Christians, because Jesus was a Jew. His coming was seen by Christians as a way to spread the covenant between God and the Jews to all the world.

The Apocrypha (see unit 6:8) consists of fourteen books of the Bible included in the Vulgate version of the Bible (the authorized Latin version of the Bible used by the Roman Catholic Church), but considered noncanonical by most Protestant groups.

The New Testament is comprised of the books that are the fulfillment of the promises of the Old Testament. The first four books—the Gospels, attributed to four inspired authors, Matthew, Mark, Luke, and John—tell the story of the Angel Gabriel's annunciation to Mary, the birth of Jesus, his life and miracles, his ultimate crucifixion and resurrection, and his final ascension into heaven. The book of the Acts of the Apostles tells about the early church in the years following Jesus' resurrection. The epistles (or letters) of some apostles, but mainly Paul, to early Christian groups are also included. The last book of the Bible is a very mystical book called "The Revelation to John" (or Revelations), which speaks of a vision of the end of the world sent by God to John on the island of Patmos.

The Christian Seasons and Holy Days

The traditional liturgical colors of the church season are white, purple, red, and green.

> *White*, signifying purity, is used for the festivals of Jesus Christ, primarily Christmas and Easter, and for All Saints' Day.
>
> *Purple* represents repentance, royalty, and suffering, and is used during Lent and Advent.
>
> *Red* symbolizes the fire of the Holy Spirit during Pentecost.
>
> *Green* is appropriate for those times of the year that are not in any specific season and signifies spiritual growth.

Advent (Latin: "coming" or "arrival") is the period just before Christmas during which Christians reflect on two different "comings" of Jesus: his first coming in humility to earth and his second coming in the future when he will come in glory as judge at the end of time.

Christmas (December 25) commemorates the birth of Jesus, although this day is likely not his birth date. The date was probably chosen at Rome during the fourth century to provide a Christian alternative to a local festival. Christians sing carols, and some celebrate the "Service of Nine Carols and Lessons" designed to trace the Bible story that recalls God's work of redemption beginning with the call of Israel and ending in the coming of Jesus Christ. In the dark of the year the light of the world came.

In the Eastern church, the festival of *Epiphany* is linked to the baptism of Jesus. In the Western church Epiphany recognizes the visit of the "wise men" to the infant Jesus. More generally the festival commemorates making Jesus known to the world.

Lent is a time of preparation for Easter based on Jesus' period of forty days fasting before the beginning of his ministry in Galilee. Traditionally, many Christians fast or deny themselves pleasures during Lent.

The final week of Lent leading up to Easter (*Holy Week*) starts with *Palm Sunday*, which commemorates the triumphal entry of Jesus into Jerusalem when crowds threw palm leaves before him (Matt. 21:1–11).

Maundy Thursday focuses on Jesus' washing of the disciples' feet (John 13:1–15). In medieval times clergy used to wash the feet of church members in accord with the example of Jesus. In England the monarch would also wash the feet of a small number of people. Now "Maundy Money" is specially minted and distributed to the elderly at cathedrals throughout England.

Good Friday marks the day Jesus died on the cross. It is a serious and solemn occasion and takes different forms, for example, the famous *Oberammergau* passion play expressing their thanks to God for delivering them from the plague in 1633. In the Philippines, the crucifixion is reenacted by young men who are briefly nailed to crosses to show their Christian commitment. In other traditions there is a practice of observing three hours' devotions from midday to 3 P.M.

The most important festival of the Christian year is *Easter Sunday*, marking the resurrection of Jesus Christ from the dead.

In liturgical churches, the "paschal vigil" is the heart of the Easter celebration during the Saturday night and Easter Sunday morning. Since the fourth century it has concentrated wholly on the resurrection of Christ from the dead, and the service is a powerful enactment of those historic events. The Eastern Orthodox rite starts with the lighting and blessing of the Paschal Candle outside the church. At one minute past midnight, on Pascha, the doors of the church are flung open and the priest calls out the ancient words, "Christ is risen," while at the same time light fills the church, symbolizing Jesus, the Resurrection, the Light of the world returning. And they proclaim each year at the Paschal midnight service the words attributed to St John Chrysostom:

> Let none fear death, for the death of the Saviour has set us free.
> Christ is risen and the demons have fallen.
> Christ is risen and the angels rejoice

Ascension Day recalls the ascension of Christ after having been raised from the dead.

Pentecost celebrates the gift of the Holy Spirit to the early church after which they were able to spread the good news of the gospel.

Reformed Liturgical Traditions

The Protestant Reformers of the sixteenth century took differing attitudes toward liturgical traditions. With their strong sense of the prime authority of scripture and of the freedom of the gospel from all legalisms in liturgical matters, they revised the church year in various ways.

Lutherans and Anglicans retained the traditional seasons but eliminated commemorations unconnected with the biblical record.

The Reformed churches, on the other hand, allowed only those feasts with a clear basis in the New Testament: Sundays, Holy Week and Easter, Pentecost, and in some cases Christmas.

The Church of Scotland and Anabaptist and Puritan groups abolished the church year entirely, except for Sundays. In recent years this attitude has been very much modified. Their protest has been a reminder to the church that all days are regarded as belonging to Christ in the freedom of his Spirit, who cannot be controlled by rigid systems of fixed special observances.

UNIT 7:6 ISLAM

In the name of God, the Merciful, the Compassionate,
Praise belongs to God, the Lord of all Being,

The All-merciful, the All-compassionate,
The Master of the Day of Doom.

Thee only we serve; to Thee alone we pray for succour.
Guide us in the straight path,
The path of those whom Thou hast blessed,
Not of those against whom Thou art wrathful, nor of those who are astray.

Qur'an 1, *The Koran Interpreted*

The word "Islam" is derived from the root *s-l-m*, with the connotation of "peace" but the secondary sense is "surrender." A central thought in Islam is the peace that comes from surrendering to God. Adherents to Islam are called Muslims.

For Muslims the religion of Islam started with God, not with the revelations of God given to Muhammad in the sixth century C.E. Muslims share a common theological background with Christianity and Judaism in their belief that God created the world. They also revere Abraham (see unit 7:4) who, anxious to continue his line, took a woman called Hagar as his second wife. She gave him a son, Ishmael, but when Abraham's first wife Sarah later conceived her son Isaac, Hagar and Ishmael were expelled from the clan. From here on, the biblical and Qur'anic accounts begin to differ. According to the Qur'an, Ishmael went to the area near what later became known as Mecca and his descendants became Muslims. The other son Isaac remained in Palestine with the Hebrews, who became known as Jews.

Muhammad

Muslims believe there were prophets before Muhammad, but he is the "Seal of the prophets." Muhammad was born about 570 C.E. in the city of Mecca, an important trading center in western Arabia. He was of the Hashim clan of the powerful Quraysh tribe. His name means "highly praised." Muhammad's early life was filled with tragedy—with the loss of his father, his mother, and his grandfather—so he was placed in the care first of his grandfather Abd al-Muttalib and, after 578, of his uncle Abu Talib, who succeeded as head of the Hashim clan. Tradition records him as a sensitive young man, always caring about the weak and people in poverty. This outlook earned him the title of Al-min: "The Upright One." At age twenty-five he married Khadijah, a rich widow of high social status in Mecca, but both their sons died at a young age. Four daughters were born.

In the year 610 C.E.—at age forty during one of his frequent times of seclusion and prayer in a cave on Mount Hira—he saw a being in a human form who told him, "Read!" Muhammad replied that he could not read. Three times this exchange continued until the angel said:

> Recite: In the Name of your Lord who created, created Man of a blood-clot.

> Recite: And your Lord is the Most Generous who taught by
> the Pen,
> Taught Man that he knew not.
>
> Qur'an 96:1–5

Later Muhammad instructed some of his companions to write down the revelations and some to learn them by heart. Muhammad ran home terrified, and his wife supposed he had been chosen as a prophet. The first revelation was on the Night of Power (*Lailat-al Qadr*). The other revelations followed from the angel Gabriel, and Muhammad began to preach about Allah, the One and the Only God. He denounced idol worship at the Ka'ba, which proved threatening to the traders who dealt in idol worship. He also claimed that all were equal in God's eyes, which contradicted the class-conscious society in Mecca. This led to the persecution, torture, and suffering of many new Muslims—especially the slaves who believed in Allah—but Muhammad was not deterred.

In order to establish Allah's rule in the world, Muhammad knew he would have to set up an independent state based on the laws of Allah. Therefore Muslims fought for the independence of Medina from Mecca.

In 630 followed the destruction of all 360 idols in Mecca, the circling of the Ka'ba, and its rededication to God. From then on the spread of Islam was profound. Muhammad was succeeded by four caliphs, the last of whom was 'Ali. The Qur'an was influential in removing idols and making the divine a single invisible God for all; thus, the essential contribution of Islam to Arabic religion was monotheism.

During the remaining years of his life, Muhammad received further revelations, which came to form the text of the Qur'an.

At first in private and then publicly, Muhammad began to proclaim his message: that there is but one God and that Muhammad is his messenger sent to warn people of the judgment day and to remind them of God's goodness.

Opposition to Monotheism

The Meccans responded with hostility to Muhammad's monotheism. As long as his uncle Abu Talib was alive, Muhammad was protected by the Hashim. About 619, Abu Talib died, and the new clan leader was unwilling to continue to protect Muhammad. At about the same time, Muhammad lost his faithful and valued wife Khadijah. In the face of persecution and with less freedom to preach, Muhammad and about seventy followers decided to sever their ties of blood kinship in Mecca and move to Medina, a city about 400 kilometers (250 miles) to the north. This move, called the Hegira, or *hijra* ("emigration"), took place in 622, the first year of the Muslim calendar. (Muslim dates are often followed by A.H., "Anno Hegirae," the year of the hegira.)

In Medina attacks on caravans from Mecca led to war with the Meccans.

Muhammad's followers obtained victory at Badr (624) but were defeated at Uhud a year later. In 627, however, they successfully defended Medina against a siege by ten thousand Meccans.

Since 624 C.E. (2 A.H.) the Muslims of Medina had been facing toward Mecca during worship, because of the presence there of the Ka'ba. This sanctuary was then a pagan shrine, but according to the Qur'an (2:124–29), it had been built by Abraham and his son Ishmael and had therefore to be reintegrated into Muslim society. In 628 Muhammad and his followers attempted to go on a pilgrimage to Mecca but it was unsuccessful. A subsequent arrangement was made allowing the Muslims to make the pilgrimage the next year, on condition that all parties cease armed hostilities. Incidents in 629 ended the peaceful arrangement, and in January 630 Muhammad and his men marched on Mecca. The Quraysh offer to surrender was accepted with a promise of general amnesty, and very little fighting occurred. Muhammad's generosity to a city that had forced him out eight years earlier is often quoted as an example of his outstanding benevolence.

A few months after a farewell pilgrimage to Mecca in March 632 he fell ill. Muhammad died on June 8, 632, in the presence of his favorite wife, Aisha, whose father, Abu Bakr, became the first caliph.

Scriptures and Authentic Texts

The Qur'an (meaning "recitation") contains the messages that Muhammad received as revelations from Allah through the angel Gabriel during a period of twenty years, beginning in 610 C.E. The Qur'an contains 114 surahs or chapters and became a book in 650 C.E. with the compilation of an official version. Unlike the other sacred books mentioned in this publication, the Qur'an was collected together by one person and has remained unchanged since its original revelation; therefore, Muslims affirm the importance of reading it in its original language.

The Hadith are the second source of information for Muslims concerning the right way to live. They are the sayings, action, or silent approvals of the Prophet Muhammad. People who memorized Hadith had to record the chain of narration (*isnad*) so that they could state from whom the saying came. The collections of the sayings of the Prophet were written down by his companions during his lifetime or by their immediate successors. Six collections regarded as fully authentic (*sahih*) are those of

- Imam Muhammad al-Bukhari (which lists 2,762)
- Imam Muslim Ibn al-Jajjaj (which lists 4,000)
- Abu Dawud
- Tirmidhi
- Ibn Majah
- An-Nasa'i

Other reliable collections are those of Darimi, Darqutni, Ibn Hanbal, and Ibn Sa'd.

God

The Unity (*tawhid*) of God is the central doctrine in Islam. This doctrine is explained through the Unity of God's Essence, the Unity of God's Absolute Qualities, and the Unity of God's works.

The Unity of God's Essence expresses the belief that God transcends all human qualities; nothing is like Him:

> He is God, one,
> God, the Everlasting Refuge,
> Who has not begotten, and has not been begotten,
> And equal to Him is not any one.
>
> Qur'an 112

The essence of God is therefore totally transcendent, which can be seen in nine different ways:

> God alone exists, therefore he can bring creation into being.
>
> God is eternal, no beginning and no end.
>
> God is essential—all essences derive from him.
>
> God is unique—not to be compared to anything or anyone.
>
> God's unsubstantiality: All substance is created.
>
> God's essence has no material body.
>
> God is without form.
>
> God's presence is felt everywhere.

God is perceived through his Absolute Qualities, e.g., Merciful, the Just, the All-Knowing, the Sustainer. The Qualities of Allah can be perceived through his names. There are 99 beautiful names applied to him. God's compassion and mercy are cited 192 times in the Qur'an. He is:

> The Holy, the Peaceful, the Faithful, the Guardian over his servants, the Shelterer of the orphans, the Guide of the erring, the Deliverer from every affliction, the Friend of the bereaved, the Consoler of the afflicted; in His hand is good . . . whose love for man is more tender than that of the mother-bird for her young. (Ameer Ali, *Spirit of Islam: A History of the Evolution and Ideals of Islam within the life of a prophet* [Prometheus Books, 1974].)

The creation reflects the Unity of God's works for he is the real cause of all that is. He sustains the universe—even natural disasters such as earthquakes are part of God's order. It all has a purpose. Note the difference between this view of creation and that of Hinduism. The Hindu texts suggest that the world emerged from the divine by a process of emanation; in Islam the world was created by a deliberate act of Allah's will (Qur'an 16:3). Like Allah's will, it must therefore be good.

Salvation

Muslims believe that human beings are born innocent and free from sin; they are also free to obey God or not. People have the chance to prove themselves by doing good deeds. All of us are God's managers (*khalifah*) on earth, and there is the responsibility to God to fulfill the task well. Most of us, however, choose to live in rebellion with God. God will not tolerate this forever. Individually every person will die at the appointed time, and on a world scale God will finally act to bring about the last judgment (*yaum al-Din*). The common word for salvation, *najah*, is used only once in the Qur'an:

> O my people, how is it that I invite you to salvation, but you invite me to the fire? (40.44)

Hell

Hell (*Jahannam*) is mentioned frequently in the Qur'an and has seven gates (Qur'an 39.71) with different levels and different punishments according to the measure of one's sins. A person's eternal destiny is mostly seen as a practical thing, resting on the believer's ability to submit to Allah and follow the teachings of the Qu'ran, especially the five pillars of Islam.

> Men and women who have surrendered,
> believing men and believing women,
> obedient men and obedient women,
> truthful men and truthful women,
> enduring men and enduring women,
> men and women who give in charity,
> men who fast and women who fast,
> men and women who guard their private parts,
> men and women who remember God oft—
> for them God has prepared forgiveness
> and a mighty wage.
>
> *The Koran Interpreted,* trans. Arberry, Oxford: Oxford University Press, 1964, Sura 33:35, 431.

Life after Death

Actions in this life will be the cause of reward or punishment in the afterlife (see unit 6:3). Between death and the last day of judgment, all spirits have to pass through a stage. If souls continue to attach themselves to this world, then they will suffer, but pure souls enjoy bliss.

Muslims believe in angels, which are seen as spiritual beings who are Allah's agents and who help to run the universe. They are invisible but can assume any form. Two angels are constantly recording human deeds. Two angels wipe out bad actions if we ask for God's forgiveness. Two angels (Munkar and Nakir) ask each dead person about his or her faith.

A number of surahs in the Qur'an describe the total destruction that will occur on the day of judgment (Qur'an 81:1–14; 69:13–37). No one, however—not even Muhammad—knew the exact time of the last day, although various signs will signal the end: the coming of Imam Mahdi (the guided one), the coming of Dajjal (the anti-Christ), and the return of Christ to kill Dajjal and to sanctify the world and preach Islam. (Christians obviously would reject such a view.)

Moral Action

Islam makes a distinction between a person who has faith in believing God exists and submits to God's guidance by believing in his law (*muslim*) and one who possesses *mu'min*, a faith that acts upon this realization. Central to the study of Islamic ethics are three disciplines: *falsafa* (philosophy), *kalam* (discourse), and *fiqh* (jurisprudence) (see unit 6:4).

The word for Islamic law, *Shari'ah*, means literally "the way to water." It is therefore a clear path to God who is the fountain of life. In the Arab world, the image of an oasis is seen at the heart of the faith for the *Shari'ah*. The *Shar'iah* derives its being from the Qur'an and the example of the prophet Muhammad. Islam distinguishes between actions that are obligatory, meritorious, indifferent, reprehensible, and *haram* (forbidden), which is in contrast to *halal* (permitted). For example, the Ayatollah Khomeini pronounced smoking as *haram* in Iran, and the people accepted that he had the authority to make this pronouncement. Shi'ite Islam often functions through such authority.

Islam values life and does not allow abortion unless the pregnancy is likely to cause the death of the mother. Euthanasia is viewed as morally equivalent to suicide. Hardships and suffering in this life are a test of a Muslim's faith.

Sin and Sins

In Islam no belief equates to the Christian belief in original sin. Human beings are born pure and lean towards goodness, so that to incline towards evil is seen as against human nature. First-order sins concern the honor of God and associating God's divine attributes with anything inferior. This is known as *shirk*. Second-order sins are acts such as murder, theft, or sexual impropriety.

The Five Pillars of Islam

The Shari'ah includes the Five Pillars of Islam, which are obligatory for all Muslims:

1. The declaration of faith, the Shahadah
2. Prayer (*salat*)
3. Almsgiving (*zakat*)
4. Fasting during Ramadan (*sawm*)
5. Hajj: the pilgrimage to Mecca

Hajj

The call to pilgrimage makes the desert city of Mecca a huge annual gathering place for people from all parts of the world. The rituals of the Hajj were established by the prophet Muhammad. They focus on repentance, resulting in forgiveness by God. The practice also strengthens the unity and oneness of mind among the faithful from all walks of life and regions of the world. Hajj occurs during the Islamic month of Dhu 'l-Hijja.

1. Early in the morning on the eighth day of Hijjah, the pilgrims (some two million people) take to the roads leading out of Mecca toward Mina Valley, starting a five-day journey into the desert. Muslims on Hajj give up the usual comforts and embark on a basic metaphor of life as a journey on the earth. They are nomads living in tents on the sand. Everyone, regardless of class or fortune, is the same, and class distinctions dissolve, binding the Hajj community closely together.

2. Dawn to midnight, Day Two. The pilgrims camp at Mina. During the Hajj season, every square inch of sand is covered with several hundred thousand tents. Hour after hour, two million pilgrims arrive. The traffic jams are legendary and last until well after midnight.

3. Day Three. The next morning a mass exodus journeys five miles east to the Plain of Arafat. This barren stretch of sand is marked by the single hill of Mount Mercy. The Hajj reaches its climax here. The Hajj is designed to deliver the pilgrim to Arafat with an open heart and an sensitive conscience. From dawn and throughout the rest of the day, the pilgrim population streams onto the Plain of Arafat. Arafat is a daylong vigil where Muslims join together to stand in the presence of God. The ceremony is slight so that normal daily prayers are shortened, and there is only a brief sermon because the heart of this event, called the Day of Standing, is simply to be there. At sundown, the entire population leaves.

Evening of Day Three. On the way, the pilgrims stop off at a patch of hills and pebbled plain called Muzdalifah to rest for the night and eat, and to gather stones for the following day.

4. Day Four. At dawn, pilgrims set out to accomplish one of the last of the Hajj rites: the ancient practice of stoning three pillars that symbolize temptation. The symbolism of the act is simple but profound. The Hajj has left its pilgrims with a clean conscience. But what about tomorrow? How will they keep pure?

The stoning is a symbolic act stressing that human error, sin, is a matter of missing the target; if your aim is right, the pillar of wrong can be brought down by the smallest right action. Now the Hajj changes ethos, and three days of restful celebration occur.

Days Four, Five, and Six. The return to Mina also marks the commencement of a three-day feast, the Id al-Adha. The celebration is observed throughout the world, but nowhere with greater vitality than in Mecca.

Prayer and Worship

The second pillar of Islam is *salat* (see unit 6:5) or prayer. In Islam you cannot perform prayer if you are unclean and impure. Muslims, therefore, perform ritual cleansing (*taharah*). This act includes a system of ablution (*wudu*), which contains rich symbolic meaning. The intention of this cleansing is to purify body and soul. *Wudu* is made invalid by deep sleep, unconsciousness, or bodily discharges. In the event of these, a Muslim has to repeat his or her *wudu*. Washing the whole body is obligatory after sexual intercourse, menstruation, postnatal periods, and wet dreams. In Islam, prayer must be said five times a day. *Morning prayer* is at dawn; *midday prayer* is between midday and halfway between midday and sunset; *afternoon prayer* is between midday prayer and sunset; *evening prayer* is after sunset and until it is dark; *night prayer* is between evening prayer and dawn. Four postures in prayer are always followed: standing, bowing, prostration, or sitting. The pray-er must have clean clothes and be in a clean place, with the right intention towards God. An *imam* leads the prayer; he is often the most elderly learned person who keeps the five pillars of Islam. The call to prayer is given (*adhan*) in a mosque, where the worshipers stand in rows, but women pray separately at the back of the mosque or in a special room or gallery above. At the commencement of prayer, the Muslim stands with head bent and arms crossed like a slave in front of the master. Wherever they are in the world they are facing the Ka'ba in Mecca and imagining that Allah is in front of them. Standing upright, the opening chapter of the Qur'an (the *Fatihah*) is recited (see the opening quotation in this unit). Muslim worship and devotion is not limited to the precisely prescribed words and gestures of the *salat*, but also in a wealth of personal prayers, in the gathering of the congregation in the central mosque on Fridays, and in the celebration of the two main festivals: Id al-Fitr, the festival of the breaking of the fast at the end of Ramadan, and Id al-Adha, the festival of the sacrifice (in memory of Abraham's willingness to sacrifice his son). The latter, observed on the tenth day of the month of pilgrimage, is celebrated not only by the participants in the pilgrimage, but also simultaneously by those who stay in their own locations.

Gender and Religion

From its inception, Islam brought great advances to the status and the safety of women. The status of Arabian women before Muhammad was of no consequence. Marriage was so loose as to be hardly recognizable. Women were like any other possession. Their fate was in the hands of fathers or husbands. There were no inheritance rights for daughters. The birth of a girl was often viewed as a calamity, and baby girls were commonly buried alive at infancy.

The Qur'an brought in sweeping reforms for women. Infanticide was forbidden, and daughters were to receive part (a half) of the inheritance in proportion to sons. But in the sanctification of marriage women were given their greatest rights. Marriage became the only lawful place for sexual intercourse, and the Qur'an states that a woman must give her free consent to wed. Divorce is allowed, but only as a last resort. In these and other respects, the Qur'an leaves open the possibility of women's full equality with men.

Theologically, Islam does not believe that women are the source of sin. In the Qur'anic creation account, Eve is not specifically named; both Adam and Eve are equally to blame for their disobedience to God.

At the present time there are four orthodox schools of Muslim law named after their founders: the Hanafi, Maliki, Shafi'i, and Hanbali schools. They agree on broad principles of legislation but differ in rulings on specific issues, including the rights and roles of women. All schools of law agree that all Muslims, whether they are men or women, are equally competent to perform all Muslim rites and that all believers are equal in the sight of God and are in direct personal relationship with God. Relatively new moves in Muslim law include the legal ruling by classical jurists (*ulama*) in Saudi Arabia that women are forbidden to drive all kinds of motorized vehicles. There are wide differences of opinion among the classical *ulama*. An example can be seen in rulings regarding the liberty of women to contract their own marriage without the permission of a legal guardian (*wali*). At its most restrictive edge, women are not legally competent to contract their own marriage, and even a virgin may be coerced into marriage by either her father or grandfather. At the liberal end, a woman who is of sound mind may legally negotiate her own marriage contact, and no one else has any legal right to intervene.

Shar'iah Law and Fundamentalism

Shar'iah (Arabic = "the path worn by camels to the water") is the Muslim religious law about how people should live. It has been criticized in the West as cruel and barbaric. For example, *zina* is unlawful sex. Premarital sex brings one hundred lashes to either male or female offenders, and adultery brings the penalty of death by stoning. Theft is punished by amputation, and drink and drug offenses are punished by flogging. For the crime of apostasy, the death sentence is pronounced, as in the famous case of Salman Rushdie, the author of *Satanic Verses*, who on February 14, 1989, was issued with a legal sentence (*fatwa*) of death by the Ayatollah Khomeini, the prominent Shi'ite specialist in ethics. This episode showed the marked differences between the Islamic view of the world and modern Western secularism. Liberals and postmodernists typically cannot understand how a modern novel could provoke a death sentence. Muslims see the issue differently. Rushdie portrayed Muhammad as a conniving, alcoholic businessman, and the names of Muhammad's wives are given to prostitutes. In the eyes of an observant Muslim, the truth of the Qur'an and prophet Muhammad should always be treated with respect. In his book *Islamic Government*, the Ayatollah Khomeini spoke out about the corruption of Western values in his country of Iran. He defends Shari'ah law and its severity as a necessity.

> Many forms of corruption that have appeared in society derive from alcohol. . . . But when Islam wishes to prevent the consumption of alcohol—one of the major evils—stipulating that the drinker should receive eighty lashes, or sexual vice, decreeing that the fornicator be given one hundred lashes (and the married man or woman be stoned), then they start wailing and lamenting, "What a harsh law it is, reflecting the harshness of the Arabs!" They are not aware that these penal provisions of Islam are intended to keep great nations from being destroyed by corruption. Sexual vice has now reached such proportions that it is destroying entire generations. . . ." (Ayatollah Khomeini, *Islamic Government*, in Hamid Algar, *Islam and Revolution: Writings and Declarations of Imam Khomeine* [Berkeley, Calif.: Mizan Press, 1981].)

Islamic Fundamentalism and Women: The Case of Afghanistan

At the time of this writing, the issue of women's rights and human dignity in Islamic Afghanistan is still a pressing one. Since the Fundamentalist Islamic Taliban took power in 1996, numerous press reports say that women are not allowed to work or even go out in public without a male relative. Professional women—professors, translators, doctors, lawyers, and artists— have been forced from their jobs and stuffed forcibly into their homes. Relief workers report that depression is becoming so widespread that it has reached emergency levels. Women have had to completely cover themselves and have been beaten and stoned in public for not having the proper attire, even for simply not having the mesh covering in front of their eyes. Homes where a woman is present must have their windows painted so that she can never be seen by outsiders. One early news report spoke of an eyewitness account of a woman beaten to death by an angry mob of fundamentalists for accidentally exposing her arm while she was driving. For the majority of Muslims—both men and women—it is hard to reconcile the cruel and callous treatment of women by the Taliban, and indeed of any other group or individual, with the dignity and honor bestowed on them by the prophet Muhammad.

Mysticism

> He who knows himself knows his Lord. . . . This Lord is not the impersonal self, nor is it the God of dogmatic definitions,

> self-subsisting without relation to me, without being experienced by me. He is the he who knows himself through myself, that is, in the knowledge that I have of him, because it is the knowledge that he has of me. (Ibn 'Arabi [1165–1240] Henry Corbin, *Creative Imagination in the Sufism of Ibn 'Arabi*)

A Muslim may follow the path of Shari'ah, the external legal and moral code of Islam. They may know the Qur'an by heart and live a devout life, but at the same time they may lack the deeper spiritual knowledge of the Unseen. Sufism (Arabic = *tasawwuf*) is generally understood by scholars to be the inner, mystical, or psychospiritual dimension where Muslims seek close personal experience of God. They follow the path of spiritual development known as *tariqah*. The root meaning of the word Sufi is wool (*suf*), which points to the woollen garments of ancient Middle Eastern ascetics in contrast to the silks and satins of worldliness and materialism of their day.

Early Movements and the Baghdad School

Sufism is often seen as a single spiritual movement, but it is made up of many different strands and styles. Its early history is somewhat unclear, but it appears to have originated in the early Muslim community among people who were determined not to be distracted from the simplicity and spirituality of their faith by the rapid Muslim expansion of wealth and territory. Hasan al-Basri was one early Sufi who combined his knowledge of Shari'ah law with a thirst for spiritual knowledge. Although the Qur'an warns against asceticism, it is proposed that early Sufis had contact with Christian Syriac monks; in early Sufi writings, Jesus is seen as the ideal representative of love, renunciation, and divine joy.

Sufis see themselves to be on a passionate spiritual journey (*tariqah* = "path") toward God. Whereas all Muslims believe they will become close to God in paradise—after death and the final judgment—Sufis believe that coming close to God and experiencing this closeness is possible in this life. Some Sufis are regarded as saints, through whom God works *karamat* (miracles of grace). These miracles can include healing or the mystical knowledge the saint has of unseen events and things, or even physical flight to distant destinations.

The early phase of Sufism began around the end of the eighth century with a mystical group called the Baghdad School, which included the poet Rabi'a al-Adawiyya (c. 713–801), an outstanding Sufi mystic. As a child she was sold into slavery, during which period she devoted the time she was not working to solitary, all-night vigils of prayer and devotion. She was later set free from slavery. Rabi'a speaks through the centuries with spiritual force and integrity. She often spoke out about the motive for loving God and that one should not worship from desire of paradise or fear of hell, but only for the love of God:

> O my Lord, if I worship you from fear of hell, burn me in it; if I worship you in hope of paradise, exclude me from it. But

> if I worship you for your own sake, then do not hold me back from your eternal beauty.

> I have two ways of loving You:
> A selfish one
> And another way that is worthy of You.
> In my selfish love, I remember You and You alone.
> In that other love, You lift the veil
> And let me feast my eyes on Your Living Face.
> That I remember You always, or that I see You face-to-face—
> No credit to me in either:
> The credit is to You in both.
>
> Rabi'a al-Adawiyya

The exploration of love is a core theme in Sufism. Sufi love poetry is famous throughout the world. Rabi'a discovered that God's love was at the heart of the universe, and the call is to steep oneself in it and reflect it outwards to others. Denial of this call is to forfeit the beauty of living. Love is never more in evidence than when the loved one is absent. Sufis down the centuries have reflected on the necessary agony of separation in order to deepen the mystic's love of God and therefore draw even closer to him.

By the ninth century new developments were taking place within Sufi belief. A broader natural theology based on the concept of *ma'rifah* (nonintellectual knowledge) is attributed to the Egyptian Dhual-Nun (d. 859), who helped to preserve in writing the utterances of the solitary ascetic al-Bistami (d. 874). Al-Bistami sought God by stripping off all human qualities, until not even the human personality remained. His thought contains imagination and paradox in which he experiences utter self-effacement and also deification and oneness with God. Even today he is much quoted by Sufis for his sensitivity to the tension that the spiritual man or woman faces between human sinfulness and the hope for grace and mercy.

Oneness with God

Sufi faith combined a strict form of discipline and asceticism with an intense love of God, giving rise in time to trance states of ecstasy. Although Sufi teaching was careful to warn against hedonistic ecstasy, teaching began to emerge that seemed to blur the distinction between God and the self, thus offending Muslims who were sensitive to the absolute transcendence of God. The controversial Sufi mystic al-Hallaj was executed in 922. He had aimed at being a bridge between humanity and God:

> I am He whom I love and He whom I love is I. We are two spirits dwelling in one body. When you see me, you see Him.

Sayings such as this appeared blasphemous, and his alleged famous phrase, "ana'l-Haqq" (I am the Truth), led to his death. It is said of al-Hallaj that on the first night in prison his jailers visited his cell but could not find him, nor on the second night, but on the third night he was there. When they asked him for an explanation of his absence, he said,

> On the first night I was in the Presence, therefore I was not here. On the second night the Presence was here, so that both of us were absent. On the third night I was sent back, that the Law might be preserved. Come and do your work! (A. J. Arberry trans. *Muslim Saints and Mystics,* 1979 paperback edition. Routledge & Kegan Paul Ltd., 1979.)

Self-Extinction and Self-Purification

Fana is the term for annihilation or the self-extinction of all human attributes. The Sufi strives for this higher state of consciousness and then returns to his or her normal state with the certainty of the truth or higher reality. Knowledge of this kind causes the believer to be indifferent towards worldly joy or sorrow and imbues them with moral virtue.

> All your agonies arise from wanting something that cannot be had. When you stop wanting, there is no more agony. (Jalal Ud-Din Rumi: *Signs of the Unseen: The Discourses of,* 135)

Spiritual Jihad

In the early part of the Middle Ages, Islam was fighting the Crusades against the Christian infidels on the basis of Muhammad's teaching on *Jihad* or "Holy War." *Jihad* means "struggle" or "strife" against something of which God disapproves. Three kinds of disapproval are a visible enemy, the devil, and a personal defect. The ultimate purpose of *jihad* is to purify the self. The first *jihads* happened to save Islam from the Quraysh and to conquer Mecca. Islam requires Muslims to be ready to defend the truth and to fight if necessary.

Sufi teaching interprets *jihad* as an internal struggle or battle to overcome self and the lower soul (*nafs*) and to surrender to God. This surrender causes you to wake up to reality and to a direct experience of Allah. This is the task of life—to leave the present sleep of this world, the limited personal self, and journey toward the identity that is in God. In the tenth century, the spiritual path was elaborated with stages of repentance, fasting, sleep deprivation, and other forms of hard spiritual straining that were controlled by the master (*murshid*; *shayk*). This activity included the practice of the constant recollection of God (*dhikr*) through the word "Allah" or a similar formula. The end of the path meant the disciple had reached self-extinction (*fana*).

Sufi Poetry

Sufi devotional poetry is famous throughout the literary world. In Iran it found its most profound expression in new poetical forms, especially the Mathnawi, which was written in rhyming couplets that could be extended and developed at will. The Afghan poet Jalal Ud-Din Rumi (d. 1273) was an academic professor who was transformed by the wandering dervish Shams-al-Din Tabrizi to leave his career and follow the Sufi path. The Whirling Dervishes were founded by Rumi. They use the name of Allah as a mantra in repetition, and to the music of drums and flutes they perform a circular, whirling dance (symbolizing all creation joyful around the center of God) and enter ecstasy with closed eyes. The love of God became the whole basis for Rumi's life and poetry:

> All the hopes, desires, loves, and affections that people have for different things—fathers, mothers, friends, heavens, the earth, gardens, palaces, sciences, works, food, drink—the saint knows that these are desires for God and all those things are veils. When men leave this world and see the King without these veils, then they will know that all were veils and coverings, that the object of their desire was in reality that One Thing. . . . They will see all things face to face. (The Sufi Path of Love: The Spiritual Teachings of Rumi, 201)

Rumi's poetry has been described as the Essence of the Qur'an rendered in Persian.

Sufism in the World Today

A *khanqah* or *zawiah* is where shaykhs meditate and train disciples in the Sufi path. Throughout the history of Islam these places have been centers of religious learning and moral thinking and reform. Many of the shaykhs are buried there. Famous shrines are the shrine of Shaykh Abdul Qadir Jilani in Baghdad, and Shaykh Muinuddin Chisti in Ajmeer, India. Today they are visited by Muslims from all over the world.

Sufism has often been criticized as backward and dangerous to the Muslim faith. A more positive view sees Sufism as saving Islam from excessive legalism or from philosophers who would turn the faith into metaphysics. In recent history, many would say that the Sufis kept Islam alive in the hearts of Muslims during the antireligious campaign of Communist Russia.

Other Muslim Beliefs

Prophets

Out of the total number of prophets, 313 or 315 of them received messages from God. These were the messengers (*rasul*). Seven of them are described as the great prophets (*ulul 'azm*). These seven great prophets are

Adam

Noah (Nuh)

Abraham (Ibrahim)

Moses (Musa)

David (Dawud)

Jesus (Isa)

Muhammad

According to Islam, none of the prophets ever deliberately committed any sins. The same reverence must be accorded to all the prophets, and all of them must be accepted by Muslims, whether their names are mentioned in the Qur'an or not.

Islam honors Jesus as a prophet and accepts his virgin birth; only the souls of Adam and Jesus were created directly by God. But Islam has no doctrine of the incarnation. The Qur'an says, "They say the God of mercy has begotten a son. Now have you uttered a grievous thing. . . . It is not proper for God to have children" (Qur'an 3:78; 19:93). Muslims claim that both Judaism and Christianity are superseded by Islam (Surah 3:3–7).

Predestination

The smallest details in a person's life are decreed by God. This is called predestination (*qadr*). Even so, God is not bound by his rules. There is freedom of choice for people, and God can change whatever he wills. Human choice and action is considered very important for everybody because we shall receive reward or punishment as a result of what we are doing. In Islam, human freedom stands in tension with God's omnipotence.

Shia and Sunni Islam

The majority of Muslims (85 percent) are Sunnis and a substantial minority (15 percent) are Shi'as. They share the same central beliefs and practices, but differ over the issue of who can interpret the Islamic religious law.

Following the death of Muhammad, disagreement arose as to the necessary qualifications and exact function of his successors as leaders (Imams) of the Muslim community. The Shi'ites are those who insisted that only members of the Prophet's clan, specifically, the descendants of Muhammad's daughter Fatima and her husband 'Ali, could qualify. The Sunnis disagreed, believing that the successor should be appointed by community consensus. Although 'Ali became the fourth caliph (655), he was murdered in 661, and the followers of 'Ali continued to regard him and his descendants as the true leaders of the Muslim community. Shi'ism has three major subdivisions as well as numerous offshoots. The majority are called Twelvers (Ithna Ashariyya), because they recognize twelve Imams, beginning with 'Ali; the twelfth disappeared in 873 but will return as the *Mahdi* (messiah). Twelver Shi'ism became the state religion of Persia (Iran) under the Safavid dynasty in the sixteenth century; it retains that position in the present-day Islamic republic of Iran.

Al-Mahdi

In Sunni Islam al-Mahdi (guided one) can refer to caliphs in the past or reformers who revive the faith, or it may apply to a future guide who will come to bring in the end of all things. Shi'ite Muslims have a strong belief in al-Mahdi as the hidden Imam (the twelfth Imam, Ali ibn Muhammad Simmari, withdrew to a secluded place and remains hidden until God allows him to show himself at the end of time). Al-Mahdi still hears the prayers of believers and intercedes for them.

Ahmadiy(y)a is the Islamic movement started by Mirza Ghulam Ahmad Qadiyani (c. 1835–1908), who claimed to be al-Mahdi. His teachings are set out in *The Arguments of the Amide*, the first volume of which appeared in 1880. Orthodox Muslims regard him and his writings as heretical. In 1889 Ahmad claimed to have received a revelation, giving him the right to receive homage and to be recognized as the Mahdhi or world teacher expected by Zoroastrians, Hindus, and Buddhists. He claimed to be an avatar of Krishna (see Hinduism, unit 7:1) who had come in the spirit of Muhammad. He defended his beliefs by claiming that Sura LXI in the Qur'an speaks of him. He is believed to have performed signs and miracles as proof of his claim. His followers believe, as do some other Muslims, that Jesus (Isa) did not die on the cross, neither did he ascend into heaven; rather, Jesus went to India and preached there until he died at the age of about 120. His tomb is a sanctuary at Srinagar visited by thousands each year. The Ahmadiyya are seen as Muslim heretics and have suffered much persecution, most recently in Pakistan.

Black Muslims

Black Muslim is a widely used name for the adherents of an American black nationalist religious movement whose self-designation changed in 1976 from "The Lost-Found Nation of Islam" to "The World Community of Islam in the West." The movement traces its beginnings to Wallace D. Fard (Wali Farad), known as "Prophet Fard," "The Great Mahdi," or "The Savior."

The movement has its headquarters in Chicago, and has expanded through Fard's successor, Elijah Muhammad, who exercised strong leadership until his death in 1975. One of the best-known Black Muslim ministers during this period was Malcolm X, converted while he was in prison in 1947, who broke with the movement in March 1964 and was assassinated eleven months later.

Festivals

Hijrah Day (New Year). Commemorating Muhammad's departure from Mecca to Medina and the spread of Islam. (September/October)

Miraj (Night of Ascent) or *Lailat-al Isra* (Night of the Journey). Commemorating the event in Sura 17 of the Qur'an when Muhammad went with Gabriel on the winged donkey-mule from Mecca to Jerusalem where he met Abraham, Moses, and Jesus and was shown heaven and hell.

Meelad ul-Nabi (The Prophet's Birthday). Held on the twelfth day of the fourth month. The Prophet's original birthday was August 20, 510. There are processions and readings that recall the life of Muhammad.

Id al-Fitr (or *Eid-Ul-Fitr*). The festival of the breaking of the fast falls on the first day of the tenth month of the Islamic year and marks the end of the fast of Ramadan. People wear new clothes and visit and give presents. Charity is given to the poor.

Ashura. Held by Shi'ite Muslims on the tenth day of the first month to commemorate Husain, who was the Prophet's grandson who died in battle. For Sunnis, the celebration remembers the birth of Adam, the saving of Noah, and the Exodus of the Jews.

Id al-Adha or *Id al-Kabir*. The Great Festival of Sacrifice occurs during the Hajj, the Muslim pilgrimage in the twelfth month. It remembers Abraham's obedience to sacrifice Ishmael (Surah 37:100–111). There are prayers and a sermon, then the sacrifice of sheep, cows, or a camel. The head of each family either slays his own offering or gets a butcher to do it for him. The animal faces Mecca and is killed in one blow to the throat while the name of God is recited. The animal is then cooked and eaten and shared with the poor.

UNIT 7:7 SHINTOISM

> *This world in which we live is progressing from chaos to order, from the confusion of contradictions to a state of harmony and unity. Just as organic life develops, so in society good order is evolving as the result of mutual aid and co-operation. Shinto believes that this world gives promise of an unlimited development of life-power.*
>
> Sokyo Ono, *Shinto, the Kami Way*

Shinto is an ancient Japanese religion. As an organized religion it evolved over time, dating from about 500 B.C.E. (or earlier). Its name was derived from the Chinese words *shin tao* (the way of the gods). On a time line, the beginning of Shinto falls between the older religion of Confucianism and the newer religion of Buddhism. Most Japanese follow two religions: both Shinto and Buddhism. Buddhism first arrived in Japan from Korea and China during the sixth century C.E. Within Shinto, the Buddha was viewed as another "Kami" (nature deity). Although important mythology and cosmology is found in ancient Japanese chronicles (the Kojiki and the Nihongi), Shinto has no sacred scriptures, no fixed system of doctrine, and a very loosely organized priesthood. Shinto creation stories tell of the history and lives of the Kami. Among them was a divine couple, Izanagi and Izanami, who gave birth to the Japanese islands. One of their daughters was Amaterasu (Sun Goddess), who is revered as the chief deity and from whom the Imperial Family of Japan traces its ancestry.

Shinto forms the foundation for many of the differing Japanese sensitivities, beliefs, and values. Shintoism is a very simple religion, focusing on one command: Be loyal to one's ancestors.

Recent History and Different Types of Shinto

The feudal Edo era of Japan collapsed in 1868, and the Meiji rulers (1868–1912) modernized the country to cope with unrest and increasing foreign trade. The outcome was to promote a positive national identity by establishing a national religion centered on emperor devotion (as the emperor was a descendant of Amaterasu). In the 1880s the government guaranteed freedom of religion to all faiths, but in the process Buddhism was separated from Shintoism and distinctions were drawn between shrine Shinto (sometimes called state Shinto) and sect Shinto.

State Shinto was affiliated with the power structure of the new state; its priests became government officials and enjoyed the attendant privileges and status. State Shinto combined Imperial House (*koshitsu*) Shinto, which centered on the rites performed by the emperor for his ancestor's spirits, and Shrine (*jinja*) Shinto. Sect Shinto became a name for the different sects that the Meiji did not wish to subsume into State Shinto. These sects have developed and become popular in recent times. A popular example is the Tenrikyo (Religion of Heavenly Truth) sect, its foundress being Nakayama Miki (1798–1887). Today the sect is visible through its impressive buildings, which are spread throughout Tenri City.

Shinto is presently divided into three main groups:

- *Jinja (Shrine) Shinto*: Jinja is the largest Shinto group. As the original form of the religion, its roots date back into prehistory. Until the end of World War II, Jinja was closely aligned with State Shinto. The Emperor of Japan was worshiped as a living God. Almost all shrines are members of Jinja Honcho, the Association of Shinto Shrines.
- *Kyoha (Sectarian) Shinto*: This group consists of thirteen sects that were founded by individuals since the start of the nineteenth century. One of these sects, Ryobu Shinto, synthesizes Buddhism and Shinto, where the kami are identified with bodhisattvas and Buddhist sanctuaries are attached to Shinto shrines.
- *Folk Shinto* is not strictly a Shinto sect; it has no formal central organization or creed, but its presence is seen in local practices and rituals, e.g.,

small images by the side of the road, agriculture rituals practiced by individual families, etc.

These three forms are closely linked. Shinto is a tolerant religion that accepts the validity of other religions. Believers commonly pay respect to other religions, their practices, and objects of worship.

God

The only deity actually recognized in higher Shintoism is the spiritualized human mind. Shinto is the way of the kami. The kami are omnipresent manifestations of the sacred. Kami is a complex concept that is applied to the various deities of heaven and earth and to their spirits residing in the shrines where they are worshiped. Kami can also apply to sacred places and beings—mountains, trees, animals . . . all things that evoke reverence for their unique powers and qualities.

Ancestors are deeply venerated and worshiped. Humanity is regarded as "kami's child." All human life and human nature is sacred. "Kami" has a whole range of meaning: "mysterious," "an invisible power," "soul," and so on. All people can become kami spirits in the end. No Shinto concepts compare to Jewish/Christian beliefs about God, his omnipotence and omnipresence, or the separation of God from humanity due to sin. Shintoists believe in no definite line that divides humans from kami spirits. A kami evokes feelings of awe or reverence. People owe gratitude to the kami and to their ancestors for life itself and for their ever-present love. Belief in the kami has two aspects:

- Certain kami, who originally were the ancestors of leading families, protect particular areas of Japan.
- Other kami protect you in specific situations, e.g., when in danger or in stressed situations.

Shinto believes that we are all in the process of becoming kamis.

Shinto scholar Motoori Wonnaga (1730–1801) referred also to malignant kami:

> They (kami) need not be eminent for surpassing nobleness, goodness, or serviceableness alone. Malignant and uncanny beings are also call Kami if only they are the objects of general dread. (W. G. Aston, *Shinto: The Ancient Religion of Japan* [London: Constable & Co. Ltd., 1910].)

Salvation

Shinto promotes no concept of sin, nor a judgment day in the future. Souls (*tama*) are not "lost" and do not need "saving." Humankind by nature is inherently good and is considered to be both earthly and divine. Evil comes from without. The source of temptation and evil is in the world of darkness, from evil spirits called *magatsuhi*. Moral evil is seen as an affliction, and human beings do evil because, although their soul is good, their senses and their body easily give way to temptation.

The Shinto soul has two parts—the *kunitama*, which joins the body at conception, and the *wake-mitama*, which arrives at birth. Death occurs when the two of these fall out with the *kunitama*, returning to earth from which it originated.

Death

Shintoism sees death as evil or a curse. Adherents to Shinto use the word *kegare* when they talk of death; the term can also mean "abnormality" or "misfortune." Traditionally Shinto has little interest in the afterlife, yet the old religious texts discuss the "High Plain of Heaven" where the kami live and the "Dark Land," which is an unclean land of the dead. A year of purification can bring the soul to the Land of Toko-yo, which is a pleasurable land of peace and prosperity. However, modern Shintoism is more concerned with what happens in this life than in the next. Because of this modern approach, Buddhism fills an important gap. The Japanese are said to see Shintoism as the religion of the living and Buddhism as that of the dead. The majority of Shintoists follow Buddhist funeral rites, although a Shinto funeral rite is usually held in the home rather than the shrine so as not to cause pollution. Everything concerned with death is considered pollution in Shinto, yet not necessarily an evil. If the deceased is polluted, then access to the Kami is denied.

Gender and Religion

Any attempt to study women and gender issues in Japanese religion is very complex. Although Buddhism and Shinto were separated, in many ways the Japanese continued to practice what had been one religious system. This situation is complicated by the addition of a folk religion that encompasses ancestor worship with its Confucian roots, astrology, spirit possession, and Taoism. There are also a number of new religions in Japan. Therefore, two recognizable areas are available for the study of the role and status of women in Shintoism: the organized religious beliefs and practices, including new religions, and folk and family religion.

The Status and Role of Women in Organized Religion

In organized religion both mythology and scholars are agreed that in early Japanese history women functioned as shamanesses so that women were seen as mediators for the deities, known as *miko*. Historians describe the miko as women who both advised political leaders and who mediated between the ordinary people and the deities. In one of the oldest texts, the Kojiki, the importance of women is demonstrated when Empress Jingu shows force and strength both in conquering the kingdoms of Korea and in giving birth. Japanese women had higher status in all aspects of life before the feudal age (twelfth to seventeenth centuries). It is debatable whether Buddhism and Confucianism held responsibility for the overall historical decline in women's rights, but the views of both of these religions were used to support later laws that stripped women of their rights to inherit property or to divorce their husbands. In both Shinto and Buddhism, women were considered to be polluting because of their menstrual blood, although scholars such as Karen A. Smyers (1983) would argue that in pre-Buddhist Shinto belief, women's menstrual blood was considered powerful rather than a pollutant. A number of scholars have seen the connection between Japanese women's concern with hygiene and cleanliness and older religious traditions of purity.

The Status and Role of Women in the New Religions and Folk Religion

Several of the hundreds of newer religions are led by women and were started by women who had supernatural revelatory experiences. In small rural areas, women are often considered the keepers of religious knowledge and wisdom. Yet studies of ancestor worship in Japan reveal that the ideal is to worship the male ancestors and that the men were the ones to attend important public occasions. Preparing offerings for the deities at the household Shinto altar is the work of the women.

Mysticism

In a general sense many aspects of Shinto practice could be seen as mystical. For example, when entering a shrine, one passes through a Tori, a special gateway for the gods that marks the demarcation between the finite world and the infinite world.

Moral Action

The virtue that is stressed constantly in Shintoism is purity, and as regards individual virtues, sincerity (*makoto*) is an essential attitude of life. Jean Herbert (1967, p. 73) quotes a modern exponent of Shinto as saying:

> Makoto is a sincere approach to life with all one's heart, an approach in which nothing is shunned or treated with neglect. It stems from an awareness of the Divine. It is the humble, single-minded reaction which wells up within us when we touch

> directly or indirectly upon the workings of the Kami, know that they exist, and have the assurance of their close presence with us.

Morality is based upon that which is of benefit to the group. Shintoism is optimistic about human nature, believing it to be essentially good and therefore capable of right practice, sensibility, and attitude. Shintoists believe that a person is born with the kami spirit within and therefore will have an inner knowledge of right and wrong. A Shintoist would not think in terms of committing "sins" but in terms of maintaining honor by being honest, tolerant, and sincere. People who fail to maintain honor can ritually purify themselves through two ceremonies:

- *Misogi* (Japanese = "pouring water over the body") is technically performed at a river or the seashore for the purpose of cleansing pollution from the body. Small quantities of simple food are also eaten, although meat, coffee, tea, and alcohol are avoided.
- *Harai* (Japanese = "to sweep or cleanse") is the Shinto rite of exorcism or purification and refers to purification that is enacted by a priest performing "offerings" on your behalf by waving a sacred wand. Sometimes this rite is performed on objects like a car or a new home to make them safe.

There are four affirmations in Shinto.

1. *Tradition and the family*: The family is seen as the main mechanism by which traditions are preserved. Their main celebrations relate to birth and marriage.
2. *Love of nature*: Nature is sacred; to be in contact with nature is to be close to the gods. Natural objects are worshiped as sacred spirits.
3. *Physical cleanliness*: People take baths, wash their hands, and rinse out their mouth often.
4. "*Matsuri*": To worship and honor gods and ancestral spirits.

Prayer and Worship

In their homes, Shintoists have a *kamidana* (godshelf) fitted with brass fixings and containing *shintai* (god emblems). This shelf honors the local kami and the ancestors. Shinto recognizes many sacred places: mountains, springs, and shrines. Each shrine is dedicated to a specific Kami who has a divine personality and responds to sincere prayers of the faithful. To overcome damaging pollution, humans reconcile to the Kami, which takes place at a shrine. Jean Herbert (1967) attempts to capture aspects of the experience of a Shinto shrine:

> The best explanation I can offer is that the Shinto shrine is a visible and ever active expression of the factual kinship—in the most literal sense of the word—which exists between

> individual man and the whole earth, celestial bodies and deities, whatever name they be given. When entering it, one inevitably becomes more or less conscious of that blood relation, and the realisation of it throws into the background all feelings of anxiety, antagonism, loneliness, discouragement, as when a child comes to rest in its mother's lap. (Jean Herbert, *Shinto: At the Fountain—Head of Japan* [London: George Allen & Unwin Ltd., 1967] 92.)

Origami ("paper of the spirits") is a Japanese folk art in which paper is folded into beautiful shapes. They are often seen around Shinto shrines. Out of respect for the tree spirit that gave its life to make the paper, origami paper is never cut.

Another form of worship is *kagura*, ritual dances performed by skilled and trained dancers and accompanied by ancient musical instruments.

Scriptures

There are no sacred texts in Shintoism, but many texts are valued nonetheless. Most works date from the eighth century C.E.:

- The Kojiki (Record of Ancient Matters)
- The Rokkokushi (Six National Histories)
- The Shoku Nihongi and its Nihon Shoki (Continuing Chronicles of Japan)
- The Jinno Shotoki (a study of Shinto and Japanese politics), written in the fourteenth century

Festivals

A secular, countrywide National Founding Day is held on February 11 to commemorate the founding of Japan; this is the traditional date on which the first (mythical) emperor Jinmu ascended the throne in 660 B.C.E. Some shrines are believed to hold festivities on that day. Other festivals include

January 1–3: Shogatsu (New Year)

March 3: Hinamatsuri (Girls' festival)

May 5: Tango no Sekku (Boys' festival)

July 7: Hoshi Matsuri (Star festival)

Followers are also expected to visit Shinto shrines at the times of various life passages. For example, the Shichigosan Matsuri involves a blessing by the shrine priest of girls ages three to seven and boys age five. This ceremony is held on November 15.

The New Year Festival is both a national holiday and a religious occasion that centers around spiritual themes of renewal, regeneration, and purification. It is customary to visit shrines and temples and to pay respect to the kami and to request good luck for the coming year. Lucky charms and talismans are sold at the temples and old charms are replaced for new. Ian Reader's colorful book, *Religion in Contemporary Japan* (1991) sets the scene:

> The old amulets and talismans from the previous year are jettisoned, and most shrines and temples at this time designate a special place where these can be left. Some time later, usually in mid-January, these will be formally burnt in a purificatory rite, generally to the accompaniment of priests chanting prayers whose powers, along with the exorcistic nature of fire, transform the impurities and eradicate the bad luck that have been absorbed by the amulets and talismans.

Reader goes on to describe the evening of December 31 in Japan as a time of special seasonal feasting with houses and shrines decked with bright lanterns. At midnight the bells of the famous Chionin Buddhist temple in Kyoto, along with other temples throughout the country, toll 108 times just before midnight. The number is symbolic of the suffering in the world; the tolling symbolically eradicates them:

> As the tolling ended and the time chimed midnight people began to flow through the arch, clapping their hands in prayer, tossing coins in to the offering box and praying. . . . Soon the entire shrine was crowded. . . .

His description sets out a scene of national celebration with music and dancing and the expectation of the transfer of the Kami's benevolence to the people.

UNIT 7:8 TAOISM

To name Tao is to name no-thing.
Tao is not the name of (something created).
"Cause" and "chance" have no bearing on the Tao.
Tao is a name that indicates without defining.

Tao is beyond words and beyond things.
It is not expressed either in word or in silence.
Where there is no longer word or silence
Tao is apprehended.

Chuang Tzu, *The Way of Chuang Tzu*

The "Tao" (or Dao) is the way of the cosmos, the natural order and flow of the universe. Taoism is sometimes called the "way of water" because it teaches that we should not resist life but, like water, surround and flow through all things. The Tao encompasses the harmony of opposites—for example, there would be no love without hate, no male without female. The heart of concern in Taoism is that people are released from the trivial, mundane activities in life and that they refocus themselves on the deep, lasting realities of life. Here are the opening verses of the *Tao Te Ching*:

> The Tao that can be trodden is not the enduring and unchanging Tao. The name that can be named is not the enduring and unchanging name.
>
> (Conceived of as) having no name, it is the Originator of heaven and earth; (conceived of as) having a name, it is the Mother of all things.
>
> Always without desire we must be found,
> If its deep mystery we would sound;
> But if desire always within us be,
> Its outer fringe is all that we shall see.
>
> Under these two aspects, it is really the same; but as development takes place, it receives the different names. Together we call them the Mystery. Where the Mystery is the deepest is the gate of all that is subtle and wonderful.

Lao Tzu

The term "Taoism" refers both to the philosophy outlined in the *Tao Te Ching* (identified with Lao Tzu) and to China's ancient Taoist religion. According to tradition, Lao Tzu lived in the sixth century and was a contemporary of Confucius. His name means "Old Master," and it is said that he was born at age sixty with white hair after his mother had carried him in her womb for twenty-eight years. Lao Tzu held the belief that civilization was the foundation for the downfall of humanity, yet his teachings formed the basis for China to survive morally and socially for centuries. Even so, he never preached or founded a religion. One day, weary of the world of his day, he set off towards the west to leave the country. Upon reaching the mountain pass at Han-ku, the gatekeeper persuaded the great sage to write down his wisdom before he left. Lao Tzu wrote down the eighty-one aphorisms that make up the *Tao Te Ching*, after which he was never seen again.

Taoism then passed through three stages of religious growth. Up to about 200 B.C.E., Taoism involved abstention from too much food, deep breathing, and learning rules for long life. The aim was to escape from the world's evils through abstinence. The second stage was a magical stage, lasting from 200 B.C.E. to 200 C.E., during which time Taoists developed alchemy, fortune-telling, and exorcism. In the third stage, a religious phase occurred that is often regarded as a corruption of Taoist philosophy. During the third stage, Taoism also developed its own concept of hell.

The Taoist religion began in the third century B.C.E. and included practices such as alchemy (the mixing of elixirs, ensuring the immortality of the body) carried out by Taoist priests—magicians at the court of Shih Huang-ti of the Ch'in dynasty (221–207 B.C.E.). These magicians were seen as spirit mediums and experts in levitation. They were heirs of the archaic folk religion of China, which had been rejected by the early Confucianists. Taoist religion retains beliefs in physical immortality, alchemy, breath control, hygiene, a pantheon of deities (including Lao Tzu as one of the three Supreme Ones or Taoist Trinity), monasticism, and revealed scriptures. The Taoist liturgy and theology were influenced by Buddhism. Its scriptures, the Tao-tsang, consist of hundreds of separate works totaling more than five thousand chapters.

Today, there are many strands of Taoism:

- *Philosophical Taoism* (*Tao Chia*) (wise thinking)
- *Religious Taoism* (*Tao Chiao*) (teaching of the Way)
- *Heavenly (Celestial) Master,* founded in West China in the second century C.E., advocated faith healing through the confession of sin and at one time recruited members as soldiers and engaged in war against the government.
- *Supreme Peace*, founded in the second century C.E., adopted practices similar to those of the Heavenly Master sect and initiated a great rebellion that went on for several years before ending in 205 C.E.
- The *Mount Mao* (*Mao Shan* [*Mao-shan*]) sect was founded in the fourth century C.E. and introduced rituals involving both external and internal alchemies, mediumistic practice, and visionary communication with divinities.
- The *Sacred Treasure* (*Ling Bao*/*Ling-pao*) sect was founded in the fourth century C.E. and introduced the worship of divinities called *T'ien-tsun* (Heavenly Lords).
- The *Completely Real* (*Chuan Zhen* [*Ch'uan-chen*]) sect was founded in the twelfth century as a Taoist monastic movement.

Eventually the Heavenly Master sect absorbed most of the beliefs and practices of the other sects and, in the twentieth century, became the most popular Taoist group. In this unit we shall concentrate on philosophical Taoism, which has created great interest in the West. Reference will also be made to religious Taoism.

God

The Chinese word for supreme one is *T'ai-i*, who is the ultimate source of all appearance. The word has been differently understood in the various schools of

Taoism. In religious Taoism, he is personified in the form of the supreme God; in philosophical Taoism, the one is impersonal—an underived source of appearance. Lao Tse did not believe in a personal creator of the world but in an impersonal Tao ("method" or "way"). The Way has a number of aspects or meanings.

The impersonal Tao is the only reality behind all existence, because there is no supernatural world. Unlike the beliefs of Jews, Muslims, or Christians, the Tao does not possess preknowledge or memory of the world's events, and is not the object of prayer. Akin to Brahman, Tao is the ultimate source, but whereas in Hinduism Brahman is eternal and timeless, the Tao is forever in flux and changing.

Tao is also the driving force of the universe that prevents chaos. Although nature is always changing, the Tao is like the cycle of the sun in that it always remains the same, operating as Yin and Yang.

Yin (dark side) is the breath that formed the earth. Yang (light side) is the breath that formed the heavens. Yin and Yang symbolize pairs of opposites in the universe: good and evil, light and dark, male and female. Yang denotes the active, masculine energy and Yin the passive, feminine one. Intervention by human civilization upsets the balance of Yin and Yang. What seems like Yin is often supported by Yang, and vice versa—e.g., to truly know good, you must know what evil is, and without good as a comparison, nothing is evil. Thus, while keeping to one end, do not shun the opposite end, but embrace both as they are. Allowing Yin to flourish, you welcome Yang. Yin and Yang often represent the following opposites:

Negative/positive

Female/male

Dark/light

Evil/good

Earth/heaven

Tao is also the Way that human beings should order their lives, to harmonize with the way the universe flows.

Salvation

All nature is united in Tao, therefore emancipation and salvation are not concerned with escaping nature, i.e., via the soul or a spiritual release, but in directing the forces of nature in your own body. Different schools of Taoism focus on different bodily functions—e.g., breathing, sexuality, moral behavior—and attend to often strenuous and focused disciplines to evoke the power of the cosmos to the whole body. One example of such a discipline is the practice of Tai Chi, which works on all parts of the body. Traditional Chinese medicine teaches that illness is caused by either blockages or the absence of balance in the body's "chi" (intrinsic energy). Tai Chi is believed to balance this energy flow.

Death

Lao Tse taught a belief in transmigration of souls, which became absorbed into Taoism, Confucianism, and the other Eastern religions as reincarnation. Chinese belief in the soul is twofold: the Hun soul is the higher spiritual soul with the Yang attributes, while the P'o soul is the earthly one with Yin qualities. When a person dies, the Hun soul takes on a spirit form (*shen*) and takes a perilous journey to the underworld. The journey of the *shen* soul is divided into seven periods of seven days each. The soul must pass through seven phases of transmigration including the second week where the Hun Soul is put on the scales of the Weighbridge to be weighed. If you are good, you are as light as air; if not you are weighed down by evil deeds. The temporary consequence of bad actions is to be torn apart or ground down to power before continuing the journey. The P'o soul stays at the grave where sacrifices are made to it to prevent it from emerging as a wicked ghost (*kuei*).

Funerals

A diviner advises when the soul will leave the body (as a vapor), what form the soul will take, and where the funeral should be. Feng Shui ("wind-water") determines the natural site for the burial. The body is washed and clothed. The feet are also tied together because Taoists believe that the body can jump about if tormented by evil spirits. Although traditionally Taoists bury their dead, in Hong Kong 50 percent of funerals are cremations.

Ancestral Worship

Taoists keep a shrine room where they place tablets with their photographs of dead members of the family. The older ancestors are placed in ancestral halls in the country.

Moral Action

The concept of Yin and Yang brings with it the message that life and therefore the way you live it is not a case of opposites, a black-and-white thing. Life is a mixture of good and evil. The power of Yang is in the firm, solid, warm things, and the power of Yin is the soft, moist, changeable things. Therefore Taoists are reluctant to say what is unchanging good and evil. Yin and Yang alternate so that "The Way to do is to be." In philosophical Taoism you ally yourself to the way, whereas in religious Taoism the priests evoke the gods to control the course of nature and its effects with their rituals.

Gender and Religion

In Tao philosophy the female is acknowledged. The Tao is both male and female:

> He who knows the male and keeps to the female
> Becomes the ravine of the world.
> He will never depart from eternal virtue,
> But returns to the state of infancy.
> He who knows the white and yet keeps to the black
> Becomes the model for the world,
> He will never deviate from eternal virtue,
> But returns to the state of the non-ultimate.
> He who knows glory but keeps to humility
> Becomes the valley of the world,
> He will be proficient in eternal virtue,
> And returns to the state of simplicity (uncarved wood).
> When the uncarved wood is broken up, it is turned into
> concrete things
> But when the sage uses it, he becomes the leading official.
> Therefore the great ruler does not cut up.
>
> Wing-Tsi Chan, *The Way of Lao Tzu Tao-te Ching*
> (New York and London: Macmillan [Collier]
> Publishing Co., 1963).

Mysticism

Chuang Tzu was a Taoist sage, living sometime before 250 B.C. The quotations here were taken from *The Way of Chuang Tzu*, which was compiled by Thomas Merton (a Roman Catholic monk) after reading four different translations of Chuang Tzu. Thomas Merton says in his introductory note to his abridged version of Chuang Tzu;

> You enter upon the way of Chuang Tzu when you leave all ways and get lost.

The following quotations give a flavor and a feeling for the wisdom of Chuang Tzu and the Taoist perception of reality.

> When he tries to extend his power over objects,
> those objects gain control of him.

He who is controlled by objects loses possession of his inner self. . . .
Prisoners in the world of object,
they have no choice but to submit to the demands of matter!
They are pressed down and crushed by external forces:
fashion, the market, events, public opinion.
Never in a whole lifetime do they recover their right mind! . . .
What a pity!
(23:8 and 24:4, pp. 202, 211)

You train your eye and your vision lusts after color.
You train your ear, and you long for delightful sound.
You delight in doing good, and your natural kindness is blown out of shape.
You delight in righteousness, and you become righteous beyond all reason.
You overdo liturgy, and you turn into a ham actor.
Overdo your love of music, and you play corn.
Love of wisdom leads to wise contriving.
Love of knowledge leads to faultfinding.
If men would stay as they really are, taking or leaving these eight delights would make no difference.
But if they will not rest in their right state, the eight delights develop like malignant tumors.
The world falls into confusion.
Since men honour these delights, and lust after them, the world has gone stone-blind.
When the delight is over, they still will not let go of it . . .
(11:1–2, pp. 103–4)

Love of colors bewilders the eye and it fails to see right.
Love of harmonies bewitches the ear, and it loses its true hearing.
Love of perfumes fills the head with dizziness.
Love of flavors ruins the taste.
Desires unsettle the heart until the original nature runs amok.

These five are enemies of true life.
Yet these are what men of discernment claim to live for.
They are not what I live for.
If this is life, then pigeons in a cage have found happiness!
(12:15, p. 118)

Taoism in the Modern World

After the Communist victory in 1949, religious freedom in China was severely restricted. Monks were forced into manual labor, temples were confiscated and robbed. During the Cultural Revolution in China (1966–1976), much of what was left of Taoist heritage was destroyed. Some religious tolerance was been restored under Deng Xiao-ping (1982 onwards).

Taoism has had a significant impact on North American and British culture through the practice of acupuncture, herbalism, holistic medicine, meditation, and martial arts.

Scriptures

The Tao Te Ching is the single most important text of Chinese Taoism. The book is now mostly considered to date from the fourth century B.C.E. It is imbued with richly poetic imagery and advocates balance, restraint, simplicity, and the avoidance of activity and desire as the means of achieving harmony with the natural currents of the universe. The harmony of opposites (*T'ai Ch'ai*) is achieved through a blend of the yin (feminine force) and the yang (masculine force); this harmony can be cultivated through creative quietude (*wu wei*), an effortless action whose power (te) maintains equanimity and balance.

Government

In Taoism, the government should also follow the way in governing the people. The Tao Te Ching describes the ideal way of governing people. To summarize:

- Do not emphasize status, intelligence, wealth, or possessions.
- Govern with least visibility and adopt an attitude of servanthood.
- Reduce laws and govern lightly.
- Take few actions that involve the populace.
- Treat other countries in a nonaggressive way.

Three Jewels

Three jewels (characteristics) that Taoists should cherish are mentioned in Tao Te Ching chapter 67:

1. Compassion—leading to courage
2. Moderation—leading to generosity
3. Humility—leading to leadership

Festivals

Festivals grounded in Taoist heritage include:

- *The Cosmic Renewal Festival.* A festival in religious Taoism involving colorful ritual to welcome the gods, drive evil spirits away, and release souls from hell.

- *Birthday of Matzu* (Queen of Heaven), who is said to honor every home that she passes in procession.

Taoists also celebrate other Chinese festivals that are not exclusively Taoist, such as

- *Hsin nien*: The New Year Festival
- *The Lantern Festival*, which ends the new year with displays of lanterns, notifying the ancestors of any new sons
- *Ching Ming*: A festival in April to honor the dead
- *Dragon Boat Festival*, in honor of Ch'u Yuan, who drowned himself in protest at the greed of the emperor
- *Mid-Autumn Festival*, during which offerings to the goddess moon are made

UNIT 7:9 CONFUCIANISM

> *The Master said, "The gentlemen is at ease without being arrogant; the small man is arrogant without being at ease."*
>
> Confucius, *The Analects*

> *Confucius said, "By nature men are pretty much alike; it is learning and practice that set them apart."*
>
> Confucius, *The Analects*

> *Confucius said, "In education there are no class distinctions."*
>
> Confucius, *The Analects*

In the West, a popular image of Confucius is as a wise man or a sage giving forth wisdom on how to live a good and moral life. Confucius has been claimed as a secular humanist, a philosopher, and a religious thinker. Whatever one's view, Confucius and the school named after him put forward a moral answer to the question of how to understand the meaning of life and what sort of society we should live in.

The founder of Confucianism was Master Kong (K'ung, Confucius, 551–479 B.C.E.). His intention was not to found a new religion, but to interpret and revive the unnamed religion of the Zhou (Chou) Dynasty. During the eighth to third centuries B.C.E., China had experienced a collapse of the Chou Dynasty's governing power. By the time of Confucius there was relentless warfare and horror involving mass executions and unthinkable barbarism. Confucius lived at a time when social cohesion had all but disappeared. The questions arose "Why couldn't the gods prevent the social upheavals?" and "How can we prevent self-destruction?" The pressing issue of the day was: "If it is not the ancestral and nature spirits, what then is the basis of a stable, unified, and enduring social order?"

The dominant answer to such questions was put forward by realists and legalists, who said that strict law, civic control, penalties, and rewards were the bases of sound policy. Confucius disagreed, believing that the basis lay in Zhou religion and its rituals (*li*). He saw these rituals not existing in sacrifices seeking the blessings of the gods, but as ceremonies enacted by human beings themselves and embodying the civilized and cultured patterns of behavior developed through generations of human wisdom.

Chinese religion, as it stands in history, has been divided into four stages named after the seasons of the year: spring, summer, autumn, and winter. Historically the two dominant religious traditions in China have been Confucianism and Taoism. Buddhism was introduced during summer flowering (206 B.C.E.–900 C.E.), but it generally did not replace the indigenous religious culture.

Confucianism has been the mainstream philosophy in China for the past two thousand years and has also influenced the cultures of Korea, Japan, and Indochina. Confucianism is both a religion and a system of social and ethical philosophy, but it is different from Western religions that believe in revealed doctrines and God. Confucius was a profound philosopher, and his teaching concentrated on a form of humanism that is open to the transcendent order of reality. His philosophy and teaching deeply probe the nature of relationships and the cultivation of virtues, both of which have bearing on political leadership.

Legends about Confucius abound, and establishing reliable information about his background is difficult. *The Analects* (*Lun-Yu*) date from the third century B.C.E. and show Confucius's reported conversations with his disciples. *The Analects* say that Confucius was born to a poor but aristocratic family in the ancient state of Lu (now Shantung Province), in China. His Chinese name was K'ung Fu'tzu, and by his early youth he had set his mind on studying. He eventually acquired a fine reputation as a teacher, leading to an appointed position in the government. He traveled for many years and visited other states in search of a ruler who could use his wisdom and thought, but his search was unfruitful. Confucianism eventually became the basis of the Chinese state during the Han Dynasty (206 B.C.E.–220 C.E.).

God

Confucius appears to have had beliefs in the existence of a supreme deity. Here is a classic statement of his teaching that rulers must pay regard to the mandate of heaven; if they do not, their reign becomes untenable.

> Revere the anger of Heaven,
> And presume not to make sport or be idle.
> Revere the changing moods of Heaven,
> And presume not to drive about at your pleasure.
> Great Heaven is intelligent,
> And is with you in all your goings.
> Great Heaven is clear-seeing,
> And is with you in your wanderings and indulgences.
>
> Confucius, *Book of Songs,* Ode 254

His philosophy was grounded in the traditional religion of the Lord-on-High. However, these beliefs expressed themselves in an implicit way, in contrast to Western religions that emphasize divine revelation in their doctrines.

Confucius moved away from the earlier Chinese focus on the supernatural. The idealist wing of Confucianism had a religious character with humanist underpinnings. The teachings showed an open attitude to transcendent realities—not in the sense that they were otherworldly (the Confucians were not interested in a far-off heavenly realm), but in the sense of the transcendent ideal of perfection.

> Absolute truth is indestructible. Being indestructible, it is eternal. Being eternal, it is self-existent. Being self-existent, it is infinite. Being infinite, it is vast and deep. Being vast and deep, it is transcendental and intelligent. It is because it is vast and deep that it contains all existence. It is because it is transcendental and intelligent that it embraces all existence. It is because it is infinite and eternal that it fulfills or perfects all existence. In vastness and depth it is like the Earth. In transcendental intelligence it is like Heaven. Infinite and eternal, it is the Infinite itself. Such being the nature of absolute truth, it manifests itself without being seen; it produces effects without motion; it accomplishes its ends without action. (Confucius, *Doctrine of the Mean* 26.)

Confucius affirmed the spiritual nature of humankind:

> Confucius said, "The power of spiritual forces in the universe—how active it is everywhere! Invisible to the eyes and impalpable to the senses, it is inherent in all things, and nothing can escape its operation."
>
> It is the fact that there are these forces which make men in all countries fast and purify themselves, and with solemnity of dress institute services of sacrifice and religious worship. Like the rush of mighty waters, the presence of unseen Powers is felt; sometimes above us, sometimes around us. In the Book of Songs it is said,
>
> > The presence of the Spirit:
> > It cannot be surmised,
> > How may it be ignored!
> > Such is the evidence of things invisible that it is impossible to doubt the spiritual nature of man.
> >
> > *Doctrine of the Mean* 16

Salvation

Rather than focusing on salvation, the emphasis on Confucianism is to reach psychic harmony, which is accomplished through the practice of moderating our emotions.

Death

The philosophy of Confucius changed direction from earlier religious preoccupations of Chinese religion that focused on the supernatural. However, his teaching aided the ancient cult of venerating ancestors and worshiping heaven, which were practiced by the rulers of China who saw themselves to be "the keepers of Heaven's Mandate of Government." Confucius was once asked about death:

> Tzu-lu asked how one should serve ghosts and spirits. The Master said, "Till you have learnt to serve men, how can you serve ghosts?" Tzu-lu then ventured upon a question about the dead. The Master said, "Till you know about the living, how are you to know about the dead?" (*Analects* 11.11)

Moral Action

Confucianism regards the original heart of man as inherently good and characterized by benevolence (*jen*); this concept is illustrated by a well-known passage from Mencius about people's spontaneous reactions to a child falling into a well: "*No matter who the man is, his heart will flip, flop, and he will feel the child's predicament*" (Mencius II.A.6). This reaction does not occur because a person expects to derive something from it or because he wants praise from his neighbors or friends, or because he is afraid of a bad name. Instead, the reaction comes from being human and having a heart that sympathizes with pain.

> The moral man's life is an exemplification of the universal order, because he is a moral person who unceasingly cultivates his true self or moral being. The vulgar person's life is a contradiction of the universal order, because he is a vulgar person who in his heart has no regard for, or fear of, the moral law. (*Doctrine of the Mean*)

Above all, Confucius was concerned with how people become humane, benevolent human beings. People who undertook this pursuit were real gentlemen, in contrast to those who had inherited rank or status. The way of benevolence is to put the self in the position of the other and then treat the other accordingly.

> Confucius said: "Do not do to others what you would not like yourself." . . . "Do unto others what you wish to do unto yourself." (*The Analects*)

Confucius also wrote:

> "Tzu-kung asked, 'What must a man be like before he can be said truly to be a Gentleman?' The Master said, 'A man who

> has a sense of shame in the way he conducts himself and, when sent abroad, does not disgrace the commission of his lord can be said to be a Gentleman.'
>
> 'May I ask about the grade below?'
>
> 'Someone praised for being a good son in his clan and for being a respectful young man in the village.'
>
> 'And the next?'
>
> 'A man who insists on keeping his word and seeing his actions through to the end can, perhaps, qualify to come next, even though he shows a stubborn petty-mindedness.'
>
> 'What about men who are in public life in the present day?'
>
> The Master said, 'Oh, they are of such limited capacity that they hardly count.'" (Confucius, *The Analects*, translated with an introduction by D. C. Lau [Harmondsworth: Penguin, 1979], 121–23.)

Ritual Propriety

Education in the rituals rests on the natural ability people have to imitate sages. The sages have mastered the *li* and are the models of behavior from which the rest of the populace learns. Social rituals give the means by which people form social and aesthetic norms that guide them in their social relations. In this way Confucianism was the affirmation of accepted values and norms of behavior in society and in relationships. Confucius taught that all human relationships involved a set of defined roles and mutual obligations, and that each person should understand and conform to his/her proper role. Starting from individual and family, people acting rightly could reform and even perfect society. The blueprint of this process was described in *The Great Learning*, a section of the Classic of Rituals:

> Only when things are investigated is knowledge extended; only when knowledge is extended are thoughts sincere; only when thoughts are sincere are minds rectified; only when minds are rectified are the characters of persons cultivated; only when character is cultivated are our families regulated; only when families are regulated are states well governed; only when states are well governed is there peace in the world. (Confucius, *Confucian Analects, the Great Learning and the Doctrine of the Mean*)

Confucius also emphasized the management of the emotions, so that there is psychic harmony in oneself, the family, the community, and the nation. At the root of all well-being is the cultivation of the person. Confucius said:

> From the Son of Heaven down to the mass of the people, all must consider the cultivation of the person the root of everything

> besides. It cannot be, when the root is neglected, that what should spring from it will be well ordered. It has never been the case that what was of great importance has been slightly cared for, and, at the same time, that what was of slight importance has been greatly cared for. (Confucius, *Confucian Analects, the Great Learning and the Doctrine of the Mean* [New York: Dover, 1971].)

Under the Han Emperor Wu (c. 140–87 B.C.E.), Confucianism became accepted as the ideology of the state. From that time on, the imperial state promoted Confucian values to maintain law, order, and the status quo. In late traditional China, emperors sought to establish village lectures on Confucian moral precepts and to give civic awards to filial sons and chaste wives. Confucianism focused on the importance of five forms of relationship, or filial piety (*Hsiao*):

Father and son

Elder and younger brothers

Husband and wife

Elder and younger

Ruler and subject

Confucianism also combines political theory and a theory of human nature that result in a *tao*—a prescriptive doctrine or way. He had a utopian vision for society that was based on the practice of the ancient sage kings. The political theory starts with a belief that political authority is based on the mandate of heaven, so that the legitimate ruler derives authority from heaven's command. The ruler therefore shoulders responsibility for the well-being of the people in the empire. Ideally, the ruler should be a model of good behavior and should appoint others who are models of *te* (virtue) to public prominence.

Confucius died at the age of seventy-three, reportedly having taught a total of three thousand disciples who carried on his teaching.

Mencius

Mencius (c. 372–289 B.C.E.) put forward a different version of Confucianism, stressing *jen* as an *innate* inclination to good behavior that does not need educating. Hsun Tzu (c. 313–c. 238 B.C.E.), on the contrary, argued that all inclinations are shaped by acquired language and other social conventions and forms.

Gender and Religion

Many ambivalent attitudes to women are apparent in traditional Chinese texts. The *Analects* of Confucius are no exception; they reflect patriarchal moral values and have had a formulative influence on Confucian thinking both in China and Japan.

> The Master said, "In one's household it is the women and the small men that are difficult to deal with. If you let them get too close, they become insolent. If you keep them at a distance, they complain." (*Analects* 17:13)

In the Confucian social order, human relationships tended to become hierarchical so that they were fixed and rigid. Under this construct, women increasingly became subordinate. A woman's sacred duty was to provide a male heir, thus ensuring the continuation of the ancestral cult. In the case of childlessness or the birth of only a daughter, men had the opportunity of taking other wives. In the Three Obediences, a woman is to obey her father while at home, her husband when married, and her son if widowed. Confucius wanted men to become gentlemen (*chun tzu*) through the cultivation of virtue (*jen*), which comes through practicing various rites (*li*). He said very little about women, however, preferring to accept the cultural norms of his day. Women should be wives or concubines, and they should learn to be good wives and how to care for their parents:

> When it (the child) was able to speak, a boy (was taught to) respond boldly and clearly; a girl submissively and low. The former was fitted with a girdle of leather; the latter, with one of silk. . . .
>
> A girl at the age of ten ceased to go out (from the women's apartments). Her governess taught her (the arts of) pleasing speech and manners, to be docile and obedient . . . to learn (all) women's work, how to furnish garments. . . . At fifteen, she assumed the hair-pin; at twenty, she was married, or if there were occasion (for the delay), at twenty-three. If there were the betrothal rites, she became a wife; and if she went without these, a concubine. . . . (*The Book of Rites,* from *The Texts of Confucianism, Sacred Books of the East,* vol. 27, trans. James Legge, ed. F. Max Muller [Oxford: Clarendon Press, 1885], 476–79.)

In Chinese popular religion a woman dying before she is married is still a serious matter. This belief shows itself in that the majority of displeased ghosts are women whose lower status and all the accompanying feelings are seen to carry over into the supernatural order of the afterlife. One of the ways to rectify this situation is to have a ghost marriage. In a ghost marriage, the woman's spirit is married either to another spirit or to a living man. The ceremony is performed using paper models of the ghosts. The woman's spirit tablet is then placed on the ancestral altar of the family into which she is marrying. This is a formal arrangement only. If the groom is a living man, he is free to marry in the normal way after the ceremony. Ghost marriages still happen in Hong Kong, Taiwan, and the New Territories.

Scripture

Confucius edited, compiled, or wrote the *Five Canons*. The *Four Books* were his teachings, compiled by his followers. The *Five Canons* (or *Five Classics*) are:

- *Book of Changes* (*I Ching*)
- *Book of History*, before 650 B.C.E. (*Shu Ching*)
- *Book of Rites* (*Li Chi*)
- *Spring and Autumn* (*Ch'un Ch'iu*)
- *Book of Poetry* (*Shih Ching*)

The *Four Books* are:

- *The Analects* (*Lun Yu*)
- *The Doctrine of the Mean* (*Chung Yung*)
- *The Book of Mencius* (*Meng Tzu*)
- *The Great Learning* (*Ta Hsueh*)

Celebrations and Festivals

Five major festivals in Confucianism are as follows:

- *The New Year Festival*—a time for family ritual, visiting, and special food.
- *Feast of the Night of the First Full Moon*—lanterns are put out and ancestors told of new sons in the family.
- *Ch'ing Ming* (second month, day sixteen)—the dead are honored with offerings.
- *Mid-Autumn Festival*—in praise of the goddess moon.
- *Winter Festival* (eleventh month, day eleven)—a family occasion.

Neo-Confucianism

What has been termed the neo-Confucian movement is the later development of Confucian thought, which avoided both extensive rationalism and the appeal of superstitions and omens and instead drew the riches of spiritual belief into mainstream philosophy—unlike the West, where spirituality (both ascetic and mystical) has never had a central place in mainstream philosophy. This new expression of Confucian thought was based on a smaller group of classical texts that were reinterpreted in response to Buddhist challenges. It was reformulated by the neo-Confucian philosophers of the Sung dynasty.

UNIT 7:10 ZOROASTRIANISM

> *In the name of God. I praise and invoke the creator Ormazd, the radiant, glorious, omniscient, maker, lord of lords, king over all kings, watchful, creator of the universe, giver of daily bread, powerful, strong, eternal, forgiver, merciful, loving, mighty, wise,*

holy, and nourisher. May (his) just kingdom be imperishable. May the majesty and glory of Ormazd, the beneficent lord, increase. (Hither) may come the immortal, radiant, swift-horsed Sun. Of all sins . . . I repent.

Khwarshed Niyayesh, "Litany to the Sun"

Zoroastrianism developed in Iran from about the sixth century B.C.E. and is generally ascribed to Zoroaster (Zarathustra). The religion of ancient Iran was derived from that of the ancient Indo-Europeans, or Aryans. The language of the earliest Zoroastrian writings is close to that of the Indian *Vedas*, and some of the mythology is recognizably the same. The date of Zoroaster's birth had been accepted as about 600 B.C.E. but Western scholars more recently place it as early as 1200 B.C.E. or even earlier. The major piece of documentary evidence associated with him is the text of his *Divine Songs*, the *Gathas*, and historians have tried to reconstruct Zarathustra's life mainly from this one source. This task has proved difficult, however, because the text is poetry describing Zarathustra's spiritual philosophy, not a historical account of his life. Such uncertainty has left fertile soil for various mythologies to surround his life. Nevertheless, scholars have pieced together information from his writings that give us access to the life and teaching of a profound spiritual master.

Zoroaster was probably the son of a pagan priest, living in Persia. At the age of thirty he had a religious experience of the one god, Ahura Mazda ("the Wise Lord"), that led to his proclamation of a prophetic message based on monotheism, the reform of sacrificial practice, and personal responsibility in religion.

Zoroaster protested against what was false and cruel in religion. He suffered persecution, partly because, as we shall see, he rejected as demonic the *daevas* ("shining ones"), a group of gods in ancient Persia. His teaching brought opposition from the priests at the time.

Later tradition reports a more detailed account of his life, in which evil forces tried to destroy him as a baby—through cattle stampeding and wolves and evil priests—but Ahura saved him from them all. During his ministry, evil priests imprisoned him, but Zoroaster persuaded a local king of the truth by performing miracles and healing the king's favorite horse. The king therefore endorsed and supported the prophet's religion, which then spread. Tradition says that Zoroaster was seventy-seven years old when he was killed by invaders when worshiping at the altar.

For Zoroastrians, the prophet Zoroaster is the true and unyielding opponent of all that is evil, the one who carries the great revelation from God.

The Spread of Zoroastrianism

By the seventh century B.C.E. Zoroastrianism had spread. When Cyrus the Great established the Persian Empire in the sixth century B.C.E., Zoroastrianism became the state religion. It also became the religion of the pre-Islamic Iranian empires of the Achaemenids (559–331 B.C.E.), the Parthians (mid-second century B.C.E.–224 C.E.), and the Sasanians (224–652 C.E.). The Zoroastrian concepts of the One God, good vs. evil, beneficent angels (*Amesha Spentas*), humanity's place in the universal fight, immortality of the soul (*urvan*), a savior (*Saoshyant*) born of a virgin, and personal and collective final judgment influenced Jewish, Christian, and Muslim thought. In time, however, in the seventh century C.E., Muslim conquest marked a steady decline of the Zoroastrian faith and eventually persecution (tenth century), the result of which caused the majority of Zoroastrians to migrate to India, where they became known as the Parsis (people from Persia). In Iran in the early twentieth century, Zoroastrianism experienced a revival and renewal due largely to the untiring work of Manekji Limji Hataria and dedicated others. As human rights conditions improved for Zoroastrians in Iran, they began to migrate back to Tehran. When the Islamic Republic under Ayatollah Khomeini came to power in 1979, many Zoroastrians feared for their future and the out-migration process started once again—to Australia, Canada, Britain, and especially the United States.

God

The deeds which I shall do and those which I have done
ere now,
And the things which are precious to the eye, through Good
Mind,
The light of the sun, the sparkling dawn of the days,
All this is for your praise, O Wise Lord, as righteousness!

Avesta, *Yasna* 50.10

In this text from the *Yasna*, there is only one true Creator, the Lord Ahura Mazda. Zarathustra proclaimed the worship of Ahura Mazda, who is uncreated, eternal, and omniscient, and who created a good world consisting of seven elements of creation: the sky, waters, earth, plants, cattle, humans, and fire.

Other Zoroastrian texts indicate dualistic accounts of creation, attributing diseases and other natural evils to the creations of the Evil One (*Yasna* 30.3–5).

This do I ask, O Lord, reveal unto me the truth!
Who is the first begetter, father of the Cosmic Law?
Who assigned orbit to the sun and the stars?
Who causes the moon to wax and again to wane?
Who other than Thee? This and else I wish to know!

Who is the upholder of the earth and of the sky?
Who prevents them from falling down?
Who maintains the waters and also the plants?
Who yoked speed to winds and clouds?
Who is the creator of the creatures?
Who is the architect of light and darkness?

Who created sleep and wakefulness?
By whom exists dawn, mid-day and night,
Which monitor the duties of men?
Avesta, *Yasna* 44.3–5

The creative aspect of Ahura Mazda is *Spenta Mainyu*. In addition, there are emanations of Ahura Mazda (*Amesa Spentas*), the most important being six heavenly forces that are created by Ahura and which each represent an aspect of Ahura while also being attributes of good Zoroastrians. The *Amesa Spentas* ("Bounteous Immortals") therefore provide a way by which worshipers can approach Ahura and likewise a means of Ahura approaching those who worship him. They are:

- *Vohu Mana*, the Good Mind who appeared to Zoroaster in his visions to lead him into the divine presence—the personification of Wisdom.
- *Khshathra*, "Realm Power." The personification of Ahura's power on earth to overcome evil and help the poor and defenseless; the guardian of sky.
- *Armaiti*, "Proper Mind" or Devotion. Represented in the feminine, the personification of obedience, harmony, and worship; the guardian of earth.
- *Haurvatat*, "Completeness/Health"; the guardian of water. *Ameretat*, "Immortality"; the guardian of plants. These two are always mentioned together in the writings. Both are feminine and both represent what salvation means to the individual person.
- Fire (*Atar* or *Adur/Adar*) is used in many Zoroastrian ceremonies and is believed to be a sacred force that is the source of all energy and the symbol of truth and righteousness. The Parsis, a branch of Zoroastrianism, are fire worshipers. Zoroastrians generally worship natural objects, such as the sun and fire.

Dualism and Belief in Evil

Zoroastrianism is dualistic in that it poses the forces of God against those of Evil. Ahura Mazda is opposed by an equal: an uncreated entity called Angra Mainyu (the "Destructive Spirit"), who created both life and nonlife and who is characterized by the doing of anger, greed, jealousy, and destruction in the world. The demonic forces of Angra Mainyu are the *daevas* (e.g., forces of war, destruction, fury); their counterparts are the ahuras. The ahuras are epitomized as good in Zoroastianism, in contrast to later Hindu thought, where they are seen as evil.

Salvation and Eschatology

The eternal consequences of personal choice are found in Zoroaster's teaching of individual judgment. Sins are not washed away but rather balanced out.

Traditional Zoroastrians believe that the righteous of every religion go to heaven, all religions are equal, and converting to another faith is therefore folly. Conversion goes against the Master Law of Ereta (righteousness) itself, because God has given us birth in our respective religions, to adore him in them, and not to mistrust his judgment by rebelling and converting to another faith. Zorastrians pray to God to cause all creatures, not just the wise man, to achieve their destiny in God's Kingdom.

> We will make offering unto thee with worship, O Lord, and to the Right, That you may achieve through Good Mind the destiny of all creatures in the Dominion. For the salvation of the man of insight among such as you, O Wise One, will hold good for everyone. (Avesta, *Yasna* 34.3)

A fundamental teaching of the prophet Zoroaster is the belief in the beginning and ending of the world. Three saviors will appear at the end of time. Equally important is the human role at the end of time because the ethical choices of each person define the final outcome of the battle between the forces of good and evil. The final battle is the first time that human beings have a role in the cosmic struggle. The final result is not predetermined, but the salvation of the world is tied up with the good use of reason and insight that each individual makes. Later Zoroastrian teaching predicted the outcome that the good would have eternal life and evil would be annihilated.

The Saoshaynt

A belief in the coming of the Saoshyant (Savior) has sustained the Zoroastrian religion through the centuries. Zoroastrians claim they are the first religion to proclaim that Ahura Mazda will send the Saoshyant, who will be born of a virgin and inaugurate the final spiritual battle between the forces of good and evil, resulting in evil's utter destruction. At that point the resurrection of the dead will take place and the world will be purged by molten metal, in which the righteous will wade as if through warm milk, and the evil will be scalded. The final judgment of all souls will commence at the hands of Ahura Mazda the Judge (*Davar*). All sinners will be punished, then forgiven, and humanity will be made immortal and free from hunger, thirst, poverty, old age, disease, and death. The world will be made perfect once again, as it was before the onslaught of the evil one. This belief is called *Frasho-kereti* ("making fresh") or the Renovation, brought on by the will of Ahura Mazda, the Frashogar.

Death

Traditional Zoroastrian funeral services include the washing of the corpse; putting the *sudre* (the white undershirt), *kusti* (a long, hollow, woven wool cord), and a white sheet over the corpse; and relatives and friends paying their last respects. According to the Vendidad—the Zoroastrian purity rules—*Dakhma-nashini* is the only method of corpse destruction. The dead body is placed in the stone-enclosed Dakhma and is destroyed, by the flesh-eating birds or the rays of the sun. This process is considered the most spiritually powerful method of disposing of the dead and was commanded by Ahura Mazda to Zaratustra. Zoroastrians argue that *Dakhma-nashini* is also very hygienic and ecologically sound, because it prevents the world from being spiritually or materially polluted by decaying dead matter. The dreaded impure state of *Nasu* resides in the corpse after death, so that the body is only touchable by the Nassesalars (corpse-bearers), who may then be purified by ritual means.

On the third and fourth days after death, prayers are offered for the safe passage of the soul.

Zoroastrians do not believe in reincarnation. Hell is a temporary place of suffering for sinners after death. When evil is finally defeated (at Frashegird), the souls of sinners will be released from hell and will be purified by the ordeal of molten metal. They will then join the congregation of God and the saints.

The belief is that after death the soul is lead by conscience (the *daena*), which is pictured as a maiden, to the Chinvat Bridge, the Bridge of Judgment. For people whose thoughts and actions are predominantly good, safe passage is provided to a wonderful existence, a place of song. The wicked fall from the bridge and land in the "House of the Lie," which is a foul place with inferior food, awful smells, and prolonged torment (*Yasna* 31.20, 49.11).

For people for whom good and wickedness are balanced, the soul passes into an intermediate state and remains there until the day of judgment. Zorastrians believe in the resurrection of the body. The creator Ormazd will triumph ultimately, at which point one undivided kingdom of God in heaven and on earth will be in place.

Moral Action

The central belief behind Zoroastrian ethics is the focus on human free will as reflected in the motto, "Good thoughts, Good words, Good actions."

> I profess myself a Mazda-worshipper, a Zoroastrian, having vowed it and professed it. I pledge myself to the well-thought thought, I pledge myself to the well-spoken word, I pledge myself to the well-done action. (Yasna 12, The Zoroastrian Creed. [Translation by J. H. Peterson, 1996–97].)

Zoroaster taught the existence of a higher moral plane where virtue is accrued by good thoughts and conduct rather than by sacrifice. The good works of each person are entered into the book of life as credits, and bad works as debits. Moral action is determined by the divine word:

> Then do I proclaim what the Most Beneficent spoke to me,
> The Words to be heeded, which are best for mortals:

> Those who shall give hearing and reverence
> Shall attain unto Perfection and Immortality
> By the deeds of good spirit of the Lord of Wisdom!
>
> Avesta, *Yasna* 45.5

Strong moral injunctions are written in the Verdidad against the acts of homosexuality and prostitution.

Prayer and Worship

In modern Zoroastrianism the *dastur* (priest) is sought out for guidance and direction on religious matters. The dastur must, above all, keep himself in a state of moral and physical purity in order to perform rituals that generate ritual power and invoke the heavenly forces.

Fire temples and rituals of the *Yasna* are considered sacred and necessary for the religion. The Nirang-din ceremony, which creates the Holy Nirang, forms the foundation of many other sacred rituals that when performed increase the power of good in this world and decrease the power of evil.

The *sudre/kusti* prayers are one of only two compulsory religious duties. They are part of the initiation ceremony called the *Naujote*. The other compulsory duty is to observe the *gahambar* (festivals).

The *sudre* is like a vest made of cotton and is worn all the time next to the skin. It is white to symbolize purity, and a small pocket is placed at the front of the neckline so that the believer can store up good thoughts, words, and deeds. The *kusti* is a long wool cord that is tied around the waist. At the beginning of prayer the cord is untied, and the worshiper holds it in both hands in front of the body while facing the source of light. Prayers are then said that reject evil (Angra Mainyu) and affirm allegiance to Ahura Mazda. As the prayers are said, the initiate ties knots at the back and at the front and vows to practice good thoughts, good words, and good deeds.

The *Fravarane* is a central Zoroastrian prayer that commences with the words, *"Come to my aid, O Mazda! I profess myself a worshiper of Mazda, I am a Zoroastrian worshiper of Mazda."*

Each worship day is divided into five Gah or Geh (times):

- *Havan* (from sunrise to noon)
- *Rapithwan* (from noon until 3 P.M.)
- *Uziren* (from 3 P.M. to sunset)
- *Aiwisruthrem* (from sunset to midnight)
- *Ushahen* (from midnight to sunrise)

The main rite is the *yasna*, which is performed daily in fire temples by a chief priest, who is assisted by another. Fire is the major purifying element in Zoroastrianism, and the *yasna* is an elaborate cosmic purification rite.

Gender and Religion

The Avesta—the collection of Zoroastrian sacred texts—has no creation myth to tell how the first man and woman were created, simply saying that Ahura Mazda created, among other things, the living world of mankind and other animals. With the advent of Zarathustra, the position of woman in society emerged more clearly. The Gathas (one of the Zoroastrian sacred texts) and supplementary texts in the Gathic dialect are explicit on the subject:

> To those who make the right choice and join the Good Religion, he says: "Wise God, whoever, man or woman, shall give me what You know to be best in life—rewards for righteousness, power through good mind—I shall accompany him and her in glorifying such as You are, and shall, with them all, cross over the sorting bridge." (Gathas Song 11; Yasna 46.10)

> We venerate the righteous woman who is good in thoughts, words, and deeds, who is well-educated, is an authority on religious affairs, is progressively serene, and is like the women who belong to the Wise God.
>
> We venerate the righteous man who is good in thoughts, words, and deeds, who knows well the religion he has chosen, and who does not know blind following.
>
> It is these people who, with their actions, promote the world though righteousness. (Aiwisruthrem Gah 9 and Vispered 3.4)

In Zoroastrianism, religious responsibilities, including initiation, are the same for men and women. Women have additional responsibility because of the purity laws. Improper contact with a corpse, menstruation, and stillbirth are considered major pollutants. The Vendidad is mostly devoted to pollution and purification rites and include the concept of menstrual seclusion: a woman is in a state of impurity during menstruation and must stay away from her husband and all religious objects, including the household fire. A menstruating woman's food was rationed, and no one could come into contact with her. At the end of menstruation, she had to wash herself ritually with bovine urine, sand, and water to regain purified status and resume normal social contacts. A woman with a stillborn child had to undergo a more rigorous purification rite over a longer period (Vendidad 5.45–56, 16.1–12). Cohabitation with a menstruating women brought physical punishment of 60 lashes for the first offense, 100 for the second, 140 for the third, and 180 for the fourth (Vendidad 16.14–16).

The Zoroastrian Gathic doctrine puts men and women on fully equal status in all religious and social affairs. In the post-Gathic period, however, women were not endowed with as high a status, at least by certain factions of the very late Avestan people. The Avesta speaks about the decline of women in favor of an egocentric man of authority, but never to a severe degree. Taboos could not rob her of her given position in the scriptures. There is no indication in the Avesta that suggests the inferior status of women, and even the Vendidad with its emphasis on seclusion does not make any negative remarks about women per se.

Mysticism

According to the historian Herodotus, the magi were originally one of six Median tribes who governed all ritual activity, i.e. sacrifices. During the Achaemenid era, when Zoroastrianism was the state religion, Babylon was the central administrative center, and the magi very likely became involved with a number of mystical beliefs (hence the word "magic") and astrology.

A modern example of the mystical tradition in Zoroastrianism came in the late nineteenth and early twentieth centuries when a Parsis called Behraqmshah Shroff (1857–1927) sought to reinvigorate traditional practices in terms of theosophy and its occult interpretations. He claimed to have been taken by a group of nomadic secret Zoroastrians to caves in the Persian mountains, where he was shown ancient treasures and teachings. When he returned he was silent for thirty years, after which he taught his followers *Ilm-I-Kshnoom*, "The Path of Knowledge." Along with Theosophy, this movement believes in vegetarianism and abstention from alcohol, rebirth, personal aura, and the occult power of prayers recited in the sacred language.

Scriptures

All the Zoroastrian scriptures are sacred, including the Gathas, Yashts, and the Vendidad. They are prayed aloud in the fire temples before the sacred fire, and they are believed to have immense spiritual power. Their very utterance in the sacred Avestan language serves to further righteousness and fight evil.

The Gathas, together with the vast Avestan literature, suffered two major catastrophes. The first catastrophe occurred when the last Achaemenid emperor Darius was defeated and Alexander the Great burned the Zoroastrian scriptures. Again in 650 C.E., the restored scriptures were destroyed by invading Arabs. The Gathas that the Zoroastrians have now inherited are the fragmented and truncated parts of the original extensive texts. The Zoroastrian scriptures are known collectively as the Avesta and contain

> The *Yasna*—hymns of Zarathustra and liturgical texts, which contain the *Gathas,* seventeen songs attributed to Zoroaster and believed to be the oldest part of the Avesta
>
> The *Yashts*—hymns of praise and prayers of the laity
>
> The *Vendidad*—purity rules and laws
>
> The *Vispered* (cult)

Nyāyishu and *Gah* (prayers)

Khorda (daily prayers)

Hadhokht Nask (Book of Scriptures)

Nirangistan (cultic regulations)

UNIT 7:11 JAINISM

Whoever conquers mind and passion, and acts with true austerity, shines like a fire into which the oblation has been poured.

Isibhasiyaim 29.17

The unwise sleep, the sages always wake. Know, that in this world the (cause of) misery brings forth evil consequences! Knowing the course of the world, one should cease from violent acts. He who correctly possesses these (sensual perceptions), viz. sounds, and colours, and smells, and tastes, and touches, who self-possessed, wise, just, chaste, with right comprehension understands the world, he is to be called a sage, one who knows the law, and righteous. He knows the connection of the whirl (of births) and the current (of sensation with love and hate). Not minding heat and cold, equanimous against pleasure and pain, the Nirgrantha does not feel the austerity of penance. Waking and free from hostility, a wise man, thou liberatest (thyself and others) from the miseries.

Akaranga Sutra, *Jaina Sutras*. Trans. Hermann Jacobi, from *Sacred Books of the East*, vol. 22, 1884.

The word *Jain* derives from the title "Jina," meaning spiritual victor. Jainism is an ancient Indian religion that, according to Jain tradition, dates back into prehistory. It arose in the sixth century B.C.E. in protest against the ritualism of Hinduism and the authority of the Vedas. Jains see Mahavira as the last of twenty-four founders, or tirthankaras, who through spiritual struggle are believed to have attained omniscience or perfect gnosis (*kevala jnana*).

Mahavira (599–527 B.C.E.) was a prince in Bihar, India. His original name was Vardhtmana, and he was a contemporary of the Buddha. At the age of thirty, after the death of his parents, he left his family and royal household, gave up his worldly possessions—including clothing—and became a monk. He spent the next twelve years in deep silence and meditation to conquer his desires and feelings, improve his speech, and clear his mind. He practiced nudity and also what was to become the Great Vows (*mahavrata*) of Jainism: to renounce killing, lying, stealing, sexual activity, and accumulating worldly goods. He went without food for long periods. He carefully avoided harming or annoying other living beings, including animals, birds, and plants.

At the end of this period, Mahavira reached complete omniscience or perfect gnosis (*keval jnana*) and became a *jina*. Two traditions exist about this state: the *kevalin* is (1) free from all the normal constraints of human nature (e.g., excretion, indigestion), which (2) makes him or her free from the state of impurity that accompanies them. After the attainment of perfect gnosis, the *jina* (conqueror) began to spread the truth.

Mahavira spent the next thirty years traveling on bare feet around India, teaching the path of purification and attracting people from all walks of life, rich and poor, princes and priests, touchables and untouchables. He organized his followers into a fourfold order:

- monks (*Sadhu*)
- nuns (*Sadhvi*)
- laymen (*Shravak*)
- laywomen (*Shravika*)

Later on they became known as Jains.

The essence of Mahavira's teaching is how one can attain freedom from the cycle of birth, life, pain, misery, and death, and thus achieve the permanent blissful state of one's self. This state is also known as liberation, nirvana, absolute freedom, or *moksha*.

According to tradition, Mahavira died at age seventy-two and passed to *moksha* ("liberation"), becoming a Siddha: a pure consciousness, a liberated soul, living forever in a state of complete bliss. Tradition claims that Mahavira left 14,000 monks, 36,000 nuns, 159,000 laymen, and 318,000 laywomen to spread his teaching.

God

Jainism believes in Godhood but does not believe God to be the first cause. This religion deifies a large pantheon of godlings, celestials, or angels who are superhuman, just like the Hindu gods. These beings are also considered mortal, just like humans. Jain philosophy and belief differs from traditional Hindu belief in rejecting the idea of God, the Vedas, and caste. Mahavira was radical in the spiritual field in that he upheld the concept of karma in place of a creator God.

Jainism conceives of karma as a substance rather than a process. The individual's soul-substance (*jiva*) mingles with karmic substance to produce each individual person. All past and present actions produce karmic principles that weigh you down and bind you to endless rebirth. In this view, humanity creates its own destiny and rises only by his or her own efforts and not by the grace of an external agency. God is devoid of attachment, hence there is no need for him to create this universe.

Jains believe that the universe and all its substances or entities are eternal. As no one created the universe, no one needs to manage the affairs of the universe, which runs on its own accord by its own cosmic laws. The universe exists as a series of layers, both heavens and hells, with no beginning and no ending in place or in time. The universe consists of

- *The supreme abode*—located at the top of the universe, where Siddha, the liberated souls, live.
- *The upper world*—thirty heavens where celestial beings live.
- *The middle world*—the earth and the rest of the universe.
- *The nether world*—seven hells with various levels of anguish and punishments.
- *The Nigoda*, or base—where the lowest forms of life reside.
- *Universe space*—layers of clouds that surround the upper world.
- *Space beyond*—an infinite volume without soul, matter, time, medium of motion, or medium of rest.

Everyone is bound within the universe by one's karma (the accumulated good and evil that one has done). *Moksha* (liberation from an endless succession of lives through reincarnation) is achieved by enlightenment, which can be attained only through asceticism. When a person destroys all karmas, that person becomes omniscient and omnipotent, a god of Jain religion. Hence Jains do not believe in one God. In Jain religion, gods are innumerable and the number continuously increases as more living beings attain liberation.

Salvation, Death, and Afterlife

Jain philosophy fundamentally distinguishes living and nonliving matter. Living souls are divided into bound and liberated. Nonliving matter consists of karman, which are very fine particles that enter a soul and produce changes in it, thus causing its bondage. This influx of karman is caused by activity and has to be burned off by experience. Karmans are of infinitely numerous varieties and account for all distinctions noted in the world. Through the practice of nonattachment, an individual prevents the influx of further karmans and escapes from the bonds of action. A soul (thought of as having the same size as its body) at liberation has lost the matter that weights it down and thus ascends to the top of the universe, where it remains forever.

In Jainism salvation comes only from the self within, and from the teachings and examples of the twenty-four tirthankaras or buddhas and bodhisattvas. Until that time, all beings are carried along in the current of their actions, born again and again to reap the fruit of their own acts.

Souls have no beginning or ending in Jainism; they are eternally individual. Jainism classifies souls into three categories:

- Souls not yet evolved
- Souls in a process of evolution

- Souls that are free, that have achieved perfection and who are thus free from rebirth

Numerous temples have been built celebrating the perfected souls; a notable example is the temple at Mount Abu in Rajasthan.

The ultimate purpose of all life and activity is to realize the free and blissful state of our true being. Following the Jain faith should result in removing all bondages (karmas) in the process of purifying the soul.

> [The soul] cannot be taken from its place of deposit; it does not perish anywhere by fire; if kings of surpassing grandeur are angry they cannot take it away; and therefore what any man should provide for his children as a legacy is learning. Other things are not real wealth. (*Naladiyar* 134)

While traveling on the path of spiritual progress, a person destroys all eight of these types of karmas in the following sequence, thus attaining liberation:

1. *Mohaniya* (delusion)
2. *Jnana-varaniya* (knowledge)
3. *Darasna-varaniya* (vision)
4. *Antaraya* (natural qualities)
5. *Nama* (body)
6. *Ayu* (life span)
7. *Gotra* (social standing)
8. *Vedniya* (pleasure and pain of the body)

Moral Action

The first step in the process of self-realization is to discard superstitious beliefs and to adopt a rational attitude in life. The Three Jewels (*ratna-traya*) that offer a graduated pathway towards *moksha* (release) are right belief, right knowledge, and right conduct.

Over time the influx of new karmic particles can be stopped and old ones can be eliminated through various disciplines and ascetic practices. Through one's deeds alone—not by caste (see Hinduism, unit 7:1)—is spiritual progress made:

> By deeds, not by birth, is one a brahmin. By deeds one is a ksatriya, by deeds is one a vaishya, and by deeds is one a shudra. (Uttaradhyayana Sutra 25.3)

Each believer can be guided by the examples of five benevolent personalities (*panch parameshthi*), which can be categorized as follows:

- Supreme human beings (*arihantas*). *Arihantas* are human beings who, like Mahavira, have attained *keval jnana*. At the end of their human life, they will be totally liberated and will become *siddhas*.

- Pure or perfect souls (*siddhas*)
- Master teachers (*acharyas*)
- Scholarly monks (*upadhyayas*)
- Ascetics (*sadhus*)

At the heart of Jainism lies a radical ascetic ethic based on the *anuvratas* (five life-long minor vows) that are followed religiously by the monks and nuns and to which the laity aspire to the best of their ability.

The central teaching of Jainism, which represents the first of these vows, is *ahimsa* (nonviolence). Jain philosophy holds that every thing has a soul. Jain philosophy further believes in a gradation of beings, from those with five senses down to those with only one sense. At this point Jainism adopts a radical break from the practice of Hindu sacrifices. Jainism aspires to avoiding all harm, including mental harm, to even the smallest being. Adherents must exercise extreme caution in all activity. Jain monks often wear cloth over their mouths to avoid unwittingly killing anything by breathing it in, and floors are kept meticulously clean to avert the danger of stepping on any living being. However, Jains believe that violent intentions or even violent thoughts are much more serious.

Aside from ahisma, the other four vows of Jainism are

- *Satya*—speaking the truth
- *Asteya*—not taking anything that has not been given
- *Brahmacharya*—chastity or abstinence of sexual activity outside of marriage
- *Aparigraha*—detachment from places, possessions, and things.

Jains also follow fruitarianism, the practice of only eating that which will not kill the plant or animal from which it is taken, e.g., milk, fruit, nuts.

The Path to *Moksha*: Nuns and Monks

The path to liberation begins when a Jain renounces the life of the home in order to become a *sadhu* (monk) or *sadhvi* (nun). They then take the *mahavratas* (the "great vows"), a stricter form of the *anuvratas*. Jains offer *puja* ("worship") at their home three times daily: before dawn, at sunset, and at night.

Jainism is unique in allowing the spiritually advanced to hasten their own death by certain practices (principally fasting). According to Jainist ethics, a monk who has practiced twelve years of severe asceticism, or who has found after long trial that he cannot keep his lower nature in control, may hasten his end by suicide.

Lay householders are expected to limit themselves by refraining from eating meat, certain fruits, or honey, or from drinking wine.

Jainism lays great emphasis on observing five rules of conduct (*Samitis*) and three rules of avoidance of misconduct (*Guptis*). *Samitis* purify the actions and make them faultless, while *Guptis* are prohibitions against sinful activities of mind, speech, and body. Collectively all eight virtues are known as *Ashta Pravachan Mata*. The five *Samitis* are

1. *Iriya Samiti*—regulation of walking
2. *Bhasa Samiti*—regulation of speaking
3. *Esnna Samiti*—regulation of begging
4. *Adana Nikshepana Samiti*—regulation of taking or keeping
5. *Utsarga Samiti*—regulation of disposal

A person must be careful in walking, sitting, standing, and lying down. He or she must speak only gentle, sweet, and pure speech, and be careful in placing and removing articles. A person must be clean and should not make oneself instrumental in the growth or death of germs and insects. The Jainist ascetic allows himself to be bitten by gnats and mosquitoes rather than risk their destruction by brushing them away. Hospitals for animals have been a prominent feature of Jainist benevolence, even to the extent that in 1834 there existed in Kutch a temple hospital which supported five thousand rats.

The three *Guptis* are

1. *Mana Gupti*—regulation of mind. Jains guard against impure thoughts such as anger, hate, and greed. They are taught to always be forgiving and devote the mind to spiritual meditation.
2. *Vachana Gupti*—regulation of speech. Jains guard their speech to avoid harsh, harmful, careless, foul, senseless, or bad language.
3. *Kaya Gupti*—regulation of bodily activity. Jains regulate the movement of their bodies, so others are not hurt. They walk with an eye on the path below so as not to harm or kill an innocent life, such as ants or other creatures. For this reason, a Jain should not daydream while doing any activity.

While Jains are taught to adhere to the call upon self-restraint and self-reliance, they also seek help from a large number of deities known as *yakshas* or *yakshines*. These deities are evoked to help assist in worldly matters. One example is Ambika, the mother-goddess of Jainism who is the patron deity of material prosperity and childbirth and the protector of women. Images of goddesses like Ambika adorn the temples to the tirthankaras and are usually connected with the supreme beings to whom the temples are dedicated.

Prayer

Meditation forms an integral part of Jain life. Jains practice a form of meditation known as *Samayika*, which focuses on establishing a peaceful state of mind.

Worship in the home as well as in temples is also important. Jain homes usually have wooden shrines that are modeled after the stone temples. Jain worship may involve the chanting of mantras or gazing upon an image of one of the gods (*puja*). More elaborate rituals in Jain worship involve the decoration or anointing of images. An important pilgrimage center for Jains in Maharashtra is Bahubali, where the Svetambaras have a temple on top of a hill, and the Digambaras have a temple lower down in which there is a giant figure of Shree Bahubali, the son of the first prophet. Kunthalgiri near Osmanabad has a Digambara Jain temple and the shrine of Shree Shantisagar Maharaj. (Digambaras and Svetambaras are described more later in this unit.)

The Namaskar Mantra is a revered prayer in Jainism in reverance of the five holy beings. The holy beings and their prayers are as follows:

- *Namo Arihantanam*: "I bow to the *arithantas*, the ever-perfect spiritual victors."
- *Namo Siddhanam*: "I bow to the *siddhas*, the liberated souls."
- *Namo Ayariyanam*: "I bow to *acharyas*, the leaders of the Jain order."
- *Namo Uvajjayanam*: "I bow to *upadhyayas*, the learned preceptors."
- *Namo Loe Savva Sahunam*: "I bow to all saints and sages everywhere in the world. These five obeisances erase all sins; amongst all that is auspicious, this is the foremost."

Gender and Religion

Jain texts point to beliefs in sexual equality and the belief that a person's deeds determine their position in society.

> The Law is that which leads to welfare and salvation. It forms conduct and character distinguished by the sense of equality among all beings. (*Somadeva, Nitivakyamrita* 1.1)

Digambara Jains, however, believe women cannot attain nirvana or heaven. The Svetambara believe that women can attain Nirvana.

Mysticism

At its inception, Jainism was earthed in the experience of the mystical through Mahavira, "The Great Hero." The extent of Jain mystical doctrines can be appreciated by studying their intricate teachings. For instance, they believe universal life is composed of an infinite number of interacting particles, each particle being in essence a *jiva* or "life"—an eternal and intrinsically individual consciousness/life that embodies karmic vehicles of its own making.

The Jains often compare the self to gold, which may be shaped, melted, and reshaped in a hundred forms without any decline in brilliance and malleability. In a similar fashion, the self loses none of its essential characteristics as it manifests itself, in a continuous flow, in and through myriad and ever-progressive forms/bodies.

Scriptures

About sixty texts—known as the Shruta, Agamas, or Siddhanta (doctrine)—contain the teachings of Mahavira and other tirthankaras, mostly written in the ancient language of Ardhamagadhi. The Purvas are believed to include oral traditions of the previous tirthankaras. Digambara Jains see some of this material as the basis for the Shat Khanda-Agama (the Scripture in Six Parts), while Svetambara Jains believe this material to have been lost. According to Digambara tradition, the twelve books of the Angas, based on the teachings of Mahavira, are no longer available in their original form. Other texts include the Tattvartha Sutra, which is believed by contemporary Jains to sum up the key features of Jain teaching and therefore provide a scheme for Jain education in the modern world.

Diversity in Jainism

Jains fall into two groups: the Sthankwasi, who do not worship idols, and the Murthipujak, who do. The latter group is split into two further groups: the Svetambara and Digambara sects. The Digambara (meaning "nude" or "sky-clad") wear no clothes and believe that absolute nudity is an essential condition for a monk to attain omniscience. Nudity is considered the ultimate detachment from worldly possessions. The Svetambara (meaning "clad in white") wear a loincloth, believing the wearing of clothes to be sometimes necessary and therefore not an impediment to the highest attainments. A further minor schism occurred in 1653 C.E., when the Sthanakavasi broke from the Svetambara to condemn idolatry and temple worship. Both groups disagree on the legitimacy of the other's scriptures, but fundamentally both sects' views on ethics and philosophy are identical.

The Jain community focuses on monastic life, which is supported by lay people. Some sects have nuns, and both nuns and monks take vows to abstain from violence, deceit, theft, and attachment to material things (including sex) and practice the Three Jewels of right belief, right knowledge, and right conduct. Monks take the wandering life seriously, but they seek refuge in monasteries or temples during the rainy season to avoid injuring small creatures that reside in the mud.

The Influence of Jainism

In southern India, Jain converts included King Samprate, ruler of Ujjayini; King Kharavela, who ruled Orrissa; the Ganga Dynasty; as well as the rulers of Karnataka, the Rashtrakutas, the Hoyasala, and the Chalukyas. Jain contribution to art and architecture is noted in carvings and design. One illustration is the colossal statue of Bahubali in Mysore. Considered a "sculptural wonder of the world," it is a fifty-seven foot statue that was chiseled out of solid rock in the tenth century C.E. and is the site of a pilgrimage. The Jain ethic of *ahimsa* gained international recognition through the life and ministry of Mohandas K. Gandhi, who was influenced in his Hindu thinking by a young Jain believer named Raychandbhai Mehta.

The contribution of Jain faith to Indian thought and life has been significant. The central themes of the teachings of Mahavira are nonviolence, nonabsolutism, and nonpossession. The doctrines of nonabsolutism (*anekantavada*) and the many-sidedness of reality have enabled a tolerant stance enabling the Jain minority (estimated at 0.5 percent of the Indian population) to survive in India. Jain doctrine is also amenable to the philosophies of a postmodern world (see this volume's introduction for a discussion of postmodernism).

In the 1970s Jains who had settled in East Africa migrated to Europe as a result of the African political climate.

UNIT 7:12 THE BAHĀ'Ī FAITH

Blessed is the spot, and the house, and the place, and the city, and the heart, and the mountain, and the refuge, and the cave, and the valley, and the land, and the sea, and the island, and the meadow where mention of God hath been made, and His praise glorified.

Bahā'u'llāh

Happy the days that have been consecrated to the remembrance of God, and blessed the hours which have been spent in praise of Him Who is the All-Wise.

Bahā'u'llāh

The Bahā'ī faith has grown at a rapid rate worldwide since its founder Bahā'u'llāh proclaimed that he was the long Expected One in 1863. It is estimated that there are some six million Bahā'īs in the world today. The question arises as to why this historically modern religion has had such appeal. One answer can be found in the familiarity and similarity of the Bahā'ī Faith to other world religions. It is a religion of the book, as is Judaism, Islam, and Christianity, and the prophets of each of these religions is given respect in the Bahā'ī Faith. The overarching theology of Bahā'īsm is the One God who sends messengers to his people throughout the ages. Christians, Jews, and Muslims would all find some common ground of shared theological culture with Bahā'ī beliefs. The Faith, with its eclectic search for truth and peace, also appeals to New Age seekers and their desire for Oneness.

In May 1844, a young Persian by the name of Siyyid 'Alí' Muhammad' (1819–1850) declared that he was the promised Mahdi, the hidden imam of

Shi'ah Islám (see unit 7:6). He assumed the title of The Bāb (Gate) and announced his mission, which was as an independent messenger who was also preparing the way for the coming of another manifestation (messenger) of God, a prophet who would show himself soon.

The followers of the Bāb increased greatly in the early years, as did the persecution of Shi'ah clergy of Iran to destroy the new religion. Some twenty thousand Bábis were eventually put to death for their beliefs. The Bāb himself was imprisoned and executed in July 1850.

Many Bábis were also imprisoned, including Mirza Husayn—'Alí' (1817–1892). 'Alí was the son of a wealthy government minister. In 1853, soon after the Bāb's death, he was imprisoned for several months in Tehran and then exiled to Baghdad. In 1863 'Alí claimed to be the fulfilment of the Bāb's prophecy and thus he was the Bahā'u'llāh, the Glory of God. The majority of the Bābis accepted his claim and became known as Bahā'īs. Soon after the declaration, Bahā'u'llāh was again banished, to Constantinople and other cities in the Ottoman Empire. Finally in 1867, Bahā'u'llāh was exiled for the last time to Akká (Acre) in present-day Israel until his death in 1892.

Before Bahā'u'llāh passed away, he appointed his eldest son, 'Abdu'l-Bahá (1844–1921), to be his successor and the interpreter of his writings. Although he is not considered to be a manifestation of God like the Bāb and Bahā'u'llāh, 'Abdu'l-Bahá's name means "'Servant of Splendor." His decisions are considered divinely guided and his writings (along with the Bāb's and Bahā'u'llāh's) form part of the Bahā'ī sacred scripture. After being released from the prison in Akká, 'Abdu'l-Bahá made several journeys to the West, including a trip to America in 1912.

'Abdu'l-Bahá willed that leadership of the Bahā'ī community was to be passed on to his eldest grandson, Shoghi Effendi (1897–1957), who became the "Guardian" of the Bahā'ī community. Under his leadership the Bahā'ī Faith spread to all corners of the world. He left no children, thus raising the issue of succession. Authority was passed to chief stewards, who had been appointed by Effendi. Some members refused to accept Effendi's authority. After his unexpected death in 1957, controversy developed over his successor. One webmaster (untitled Web site by Robert Wright at members.aol.com/peace144) states that there are now seven faith groups in the world who claim to be the "true" Bahā'ī Faith. Today, the Bahā'ī international headquarters is in the Universal House of Justice in Haifa, Israel. Perhaps the one most distinctive religious concept of the Bahā'ī faith is that of continuous prophecy and that each new age requires a new message. Even Bahā'u'llāh himself is not the last. Bahai itself will be superseded, though not for a thousand years.

The Oneness of God

God in his essence is completely transcendent and unknowable. He is one, and there is one God for all the world. Bahā'īs believe that Eastern and Western religions are really one and the same thing, not different versions of reality. The differences are just the result of looking at God from a different perspective, and no one faith can claim absolute truth.

> There can be no doubt that whatever the peoples of the world, of whatever race or religion, derive their inspiration from one heavenly Source, and are the subjects of one God. The difference between the ordinances under which they abide should be attributed to the varying requirements and exigencies of the age in which they were revealed. All of them, except for a few which are the outcome of human perversity, were ordained of God, and are a reflection of His Will and Purpose. (*Gleanings from the Writings of Bahā'u'llāh* trans. Shoghi Effendi. [Wilmette, Ill.: Bahā'ī Publishing Trust, 1939; 3rd ed. 1976], 111.)

Likewise, all attempts to define God are doomed to fail. Although God is characterized as "He," this is more to conform to linguistic conventions of Arabic. Bahā'u'llāh taught that God is beyond any comparison to human form or gender.

Bahā'īs believe that there is only one God who is the source of all creation. God is transcendent and unknowable. He has sent, however, great prophets to humanity, through which the Holy Spirit has revealed the "Word of God." The Great Manifestations of God up to this time have been:

1. Abraham
2. Moses
3. Krishna
4. Zoroaster
5. Buddha
6. Jesus Christ
7. Mohammad
8. The Bāb
9. Baha'u'llah

> It is not for him to pride himself who loveth his own country, but rather for him who loveth the whole world. The earth is but one country and mankind its citizens. (*Gleanings from the Writings of Bahā'u'llāh*)

Salvation

According to the Bahā'ī scriptures, Satan or the devil is a symbol for the animal side of human nature. This animal side constantly tempts us and keeps us from fulfilling our spiritual potential. Bahā'īs view life as a kind of workshop, where it is possible to develop and perfect the qualities that will be required in the next life. Heaven is conceived of partly as a state of nearness to God, and hell is a state of remoteness from God. Both heaven and hell follow as a natural consequence of the spiritual efforts an individual either makes or does not make. Nevertheless, God desires a universal salvation for all.

> I testify that Thou art the Lord of all creation, and the Educator of all Beings, visible and invisible. I bear witness that Thy power hath encompassed the entire universe, and that the hosts of the earth can never dismay Thee, nor can the dominion of all peoples and nations deter Thee from executing Thy purpose. I confess that Thou hast no desire except the regeneration of the whole world, and the establishment of the unity of its peoples, and the salvation of all them that dwell therein. (*Gleanings from the Writings of Bahā'u'llāh* 115)

Death

Bahā'īs believe that there is life after death but that our knowledge of what it is like is limited. The emphasis is on preparing the soul in this world for its future existence through prayer and meditation and obedience to God's laws. Every person has an immortal soul. Unlike the rest of the created order, the soul is not subject to decomposition. At death, the soul is freed to travel through the spirit world, which is seen as timeless and placeless. The spirit world is an extension of our own universe and is not physically remote or removed from it. After death the soul may pass though many other worlds before it reaches God. Prayers are said for the dead, as these can help departed souls to progress towards God. The concept of reincarnation is rejected.

Moral Action

The Bahā'ī faith focuses on a number of specific issues for the present age, including:

- *The development of international auxiliary language*. Bahā'īs believe that there will eventually be a single world government, to be led by Bahā'īs, and based on the Faith's administrative framework. All children should be taught one universal language (the same for all the world), as well as his or her own national language.
- *Universal education*. If there are insufficient resources to provide education for everybody, then women should be given priority because they are the ones who will influence and educate the next generation.
- *The elimination of all forms of prejudice*. All other religions warrant respect. Bahā'ī teaching, however, disapproves of homosexuality.
- *The abolition of the extremes of wealth and poverty*. Bahā'u'llāh taught that justice was the most beloved of all things. This sense of justice

extends to economic justice, and Bahā'īs strive to eliminate the extremes of wealth and poverty. This is in contrast to promoting egalitarianism. Members of the faith contribute a voluntary wealth tax out of the surplus of their income, which goes to the World Center of the Faith. Gambling and begging are forbidden.

- *Stable family life is emphasized* in the form of monogamous marriage, while divorce is strongly discouraged but permitted after a set "year of waiting." All extramarital sexual relations are forbidden, as are homosexual relationships.

Unlike many other religions, Bahā'īs put forward scientific inquiry as essential to expand human knowledge and deepen their members' faith. They believe that science needs to be guided by spiritual principle so that its applications are beneficial to all humanity.

Prayer

There are no priests or set liturgy in the Bahā'ī faith, and its outlook is democratic.

Bahā'īs are exhorted to pray each day, observe the nine holy days, fast nineteen days a year, and work to abolish prejudice. They regard work as a form of worship and make at least one pilgrimage, if they can, to the Shrine of the Bāb and the houses in which Bahā'u'llāh lived, which are situated near the Bahā'ī world headquarters. Reminiscent of their origins in Shi'ite Islam, Bahā'īs do not consume alcohol.

Bahā'u'llāh and his followers composed many prayers that are thought to be potent.

> Know thou that in every word and movement of the obligatory prayer there are allusions, mysteries and a wisdom that man is unable to comprehend, and letters and scrolls cannot contain. ('Abdu'l-Bahá, *Prayers, Meditation and the Devotional Attitude*, to be recited once in twenty-four hours, at noon.)

> I bear witness, O my God, that Thou hast created me to know Thee and to worship Thee. I testify, at this moment, to my powerlessness and to Thy might, to my poverty and to Thy wealth.
>
> There is none other God but Thee, the Help in Peril, the Self-Subsisting. (Medium obligatory prayer)

Gender and Religion

Men and women are equal, being the "two wings" of humanity. Women can hold positions in the faith but are excluded from serving on its highest religious court, the Universal House of Justice. Other areas reflecting different treatment of women can be noted, such as the prohibition of women on Bahā'ī pilgrimages and the fact that women receive less inheritance. Women's belongings also are seen as belonging to their husbands, unless formal declaration has been made to the contrary.

Mysticism

While in Baghdad, Bahā'u'llāh's written works were primarily concerned with ethical, mystical, and doctrinal themes. During this time he wrote several works, including *Hidden Words*, *Seven Valleys* and *Book of Certitude*. Below are two examples of the depth and mystical quality of his writings.

In the spiritual world that Bahā'u'llāh envisaged, everything is anew and the individual is lost in wonderment. Here the mystical traveler enters a new realm of being:

> Pleasant is the realm of being, wert thou to attain thereto; glorious is the domain of eternity, shouldst thou pass beyond the world of mortality; sweet is the holy ecstasy if thou drinkest of the mystic chalice from the hands of the celestial Youth. Shouldst thou attain this station, thou wouldst be freed from destruction and death, from toil and sin. (Bahā'u'llāh, *Hidden Words*, Persian no. 70.)

The aim is to achieve a spiritual station where the self of the individual vanishes completely, allowing the divine nature to shine out brightly. This station is one of true poverty and absolute nothingness.

> This station is the dying from self and the living in God, the being poor in self and rich in the Desired One. Poverty as here referred to signifieth being poor in the things of the created world, rich in the things of God's world. For when the true lover and devoted friend reacheth to the presence of the Beloved, the sparkling beauty of the Loved One and the fire of the lover's heart will kindle a blaze and burn away all veils and wrappings. Yea, all he hath, from heart to skin, will be set aflame, so that nothing will remain save the Friend. (Bahā'u'llāh, *Seven Valleys*)

Scripture

Bahā'u'llāh devoted the last years of his life to writing. These writings are regarded as revelations from God. Bahā'ī scripture comprises the writings of the Bāb and Bahā'u'llāh, together with the writings of 'Abdu'l-Bahá. Among the better known writings of Bahā'u'llāh are *The Most Holy Book*, *The Book of Certitude*, *Gleanings from the Writings of Bahā'u'llāh*, *The Hidden Words* and *The Seven Valleys*. Many others books of Bahā'ī scripture have also been composed.

Status and Persecution

Bahā'īsm is regarded as heretical by Islamic authorities. About 350,000 Bahā'īs in Iran are under persecution for their religious beliefs. They are regarded as heretics, because of Bahā'u'llāh's claim to be the latest prophet of God. Muhammad, the founder of Islam, declared himself to be the final prophet centuries earlier. Bahā'īs have also been subject to persecution especially for their Western ideology. Bahā'īs claim that the faith is a world religion, but the world's religious scholars disagree as to whether Bahā'īsm can be regarded as a world faith, a new religious movement, or an Islamic sect.

Festivals

The Bahā'īs have a new calendar. The new year begins on March 21, the spring equinox. Other seasonal days of celebration or commemoration are as follows:

April 21 and 29; May 2: Ridvan festival to mark Bahā'u'llāh's public declaration of his mission

May 23: The Bāb's declaration of his mission

May 29: Passing of Bahā'u'llāh

July 9: Martyrdom of the Bāb

October 20: Birth of the Bāb

November 12: Birth of Bahā'u'llāh

Chapter 8
Some Alternative and Indigenous Religions

UNIT 8:1 ELAN VITAL (THE DIVINE LIGHT MISSION)

"Don't make a problem where there's no problem, or then you've got a real problem."

Maharaj Ji

"If you win the rat race, you're still a rat."

Maharaj Ji, www.some-guy.com/quotes/maharaji.html

Elan Vital came from the Hindu Santa Mat (the way of the saints) tradition, a nineteenth-century spiritual movement that developed in Northern India. One of its goals was to instruct the world in a type of yogic meditation technique that was said to connect the devotee to the universal primordial force. This was achieved through meditation on the Holy Name (Word) and on the Divine Light, which pervade everything.

Founding and Development

The Divine Light Mission was founded by Shri Hans Maharaj Ji. He died in 1966 and was succeeded by his youngest son, Prem Pal Singh Rawat who is reported to have said at his funeral, "You have been deceived by maya (illusion): Maharaj Ji is here in your midst: recognize him, worship him and obey him." Maharaj Ji had already become a spiritual adept at the age of six, and at age nine he gave himself the title of Perfect Master at his father's funeral. He was two years later recognized as the new "Perfect Master," an embodiment of God on earth and therefore worthy of veneration. He assumed the title of Maharaj Ji. In 1971 an American who had begun to worship Maharaj Ji invited him to the United States. The same year he also made his first visit to Britain. In Colorado, a number of people were initiated, and the American headquarters of the Mission was established in Denver. After only two years, several hundred centers and over twenty ashrams had been founded, but in November 1973 the Mission suffered the failure of "Millenium '73," which had cost thousands of dollars and had been organized to celebrate the birthday of Maharaj Ji's father and the commencement of a thousand years of peace. The movement is reported to have suffered deep debt and the loss of many people from the movement. Ex-members became critical, and accusations of brainwashing and mind control were levied.

The movement also suffered from family problems. The guru's mother, Mataji, disapproved of his marriage to his twenty-four-year-old secretary Marolyn Johnson in 1974, who presented a challenge to her. Maharaj Ji had claimed that she was the incarnation of the Hindu goddess Durga. Press reports of the day also said his mother disapproved of his lifestyle, which included a number of Rolls-Royces and luxury homes. Mataji accused her son of breaking his Hindu spiritual disciplines, and she took control of the mission in India by replacing him with his oldest brother. In 1975 Maharaj Ji took his family to court. As a result, he was able to control the movement worldwide, except in India, where his brother remained in authority. In the early 1980s Maharaj Ji ordered all ashrams to be disbanded, and he renounced his almost divine status. His teaching had become increasingly universal rather than reflecting Indian religious tradition. After this action, the organization Elan Vital was created to support Maharaj Ji's ongoing teaching of his students on a one-to-one basis and worldwide travel. The instructors ceased to be called *mahatmas*. Today the group maintains a low profile, publishing two newsletters and continuing the initiation rituals.

In its earlier existence Divine Light teaching derived mainly from Hinduism. Maharaj Ji, as the guru, imparted wisdom upon his followers. Devotees practiced *siddha yoga* and sometimes use a T-shaped baragon as an aid to meditation.

In the Divine Light Mission the guru taught that humanity is inherently divine. For people to attain this divinity, they must gain knowledge, which came from the teachings of the Guru Maharaj Ji, who is of the line of Perfect Masters.

Teaching, Beliefs, and Practices

The movement that originally started as the Divine Light Mission is now reformed in its beliefs and teachings. Elan Vital bears little or no similarity to traditional Indian religious concepts such as reincarnation or heaven. The emphasis is on present-tense experience of life in the here and now. At the heart of his teaching, Maharaj Ji believes that great masters such as Krishna, Buddha, Christ, Muhammad, and other lesser masters have all taught what is known as Knowledge.

Maharaj Ji now teaches a simple self-discovery process, involving four simple techniques to turn the senses within and appreciate the joyful basis of existence beyond thoughts and ideas. He denies the criticism that his teachings represent instant gratification, but he sees it instead as an ongoing learning process that can enrich an individual's life.

The four secret meditation procedures involved in the journey to Knowledge are

Light

Music

Nectar

Word

The emphasis is on seeking what is already within.

A preparation time of several months is suggested for those (the premies) who wish to understand Knowledge. Maharaj Ji's talks are videotaped and made available through screenings in many locations around the world as well as through direct sales. The movement enjoys favorable tax conditions in various parts of the world as it is registered as a charity. The British organization of Elan Vital was established in 1991 and registered as an educational charity in 1992. According to Elan Vital in the United Kingdom, roughly ten thousand people "practice the techniques of Knowledge" (Barrett [1996]). Outside of India, at the time of this writing, Elan Vital claims some seventy-five thousand followers in the rest of the world.

UNIT 8:2 ISKCON (HARE KRISHNA)

The International Society for Krishna Consciousness (ISKCON) is more popularly known as Hare Krishna. This Hindu religious movement is derived from Vaishnavism, or devotion to the Hindu god Vishnu, although devotees focus on the Hindu god Krishna who is an incarnation of Vishnu. Whereas mainstream Hinduism regards Krishna to be the eighth incarnation of Vishnu (the Preserver and one of the Hindu trinity of deities), ISKCON regards Krishna to be the supreme Lord over all deities, including Vishnu. ISKCON is therefore a monotheistic faith group that stresses *bhakti*, the way of devotion.

The ancient faith was revived by sixteenth-century Guru Caitanya Mahaprabu, who many Hindus believe is an incarnation of Krishna in the form of his own devotee. Caitanya followed doctrines taught by thirteenth-century philosopher Nimbarka, who taught a form of dualistic nondualism—that is, the belief that God was the same as, and yet different from, individual souls. Caitanya also taught both that Lord Krishna was the principle deity, God himself, and devotion to Krishna through *sankirtana* (congregational chanting of God's names, specifically the Hare Krishna mantra). After Caitanya's death, the movement continued, though not with the same enthusiasm. (The story is documented in detail by Kim Knott in *My Sweet Lord*, Aquarian Press, 1986.)

The present Hare Krishna movement was founded in 1965 in the United States by A. C. Bhaktivedanta Swami Prabhupada (1896–1977), who was born Abhay Charan De in Calcutta and became a *sannyasin* in 1959. His guru was Bhaktisiddhanta Sarasvati, who had a vision of Caitanya's teaching reaching beyond Bengal and India into the English-speaking world. Just before his death he entrusted the work to his disciple Praphupada. In 1965 he arrived in America—his simple robe, sandals, and begging bowl appealed to the hippie community in New York and afterwards in San Francisco. In 1968 ISKCON members arrived in Britain, and a year later George Harrison helped to record the song "My Sweet Lord," which was based on Hare Krishna Chant. The song was an instant hit on the pop charts, bringing with it enormous publicity.

After the successful promotion of Krishna Consciousness, the Master died in 1977. His main writings were word-for-word translations and commentaries on the *Bhagavad-gita*, the *Bhagavata Purana*, and the *Caitanya Caritamrita* ("The Life and Teachings of Caitanya Mahaprabhu"). Before his death, Prabhupada appointed eleven commissioners (some sources argue there were twenty) to accept disciples and extend the organization internationally.

ISKCON's headquarters are based in Los Angeles. They publish a magazine called *Back to Godhead.*

Sacred Text

The central text of Hare Krishnas is Prabhupada's translation of the *Bhagavad-gita* with his own commentary on the text. Followers believe all other translations to be inaccurate or "motivated," in contrast to the pure text. The *Gita* is an episode in the ancient Sanskrit epic, the *Mahabharata*. They also use other important texts, especially the *Bhagavata Purana.*

Beliefs and Practice

Krishna Consciousness differs from many other forms of Hinduism in that it teaches a relationship between its followers and a personal god, Krishna. This is a monotheistic form of Hinduism (Vaishnavism), where Krishna is seen as the Supreme Godhead who is omniscient, omnipresent, omnipotent, eternal, and the energy that sustains the universe and the created order. Even so, unlike many other forms of Hinduism, God can be conceived of as personal rather than unknowable.

Still, ISKCON has much in common with conventional Hinduism:

- Their sacred text, *Bhagavad-gita*, contains conversations between Lord Krishna and a soldier Arjuna.
- A common ISKCON saying is, "We are not this body," meaning that we are all spirit souls who are temporarily trapped in a material body

with its problems. Their goal is release from *samsara* (endless repetitive reincarnations) and return to the kingdom of God.

- Bhakti Hinduism has been a widely practiced and respected form of Hinduism since the death of the Bengali saint, Caitanya Mahaprabhu (1486–1533). A religion that is effectively monotheistic, Krishna is venerated as the Supreme Godhead and worship of him involves loving devotion and surrender, singing the names of Krishna, and ecstatic dancing.

The main aim of ISKCON is to help those who are living in this present evil age (the age of *Kali-yuga*) to attain salvation through having permanent Krishna-consciousness. This state is pure and blissful, and repeating the names of God in the mantra aids the spiritual life of devotion and love. The worshiper can even gain a foretaste of eternal union with Krishna by way of Bhakti yoga and especially through the mantra. The Mahamantra of ISKCON is:

> Hare Krishna, Hare Krishna; Krishna Krishna, Hare, Hare;
> Hare Rama, Hare Rama; Rama, Rama, Hare, Hare.

Eating food prepared and offered to God represents an act of communion with Krishna where Krishna's energy purifies the body of the devotee.

The main differences from other forms of Hinduism are as follows:

- Liberation from *samsara* is attained through *sankirtana*, which is communal singing of God's names leading to Krishna Consciousness.
- Krishna is worshiped as the Supreme God; the worshiper can aspire to a personal relationship with Him.
- ISKCON teaches hell as a temporary destination after death for people who have sinned greatly while on earth.
- ISKCON teaches that every person is an individual, unlike, for example, the teaching of Shankara where the *atman* (higher soul) of every person is the same.
- Devotees need a spiritual master in line of succession from the guru Caitanya (or one of three other lines of disciple succession who worship Krishna as the Supreme God).

Practices

One of the distinctive features of ISKCON is its requirement for its members to engage in a disciplined lifestyle, to abstain from alcohol, tobacco, and drugs, and to be vegetarian. Members who live communally in the ashrams rise at 3 or 4 A.M. for worship. The members are divided into two classes: *brahmacarin* ("students"), who live in temples and vow to abstain from sex, meat, gambling, and drugs; and *grihasta*, or lay members who marry and have families. Communal members wear regular clothing and work in regular jobs. Many live near a temple, follow a vegetarian diet, do some prayer and chanting at home, and come to the temple at least once a week, often to attend the Sunday Feast. Sunday Feasts are held at Hare Krishna temples internationally and are open to all to come and participate in the chanting, dancing, and feasting on vegetarian food offered to Krishna.

Monks and Temples

Adherents in the West who choose to live in the temples purify their consciousness by performing *japa*, which is chanting the Hare Krishna mantra for a period of about two hours.

Male monks shave their heads, except for a central patch called a *sikha*, and receive a Sanskrit name (one of the many names of God) plus the suffix "dasa," which means "servant of." They are identified in the West by their saffron-colored robes, *dhotis*, which signify celibacy. Married monks wear white *dhotis*.

Female residents of a temple wear traditional *saris* and do not shave their heads. Celibacy is preferred and is mandatory for single devotees; sexual activity for married couples is only for the purpose of procreation.

The Ongoing Development of the Movement

Since the death and at the request of its founder, the movement has been governed by a Central Governing Board Committee, which appoints a swami or representative to have spiritual and administrative control over different temples around the world. In common with many other religious movements, ISKCON has been criticized for its attitudes towards women, although the movement has had women priests. A number of temple presidents at the time of this writing are women. In the United States and Britain, the movement was troubled by charges of sexual impropriety and internal disputes that reportedly led to several killings. Critics made accusations of other illegal activities as well. Ravindra Svarupa, chairman of the North American Governing Body Commission Continental Committee, cites the movement's early explosive growth as one of the factors that has led to internal strife and the lack of moral discipline that has discredited the movement. He says, "New people, without much material or spiritual maturity or even training, had to assume positions of leadership and responsibility" ("Cleaning House and Cleaning Hearts: Reform and renewal in ISKCON," Part 1, in *ISKCON Communications Journal* 3 [January-June 1994], 47.)

ISKCON is now not attracting the large numbers it once did, but the decline in its novelty appeal has been replaced by a more respected established Hindu movement whose educational services are widely available, especially in the United Kingdom.

UNIT 8:3 NICHIREN SHOSHU/ SOKA GAKKAI

Nichiren Daishonin was born on February 16 in the first year of Jo'o (1222–1282) in Japan. His name means "Sun Lotus"; "sun" represents Japan and "lotus" stands for "*Lotus Sutra.*" At age twelve, his family put him in the care of the local Tendai Buddhist temple at Seichoji. At the age of sixteen, he left and devoted the next ten years of his early life to complete a thorough and entire study of Buddhism. This education included studying the Pure Land school of Buddhism and Zen. Nichiren was anxious to discover the true teaching of the Buddha and not to accept the many variations that were available in his day. His ideas were radical and he encountered opposition to them, so he eventually moved to Mount Koya to study the esoteric beliefs of the Shingon (True Word) school of Buddhism. His ultimate realization was that the only true form of Buddhism was that taught by Saicho (eighth century) and that the Buddha's purest teachings could be summed up in the *Lotus Sutra*, which he wrote six years before his death. All the other teachings of the Buddha were superseded by the classic Mahayana text of the *Lotus Sutra.* Nichiren taught common people that by chanting just the title of this Sutra they are in effect chanting the whole of the *Lotus Sutra* and therefore could attain enlightenment.

In February 1260 Nichiren wrote his famous article, *Rissho ankoku-ron* ("Treatise on the Establishment of Righteousness to Secure the Peace of the State"). His political statements against the government and his condemnation of all other religious teachings other than his own evoked much opposition. He encountered persecution, which included a night assault on his life in Kamakura, an execution attempt at Tatsunokuchi and two sentences of exile. During his second exile (1271–1274) on the island of Sado, he wrote *Kaimokusho* ("Treatise on Opening the Eyes") and *Kanjin Honzonosho* ("Treatise of Contemplating the True Object of Worship"). In the letter he wrote:

> I am living now in loneliest isolation. Yet in my heart, in Nichiren's body of flesh, is hidden the great mystery which the Lord Sakyamuni (Buddha) revealed on Vulture Peak and has entrusted to me. My heart is the place where all Buddhas are immersed in contemplation, turning the wheel of truth on my tongue, being born from my throat, attaining enlightenment in my mouth.

Nichiren died on October 13, 1282. Since his death, over the centuries Nichiren's teaching has diversified into different sects, among them several new religions related to Nichiren such as Reiyukai, Soka Gakkai, and Nichiren Shoshu.

Nichiren Shoshu was founded by Nikko Shonin (1253–1314), who had founded the Daisekiji temple to preserve the true and authentic teaching of Nichiren. Eventually Nikko's version of Nichiren's teaching acclaimed itself as the Orthodox Nichiren Sect, otherwise known as Nichiren Shoshu (1913). It acknowledges Nichiren as the religious founder but Nikko as the authentic sect founder.

In the twentieth century, two devotees of Nichiren Shoshu, Tsunesaburo Makiguchi (1871–1944) and Josei Toda (1900–1958) founded the lay movement of Soka Kyoiku Gakkai, literally the "Value Creating Education Society," which was primarily aimed at educational reforms. During the Second World War, the Japanese government ordered that Shinto shrines should be installed in every home for worship of the emperor. Nichiren Shoshu Buddhists declined to follow this order, and a number of their leaders, including Makiguchi and Toda, were sent to prison. Makiguchi died in prison and left Toda as the sole leader of the movement. Toda renamed the organisation as Soka Gakkai ("Value Creation Society") and began an intensive recruitment drive that led to the controversial method of proselytizing called *shakubuku* (break and subdue), which emphasizes refuting the teachings of rival Buddhist groups. Rumors of physical violence in attempts to win converts have been denied. Under the leadership of Daisaku Ikeda (b. 1928), the movement has spread to the West.

Beliefs and Practices

The *Gohonzon* (meaning "respected or honored object") is a scroll, hand-copied by one of the Nichiren Shoshu high priests. The original goes back in time to Nichiren himself and is revered in a shrine at the main temple at the bottom of Mount Fuji. The words on it are the phrase, *Nam myoho renge kyo Nichiren*, and also the names of enlightened ones.

Nam is Sanskrit for "devotion," and *Myoho* means "enlightenment of the law." The whole of the phrase translated means, "Devotion (or homage) to the enlightenment of the law of the Lotus Sutra."

The Lotus Sutra

According to the *Lotus Sutra,* the teachings of Gautama, the historical Buddha, did not embody the whole truth about Buddhism, but rather only what people of the sixth century C.E. were ready to hear and accept. On this view Buddhists need to develop their skills to make spiritual progress within their historical time and place, and when people are ready then the new truths can be delivered. This is the purpose for which the *Lotus Sutra* was given.

Beliefs about Nichiren Diashonin

The *Lotus Sutra* teaches that the Buddha was already enlightened before his realization under the Bodhi tree at Bodh Gaya. He assumed the role of the unenlightened to teach his followers by his own life and teaching the way to nirvana. The Buddha was therefore a physical emanation of a primal buddha (*adi-buddha*) who assumed a body for this task.

Devotees of Nichiren Buddhism believe that the primal buddha was actually Nichiren himself, and he therefore is worthy of greater veneration than even the Buddha. Devotees always show their respect by calling him "Nichiren Daishonin." *Diashonin* means "great sage."

Trust

The first requisite of "Faith" involves placing absolute trust in the Gohonzon and in the teachings of Nichiren Daishonin; one must also have absolute confidence in the validity of one's practice in the Supreme and Only True Law.

Gongyo

Another requisite of the practice of Nichiren Shoshu is morning and evening Gongyo ("diligent practice") every day, in front of the Gohonzon, and chanting the *daimoku* of "Nam-Myoho-Renge-Kyo" in order to purify one's life. The pure life force (or the ninth level of consciousness) is purified through Gongyo. The ninth level is unaffected by cause and effect, and by chanting Nam Myoho Renge Kyo, every other level of consciousness is purified so that the ninth level, that of Buddha consciousness, is able to permeate the whole of one's being. The chant is seen as powerful and able to attract material and spiritual benefits to the devotee.

The Teachings

The third and final requisite study is of the teachings of Nichiren Daishonin as well as the various sermons preached by the successive high priests. This practice deepens the understanding of the Buddhist teachings transmitted down since the Daishonin's time.

Differences and Distinctions between Nichiren Shoshu Buddhism and Traditional Buddhism

- There is very little similarity between traditional Buddhism and Soka Gakkai. Soka Gakkai is a lay movement and members are in normal work situations rather than the priesthood.
- The Four Noble Truths, the Eightfold Path, and other teachings of the Buddha are given little significance.
- Traditional forms of Buddhism (see unit 7:2) focus on the impermanence of life and the suffering that comes from craving. The realization of this impermanence leads the follower to eliminate desire and illusion and achieve a level of selflessness (nirvana). Later thinkers pointed to the truism that to seek nirvana is a strong desire in itself. Nichiren Daishonin believed that illusion and earthly desires should be therefore

transformed into enlightened wisdom rather than extinguished. Instead of focusing on the eradication of desire, he taught that the transformation of innate desires was a positive force. The belief that Buddhist practice can satisfy desire rather than eliminate it departs from the core teaching of Gautama Buddha, who taught that unsatisfactoriness (*dukkha*) is caused by desire.

Recent Developments

Nichiren Shoshu is criticized because of its exclusive claim to be the only true form of Buddhism. Traditional schools of Buddhism accuse the movement of departing from the true teaching of the Buddha, as shown previously. More recently, there has been a split between Nichiren Shoshu and Soka Gakkai. The lay movement of Soka Gakkai is international and therefore sees the need to relate and grow in relevance to today's world. In contrast the Nichiren Shoshu priesthood focuses on maintaining the traditions. Fragmentation between the two has been ongoing, largely due to Soka Gakkai carrying out the functions of both priests and lay believers. Among other issues this fragmentation resulted in Soka Gakkai being barred from visiting the Taiseki-ji Temple as pilgrims and being deprived of the services of the Nichiren Shoshu priesthood, thus forcing ongoing independence. Mutual antagonism has continued with force, and because of the schism between lay members and priesthood, *gohonzons* are no longer inscribed or given to Soka Gakkai members. This withholding inevitably forces a reappraisal of the material importance and spiritual significance of the *gohonzon* itself.

UNIT 8:4 OSHO INTERNATIONAL (BHAGWAN SHREE RAJNEESH)

> *We are continuously moving on the circumference, always somewhere else far away from our own being, always directed towards others. When all this is dropped, when all objects are dropped, when you close your eyes to all that is not you—even your mind, your heartbeats are left far behind—only a silence remains. In this silence you will settle slowly into the center of your being, and then the roots will grow on their own accord, and the wings too. You need not worry about them. You cannot do anything about them. They come on their own. You simply fulfill one condition: that is, to be at home—and the whole existence becomes a bliss to you, a benediction.*
>
> (Bhagwan Shree Rajneesh, on www.peripheral.org/pages/sketch.html)

Osho (formally Rajneeshism) was founded by Bhagwan Shree Rajneesh (1931–1990). He was born Rajneesh Chandra Mohan in Kuchwara, a town in central India. "Bhagwan" is variously translated as "God" or "The Blessed One," or even controversially by some as "Master of the Vagina." He eventually took the name "Osho," meaning "'friend."

Rajneesh was raised in the Jain faith. By his own account he received *samadhi* (enlightenment in which his soul became one with the universe) at the age of twenty-one. Rajneesh obtained a masters degree in philosophy from the University of Saugar and taught philosophy at the University of Jabalpur for the next nine years. In 1966 he left his teaching post and began to travel around India promoting spiritual teaching, meditation, and free love.

In 1974 local opposition from the authorities prompted his move to an isolated ashram in Poona. Some accounts suggest that as many as fifty thousand Americans spent time seeking enlightenment with the guru.

In 1981 facing rumors of income tax evasion and insurance fraud, and fearing for his own security, he left India and settled on the sixty-five-thousand-acre Big Muddy Ranch near Antelope, Oregon. He renamed the place Rajneeshpuram ("City of Rajneesh" or "Essence of Rajneesh"). His devotees built the city for little or no payment. The influx of Rajneesh followers boosted his influence in the town but brought accusations of local elections being rigged and prospective voters' food being poisoned. Rajneesh took a vow of silence for several years, resulting in an Indian devotee named Ma Anand Sheela overseeing the religion and the community. Matters escalated and came to a head in 1985 when Sheela was denounced by Rajneesh and expelled. He attempted to leave the country but was apprehended when the plane stopped to refuel. He was fined and given a suspended jail sentence on the condition that he leave the United States. Sheela was extradited from Germany and served four years of a twenty-year jail sentence for attempted murder, immigration offenses, firearms illegalities, and financial corruption. Two British women (Sally-Anne Croft and Susan Hagan) were eventually convicted of conspiracy to murder lawyer Charles Turner in an attempt to prevent closure of the ranch. Both women received a five-year sentence. They both returned to Britain and managed to fight extradition to the United States for several years. However new fears were justified in 1995.

Rajneesh resettled in Poona as Osho. After his death in 1990 rumors spread that he died of AIDS, was poisoned, or had heart failure.

At its peak, Rajneeshism had about two hundred thousand members and six hundred centers internationally. The Rajneesh Foundation has declined since his death, but even so his work continues and his followers in Poona offer courses in his teaching. There are also about twenty meditation centers around the world. Rajneesh's main influence now is through his many writings.

Beliefs and Practices

Rajneesh taught a syncretistic religion that combined elements from a number of religious traditions, including Hinduism, Zen Buddhism, Christianity, Jainism, ancient Greek philosophy, and meditations from Gurdjieff (see unit 11:2). His followers give testimony to a man of deep spiritual insight. His teachings are very diverse and difficult to list in a detailed way, but they included the following beliefs:

- A monistic interpretation of reality, that there is only one source of energy called "life" or "love" or "light."
- The reunification of spiritual and material life. There are no contradictions in life, just complementarities—like death to life or summer to winter.
- An emphasis on the existential, experiential realities of life. His message cannot be understood intellectually.
- An emphasis on awareness: anything you do with awareness leads to the same goal.
- Elements of classical Indian yoga (*sash*), so that awareness of the inner life causes us to stand apart from it and eventually to observe it impartially.
- Every part of life can be communion with God. There is no inner or outer life, no separation. God and the world are mixed together and inseparable. People, even at their worst, are divine.

His followers practiced intense meditation, chanting, primal screaming, extreme forms of exercise, shouting mantras, and free love. Although some of these activities led to violence and injuries, Rajneesh put a stop to these harmful effects early in the movement. The aim of such practices was to achieve personal transformation by overcoming repression, lowering inhibitions, developing emptiness, and attaining enlightenment. This transformation would lead the devotee to have "no past, no future, no attachment, no mind, no ego, no self."

Criticisms of the movement are typical to those aimed at many cults. They have centered around the contrast of the members, who lived a frugal, simple lifestyle, and the founder Rajneesh himself, who lived in luxury. His collection of Rolls Royce cars was well known (some sources say he owned as many as one hundred cars). His critics also accuse him of opposing family relationships and ties. His followers tended to sever their connection to family when they joined his group.

Bhagwan Shree Rajneesh remains one of the most eclectic, diverse, and controversial religious teachers of recent times. His comments and thoughts on society, Eastern religion, and Western religion in the 1980s could be penetrating and evocative. In his book, David V. Barrett (1996) points to an early (1983) publication, *Rajneeshism: An Introduction to Bhagwan Shree Rajneesh and His Religion,* which was withdrawn but which quotes the Bhagwan as saying:

> The East is against love. That's why Eastern spirituality is sad, dull, dead. No juice flows through the Eastern saint. He is

afraid of any flow, any vibration, any streaming of his energy. He is constantly controlling himself, repressing himself. He is sitting upon himself, on guard. He is against himself and against the world. He is simply waiting to die, he is committing a slow suicide. . . .

The Western man has lost all idea of who he is. He has lost track of consciousness, he is not aware. He has become more and more mechanical because he denies the inner. So laughter is there but laughter cannot go deep, because there is no depth. The depth is not accepted. So the West lives in a shallow laughter and the East in a deep sadness. This is the misery, the agony that has happened to man.

UNIT 8:5 TRANSCENDENTAL MEDITATION

My Vedic Approach to Health is the approach of Natural Law, which is inscribed in every grain of the human physiology and is easily accessible to anyone within the intelligence of his own body.

This has provided a direct path for prevention, restoration, and maintenance of balance in the natural relationship between intelligence and the physiology—between the body and its own inner intelligence.

With this, the possibility has arisen for the individual to really enjoy balanced, healthy life in happiness—the goal of an affluent society.

Maharishi Mahesh Yogi, www.lisco.com/wuebben/TM

Guru Maharishi Mahesh Yogi (meaning "Great Sage" or "Seer") was born at Jabalpur, India, in 1911, as Mahesh Prasad Warma. He studied physics at Allahabad University and gained his degree in 1940; after his formal schooling he went to study under Guru Dev, who died in 1953. Mahesh went into the secluded life for two years until 1956. He then appeared out of seclusion and began his mission of bringing to the world the mystical Hindu techniques taught to him by Guru Dev.

Mahesh established the Spiritual Regeneration Movement in Madras in 1958 but received little response, and he expanded his influence to America in 1959. The TM movement has become the largest and fastest growing of the various Eastern spiritual disciplines that have taken root in the West. He gave a series of lectures at Caxton Hall in London in 1960. In 1961 the Maharishi announced a nine-year plan to spread the message of the Spiritual Regeneration Movement via The International Meditation Society. Later, the movement's name was changed to the Science of Creative Intelligence.

With the help of George Harrison and the Beatles in the 1960s, he gained international publicity. Reports state that he was making $20 million a year in the 1970s. He founded the Maharishi International University in Fairfield, Iowa, in the United States in 1971. In 1972 the Mararishi announced a world plan for one teaching center for each million people in the world and the long-term goal of one TM teacher per thousand population. TM was taught in schools and colleges in the United States until court cases in 1977 and 1979 were brought by evangelical Christians. The court agreed it was advancing Hinduism and therefore was a state-sponsored religious activity that as such contravened the American Constitution. In 1977 the TM movement bought Mentmore Towers in Buckinghamshire, England, where the Maharishi sought to create a "world government" to administer "the age of enlightenment." In 1994 the name was changed to the Maharishi Foundation.

Teaching, Beliefs, and Practices

Transcendental Meditation is part of the monist tradition, which believes in the essential oneness of all reality and therefore the possibility of human unity with the divine.

Meditation

Maharishi has introduced and marketed a simplified and Westernized set of yoga techniques that is presented as a nonreligious practice designed to enable a person to make use of his/her full mental potential while at the same time achieving deep rest and relaxation. TM offers its followers happiness, perfect bliss, and "restful alertness" through a technique that requires a minimum of twenty minutes meditation twice a day.

The practice of TM is founded on the classic Hindu religious meditation practice of the *mantra*. This mental technique is said to lead those who practice it to "the field of pure consciousness" and is akin to classic Hindu religious practice in that it attempts to calm the restlessness of the physical body through the simple practice of concentration, which elevates the spiritual self. More advanced techniques such as Yogic Flying are also taught. The meditator is promised clarity in thought, peace, and tranquillity through his or her perception of the world's underlying truth. In addition, TM adherents claim to enjoy increased creativity and productivity in work or study. The emphasis here is that people function in accordance with natural law and move beyond the "ruts" of thought that rule society into a deep level of transcendental creative intelligence.

TM has also claimed that, through the advanced Sikhi program, when Transcendental Meditation is done with significant numbers of meditators, a radiance is transmitted which is powerful enough to reduce crime, accidents, and illnesses over a wide area.

Initiation

At initiation, the candidate is given a "secret" mantra, a Sanskrit word or syllable that is believed to possess special vibrational qualities and which the meditator is to use in meditation.

Is Transcendental Meditation a Religion?

The TM movement does not claim to be a religion. Other commentators disagree with this self-analysis on a number of grounds:

- At the TM puja ceremony, Sanskrit words are given with no translation. They are asking Hindu gods for help, and Guru Dev is identified as a divine incarnation.
- The mantra is chosen according to ancient Hindu tradition.
- The Maharishi himself is a Hindu bhakti monk, and his techniques came from studying the Hindu Vedic sacred texts.
- TM, like Hinduism, teaches that life is a cycle of rebirths, and human perfection can be obtained through meditation.

UNIT 8:6 RASTAFARIANISM AND VOODOO

O God, You are great,
You are the one who created me,
I have no other.
God, You are in the heavens,
You are the only one:
Now my child is sick,
And You will grant me my desire.
African Traditional Religions.
Anuak Prayer (Sudan)

While it is most often associated with dreadlocks, smoking of marijuana and reggae music, the Rastafarian religion is much more than simply a religion of Jamaica. With its beginnings in the Jamaican slums, Rastafarianism has spread throughout the world and currently has a membership of over 700,000.

Leonard E. Barrett Sr., *The Rastafarians: Sounds of Cultural Dissonance*

Rastafarianism is more commonly called Rasta and journeys back to the teachings of Marcus Garvey. Jamaican-born Garvey was a black nationalist leader whose Universal Negro Improvement Association (UNIA) was the most prominent black power organization of the 1920s. Although he was a Roman Catholic, Garvey encouraged his followers to imagine Jesus as black and to organize their own church. To emphasize that the new church was neither Catholic nor Protestant, the name "Orthodox" was adopted. In the 1930s Garvey preached a message of black self-empowerment and initiated the "Back to Africa" movement. This movement identified blacks as the true biblical Jews, who were superior to whites and who were existent in either Ethiopia or Jamaica where they had scattered and were exiled because of divine punishment. Garvey called for all blacks to return to their ancestral home, Ethiopia. He advanced a "back to Africa" consciousness, which encouraged black pride. This movement rejected the focus on a eurocentric worldview and what it considered to be white colonial indoctrination, which caused blacks to feel shame for their African heritage. In Rastafarianism, Zion refers broadly to Africa and more specifically to Ethiopia as the ancestral homeland of all black peoples.

As early as the 1920s Garvey was exhorting people to "Look to Africa, when a black king shall be crowned, for the day of deliverance is at hand." Many people thought the prophecy was fulfilled when in 1930 Crown Prince Ras Tafari was crowned emperor Haile Selassie I of Ethiopia, taking this as the sign that the punishment had ended, the millennium was at hand, and the return to Africa was beginning. Ras is an Amharic term equivalent to duke or lord. Rastafari is the same name taken by members of the Rastafari movement who regard the Ethiopian Emperor as the reincarnation of Christ as well as the embodiment of the Godhead. At his coronation, the emperor claimed for himself the titles of "Emperor Haile Selassie (Power of the Trinity) I, Conquering Lion of the Tribe of Judah, Elect of God and King of the Kings of Ethiopia."

Haile Selassie claimed to be one of the direct descendants of King David, the 225th ruler in an unbroken line of Ethiopian Kings from the time of Solomon and Sheba. Rasta theology centered on the divinity of Selassie as a living manifestation of Jah, the all-knowing and all-loving God. "Jah" is the term used as a synonym for Emperor Haile Selassie as the manifestation of the Godhead. The term derives from the Old Testament where it appears as an archaic form of "Jehovah" (see Ps. 68:4). For Rastafarians, the Old Testament is about black Africans who descended from Abraham and Jacob. But white Christians altered this fact to keep Africans in a substandard position. Rastafarians refer to this oppression as "Babylon," with references to slavery and cultural tyranny that all blacks must overcome. In a Rasta context Babylon is the historically white, European, colonial and imperialist power structure that has oppressed blacks and other peoples of color. The poet Joe Ruglass writes:

> As a spiritual philosophy,
> Rastafarianism is linked
> to societies of runaway slaves, or maroons,

and derives from both the African Myal religion
and the revivalist Zion Churches.
Like the revival movement,
it embraces the four hundred year old
doctrine of repatriation.
Rastas believe that they and all Africans
who have migrated are but exiles in "Babylon"
and are destined to be delivered out of captivity
by a return to Zion or Africa—
the land of their ancestors
and the Seer of Jah Rastafari himself,
Haile Selassie I,
the former emperor of Ethiopia.

OneWorld Magazine

The Rastafarian movement first became visible during the 1930s when members started living in communes on the Kingston garbage sites of Jamaica. One of its early leaders, Leonard Howell, was arrested in 1933 for preaching "a revolutionary doctrine" (Crim, *The Perennial Dictionary of World Religions*).

Haile Selassie visited Jamaica on April 21, 1966, to an ecstatic reception. He convinced the Rastafarian movement not to immigrate to Ethiopia until they had liberated the Jamaican people. Since then April 21 has been commemorated "Grounation Day" as a holy day among Rastafarians. Contrary to the widely repeated claim that the emperor was amazed at the existence of the Rastafarians (most of whom by 1966 believed him to be God in essence), there is much evidence that Haile Selassie's whole purpose in visiting Jamaica was to meet the Rasta leadership. He was greeted at the airport by thousands of dreads in white robes chanting "Hosanna to the Son of David." Haile Selassie gave audience to a delegation of famous Elders, including Mortimo Planno. The details of this historic occasion are not available, but almost certainly Selassie urged the elders to become Orthodox and held out the possibility that Jamaican settlers could receive land-grants in South Ethiopia. Most of the well-established versions of the meeting say that he also gave the elders a secret message, very much in keeping with the Emperor's known policies on Third World development: "Build Jamaica first."

Haile Selassie died on August 27, 1975, although many people were disbelieving of his death.

Beliefs and Doctrines

More than one scholar has observed that from its beginnings the Rastafarian movement has been so loosely defined that doctrine has often been a matter of individual interpretation. Nevertheless, early on Leonard Howell gave the Rastafarians six principles:

1. a hatred for the White race
2. the superiority of the Black race

3. revenge on Whites for their wickedness
4. the negation, persecution, and humiliation of the government and legal bodies of Jamaica
5. to go back to Africa
6. acknowledging Emperor Haile Selassie as the Supreme Being and only ruler of Black people (Barrett, *The Rastafarians*)

In addition, "true" Rastafarians only eat "I-tal" food, which is organic food that never touches chemicals or comes out of cans. Salts, condiments, or preservatives are prohibited, as are flesh, blood, or "white blood" (as Rastafarians call milk). Alcohol is prohibited, as are all other nonherbal drinks. Rastafarians use ganja (marijuana) in much of their cooking.

Babylon

"Babylon" refers to the Jamaican government, the establishment, or white oppressors in general.

I and I

The concept of "I and I" is of core importance to Rastafarian doctrine and belief.

> I and I is an expression to totalize the concept of oneness. "I and I" as being the oneness of two persons. So God is within all of us and we're one people in fact. I and I means that God is in all men. The bond of Ras Tafari is the bond of God, of man. But man itself needs a head and the head of man is His Imperial Majesty Haile Selassie of Ethiopia. (Cashmore, *Rastaman*, 67)

Other Doctrines

Some other, more loosely taught doctrines are as follows:

- Rastafarians have a doctrine of avatar similar to that of Hinduism (see unit 3:1):

  > God revealed himself in the person of Moses, who was the first avatar or savior. The second avatar was Elijah. The third avatar was Jesus Christ. Now the advent of Ras Tafari is the climax of God's revelation. (Barrett, *The Rastafarians,* 112.)

- The devil is the god of the white man, and white men are devils.
- Rastafarians are the reincarnations of the ancient tribes of Israel who had been enslaved and kept in exile by their white oppressors, the agents of Babylon.

- The Bible was originally written by and for black people. Rastas accept the Bible as their central text, although they believe that much of its original material has been distorted during its translation into English. They take an allegorical approach to Bible interpretation, claiming that the pages of scripture should be searched for "hidden meanings and directives" (Cashmore, *Rastaman*, 74).
- A physical feature that identifies Rastas is wearing their hair in dreadlocks. Dreadlocks were inspired by a biblical injunction against the cutting of hair. In 1976 all Orthodox Rastas were required to cut their locks and make a formal repudiation of heretical emperor worship (*latreia*). This decree forced people to make a sudden decision about the cutting of locks, which seemed to many a repudiation of the movement's history.
- Ganja (marijuana) is also known as the "holy herb." Ganja took on the role of a religious sacrament for the Rastas in the 1930s, symbolizing a protest of the oppressive white Babylon, or power structure, which had deemed its use illegal. Rastafarians emphasize the smoking of marijuana. Barrett says that by using ganja, the Rastafarian reaches an altered state of consciousness where he or she experiences *"the revelation that Haile Selassie is God and that Ethiopia is the home of the Black. . . . The herb is the key to new understanding of the self, the universe, and God. It is the vehicle to cosmic consciousness"* (Barrett, *The Rastafarians*, 254–255).
- Serious Rastafarians are also vegetarians.

Reggae and Rastafarianism in Recent Times

Reggae is called "the King's music." It is the music of black protest that emerged in Jamaica during the late 1960s. During the 1970s, reggae themes became central to the emergent national consciousness of Jamaicans, both Rastafari and non-Rastafari alike.

The period from about 1975 to the present day has been a time of real growth for the Rastafarian movement. This growth can be attributed to Bob Marley, reggae artist, and the worldwide acceptance of reggae as an acceptable mode of Rastafarian self-expression. Bob Marley's family was mostly Orthodox Rastafarian, although Marley himself was for most of his career a member of the Twelve Tribes sect. The Twelve Tribes of Israel, founded by Vernon Carrington, has its headquarters in New York. This group is closely tied to the Royal family of Ethiopia in exile and is working to restore to the throne Zere Yacob, Haile Selassie's grandson.

In his final years, dying young of cancer, Marley underwent a remarkable spiritual transformation, reverting back to his spiritual roots. This movement was evident in his music around the time he was converting to Orthodoxy from the Twelve Tribes.

His Orthodox funeral in 1981 was attended by tens of thousands of mourners.

Aside from the Twelve Tribes, other groups claiming allegiance to Ras Tafari are the Ethiopian Coptic Church and the Ethiopian World Federation.

The Zion Coptic Church is a Garveyite Orthodox denomination, revitalized by white hippie converts in the 1960s.

Scriptures

Rastafarians follow no official publication, but they use various quotes from the Bible. Rastafarians disagree with parts of the Bible, however, which are said to have been changed by Babylon (the white power structure). Rastafarians speak of the Holy Piby, an occult bible allegedly translated from Amharic, the Semitic language that is the official language of Ethiopia. The Piby focuses on the destruction of white Babylon and the return of the Israelites to Africa. Another volume, known as the Kebra Negast, compiles the history and traditions of the Ethopian Orthodox faith. It focuses on the transfer of the authority from Jerusalem to Ethiopia and explains the existence of the Israelite "ark of the covenant" in Axum, Ethiopia.

Voodoo

The word "voodoo" comes from the West African word "vodun," meaning deity or spirit. Voodoo, as we know it today, was born in Haiti during the European colonization of Hispaniola. Most likely, the enforced immigration of enslaved Africans from different ethnic groups provided the conditions for Voodoo, which began as the clandestine religion of the African sugar-plantation workers in Haiti in the seventeenth century. Most of the early history of Voodoo is known through the remnants of eighteenth-century colonial records, which report variously on secret meetings, funeral practices, dances, and trancelike possessions.

Voodoo Beliefs

In Voodoo, God is manifest through the spirits of ancestors who can bring good or harm and must be honored in ceremonies. A sacred cycle exists between the living and the dead. Believers ask for their misery to end. Rituals include prayers, drumming, dancing, singing, and animal sacrifice.

Voodoo is an animist faith. Objects and natural phenomena are believed to be sacred and to possess a soul.

The supreme deity in Voodoo is Bon Dieu. Music and dance are key elements to Voodoo ceremonies. The dance is an expression of spirituality, of connection with divinity and the spirit world. The divine spirits or *Loa* represent ancestors, African deities, or Catholic saints. They control nature, health, wealth, and happiness of mortals. The Loa form a pantheon of deities that include Damballah, Ezili, Ogu, Agwe, Legba, and others. They can communicate during dreams or possess the body during Voodoo ritual. Loa appear by "possessing" the faithful, who in turn become the Loa, relaying advice, warnings, and desires. The Loa divides into pantheons or nations of spirits. The Rada are generous spirits of benevolence, but the Petro are terrible powers that dominate. Individual worshipers are often drawn to spirits by necessity or similarity or because they have been venerated by the family.

The serpent occupies a central part in the Voodoo faith. The high priest and/or priestess of the faith (often called Papa or Maman) are the vehicles for the expression of the serpent's power. The spiritual leaders in Voodoo communities are the hungans (male) and the mambos (female), who perform divination and healing rituals for worshipers, including the possession trance dances. These ceremonies allow divine spirits to be present among the worshipers.

Voodoo in the Modern World

During the French colonization of Haiti, African religion was prohibited and punished by imprisonment, lashings, and hangings. This religious struggle continued for three centuries, causing Voodoo to grow under harsh cultural conditions.

Modern films and the media have sensationalized Voodoo rites, focusing on evil potions, cannibalism, and sorcery. Voodoo followers acknowledge that like all religion, spiritual power can be manipulated for bad intent. They recognize the work of "the left hand"—malevolent practice undertaken purely for personal gain.

Voodoo survives as a legitimate religion in a number of areas of the world, including Brazil where it is called "Candomblé" and the English-speaking Caribbean where it is called "Obeah." The recent history of Voodoo has seen several attempts of its suppression by the Roman Catholic Church in Haiti, including increasing politicization though the infiltration and co-opting of its leaders.

UNIT 8:7 NATIVE AMERICAN RELIGION

Treat the earth well: it was not given to you by your parents, it was loaned to you by your children. We do not inherit the Earth from our Ancestors; we borrow it from our Children. We are more than the sum of our knowledge; we are the products of our imagination.

Ancient Proverb

Sometimes dreams are wiser than waking.

I cured with the power that came through me. Of course, it was not I who cured, it was the power from the Outer World, the visions and the ceremonies had only made me like a hole through which the power could come to the two-leggeds.

If I thought that I was doing it myself, the hole would close up and no power could come through. Then everything I could do would be foolish.

Black Elk (Holy Man of the Oglala Sioux)

The arrival of Europeans marked a major change in American Native society. Tens of millions died in the wake of sickness and programs of slavery and enforced socialization by a number of different groups, including Dutch Calvinists and the British.

Foreigners commonly thought of Native spirituality as worthless superstition or a product of the devil. Many Native American survivors were forcibly converted to Christianity, and government policies forced Natives onto reservations in a policy of assimilation.

Native American religious traditions are extremely varied, rich, and diverse. Only a few can be referred to in this unit. The origin of North American Indians has long been the object of debate. Because of the wide range of habitats in North America, different native religions evolved to match the needs and lifestyles of the individual tribes.

- In the *far north* were peoples who belonged to two different linguistic families: the eastern Algonquins (e.g., Ojibwa) and the Athapascans (e.g., Yellowknife and Chippewan). The Navajos and the Apaches are Athapascan Indians who emigrated from Canada before the colonists arrived.
- The *northwest coast* was in three units: northern, central, and southern, with tribes such as the Haida, the Bella Coola, and the Chinook.
- To the *east and south of the Great Lakes* were the Iroquois and Sioux, Cree, Cheyennes, Blackfoot (all of the Algonquin languages); Apaches (Athapascan languages); Pawnee, Arikaras (Caddoan), Comanches, and Utes (Kowa-Tanoan, Tonkawan, and Uto-Aztec languages).
- The *great basin* sheltered the Shoshones and the Paiute.
- The *far south* included a variety of tribes belonging to different linguistic communities of Tanoan, Zuni, Uto-Aztec (Hopi), Athapascan, Hokan, and Keres.

Anthropologists have collected detailed information of the practices and beliefs of these many different groups. The popularized versions of Native American spirituality often bear little or no resemblance to the traditional tribes or their members. Along with an infusion of Christianity, more recently New Age beliefs and practices have modified traditional beliefs. Native American religion has developed from the taboos, animal ceremonies, beliefs in the spirit world, and shamanism of their ancestors. In their beliefs North American traditions acknowledge the priority of the soul and the spiritual dimensions of life over the physical, visible world. For many in our materialistic, technological world these viewpoints are invalid and hastily dismissed as superstition.

Even though the vast number of groups and enormous diversity of beliefs restrict this study to a superficial level of inquiry, some common tendencies among types of Native spirituality can be listed.

When Europeans first made contact with the indigenous cultures in North

America all but a few had developed coherent religious systems of belief. These systems included cosmologies and creation myths, which were transmitted orally from generation to generation to explain the beginning of each tribe and community.

God

Creation stories and myths on the whole tell of spiritual entities with good and evil motives. Spirits also control weather and interact with humans and others who inhabit the underworld. Simultaneously, the Creator and the spirits may be perceived as a single spiritual force, as in the unity called Wakan-Tanka by the Lakota and Dakota.

Some Native American traditions—for example, the Plains Pawnee and the Beaver in British Columbia—say that creator figures in their myths brought the world into being. The Pawnee creator is Tirawahat, who established heaven and then positioned in it a hierarchy of the natural powers: Sun, Moon, stars, and the constellations in the heavens. Tirawahat then performed a number of primordial actions—breathing, lightning, thinking, making gestures—and in so doing brought life into the entire world. Such beliefs in a hierarchical superior are exceptional in the Native American tradition; more generally, mythical figures reflect the same personal nature as people themselves and a range of motives.

Nature

Religion was closely allied to the natural world. The land was thought to be imbued with supernatural meaning, and natural objects associated with sacred presences. Also, certain animals and other aspects of nature embody spiritual significance for the tribal people across the length and breadth of the Americas.

Ceremony and Ritual

In Native American cultures, there is a reciprocity between human beings and the spirit world that involves the giving of gifts and gratitude. Underlying such ceremonies is a basic recognition that human beings have a crucial role to play in "mediating" between the human world, the spirit world, and the natural world. This role can involve healing rituals. Rituals and ceremonies are very diverse, ranging from mask dances to sun dances, but some common principles underly the rituals:

The use of dance and drum

Chanting and singing

Ritual cycles: celebrations of solstices or equinoxes

Initiations

Seeking a guardian spirit who will be supportive for life

In particular the ceremony of the sweat lodge is practiced by the Plains tribes. This structure generates hot, moist air—similar to a Finnish sauna—and is used for rituals of purification, spiritual renewal and healing, and education of the youth. The lodge symbolizes a rebirth or purification for the worshiper. In effect the sweat lodge is a microcosm of the cosmos. The lodge itself is an enclosed space, often sunk into the earth. Everything is significant in the sweat lodge ceremony. In his explanation of one part of the ceremony, Black Elk tells us:

> The sweat lodge is made of from twelve to sixteen young willows, and these too have a lesson to teach us, for in the fall their leaves die and return to the earth, but in the spring they come to life again. So, too, men die, but live again in the real world of Wakan-Tanka, where there is nothing but the spirits of all things, and this true life we may know here on earth if we purify our bodies and minds, thus coming closer to Wakan-Tanka, who is all-purity. (Black Elk, *The Sacred Pipe*, ed. J. E. Brown [Penguin USA, 1972], 31–32.)

In about the year 1870 the millennarian cult called the Ghost Dance spread among the Plain Indians. This cult was encouraged by the Mormons of Utah, whom the Indians believed were the ten lost tribes of Israel. A prophet called Wovoka said that the Indians must cease fighting against the colonists. Instead they should purify themselves and dance to the Great Spirit, because the Spirit was about to destroy the colonists and spare the natives. The colonists opposed the Ghost Dance movement, which eventually resulted in the government sending in troops in 1890 to slaughter 260 Sioux who were on their way to Wounded Knee Creek in South Dakota to perform rituals.

Warriorship

Warrior cultures are found worldwide and are founded on basic common principles—especially their belief in the afterlife. Here the belief is that this life is a place where you are proved and tested, especially in war. Heroic feats of bravery are possible because of the belief that the spiritual world takes precedence over the physical world. This belief leads to a number of practices and customs, including the Sioux belief that by wearing "ghost shirts," warriors would be invincible during battle. The Sioux warrior, Black Elk, tells of how he put on his sacred shirt just before the battle at Wounded Knee and was protected from harm. The shirt was decorated with images of his sacred vision and, therefore, although the bullets were all around, they did not find him. He said:

> All the time the bullets were buzzing around me and I was not Hurt. I was not even afraid. It was like being in a dream about shooting. (J. Neihardt, ed. *Black Elk Speaks,* Pocket, 1972.)

But he hesitated, his dream disappeared into thin air, and he felt fear. In that moment he was wounded by a bullet.

Life after Death

Some Native Americans believe in reincarnation, with a person being reborn either as a human or animal after death. Others believe that humans return as ghosts, or that people go to another world.

The Native American Church

Many Native families today have been devout Christians for generations. Others, particularly in the Southwest, have retained their aboriginal traditions more or less intact. Many follow a personal faith combining traditional and Christian elements. Pan-Indianism is a recent movement that encourages a return to traditional beliefs and seeks to create a common religion. At the time of writing, membership of the Native American Church is estimated at 250,000. Although its roots and practices can be traced back in time, the Native American Church was only founded in 1918. Worship included the practice of generic religious rites, Christianity, and the use of the peyote plant. The peyote ritual is comprised of four parts: praying, singing, eating peyote, and quietly contemplating.

Native American Groups

Lakota

The Lakota were nomadic Plains Indians who lived in tipis and hunted buffalo. History records them destroying Custer's forces at the Battle of the Little Bighorn in 1876. Today they live on reservations. Their religious system traditionally focuses on cosmology and the appeasement of supernatural beings to ensure successful buffalo hunts. The "Seven Sacred Rites" at the heart of their religion include: The Sweat Lodge, The Vision Quest, The Sun Dance, Making Relatives, Puberty Ceremony, Ghost Keeping, and Throwing the Ball.

The Inuit

The traditional Inuit (Eskimo) culture recognizes that life is precarious, given the challenge of extreme cold and the ongoing threat of starvation. Their religion is grounded in the belief that *anua* (souls) exist in all people and animals. Everyone must avoid a complex system of taboos so that animals will continue to make themselves available to the hunters. Many rituals and ceremonies are performed before and after hunting expeditions to guarantee hunting success.

The underwater Goddess Sedna or Takanaluk is part human and part fish. She keeps charge of the sea mammals and takes notice of how the tribe obeys the taboos, thus releasing her animals to the hunters accordingly. Other deities release land mammals; these are Keepers or Masters, one for each species.

Navajo

The Navajo mostly live on a reservation in northern Arizona and New Mexico. In the 1980s, their population was approximately 175,000. The Navajo creation myth speaks of their emergence onto the Earth from a series of underworlds. The underlying force of the myth is that the natural and supernatural interact and coexist.

Apache

Apache tribes live in the American Southwest. Their religion centers on the existence of a supernatural power that manifests itself at all levels of Apache existence. They believe good relationships with this power can offer help to the Apache through visionary experiences. In shamanistic ceremonies, the practitioner interacts with his own particular power. Other rituals require a priest to officiate. The Apache perform life-cycle rites, including the rite for a child who takes his or her first steps and a girl's puberty rite.

Historians Debate

During the last twenty years the central development in the field of Native ethnohistory is the growing awareness that a "new world" was created for both whites and Indians in the interactions they both had with each other. Earlier relations were more polarized: either Euro-American "civilized peoples" were overcoming Indian "savagery," or Native peoples were suffering decline and defeat through military conquest and disease. Both historical models make the assumption of Native people being passive victims. More recent scholarship emphasizes the ongoing Indian resistance to white supremacy and also the many different ways in which cultural adaptation took place on both sides of the frontier. Richard White's detailed and erudite study, *The Middle Ground: Indians, Empires, and Republics in the Great Lakes Region* (Cambridge/New York: Cambridge University Press, 1991), concentrates on the Ohio Valley and the way in which a common cultural world evolved as indigenous peoples interacted with the many different settlers, first the French and later the English.

Frank Fools Crow

Frank Fools Crow was a spiritual and civic leader of the Teton Sioux. He was a gentle man who believed in personal discipline. He also believed in the old customs of his people. When he saw the social problems of the new era, he was brave and courageous in denouncing them. He died in 1989 at the Pine Ridge Reservation in South Dakota, much loved and widely respected as a holy man. During interviews given to author Thomas E. Mails, conducted in the 1970s, Fool's Crow spoke of the early days of reservation life—as the Sioux learned to farm the land—and later times when alcoholism, the changing economic climate, and World War II were fast eroding the old way of living. He described his own visionary experiences and life as a medicine man. Fool's Crow also gave details of the Yuwipi and sweat lodge ceromonies, the Sun Dance, and examples of physical healing. Fool's Crow traveled abroad and was with Buffalo Bill's Wild West show. He was involved in mediation between the U.S. government and Indian activists at Wounded Knee in 1973, and he appeared before a congressional subcommittee to ask for the return of the Black Hills to his people. (Thomas E. Mails, *Fools Crow* [Doubleday, 1979].)

Native American Women

Julia C. White

Julia C. White was born in North Carolina of Cherokee/Sioux heritage and lives in Southern California. She received her MBA in Florida and has worked as a certified teacher and a paralegal. Julia is the author of the book *The Pow Wow Trail.* In her work she cites that many of the Native women have been a driving force in their cultures but also that little has been written about these women, and little is known. Her Web page, Woman Spirit, is dedicated to the noble Native women of all cultures, who continue to impact the world. Here we briefly look at the story of one of many remarkable Native women, Susan La Flesche.

Susan La Flesche—Omaha

Iron Eyes was the last Omaha chief to foresee that the white man was here to stay. He concluded that the only way for his people to survive was for his people to be educated and learn to balance Native ways with the white ways. His children became authors, politicians, orators, and anthropologists. His daughter Susan became the first Native American woman to gain a medical degree and work as a practicing M.D.

After completing her degree, Susan returned to Nebraska to work as a government physician. She is described as riding on horseback from reservation to reservation, from family to family, treating the sick.

Susan married and settled in Bancroft, Nebraska, where she had a private practice treating both Native and white patients. She adopted Christian faith and became a missionary of the Omaha Blackbird Hills Presbyterian Church and founded a hospital in Walthill, later leading a delegation to Washington, D.C., to fight against the sale of liquor in Nebraska. Her success meant that covenants were placed in land sale documents of that time prohibiting the possession of liquor on any land purchased from Omaha. Susan died at the age of 50 and is buried in Bancroft, Nebraska.

Chapter 9
Christianity: A Brief History

In chapters 1 through 8, this book has provided a brief overview of various faiths and movements to give the general reader and the new student a conceptual grasp of some of the central beliefs and practices of a faith. The author is only too aware of the finer details and the complex theological and religious developments that are necessarily omitted in a book of this sort, where there is neither the space nor sufficient author expertise to do justice to all the world faiths included.

Chapter 9 of this book focuses in some detail on the history and development of the Christian faith throughout the centuries. Aside from the information presented, a purpose of this chapter is to provide an example of a further level of study that readers and students can, if they wish, pursue for the other faiths.

Key Issues in the First-Century Church

- Jesus ascends into heaven and God's spirit descends on the church at Pentecost.
- Saul of Tarsus was converted to Christianity, becoming Paul—the apostle to the Gentiles and the greatest earliest theologian.

- The earliest followers of Jesus did not think of themselves as separate from the Jewish religion and culture, even though Jesus had spoken severely to the Pharisees (as did the Talmud).
- The words and sayings of Jesus are collected and preserved, and New Testament writings are completed.
- Christian gatherings were in or connected to Jewish synagogues.
- The Christian Church has to work out how to relate to its Jewish roots and how to relate to the Greek world of ideas (Roman culture) in which it lived.
- The expectation of the early Christians is that the Lord may return at any time. The end is near.
- 90 C.E. The Jews at Jamnia affirm the canon of the Hebrew scriptures. The same books are recognized as authoritative by Christians.
- The Christian Church begins to taste persecution, especially under Nero in Rome, who blames Christians for the famous fire that destroyed the city in 64 C.E. He used Christian live bodies as human torches to illumine his gardens.
- Persecution continues under the Emperor Domitian, who demanded to be worshiped as "Lord and God."
- Despite opposition, the gospel is preached throughout the Roman Empire and beyond. The early martyrs die for faith.

UNIT 9:1 THE EARLIEST CHRISTIANS

The Birth of the Christian Church: Pentecost

Following the death and resurrection of Jesus, the early disciples (who were Jews) are recorded as waiting in Jerusalem as instructed by the risen Jesus before his ascension into heaven (Luke 24:49). At the time of the Jewish Feast of Pentecost the disciples of Jesus were "all together in one place" (Acts 2:1) when God's Holy Spirit came upon them empowering them with "tongues, as of fire" and "other languages, as the Spirit gave them ability" (Acts 2:4). On this occasion Peter preached to the huge crowd that was gathered. The sermon, as recorded by Luke in his second work, The Acts of the Apostles, reflects the beliefs of the early Christian community that:

- The prophecy of the Jewish prophet Joel is now being fulfilled.
- Jesus was a descendant of King David, and he has been raised from the dead by God.
- Jesus is now seated at God's right hand.
- God has made Jesus "both Lord and Messiah."
- The Jewish nation has crucified Jesus.
- All could be forgiven if they repented and were baptized.

The book of Acts says that about three thousand people responded to Peter's sermon on the day of Pentecost and also describes the lifestyle of the early followers, centering around the teaching of the apostles, prayer, fellowship with each other, breaking bread together, sharing possessions, and joyfulness. (Note that there was no recorded concept of a priesthood in the earliest days of the church.)

Early Christianity and Judaism

The rapid rise of the Christian movement caused unrest among Jewish leaders, and there was threat and persecution, which included Peter's imprisonment, Stephen's stoning and death, and James, the brother of John, was beheaded by King Herod. But the courage and joy of the early church resulted in the spread of the gospel (Acts 8:4). Saul of Tarsus was a Jew and a Roman citizen who zealously opposed the early Christian movement and was a witness to the stoning of Stephen. His famous conversion is described in Acts 9:3–6, where he heard the voice of Jesus on the road to Damascus, resulting in his loss of sight and his subsequent conversion to Christianity. His name changed to Paul, and he claimed to have been given by God the task of taking the gospel to all Gentiles, kings, and all people of Israel, regardless of their race or their rank.

For Paul the good news of the gospel of Christ abolished such distinctions for those who were baptized into Christ: "There is no longer Jew or Greek, there is no longer slave or free, there is no longer male and female; for all of you are one in Christ Jesus" (Gal 3:28). Hence, though at first Jews joined the Christian movement, soon Gentiles were converted to Christ, and in Antioch (Syria) the believers were first called "Christians."

The inclusion of Gentiles raised a number of issues for the early church. One of the most important questions was whether or not it was necessary to become a Jew before following the Jewish Messiah. Controversies ensued between people who thought that new believers had to become devout Jews first and keep the Jewish law and others who said that salvation was a matter of being saved or put right with God through faith in Jesus Christ and what he had done for humanity. These controversies led to the Council of Jerusalem in about 49 C.E., where the views of Paul, Peter, and Barnabas triumphed: Salvation was not a matter of being a Jew but a matter of believing in God's provision for human sin through his son, Jesus. Without this missionary emphasis to the Gentiles, Christianity may not have crossed cultural and national boundaries. Christianity could well have remained a Jewish sect.

The Gospel and Greek Philosophy

The background of Christianity is Judaism, but the question of how much modern Christianity reflects its Jewish roots is a complex one. From the time of the first Christians, the faith has absorbed other elements, especially those of Greek philosophy. The early Christian fathers were Greeks, Gentiles, and Romans who sought to communicate their faith to the generation of their day. In so doing they related it according to the prevailing conceptual world of Greek philosophy.

The early Fathers had to wrestle with the inherent contradictions between the Greek idea of God and the biblical (Jewish) concept of God. By the time of Jesus, Greek philosophy relied on the ideas of Plato and Aristotle, believing in one transcendent God who is unchanging and immutable (Being). This high transcendent view meant that God, in Greek thought, could have no direct contact with the created world of change (Becoming). Such a belief also does not attribute to God any feelings, because feelings belong to the world of change.

The Logos

Greek thought recognized the need for a mediator between God and humankind through the idea of Logos, which was seen as the powerful principle of Reason or Word. In the prologue of St. John's Gospel there are parallels with this worldview: "In the beginning was the Word (Logos), and the word was with God, and the Word was God" (John 1:1). John saw the obvious common ground between Christianity and Greek thought in presenting his gospel. But the Greek idea of Logos is inferior to God and separate from him; the main function of Logos was to preserve God's distance from a changing world. The Greek concept has little to do with the Christian faith, which came to see the human Jesus (The Word Incarnate) as divine. Any Greek thinker who held to ideas of the logos and who read John's Gospel would conceptually part company in John 1:14, where John declares: "And the Word became flesh and lived among us, and we have seen his glory, the glory as of a father's only son, full of grace and truth."

The Greek world despised the material world because it was always subject to change; hence, the Jewish-Christian belief in the resurrection of the body would have been untenable in Greek thinking. Paul discovered this outlook when he was in Athens (Acts 17:3–20). Greek views of human nature were seen in terms of opposites, i.e., body and soul. The body belongs to the material world of Becoming and change, and the soul is the divine spark from the world of Being, which is a rational world. Each body is controlled by a small logos (word or reason), which is the soul. The soul is the real essence of the person, and the body is merely a house in which the soul lives. This explains the Greek belief in the immortality of the soul: at death the soul is released, free at last from the changing world of feeling and emotion.

The Quest for Orthodox Christianity

This distinction from Greek philosophy is an important starting point for understanding so much of the subsequent quest for an orthodox Christian doctrine. In the early days, the small Christian churches had to work out which aspects of Greek philosophy or Jewish religion should be adapted and which parts were unacceptable. The Apostolic fathers were the earliest to write outside of the New Testament. They preserved the teaching of the first apostles between the time of the late first century until the late second century. Their task was to live out and teach their Christian faith in relation to their Greek background and the world in which they lived.

The Apostolic Fathers: Controversy and Martyrdom

1 Clement

In 1628 an ancient manuscript of the Greek Bible was given to King Charles I by the Patriarch Cyril of Constantinople. The manuscript included two documents known as the Epistles of Clement. The second of these turned out to be part of a sermon that is now held to be the earliest and most valuable surviving example of Christian literature outside the New Testament. 1 Clement was a letter written around 96 C.E. from the church of Rome to the church at Corinth. The letter is ascribed to Clement of Alexandria, a well-known leader in the Roman church, but his name is not mentioned in the actual text. The church at Corinth was in chaos, and this letter emphasizes the need for order. The letter cites the natural order of things: God sent Christ, who sent the apostles, who then appointed bishops and deacons. People who have been so appointed should not be removed, but must be restored to office as soon as possible.

Ignatius of Antioch

Saint Ignatius of Antioch was the third bishop of Antioch. In the year 107 he was brought to Rome, which was under the rule of the emperor Trajan, and thrown to wild beasts. On the way to Rome he wrote to the Christians at Ephesus, Magnesia, Tralles, Rome, Philadelphia, and Smyrna, and to Polycarp, bishop of Smyrna. These seven letters illumine our understanding not only of the beliefs and internal conditions of early Christian communities, but also of the character of Ignatius himself.

Ignatius wrote about the virgin birth and divinity of Christ, but he stressed especially Christ's human nature. His letter to Tralles is an important early witness to the challenge of Docetism (Greek = "to seem"), which said that Christ did not really suffer, but only seemed to suffer, and was thus not truly human.

> So do not pay attention when anyone speaks to you apart from Jesus Christ, who was of the family of David, the child of Mary, who was truly born, who ate and drank, who was truly persecuted under Pontius Pilate, was truly crucified and truly died, in full view of heaven, earth and hell, and who was truly raised from the dead. . . . But if, as some godless people, that is, unbelievers, say, he suffered in mere appearance—being

> themselves mere appearances—why am I in bonds? (*Ignatius, letter to the Trallians* 98–10)

Ignatius was among the first to call the church "catholic." He saw it as a society of love, presided over in love by a bishop with his presbyters and deacons, and assembled in grace, in one faith, and in one Jesus Christ (Ephesians 2). Ignatius considered martyrdom a great honor and asked the Roman Christians not to save him. In his letter to Polycarp, he wrote:

> Men that seem worthy of confidence, yet teach strange doctrines, must not upset you. Stand firm, like an anvil under the hammer. It is like a great athlete to take blows and yet win the fight. For God's sake above all we must endure everything, so that God, in turn, may endure us. Increase your zeal. Read the signs of the times. Look for Him who is above all time—the Timeless, the Invisible, who for our sake became visible, the Impassable, who became subject to suffering on our account and for our sake endured everything.

Letter to Polycarp

Polycarp of Smyrna (c. 69–155 C.E.) was another early church leader known as an Apostolic Father, one of the bishops who were appointed and instructed by the apostles themselves. According to Irenaeus, Polycarp was a disciple of John the Evangelist and was appointed the Bishop of Smyrna (now Izmir, Turkey). When St. Ignatius passed through Smyrna on his way to martyrdom, Polycarp kissed his chains. Ignatius therefore entrusted his churches in the east to the pastoral care of Polycarp. Only one letter of Polycarp survives, written to the church in Philippi showing his own deep faith and compassion. Very little is known of his life before his martyrdom, except that he once journeyed to Rome, to discuss, among other things, the date of Easter.

Authentic records of Polycarp's death are, however, available. In 155 the Roman Emperor began intensive persecution of Christians. (The historian Eusebius identifies the emperor as Marcus Aurelius, although difficulties arise in trying to match the relevant dates.) Polycarp went into hiding but was betrayed by a slave. At the time of his arrest at age eighty-six, he refused to flee again, saying that he would put himself in God's hands. The proconsul showed some reluctance to deal violently with such an old man and urged him to renounce Christ and swear by the spirit of Caesar. Polycarp replied,

> I have served Christ for eighty-six years and he has done me no wrong. Should I now renounce him? I am a Christian, and if you want to learn of Christ, I will teach you. (From "The Encyclical Epistle of the Church at Smyrna Concerning the Martyrdom of The Holy Polycarp," from *Early Church*

> *Fathers: Ante-Nicene Fathers to A.D. 325*, vol. 1, eds., Alexander Roberts and James Donaldson)

The proconsul hesitated and replied that if Polycarp could convince the people, he would let him go. In the face of a zealous mob, however, the proconsul agreed to his death. The mob wanted him thrown to the lions, but the proconsul refused so they cried out for him to be burned. Nailing victims to the stake was the custom, but the proconsol ordered him to be tied instead, and Polycarp promised not to try to escape. With flames surrounding him, he cried a prayer that he might be a worthy martyr, thanking God for all the blessings that had been given him by Christ. He died at 2:00 P.M. on February 23, 155 C.E.

Justin Martyr

Justin Martyr was born around 100 C.E. at Flavia Neapolis (modern Nablus) in Samaria (between the north and south of Israel). His parents were Pagan Greeks who gave him a good education in rhetoric, poetry, and history. He studied Greek philosophy in Alexandria and Ephesus, and allied himself first to Stoicism, then Pythagoreanism, then Platonism. While at Ephesus, he greatly admired the Christian martyrs. One day he met an old Christian man by the sea who spoke to him about Jesus, who was the fulfilment of the promises made through the Jewish prophets. Justin was overwhelmed. "Straightway a flame was kindled in my soul," he writes, "and a love of the prophets and those who are friends of Christ possessed me."

Justin started with the view that Pagan philosophy, especially Platonism, is not simply wrong, but is only a partial grasp of the truth, and serves as "a schoolmaster to bring us to Christ." He debated with Pagans, Jews, and heretics and founded a school of Christian philosophy. There he argued with the Cynic philosopher Crescens in debate, but was later arrested on the charge of practicing an unauthorized religion. The Roman prefect Rustics tried him, and he refused to renounce Christianity. Justin Martyr was put to death by beheading along with six of his students, one of them a woman. A record of the trial, probably authentic, exists and is known as *The Acts of Justin the Martyr.*

There are three works of Justin Martyr, as follows:

- His *First Apology* (around 155), addressed to the Emperor Antoninus Pius and his adopted sons, defends Christianity as the only rational creed. He includes an account of current Christian ceremonies of Baptism and the Eucharist (probably to counteract distorted accounts from anti-Christian sources).
- The *Second Apology* is addressed to the Roman Senate. It is chiefly concerned about rebutting specific charges of immorality and the like that had been made against the Christians. He argues that good Christians make good citizens, and that the notion that Christianity undermines the foundations of a good society is based on slander or misunderstanding.

- The *Dialog with Trypho the Jew* is an account of a dialogue between Justin and a Jewish rabbi named Trypho (whom he met while promenading at Ephesus shortly after the sack of Jerusalem in 135). Trypho had fled from Israel, and the two men talked about the Jewish people and their place in history, and then about Jesus and whether he was the promised messiah. A principal question is whether the Christian belief in the deity of Christ can be reconciled with the uncompromising monotheism of the scriptures. The dialogue is a valuable source of information about early Christian thought concerning Judaism and the relation between Israel and the Church as communities having a covenant relation with God. Toward the end of the dialog, Trypho asks, "Suppose that I were to become a Christian. Would I be required to give up keeping kosher and other parts of the Jewish law?"

  Justin replies, "Christians are not agreed on this. Some would say that you must give them up. Others, such as myself, would say that it would be quite all right for you, as a Jewish convert to Christianity, to keep kosher and otherwise observe the Law of Moses, provided that you did not try to compel other converts to do likewise, and provided that you clearly understand that keeping kosher will not save you. It is only Christ who saves you."

  They finally part friends, with Trypho saying, "You have given me food for thought. I must consider this further." (*Dialog with Trypho*).

UNIT 9:2 THE SECOND CENTURY: HERESIES AND MARTYRS

Key Developments in the Second-Century Christian Church

- The Lord has not returned as soon as many believed, and church leadership (especially bishops) during perilous times becomes more necessary and more developed.
- The early church defends its faith and its beliefs about Jesus from heresies such as Gnosticism, Docetism, Marcionism, and Montanism.
- Christian apologists (those who defend the faith) continue to emerge.
- Christians continue to be put to death because they refuse to deny the faith at any cost.
- By the end of the second century the four Gospels and Paul's letters were recognized as authentic texts.
- Asia Minor and North Africa are strong in Christian influence, as is Rome.

The church fathers—sometimes called the patristic fathers—were church leaders and theologians who wrote from the period between the end of New Testament times up until the sixth and seventh centuries. We cannot address all of them, but included in this unit are some of the main figures who shaped the development and thought of the early church in its struggle with early heresy.

The term "heresy" is derived from the Greek, meaning "to choose," and refers to the willful rejection of official doctrine. Gnosticism was an early Christian heresy. This modern theological term refers to a number of second-century sects that all had some common element of belief. Gnostics used the Bible and taught from it, and Jesus was given significance but Gnostic theology was different from mainstream Christianity. Gnostics believed in God, but in a God who was removed and remote from this world. The world as we know it was created by a lesser god, who was responsible for the imperfect material world—sometimes identified as the God of Judaism or of the Old Testament. The interpretation of God that finally emerged and won the doctrinal struggles of the early church became identified as the "orthodox," from the Greek meaning "straight thinking."

By the fourth century, orthodox proponents were established and well advanced in eliminating all unsuccessful pretenders to the doctrinal throne. By establishing themselves as the one and only "true" interpreters of the Christian message, they decided what came to be the official scriptures, most importantly the Gospels. The final affirmation of orthodoxy came in the fourth century when Athanasius, Bishop of Alexandria, defined what he claimed to be the four "true" gospels of the New Testament. Athanasius proclaimed: "I bring before you the books included in the Canon, and handed down and accredited as Divine. These are the fountains of salvation. In these alone is proclaimed the doctrine of godliness. Let no man add to them, neither let him take away."

The Gnostics

For the Gnostics, the source of divine truth and wisdom is through the Gnosis, or knowledge, that people are able to discover within themselves. This view contrasts with the orthodox, who saw knowledge of God and salvation through faith handed down from Christ and the early apostles, interpreted by the Pope and the other bishops, and transmitted to the populace primarily by priests and deacons. While not wholly disagreeing with this process, Gnostics felt that for spiritual knowledge to be legitimate, it must move beyond social and religious structures to one's own unique inner knowing. With a clear mind and a pure heart, one can come to Gnosis (knowledge).

One main source of understanding of Gnosticism was based almost exclusively on the reports of early theologians and bishops who opposed it. The most prolific and powerful of these was Iranaeus (Bishop of Lyons), writing in the second century. His five volumes, called *The Destruction and Overthrow of Falsely So-called Knowledge,* begin with his promise to

> Set forth views of those who are now teaching heresy . . . to show how absurd and inconsistent with the truth are their

> statements. . . . I do this so that . . . you may urge all those with whom you are connected to avoid such an abyss of madness and of blasphemy against Christ.

The Nag Hammadi Texts

In December 1945, at a place called Nag Hammadi in upper Egypt, a local peasant quite accidentally found an earthenware jar containing forty-nine treatises (five duplicates), which were Coptic translations of original Greek documents dated to about 120 C.E. The Nag Hammadi documents themselves have been variously dated between the third and fifth centuries C.E.

The Nag Hammadi texts include a fragment of Plato's *Republic*; hermetic (Gnostic) tracts; the Gospel of Philip; the now well-known Gospel of Thomas (which claims to be sayings of Jesus); an essay on Gnostic liberation in a world of tragedy; the Book of Thomas the Contender; a work called the Apocrypohon (literally, "secret book") of John, in which we find what are called "the mysteries, [and the] things hidden in silence" that Jesus taught to his disciple John; and the Gospel of Truth, a meditation on personal religious experience. The Nag Hammadi texts show Gnosticism to be a very different religion from orthodox Christianity. Different Gnostic groups had their own scriptures and teachings; they also believed in secret traditions that they claimed they had learned or received from the early apostles. Jesus was seen as an emissary of the supreme God in docetic (seemingly) human in form.

Irenaeus

As a young man in Smyrna (near Ephesus, in what is now western Turkey), Irenaeus (c. 125–c. 202) heard the preaching of Polycarp, who as a young man had heard the preaching of the apostle John. Irenaeus was also influenced by Justin Martyr (see unit 9:1) and is thus an important link between the apostolic church and later times. Irenaeus also provides an important link between early Greek theology and Western Latin theology. His major work is the *Refutation of Heresies*, a defense of orthodox Christianity against its Gnostic rivals.

- Gnostics were dualists, teaching that there are two great opposing forces: good against evil, light versus darkness, knowledge versus ignorance, spirit versus matter. Arguing that the world is material, evil, and imperfect, they denied that God had made it. "How can the perfect produce the imperfect, the infinite produce the finite, the spiritual produce the material?" Gnostic beliefs were a mix of Christianity, Judaism, Platonism, and later Zoroastrianism. They rejected the Christian belief in the resurrection of the body in favor of the immortality of the soul.

- Gnostics claimed to be Christians. They said that Jesus had had two doctrines: one doctrine for the common person and preached to everyone, and the other an advanced teaching, kept secret from the crowds and only for the spiritually elite, the chosen few. They claimed that for the real knowledge and the real truth, one must turn to the Gnostics.

In opposition to Gnosticism, Irenaeus preached that the gospel message is for everyone. He was, with Ignatius, among the first to speak of the Church as "catholic" (universal). In using this term, he contrasted Gnosticism and orthodox Christianity by pointing to the different churches founded by the apostles and the open, continuous public teaching and preaching in them. His main appeal against Gnosticism was in the authenticity of apostolic scripture (the New Testament) and to apostolic teaching handed down in the churches. The Gnostics did not accept the New Testament and so Irenaus appealed to the apostolic religion. Later, as we shall see, apostolic Christianity was summarized (e.g., in the Apostles Creed) precisely to oppose Gnosticism.

The Formation of the New Testament

Jesus and his first disciples were almost certainly thought to speak or have knowledge of three languages: Aramaic (the common Semitic language), Hebrew (the language of their Jewish Scriptures), and Greek (spoken throughout the Roman Empire). The original New Testament documents were written in Greek.

For Irenaeus and the early church the two important questions were: How do we know what is true? and Where is the source for believing what is true about Christianity? Their answer was based mainly on apostolic authority. If a book was recognized as having been written by an apostle or by someone closely associated with an apostle, then it was authentic. On this basis, the four Gospels of Matthew, Mark, Luke, and John were immediately admitted. Writings such as The Shepherd of Hermas, the first epistle of Clement to the Corinthians, and the Didache were excluded. They had been written too late to be apostolic. The Gospel of Philip and The Gospel of Peter were excluded for the same reasons. Scholars recognize that a great difference in quality exists between these later writings and the Gospels and other writings that found their way into the New Testament. By the end of the second century, the four Gospels and Paul's letters were settled. In 367 C.E. Bishop Athanasius wrote a letter in which he listed the twenty-seven books of the New Testament as being canonical, i.e., official scripture. In the Armenian Church, however, the inclusion of Revelation was resisted until the twelfth century.

Tertullian, Montanism, and Monarchianism

In the latter half of the second century, the heresy of Montanism grew. Montanus was a self-appointed prophet who attracted followers through his principal message that the end of the world was imminent. Montanists were led by prophets (men and women) who were ascetics, practicing severe fasting, prohibition of second marriages, and no flight from martyrdom (in contrast to Matt. 10:23).

The movement initially won the support of Tertullian (c 160–220 C.E.), a brilliant lawyer who converted from Greek Paganism sometime before the year 197 C.E. Tertullian was the first well-known Christian to write in Latin, with a long and very varied list of publications. In his *Apology*, the faith is summarized as, "The blood of the martyrs is the seed of the church." He wrote, *"As often as you mow us down, the more we grow in number."* Tertullian insisted on the separation of the church from pagan society. He was a strong critic of Greek philosophy in contrast to Justin and the earlier apologists, although his own training in philosophy, especially Stoicism, shows through his writings. The theological works he wrote are mainly polemical against heresies, and like Irenaeus he argued against Gnosticism. His longest book is called *Against Marcion*. Marcion was the greatest of the second-century heretics who mixed Gnostic beliefs with the teaching of Paul.

Tertullian also argued against Monarchianism, which taught the "monarchy" or sole rule of God. In so doing, Monarchians ignored the Trinity by teaching that the Father, the Son, and the Spirit are three different names for the same being. Instead of the Christian belief in the difference of three persons within the Godhead, they spoke of a succession of different modes of operation. Tertullian condemned Monarchianism for threatening the independence of the Son. In his work *Against Praxeas*, he stated that God is one substance in three persons, thus voicing the language for the Trinity that was to form the basis for later definitions of the doctrine of the Trinity and the Incarnation.

Origen, the Father of Eastern Christianity

Tertullian exerted great influence in Western Roman Theology, whereas Origen (c. 184–254) was a leading early theologian of the Eastern Greek-thinking world. He was born of Christian parents in Alexandria. His father Leonides was martyred. As a young man he devoted himself to an austere life and scholarship and was eventually head of a catechetical school. He moved to Caesarea in Palestine after a falling out with the bishop. In the Decian persecution (249–251), he was imprisoned and tortured, dying a few years later from injuries suffered at that time.

Origen employed the Alexandrian method of biblical interpretation using allegory. For Origen, everything had both a bodily aspect that everyone can see and understand and a spiritual aspect that is only understood by people who are perfect. This two-tier view, then, presented Christians as either simple or perfect. He taught that the Persons of the Trinity are at different levels: the Father greater than the Son, and the Son greater than the Spirit. The Father is, therefore, the one "true God" and the Son is God, but at a lower level. He also believed in a fourth level, that of rational beings. Each level participates in the level above. In the next century, Arius expanded ideologically from these views by stating that only the Father is really God and teaching that the Son and the Spirit are merely creatures.

Origen also believed that being saved means becoming like God. The Christian becomes saved by fixing his or her mind on God and becoming 'deified' through contemplation. The human soul has to rise through the earthly Jesus from the world of becoming to the world of being, and then to the eternal world through Jesus, the Word of God. These ideas drew heavily on neo-Platonism and Gnosticism. Origen's theology was opposed in the fourth century and finally condemned at the Second Council of Constantinople in 553 C.E.

Cyprian, Bishop of Carthage, and the Decian Persecution

Cyprian (d. 258) was born early in the third century to a pagan family, but in the year 245/46, his critical reflection on the Roman world and his search for moral and spiritual renewal led him to become a Christian. Cyprian was appointed as Bishop of Carthage, in the Roman province of Africa, soon after his conversion. Intellectually, he was a follower of Tertullian and is said to have read his works daily. The ten years of his office saw some of the worst persecution and struggle the church has ever known in the Decian attack on the church, which began with the murder of the bishops of Rome, Antioch, Jerusalem, and Caesarea. Christians were then forced, upon pain of death, to sacrifice to the gods. Large numbers of Christians succumbed and were given certificates of proof; others bribed officials for falsified certificates. Cyprian went into hiding and led the church through exile, writing letters to the faithful. After his return he set about reconciling people who had lapsed and fallen into apostasy during the persecution. A council at Carthage in 251 decided that after appropriate penance and delay, these people were allowed to return and be readmitted to the Church. At this time in Rome, Cornelius was appointed as bishop, but his authority was challenged by a rival called Novatian who refused to readmit people who had lapsed.

For Cyprian, the issue of the division of the church was paramount. In his most important work, *The Unity of the Church*, he stated the impossibility of dividing the Church; one can leave it, but the only true Church is the catholic church handed down from the apostles. He put forward the view that, *"No one can have God as Father who does not have Church as Mother."* One of his letters contains one of the first expressions of the belief that "Outside the Church there is no salvation." Ironically Cyprian, who insisted on rebaptism for people who lapsed, brought this issue into conflict with the policy of Rome. Eventually Rome and Africa went their own ways over rebaptism, Africa following Cyprian. But in his focus on the nature and unity of the Church (which accepts the authority and authenticity of the office of bishops) he had his greatest influence on Christian thought in the West. As the successors of the apostles, bishops had authority over more charismatic theologies of the martyrs, the lower clergy, or the laity. This structure laid the foundation for the later hierarchy in the Roman Catholic Church.

UNIT 9:3 CONSTANTINE, CREEDS, AND COUNCILS

Key Developments in the Third- and Fourth-Century Christian Church

- North Africa becomes important for the growth of Christianity. Carthage and Alexandria are centers of Christian theology with famous thinkers such as Origen, Tertullian, and Clement of Alexandria.
- The persecution ordered by Decius in 250 C.E. was throughout the Roman Empire. Pagan sacrifice was enforced and the church continues to think about how to treat "lapsed" Christians who gave in to persecution but want to come back to faith.
- The Church engages in the study of "Christology"—how to understand Jesus' humanity and divinity existing both in the same person.
- Early in the third century, Anthony enters the desert as a hermit. This marks an early move to monasticism.
- The historian Eusebius wrote his Church history, included an account of the vision of Constantine.
- 323: Eusebius wrote his "Ecclesiastical History."
- 325: First Ecumenical Council at Nicaea, condemning Arianism and producing the Nicene Creed (Athanasius).
- 367: Athanasius's letter contains definitive (twenty-seven books) of the New Testament canon.
- 387: The conversation of Augustine.

Jesus whom I know as my Redeemer cannot be less than God.
St. Athanasius

At its heart Christianity is based on a very simple premise that humanity is alienated from God and from each other, and that this acute condition has been healed through the life and saving death of a single man, Jesus of Nazareth. Therefore, at its core, Christianity believes not in a philosophy but in a person. Looking, as we will, at the early creeds and councils, forgetting this fact is easy because the language and the debate often grow complex. From the earliest days, belief about the person of Jesus was a central issue for faith and doctrine. How to understand his humanity and his divinity as existing both in the same person gave way to a vast field of what has been termed *christological* study that continues unabated to the present day. Broadly speaking, Christology falls into two major extremes (both to be rejected later as error):

- "Low" Christology represents a theological "low" trend of Jewish background, believing that Jesus is only a messenger or prophet, with nothing divine in him. Groups, individuals, and beliefs with varying "low" Christologies included: the Ebionites, Adoptionism, Origen, Nestorianism (two separate natures of Christ), and Antiochene Christology.
- "High Christology" often relies on Platonic ideas and admitting only the divine nature of Christ at the expense of his humanity. High Christology is often associated with the partriarch Cyril of Alexandria (d. 444). Other groups, individuals, and beliefs with a "high" Christology include Apollinarius of Laodicaea (c. 310–390), Eutyches of Constantinople (c. 378–454), and Monophysitism (of one nature solely—Christ's two natures were mixed, so that he was a new species, neither divine nor human).

Both low and high Christology were refuted at the Council of Chalcedon (451), which declared that Christ had two natures: human and divine. At the Council of Nicaea (325 C.E.), the profession of faith was that Christ was of the same substance as the Father.

Persecution in the Early Church

As we have seen in units 9:1 and 9:2, Christianity in the first two centuries suffered bouts of external persecution from Judaism and the Roman Empire and theological/ideological attacks by Docetists, Gnostics, and others on its main doctrines of the Trinity (God in three persons) and the Incarnation (God come in human form in the person of Jesus).

Politically there was no wholesale systematic persecution of Christians until 250 C.E. under the emperor Decius. The suffering endured by the early church exercised influence on the Christian imagination. Even before the fourth century evidence exists of martyrs' shrines becoming places of pilgrimage with churches being built over their tombs. In the first four centuries Christianity grew most vigorously in the cities of the Roman Empire or their colonial outposts. Christianity was eventually given patronage by the emperor Constantine, in the Edict of Milan in 311.

Constantine the Great

Constantine the Great (c. 288–337) was the first Roman emperor to accept the Christian faith. His father died in 306, and he was declared emperor in the West but this could only be claimed by fighting Maxentius. In 312 on the evening before the battle of Milvian Bridge, the historian Eusebius reports that Constantine had a vision. It was of a cross bearing the inscription, *"In hoc signo vinces,"* which means

Landmarks in Early Christology	
c.100–165	Justin Martyr: apologist
c.177–200	Irenaeus of Lyons
c.185–254	Origen: from Alexandria
196–212	Tertullian: active from Carthage
d. 336	Arius: opposed Christ's divinity
c.296–373	Athanasius: defender of the Trinity
b. c.310	Apollinarius: from Antioch—Jesus controlled by a divine mind
313	Roman Empire espouses Christianity
325	Council of Nicea
354–430	Augustine: father of Western theology
c.381–451	Nestorius: distinguished the two natures
381	First Council of Constantinople
431	First Council of Ephesus
d. 444	Cyril of Alexandria
	Council of Chalcedon

"In this sign you will conquer." After the victory he established a new capital for the empire on the site of Byzantium, which then became Constantinople.

Eusebius and the History of the Church

Much of what we know of the first three hundred years of the church comes from the writings of Eusebius of Caesarea, who wrote the only surviving history of the Church during the first crucial three hundred years. His theme throughout is the way providence works through the apostolic succession. His history records the ordeals of 146 martyrs, the theology of 47 heretics, and the events leading up to the great Church Councils in the third and fourth centuries. The history of the Church preserves many early documents that would otherwise be unknown.

Eusebius was a strong admirer of Origen and a close friend and ally of the emperor Constantine. When he supported Arius, he was temporarily excommunicated at the Council of Antioch in 325. At the Council of Nicaea in the same year he explained himself and was reinstated but not without paying the price of having to sign the Nicene Creed itself. This alliance was uneasy for Eusebius. He had written a letter to his church in Caesarea (which still survives today) explaining to the flock his interpretation of the creed, which is clearly in theological disagreement with its main tenets and beliefs.

The Council of Nicaea (325 C.E.)

The Council of Nicaea (modern Iznik in northwest Turkey) was the first ecumenical council of the Christian Church that met in response to the teaching of Arius. Arius's theological opponent was Athanasius.

Athanasius contra Arius

Athanasius was born around 298 C.E., and lived in Alexandria, Egypt, the chief learning center of the Roman Empire. Arius of Alexandria began to teach concerning the Word of God (John 1:1) that "God begat him, and before he was begotten, he did not exist." Arius was of the view that it was impossible for God to be present in a human life. If Christ is "divine" it is only because God has done it, not because he is equal with God. Athanasius was at that time a newly ordained deacon and secretary to Bishop Alexander of Alexandria. His reply to Arius was that the begetting of the Word by the Father is an eternal relation between Them, and not a temporal event. Arius was condemned by the bishops of Egypt (with some exceptions). He went to Nicomedia, and wrote letters to bishops throughout the world, stating his position.

The Emperor Constantine resolved to solve the dispute by calling a council of bishops from all over the Christian world. This council met in Nicaea, just across the straits from Constantinople, in the year 325. The council consisted of 317 bishops. Athanasius accompanied his bishop to the council and was seen as a chief spokesman for the view that the Son was fully God, coequal and coeternal with the Father.

Attendees in favor of Athanasius were in the majority. Athanasius set himself to confront the Arian belief that the Son was merely a creature however unique or perfect. The challenge was to formulate a creed and find a formula from holy scripture that would express the full deity of the Son, equally with the Father. However, the Arians agreed to all such formulations, having made their own interpretations already. Finally, the Greek word *homoousios* (meaning "of the same substance, or nature, or essence") was introduced, because it was one word that could not be understood to mean what the Arians meant.

- It was a word that was agreeable to the West (Tertullian had seen the Trinity as three persons in one substance).
- It was agreeable to the Antiochenes (the minority school in the East who affirmed the unity of the Godhead, but were less clear about the distinctness of Father, Son, and Holy Spirit).
- But it was not acceptable to the followers of Origen (especially Eusebius) and the majority in the East.

Some bishops hesitated in using a term not found in the scriptures, but came to see that the alternative was a creed that both sides would sign. Furthermore, the Church could ill afford to leave the question of whether the Son is truly God (the Arians said "a god") undecided. The conclusion was that the Council adopted a creed that is a shorter version of what we now call the Nicene Creed, declaring the Son to be "of one substance with the Father."

In 328, Alexander died, and Athanasius succeeded him as bishop of Alexandria. His life was spent defending the full deity of Christ against emperors, bishops, and theologians. For this, he was regarded as a trouble-maker by Constantine and his successors, and was banished from Alexandria on several occasions (this opposition lead to the expression *Athanasius contra mundum*, or, "Athanasius against the world"). Eventually, Christians who believed in the deity of Christ came to see that once they were inclined to abandon the Nicene formulation, they were in danger of relegating the Logos (the eternal word, see John 1:1) to the status of a high-ranking angel. Only the Nicene formulation would preserve the Christian faith in any meaningful sense, and so they reaffirmed the Nicene Creed at the Council of Constantinople in 381, a final victory that Athanasius did not live to see. Part of the creed reads: "I believe in one Lord Jesus Christ, the only-begotten Son of God, begotten of his Father before all worlds, God of God, Light of Light, very God of very God, begotten not made, being of one substance with the Father, by whom all things were made. . . ."

Athanasius struggled all his life against Arianism. Arius was condemned at Nicaea, but the creed was not accepted by followers of Origen in the East. Athanasius saw the divinity of Jesus Christ as the foundation of the Christian faith; only a divine Christ could save the world. This theme permeates all he wrote. In his *Incarnation of the Word,* Athanasius argues against those who said that the incarnation and crucifixion of God's Son is degrading. Athanasius said that only the one through whom the world was created could restore it,

> We were the cause of his becoming flesh. For our salvation he loved us so much as to appear and be born in a human body. . . . No one else but the Saviour himself, who in the beginning made everything out of nothing, could bring the corrupted to incorruption; no one else but the image of the Father could recreate men in God's image; no one else but our Lord Jesus Christ, who is Life itself, could make the mortal immortal.

Nicaea split the church into two major groups: the Nicene party and the Origenists. The Origenists were not Arians—i.e., they did not see Jesus Christ as a creature, made out of nothing like the rest of humanity, but they saw him as inferior to the Father. The misunderstandings between the two groups came to be called "The Arian controversy" and continued for nearly half a century.

Apollinarius

Later in the fourth century Apollinarius taught that Jesus was controlled by a divine mind. His flesh was human but his mind was divine. Debate about the nature of Christ (christological debate) continued well into the fourth and fifth centuries, and two different approaches to the person of Jesus developed focused on two different centers: Antioch and Alexandria.

Antiochene Christology

In Antioch, theology focused on the importance of Christ's life as a full human being so that just like everyone else he had been tempted to sin and self-interest but unlike anyone else had not given in to it. Antiochene expositors included John Chrysostom, Theodore of Mopsuestia, and Nestorius. They stressed that Christ's human nature was distinct from his unity with the Son of God. In this view Jesus had two natures, and the problem was how to speak of a unity in Christ's person. Antioch is now the see of five patriarchs, the Greek Orthodox, Syrian Orthodox, Maronite, Melkite, and Syrian Catholic.

Alexandrian Christology

Alexandrian theology—represented by Origen, Athanasius, and Cyril—emphasized God coming down to rescue humanity. They affirmed the unity of Christ's person but had to imply a fusion or mixture of his two natures into one. His human nature tended to be restricted to the flesh, which was a vehicle for the divine. The patriarchs of Alexandria today have jurisdiction over Catholic Copts, Coptic Christians who do not accept the Chalcedon Creed, and Orthodox Copts who trace their tradition back to 567.

The Council of Chalcedon

The ongoing struggle between these views led to the Council of Chalcedon (451 C.E.), which was called by the emperor Marcian. The Creeds of Nicaea and Constantinople (381) should have sufficed for the unity of the church, the latter having further condemned Arianism and Apollinarianism. But Nestorius, from the Antiochene school, perpetuated the controversy by dividing Jesus Christ into God the Word and Jesus the man. He was opposed by Cyril (bishop of Alexandria, 412). Then came Eutyches, from the Alexandrian school, who in his efforts to oppose Nestorianism was perceived as guilty of the opposite error, that of confounding or blurring the two natures of Christ. The creed agreed upon by the council at Chalcedon made sure that Christian Orthodoxy saw Jesus Christ as both fully God and fully man. In him, "two natures" were united in one "person" but remained distinct:

> Following the holy fathers, we confess with one voice that the one and only Son, our Lord Jesus Christ, is perfect in Godhead and perfect in manhood, truly God and truly man, that he has a rational soul and a body. He is of one substance with the Father as God, he is also of one substance with us as man. He is like us in all things except sin. He was begotten of his

> Father before the ages as God, but in these last days and for our salvation he was born of Mary the virgin, the "God-bearer," as man. This one and the same Christ, Son, Lord, Only-begotten is made known in two natures, without confusion, without change, without division, without separation. The distinction of the natures is no way taken away by their union, but rather the distinctive properties of each nature are preserved. . . . They are not separated or divided into two persons but they form one and the same Son, Lord Jesus Christ.

The Decline of the Roman Empire

As we have seen, Christianity emerged as the religion of the Roman Empire, but at the same time that empire was in decline. Early in the fifth century, the city of Rome fell to the Barbarian invasion. Eastern Christendom, with its center at Constantinople, slowly became separated from the West and in so doing developed its own particular theology and practice. In time, these differences would culminate and create a schism so that in the eleventh century they parted company. That division, between the Orthodox Church in the East and the Roman Catholic Church in the West, has been in place up to the present, nearly ten centuries later.

St. Augustine

Augustine (354–430) was one of the foremost philosopher-theologians of early Christianity and as bishop (396–430) of Hippo (Modern Bone, Algeria) was the leading figure in the church of North Africa. He had profound and lasting influence on the subsequent development of Western thought and culture. More than anyone else, Augustine shaped the ideas and defined the issues that have characterized the Western tradition of Christian theology. He wrote vigorously; two of his major works are his semiautobiographical *Confessions*, which includes elements of mysticism, and *City of God*, a Christian vision of history.

The first part of Augustine's life (to 391) seems to have been an attempt to reconcile his Christian faith with classical culture. He was driven with enthusiasm for the philosophic life and adopted Manichaeism, a Christian heresy that claimed to provide a rational form of Christianity on the basis of an edited text of scripture. His search for truth led him eventually through neo-Platonism and a dramatic conversion to Christianity.

Augustine's ordination was unexpectedly forced upon him by popular acclamation during a visit to Hippo in 391. His subsequent career as priest and bishop was to be dominated by controversy and debate, focused for much of the time around the Donatists and with the British theologian Pelagius. The Donatists were Christian separatists, maintaining that only they were the true church and therefore only their sacraments were valid. Augustine's reply was to emphasize unity, not division, as the authentic mark of Christianity. He also stated that the validity of the sacraments depended on Christ himself, not on any human group or institution.

Pelagianism was an early fifth-century Christian reform movement which believed that no person could be excused from meeting the full demand of God's law. Pelagians stressed the freedom of the human will and its ability to control motives and regulate behavior. In contrast, Augustine argued that because everyone inherits sin (the doctrine of original sin), nobody entirely governs his or her own motivation. Only with the aid of God's grace is it possible for persons to will and to do good. But even when we have received grace, Augustine pointed out that without God's help we would soon lapse from grace. Human beings are so undermined by sin that they do not have the capacity even to seek salvation. If faith is to be constant, then the *gift of perseverance* is needed. God does not give this gift to all freely but only to those whom he has elected to receive it. This approach led to a belief in *predestination*, which is the view that God foreknows and predetermines the outcome of all things, including one's individual destiny. In contrast, Pelagius believed that human beings had the freedom to choose or deny God. In these controversies, Augustine opposed forces that divided Christians on grounds either of religious exclusivism or of moral worth.

Augustine died in 430 in the wake of a barbarian army about to take the city of Hippo. At the same time the Western Roman Empire was crumbling. But his theological thought dominated the Middle Ages, so that he has become thought of as the Father of the Western Church. This title was affirmed by the Reformers of the sixteenth century (see unit 9:6) who, for good or ill, rediscovered Augustine's doctrine of grace and used it for their own purposes.

Monophysitism

Monophysitism (sometimes known as Eutychianism) is the doctrine that Jesus Christ had only one nature, rather than two. Eutyches, in the mid-fifth century, taught that in Jesus Christ the humanity was absorbed by the divinity, "dissolved like a drop of honey in the sea." He opposed the Nestorian doctrine that the two natures of Christ represented two distinct persons, but Nestorianism was condemned as heretical at the Council of Chalcedon in 451.

Strict Monophysitism explains the one nature in Christ in one of four ways:

- The human nature is absorbed by the divine
- The divine Word (Logos) disappears in the humanity of Christ
- A unique third nature is created from the combination of the divine and human natures
- A composition (a natural whole) of humanity and divinity exists without confusion.

Severus (c. 465–538), patriarch of Antioch, put forward a less extreme version of Monophysitism but all Monophysites rejected the formulas of Chalcedon, and efforts to compromise failed. By the sixth century Monophysitism had a strong influence in the Armenian Church, the Coptic Church, and the Jacobite Church, all three of which retain a nominal Monophysitism today.

UNIT 9:4 THE EASTERN CHURCH

Key Developments in the History of the Fourth-Century to Fifth-Century Orthodox Church

- 314: Council of Arles, summoned by Constantine against the Donatists. Capital of Empire moves to Constantinople. In 324 the city was founded, and Rome is no longer the power base for the empire.
- 330: Constantinople named the capital of Christian Empire.
- 340–430: Period of the Church Fathers (Ambrose, 340–397; Jerome, 340–420; Augustine, 354–430; etc.).
- 358: Basil of Caesarea (Nicene Cappadocian Fathers) founded monastic community (and Greek Orthodox monastic rule).
- Iconoclastic controversy over the veneration of images divides the Byzantine Emperor and the Pope.
- 382: The Second Ecumenical Council: Constantinople I—against Apollinarius's christological heresy and Macedonius's heresy of the Holy Spirit.
- 398: John Chrysostom consecrated bishop of Constantinople.

> *The Church is one and the same with the Lord—His Body, of His flesh and of His bones. The Church is the living vine, nourished by Him and growing in Him. Never think of the Church apart from the Lord Jesus Christ, from the Father and Holy Spirit.*
>
> St. John of Kronstadt

The Eastern Orthodox Church

In this unit we follow through some of the main events and beliefs of the Eastern Orthodox Church from the fourth century until the present time. The next unit (9:5) then picks up the broad historical line of church history from the fifth century onward.

The Orthodox Church claims that it was founded by the Lord Jesus Christ and is the living manifestation of his presence through the ages. Orthodoxy, whether in its Greek or Roman forms, is recognized by its rich liturgical life and its faithfulness to the apostolic tradition. Whereas Catholicism and later Protestantism focus on doctrine and teaching, the Orthodox tradition emphasizes worship as the most important area of religious experience.

In addition, Orthodox Christians believe that their Church has preserved the tradition and continuity of the ancient Church in its fullness, compared to other Christian denominations who have moved away from the common ground of the Church of the first ten centuries who followed the faith and practices that were defined by the first seven ecumenical councils. The word "orthodox" means "right belief and right glory." Today, approximately 300 million Christians belong to the Orthodox Church.

Historical Background of Eastern Orthodoxy

The fourth century was a pivotal time in the history of the Christian Church. The century witnessed major changes and transitions in church relations with state and society which included:

- *The Empire persecuting the Church.* At the beginning of the century, the church went through the "Great Persecution" by Emperor Diocletian (305), although that movement failed to exterminate the church.
- *The Empire legitimizing the Church.* The Emperor Constantine professed Christianity and the church was given legal status.
- *The Empire undermining the Church.* Paganism was the indigenous religion of most of the Empire, and the Emperor Julian (361–363) attempted unsuccessfully to reestablish paganism.
- *The Empire adopting the Church.* Christianity was officially made the state religion under Emperor Theodosius IX in 381.
- *The Church challenging the Empire.* In a dramatic confrontation that foresaw further confrontation between two opposing forces, Bishop Ambrose of Milan defied the emperor. By the end of the century the persecuted church in its turn became the persecutor. It believed itself to be combating heresy and evil forces.

By the end of the fourth century there were five leading churches: Rome, Constantinople, Alexandria, Antioch, and Jerusalem. The bishops of Alexandria and Rome were called "popes," while the bishops of the other three were called "patriarchs." By the fifth century, the Roman Empire had been divided into east and west.

For centuries after the Council of Chalcedon (451) the Eastern Church continued with controversy over the person of Jesus Christ. In Egypt and other areas, the Council was never accepted, which presented the emperors of the East with a problem of unity. Their options were limited. They could be reconciled with the non-Chalcedonians by ceasing to adhere to the Chalcedonian Creed, but that would incur further disunity with Rome. The alternative was to keep unity with the West by continuing to accept Chalcedon, but live with schism in their own

Eastern Church. In time the dilemma was resolved by external forces. The Muslim invasions removed the non-Chalcedonians from the Empire, and Eastern Orthodoxy held to Chalcedon and union with Western Christianity.

The non-Chalcedonians were independent, as they have been ever since. They are now the Oriental Orthodox Churches—namely, the Syrian, Coptic, Ethiopian, and Armenian Orthodox Churches, which have in common their historic rejection of the Council of Chalcedon, and its Christology of two natures in Christ. (Since the 1960s the Oriental Orthodox Churches have organized conferences to pursue theological reconciliation with the Orthodox and Roman Catholic Churches.)

The Byzantine Church

During the fifth century, many of the western territories of the Christian Roman Empire had been lost to Germanic tribes. Emperor Justinian undertook a military campaign to restore the territories and unify the church. The theoretical basis for absolute rule under a Christian monarch was formulated in the fourth century by the apologist Eusebius of Caesarea (see unit 9:3). Eusebius wove together Christian ideology and imagery with Hellenistic concepts of divine kingship in order to innovate a Byzantine political ideology where the religious and secular spheres were closely integrated. The word Byzantine refers to the church and the patriarch of Constantinople, although it is often used to refer to the whole of the Eastern Orthodox Church.

In the Byzantine Empire the emperor was responsible for ensuring that Orthodox belief was enforced. During the reign of Justinian, the Byzantine rite became imperial and elaborate. One of the most impressive features of the imperial rite in Constantinople would have been the processions from one holy place to another, where often the emperor in his imperial vestments, the clergy, and the people all participated. One of the notable achievements of the reign of Justinian was the building of churches, especially St. Sophia in Constantinople. There was also a rich flowering of liturgy, literature, and art.

A majority of non-Greek-speaking Christians of the Middle East rejected the Council of Chalcedon (see unit 9:3). After the eighth century, most of the area where Christianity was born remained under the rule of Muslims, so that the Orthodox patriarchates of Alexandria, Antioch, and Jerusalem kept only a shadow of their former glory. During most of the Middle Ages, Constantinople remained the most important center of Christendom.

The famous Byzantine missionaries, St. Cyril and St. Methodius, translated (c. 864) scripture and the liturgy into Slavonic, and many of the Slavic nations were converted to Byzantine Orthodox Christianity. The Bulgarians also embraced the Christian faith in 864 and the Russians, baptized in 988, remained in the ecclesiastical jurisdiction of the patriarchate of Constantinople until 1448.

The Seeds of Monasticism

One form of resistance to Roman culture came in the late third century when certain Christian groups fled the cities and urban areas for the deserts in order to live religious lives centered on regular prayer, self-denial, and asceticism. These practices formed the foundation for later monasticism, which exerted great influence on Christianity in Syria, Palestine, North Africa, and the world of Byzantia. The disciplinary order of the Roman Catholic clergy (e.g., celibacy) has roots in the early Christian monastic movement of Eastern monasticism. Monasticism has taken three chief forms, all of which would be seen in Egypt by the year 350, and which are still found in the Orthodox Church today:

- *The eremitic life.* Hermits or ascetics led the solitary life in caves, in tombs, or on the tops of pillars! The great example of eremitic life is the father of monasticism, St. Antony of Egypt (251–356).
- *The community life.* Monks live together under a common rule. St. Pachomius of Egypt (286–346) was author of a rule later used by St. Benedict in the west. Basil the Great, whose ascetic writings have had a lasting influence on Eastern monasticism, advocated community life. He gave a social role to monastics, urging them to care for the sick and poor, and to maintain hospitals and orphanages. In general, though, Eastern monasticism has been less involved in active work; in Orthodoxy, a monk's primary task is the life of prayer, by which he serves others.
- *The semi-eremitic life.* This form of monasticism is known as the "middle way." In the place of a single, highly organized community there is a loosely knit group of small communities, each with a few members under the guidance of an elder. The great centers of the semi-eremitic life in Egypt were Nitria and Scetis, which by the end of the fourth century had produced many outstanding monks: Ammon, the founder of Nitria; Macarius of Egypt and Macarius of Alexandria; Evagrius of Pontus; and Arsenius the Great. From the start monastic life was seen as a vocation for women as well as men, and throughout the Byzantine world there were many communities of nuns. This semi-eremitic system can also be found in the West in Celtic Christianity.

Fourth-century Egypt was regarded as a second Holy Land, and travelers to Jerusalem also made pilgrimages to the ascetics located on the Nile. In the fifth and sixth centuries, leadership in the monastic movement shifted to Palestine, with St. Euthymius the Great (d. 473) and his disciple, St. Sabas (d. 532). The monastery founded by St. Sabas in the Jordan valley can claim an unbroken history to the present day; John of Damascus resided there. The monastery of St. Catherine at Mount Sinai has the same unbroken history. It was founded by the Emperor Justinian. Since the tenth century, the chief center of Orthodox monasticism has been

Athos, a peninsula in Northern Greece jutting out into the Aegean and culminating at its tip in a peak 6,670 feet high, known as "the Holy Mountain."

There are no "Orders" in Orthodox monasticism. In the West, a monk belongs to the Franciscan, the Cistercian, or some such order; in the East he is just a member of the one great fellowship that includes all monks and nuns. The monastery of Studion was a community of over one thousand monks who frequently opposed both government and ecclesiastical officialdom, defending fundamental Christian principles against political compromises. The Studite Rule (guidelines of monastic life) was adopted by other monasteries, particularly the famous Monastery of the Caves (*Pecherskaya Lavra*) in Kiev (in Russia).

The writings of St. Symeon the New Theologian (949–1022), abbot of the monastery of St. Mamas in Constantinople, are a most remarkable example of Eastern Christian mysticism. He was the first systematic exponent of the way of inner prayer. He also was unique in medieval mysticism for he spoke freely and passionately of his own spiritual experiences:

> So I entered the place where I usually prayed and, mindful for the words of the holy man (Simeon the Studite) I began to say "Holy God." At once I was so greatly moved to tears and loving desire for God that I would be unable to describe in words the joy and delight I then felt. I fell prostrate on the ground, and at once I saw, and behold, a great light was immaterially shining on me and seized hold of my whole mind and soul, so that I was struck with amazement at the unexpected marvel and I was, as it were, in ecstasy. . . . (St. Symeon Catechetical Discourses 16:3)

John of Damascus

In the fifth century the Eastern Church was passionately concerned to preserve the orthodox tradition without even slight variation in its belief or liturgy. Quotations and writings of the Fathers were collected, and John of Damascus (c. 675–749), who has been called the last of the Greek Fathers, finally drew together the earlier teaching of the Fathers into a systematic manual. He expressed his motives in this way:

> Like a bee I shall gather all that conforms to the truth, even deriving help from the writings of our enemies. . . . I am not offering you my own conclusions, but those which were laboriously arrived at by the most eminent theologians. . . . (*Dialectic*, Prologue)

John of Damascus was a Syrian theologian brought up at the court of the caliph in Damascus, where his father was an official. He was educated by a Sicilian monk. He spent his life writing for orthodoxy against iconoclasm (a breaker of icons or images used in religious worship). His major work is *The Fountain of Wisdom*, a Greek work in three parts—a theological study of Aristotle's categories; a history of heresies with supplementary material on iconoclasm (Greek = image "breaking") and Islam; and a formal exposition of the Orthodox Christian faith, *De fide orthodoxa* (trans., F. N. Chase, 1958), which concentrates especially on the doctrines of the Trinity and the person of Jesus Christ.

On the doctrine of the Trinity John of Damascus supports the teaching of the Cappadocian Fathers, who were three fourth-century Christian theologians: Basil of Caesarea; his brother, Gregory of Nyssa; and Gregory of Nazianzus. Together they opposed Arianism after the Council of Nicaea and were instrumental in its defeat at the Council of Constantinople. Their doctrine of the Trinity was canonized. In it they defended the deity of the Holy Spirit with the Father and the Son as three persons in one substance. The theological orthodoxy of John of Damascus was used by the scholastics and is still a major source for the dogmatic opinions of the Eastern Fathers. John was also a hymnist, and he regulated the choral parts of the Byzantine liturgy. In addition, he encouraged and energized the production of Byzantine painting.

The Great Schism

Between the fourth and eleventh centuries, Constantinople, the center of Eastern Christianity, was also the capital of the Eastern Roman, or Byzantine, Empire. Rome, after the barbarian invasions, fell under the influence of the Holy Roman Empire of the West, a political rival.

The Great Schism between the Eastern Church and the Western Church (1054) was the culmination of a gradual process of alienation between the East and West that started in the first centuries of the Christian Era and continued down through the Middle Ages. Gradually, the Church of Rome began to assume preeminence over the rest of Christianity, but not necessarily with the cooperation of the Eastern churches. Eventually, doctrinal differences and questions regarding papal authority led to the "Great Schism" of 1054, when Rome excommunicated the Patriarch of Constantinople, Michael Cerularios. As a result, if asked when Orthodox Christianity was founded, an Orthodox Christian might say around 33 C.E., but a Roman Catholic would say 1054.

A number of circumstances contributed to the estrangement between East and West, including linguistic and cultural differences and political events such as the coronation of Charlemagne by Pope Leo II as emperor of the Holy Roman Empire in opposition to the Roman Emperor of Byzantium. Debates over clerical celibacy and the practice of the Eucharist also widened the division. Orthodox doctrine was and is mostly in agreement with other high liturgy churches such as Roman Catholicism and the Anglican Church. The major cause of the Great Schism was the addition of the filioque to the Nicene Creed (see unit 9:3) by the Roman Church. The Nicene Creed stated that the Holy Spirit proceeds from the Father alone, whereas the filioque teaches that the Holy Spirit proceeds from both the Father and the Son. Another issue of contention with the Roman Church is the authority of the Pope over all of Christendom, with which the Orthodox Church does not agree. A focus of Orthodoxy is the veneration of icons, with which many Western Christians, especially Protestants, cannot agree.

West and East

In the West, theology remained under the influence of St. Augustine of Hippo and gradually moved away from meaningful engagement with the rich theological tradition of the Christian East. At the same time the Roman See was almost completely overtaken by Franks. Even with these different circumstances, theological differences may well have been agreed upon but for two different concepts of church authority. The growth of Rome insisted on church primacy based on the concept of the apostolic origin of the Church of Rome. This assertion was not just an empty title; Rome insisted on jurisdictional authority above all other churches, which was clearly incompatible with traditional Orthodox ecclesiology. The Eastern Church considered all churches as sister churches. In the East, it was inconceivable that the authority of a single church or a single bishop should determine vital matters of faith and doctrine. In the course of time (see unit 9:11) the Church of Rome finally proclaimed the pope's infallibility when teaching *ex cathedra*, which widened the gap even more between the Christian East and West. The Eastern Orthodox Church sees the Protestant denominations (which departed from Rome during the Reformation and afterwards) as even further away from the original teaching of the Holy Fathers and the Holy Ecumenical Councils. Because of these differences, the Orthodox Church is in communion with neither the Roman Catholic nor the Protestant communities.

The Tenth-Century Expansion of Byzantine Christianity

For Eastern Orthodoxy the most significant historical event was the missionary expansion of Byzantine Christianity throughout Eastern Europe. In 988 the Kievan prince Vladimir embraced Byzantine Orthodoxy and married a sister of the Emperor Basil. After that time, Russia became an ecclesiastical province of the church of Byzantium, headed by a Greek or, sometimes, a Russian metropolitan from Constantinople. This statute of dependence was not challenged by the Russians until 1448. During the entire period, Russia adopted and developed the spiritual, artistic, and social heritage of Byzantine civilization.

The Fall of the Byzantine Empire

In 1204 the fourth crusade resulted in the sack of Constantinople. The Venetians insisted on this new target, and Pope Innocent III (1198–1216) agreed. Churches were desecrated, nuns were raped. The city remained under Western control until 1261 when the East Romans under Michael VIII Palaeologus conquered Constantinople, taking it back from the crusaders.

The fall of Constantinople to the Turks on May 29, 1453, was the end of a process of disintegration that had begun much earlier, but it was seen as a tragic end of the second Rome—that is, the imperial city founded by Constantine in 330 C.E. The Western Latin Church had failed to come to the aid of the Byzantine empire despite the persistent presence of embassies staffed by successive emperors. In any case the price of such aid would have meant papal supremacy for the Byzantines, which was unacceptable to the majority of the Greek clergy. One grand duke allegedly said it would be preferable to see the turban of the Turk in the city rather than the mitre of the Latin. During the three days of siege and plunder by the Sultan's army, many manuscripts and icons were destroyed, and after the siege Constantinople became the capital of the Islamic Ottoman Empire. However, the religious, spiritual, and political traditions of the Byzantine Empire lived on to a large extent in the Slavic churches of Serbia, Rumania, Bulgaria, and Russia.

During the subsequent centuries, the Greeks in Constantinople were able to keep track of developments in the rest of Europe. During the Protestant Reformation and the Catholic Counter-Reformation, some contact occurred between Protestants and Orthodox that focused on developing common ground on what might be called a non-Catholic identity (as described by Nicholas Zernov in *Eastern Christendom*).

In 1782 *The Philokalia* (*Love of [Spiritual] Beauty*), an anthology of ascetic and mystical texts from the fourth to the fifteenth centuries, was published in Vienna. The collection was compiled by St. Macarius, Metropolitan of Corinth, and St. Nicodemus of the Holy Mountain.

From 1800 onwards Orthodox influence in the Holy Land began to rise dramatically. Catholic monks were lamenting that the Church of the Nativity had been in Greek hands for forty or fifty years. A flow of financial aid and pilgrims streamed into the Holy Land from Russia.

The Crimean War (1853–1856) resulted from a French demand that the Turks restore Latin rights in the Holy Land as stated in a treaty of 1740. The Turks complied and, in so doing, dispossessed the Orthodox Christians of their acquired rank. The Russian tsar, Nicholas I, reacted and demanded the restoration of Orthodox privileges and, in addition, he wanted to be guaranteed a protectorate over all Orthodox Christians (estimated at twelve million people) in the Ottoman Empire. The demand for a protectorate over the laity caused the Turks, backed by the British and the French, to refuse, which led to the war.

The Roman Catholic church influenced the British and French against the Russians.

In the next century in 1917, the first phase of persecution began against the Orthodox Church in Russia. To begin with, this persecution was done in a nonsystematic manner by individual Bolshevik "war lords." But Lenin wished to destroy the Church by abolishing private property, and thus eliminating the Church's income.

In 1921, the second phase of the persecution began. The Orthodox Church was stigmatized as a subversive element loyal to the old tsarist regime, while other religions were tolerated. Later, clergy were not allowed to vote or serve in the armed forces, but at the same time were taxed for failing to do so. These taxes, in addition to the tax on private enterprise (up to 81 percent), often resulted in clergy being taxed in excess of their income. In the period between 1927 and 1940, it is estimated that the number of Orthodox churches in the Russian Republic fell from 29,584 to under 300. Approximately 40,000 Orthodox clergy and millions of laymen were killed for their faith between 1917 and 1940. Under Bolshevik rule (1917–1991), all church buildings were confiscated by the state, and only a few were leased back to the church for use.

Central Orthodox Christian Beliefs

Like the Roman Catholic Church, Orthodoxy adheres to a hierarchical structure based on Apostolic Succession, the episcopate, and priesthood. Believers also pray to the saints for help and intercede for people who have died. But unlike Rome, Orthodoxy looks to the five patriarchs and the ecumenical councils as ultimate authority rather than papal infallibility.

The Orthodox maintain that the ecumenical councils of Nicaea (325), Constantinople I (381), Ephesus (431), Chalcedon (451), Constantinople II (553), Constantinople III (680), and Nicaea II (787) provide an infallible guide to Christian doctrine and the organization of the Church.

The Orthodox Church understands itself as essentially a eucharistic community rather than an institutional organization. The Orthodox belief is that the church is the body of Christ through which a Christian participates in the divine life and encounters salvation. Therefore every local gathering of believers that congregates and shares the Eucharist is actually the whole body of Christ uniting heaven and earth. Bishop Kallistos Ware says:

> Just as each person is made according to the image of the Trinitarian God, so the Church as a whole is an icon of God the Trinity, reproducing on earth the mystery of unity in diversity. (Timothy Ware [1979])

Mystical Theology

From the fourth century onwards the Orthodox spiritual practices contain deep inner wisdom. Saints such as Gregory Palamas (1296–1359) and Metropolitan of Thessalonika in the fourteenth century were not condemned for their innovative teachings but accepted within the tradition. Palamas defended the Orthodox doctrine of *hesychast* (solitary) prayer and the use of the Jesus Prayer, and he elaborated on the concept of *theosis* or deification in this life. He distinguished between the unknowable essence of God and the energies of God, which may be perceived and even participated in by saints who have attained complete union with God. Gregory is commemorated on the Second Sunday of Great Lent.

Churches

Churches are autocephalous (self-governing), gathered around bishops who are responsible for teaching the faith and celebrating the sacraments in their own communities. Bishops are recruited from the monastic clergy, who have taken vows and are not permitted to marry. However, unlike the Roman Catholic Church, priests (and deacons) can be married men.

Sacraments

Seven sacraments are recognized: baptism, chrismation (confirmation), Eucharist, confession, holy orders, marriage, and anointing the sick.

Divine Liturgy

At the center of Orthodox worship is the divine liturgy (Mass). There exist four different eucharistic liturgies, the most popular being the Liturgy of St. John Chrysostom. Liturgies are said in the common language and always sung by either the choir or on occasion with the congregation.

Icons

Orthodoxy is known for its use of icons in both private and public worship. Icons are images of Christ, the *Theotokos* (Mother of God [literally, "bearer of God"]), or a saint. Believers give honor to the person represented by the icon. The great iconoclastic controversy of the eighth and ninth centuries centered around a theological dispute concerning the relation between humanity and divinity in understanding the person of Christ and his work of sanctifying the saints. The Orthodox faith was triumphant in affirming that God became visible in the Incarnation of Christ and that through Christ God can make human beings godly.

The Eastern Orthodox Church Today

Divisions do not tend to occur along doctrinal lines, as is common in Protestant churches, but rather for reasons of national, ethnic, and linguistic differences. Relations between the various churches are for the most part cordial.

The Orthodox Church today is the local churches (dioceses) in communion with the patriarchs of Constantinople, Alexandria, Antioch, and Jerusalem, and the newer patriarchs that appeared later—e.g., Moscow, Bulgaria, Romania, Belgrade.

Some features of the Orthodox Church are notable:

- Since the seventh century, Orthodox Christianity has been part of an oppressed and subjugated group. Alexandria, Jerusalem, and Antioch have been under Arab and Turkish Muslim rule for much of this time.
- Orthodox Christianity spread to the Slavic lands—Bulgaria and Russia—in the ninth and tenth centuries, but no sooner was it established than most of Russia fell under Tartar rule for some two centuries.
- From the fifteenth to the nineteenth centuries, Russia was the only Orthodox country in which Christians were free to engage in mission. In the nineteenth and twentieth centuries, Greece and other Balkan countries threw off the Turkish regime and Russia came under the atheist Bolshevik regime. In comparison, Western Christians seem to have had a less turbulent existence.

The largest of the Orthodox churches is the Russian Orthodox Church under the Patriarchate of Moscow. After two generations of persecution, the Orthodox Church in Russia is experiencing a revival, but not without problems. At the time of this writing, the state has returned many more of the confiscated churches, but many are in dire need of repair, and some have to be totally rebuilt.

The Orthodox Church Patriarchates

The Patriarchate of Constantinople is now in Turkey, and most of the Orthodox Christians left Turkey after a war between Greece and Turkey in the 1920s. The patriarchate does, however, include groups of Christians in Western Europe, the Americas, Australia, and some other places in Asia. A group in the Philippines recently joined the Orthodox Church, and new Orthodox Churches have been formed in Indonesia.

The Patriarchate of Alexandria and All Africa traces its history back to the first century and St. Mark's establishing the Church in Alexandria, Egypt. The Church of Alexandria has been influential in shaping Christianity throughout the world, as we have seen (see unit 3:3, St. Athanasius). The Patriarchate of Alexandria had its center shift from Egypt to the south during the twentieth century. In the first three centuries it was confined to Egypt and the coast of Libya, and only in the fourth century did it spread as far as Ethiopia. Some people from further south did join the Church, however. One of the best-known figures from this patriarchate is St. Moses the Black, a runaway slave who became a thug, then repented and founded a monastery. Today most Christians in Egypt itself belong to the Coptic Orthodox Church, which split off in the sixth century.

The Greek Orthodox Patriarchate has most of its members in Kenya, Uganda, and Tanzania, and is also growing in other places in tropical Africa.

The Patriarchate of Antioch is now based in Damascus, Syria (Antioch itself is actually in Turkey). Most of the Orthodox Christians are Arabic-speaking, and the patriarchate has also established churches in other countries for Syrian and Lebanese emigrants. Recently, a group of former Protestants in North America—who had formed the Evangelical Orthodox Church—were admitted, and more recently groups in Britain that had left the Church of England have joined.

The Patriarchate of Jerusalem is largely Arabic-speaking, though much of the leadership of the patriarchate falls to Greek-speaking monks.

There are also patriarchates of Belgrade, Sofia, and Romania, and autocephalous churches (independent churches choosing their own head) in Cyprus, Greece, Poland, and a few other places. Russian missionaries went to China, Japan, Korea, and North America in the eighteenth and nineteenth centuries and established churches.

UNIT 9:5 THE WESTERN CHURCH IN THE DARK AGES AND MIDDLE AGES

Key Developments in the Christian Church of the Dark and Middle Ages

- The spread of the heresy of Nestorianism.
- 405: Jerome completed The Vulgate (Latin version of the Bible).
- 410: Fall of Rome, sacked by Visigoths, who ruled in Spain up to the Moslem invasion in 711.
- Barbarians attacked the Empire, sacking the city of Rome. Augustine wrote *City of God* (413–426), showing that the true movement of history was the unseen conflict between sin and salvation, between the city of man and the kingdom of God.
- 416: Council of Carthage condemned pelagianism.
- 431: Third Ecumenical Council of Ephesus—to confront the heresy of Nestorianism.
- 432: Patrick began his mission to Ireland.
- 440: Leo (the Great) was consecrated as bishop of Rome.
- Pope Leo I (440–461) saved Rome from Attila the Hun (452) and asserts authority over other bishops, claiming that the bishop of Rome is the successor to the Apostle Peter.
- 445: Valentinian's Edict strengthened primacy of Rome.
- 450: Anglo-Saxons invaded England.
- 451: Fourth Ecumenical Council at Chalcedon (Pope Leo the Great) condemned Monophysitism.
- 476: Traditional date for the end of Roman Empire.

- Various "features of the Church" begin: the Church calendar, the cult of martyrs and relics, and growth in the glorification of the Virgin Mary.
- Benedict's "Rule" for monks (c. 540) established.
- Barbarians are converted to Christianity: Recared, the Visigoth king in Spain and an Arian, became Roman Catholic.
- Islam is founded by Muhammad (c. 570–629) and begins to supplant Christianity across the Middle East and North Africa.
- 638: Islam captures Jerusalem
- 648: Emperor Constans II issued "The Typos" limiting Christian teachings to those stated in the first five ecumenical councils. Pope Martin I (d. 655) refuses to sign Typos and is banished to Crimea, where he dies.
- 664: The Synod of Whitby in England adopts the Roman Catholic faith despite conflict between the original Celtic Church and the Roman evangelists.
- Papacy asserts its earthly rule and establishes the papal states in Italy. Pope Leo III (d. 816) separates from the Eastern Empire and becomes supreme bishop in the West.
- 800: Charlemagne (Charles the Great, c. 742–814) was crowned "Holy Roman Emperor," establishing his dream of a kingdom with a Christian king.
- The theologian John Scotus Erigena (c. 810–877) paves the way for scholasticism.
- 993: Saints begin to be officially canonized by the Roman church.
- 1009: Muslims sack The Holy Sepulchre in Jerusalem.
- 1066: William of Normandy conquers England, appointing Lanfranc as the Archbishop of Canterbury in 1070. Lanfranc reforms the English church.
- 1095: Pope Urban II announces First Crusade to reclaim Jerusalem from the Muslims.
- 1099: The Crusaders capture Jerusalem.
- Anselm appointed as Archbishop of Canterbury in 1093.
- 1115: St. Bernard establishes the monastery at Clairvaux.
- 1147: Second Crusade (supported by Bernard of Clairvaux) fails, with most Crusaders dying in Asia Minor.
- 1187: Loss of Jerusalem by the Crusaders
- 1204: Europeans capture Constantinople.
- 1209: Francis of Assisi establishes Franciscans.
- Papacy grows in power with Pope Innocent III (1198–1216) approving the fourth Crusade and forming the Inquisition, which enlisted both church and state to punish heretics.
- Thomas Aquinas summarizes scholastic theology in his *Summa Theologica* (1271), writing, "*intelligo ut credam*" ("I understand, in order that I may believe").

- Mysticism flourishes, especially in Germany.
- 1382: John Wycliffe translates the Bible into English, and trains lay preachers to spread the scripture.

Early Christianity often voiced a protest of counterculture to the norms of its day. For the first disciples no place was inherently seen as sacred, so Paul could say at Athens, "The God who made the world and everything in it, he who is Lord of heaven and earth, does not live in shrines made by human hands" (Acts 17:24). As we have seen (unit 9:1), Paul was a converted Christian, a Jew, and a Roman citizen. Along with the early Christians he saw the pagan nature of temple worship. Christian churches at that time housed no divine God, for they themselves were "the temple of the living God" (2 Cor. 6:16). The place of worship was not holy in itself but only because Christ was worshiped there.

In the fourth century this position changed. The emperor Constantine had sponsored the building of a cathedral and great memorial churches. His successors continued to do likewise, so that in the fifth century the popes in alliance with the aristocracy were changing the landscape of urban towns.

Important Events for the Church in the Dark Ages (c. 450–1000) and the Middle Ages (c. 700–1500)

In 410 C.E., the unbelievable happened: Rome was taken. In the years that followed, the West was besieged with invasions from Islam in the south and from Norse and Danes from the north. The years from about 450 to 1000 have been called by some "The Dark Ages." This era is the longest in Christian history and also the most difficult to grasp and interpret.

They were times of acute social turbulence and anarchy that occasionally came perilously close to the collapse of European civilization. The Western Church provided most of the learning and thought that did exist, primarily through the monasteries, which continued to be a source of stability. Theology during this period is referred to as monastic theology; Christians in the West were rethinking the culture they had inherited from the ancient world.

Christianity was spread through the work of countless holy men, monks, ascetics, and wonder-workers. The evangelism of the monks was crucial in the rural conversion of Europe at the time, and many bishops of the day would have considered themselves to be monks. For example, St. Cuthbert of Lindisfarne (d. 687) could claim a theological ancestry back to St. Martin of Tours (d. c. 397). But it would be incorrect to claim in the year 700 that any sense of a homogenous Christian community was aspiring to be called "Western Christendom." The thesis of Henri Pirenne's *Mahomet et Charlemagne* (1937) was that the ancient Mediterranean civilization of Christendom was disrupted not through the European Germanic invaders but only through the spread of Muslim power. Taking only one facet of Muslim expansion, the Islamic occupation of North

Africa, meant a vital loss to the Western Church. The North African Church had long been autonomous and provided challenge to both popes and emperors, but with Islamic rule it became annexed off from the West along with Carthage, thus leaving the see of Rome as the sole religious authority and the Christian center of a barbarian West. In this way Pirenne cites Muhammad and Islam as the creator of medieval Western Christendom.

When Charlemagne (c. 742–814) became emperor in 800, stability and unity returned, bringing with them a renewal of scholarship, namely in the work of John Scotus Erigena, an outstanding, original thinker in the world of the Dark Ages.

The Middle Ages: John Scotus Erigena: Irish Theologian and Neo-Platonist Philosopher

John Scotus Erigena (c. 810–877) was one of the few Westerners of his day who knew Greek. He translated the words of Dionysius the Areopagite and Maximus the Confessor's commentary on him. This work of translation was very influential for a number of later medieval theologians, including St. Thomas Aquinas. Though born in Ireland, Erigena later moved to France (c. 845), where he took over the Palatine Academy at the invitation of King Charles I (Charles the Bald, 823–877). Erigena was thus the first to introduce the ideas of neo-Platonism from the Greek into the Western European intellectual tradition, where they were to have a deeply formative influence in the world of Christian theology.

His freethinking writing remained the subject of controversy for centuries. His work *De divina praedestinationa* (*On Divine Predestination*) was written around 851 to support Hincmar (c. 806–882) in the predestination debate with Gottschalk (c. 820–868). The book was seen as extreme by some and was therefore condemned by the Councils of Valence (855) and Langres (859) as "*pultes Scotorum*" ("Irishman's porridge") and "the invention of the devil."

Erigena's major work (865–870) was *De divisione naturae* (*On the Division of Nature*), where he classified nature into four parts:

1. That which creates but is not created: God
2. That which creates and is created: the Word or Logos
3. That which is created but does not create: the sensible world
4. That which does not create and neither is created: God as supreme end

John Scotus Erigena conceived of humanity as a microcosm of the wider universe, having senses and reason to determine causes and mechanisms. Erigena tried to fuse reason with faith. His ideas come from neo-Platonists like Plotinus, whose thinking was akin to pantheism, and interestingly also modern rationalism. His work is largely based upon Augustine, Pseudo-Dionysius, and the Greek Fathers, and is clearly neo-Platonist.

Erigena was condemned in his day for his tendency toward pantheism and thus to accessing God through direct revelatory experience, rather than through the dogmas of Church orthodoxy. In this way, his thinking is related to later Christian mystics such as St. Teresa and St. John of the Cross.

Erigena did not submit his work for papal approval and therefore went out of favor; then, at the Council of Sens in 1225 and by Pope Gregory XIII in 1585, his works were condemned as heretical.

Tradition or myth has it that Erigena returned to Britain in the latter part of his life to become Abbot of Malmesbury in southern England, but was stabbed to death by his scholars with their pens for "trying to get them to think." Yet John's bold and creative thinking determined the ethos of Christian thought for centuries. It proved seminal to many later thinkers and was enormously influential, despite lack of official recognition.

The Growth of Scholasticism

Despite a brief flowering of intellectual thought, Charlemagne's empire soon fragmented and Viking raids once again brought havoc. By this time, much of Western Europe (except the Jewish ghettoes and the Muslims in Spain) held a nominal Christian faith, the invaders having been Christianized and converted. The eleventh century, therefore, saw many new religious movements. The theological debates and thinking of the first to fourth centuries—where Greek philosophy and Christian faith had been in dialogue with each other—were reopened. This time the impact of philosophical thinking and methods (the use of reason) was more forceful and appealing, resulting in a new approach to theology called Scholasticism—so called because it was taught by scholars in medieval universities. From this period on, philosophy found its natural home in the university and became less and less exclusively associated with the church.

The Eleventh and Twelve Centuries of Scholasticism

Anselm (see chapter 2) graphically depicted the effect of philosophy on theology when he sought to provide a "proof" of God that would work according to reason and at the same time be in accordance with his Christian faith. He said, "The rational mind alone of all creatures is able to mount an investigation of the supreme being." At the time of Anselm, reason was not yet employed to investigate and define Christian doctrine (which was grounded in divine revelation) but to understand faith. Later in the twelfth century, Peter Abelard (1079–1142), grounded in the teachings of Aristotle, was to take philosophical methodology further into theology. He was one of the most brilliant and also controversial theologians of his day, challenging both prevailing philosophical orthodoxy and theology.

Philosophically, the issue of the day was over what is truly real: individuals or universals? Nominalism argued that individuals are real (e.g., the pen I am holding) and that universals (the idea of pens) are only concepts taken from our experience of individuals. Opposing this, realists argued that particular pens come and go, but the idea of "a pen" continues whereas individuals do not. Such an example was meant to illustrate that the idea of the pen is more real than the means of illustrating its existence.

Abelard took a middle path between nominalism and realism, seeing universals as mental concepts—that is, they have no existence of themselves outside of particular individuals. In 1122 Abelard wrote his major work entitled *Sic et non* (*Yes and No*), in which he used philosophical methods to decide between conflicting theological views and documents of revelation. Anselm had followed the monastic faith, where faith is the starting point and it then seeks understanding: "I believe in order that I may understand." But Abelard reversed the order of things by using the philosophical method of doubt as the starting point, then asking questions in order to find faith. In this way Abelard foreshadowed the use of the modern scientific method. He also applied this method to the doctrine of the atonement, which he saw as the supreme example of the love of God. But his work was to later be condemned at the Council of Soissons in 1121. Bernard of Clairvaux was radically opposed to Abelard's teaching and accused him of inventing a fifth Gospel.

Bernard of Clairvaux

Bernard (1090–1153) has been called the Last of the Fathers, because he was the last great theologian of the early medieval monastic tradition. He preached around Europe gaining support for the second crusade, whose failure he felt deeply. He wrote vigorously. His works include *Grace and Freedom*, in which he follows St. Augustine in maintaining that our good works are also entirely the work of God's grace. He also wrote a book on *Loving God* and another on *The Steps of Humility and Pride*, in which he reflects deeply on human nature:

> Humility is a virtue by which a man has a low opinion of himself because he knows himself well. . . . You will never have real mercy on the failings of another until you know and realize that you have the same failing in yourself. . . . (The round man's) eyes are closed to anything which shows his own vileness or the excellence of others, wide open to what flatters himself. . . . His aim is not to teach you nor to be taught by you, but to show you how much he knows. . . . He wants not so much to be better as to be seen to be better. (*Humility and Pride* 1:2; 3:6; 12:40; 13:41–42)

In his opposition to Abelard, amongst other issues, Bernard confronted a view of the atonement that reduced the act to an example of God's Love:

> I was made a sinner by deriving my being from Adam. I am made just by being washed in the blood of Christ. . . . Such is the justice which man has obtained through the blood of the

> Redeemer. But this "son of perdition" (Abelard) disdains and scoffs at it. . . . (*The Errors of Peter Abelard* 6:16f)

The point Bernard is making is that Abelard believed that Christ lived and died solely for the purpose of showing humanity how to live by his words and example. For Bernard this reduced the sacrifice Christ had made and departed from the mainstream of Christian faith.

Several Latin hymns are ascribed to Bernard including, "Jesu, the very thought of thee/ with sweetness fills my breast," and, "O Sacred Head now wounded."

St. Thomas Aquinas

The greatest of the scholastics was St. Thomas Aquinas (1225–1274), whose type of philosophy is known as Thomism. His achievements were enormous in that he made the works of Aristotle known and acceptable to the scholars of his day. By doing this he displaced Plato. He originated a vast metaphysical system with a glossary of technical terms, and he put forward the famous "five proofs" for the existence of God and dealt with the problem of religious language—that is, how we can talk about God and mean something. Aquinas became the official theologian of the Roman Catholic Church through a pronouncement by Pope Leo in 1879. His *Summa Theologica* alone contains more than two million words. Yet even such genius had its doubts. In December 1273, while saying Mass, Aquinas had an experience which caused him to stop writing. He was later to tell his secretary, "I cannot, because all I have written now seems like straw."

Aquinas emphasized the use of reason, which led to a gradual severing between "natural" reason and "supernatural" faith. He believed that reason could discover limited truths about God, but doctrines such as the Trinity and the Incarnation could only be comprehended through revelation. Reason traveled in various forms through the Middle Ages, by way of the Renaissance and the Reformation to the Enlightenment and the emergence of modern, autonomous humanity.

The Rise in the Power of the Papacy

During the later Middle Ages there was a consolidation of papal authority, partly due to the death of emperor Henry IV in 1197, who left his throne to his three-year-old son. The chaos and disarray that followed left a weak and divided empire. In 1198 Pope Innocent III used this political situation to reestablish the authority of the papacy, but to an unprecedented level of power in which he adopted the title of "Vicar of Christ." In his decree *Sicut universitatis conditor* (1198), Innocent declares the subordination of the state to the church.

> Just as the creator of the universe established two great lights in the firmament of heaven . . . so he also appointed two dignitaries for the firmament of the universal church. . . . The

> greater of these rules souls and the lesser of them rules bodies. These dignitaries are the authority of the pope and the power of the king. And just as the moon derives her light from the sun, and is inferior to the sun in terms of its size and its quality, so the power of the king derives from the authority of the pope.

The Medieval Growth and Expansion of Religious Orders

By the dawn of the fourteenth century, estimates are that some six hundred Cistercian monasteries or convents had been founded. Two major orders were founded during this time, the Franciscans and the Dominicans. St. Francis of Assisi (c. 1181–1226) founded the Franciscans. He renounced his wealthy life for one of prayer and poverty. The order was referred to as "the gray friars" because they wore dark gray habits and emphasized love of humanity, creation, and communal poverty. Franciscans have often been labeled "anti-intellectual" because of their theological simplicity, but one of the finest theologians of this era, Bonaventura (1221–1274) was a member of the order.

The Dominicans or "Black Friars" were founded by the Spanish priest Dominic de Guzman (1170–1221), who emphasized the use of the intellect in matters of faith. St. Thomas Aquinas was a Dominican. This expansion in Scholastic intellectual theology was mostly located in Northern Europe. Not until the Renaissance did Italy undergo such far-reaching conceptual changes in belief and thought.

The Venerable Bede (673–735 C.E.)

Bede was a monk at the English monastery of Wearmouth and Jarrow, in Northumbria. From the age of seven, he spent all his life at that monastery, except for a few brief visits to nearby places. He wrote: "I have devoted my energies to a study of the Scriptures, observing monastic discipline, and singing the daily services in church; study, teaching, and writing have always been my delight."

Bede was the first to write scholarly works in the English language, but only fragments of his English writings have survived. His works of translation are famous. He translated the Gospel of John into Old English, which he completed the day he died. He also wrote commentaries on the Pentateuch and other Biblical passages. Bede's best-known work is his *History of the English Church and People*, a classic that gives a history of Britain up to 729. This book records the Celtic peoples who were converted to Christianity during the first three centuries of the Christian era, and the invasion of the Anglo-Saxon pagans in the fifth and sixth centuries along with their subsequent conversion by Celtic missionaries from the north and west and Roman missionaries from the south and east. His work is the main source for the history of the British Isles during this period. Bede also wrote hymns, the first record of martyrdom with historical notes, letters, and works on grammar and astronomy: he was aware that the earth is a sphere. Bede was the first historian to date events *Anno Domini* and the earliest known writer to state that the solar year is not exactly 365 and a quarter days long, so that the Julian calendar (one leap year every four years) requires some further adjusting if the months are not to fall out of step with the seasons.

UNIT 9:6 RENAISSANCE AND REFORMATION

Key Developments in the History of the Fifteenth-Century and Sixteenth-Century Church

- Thomas à Kempis wrote the classic book *The Imitation of Christ.*
- 1431: Joan of Arc is burned at Rouen as a witch.
- 1453: The Turks capture Constantinople and turn St. Sophia Basilica into a mosque. Hundreds of scholars flee west and inspire a revival of classical learning: the Renaissance.
- 1453: Johannes Gutenberg developed the printing press and prints the first Bible.
- 1479: The Inquisition against heresy in Spain is instituted by Ferdinand and Isabella with the approval of the pope. Jews have to become Christians or leave the country.
- Florence fell under the control of the Medicis and flowers as the center of Renaissance humanism. Brunelleschi, Donatello, Michelangelo, Botticelli, and Leonardo da Vinci all paint paying attention to Christian themes, the natural world, and especially the human form.
- 1517: Luther nailed the famous ninety-five theses to the door of Wittenburg Cathedral.
- The Reformation is expressed in different ways by Luther, Zwingli, Calvin, Tyndale, and the Anabaptists.
- The printing press spreads the Reformation message as the Bible becomes more available via translations. Luther translates into German and Tyndale into English in the 1520s.
- Henry VIII's quest for an heir to the throne caused him to separate from Rome and establish himself as head of the Church of England.
- The Counter-Reformation defends traditional Catholicism against Reformation ideas. The Council of Trent (1545–1563) reaffirmed Catholic doctrine.
- Both Catholics and Protestants are martyred. Foxe's *Book of Martyrs* records the persecution believers in Christ have endured through the centuries.
- In England, Puritans base their church and their faith more on the Bible than on church tradition.

By 1500 the Pope's influence on Western Christendom looked unshakeable in terms of wealth and influence, but it was soon to be rocked to its foundations by the Protestant Reformation. An increasingly literate Europe was producing original thinkers who questioned the doctrine and authority of the Church in Rome. As a result of the invention of the printing press, the Holy Scriptures became widely available to the common person for the first time. Great discrepancies became clear between what was read in scripture and what was practiced by the Roman Catholic Church. They began to demand reform of the Church, and when this did not happen, open dissent became the Reformation.

Protestantism was founded on the belief that God deals directly with men and women as persons, so that salvation is gained "by faith alone." As a form of Christian religion Protestantism originates from the Reformation and especially from the work of Martin Luther and John Calvin. Four hundred years have brought change in Protestantism, but the years have not effaced the theological emphases first created by the Reformers in the sixteenth century. Many factors prepared the ground for a Reformation of the Christian faith in the West; one of these was the rise of humanism (not to be confused with atheist or agnostic humanism) in what has been called the Renaissance.

The Rise of Renaissance Humanism

As the church in the East crumbled and Constantinople finally fell to Islamic invaders (1454), an exodus of Greek-speaking intellectuals went westward. Italy was geographically close to Constantinople and became a refuge for emigrants who revitalized interest in the Greek language and its classical culture. Italy had many ruins that were visible reminders of the ancient Roman civilization, which acted as a stimulus in rediscovering the glories of Rome.

Historian Jakob Burckhart said that the Renaissance was the coming of age of man as a spiritual individual. Two ideals seem to capture the mood of change and the humanist agenda of this period. The first was a return to the original sources of Western European culture in classical Rome and Athens. This movement happened in Southern Europe where, for example, in sculpture, Michelangelo's "Bacchus" was such a fine imitation of classical style that it was believed for some while to be a genuine antique. In architecture, men like Filippo Brunelleschi (1377–1446) and Donato Bramante (c. 1433–1514) went to Rome to observe and measure classical buildings. In literature and philosophy, Marsilio Ficino (1433–1499) translated all the dialogues of Plato and other Greek works, and the classical Latin language was revived along with principal literary forms of ancient Rome—the comedy, the epic, and the tragedy.

In Northern Europe, the humanism was distinctly Christian, with a theological return to the primary sources of the original New Testament scriptures. It became increasingly clear to humanist theologians that existing Latin translations of the Bible, especially the Vulgate that had gained such prominence in the Middle Ages, were inadequate and unreliable. Access to the New Testament in its original language of Greek was needed.

Desiderius Erasmus: Christian Humanist

As a youth Desiderius Erasmus (c. 1466–1536) was educated in classical ideas. He studied in Paris, and for a time he was a professor at Cambridge. Erasmus hated Scholasticism, which was based in Aristotelian philosophy, and he derided it by publishing satirical works including *In Praise of Folly* (1509), which was directed against the corruption in the church:

> The apostles went everywhere baptising people, and yet they never taught what the formal, material, efficient and final causes of baptism were, nor did they mention that it was both a delible and an indelible character. . . . Furthermore, the theologians draw exact pictures of every part of hell, as though they had spent many years in that region.

Erasmus believed that the best way to revive the church was by real scholarship, which included going back to the sources, the Hebrew and Greek Bible and the early Christian Fathers. He became tireless toward this end. The first printed Greek New Testament was produced by Erasmus in 1516, a literary milestone. For the first time, theologians could compare the original Greek text of the New Testament with the later Latin Vulgate translation. Erasmus also wrote his *Handbook of the Christian Soldier* (1503), where he emphasized inward faith in which the believer deepens his or her knowledge of God by the reading of scripture and also the attractive idea that the church could be reformed and renewed by the laity. This book had enormous appeal to educated laypeople and underwent numerous editions.

Theologically, Erasmus was a true humanist in the old sense of the word, for he believed in the dignity of humankind. Against Scholastic theologians, he believed that human free will was capable of responding to God. He even fell out with Martin Luther who, schooled in Scholasticism, believed that the fallen human will is in bondage.

Erasmus's impact on the history of ideas needs much more attention than this short section affords. He represents the link between humanism and theology that flowered in the first two decades of the sixteenth century. His satirical teaching against the corruption of Rome was so effective that all his works were included on the *Index of Forbidden Books* in 1559. He laid the foundation for the Protestant Reformation, such that it was said of him that, *"Erasmus laid the egg but Luther hatched it."*

In the early Middle Ages, literacy was restricted to the clergy. At the beginning of the sixteenth century, however, adult literacy was increasing, made possible by the development of printing. The clerical monopoly on literacy was broken, and there simultaneously arose a mood of anticlericalism where an increasingly articulate laity spelled out their contempt. Spelling out the causes of the Reformation is virtually impossible because of the countless varieties of protests among groups of Christian people in Western Europe regarding the theory and practice of traditional religion. The original protestors became known as Protestants.

The Protestant Reformation

The Reformation began with a spark and ended with a raging fire.

By the year 1513, Pope Leo X owed 125,000 ducats and was facing bankruptcy. Money was required to pay for St. Peter's Church in Rome, so the practice of selling indulgences was implemented. The Roman Catholic doctrine of purgatory meant that the souls of the dead went to a place where they could be "purged" for heaven. By buying an indulgence, ordinary people were told they would spend a shorter time in purgatory and that the souls of the dead could be freed and go straight to heaven. The Dominican friar John Tetzel was commissioned by the Archbishop Albert of Mainz to sell indulgences, claiming that, "As soon as the coin in the coffer rings, the soul from purgatory springs."

Martin Luther and the Doctrine of Salvation

Martin Luther (1483–1546), professor of Holy Scripture at the University of Wittenberg, was appalled at the spiritual competitions in the Church. On October 31, 1517, he attached a placard to the door of the castle church at Wittenberg inscribed with "Ninety-five Theses upon Indulgences." Unbeknown to anyone including himself, Luther had lit the spark of the Reformation. Within ten years, every major difference from the Roman Church had been stated by Luther. His basic principle was an appeal to a belief in human conscience, personally enlightened by the Holy Spirit, against what he called the "accretion of the Roman Church." Luther's theory of conscience was that it was bound up with the Word of God in the scriptures. Therefore, instead of popes and councils, the scriptures alone became the source of religious knowledge. Luther also rejected all but two of the Roman Catholic Church's seven sacraments. Most Protestant denominations today limit the number to two, as did Martin Luther, to include only baptism and the Eucharist (Holy Communion or Lord's Supper).

Martin Luther loved music. Another innovation that has since become a part of most Protestant churches is the singing of hymns by the congregation. Luther said, "Next after theology, I give to music the highest place and the greatest honor." In 1524 he published a hymnbook called *The First Evangelical Hymnal.* Based on the Vulgate version of the Forty-sixth Psalm, Luther's now-famous hymn, "A Mighty Fortress Is Our God," was written during a period of deep depression.

Luther's theses were printed and distributed, and his views gained wide public support. Luther gained the protection of Frederick, Elector of Saxony, who enjoyed displeasing the Archbishop and had no love of popes interfering in German affairs. Luther was mainly concerned with biblical issues, which he considered to be obscured by scholastic theology. He personally struggled spiritually to know how he, a sinner, could be saved. After much seeking and self-denial, he eventually resolved his conscience by understanding Paul's doctrine of justification by faith. Salvation was not a gradual process, neither is it accumulation of righteousness; instead, the unmerited grace of God is given to sinners because of the atoning work of Christ on the Cross (*Sermon of the Threefold Righteousness* [1518]).

At the Diet of Augsburg in 1518 Luther refused to withdraw his views, and he was presented with choosing either the Pope's authority or rebellion. He chose the latter, and his friends smuggled him out of Augsburg for his own safety. By 1520 he was famous through his pamphlets, which had been already published in German and Latin and were read by many. In them he sought to recruit the secular authorities and sympathetic clergy:

- "To the Christian Nobility of the German Nation" likened his work to the blast of the trumpet that brought down the walls of Jericho and called on the nobles of Germany to reform the church.
- In "The Babylonish Captivity of the Church," Luther assaulted the seven sacraments of the Church.
- His third tract was "Treatise of the Liberty of a Christian Man" (1520), where he commended the belief in justification by faith to those who would know Christ.

On June 15, 1520, Luther was condemned as a heretic with the mandate for all the faithful to burn his books. By way of reply, Luther burned the papal document at a public meeting. Charles V, the Holy Roman Emperor, wanted peace and summoned Luther to the Diet of Worms in 1521. In front of the emperor, Luther said, "Unless I am proved wrong by scriptures or by evident reason, then I am a prisoner in conscience to the word of God. I cannot retract and I will not retract. To go against conscience is neither safe nor right. God help me. Amen."

Luther and the Translation of the Bible into German

Soon after, Luther was outlawed and went into hiding, during which time he began the huge task of translating the Bible into German. He completed this project in 1534 and also wrote hymns, lectures, and liturgy. As a preacher he deplored the mediatory power of the priesthood. Luther stood against the Peasant Uprisings of 1524–1525, which strengthened the German princes and their power. Germany became divided between people who supported Rome and people who did not.

In 1531, the Protestant princes and cities formed the Schmalkaldic League, representing a new power in Europe. Meanwhile, the Reformation spread further into most of Europe. In Zurich, Zwingli began to preach reform at about the same time as Luther. He was influenced by Luther but did not hold to all his views. Before long Protestantism was split into two strands: Lutheran and

Reformed (or Swiss) Protestantism. Zwingli died young, and John Calvin took his place as the leading Reformed theologian. Thus, the Reformed faith is often known as Calvinism.

John Calvin and Geneva, the City of God

John Calvin (1509–1564) was born in Noyon, France. He studied the methods of medieval scholasticism and also various schools of humanist thought. In Paris he came under Protestant teaching, where he experienced a change of heart: "God by a sudden conversion subdued my heart to teachableness." Under personal threat Calvin left Paris in 1533 and went to Switzerland, where he wrote his finest work, *The Institutes of the Christian Religion* (1536). He passed through Geneva in 1536 and was persuaded to stay by Guillaume Farel. Soon forced to flee, Calvin was in exile from 1538 to 1541, until the magistrates of the city begged him to return.

In the vacuum left by the collapse of Roman Catholicism, the Protestant Church had to find new methods of organization. Calvin drew up reforms to bring order and decency to the city. Geneva was to become the City of God. Calvin was influential in persuading the city council to impose the "Ecclesiastical Ordinances" on the city. Rules were written about clothing and prohibition of dancing. There was a plan to close the bars, which the people of Geneva did not accept and they had to be reopened. Calvin appointed elders to supervise Genevan morals, including barring sinners from taking Holy Communion. Punishments were common and often severe. Calvin was inflexible and never popular; he was either admired and followed or hated and opposed. But his approach to Church life in the Ordinances showed his grasp on the importance of structure and discipline for the church when it was threatened with hostile conditions.

During the 1550s a flood of Protestant refugees swept into the city, helping his power to continue. He never held a public office, however, and efforts to see him as some sort of dictator failed, for he was always answerable to the City Council. Calvin nonetheless transformed Geneva. The Scots reformer John Knox said that it was

> the most perfect school of Christ that ever was in the earth since the days of the apostles. In other places I confess Christ to be truly preached. But manners and religion to be so sincerely reformed, I have not yet seen in any other place.

Calvinism

Calvin is often held responsible for the doctrine of predestination, which was clearly taught by St. Augustine, the vast majority of medieval theologians and all of the Reformers. Historians and theologians now generally distinguish Calvin's theology from the Calvinism that followed, for predestination was never the central focus of Calvin's thought. However, Calvin did set out the doctrine of "limited atonement," stating that Christ did not die on the cross for everybody, but only for the elect. Theodore Beza and other early Calvinists were quick to establish the divine decree to eternal life or death as the leading principle from which all other thought followed. They were anxious to distinguish Calvinism from the Lutheran wing of the Reformation and also from the rise in interest in Aristotelian thought that was happening at the time.

By 1566, Calvinist theology was powerfully expressed in the Helvetic Confession, and at the Synod of Dort (1618–1619) the five points of Calvinism were expounded: total depravity, unconditional election, limited atonement, irresistible grace, and the final perseverance of the saints. By the middle of the seventeenth century, Calvinism had spread to England and Scotland, where it was firmly grasped and preached by many Puritans and transported along with them to New England. But not every reformer agreed with the doctrine of predestination. Jacobus Arminius (1560–1609), who studied with Beza, set out to defend the doctrine of predestination against its critics, but after deep reflection he agreed with its critics—that the ultimate choice regarding salvation is made by man himself.

Calvin died at the age of fifty-five, a man of incalculable influence in Western culture.

Roman Catholic Reaction and Reform

Scholars often say that the Roman Catholic Church was somewhat unprepared for the Reformation. But from 1545 to 1563, three phases of the Council of Trent met where leading Protestant and Catholic theologians tried to reach an understanding:

- Agreement was reached at Regensburg in 1542 on justification by faith.
- There was no compromise on the doctrine of transubstantiation (Catholic belief that the bread and wine of the Eucharist changes into the substance of the body and blood of Christ) and papal authority.

This failure to reconcile Protestantism meant that the Catholic zealots influenced the Council of Trent to determine doctrine in an anti-Protestant way.

The counterattack on Protestantism was led by Ignatius Loyola, who in 1534 founded the Society of Jesus, which became the Jesuits. Their three major aims were to reform the church from within, focusing on education, fighting the heresy of Protestantism, and preaching the gospel to the world. During this period also, the two great Spanish mystics, Teresa of Avila and St. John of the Cross, were beginning their spiritual journeys.

While the Council of Trent was called ecumenical, in actuality more than two-thirds of the bishops in attendance were Italian and therefore not free of papal control. Even though the Council was not even representative of the Roman Catholic Church, Trent became the normative statement of anti-Protestant counter-reformation belief for the next four hundred years. Its reign was brought to an end by the Second Vatican Council (1962–1965), which breathed a very different spirit, including a program for reunion with other Christians.

Radical Reformers

Luther and Calvin were magisterial reformers in that they worked in cooperation with the rulers of their day. Their approach to change was to reform the old church, not to start a new one. The reform was one of doctrine rather than the division of church and state. Certain groups were more radical in their desire for reform. The Anabaptists, for example, were diverse in their doctrinal focus. Anabaptism was a movement that owed its origins to Huldrych Zwingli, and it centered on the belief that only people who had made a personal profession of faith should be baptized. Some Anabaptists stressed inward experience as being the most important aspect of faith. Some were apocalyptic, believing that the prophecies about the tribulation in the book of Revelation were about to take place. All tended to be distrustful of external authority.

One of the most infamous Anabaptists was John of Leyden who introduced polygamy in the city of Munster, which was eventually besieged, further discrediting the Anabaptist cause. This reaction led to redefinitions of the movement, especially by Menno Simons. Simons was a pacifist with high social ideals and a deep spirituality that are still treasured by the Mennonites, who bear his name. Generally, the Anabaptists were united by their separation from the world, which included refusal to do military service or take oaths, their call to simplicity and holiness, and most of all the application of Love, for Love is God Himself.

The evangelicals were another large group of radical reformers. They rejected the idea of a state church and the sacrament of infant baptism. They too were called Anabaptists because they rebaptized people baptized as infants. Rebaptizing was already a capital offense, and evangelicals suffered severe persecution, although their ideas have survived.

UNIT 9:7 THE ENGLISH REFORMATION AND THE EVANGELICAL AWAKENING

Key Developments in the English Reformation, the Sixteenth- through Eighteenth-Century Church

- 1524: William Tyndale's translation of the New Testament into English.
- 1531: Henry VIII is recognized as Supreme Head of the Church in England.
- 1534: The Act of Supremacy: The King is declared head of the Church in England.
- 1535: Thomas More is executed for refusing to take the oath of the King's supremacy.

- 1536: Henry VIII dissolves 376 Roman Catholic monasteries and nunneries.
- 1539: The Six Articles.
- 1547: Edward VI (r. 1546–1553) becomes King of England.
- 1549: Thomas Cranmer issues the *Book of Common Prayer*.
- 1553: Mary I (r. 1553–1558), a Roman Catholic, becomes Queen of England.
- 1554: The Roman Catholic Church is restored to power in England.
- 1555: Thomas Cranmer and Nicolas Ridley are burned at the stake.
- 1558: Elizabeth I (r. 1558–1603) becomes Queen of England.
- 1559: Elizabethan (Protestant) *Book of Common Prayer* issued.
- Voltaire develops the rationalism of the "Enlightenment," which attacks Christianity by asserting that man (humanity) is the center of all things.
- An evangelical awakening spreads throughout England and America under the preaching of George Whitefield, the Wesley brothers, and Jonathan Edwards.
- Pietism brings new life to German Lutheranism, and Count Zinzendorf establishes Herrnhut as a Moravian settlement in Saxony, from where the Moravian Brethren start their missionary work.
- Classical works of Christian literature written during this period include William Paley's *Principles of Moral and Political Philosophy* and William Wilberforce's *Practical View of the Religious System*.
- The era of modern missions expands and develops with England's Baptist Missionary Society and the mission of William Carey to India.

> *God himself has condescended to teach the way: for this very end he came from heaven. He hath written it down in a book. O give me that book! At any price give me the Book of God!*
>
> John Wesley, Preface to *Standard Sermons*

> *One man with God is always in the majority.*
>
> John Knox, inscription on the Reformation monument in Geneva

During the Reformation, King Henry VIII (1491–1547) supported the Catholic Church and ordered the burning of Protestant media. For this, for various wars against the French Protestants, and for his written refutation of Lutheran ideas, he received the title "Defender of the Faith" by Pope Leo in a ceremony at St. Paul's Cathedral. Henry was unhappy, however, with his Spanish wife, Katherine of Aragon, because she bore him no male heir. He had been granted a papal dispensation to marry (she was his brother's widow), but Henry saw the lack of a male heir to his throne as God's judgment on an unlawful union. He sent Cardinal Wolsey to Rome to secure a decree of divorce. The Pope, afraid of Spain's reaction, refused. This refusal caused Henry to repudiate Roman canon law and ultimately the papacy. Henry used the Reformation Parliament (lasting from 1529 to 1536) to remove England from the authority of the Roman Catholic Church, and he made strategic appointments of Thomas Cromwell (c. 1485–1540) and Thomas Cranmer (1489–1556) to carry out his reforms. Cranmer was a theologian who had suggested that university theologians, not the Catholic Church, should decide Henry's claim for divorce. Together, Cromwell and Cranmer steered a somewhat reluctant king towards the dissolution of the monasteries, doctrinal reform, and the declaration that an English Bible should be placed in every church in the realm.

Historians often claim that the state of the British monasteries was scandalous in their corruption, ineffectiveness in pastoral care, and huge economic influence (they controlled about one quarter of England's lands and wealth). Critics of this view point to the fact that such accusations come all too easily from people with vested interest against the monasteries. Regardless, Henry began methodically closing the monasteries in 1535. Sir Thomas Cromwell began gathering evidence against the monasteries, and, in 1535, Parliament closed 376 of the smallest and confiscated their lands and treasures. The lower classes were devastated, no longer having places to turn to for economic support, and they rioted several times with the support of the homeless monks and nuns.

The Book of Common Prayer

Henry VIII died in 1547. Edward VI succeeded to the throne, and serious reform began. Cranmer was able to publish the first English *Book of Common Prayer* (1549), written with care so as not to offend traditional Catholics, but revised in 1552, with the help of intellectuals Martin Bucer and Peter Martyr, to avoid ambiguities that were perceived as Catholic. Cranmer had persuaded Martyn Bucer to come to England. He was a significant first-generation reformer, and his appointment as Regius Professor of Divinity at Cambridge brought German and Swiss theology into Britain. The 1559 prayer book revised by Elizabeth I was in use for the next three hundred years in the Church of England. Elizabeth had a famous verse removed to avoid Catholic antagonism:

> From the tyranny of the Bisshop of Rome and al hys detestable enormities . . . Good Lorde, delyver us!

Protestant Martyrs

Edward was succeeded by Mary, who was the daughter of Katherine of Aragon. She set about gradually reinstating the power of the papacy and the medieval Latin liturgy. But in 1555 she began to burn Protestant heretics. On October 16, 1555, the very popular Hugh Latimer (Bishop of Worcester) and Nicolas Ridley (Bishop of London) were burned at the stake in Oxford. Latimer encouraged Ridley with the words:

> Be of good comfort master Ridley and play the man. We shall this day light such a candle by God's grace in England as (I trust) never shall be put out.

Cranmer was "persuaded" to recant his Protestant beliefs, which under pressure he did. But then Mary decided he should be burned and publicly renounce his faith at the execution on March 21, 1556. Cranmer did no such thing. Given the opportunity to speak, he renounced his recantation and affirmed with conviction his Protestant beliefs. He held fully in the fire till it burned the hand that signed the recantation.

Over two hundred Protestant martyrs were burned at Mary's command. These actions and her unpopular marriage to Philip of Spain did not further the cause of Catholicism in England. She was given the title "Bloody Mary."

The Elizabethan Settlement

Elizabeth I came to the throne in 1558. She had been imprisoned by Mary and had escaped almost certain death. Elizabeth owed her very existence to her father Henry's repudiation of Rome, and she wasted no time in establishing a Protestant Settlement of religion and the doctrine of the Thirty-nine Articles with the help of Parliament and Matthew Parker, the Archbishop of Canterbury, and John Jewel, who defended it against Rome. Under Elizabeth, the Church was to be religiously governed under the Monarch and Parliament. The role of the Sovereign in the Church was opposed on the one side by the Catholics because it clashed with papal authority, and on the other side by the Puritans because of their view of scripture and because it took Protestantism away from the European Reformation movement. The third response to the settlement was to wholeheartedly accept it as the preferred form of Protestantism. Richard Hooker (c. 1553–1600), who defended the settlement against Puritanism, took this view.

Puritans and Their Beliefs

Some Protestants, especially those who had been in Geneva during Mary's reign, were not prepared to accept Elizabeth's Settlement. They had seen how Geneva functioned, and they saw no reason that the Church should be subservient to the ruler or the state. They also, however, opposed many of the Catholic practices retained by the Church of England. Many of these people eventually came to be known as Puritans. They encouraged direct personal religious experience, sincere moral conduct, and simple worship services. Worship was the area in which Puritans most desired change; their aims were accompanied by intense theological convictions and the conviction about how seriously Christianity should be taken as the focus of human existence.

After James I became king of England in 1603, Puritan leaders asked him to grant several reforms. At the Hampton Court Conference (1604), their requests, which included the abolition of bishops, were rejected. Puritanism, as expressed by William Ames, and later Richard Baxter, grew in popularity early in the seventeenth century. The government and the church under Archbishop William Laud became increasingly repressive, causing many Puritans to emigrate. The

Puritans who stayed formed a powerful element within the parliamentarian party that defeated Charles I in the English Civil War. After the war, the Puritans dominated England until 1660, but internal strife meant that their influence gave way to Independent, or congregational, control under Oliver Cromwell, who proved even more intolerant than the old hierarchy. The restoration of the monarchy (1660) also restored Anglicanism. Puritan clergy were expelled from the Church of England under the terms of the Act of Uniformity (1662). Thereafter, English Puritans were called Nonconformists.

Further Factionalization

In the course of time the English Reformation ushered in Anglicanism, a particular brand of Protestantism that is far more open to Catholic thought and teaching than the Reformed or Lutheran Churches. In Scotland, the picture was very different, partly because of the influence of John Knox. During the sixteenth century, the word "Protestant" was used mainly to describe the two primary Reformation traditions: the Lutheran and the Reformed. Protestants were Christians who accepted the basic early Christian creeds (statements of belief), accepted the Bible as the supreme authority in all matters of faith and practice, believed in salvation by faith alone, and accepted only two sacraments instead of the seven insisted on by Roman Catholics.

John Knox and the Scottish Reformation

John Knox (1505–1572) was the leader of the Reformation in Scotland. At about thirty years of age he was won over to Protestantism, having been influenced by the courageous preaching of George Wishart, who had been burned at the stake. In 1551, Knox became chaplain to Edward IV and helped in the revision of the *Prayer Book*. When Mary came to the throne, Knox fled to Frankfurt, where he engaged with Swiss reformers and his theological views became thoroughly reformed and too radical for the more moderate wing. They sent Richard Cox and others to try to convince him of moderation. They argued that "they would have the face of an English church." Knox's reply was, "The Lord grant it to have the face of Christ's Church." Cox orchestrated Knox's expulsion from Frankfurt, causing him to go to Geneva, where he wrote his famous "First Blast of the Trumpet against the Monstrous Regiment of Women" (1558). In this publication, Knox argued that female sovereignty contravened natural and divine law. When Elizabeth I came to the throne, his work naturally fell into disrepute. In 1559, Knox returned to Scotland and continued to preach and write. He helped to draw up the Scots Confession and the First Book of Discipline, and he wrote his "Treatise on Predestination" (1560). His major work was his *History of the Reformation of Religion within the Realm of Scotland*, which appeared in full in 1644, seventy-two years after his death. He was a man of strong conviction, compassion, and deep spirituality. The Reformation Monument in Geneva has immortalized the words he inspired: "One man with God is always in the majority."

Protestantism

Protestantism under Charles I suffered a serious theological divide between people who accepted Calvinist predestination and people who did not, the Arminians (although different from Arminius himself). The theological views of Arminians were summarized after the death of Jacobus Arminius (1560–1609) by the Remonstrance of 1610, in which five points were designed to counter the prevailing Calvinist Orthodoxy of the day. The five main tenents of Arminianism are:

1. Christ died for all mankind, not only the elect.
2. Humans may resist God's saving grace.
3. Christians may fall from divine grace.
4. The Holy Spirit is necessary to help us achieve what is good.
5. Salvation is for those who trust and believe in Christ, and who continue to live a life of holiness, faith, and obedience.

Only in the sense that God could foresee whether people would believe or not did Arminius believe that God had predestined some to salvation and others to damnation; it was God's will that all should be saved, but not everyone would accept God's grace. At the Synod of Dort, Arminian teachings were condemned as heretical by orthodox Calvinists. (In the twenty-first century, Arminianism is a major theological force among North American evangelical Christians.)

The Arminians promoted church ritual and the sacraments as the vehicle to salvation. They became known as "high church." Later, in 1637, Charles I and Archbishop William Laud tried to impose the *Book of Common Prayer* and high church on Presbyterian Scotland, a move that eventually led to the civil war between Charles and Parliament and the execution of both the monarch (1649) and his archbishop. Radical change was now the order of the day, with the Scots urging the Church of England to adopt a more thorough Reformed theology and for the whole of Britain to be Presbyterian. The Westminster Assembly was convened, which produced the Westminster Confession, a stricter form of Calvinism (differing in key respects from the teaching of John Calvin himself) intended to replace the moderate Calvinism of the Thirty-nine Articles. The Westminster Confession was never adopted by the Church of England, but the Church of Scotland adopted it in 1647 to replace the Scots Confession of John Knox and the other reformers of his day.

Nonconformist and Free Churches

In the seventeenth century, some Protestants separated from the established Church of England to form their own Christian denominations, otherwise referred to as Free Churches. Catholics fared better than Puritans under Charles II. His "Cavalier Parliament" of 1662 passed an Act of Uniformity depriving of their offices all clergymen who did not accept everything in the Anglican Prayer Book. This act tended to group all nonconformists (Independents, Baptists, Presbyterians, and the new Quaker sect) into a single class, called dissenters. To support Catholics, Charles issued a Declaration of Indulgence in 1672. Parliament forced him to retraction and passed a Test Act (1673), which made it impossible for Catholics to hold public office.

Baptists and Congregationalists

Baptists and Congregationalists were both initially dissenters. They shared the common belief in the autonomy of the local congregation. The Baptists rejected infant baptism for the belief that only people who could claim a personal confession of faith could be baptized. In 1644, the first London Confession of Faith was written by just seven Baptist congregations. In 1677, the Baptists revised the Westminster Confession but omitted their names for fear of reprisal. In 1689 the second London Confession was put forward by the representatives of over one hundred Baptist congregations. The Baptist Association accepted this confession at Philadelphia in 1742, which is now known as the Philadelphia Confession.

Pietism

Pietism was originally a German Lutheran religious movement of the seventeenth and eighteenth centuries that emphasized deep religious devotion, ethical purity, charitable works, and pastoral theology in contrast to sacramental or dogmatic precision. In his *Pia Desideria* (1675), Philipp Jakob Spener proposed a "heart religion" to replace the dominant "head religion" (Stoffler, 1971). Pietism began with religious meetings in Spener's home. The movement grew rapidly, enabled by August Hermann Francke (1663–1727), who made the new University of Halle a center for Pietism. Nikolaus Ludwig Graf von Zinzendorf was a student of Francke's and godson of Spener. His Moravian Church promoted evangelical awakenings throughout Europe and in North America in the eighteenth and nineteenth centuries. John Wesley and Methodism were profoundly influenced by Pietism. What Wesley saw of their behavior and what he heard of their faith after returning to England led to his own evangelical awakening [F. E. Stoffler. *The Rise of Evangelical Pietism* (1971)].

Outside of Protestantism, pietistic elements can be seen in both contemporary Roman Catholicism and Judaism. The Jansenist movement in seventeenth-century France stressed the concern for heart religion as did Spener. The work of Baal Shem Tov (1700–1760), who founded the Hasidic movement in Judaism, also moved beyond orthodox ritual to a sense of communion with God.

Pietism shared in both the mysticism of the late Middle Ages and the Reformation commitment to scripture. Opposing formalism and heartless orthodoxy, it stood apart from the theological establishment. The main concern was for authentic personal experience. Pietism provided a Christian version of individualism and practical thinking that foreshadowed a changing Europe in its transition to modern times.

John Wesley (1703–1791) and the Evangelical Awakening

John Wesley studied at Christ Church Oxford and was ordained to ministry in 1725. While in Oxford he cofounded the Holy Club, which was also called "Methodist" because of the emphasis on discipline and self-examination. In 1735, he went on a missionary journey to Georgia, but the mission was a failure. In 1738, he wrote, "I went to America to convert the Indians, but oh who shall convert me?" Wesley was then influenced by a Moravian pastor. In his journal he wrote:

> He said (the pastor), "my brother, I must first ask you one or two questions. Have you the witness within yourself? Does the Spirit of God bear witness with your spirit, that you are a child of God?" I was surprised and knew not what to answer. He observed it, and asked, "Do you know Jesus Christ?" I paused and said, "I know he is the Saviour of the world." "True," he replied, "but do you know that he has saved you?" I answered, "I hope he has died to save me." He only added, "Do you know yourself?" I said, "I do." But I fear they were vain words. (*Journal*, February 7, 1736)

He went on to experience conversion at a meeting at Aldersgate Street, London ("I felt my heart strangely warmed"). This assurance of salvation became an essential element in his subsequent preaching so that the inward witness of the Holy Spirit became the foundation of Methodist orthodoxy and of other evangelical denominations. Wesley became a passionate and tireless open-air preacher; he is said to have preached 40,000 sermons and to have traveled 250,000 miles on horseback during his lifetime. On the advice of Calvinist evangelical George Whitefield, Wesley undertook open-air, or field, preaching, first in Bristol, then elsewhere. Because of his Arminianism, and his belief in Christian perfection, Wesley repudiated (c. 1740) the Calvinist doctrine of election. This led to a break with Whitefield, although the personal friendship of the two Methodist leaders remained firm. Together with his brother Charles (1707–1788), the message of salvation by faith in Jesus Christ was preached to the working classes, but not without hostility from his audiences. Wesley was increasingly barred from parish pulpits. *"I look on the world as my parish,"* he said.

Wesley possessed organizational skill. He convened an annual conference for preachers who were appointed to care for the converts. He wrote vigorously—letters, tracts, expositions of scripture, his famous sermons, and abridgements of important devotional works. He had little desire to part from the Church of England but increasing hostility brought its own division. Through Methodist preaching, Britain experienced the Evangelical Revival and in time the Evangelicals, insisting on the same personal assurance of faith, became the major group of believers in the Church of England. Such was the evangelical influence that all sections of society were affected in faith and morality.

One scholarly theory even holds that, without the revival, Britain may have had to face a revolution like the French. The nonconformist conscience later brought about sweeping national reform, including the abolition of slavery (1833, through John Newton and William Wilberforce) and the exploitation of child labor (1847, Earl of Shaftesbury). In America, Francis Ashbury (1745–1816), a convert and disciple of John Wesley, introduced Methodism. He was an itinerant preacher on horseback who traveled from Maine to Georgia (almost 300,000 miles in total).

The basic beliefs of Evangelicalism can be summarized from one of the many hymns written by Charles Wesley:

And can it be that I should gain
An interest in the Saviour's blood?
Died he for me, who caused his pain?
For me, who him to death pursued?
Amazing love! How can it be
That thou, my God, shouldst die for me?

He left his Father's throne above,
So free, so infinite his grace;
Emptied himself of all but love,
And bled for Adam's helpless race;
'tis mercy all, immense and free;
For O my God it found out me.

Long my imprisoned spirit lay
Fast bound in sin and nature's night;
Thine eye diffused a quickening ray,
I woke, the dungeon flamed with light;
My chains fell off, my heart was free;
I rose, went forth and followed Thee.

No condemnation now I dread.
Jesus and all in him is mine
Alive in him, my living head,
And clothed in righteousness divine,
Bold I approach the eternal throne,
And claim the crown, through Christ my own.

UNIT 9:8 THE RISE OF PURITANISM AND SEPARATISM

Key Developments in the Seventeenth-Century and Eighteenth-Century Christian Church (continued)

- In England, the Puritan (Protestant) Revolution removes King Charles (1649) and executes him while attempting to establish a Puritan Commonwealth.

- England began to establish colonies in North America: Jamestown (1607), Pilgrims land in 1620, Massachusetts Bay Colony established by Puritans in 1630.
- 1618–1648: In central Europe, the Thirty Years' War brought destruction as Protestants and Catholics wrestle for power.
- 1633: Galileo forced by the Inquisition to reject Copernicus's theories. New scientific studies: Johann Kepler, Isaac Newton, Francis Bacon.
- "Enlightenment" writers—Leibnitz, Hobbes, and Descartes—begin to base knowledge on human reason.
- Voltaire further develops rationalism of "Enlightenment," attacking Christianity and trusting human reason as the basis for knowledge.
- An evangelical awakening spread throughout England and America under the preaching of George Whitefield, the Wesley brothers, and Jonathan Edwards.
- Pietism inspires German Lutheranism, and Lutheran J. S. Bach composed music "only for the glory of God."
- Count Zinzendorf established Herrnhut as a Moravian settlement in Saxony, from which the Moravian Brethren begin their missionary work.
- Christians Handel and Haydn compose classical music, and Isaac Watts and the Wesleys write hymns for congregational singing.
- Christian classics written during the century include William Paley's *Principles of Moral and Political Philosophy* and William Wilberforce's *Practical View of the Religious System.*
- Religious freedom gains ground. In the United States, religious tests for government positions are abolished.
- Modern missions emerge, with the establishment of London's Baptist Missionary Society and the sending of William Carey to India.

This unit looks at a similar chronological period of Church history as the previous unit, with a slight overlap and an additional emphasis on the United States. During Elizabeth I's reign, Christian ministers who were not content to accept the state of affairs were faced with the decision of either separating from the national church and gathering congregations of true believers, or staying in the national church and working for the introduction of spiritual discipline. People who left were the "Separatists"; one of the most notable was John Robinson, who led his persecuted congregation to Holland. A larger number of Christians stayed in the Church, gaining the derogatory name of "Puritan." Among other things, Protestants held strong views about worship and what they saw as "unscriptural" practices, such as the wearing of vestments. At the beginning of the seventeenth century the landscape darkened. The center of the Puritan movement was the University of Cambridge. In 1602 William Perkins (1558–1602), the leading Puritan preacher in Cambridge, died at the age of forty-four. The next year James I came to the throne with the aim that he would "make them (the Puritans) conform or harry them out of the land." Perkins had left two courageous followers:

William Ames and Paul Bayne. Within a few years both these preachers were silenced, but not before stirring up others. Richard Sibbes was converted under Baynes, and John Cotton was struck with conviction of sin under the preaching of Sibbes. John Cotton (1584–1652) was to have a foremost place among the band of men who were to cross the Atlantic.

The Pilgrim Ethos

The Pilgrim ethos can be traced to Robert Browne's book, *Reformation Without Tarrying for Any*, first published in 1580. Browne was a disillusioned Puritan. After more than a decade of pursuing revival within the English Church, he formed the conclusion that it was not going to happen, so Browne "separated from" the English Church and, with the like-minded Robert Harrison, started his own congregation in Norwich in 1581. The term "separatist" was thus first applied to Congregationalist groups who dissented from the authority of the Church of England, whereas now "separatist" is a general term for a variety of Protestant denominations. Puritans, Separatists, and Independents (another name for Congregationalists) all opposed the idea of a national church.

The Separatism movement had begun with a number of key figures, including John Smyth (regarded by some as the father of English Baptists), John Robinson, William Brewster, and William Bradford. The latter three were part of the group of Separatists who, in 1608, left England for the Netherlands, and then later emigrated to the New World, landing at Plymouth, Massachusetts, in 1620. Most Puritans chose to remain within the English Church working for reform, although they later formed a much larger group of emigrants who left for New England in the late 1620s, and founded their own colony at Massachusetts Bay.

Spiritual Characteristics and Founding Beliefs of the Congregationalists

The Pilgrims were actually Congregationalists who wanted to achieve "reformation without tarrying," even if it meant separating from their church and their nation. They continued to think of themselves as English, but their emphasis was on their new political and spiritual ethos. They had passionately committed themselves to an uncompromising reformation, with the emphasis on individual righteousness before God and the autonomy of the local congregation.

When the Mayflower began her nine weeks' voyage across the Atlantic in September 1620, the intention of her passengers was to "plant the first colony in the Northern parts of Virginia," but because it was too late in the year to make a further voyage southwards, they ignored the patent from the Virginia Company, which had authorized their voyage, and became the first white settlers in what was to be New England. Englishmen of various kinds had settled in Virginia since 1607, and the Dutch had been on the Hudson since 1609. If the people of the

Mayflower had landed in either of those places, they would have had to engage people with a very different outlook from their own. New England, however, presented the opportunity for a distinct and separate society, and the Plymouth colony of Massachusetts was born. The Pilgrims of Plymouth in December 1620 numbered 102 (a baby was born) and had a mere fifty-three adult males, yet within fifteen years New England had taken over as the leading colony in North America. Some ten thousand had settled there by 1634 and eighteen thousand by 1643. Their social and political program included the building of towns and churches, the founding of free schools in townships and of Harvard College (1638), and the establishing of the first printing press in the English colonies. The expansion came through the mass immigration of Puritans from England. Over a period of twelve years, in about 198 ships, men and their families arrived in Massachusetts Bay. Cotton Mather (1663–1728) writes:

> The God of heaven served as it were a summons upon the spirits of his people in the English nation; stirring up the spirits of thousands which never saw the faces of each other, with a unanimous inclination to leave all the pleasant accommodations of their native country, and go over a terrible ocean, into a more terrible desert, for the pure enjoyment of all his ordinances. . . . The design of those refugees was that they might maintain the power of godliness and practise the evangelical worship of our Lord Jesus Christ, in all parts of it. (Cotton Mather, *The Ecclesiastical History of New England* [1702])

For eight years the Pilgrim Separatists of New England had lived in harmony with each other, but then came the challenge of living with the immigration of Puritans.

Puritan Belief in the Uniformity of Religion

Although they were victims of religious persecution in Europe, the Puritans supported the theory that sanctioned it: the need for uniformity of religion in the state. For years, controversy erupted between the Separatists and the Puritans. Separatists had accused Puritans of compromising, and Puritans had said that the Separatists caused schism. Considering this opposition, the response of the Pilgrim leaders to the new arrivals was initially charitable. Governor Bradford declared that their great hope in coming to America had been to advance the kingdom of Christ, and they were happy in this "though they should be but as stepping-stones unto others for performing of so great a work."

The Puritans were anything but tolerant of Pilgrim Separatism. John Brown writes of the New England leaders in *The Pilgrim Fathers of New England and Their Puritan Successors*:

> The question as it presented itself to them at that particular time was not whether they were to tolerate others, but whether

> they were to give to others the opportunity of being intolerant to themselves. The cases, therefore, are not parallel between a strong government harrying out of the land a little community of conscientious men, far too weak to be dangerous, and that little community fighting as for dear life to guard the liberty which has cost them so much, and which might easily be taken from them again.

New Englanders were commonly believed to be nontolerant of Baptists, hence the expulsion of Roger Williams from New England in 1636. However Cotton Mather says that at least one congregation *"questioned and omitted the use of infant baptism"* in Massachusetts prior to 1636, but *"there being many good men among those that have been of this persuasion, I do not know that they have been persecuted with any harder means than those of kind conferences to reclaim them."* The conclusion, therefore, is that Williams was expelled because of his denial that the magistrate has any religious duty. This denial, in addition to his opposing laws on such things as blasphemy and the public abuse of the Lord's Day and his toleration of pagan, Jewish, or Turkish worship was untenable for those who had settled to advance the kingdom of the Lord Jesus Christ.

The Puritans did not have an attitude of hostility to all nonconformists. Their primary concern was for a union of all righteous and godly people. Edward Winslow, one of the first governors of the Plymouth Colony, spoke on this matter. He said, *"We ever placed a large difference between those that grounded their practice on the Word of God, though differing from us in the exposition and understanding of it, and those that hated such reformers and reformation, and went in anti-Christian opposition to it, and persecution of it."* This attitude goes a long way in explaining why New England Puritans could treat righteous Baptists who followed the rule of scripture with respect, yet were so opposed to the Quakers who they saw as setting aside the rule of scripture and overturning the foundations of historic Christianity.

Roger Williams and Belief in the Freedom of Conscience

Having been expelled from Massachusetts in the winter of 1636, former Puritan leader Roger Williams (1603–1683) gave a powerful plea for freedom of conscience. He wrote, *"God requireth not an uniformity of Religion to be inacted and inforced in any civill state; which inforced uniformity (sooner or later) is the greatest occasion of civill Warre, ravishing of conscience, persecution of Christ Jesus in his servants, and of hypocrisy and destruction of millions of souls."* Williams later founded Rhode Island on the principle of religious freedom. He welcomed people of diverse religious belief, for he believed that *"forced worship stinks in God's nostrils."* Roger Williams quotes from *The Bloudy Tenent of Persecution, for cause of Conscience, discussed in a Conference between Truth and Peace. . . . (1644).* (Rare Book and Special Collections Division, Library of Congress.)

Intolerance in Virginia

In his "Notes on the State of Virginia," Thomas Jefferson reflected on the religious intolerance in seventeenth-century Virginia, notably on the anti-Quaker laws passed by the Virginia Assembly from 1659 onward. Jefferson apparently believed that it was not moral superiority but a historical accident that Quakers had not been physically punished or even executed in Virginia as they had been in Massachusetts. Beginning in 1659, Virginia enacted anti-Quaker laws, including the death penalty for Quakers. Jefferson surmised that "if no capital execution took place here, as did in New England, it was not owing to the moderation of the church, or the spirit of the legislature."

Anne Hutchinson

Anne Hutchinson (1591–1643) was one of the first New England colonists to challenge the authority of the Puritan leaders. She preferred following her conscience rather than blind obedience. Her protest helped to establish the principle of freedom of religion. Born Anne Marbury in Alford, England, her father was an English clergyman who was imprisoned for preaching against the established Church of England.

When Marbury was twenty-one years old, she married William Hutchinson, and they had fourteen children. Despite her busy domestic life, Anne was active in religious thought and practice. She often made the twenty-four-mile journey to Boston, England, just to hear John Cotton preach. In 1633, Cotton was forced to leave England because of Puritan persecution. He fled to New England. The Hutchinsons with their other children followed the next year and settled in Boston, Massachusetts.

Anne established weekly prayer meetings for the women of the colony and became critical of the clergy. She believed that the Lord dwelt within each individual, and she felt that faith alone would win salvation. Such beliefs opposed the teachings of the Puritan fathers. By 1636, many had converted to her views, including her brother-in-law, the Rev. John Wheelwright, and the governor, Henry Vane. John Cotton supported her at first, but later he publicly renounced her teachings.

When Governor Vane converted, the leaders feared civil disobedience and tried to regain control. When Vane returned to England in 1636, they obtained the governorship for John Winthrop. He immediately banished Wheelwright to New Hampshire and put Anne Hutchinson on trial. She was banished in November 1637. Cotton and other clergy tried to convince Anne to deny her beliefs. Upon refusal, she was excommunicated from the church. She and her family and friends moved to Aquidneck, Rhode Island, in 1638 and helped found a new colony. After her husband's death in 1642, Hutchinson moved with her younger children to Pelham Bay in New York. In 1643, she and most of her family were killed by Indians.

Jews Take Refuge in America

For some decades, Jews had flourished in Dutch-held areas of Brazil, but when the Portuguese conquered, the prospect of the introduction of the Inquisition confronted them. A Brazilian Jew had already been burned at the stake in 1647. A shipload of twenty-three Jewish refugees from Dutch Brazil arrived in New Amsterdam (to become New York) in 1654. By 1658 Jews had arrived in Newport, Rhode Island, also seeking religious liberty. Small groups of Jews continued to arrive at British North American colonies, settling mainly on the coast. At the time of the Declaration of Independence, Jewish settlers had established several thriving synagogues.

The Quakers and Belief in the "Inner Light"

George Fox (1624–1691) was discontented with both the Church of England and also the Puritan and other sectarian movements of his day. Through his prophetic words and deeds, he attracted a radical group of people to follow him. One tradition has it that they were called Quakers because they refused to swear oaths or respect the law courts, instead telling court officials to tremble before God rather than the law. They differed from the mainstream Christian beliefs of their day through their doctrine of the Inward or Inner Light that was the divine within each person. If recognized and nurtured, this light would lead to truth.

Quaker beliefs came to New England via William Penn in 1662. The Pennsylvania colony was founded on principles of consensus and justice. The capital, Philadelphia, literally means "city of brotherly love," and the name reflects Quaker hopes for peaceful living among people. Historically, Quakers have aspired to peacemaking and pacifism, which led to suffering. Their doctrine of the inner light also meant that women enjoyed equal spiritual status to men.

The first group of Germans to settle in Pennsylvania arrived in Philadelphia in 1683 from Krefeld, Germany. During the early years of German emigration to Pennsylvania, most of the emigrants were members of small sects that shared Quaker principles: Mennonites, Dunkers, Schwenkfelders, Moravians, and some German Baptist groups—all of whom were fleeing religious persecution. In his famous charter of religious liberty, William Penn pledged that all citizens who believed in "One Almighty and eternal God . . . shall in no wayes be molested or prejudiced for their Religious Persuasion or Practice in matters of Faith and Worship, nor shall they be compelled at any time to frequent or maintain any Religious Worship, Place or Ministry whatever."

Roman Catholicism in Maryland

Catholics continued to be harassed and persecuted in England throughout the seventeenth century. George Calvert (1580–1632) obtained a charter from

Charles I in 1632 for the territory between Pennsylvania and Virginia. In 1634 two ships, the Ark and the Dove, brought the first two hundred settlers. Catholic fortunes fluctuated in Maryland during the rest of the seventeenth century. After the Glorious Revolution in England, the Church of England was legally established in the colony and English penal laws, which deprived Catholics of the right to vote, hold office, or worship publicly, were enforced.

Anglicanism in Virginia

Virginia was settled by businessmen who were operating through a joint-stock company, the Virginia Company of London. They also supported the Church of England in their colony and provided financial means for it. Everyone was required to attend church and be catechized by a minister. People who refused could be executed or sent to the galleys. Unlike the colonies to the north, where the Church of England was regarded with suspicion, Virginia was a stronghold of Anglicanism. Her House of Burgesses passed a law in 1632 requiring that there be a *"uniformitie throughout this colony both in substance and circumstance to the cannons and constitution of the Church of England."*

Congregationalism

Congregationalists share with the wider Protestant Church their beliefs in the sovereignty of God, the Bible as the word of God, justification by grace through faith alone, the redemptive power of the Holy Spirit, and the efficacy of the sacraments of Baptism and the Lord's Supper. They are distinctive in their convictions about their rejection of creeds, the self-governance of the local congregation, and the role of individual conscience in the life of faith. Congregationalism had its greatest following in the United States. It eventually became the established church of Connecticut and Massachusetts. One of its greatest exponents was Jonathan Edwards, who in 1734 ushered in the First Great Awakening in America.

Jonathan Edwards

Jonathan Edwards (1703–1758) entered the collegiate School at New Haven in 1716 (which became Yale College in 1718). Here he read and was stimulated by the Enlightenment philosophers Locke and Newton. In 1727, he married Sarah Pierpoint, whom he greatly respected spiritually. Edwards succeeded his grandfather as a minister, and both he and his wife seemed destined for an uneventful life of ministry, until the Revival.

In 1734, Northampton was transformed when Jonathan Edwards preached a series of sermons on justification by faith, which led to a spiritual renewal. Edwards recorded this remarkable response in his publication *The Faithful Narrative of the Surprising Work of God* (1737).

In *Faithful Narrative* he wrote, "There was scarcely a single person in the town, old or young, left unconcerned about the great things of the eternal world," and also, "I hope that more than 300 souls were savingly brought home to Christ in this town." However, the suicide of his uncle, Joseph Hawley, seemed to increase the number of backsliding converts and brought revival to a halt. Edwards reflected deeply on these things so that *Faithful Narrative* is much more than a chronicle of events but an empirical and analytical piece of writing. He attempted to look carefully at what people said before interpreting it. The influence of Locke and Newton as well as that of the Puritans was in evidence.

Between 1740 and 1741, the Awakening swept the colonies, aided by the ministry of George Whitefield from England. Edwards held profound sympathy for the revival and a respect for Whitefield but disagreed with the emotionalism of the meetings. Edwards could not believe it was a necessary proof that God was at work. On the other hand, he did not side with critics who saw revival as emotional froth without spiritual substance.

His *A Treatise concerning Religious Affections* (1746) was an important work in which Edwards argued that Christian experience does not lie in distinguishing the "heart" from the "head," as though experience and reason are opposites, at war. The opening passages of the book give conceptual tools to dissect religious experience and to give a rationale for his stand between the enthusiasts and the critics of revival. He sets out evidence that he cites as necessary to determine if genuine religious faith is present. He was critical of excessive emotional expression like fainting and falling down but not surprised by it. Conversion was not settled by physical manifestations nor words. Edwards said, *"Tis a great deal easier to get 'em to talk like saints than to get 'em to act like saints."* The real issue was that of what was true religious affection; he of course admitted that could not be judged by another human being. The list of signs regarding genuine faith in part 3 of *Religious Affections* was meant as a guide to self-examination, especially for signs of holy living.

Against this background of careful analytical support for revival we should understand the most infamous of Edwards's twelve hundred sermons: *Sinners in the Hands of an Angry God*. On this basis he was called a hell-fire preacher, but the title does him no justice. His manner in the pulpit was formal. He read his sermons out and seldom preached on hell. He had previously preached the famous sermon to his own flock but with little result. But in 1741 at Enfield, Connecticut, graphic descriptions of the sinner held by God over a bottomless pit of hell, "much as one holds a spider or a loathsome insect over the fire," produced fainting and shouting and emotionalism.

As his fame grew in the 1740s, his own relationship with his congregation declined. A series of disagreements between Edwards and the local community led to the final breach in 1748, when he refused to admit a man to church membership who could not make *"a profession of things wherein godliness consists."* The Church split into factions, and two different visions of the church were at stake. In 1750, the church council dismissed him.

Edwards moved to Stockbridge Settlement and worked as a minister and missionary to the Mahican and Mohawk Indians. In this latter period, he wrote three important publications: *Freedom of the Will* (1754), *The Nature of True Virtue* (1755, published 1765), and *Christian Doctrine of Original Sin Defended* (1758). In each of these he engages with critics of classic Calvinism. Edwards was dealing with new arguments about the essential goodness and perfectability of human nature. In these later polemical works, he showed himself able to meet the Enlightenment challenge with ideas which, although soundly Calvinist in tendency, were in some respects novel and innovative.

In 1757, Edwards was invited to become president of the College of New Jersey (Princeton). He arrived during a smallpox outbreak and succumbed to the effects of vaccination in March 1758. He was unmistakably an American Puritan, but Edwards's contribution to Christian theology goes far beyond the mere restatement of tradition. In his hands, the Calvinist tradition was infused with new thinking in the areas of religious psychology and human nature. The claim that he is America's greatest theologian is a worthy one, even two and a half centuries after his death.

UNIT 9:9 MILLENNARIANISM

Key Events and Developments of the Nineteenth-Century Western Church

- The nineteenth century has been referred to as the Protestant Century. It was an era of Protestant mission and the founding of a number of groups and organizations, e.g., The British and Foreign Bible Society, The American Bible Society, The Salvation Army, The Exclusive Brethren, and the Sunday School Union.
- It was an era of mission. David Livingstone and others evangelized Africa, and Hudson Taylor founded the China Inland Mission.
- In America, sects and groups including the Jehovah's Witnesses, Christian Scientists, Christadelphians, Seventh-day Adventists, and Mormons were established.
- 1809: Members of Thomas Campbell's Christian Association of Washington, Pennsylvania, formed a church. Working with Walter Scott, who developed a five-step plan of salvation, and Barton Stone, who put forward a simple and noncreedal form of Christianity, Alexander Campbell began the "Restoration Movement." Groups that derive from this origin include the Disciples of Christ, the Churches of Christ, and the Christian Churches.

- 1819: After William Ellery Channing's sermon on "Unitarian Christianity," many New England Congregationalist bodies became Unitarian.
- 1820: Joseph Smith had a vision in Palmyra, New York, that led to the founding of the Mormon religion.
- New philosophies came into being that opposed traditional Christian belief—e.g., Darwin's theory of evolution, Marx's communism, and Freud's psychoanalytic psychology.
- In theology the German "higher critics" attack the historical validity of the scriptures.
- Revival leader Charles Finney put forward "new measures" in his revival meetings, trusting that conversions would result if right approaches and techniques were employed.
- Dwight L. Moody and Ira Sankey led huge revival meetings, and others poured out hymns of faith and devotion on both sides of the Atlantic. Charles Spurgeon preached to packed congregations at London's Metropolitan Tabernacle.
- 1854: Rome defined the doctrine of the Immaculate Conception.
- 1870: Roman Catholicism, through the First Vatican Council, declared the pope infallible. Pope Pius IX condemned liberalism, socialism, and rationalism and announced belief in the Immaculate Conception of the Virgin Mary.
- 1889: Dutch Catholics who had separated from Rome early in this century and German and other European Catholics who rejected the dogma of papal infallibility formed the Old Catholic Church in the Union of Utrecht.

The nineteenth century was fertile with new religious movements, especially in America. At the forefront of new religious movements was millennarian belief in a future millennium (also called Millennialism), or the thousand-year reign of Christ, in which he would establish his earthly kingdom. The source of this belief comes from Revelation 20. Millennarians divide according to whether they believe in the second coming of Christ (parousia) before or after the millennium (premillennialism vs. postmillenialism). Christian attitudes toward the millennium can be classified as premillennial, postmillennial, and amillennial. These categories involve much more than the arrangement of events surrounding the return of Christ. The thousand years expected by the premillennialists is quite different from that anticipated by the postmillennialist.

Premillennialist Beliefs

The premillennialist believes that the return of Christ will be preceded by signs including wars, famines, earthquakes, the preaching of the gospel to all nations, the great apostasy, the appearance of the Antichrist, and the great tribulation.

These events culminate in the second coming, which will result in a period of peace and righteousness when Christ and his saints control the world. Many premillennialists believe that, during the thousand years, dead or martyred believers will be resurrected with glorified bodies to mix with other inhabitants of the earth. Premillennialism holds an historical place in the development of Christian fundamentalism. It is characterized by an avid interest in apocalyptic literature and events such as Armageddon. Hal Lindsey and C. C. Carlson's *The Late Great Planet Earth* (1970) shows a wide audience for its readership.

Postmillennialism

In contrast to premillennialism, the postmillennialists concentrate on the present aspects of God's kingdom, which will reach fruition in the future. They believe that the millennium will come through Christian preaching and teaching.

In America, postmillennialism was first expressed in the works of certain Puritan scholars, especially in the writings of the Anglican writer Daniel Whitby. For Whitby the kingdom of God was coming ever closer and would arrive through the same kind of effort that had always made progress in the past. Whitby influenced the views of Jonathan Edwards, who also emphasized the place of America in the establishment of millennial conditions upon the earth.

Generally, however, the term "millennialist" describes any religious movement that prophesies the imminent destruction of the present order and the establishing of a new order, which usually reverses the status of the oppressor and the oppressed.

The Roots of Millennialism

Christian millennial beliefs can be traced back to Jewish apocalyptic traditions current in the centuries just before and after Jesus Christ. Some historians have suggested that Christianity originally related to such millennarian groups as the Essenes. As Christianity developed after Jesus, millennarian activity was less mainstream and associated with reform movements such as Montanism and, in the thirteenth and fourteenth centuries, Joachimism and radical Franciscan movements. In the sixteenth century, Reformation millennarianism increased and was found, for example, among the Anabaptists and the Moravian and Bohemian Brethren. In the seventeenth and eighteenth centuries, millennarianism emerges in the beliefs of the Pietists, the Catholic Apostolic Church, the Plymouth Brethren, and Seventh-day Adventist Churches.

The Shakers

Among millennialists, the Shakers in particular are worthy of mention. The sect was formed by Ann Lee (1736–1784) from Manchester, England, who was converted to the Shaking Quakers (who trembled and danced) in 1758. She became Mother Ann and received revelations such that she was perceived as the female counterpart of Christ. A small group of followers formed around her charismatic personality, and she believed that she was to take them to the New World in order to await the millennium of Christ. To escape persecution they moved to America in 1774. By about the year 1840, they had around six thousand members, but in 1947 the Mother Church at Mount Lebanon in New York was sold. Membership officially ceased in 1965, although today a small gathering of believers still resides in Maine. Many of the new American religions of this time were directly or indirectly the spiritual descendants of the Shakers.

The Catholic Apostolic Church

Not all the new religious movements arose in the United States. In 1831, Presbyterian minister Edward Irving formed in London the Catholic Apostolic Church, an inspiring blend of churchmanship and beliefs. The Catholic Apostolic Church was millennialist in belief, but it organized itself along the lines of the Early Church. Doctrinally it preached evangelical beliefs but in a manner that used Anglican Catholic and Orthodox liturgy in its services. The Church ceased to survive the failed forecast of Christ's return by 1855. However, Irving published vigorously on the subject of prophecy and masterminded the Albury Park prophecy conferences, which encouraged other gatherings of premillennarians during the nineteenth and twentieth centuries. Irving's apocalyptic exposition found support among the Plymouth Brethren and led many in the group to become enthusiastic teachers of dispensational premillennialism. Dispensationalism is a millenial method of biblical interpretation, dividing history into seven "dispensations" in which God deals differently and progressively with the human race.

The Exclusive Brethren

In 1840, the Exclusive Brethren, led by dispensationalist J. N. Darby, broke away from the recently formed Brethren Movement. He believed that the second coming of Christ consisted of two stages. The first stage was a belief in a secret "rapture" of the saints, which was to remove the church from the world before a seven-year period of tribulation devastated the earth. In the second stage, Christ appears visibly with his saints after the tribulation to rule on earth for a thousand years.

However, most premillennialists during the early nineteenth century were not dispensationalists. Darby's interpretation was accepted because of the work of individuals such as Henry Moorhouse, who convinced many people to accept dispensationalism. William E. Blackstone, "Harry" A. Ironside, and C. I. Scofield all propagated Darby's eschatology. These beliefs spread through Scofield and his Scofield Reference Bible. This version of biblical text, which made the new eschatological interpretation central through an elaborate system of notes printed on the same pages as the text, proved extremely popular, selling millions of copies. The Moody Seminaries, the Bible Institute, Dallas Theological Seminary, and Grace Theological Seminary have all made this interpretation popular among millions of conservative Protestants.

Other Postmillennialist Movements in the Nineteenth Century

During the nineteenth century, a form of postmillennialism that equated the United States with the kingdom of God became very popular. Many Protestant ministers promoted nationalism by presenting the coming of the golden age as dependent upon the spread of democracy, technology, and the other blessings of Western civilization. This movement was called "civil millennialism." One exponent was Hollis Read of the Congregationist Park Street Church, Boston. His two-volume book *The Hand of God in History* puts forward the belief that God's millennial purposes were finding fulfillment in America. He believed that all facets of society pointed to the coming of the millennium to America in the nineteenth century. From this base, the new era would go into the whole world. Read supported imperialism because of the belief that the extension of Anglo-Saxon control over nations guaranteed the spread of the gospel.

From time to time, especially during times of crisis, civil postmillennialism is revived to encourage a community. An example can be found in the Civil War where there was support for Julia Ward Howe's "Battle Hymn of the Republic," and the vision of God working through the Northern forces to accomplish his ultimate purpose:

> Mine eyes have seen the glory of the coming of the Lord,
> He is trampling out the vintage where the grapes of wrath are stored;
> He hath loosed the fateful lightning of his terrible swift sword,
> His truth is marching on.
>
> Glory, glory hallelujah!
> Glory, glory hallelujah!
> Glory, glory hallelujah!
> His truth is marching on.
>
> I have seen Him in the watch fires of a hundred circling camps;
> They have builded Him an altar in the evening dews and damps;
> I can read his righteous message by their dim and flaring lamps;
> His day is marching on.
>
> . . .
>
> He has sounded forth the trumpet that shall never call retreat;
> He is sifting out the hearts of men before His judgment seat;
> Oh, be swift, my soul, to answer Him, be jubilant, my feet!
> Our God is marching on.

Since World War II, civil millennialism has been revived in opposition to communism and to counter social changes, such the equal rights movement for women.

In addition to premillennial, amillennial, and postmillennial beliefs, groups such as the Christadelphians, Seventh-day Adventists (see unit 10:3), and the Latter-day Saints (Mormons, see unit 10:6), tend to equate the activities of their own sect with the coming of the millennium.

Amillennialism

Amillennialists do not believe that the Bible predicts a period of the rule of Christ on earth before the last judgment. Instead, ongoing good and evil will exist in the world until the second coming of Christ, when the dead shall be raised and the world judged.

Amillennialists believe that the kingdom of God is now present in the world, as the victorious Christ rules his Church through the Word and the Spirit. The future, perfect kingdom refers, therefore, to the new earth and life in heaven. Revelation 20 is thus a description of the souls of dead believers reigning with Christ in heaven.

UNIT 9:10 THE TWENTIETH CENTURY: PROTESTANTISM AND THE RISE OF FUNDAMENTALISM AND EVANGELICALISM

Key Events and Developments in the Twentieth-Century Christian Church

- 1909: Conservative American scholars publish a series of twelve booklets defending fundamentalism under the title, *The Fundamentals: A Testimony of Truth.*
- 1917: The first phase of the persecution of the Orthodox Church in Russia begins. Lenin sets out to destroy the Church by abolishing private property, and thus eliminating the Church's income. Some eight thousand priests and nuns were killed during Lenin's reign of power, and persecution continued under Stalin (1877–1953).
- 1923: An Inter-Orthodox Congress authorizes local churches to adopt the Gregorian calendar for most feast days.
- 1925: The Scopes trial held in Dayton, Tennessee. John Thomas Scopes is found guilty of violating a state law which required that only creationism be taught in the state's public schools. Clarence Darrow's defense of Scopes and press coverage favorable to the defendant turns public opinion in his favor.
- 1929: The Soviet government begins serious opposition of religion. In the period between 1927 and 1940, the number of Orthodox Churches in the Russian Republic fell from 29,584 to under 300. Approximately

40,000 Orthodox clergy and millions of laymen were killed for their faith between 1917 and 1940.

- 1939–1945: The Second World War meant that both the Catholic and Protestant Churches and their leaders suffered and were also martyred, but some Church leaders were weak and ineffectual in their stance against the evil Nazi regime.
- 1945: The Nag Hammadi library is discovered. It consists of twelve papyrus books and eight leaves from a thirteenth book. The fifty-two tractates these books contain cover a variety of religious subjects, many from a Gnostic perspective.
- 1948: The World Council of Churches forms to move the Church forward into further unity.
- 1962–1965: The Second Vatican Council brings serious reform to the Roman Catholic Church. In 1965 both churches lift the anathemas and excommunications placed against one another in 1054.
- Crises in Darwinism revive Christian attacks on evolutionary theory and development of scientific models from a Christian perspective.
- 1995: Pope John Paul II issues the encyclical *Orientale Lumen*, encouraging reunion between East and West.
- New translation methods put the Bible into the languages of 95 percent of humankind. There are an estimated 1.9 billion "Christians," about 33 percent of the world population.
- More Christians are said to have been martyred in the twentieth century than in all the earlier centuries combined together.
- Decline of church attendance becomes marked in a large section of the Western world.
- Rise of the Internet and mass media lead to wide dissemination of the gospel by new means.
- Explosive growth of Chinese, Korean, and African Christianity.
- Emergence of charismatic Christian sects. From the 1960s to the present, the Charismatic movement has an impact on both Protestant and Catholic Christians, emphasizing "baptism in the spirit," "speaking in tongues," and the gifts of the Holy Spirit.

Throughout the twentieth century, the Church has moved towards unity and togetherness through the Ecumenical Movement. The word "ecumenical" comes from a Greek word meaning "the whole inhabited earth." In Edinburgh in 1910 an international missionary conference was led by the American Methodist John R. Mott. The main theme was Christian unity. Structures were established that eventually gave rise to the formation of the World Council of Churches (WCC), which is an international, interdenominational organization of Protestant and Orthodox churches. In 1948, the first General Assembly met in Amsterdam with 351 delegates from 147 denominations and 44 different countries. The council has no power over the 335 member churches, but provides an opportunity for cooperation in matters of common concern. The headquarters are at Geneva, Switzerland.

In 1961 The Russian Orthodox Church joined the Council, and a formal Confessional Basis was adopted, stating that:

> The World Council of Churches is a fellowship of Churches which confess the Lord Jesus Christ as God and Saviour according to the scriptures and therefore seek to fulfil together their common calling to the glory of one God, Father, Son and Holy Spirit.

In the 1960s the WCC became controversial because of its involvement in political issues, especially the giving of grants to so-called "freedom fighters" in national struggles. The Council undertook these actions believing that the grantees were oppressed minorities involved in "just wars." The Roman Catholic Church was largely absent from these initiatives. Since 1961, however, senior Roman Catholics have attended WCC Assemblies as official observers, and the Catholic Church itself has entered into ecumenical change since the 1960s through The Second Vatican Council (1962–1965). Vatican II opened the door to closer ecumenical activity, and for the first time the Roman Catholic Council acknowledged authentic Christians outside the Roman Church.

At the same time as the rise of ecumenism, the ongoing legacy of textual and literary criticism of the Bible has continued to challenge many of the long-held Christian beliefs about the authorship of the Bible and its historicity.

In the twentieth century, Europe was not the only continent to feel the waves of Enlightenment and the fruition of now long-held beliefs in the autonomy of human reason as the driving force in deciding about life's realities. In America the twentieth century was one of the most turbulent in terms of its religious belief and practices. From the 1960s to the 1980s, the Civil Rights movement, the "Sexual Revolution," Vietnam, Women's Liberation, and new "alternative" religions (e.g., yoga, Transcendental Meditation, Hinduism) all challenged the beliefs and values of the traditional church. One response to this challenge has been the rise of Christian Fundamentalism.

The Rise of American Fundamentalism

Fundamentalism has been given serious attention by historians, theologians, and social scientists. Two influential historical treatments are Ernest R. Sandeen, *The Roots of Fundamentalism* (1970) and George M. Marsden *Fundamentalism and American Culture* (1980). The former sees fundamentalism as an intellectual movement concerning the nature of the Bible and the direction of human history, energized by a small number of well-educated people on both sides of the Atlantic. The latter book sees fundamentalism as a broadly based social and religious protest against modernity's threats to traditional Christianity. In this unit, we steer more towards the latter view.

Modern fundamentalism developed in the United States in the late nineteenth century as a reaction to liberal protestantism (see also postmodernism, chapter 1). This stance was reflected in such early declarations as the fourteen-point creed of the Niagara Bible Conference of 1878 and the five-point statement of the Presbyterian General Assembly of 1910, which were

1. Literal inerrancy of the autographs (the originals of each scriptural book)
2. The virgin birth and deity of Christ
3. A substitutionary view of the atonement
4. The bodily resurrection of Christ
5. The imminent return of Christ

A series of twelve tracts entitled *The Fundamentals* (1910–1914) were sent to "every pastor, evangelist, missionary, theological student, Sunday School Superintendent, YMCA and YWCA secretary." About 3 million copies were distributed widely in the English-speaking world, and they provided a wide listing of listed enemies such as Romanism, socialism, modern philosophy, atheism, Eddyism, Mormonism, and spiritualism. Chief among the enemies cited were liberal theology, which rested on a naturalistic interpretation of the doctrines of the faith, German higher criticism, and Darwinism, which appeared to undermine the Bible's authority.

The ideas of the fundamentals had been in circulation for some time in the work of A. A. Hodge, a professor of theology at Princeton, and B. B. Warfield, a professor at Western Theological Seminary. Both argued that the scriptures were inerrant, but limited that inerrancy to the original manuscripts of the Bible. As such they were "absolutely errorless" because of their divine origin, although Hodge and Warfield conceded that some "apparent inconsistencies and collisions with other sources of information are to be expected in imperfect copies of ancient writings. . . ."

Belief in the fundamentals was not exclusively Protestant. Some of these beliefs were also held by Roman Catholics. Initially the main centers of fundamentalism were Philadelphia, Fort Worth, Minneapolis, Denver, and Los Angeles, and also Princeton University, which disseminated the beliefs and teachings among its students.

In the aftermath of the American Civil War, at least three main religious responses can be seen:

1. The Modernists, who sought to adjust their inherited faith tradition to the new social and intellectual climate.
2. Fundamentalism, with its rejection of science and scientific method and its strict adherence to the worldview of the Bible.

3. The views of Henry Ward Beecher and other Christocentric liberals who argued that there were two revelations from God—one in scripture and one in the natural world—and that these are compatible with one another on a deep spiritual level. Beecher and his followers stressed the fact that the Church preceded the Bible rather than vice versa, and because the Bible was recorded and written by human beings, its understanding of reality might be contingent upon human understanding.

The fundamentalist movement produced a number of notable characters and events. Frank Norris of Fort Worth, Texas, drew huge crowds when he preached on sermons such as "The Ten Biggest Devils in Fort Worth with Names Given." When he verbally attacked the mayor of Forth Worth, a friend of the Catholic mayor of Fort Worth came to see him. Norris shot the friend with a pistol he kept to kill "critters."

Billy Sunday was a professional baseball player turned evangelist. He had no use for the "bastard theory of evolution." His version of Christian faith was both masculine and muscular, "the man who has real, rich, red blood in his veins instead of pink tea and ice water," was a real Christian and a real American. Sunday believed Christianity and patriotism to be the same thing. He and his followers coined the famous slogan "Back to Christ, the Bible, and the Constitution."

The most famous and active exponent of fundamentalism was William Jennings Bryan.

The Challenge to American Fundamentalism: The Scopes Trial

From the 1870s, Southern evangelicals led the fight against evolutionary teaching (commonly and somewhat misleadingly called Darwinism following the publication in 1859 of Charles Darwin's *On the Origin of Species*). Fundamentalists attempted to get state laws passed that would ban the teaching of evolution in schools.

To challenge laws against evolutionary teaching, a test case was planned. The American Civil Liberties Union had offered to support any Tennessee teacher willing to defy the statute. The challenge was taken with John Scopes, a young high school science teacher as the defendant, in what came to be known as the "Monkey Trial." William Jennings Bryan, an attorney and prominent Presbyterian layman, volunteered his services as counsel for the state. Since the early 1920s Bryan had been waging a highly publicized battle against evolutionary thought, which he considered the enemy of Christian civilization. Instead of focusing on the public right to insist on the content of state education, Bryan's decision was to focus attention around whether the Bible was literally true. This 1925 trial caused international interest.

Clarence Darrow was the defense lawyer and H. L. Mencken was the most famous journalist of his day. They both helped to discredit fundamentalism. Bryan was tricked into taking the stand to defend God and the Bible. Subsequently some observers felt that Bryan acquitted himself ably, while others believed that he disgraced conservative Protestant Christianity by his inability to answer some of Darrow's questions about the Bible's consistency and accuracy. Scopes lost and was fined one hundred dollars. But through this event, Bryan lost the sympathy of many people as his version of scripture appeared inadequate and intellectually discredited.

Fundamentalists and Modernists

Bitter controversies persisted and erupted between fundamentalists and modernists. Fundamentalists were determined to eject liberals from places of influence within mainstream denominations. The struggle between fundamentalists and modernists was fought in the years after World War I. The appeal of fundamentalism was hindered by a number of things, including the caricature of fundamentalism arising from the Scopes Trial, the popularization of the liberal response, well-publicized divisions among fundamentalists themselves, and preoccupations with the Depression of the 1930s and World War II. Fundamentalists enjoyed some success in their efforts to purge people who did not profess faith in the five fundamentals, but they were unable to seize control of any of the major denominations.

Another consequence of the Scopes Trial and its aftermath was a growing awareness of the inability of Protestantism to shape and inform American opinion. There were several triumphs regarding prohibition and the passing of Blue Laws to protect the Sabbath. But modern attitudes towards alcohol and recreation persisted despite such opposition. As a disillusioned public perceived leaders to be ineffectual and hypocritical, respect declined and intellectuals left the church en masse. By 1925 H. L. Mencken could claim: "Every day a new Catholic church goes up; every day another Methodist or Presbyterian church is turned into a garage."

From the start fundamentalism relied on central doctrinal affirmations to define itself and its cultural boundaries, resulting in a separatist attitude to what they considered secular culture. When the new form of evangelicalism arose after the Second World War, credibility began to be regained.

Twentieth-Century Protestantism

The distinction between Evangelicalism and Fundamentalism

Evangelicals like Alister McGrath (1997) argue that fundamentalism and evangelicalism can be distinguished at three different levels:

1. While fundamentalism is committed to a literal interpretation of scripture, evangelicalism accepts the principle of biblical criticism (used

responsibly) and recognizes the diversity of literary forms within scripture.
2. Although there is an overlap of beliefs between the two, such as in the authority of scripture, these similarities often mask profound differences in outlook—for example, the narrow commitment to doctrines such as dispensationalism that most evangelicals regard as peripheral.
3. Sociologically, fundamentalism is a reactionary movement against culture with tight criteria of membership. Evangelicalism is a cultural movement with increasingly loose criteria for self-definition.

Evangelicalism has produced significant writings in areas of philosophy, religion, apologetics, philosophy, and theology. One notable writer is Donald G. Bloesch (b. 1928) who in his *Essentials of Evangelical Theology* (1978–1979) carefully distinguishes and discusses the difference between evangelical theology, liberalism, and fundamentalism.

In the late 1940s and early 1950s a new evangelical style came into public view with the ministry of well-known figures such as Billy Graham, whose ministry was enormous and influential internationally.

Televangelism

In the 1970s and 1980s, different brands of fundamentalism again became influential in the United States, promoted by popular television evangelists and represented by such groups as the Moral Majority, and the new, politically-oriented "religious right." By the 1980 campaign of Ronald Reagan for the American presidency, fundamentalists entered a new phase. They became nationally prominent when they offered an answer for what many regarded as a supreme social, economic, moral, and religious crisis in America. Fundamentalists identified a new and more sinister enemy in secular humanism, which they believed was responsible for eroding churches, schools, universities, good government, and above all families. They cited and fought evolutionism, political and theological liberalism, communism, permissive morality, sexual perversion, socialism, and any loosening of the absolute, inerrant authority of the Bible. They called Americans to return to the fundamentals of the faith and the fundamental moral values of America.

The public face of this phase of fundamentalism was the new generation of television and print fundamentalists, notably Jerry Falwell, Tim La Haye, Hal Lindsey, and Pat Robertson. They were primarily Baptist and Southern, but their influence extended to all denominations.

Pentecostalism

The origins of the Pentecostal movement were in the post–Civil War period and appealed to the poor and less educated members of American society who no longer felt welcome in traditional Protestant congregations that had become prosperous middle-class institutions. It was an era of industrial expansion and urban isolation, and as the Pentecostals gathered in their tents and small tabernacles, worship for many congregants became more local and meaningful. Both in Britain and the United States during the late nineteenth and early twentieth centuries, many Christians believed it was necessary to go back to the experience of the early disciples. This feeling led them to seek post-conversion experience of God in the baptism of the Holy Spirit, which would empower them with gifts of speaking in tongues and healing.

Pentecostals emerged into different groups according to their beliefs, organization, and ways of worship. Some of the larger denominations are the Assemblies of God, the Church of God in Christ, the Church of God, the International Church of the Foursquare Gospel, the Pentecostal Church of God in America, the Pentecostal Holiness Church, and the United Pentecostal Church.

One of the early associations of Pentecostals with far-reaching influence was inspired by Charles Fox Parham (1873–1929) from about 1900 at Bethel Bible College in Topeka, Kansas. He linked baptism in the Spirit with speaking with tongues (glossolalia) and saw the revival as a restoration of the gifts promised in the latter days on the day of Pentecost (Acts 2). The national expansion of the movement was led by the black former holiness preacher William Seymour and began in Los Angeles at the Apostolic Faith Gospel Mission on Azusa Street in 1906. The Azusa Street movement seems to have been a merger of white American Holiness religion with worship styles derived from the African-American Christian tradition, which had developed since the days of chattel slavery in the South. The mixture of tongues and other gifts with black music and worship styles created a new and indigenous form of interracial pentecostalism. The Pentecostal movement in Los Angeles stood out as a striking exception to the racism and segregation of the times. Later well-known Pentecostal leaders included Aimee Semple McPherson, Oral Roberts, Jimmy Swaggart, and Pat Robertson.

The Charismatic Movement

From the 1960s the charismatic movement attracted followers within traditional denominations. Until then, the charismatic experience, or being "baptized in the Spirit" had been almost the total domain of the Pentecostal denominations. The Reverend Dennis Bennett in Van Nuys, California, brought the impact of the charismatic movement within mainline Christianity to public attention in the early 1960s. He told his Episcopal congregation that he had been filled with the Holy Spirit and had spoken in tongues. Reaction was mixed, with the bishop banning speaking in tongues from his diocese. However, news spread and it became clear that others inside and outside of the Episcopal Church had experienced the phenomena. Christians who are baptized or renewed in the Spirit believe and manifest the gifts of the Spirit that Paul listed in 1 Corinthians 12:8–10:

> To one is given through the Spirit the utterance of wisdom and to another the utterance of knowledge. . . . to another faith . . . to another gifts of healing. . . . to another the working of

> miracles, to another prophecy, to another the discernment of spirits, to another various kinds of tongues, to another the interpretation of tongues.

The movement distinguished itself through an exuberant expectation of the dynamic and empowering presence of the Spirit both personally in the life of the believer and corporately in big gatherings. The charismatic movement has developed its own style of corporate worship, specifically though new music, worship songs, and informal styles of prayer that have not been confined to the movement itself. In his *World Christian Encyclopaedia* (1989), D. B. Barrett estimated that over 300 million people in over 230 countries were part of the movement, which at its zenith in the 1980s grew annually at the rate of some 19 million members, many of whom have stayed within the traditional denominations.

Healing Deliverance and the Rise of the Media Churches

In the 1980s there were further developments in the charismatic movement including a revival of the practice of healing and deliverance from evil spirits. The ministry of John Wimber (d. 1997) and the Vineyard Christian Fellowship (Anaheim, California) brought a third wave of signs and wonders upon many churches in the United States and Britain. In 1994 the British churches coined the phrase "Toronto Blessing" for another wave of the Holy Spirit beginning at the Airport Vineyard Church in Toronto. Believers claimed a continual daily experience of the outpouring of the Spirit, which has led the church to be recognized by many as a "worldwide renewal center." Various phenomena are in evidence at meetings including laughter, falling or resting in the Spirit, shaking, howling, or dropping unconscious to the floor. Various sociological and psychological explanations have been offered for this behavior by noncharismatics, but people who have witnessed or experienced it mainly agree that it is a spiritual blessing which leads to a new sense of the joy of the Lord, a renewed love for Jesus and the Bible, and a desire to spread the gospel to the wider community. Its effects have been felt in mainstream denominations in the United Kingdom, South Africa, East Asia, and North America, but the movement is not without its charismatic and noncharismatic critics. Pentecostal churches do not condone the emphasis on renewal by the Spirit rather than baptism in the Spirit. In December 1995, John Wimber, the founder of the Vineyard Churches, released the Airport Vineyard from the Vineyard denomination. There was an escalation of concern and unhappiness regarding the extraordinary manifestations of the Spirit, and he was no longer able to oversee the activities of its members.

The Word/Faith Movement and the Prosperity Gospel

Kenneth Copeland is considered to be the most prosperous and well-known in the "Word/Faith"/"Positive Confession" movement. At the time of this writing, his nationwide television program is on the Trinity Broadcasting Network, and he is the author of numerous charismatic-oriented books and articles. The *Believer's Voice of Victory* magazine carries his teachings, which many Christians view as heretical. For example:

> Jesus didn't claim to be God when he lived on earth (8/88) (12/88)
>
> Healing is for every believer (2/93)
>
> Tongues are for the entire Body of Christ (1/93)

Copeland also says: "It would have been impossible for Jesus to have been poor!" (9/90). (Reported in the *Calvary Contender* [Feb. 15, 1993].)

The Word/Faith movement teaches that faith is a matter of what we say more than the God in whom we trust or the doctrines and truths we truly believe. A favorite term in the Word/Faith movement is "positive confession." It refers to the belief that words have creative power. What Word/Faith teachers claim is that there is a direct correlation between what you say and the events that happen in your life, and that your "confessions"—especially the demands you make of God—must all be stated positively and without wavering. Then God is required to answer.

Word/Faith is the fastest-growing strand of the charismatic movement. It involves two branches: the Peale/Schuller Positive/Possibility thinkers, and the Hagin/Copeland Positive Confession and Word/Faith groups, whose religious roots can be found in E. W. Kenyon (1867–1948), William Branham (1909–1965), and the Manifest Sons of God/Latter Rain Movement. Kenneth Hagin's book, *Having Faith in Your Faith*, teaches that anyone can develop universal "laws of faith" to obtain the things they desire. Hagins's teaching also decries poverty. If a Christian drives a Chevrolet instead of a luxury car, it is seen as being "ignorant" of God's "law of prosperity" that works for "whoever you are," saint or sinner. This approach is called the "name-it-and-claim-it" gospel. At the heart of the Positive Confession Movement is the cry of "Have faith in your faith." Critics say that the movement has come a long way from what Jesus taught his disciples, that is, to "Have faith in God." Copeland's talk of Christians who "are still living in sickness, bondage, and lack" has been a major source of contention to the historical churches who honor so many saints through the ages whose faith stood firm despite such suffering and infirmity.

As the heirs of the Reformation, the Protestant Church and the charismatic movement, move into the twenty-first century it remains to be seen whether they will allow their own reformation.

Into the Future

At the start of the third millennium many thinkers are looking for explanations to account for the cultural shifts and the subsequent state of religion during the last three decades of the twentieth century. The declining membership of mainstream denominations and the rise of conservative (fundamentalist, evangelical, charismatic, Pentecostal) and alternate religions (seekers, New Agers, Eastern religions) all point to a profoundly different religious landscape from that of fifty years ago. Historians like Thomas Tweed, Catherine Albanese, Joel Martin, and Peter Williams argue for a new type of narrative for American religious history. The introduction to Thomas Tweed's *Narrating U.S. Religious History* (1997) provides an stimulating discussion on the changes the study of religious history is undergoing in academic circles.

UNIT 9:11 ROMAN CATHOLICISM

He who acts against his conscience loses his soul.
John Henry Newman

Theology has to stop explaining the world and start reforming it.
Gustavo Gutiérrez

Chapter 9 branched off in unit 9:7 to study the English Reformation and the subsequent development of the Protestant church in America. In this last unit of the chapter we backtrack to trace some of the important events in Roman Catholic history that have shaped the faith. Roman Catholicism is by far the largest of the Christian denominations, with about one billion members. The denomination maintains a strong presence in Western and Central Europe, for example, in Southern Ireland, Italy, and Poland, and in parts of North America, South America, and southern India (e.g., Goa). The Catholic Church reputedly started with the commissioning of the apostle Peter as the rock on which the church is to be built (Matt. 16:18). The word "Catholic" means universal. The adjective "Roman" was added in all probability due to the Church's adoption of the organizational grid of the Roman empire and because of the tradition that Peter had founded the Church in Rome.

During its first five centuries, the Church of Rome gradually gained preeminence among the churches of the Mediterranean region (see also unit 9:4). A number of important dates and events in the history of the Catholic Church are as follows:

- In 314, the Edict of Milan recognized Roman Catholicism as a legal religion. By the end of the fourth century, Roman Catholicism was made the official religion of the Empire.
- A monastic movement developed in which monks became directly involved in the missionary expansion of the Church in Ireland, Scotland, Gaul, and England between the fifth and seventh centuries.
- The western empire fell in 476 C.E., and the pope was the only effec-

tive force left for order in the West. In the ensuing centuries, the monks worked at Christianizing the [Germanic] invaders and cemented ties between a Roman form of Christianity and a more western European culture.

- In 1054, the Great Schism occurred as the Eastern churches separated from the Western churches (see unit 9:4). The Patriarch of Constantinople, Michael Cerularios, was excommunicated by the Roman Church.
- Between the years of 1378 and 1417, there was the Western Schism, with three different men making claims to the papal throne. This schism ended in 1414 by the Council of Constance through the principle of conciliarism, which stated that a general council of the Church, not the pope, was the highest ecclesiastical authority. The Council elected Martin V (not one of the three) as the new pope in 1417.
- In the sixteenth century, reform swept through the Christian West as the reformers Luther, Calvin, and Zwingli attacked the corruption in the Church. The Reformation resulted in Protestantism (see unit 9:6).
- The Roman Catholic Church went through the Counter-Reformation under the Council of Trent from 1545 to 1563. The Council of Trent condemned most of the Protestant issues of dissent:

    Justification was not by faith alone

    The tradition of the church was given equal place alongside the Bible so that no one was free to interpret scripture "contrary to the sense in which Holy Mother Church, who is to judge the true sense and interpretation of the Holy Scriptures, has and does hold."

    The Vulgate (Latin version of the Bible) was declared the canonical text.

    The Mass continued in Latin and not in the vernacular.

Since the Protestant Reformation there have been a number of developments in the Roman Catholic Church.

The Influence of the Pope

In the decades prior to the French Revolution the popularity and influence of the pope seem to have been in decline, but in the nineteenth century the pope reemerged as a major figure within Catholicism. Napoleon had treated him with contempt, which ironically worked in the pope's favor as, in the light of this, both Catholics and the governments of Europe treated him with new respect. This led to increased papal authority—known as "ultramontanism"—and led to Pope Pius IX (1846–1878) opening the First Vatican Council in 1869. This Council gave formal expression to the famous dogma of papal infallibility (1870), which is best seen against the broader background of liberal and modern ways of thinking about the Church that threatened the faith at the time.

Eighteenth- and Nineteenth-Century Liberalism and Catholic Modernism

Liberal Catholicism was a response by a minority of Catholic intellectuals to the French Revolution and nineteenth-century European liberalism. The Catholic majority had a long tradition of conservativism and authoritarianism. The pioneer of the movement was the French priest and prophet H. F. R. de Lamennais (1782–1854). He developed a new apologetic for Catholicism, maintaining that it is not evidenced chiefly by miracles and fulfilled prophecies but rather by its ability to perpetuate beliefs that are essential to an ordered social life. These beliefs included monotheism, the difference between good and evil, the immortality of the soul, and reward or punishment in a future life. Modernism emphasized the use of general reason, consisting of the collective judgments derived from custom, tradition, and education. Lamennais's apologetics led to political ends. He aimed at promoting the social regeneration of Europe. His revolutionary program included the abolition of concordats between the papacy and civil governments; the cessation of state payment of clergy and of state intervention in the appointment of bishops; freedom (instead of monopoly) for the church in education; liberty of the press; freedom of association; universal suffrage; and decentralization of government.

The majority of liberal Catholics stayed orthodox and looked to modernize the church through the emancipation of the laity and the separation of church and state. A later generation of liberal Catholics, which included Lord Acton (1834–1902), Alfred Loisy (1857–1940), George Tyrrell (1861–1909), and J. J. I. von Dollinger (1799–1890) in Germany, advocated autonomy for the laity in doctrinal matters.

Diversity in the Catholic Faith: The Oxford Movement

The Roman Catholic Church is often perceived as a traditionalist faith without significant divisions in doctrine, faith, or practice. This picture is inaccurate, especially today when diversity is often in evidence. John Henry Newman, often cited as the greatest Catholic figure of the nineteenth century, took a significant dissenting stance and suffered the consequences.

John Henry Newman (1801–1890) was born in London to a Huguenot mother and a father who were religiously broadminded. While a member of the Church of England, his views began to move from low-church evangelical to high-church Catholic until he finally converted to Roman Catholicism in 1845. He was ordained a Catholic priest and was made a cardinal by Pope Leo XIII in 1879.

Newman was a Fellow at Oriel College (Oxford) and Vicar of University Church of St. Mary. He fought a form of liberalism he called the "anti-dogmatic principle": "Liberalism in religion is the doctrine that there is no positive truth in religion. . . ." He supported the Catholic Emancipation of 1829 and, as the leader of the Oxford movement, opposed the strong link between church and state, believing that state control of the Church could never serve the interests of religion.

After his conversion to Roman Catholicism, he took up a defense of lay rights against clericalism. He wrote an article saying that the British bishops should seek the counsel of lay Catholics on important issues. He also defended the liberal arts against fellow clergy who desired to restrict student access to knowledge and information for fear such things would undermine faith. Newman received strong criticism and disapproval for these views, but he responded by writing a long article entitled "Consulting the Faithful on Matters of Doctrine," thus establishing himself directly in opposition to long-held views.

In his study, Newman wrote on the subject of his expertise: the fourth-century Arian heresy (see unit 9:2). Arius claimed that Jesus is not God, only God's greatest creation. Newman reviewed in detail the sixty-year period following the Council of Nicaea in 325 where the council had condemned Arianism and formulated, in its place, the Nicene Creed. He illustrated in detail how the vast majority of bishops and dozens of regional church councils ignored the Nicene Creed and embraced Arianism. Even Pope Liberius (under pressure) signed a pro-Arian statement.

In this article, Newman argued that so great was the move to embrace Arianism that it may well have become predominant had it not been for the Catholic laity, the ordinary believers whose instincts and faith were in tact. All over Christendom, ordinary lay people dissented from what the priests, bishops, and even the pope doctrinally advocated. In the face of excommunication and persecution, even under the threat of martyrdom, they held the belief that Jesus is the true God. Such was lay influence that at the First Council of Constantinople in 381, the Arian heresy was finally laid to rest, and the priesthood and hierarchy of the Church bowed to the will of the people. In his summary, Newman was scathing:

> The Nicene dogma was maintained during the greater part of the fourth century not by the unswerving firmness of the Holy See or councils of bishops but by the consensus of the fidelium [the faithful].
>
> On the other hand, I say that there was a temporary suspension of the functions of the *ecclesia docens* [teaching church]. The body of the bishops failed in their confession of the faith. They spoke variously against one another. There was nothing after Nicaea of firm, consistent testimony for 60 years. There were untrustworthy councils, unfaithful bishops . . . misguidance, delusion, hallucination . . . extending itself into nearly every corner of the Catholic Church. (John Henry Newman, *On Consulting Matters of Doctrine*)

Newman's conclusions were that the laity had an "instinct" for the truth, and that this "sense of the faithful" must never be dismissed by the hierarchy of the

Church. Authentic Church teaching is a cooperation on the part of both laity and hierarchy. Lapses (or "suspensions") occur when one side or the other of this living body is missing or out of action.

This radical protest was fiery. Newman was adamant in his views arguing that the promise of the Holy Spirit was given to the whole Church, and therefore the whole Church was responsible for its decisions. Newman refused to recant and charges were brought against him before the Vatican's Office of Propaganda by several English bishops, but Rome did not focus at any depth on the issue. In later life Newman was made a cardinal for his lifetime contributions to the church.

Newman left a theological legacy in believing the Church to be an organism of interactive parts. His theology of the Church was recognized at Vatican II. The Dogmatic Constitution on the Church declared, "Christ, the great prophet . . . continually fulfils his prophetic office . . . not only through the hierarchy who teach in his name . . . but also through the laity."

The thought and writings of John Henry Newman show how dissent can help reform a religious tradition.

The Second Vatican Council

The Second Vatican Council (1962–1965) was called by Pope John XXIII, who sadly lived only to see the first session. The Council's work was concluded under his successor Pope Paul VI, and it produced the great changes and proposals for reform in the Roman Catholic Church.

Sixteen documents were finally produced, representing deep thought, analysis, and programs for reform on a number of crucial twentieth-century issues including: the nature of the church, the authority of bishops and the position of the laity, the nature of revelation and the need for greater use of the Bible in theology. The Pastoral Constitution of the Church in the Modern World (*Gaudium et Spes*) dealt with the Church's attitude toward marriage, economics, war, and a range of other social issues. The Constitution on the Liturgy urged greater use of the vernacular language and the Decree on Ecumenism outlined a program for reunion with other Christians worldwide. The Second Vatican Council produced an aftermath of turbulent debate and disagreement for many, but it represents a courageous and modern attempt to reform an ancient church in the twentieth century.

Current Issues

In modern times, the Roman Catholic Church has been characterized by taking strong positions on some controversial issues. Beginning with Pope Leo XIII's encyclical *Rerum Novarum* (1891), the popes have spoken against the injustices of the economic and social conditions created by modern industrial societies and also proposed remedies to address these situations. The Church has opposed nuclear warfare, repeatedly urged an end to the arms race, and attempted at times to halt the exploitation of poor nations by rich ones.

On certain other issues the Church has been more conservative. The prohibition of artificial means of birth control was reiterated by Pope Paul VI in his encyclical *Humanae Vitae* (1968), which was a very provocative document that raised strong objections in some theological and even Episcopal circles. The Roman Catholic Church has continued in its fierce opposition of liberalized abortion laws.

Although the Church permits women under certain circumstances to administer the Eucharist and undertake other ministries, it prohibits them to be ordained priests or deacons.

Catholic Beliefs and Ethos

Catholicism is a very diverse worldwide Christian movement, and any simple analysis will be far short of accurate explanation. With that in mind, it is possible to point to a number of key features.

A Strong Hierarchical Structure

The pope is the religious head of the Roman Catholic Church; he is also known as the bishop of Rome and is elected by the College of Cardinals, who rank next to the pope in ecclesiastical authority. New popes are elected on the death or retirement of a current pope. In order to be elected, a new pope must be named on two thirds of the ballots cast, and each member of the College of Cardinals must vote. When elected, the pope must formally accept the appointment and then choose a name for himself. The custom of a pope changing his name upon election originated shortly before the year 1000. Roman Catholics believe the pope to be the successor of the apostle Peter, a belief grounded in the claim of "The Petrine theory" (which was affirmed by the Council of Florence in 1439, defined by the First Vatican Council in 1870, and endorsed by the Second Vatican Council in 1964) that Jesus Christ conferred the position of primacy in the church upon Peter alone. The First Vatican Council cited the three classical New Testament texts long associated with this position: John 1:42, John 21:15ff., and, above all, Matthew 16:18ff.

A Sacramental Church

The Church believes in seven sacraments:

1. *Baptism* brings the infant into the supernatural order of existence by planting God's first special grace in its soul. Baptism also washes away the original sin a person is born with due to Adam's fall from grace in the Garden of Eden.

2. *Penance*: If sin is committed, then penance is needed if you are to be restored

to the human and divine fellowship. The Church teaches that if one confesses one's sins to God in the presence of a priest, and truly repent, then sins are forgiven.

3. The *mass* is the central sacrament of the seven. Catholics see it as a reenactment of Christ's last supper with his disciples, not as a commemoration, as is the Protestant view. The consecrated bread and wine become Christ's human body and blood and are actually present during the service even though no actual physical change takes place in the bread and wine. They are transubstantiated into the actual body and the actual blood of Christ.

4. *Confirmation*: A child reaches the age of reason (between twelve and fourteen) and is through an act of consecration eligible for responsible action as a soldier of God. At the time of confirmation, the child takes on the name of a saint of his or her own choosing.

5. *Marriage*: Marriage is the sacred joining of two adults with the grace of God for lifelong companionship and procreation.

6. *Holy Orders*: When a man takes this sacrament, he may become either a priest or a monk. He is considered married to the Church and is bound by the same laws as a married person. Roman Catholic priests may not marry in the conventional sense and take a vow of celibacy. Women who take this sacrament become nuns in the Church and also a bride of Christ bound by a vow of celibacy.

7. *Last Rites*: Last rites are also called Extreme Unction and Sacrament of the Sick. They are received at the end of life so that the soul is prepared for its last passage to the afterlife.

A Liturgical Church

In Catholicism the forms of worship are decided centrally, pointing to the belief that doctrine and belief should be clearly linked to worship and prayer.

Beliefs about Mary, the Mother of Jesus

In Roman Catholicism a special place is accorded to Mary, the mother of Jesus. Titles given to Mary sometimes exceed the official teaching of the Church and include Mother of God (*Theotokos*), Queen of Heaven, Mother of Humanity, Mother of Angels, and even Co-Redeemer with Christ. Other beliefs that have been put forward during the centuries include

- The Immaculate Conception of Mary (also known as the Virgin Birth)
- Her perpetual virginity
- Her assumption (body and soul) into heaven

These beliefs are official doctrines in the Roman Catholic Church. Apart from their belief in the virgin birth, Protestant Christians disagree with these doctrines because they see no historical evidence for such views. Protestants stress the humility and obedience of Mary and focus on her qualities of loyalty to Jesus during his final suffering at the cross.

Beliefs about Saints

The Roman Catholic Church continues to canonize individual men and women and make them official saints. One recent saint to be canonized was a Polish Franciscan priest, Maximilian Kolbe, who in the infamous German concentration camp of Auschwitz showed remarkable courage and dignity in volunteering to change places with a married man who was sentenced to die of starvation because of his escape attempt. The exchange was granted and Maximilian was locked away with other would-be escapees to suffer a long and painful death. Two weeks later only four men were found alive, and Maximilian was the only one who was still conscious. He was subsequently poisoned on August 14, 1941, and in 1982 he was declared an official saint by the Polish Pope John Paul II. The occasion was attended by the man he had saved: Francis Gajowinczek.

The Monastic Life and Religious Orders

In the Christian tradition, religious orders are associations of men or women who seek to lead a life of prayer and pious practices. Members usually bind themselves by vows of poverty, chastity, and obedience.

In the Roman Catholic Church, religious orders narrowly include monastic orders (of which the largest is the Benedictines), mendicant orders or friars (such as the Franciscans or Dominicans), and canons regular (priests living in a community attached to a specific church).

Clerks regular are societies of priests who make vows and are joined together for the purpose of priestly ministry; the Jesuits are a well-known example.

Roman Catholic orders of nuns or sisters are often smaller in size but more numerous than those of their male counterparts and are devoted primarily to teaching. Some monastic communities are enclosed—the monks or nuns rarely leaving their monastery or convent—and devoted to the contemplative life.

Scriptures and Writings

Roman Catholics recognize the New Testament and the Old Testament (the Hebrew scriptures of Judaism). In addition Catholics recognize several other books as canon, traditionally not recognized by Protestants. These books are known by Protestants as the Apocrypha, and to the Catholic Church as the Deuterocanonicals. In addition, tradition, canon law, and the infallible authority of the pope are regarded as sources of divine truth.

Liberation Theology

The beginnings of the liberation theology movement is generally dated to the second Latin American Bishops' Conference, which was held in Medellín, Colombia, in 1968, where attending bishops issued a document that stated the rights of the poor and criticized industrialized nations for prospering at the expense of third world countries. The movement's central text was *Teología de la liberación* (*A Theology of Liberation* [1971]), written by Gustavo Gutiérrez, who was a Peruvian priest and theologian. He wrote:

> "As a sign of the liberation of humankind and history, the Church itself in its concrete existence ought to be a place of liberation. . . . The point is not to survive, but to serve. The rest will be given."

Liberation theologians view the Bible as a practical book that is concerned with freedom from physical and social oppression. Liberation theology focuses on reflection and action ("praxis") and raising the awareness of the poor in confronting issues of justice. Other leaders of the movement included Brazilian theologian Leonardo Boff, Jesuit scholar Jon Sobrino, Archbishop Helder Câmara of Brazil, and Archbishop Oscar Arnulfo Romero of El Salvador who was assassinated in 1980. Romero became unpopular in Rome after the accession of Pope John Paul II and the movement away from Vatican II. The facts are disputed but it appears that John Paul asked Romero to speak more in general terms about oppression and poverty rather than directly and specifically. The Vatican appointed an administrator to oversee his work in El Salvador, but when he returned from Rome he was killed as he said mass in the chapel of the Divine Providence Hospital.

Liberation theology grew in Latin America during the 1970s. By the 1990s the Vatican, under Pope John Paul II, had started to curb the movement's influence by appointing more conservative prelates in Brazil and elsewhere in Latin America.

Roman Catholicism in America

A small Catholic presence had been in the American colonies since the 1630s, but by the 1850s Catholics represented the largest single Church body in America, comprising a vast number of immigrants from Germany and Ireland who left Europe due to the failure of the potato crops. (During the 1840s it is estimated that some 2.5 million Irish Catholics emigrated to the east coast of the United States.) A number of notable converts were drawn to Catholicism as an alternative to evangelicalism. Among them were Elizabeth Seton, the first American-born canonized saint, and Orestes Brownson, the transcendentalist. The rapid rise in the Catholic community created tension and alarm among many Protestants, which at times resulted in acts of violence such as the burning of an Ursuline convent near Boston in 1834, and ongoing debates occurred over the nature of education. Catholics participated in the struggle of the Civil War, which played a part in their growing social acceptance. Like Protestants, Catholics had to respond to the new theological and social challenges of the nineteenth and twentieth centuries. But significantly, the pope condemned "Americanism" in the papal bull *Testem Benevolentiae* (1899). The subsequent papal condemnation of modernism in 1907 effectively meant that, for the most part, American Catholics and Protestants lived and functioned in very different intellectual worlds, until the 1960s when the election of the Catholic John F. Kennedy to the presidency saw many people believe in the beginning of an end to Protestant supremacy and minority status.

According to the Encarta Online Encyclopedia,

> In the early 1990s the estimated Roman Catholic population of the United States had reached a figure of about 59,858,000. During the same period, the U.S. Catholic hierarchy was composed of 9 cardinals, 45 archbishops, 344 bishops, and 50,320 priests. The total number of Roman Catholic parishes was 19,787. The church maintained 226 seminaries for the training of the clergy. Other educational institutions under Roman Catholic sponsorship were 7,292 elementary schools, 1,360 high schools, and 232 colleges and universities; the total number of students enrolled in these institutions was about 3,336,000. ("Roman Catholic Church," Microsoft® Encarta® Online Encyclopedia 2000 http://encarta.msn.com © 1997–2000.)

Diversity in Roman Catholicism

Latin Rite Catholics practice a liturgy that has historically been in Latin. Roman Rite churches have split from the Roman Catholic Church but have kept many of its rituals and doctrines. The Old Catholic Churches originated in Europe after the First Vatican Council (1869–1870) where the pope was declared infallible. Old Catholic Churches reject the authority of the pope and are in communion with the Anglican Church. Their priests are married. At the time of writing there are about three hundred thousand adherents. Their headquarters are in Utrecht, Germany. Other independent episcopates trace their spiritual ancestry back to legally consecrated bishops who rebelled against Church hierarchy and dogma.

Eastern Catholic jurisdictions have differing liturgies, languages, and rules, and include: Ruthenian, Ukrainian, Melkite, Maronite, Chaldean, and Armenian dioceses. Other Eastern Catholic Churches under the authority of Roman Catholic bishops include the Syrian, Russian, White Russian, and Romanian Churches. All of these churches are distinguished from native Orthodox churches usually only by the fact that they acknowledge the primacy of the pope.

The Fraternity of St. Pius X was founded after Vatican II by Archbishop Marcel Lefevbre of France (1905–1991). He was suspended from exercising his priestly ministry by the pope in June 1976 when he unlawfully ordained thirteen priests. The Fraternity is a traditionalist movement that keeps the form of mass that was established after the Council of Trent in 1545–1563 instead of the revised rite instituted in 1969. Lefebvre's concern was to keep true to the faith in a world of change. He said:

> At the hour of my death, when our Lord asks me, "What have you done with your episcopate. . . .?" I do not want to hear from His lips the terrible words, "You have helped to destroy the Church, along with the rest of them." (*Open Letter to Confused Catholics*, 1986)

Opus Dei

Opus Dei is a Roman Catholic organization founded in Spain in 1928 by Josemaria Escriva de Balaguer. The stated aim of Opus Dei is to spread throughout society "a profound awareness of the universal call to holiness and apostolate" through members of Opus Dei. Opus Dei is also known as the Priestly Society of the Holy Cross and the Work of God. In 1982 its status was that of a personal prelature where the superior exercises over members authority similar to a bishop's, but not in terms of geographical location, as the members are scattered over the world. The society therefore attracts criticism, not least of all because local bishops have little if any say over its activities.

Despite its outward noble intentions, Opus Dei has stirred up a number of other concerns and accusations that echo those more generally reserved for alternative cults and sects—for example, in their recruiting tactics and the exercise of strict penances. Controversy has also raged over the effort to canonize de Balaguer, who died in 1975 and was beatified amidst substantial controversy in 1992. The accumulation of wealth in business dealings and property and the disproportionate influence Opus Dei wields in the Vatican have also evoked concern.

Eighty thousand Opus Dei members are estimated worldwide in over eighty countries. Members are indebted to the society for the opportunity to integrate their daily working life with their religious life as one. They feel that their commitment to Christ and the Christian faith has a focus and a purpose. The spiritual focus of members is based on the writings of the founder, and his 999 maxims, entitled *The Way*.

The association is authoritarian in style and, despite widespread criticism because of that style, Opus Dei was declared blessed by Pope John Paul in 1992.

Festivals and Holy Days

In addition to the holy days celebrated by most other Christians, Roman Catholics observe a number of other holy days and saints days signified by special masses, fasts, or feasts. The major ones are All Saints Day, Annunciation, Ascension Day, Epiphany, Feast of the Blessed Virgin Mary, Feast of the Immaculate Conception, and The Nativity of St. John the Baptist (observed especially in Latin culture).

Chapter 10
Some Alternative Christian Movements

UNIT 10:1 CHRISTIAN SCIENCE

The Healing Truth dawned upon my sense, and the result was that I rose, dressed myself, and ever after was in better health than I had before enjoyed.

Mary Baker Eddy (on experiencing healing),
Miscellaneous Writings

Christian Science was founded by Mary Baker Eddy (1821–1910). She was born into a Congregationalist family with strict Calvinist beliefs. Her first husband died soon after their marriage in 1843, and her second husband treated her badly and left her. She married her third husband, Asa Eddy, in 1873 when she was fifty-six years old. From her childhood until mid-life she suffered ill health. In 1862, while suffering from an illness, she visited Phineas P. Quimby, a hypnotist and faith-healer. He taught a system of healing dealing with the mind, including the belief that the mind had the power to heal the body. For Quimby all disease was the result of incorrect or faulty reasoning on the part of the sufferer. He exerted a strong influence on her spiritual thinking, having healed her of crippling spinal disease.

Soon after Quimby's death in 1866, she fell and was seriously injured and not expected to recover. During this time she apparently read Matthew 9:2–8, the story of Jesus healing the man sick with palsy. ("And just then some people were carrying a paralyzed man, lying on a bed. When Jesus saw their faith, he said to the paralytic, 'Take heart, son; your sins are forgiven'"). Upon reading this passage, Mrs.

Eddy experienced a miraculous cure. This experience convinced her of the truth of Christian Science. She subsequently commited herself to the recovery of the emphasis on healing in early Christianity.

Use of the Bible and Other Scriptures

Mary Baker Eddy first published *Science and Health with Key to the Scriptures* in 1875 when she was fifty-four, claiming her work was inspired of God and was the final revelation of God to the world. The word "Key" in the title of her book is in reference to her being the woman of Revelation 12, that she is the key to unlocking the Bible, which she called a dark book. She claimed the Bible had many mistakes and that her writings provided the "Key" spoken of in Revelation 3:7. According to Mrs. Eddy, "No human pen nor tongue taught me the Science contained in this book, *Science and Health*." The publication is read alongside the Bible in Christian Science services. There has been speculation as to how much of Mrs. Eddy's teaching relies on that of Phineas Quimby; Christian Scientists emphasize, however, the differences between Quimby's teachings and those of Mrs. Eddy rather than the similarities.

The First Church of Christ Scientist

In 1879, four years after the first publication of *Science and Health*, the Church of Christ Scientist in Boston, Massachusetts, came into being. In 1881 Mrs. Eddy opened a metaphysical college and charged three hundred dollars for twelve healing lessons and three dollars a copy for *Science and Health*.

The Church was reorganized in 1892, and the Church Manual that provided the structure for church government and missions was first issued in 1895. The Bible and Mrs. Eddy's works are the main source of guidance, along with the *Christian Science Monitor*. Reading rooms were established where these works could be studied and make their appeal to the reader. In 1910 she died a millionaire at the age of eighty-nine.

Beliefs and Teachings: The Emphasis on Healing

At the heart of Christian Science is the emphasis on healing. It shares with some Eastern religions the belief that ignorance is at the root of human disease and suffering. Christian Scientists prefer not to use doctors, medicine, or immunizations but prefer to help people overcome the false reality of illness. Proper prayer and training are employed to battle the "nonreality" of illness. The church does not celebrate the sacraments of Lord's Supper or baptism. Mary Baker Eddy is highly regarded as a revelator of God's word, alongside others such as Jesus. The basic beliefs of Christian Science are as follows:

1. As adherents of Truth, we take the inspired word of the Bible as our sufficient guide to eternal Life.
2. We acknowledge and adore one supreme and infinite God. We acknowledge His Son, one Christ; the Holy Ghost or divine Comforter; and man in God's image and likeness.
3. We acknowledge God's forgiveness of sin in the destruction of sin and the spiritual understanding that casts out evil as unreal. But the belief in sin is punished so long as the belief lasts.
4. We acknowledge Jesus' atonement as the evidence of divine, efficacious Love, unfolding man's unity with God through Christ Jesus the Way-shower; and we acknowledge that man is saved through Christ, through Truth, Life and Love as demonstrated through the Galilean Prophet in healing the sick and overcoming sin and death.
5. We acknowledge that the crucifixion of Jesus and his resurrection served to uplift faith to understand eternal Life, even the allness of Soul, Spirit and the nothingness of matter.
6. And we solemnly promise to watch, and pray for that Mind to be in us which was also in Christ Jesus; to do unto others as we would have them do unto us; and to be merciful, just and pure.

Mary Baker Eddy, *Science and Health*, 497

Differences between Mainstream Christianity and Christian Science

A number of differences exist between traditional Christian thought and belief and Christian Science belief. The following statements indicate Christian Science beliefs that disagree with mainstream Christianity:

1. God is Universal Principle (*Science and Health* [*S&H*] 331:18–19).
2. God cannot dwell within a person (*S&H* 336:19–20).
3. God is Mind (*S&H* 330:20–21; 469:13).
4. Belief in the traditional doctrine of the Trinity is polytheism (*S&H* 256:9–11).
5. Christ is the spiritual idea of sonship (*S&H* 331:30–31).
6. Jesus was not the Christ (*S&H* 333:3–15; 334:3); "Jesus Christ is not God, as Jesus himself declared . . ." (*S&H* 361:12–13).
7. Jesus did not reflect the fullness of God (*S&H* 336:20–21).
8. Jesus did not die (*S&H* 45:32–46:3).
9. The Holy Spirit is divine science (*S&H* 331:31).
10. The devil does not exist (*S&H* 469:13–17).
11. There is no sin (*S&H* 447:24).
12. Evil and good are not real (*S&H* 330:25–27; 470:9–14).

13. Matter, sin, and sickness are not real, but only illusions, (*S&H* 335:7–15).
14. True healings are the result of true belief (*S&H*, 194:6).

Internal Battles

After the death of Mrs. Eddy internal battles for the right of succession led to various splinter movements, including the Christian Science Parent Church founded by John V. Dittemore and Annie C. Bill. More recently, the International Metaphysical Association provides the teachings of Mrs. Eddy for those "independent" Christian Scientists who have broken away from the mainstream church. In the 1970s another splinter group, the United Christian Scientists, left the mainstream in protest over the strict authoritarianism that they claimed characterized the leaders of the movement.

Christian Science Today

The compulsory purchase of reading material is a central practice within the movement. Members are required (unless financially unable) to subscribe to the daily newspaper, *Christian Science Monitor*; the weekly publication, *Christian Science Sentinel*; the monthly *Christian Science Journal*; and the *Christian Science Quarterly*.

The Christian Science Church is nonaggressive in recruiting new members, who are free to enter and leave the movement. The concern of the modern church is for ethical thinking and high moral standards, as well as devotion to God and a central and abiding commitment to the healing ministry. Health and happiness are restored not by going to doctors or mental health specialists but by applying to all of life attitudes in line with the already existing divine harmony. For the Christian Scientist, both sickness and sin are the result of error.

UNIT 10:2 THE UNIFICATION CHURCH (THE MOONIES)

> *Our motto this time is for each of the fundraising teams to earn $12,000.00 a month, a high goal. . . . If I mobilize 1,000 members, each earning $10,000.00, then we will make three million dollars a month, which is a usable sum. I will train the fund-raising team to make at least $3,000.00. When I mobilize 10,000 members, it means $30 million a month. Then we can buy Pan American Airlines and the Empire State Building. We shall buy Ford Motor Company, not to speak of the Empire State Building. That's possible.*
>
> Sun Myung Moon, *Master Speaks, Where We Are Situated Now.*

The Reverend Sun Myung Moon was born as Yong Myung Moon in North Korea in 1920. When he was a boy, his parents converted from the traditional religion of Confucianism to Presbyterianism. When he was sixteen Moon had a vision of Jesus Christ, who commissioned him to build the kingdom of God on earth. This experience was the first in a series of revelatory encounters with God in which Moon believes that he received new truth for a new age. After this he began an intensive period of prayer and study so that he could become a Presbyterian minister, and in 1946 he began to proclaim his own version of Christianity, which was both radical and unacceptable to mainstream churches. In 1948 he changed his name from Yong Myung Moon to Sun Myung Moon meaning, "Someone who has clarified the truth" or "Shining, Sun and Moon." The teachings of Rev. Moon were subsequently laid out in the *Divine Principle*, first published in 1957.

In 1954, despite strong opposition, past imprisonment, and torture from the Communists, he founded the Unification Church. The Holy Spirit Association for the Unification of World Christianity was established two years later and rapidly won converts in Korea and Japan, and later in the 1960s in the United States.

Growth and Controversy

In 1959 Moon sent Young Oon Kim to the United States, where she recruited a small group of followers. Ms. Kim settled first in Eugene, Oregon, and then moved to San Francisco. During the formative years in the Bay Area, two graduate students from the University of California, Berkeley—John Lofland and Rodney Stark—discovered the group and commenced to chronicle the group's activities in the United States.

The young Unification church was slow to expand. The tide turned dramatically when Reverend Moon conducted a "Day of Hope" tour of the United States in 1971 and early 1972. The event energized the movement, and young people began joining in large numbers.

Reverend Moon's support of President Richard Nixon during the Watergate scandal heightened his public visibility. In late 1973 Moon published an advertisement in twenty-one major U.S. newspapers in support of Nixon. The gist of the message was that because God had chosen Nixon to lead, only God should remove him. Moon's subsequent invitation to the White House created frenzied controversy, giving further publicity to the movement and benefiting recruitment.

The same pattern followed in Britain: a slow start, and then in 1978, eight hundred missionaries arrived in Britain for the One World Crusade. Small groups and communities were set up nationwide. This activity began a wave of controversy in which the Unification Church became the focus of attention for anti-cult feeling, mainly on two accounts—the first being accusations of classic brainwashing techniques including lack of food, sleep deprivation, indoctrination, and authoritarianism. In 1980 the Church sued the British newspaper, the *Daily Mail*, for libel. After a long and costly court case, the Church lost. Moon himself has been charged with financial irregularities and illegal political activities on behalf of the South Korean government. The church has attracted frequent lawsuits, and in 1982, Moon was convicted of tax evasion by a U.S. court and subsequently sentenced to an eighteen-month prison term. The church has also been criticized on a number of other commercial and political fronts: its involvement in big business, its support of right-wing politicians such as General Garcia Mesa in Bolivia and Jean-Marie Le Pen in France, its ownership of the right-wing paper the *Washington Times*, and the accusation that it hides behind a number of front organizations. Among these supposed front organizations were major international conferences on peace and religion promoted by the movement's International Religious Foundation, which has several different branches of its operation. Second, controversy has centered around the main beliefs of the Church.

The Central Beliefs and Doctrines of the Unification Church

Jesus

According to *The Divine Principle*, God finally found an obedient man, Jesus, who came in Adam's place, not to be crucified but to re-create the lost ideal. Moonies deny the Incarnation. Jesus was not God, but a perfect man without original sin. God's intention was for Jesus to take a perfected bride in Eve's place, marry, and produce sinless children. But this did not happen as Jesus was not recognized for who and what he was, but instead was crucified; his resurrection brought about only partial salvation to the world. To complete the job it is necessary for the Messiah to come again and marry and establish the Trinity both spiritually and physically.

> After the crucifixion, God gave Jesus the Holy Spirit as a mother spirit, or feminine spirit, to work with the risen Christ in Eve's place. Making restitution for Eve's part in the Fall, the Holy Spirit inspires and comforts the human heart, leading us back to God. Reflecting her feminine essence, the Holy Spirit is traditionally known as the "Comforter." As children are born through the love of parents, so through the give and take of love Jesus and the Holy Spirit give spiritual rebirth to all those who follow them. (*The Divine Principle Home Study Course*, 3—Mission of the Messiah, 1980, 37)

Therefore:

- Sun Myung is God's agent; he is sinless.
- Moon and his wife are the first couple since Adam and Eve with the ability to produce sinless offspring. Through the Messiah's perfect marriage, the fallen nature of humankind can be transformed into the ideal Trinity of God, man, and woman again.
- Moon is the Messiah, called to complete the mission Jesus could not.

The Bible

The Unification Church believes that the Judeo-Christian Bible is the inspired word of God. Moon's own book, *Divine Principle*, is given equal authority and used alongside the Bible. The use of biblical and Christian terminology in Unification belief has led casual onlookers to conclude that Moon's church is just another variant of Christianity. He has, however, admitted that his teachings deviate from the standpoint of traditional Christianity. Moon argues that because conventional churches are unable to meet the needs of today's modern world, God has communicated a new revelation of truth which, assisted by the spirit world and the movement's loyal followers (the "Moonies"), will bring about a spiritual revolution. This movement will culminate in the true, lasting unification of the family of man and the world.

The Fall

The center of Unification theology is Moon's teaching on the fall of Adam and Eve. Lucifer seduced Eve, and this sexual union caused the spiritual fall of mankind as well as the fall of Lucifer. Eve then tells Adam what she has done and enters into a sexual relationship with him to try and rectify the situation, but this action resulted in the physical fall of man.

God's Plan of Salvation

The key steps toward restoration according to the Unification Church are as follows:

1. Recognizing Moon's special status
2. Joining the Unification Movement
3. Paying personal indemnity
4. Receiving Moon's blessing in marriage
5. Bearing sinless children
6. Leading lives that will produce a sinless world

In the Unification Church, indemnity is paid by raising money and winning converts. Ensuring financial viability and recruiting new members are critical to the survival of any new religion, and in Unification theology, both duties are sacred.

The dual aspect of the fall, spiritual and physical, requires a restoration to God (salvation) that is likewise both spiritual and physical in nature. God's original intention for humankind at the time of creation was for men and women to mature to perfection in God, to be united by God in a marriage centered on God's love, thus producing perfect children and bringing about a sinless family and therefore ultimately a sinless world. God's plans were thwarted by the fall and necessitated a messiah.

Because Jesus saved mankind spiritually but not physically, another messiah, the Lord of the Second Advent, is needed to bring about physical redemption. *The Divine Principle* says that Christ will return as a physical man after the First World War, in Korea. Moon's followers have believed him to be the Messiah, and in 1992 he formally announced his messianic status.

Mass Weddings

Through the perfect marriage of the Messiah, humankind can be transformed into the ideal trinity: God, man, and woman. This process comes through the well-documented mass wedding ceremonies, where the couples are blessed by God through Moon and therefore are now in a perfect and right relationship. If they continue to live a good life, their children will be born sinless and humankind can eventually be transformed so that God's plan is established.

Sun Myung Moon is said to pray over the photographs of prospective couples and seek God's guidance in pairing them together. Many couples have never met before, but wherever possible couples are given time to get to know each other and can decline to marry if they so wish. In August 1995 there was a linkup of 364,000 couples who were blessed by Moon at fifty-two different locations in the world. Twenty-five thousand couples were members of the Unification Church being married in Seoul in Korea. The others were members of other religions who were acknowledging the sanctity of their marriage.

The mass weddings have attracted world publicity and strong criticism, especially from the West where the notion of "arranged marriages" of such magnitude (between people of different nationalities who have often not even met) and resting in the hands of one man, are viewed with disdain. The Unification Church sees it very differently. Their faith rests on their admiration and respect for Sun Myung Moon and the spiritual depth of his relationship with God. He is therefore qualified to choose for them.

At the time of this writing, Sun Myung Moon is eighty years old, and the Unification Church has approximately a quarter of a million members in the world, mainly in South Korea, Japan, and the United States. The U.S. membership appears to be stable at about five thousand members.

The Future of the Unification Movement

Few founding leaders have planned their succession with such forethought. Hak Ja Han, his wife, is the successor designate. The process of her succession began on January 1, 1993, with the declaration that the Age of Restoration is completed. Until this point in time, Moon had never declared that he was, indeed, the Lord of the Second Advent (Christ returned). Korea was chosen as the site of the announcement. It scarcely made the news in the United States, thus successfully avoiding any frenzied adverse publicity. The declaration of his divinity and the naming of his successor while alive strategically reduces the likelihood of a struggle for succession after his death.

The Unification Church is a vast financial as well as spiritual empire. Whether it can hold on in the future to a fundamental unity of thought and purpose remains to be seen.

UNIT 10:3 SEVENTH-DAY ADVENTISTS

> *All true obedience comes from the heart. It was heart work with Christ. And if we consent, He will so identify Himself with our thoughts and aims, so blend our hearts and minds into conformity to His will, that when obeying Him we shall be but carrying out our own impulses. The will, refined and sanctified, will find its highest delight in doing His service. When we know God as it is our privilege to know Him, our life will be a life of continual obedience. Through an appreciation of the character of Christ, through communion with God, sin will become hateful to us.*
>
> Ellen G. H. White, *Desire of Ages*

The history of the Seventh-day Adventists can be traced to the Millerite (Adventist) Movement of the nineteenth century, which was largely responsible for what has been called the Great Second Advent Awakening. William Miller (1782–1849) was originally a deist (a person who believes that God created the universe, but has not been actively involved since). After two years of study, Miller converted to Christianity and became a Baptist lay leader, convinced that the Bible contained coded information about the end of the world and the second coming of Jesus.

In 1831, Miller began to preach and write articles attracting thousands of followers with his message—based on prophecies in Daniel and Revelation—that the return of Christ would occur sometime between two spring equinoxes: March 21, 1843, and March 21, 1844. The end did not happen. Samuel Snow, a Millerite, then interpreted the tarrying time referred to in Habakkuk 2:3 as equal to seven months and ten days, delaying the end time to October 22, 1844. Followers sold their properties and possessions to be ready for the event, although the well-known story of them sitting on their rooftops in ascension robes has no historical foundation. That prophecy also did not come to pass. Many believers left the movement or regrouped in what has become known as The Great Disappointment. Miller died in 1849 without supporting or endorsing any of the various groups. His followers called themselves Adventists; the group was often referred to as Millerites by others.

Seventh-day Adventism was founded on doctrines that arose from different Adventists in the immediate time following Miller's death. Three main doctrines prevailed:

1. Christ had not returned to earth in 1844 because he had entered his heavenly sanctuary to cleanse it and sort out the sheep from the goats

in order to be ready for the Judgment. Hiram Edson had this revealed to him the day after Miller's death.

2. An emphasis on obeying the Ten Commandments, including keeping the Sabbath.
3. A belief that in these last days the divine gift of prophecy would be given to the Church; this belief came from the visions and teachings of Ellen G. White.

Ellen Harmon (1827–1915, later known by her married name Ellen White) was initially a Methodist, joining the Adventists when she was seventeen. Her first vision came in December 1844, telling her that that the October 1844 date was not a mistake. She believed that the 1844 prediction was correct, but that it referred to the start of an investigative judgment during which Christ is judging the dead and the living on earth for righteousness. She subsequently wrote these visions and her interpretations of them in *The Great Controversy* and the *Desire of Ages*. These books are regarded as inspirational, but they do not replace the Bible or its teachings.

White inspired many of the followers of Miller to form a movement, which set up its base in Battle Creek, Michigan, in 1855 and which in 1860 became known as the Seventh-day Adventists. The church was formally organized in 1863. She predicted that this action would soon be followed by Jesus' second coming. Late in her career, the church voted her the credentials of an ordained minister, although she was never actually ordained. The Church moved its headquarters to Takoma Park, Maryland, in 1903.

Victor Houteff joined the Seventh-day Adventist Church in 1919. His beliefs deviated from mainline church doctrine, and he formed a new sect in 1929 called the Davidian Seventh-day Adventists. Further splits eventually led to the organization of the Students of the Seven Seals, popularly known as the Branch Davidians. In 1993, after a long standoff with the FBI, the Branch Davidians' compound in Waco, Texas, burned down with major loss of life (see unit 10:4).

Beliefs and Practices

Seventh-day Adventists follow most of the conservative (and even fundamentalist) beliefs of Christianity: the fall of humanity in the Garden of Eden; original sin; the virgin birth; the divinity of Christ; the Trinity; belief in Satan as a rebellious, created being; the inerrancy of scripture as they were originally written; the bodily resurrection of Jesus from the dead; and salvation by the atoning blood of Christ. Critics of Seventh-day Adventism tend to concern themselves with the works of Ellen G. White and other writings from the early years of the movements, which are viewed as heretical. Within Seventh-day Adventism, though, some adherents see the written works of Ellen White as "a continuing and authoritative source of truth which provide for the church comfort, guidance, instruction, and correction" (see "The Gift of Prophecy" at www.adventist.org/beliefs). This view produced some conflict within the Church when research in the 1980s showed that she had borrowed heavily from contemporary writers. However, the SDA church itself does not regard Ellen G. White's books as infallible or scriptural, and there is little public emphasis on her today.

Death and the Afterlife

Seventh-day Adventists believe that when a person dies, they remain unconscious until they are resurrected. Eternal life in a new world is a gift that God will give only to righteous Christians; everyone else will be annihilated. Thus, they do not believe that a person goes to heaven or hell immediately upon death.

SDA members also believe that the second coming of Christ is imminent. Believers should be ready at all times to be transported from earth to be with God in heaven. Righteous Christians who have died in the past will be resurrected at that time and taken to heaven. For the one thousand years after that time, only Satan and his angels will be living on earth. A second resurrection will mark the end of that period. The righteous will then return to a cleansed earth, and the New Jerusalem will be established. The unrighteous who died before the second coming will be resurrected and consumed by fire and by God, along with Satan and his angels, leaving the universe free of sin and sinners. Hell exists as a lake of fire where the unrighteous are burned and destroyed; they cease to exist forever. Hell is not a place of eternal torment.

Sabbath

Perhaps the most obvious practice is that Seventh-day Adventists continue the Old Testament (Jewish) practice of observing Saturday as their Sabbath (from Friday sunset to Saturday sunset).

Baptism

Baptism is by full immersion preceded by instruction, a personal acceptance of the scriptures, repentance of sins, and confession of sins.

Abstention

Seventh-day Adventists are expected to abstain from alcohol, coffee, tea, tobacco, and every habit that is thought to defile the soul.

Marriage and Divorce

Interfaith marriages are discouraged. The Adventist World Session in 2000 modified the grounds for divorce to adultery/fornication or abandonment by an unbelieving spouse or physical violence. Adultery/fornication includes incest, child sexual abuse, or homosexual behavior. However, abandonment by a believing spouse would not be grounds for divorce. (A believing spouse means a fellow SDA member; Roman Catholics and other Protestants are considered unbelievers.)

Remarriage is only allowed if one's spouse is guilty of adultery/fornication. Divorce and remarriage amendment discussions at the year 2000 meeting are covered in http://session2000.adventist.org/news/data/.

The Role of Women

In common with many conservative Christian churches, the question of ordaining women is debated within the SDA church. Despite the special role of the SDA founder, Ellen White, and the ordination of women as elders for many years, no women are eligible to be pastors. The North American Division (NAD) of the Seventh-day Adventist Church proposed to the 1995 General Conference in Utrecht, the Netherlands, that each World Division be allowed to decide independently whether to ordain women to the pastorate. The proposal was defeated. Even so, a few NAD congregations ordained women pastors.

Homosexuality

The Seventh-day Adventist Church believes that the Bible consistently condemns homosexuality as a sin. Gay candidates are not permitted to be ordained as pastors.

Seventh-day Adventism In the Modern World

In recent years, Seventh-day Adventist theologians have tended to regard Mrs. White's prophecies as subject to judgment by the canonical scriptures and have put forth a more evangelical understanding of justification by faith. As a result, some evangelical leaders—although by no means all—have begun to include the Seventh-day Adventists within the parameters of orthodox belief.

The Seventh-day Adventist Church has experienced rapid growth since World War II. This church now tends to be insular, focusing on educating its own children. The Adventists have been well known for their dietary concerns, such as their taboo on coffee and tea, and their support for vegetarianism long before such things became fashionable.

The Seventh-day Adventists have produced many offshoots. One of the most infamous offshoots of the movement has been that of David Koresh and the Branch Davidians, the subject of the next unit. Many less notorious groups, however, have also emerged from the SDA Church, one of which is the Worldwide Church of God, which will be explored in a later unit of this book.

UNIT 10:4 DAVID KORESH AND THE BRANCH DAVIDIANS

> *April 10: I OFFER TO YOU MY WISDOM, I OFFER TO YOU MY sealed secrets. How dare you turn away? My invitations of mercy . . . Who are you fighting against? The law is Mine, the Truth is Mine. . . . I AM your God and you will bow under my feet. . . . I AM your life & your death. I AM the Spirit of the prophets and the Author of their testimonies. Look and see, you fools, you will not proceed much further. Do you think you have power to stop My will? . . . My seven thunders are to be revealed. . . . Do you want me to laugh at your pending torments? Do you want Me to pull the heavens back and show you My anger?! . . . Fear Me, for I have you in My snare. . . . I forewarn you, the Lake Waco area of Old Mount Carmel will be terribly shaken. The waters of the lake will be emptied through the broken dam.*
>
> David Koresh, quoted in *Time* magazine

On April 19, 1993, some eighty members of the Branch Davidian sect of the Seventh-day Adventist Church died in a raging inferno after an FBI seige at their campus in Waco, Texas. What was the spiritual and theological journey that brought them to this end?

Background of the Seventh-day Adventists and the Branch Davidians

The history and theology of the seminal Seventh-day Adventists are reviewed in unit 10:3 in this volume. The splintering of the SDA Church that eventually resulted in Koresh's Branch Davidians occurred as follows:

- *1929–1931.* Victor Houteff (1886–1955) was a Seventh-day Adventist who taught at a Sabbath school until his apocalyptic teaching of Daniel and Revelation prompted the church to expel him. With a dozen or so families he formed his own organization: the Davidian Seventh-day Adventists, more popularly known as "The Shepherd's Rod." The key Davidian teaching is that God will establish a literal kingdom in Israel, ruled by Jesus Christ and his lieutenant, the Antitypical David.
- *1955.* Victor Houteff died, and his widow Florence Houteff succeeded him. She announced that the second coming would occur in 1959. When this prophecy was not fulfilled, many members left to form different groups. Benjamin Roden, who claimed he was God's new prophet, founded one of these offshoots, the Branch Davidian Seventh-day

Adventists (BDSDA). Roden would tell his followers to "Get off the dead Rod and move on to a living Branch."

- *1962.* Ben Roden and his followers take over New Mount Carmel, formerly headquarters of the Davidian Seventh-day Adventists.
- *1978–1984.* Ben Roden died and was succeeded by his wife, Lois, who became president of BDSDA. She travels widely and attracts many believers. The BDSDA launches a magazine called *Shekinah.*
- *1981.* Vernon Howell (David Koresh) arrives at Mount Carmel Center as a helper.

David Koresh

David Koresh was born to a fifteen-year-old single mother as Vernon Wayne Howell in Houston, Texas, in 1959. He was raised by his grandparents. Dyslexic and a poor student who eventually dropped out of high school, his main strengths were his musical ability and a strong interest in the Bible. By the age of twelve, he had memorized large portions of the scripture.

At the age of twenty, Koresh turned to the Church of Seventh-day Adventists, his mother's church, but before long he was expelled for his bad influence on the young people. In 1981 he arrived in Waco, Texas, where he joined the Branch Davidians, a religious sect that had settled ten miles outside of Waco. Koresh had an affair with then-prophetess Lois Roden, who was in her late sixties. Lois died in 1986, and a power struggle ensued between Koresh and Lois Roden's son, George, who forced Koresh to leave under gunpoint. As part of his battle for power, Koresh challenged Roden as to who had the greater divine power and persuaded him to exhume the body of a Davidian to see whether he could bring it back to life. He then had Roden arrested for corpse abuse. Roden was eventually jailed on unrelated contempt of court charges.

By 1990 Koresh had become the leader of the Branch Davidians and had legally changed his name, saying on the court document that the change was "for publicity and business purposes." This statement arose from his belief that he was now head of the biblical House of David. ("Koresh" is a Hebrew transliteration of Cyrus, the name of the Persian king who gave permission for the Jews held captive in Babylon to return to Israel.) Once in charge of the Davidians, Koresh began recruiting in Britain with considerable success: thirty-three of the eighty-two followers who eventually died at Waco were British.

Koresh was a handsome, charismatic figure who played rock guitar. The members of the Waco community were impressed by his vast knowledge of the Bible and the way he could preach for hours without the aid of notes. His influence over his followers was evidenced in the acceptance of most members of his announcement that he had the right to sleep with any woman so that his holy seed could be spread. Some observers contend that Koresh suffered from the delusional Jerusalem Syndrome following a pilgrimage to Jerusalem in 1985, a year before he declared himself the "sinful Messiah."

In the Branch Davidian community, men and women were segregated even if they were married. The movement adapted many of the common features associated with a cult following: poor diet, sleep deprivation, and repeated and long exposure to doctrine and dogma.

The Siege of Mount Carmel

Koresh was a registered arms dealer and made money from trading weapons. It was therefore not difficult for the Waco community to pile up stocks of weaponry and food in preparation for the Apocalypse. On February 28, 1993, the Bureau of Alcohol, Tobacco, and Firearms (ATF) raided Mount Carmel, searching for illegal weaponry and stockpiles of arms. Four ATF agents were killed and many people were wounded, including Koresh who was shot in the wrist and the waist. Six cult members are believed to have died at that time, including Koresh's two-year-old daughter. The FBI was then called in and a siege ensued. After fifty-one days the siege was ended by the FBI firing CS gas (prohibited for military use by international convention) into the compound. Soon after, the campus erupted into flames, fueled by the explosion of the weaponry and ammunition.

The reason for the series of events is controversial. The FBI claims the destruction was the work of the Branch Davidian community, and the nine members who escaped claim it was sparked by the FBI attack. About twenty children were killed, and over eighty people died in all. Many observers believe that the whole scenario was badly handled by the ATF and the FBI. The ATF alleges that Koresh had embedded himself by hiding within the compound, and thus they had to take their initiative to arrest him. Local townspeople and traders disagree, saying that Koresh visited the town most days and was therefore publicly available to be questioned. While the blame and responsibility for the Mount Carmel siege will likely be debated in perpetuity, in 1995, the ATF was cleared of any misdeed.

Since officers of the Alcohol, Tobacco, and Firearms Bureau stormed the compound on February 28, 1993, the desolation at Waco has drawn militia groups and cults opposed to the federal government. Convicted Oklahoma City bomber Timothy McVeigh was recorded on video prowling through the ruins of the compound's bunkers; the bomb that destroyed the Murrah federal building in Oklahoma City exploded on the anniversary of the final Waco conflagration. All that remains of the Mount Carmel site are three burned-out buses and a compound area of concrete slabs partly submerged in a reed-covered swamp—a haunting epitaph to cult extremism in the twentieth century.

UNIT 10:5 ARMSTRONGISM AND THE WORLDWIDE CHURCH OF GOD

Does it make sense to you—when humanity has been endowed with such tremendous mental power—that more than HALF of all

> *people on earth should be illiterate, living in abject poverty, near starvation, in filth and squalor; that in one country of 26 million people, only 3 percent can read and write and per capita income is only $69 per year?*
>
> *Does it make sense to you that human civilization has developed modern science, higher education, the world's religions and its great governments, yet all these are in total ignorance of the way to world peace? None of these can tell us what man is, whether he was put on earth for a purpose, what that PURPOSE IS, where he is going or how to get there.*
>
> *Does it make sense to you—with man endowed with such great powers—that the world should be filled with so much unhappiness, troubles and evils?*
>
> *Did God Almighty the Creator purpose and ordain all of this? We may blame it all on human nature, but did God create man with this evil to harass him?*
>
> *It's time to clear up this mystery. It's time we understand. It's time we come to the answer of these supposedly unanswerable questions that seem to baffle all human thought.*
>
> Herbert W. Armstrong, *Incredible Human Potential*

Herbert W. Armstrong (1892–1986) was born into a Quaker family in Des Moines, Iowa. In 1927 his wife, Loma Armstrong, became convinced of many of the teachings of the Seventh-day Adventist Church. Armstrong began to study the Bible and eventually came to agree with his wife. He gave importance to the fact that the true biblical name for groups of Christian believers is the Church of God, and so he began to search out denominations that ascribed to that name.

In the nineteenth century, some of the Seventh-day Adventist Churches had preferred the title "Church of God," yet the movement—including Ellen G. White—had voted on the issue at a conference in Michigan in 1860 to reject "Church of God" as a leading descriptor of the Church. Some of those who lost the vote kept to the name "Church of God," rejecting White's mainstream SDA theology. One such church was based in Stanberry, Missouri, and its daughter church in Oregon was selected by Armstrong and his wife in 1927. He began to preach there and was ordained as a minister in 1931.

In 1934 Armstrong began preaching on The Radio Church of God and published the first issue of *The Plain Truth* magazine. At the height of its publication in 1988, it had a worldwide circulation of 5,813,000. *The Plain Truth* ran regular features about Armstrong's travels and influence, almost always showing photographs of Armstrong with the great world leaders. This was expensive publicity, evoking criticism from his son, Garner Ted Armstrong, who referred to the pictures as evidence of "the world's most expensive autograph hunt." (Armstrong [1992]).

The elder Armstrong's preaching and doctrines derive from British Israelitism.

In 1938 Armstrong was stripped of his Church of God Seventh Day ministerial license for teaching that the Jewish Feast days were binding on the church. Armstrong, however, retained his Oregon church and his radio ministry. He believed in the middle-class message of success. His Seven Laws of Success echo doctrines of the more recent prosperity gospel, saying that if you give God your best, he will give you his best.

During the war years, Armstrong taught that Armageddon was imminent and that Mussolini and later Hitler were both the antichrist.

In 1947 he relocated the ministry to Pasadena, California. and founded Ambassador College, a liberal arts college that offered *"the missing dimension."* A campus in the United Kingdom opened at St. Albans in 1960 and another in Texas in 1964. In 1968 the name of his organization was changed to The Worldwide Church of God.

Dissension in the Church

In 1974 forty ministers and several thousand members left the church because of doctrinal disputes and resulting malfunction. As Armstrong aged, more responsibility fell to his son Garner Ted, but the ministry went amiss. In 1972 Armstrong prevented his son from preaching on his radio program, *The World Tomorrow*. Church income began to fall drastically as a result and the senior Armstrong was brought back, but not before the *Los Angeles Times* reported Armstrong referring to his son as "in the bonds of Satan" and having confessed to sinning against his wife, his children, and the Church. In 1974 there were allegations of sexual impropriety aimed at Garner Ted Armstrong. Then in 1978 Garner Ted clashed with his father over disagreements regarding organization and doctrine. Garner Ted formed his own church, The Church of God, International, based in Tyler, Texas.

At about the same time ministers and thousands of members left the Church, having been disaffected by internal disputes regarding the remarriage of divorcees (Armstrong had opposed it) and the date of the Feast of Pentecost. By the mid-1970s, Armstrong was constantly referring to himself as God's apostle for the last days. In 1979, amid allegations of financial abuses, the State of California placed the church in receivership. After lengthy court battles, the courts removed the church from receivership. Herbert Armstrong died in January 1986 at the age of ninety-four. He was succeeded by Joseph W. Tkach as pastor general.

Doctrines and Beliefs of Armstrongism and the Worldwide Church of God

In the August 25, 1986, issue of *The Worldwide News*, there was an article entitled, "God Restored These 18 Truths: How Thankful Are You For Them?" The article stated that, "The Editorial Services staff has compiled here, for the first time in any of the Church's publications, 18 essential, basic truths that God restored to His Church through Herbert W. Armstrong." Since then, most of those "Truths" have been refined, reformed, or abandoned by the church under Tkach's leadership. As a result, thousands of Worldwide Church of God members have left to form new churches that adhere to the old ways.

The doctrines of the Worldwide Church of God derived from Seventh-day Adventists through the Church of God—7th Day. Armstrong added the Identity of Modern Israel theory, the Jewish Feast Days, church eras, the Saturday Sabbath, and the "true name" of God's church. In addition, the following beliefs were held.

The Bible

> The revelation of these mysteries was lost, even to the Church of God, although the revelation of them has been preserved in the writings of the Bible. Why, then, has the world not clearly understood? Because the Bible was a coded book, not intended to be understood until our day in this later half of the twentieth century. (*Mystery of the Ages*, 12)

God (under Armstrong)

> The Hebrew for God is Elohim, a uniplural noun, such as the words family, church, group. . . . And so, in truth, God is not merely one personage or even limited to a "Trinity," but is a family. (*The Good News*, February 1979, 1)
>
> God is a Family, a Kingdom, not a limited trinity. (*The Plain Truth*, August 1958, 17)

The Doctrine of the Trinity

> The doctrine of the Trinity is false. . . . Elohim is the divine family—only one family, but more than one divine Person. . . . So the eternal Father is a Person, and is God. Jesus Christ is a different Person—and is God. They are two separate and individual Persons. (*The Missing Dimension in Sex*, 32)
>
> At the present time there are only two beings in the God Family, 1) God the Father, Father of Jesus Christ, 2) God of Abraham, Isaac and Jacob, the One who became Jesus Christ, God the Son. ("The God Family" in *Tomorrow's World*, May 1971)
>
> However, quantitatively, man will never equal God the Father, just as surely as God the Creator (Jesus Christ) will Himself never quantitatively equal God the Father. (*What It Means to Be Equal with God*, 44)

Beliefs about Jesus Christ

> Jesus was conceived by Mary, He was not the Son of God. ("Just What Do You Mean—Born Again?" in *Tomorrow's World*, October 1971, 43)

The Resurrection of Jesus from the Dead

> God the Father did not cause Jesus Christ to get back into the body which had died. Jesus Christ was dead . . . and the resurrected body was no longer human. (*The Plain Truth*, April 1963, 10, 40)
>
> Christ's body disappeared. Christ was raised as a divine spirit being. (*If You Die, Will You Live Again?*, 6)

Holy Spirit

> (Christian) theologians adhere to the false doctrine that the Holy Spirit is a third person—the heresy of the trinity. This limits God to Three Persons! (*Just What Do You Mean—Born Again?*, 17, 19)

Sin

> Jesus Christ and His inspired apostles teach absolute obedience to all ten of the Ten Commandments. (*The Plain Truth*, November 1959, 18)
>
> Sickness is the penalty for physical transgression. Healing is the same as forgiveness of sin. Medicine has a pagan origin. (*Does God Heal Today?*, 8)

Salvation

> Jesus alone, of all humans, has so far been saved. (*Why Were You Born?*, 11)
>
> The blood of Jesus Christ does not finally save anyone. It saves merely from the death penalty (of sin). (*All about Water Baptism*, 1–3)
>
> Baptism is an essential ordinance for salvation. You must be baptized to become a true Christian. ("This Is the Worldwide Church of God," in *Tomorrow's World*, February 1971, 16–17)

Armstrong taught that a believer could lose salvation by disobeying "God's command through His chosen Apostle." He wrote, "Do you want to let resentment against God's government over you NOW disqualify you—snatch you from God's GRACE and PURPOSE for you, and cast you into a lake of fire?" (*Dear Brethren Letter*, May 2, 1974, 7).

The Second Coming of Christ

> When Jesus Christ returns to this earth, He will for the first time reach out to save the world. A majority of those who die without Christ will be resurrected and gain opportunity to believe during the Millennium. (*Predestination—Does the Bible Teach It?*)

Redemption

> The purpose of life in us is that God is really creating His own kind. At the time of the resurrection we shall be instantaneously changed from mortal to immortal. (*Why Were You Born?*, 21–22)

Life after Death

> When a human being dies, he is dead, he or she simply stops being. (*Do You Have an Immortal Soul?*, 41)
>
> The wicked will be resurrected at the close of the Millennium, but only to be annihilated. (*Lazarus and the Rich Man*)
>
> The concept of "hell" is believed to be a place of punishment and torture of the wicked. (*Tomorrow's World*, 14, 18)

Recent Reform in the Worldwide Church of God

Under the leadership of Joseph W. Tkach, the Worldwide Church of God committed itself to doctrinal reform, as can be seen graphically in their reformulation of doctrine concerning the Trinity. Armstrong taught that the concept of the Trinity was invented in the first centuries of Christianity and was a deceit of Satan. Now, the triune nature of God is accepted, and the Holy Spirit is "The third person of the Godhead."

> Do let me summarize, and I hope to make this crystal clear. Our old literature taught that there are two god beings in one God Family, each composed of Holy Spirit. That teaching, which implied that there are two Gods, is not biblical. The Bible teaches that there is one God, not two. The Bible does not teach that God is a family name, with two God Beings in that family right now, and billions to come later. The Bible

> teaches that the one and same God is Father, Son, and Holy Spirit. (Pastor General's Report, July 27, 1993, 4)

Tkach spoke to a large gathering of ministers and members in Atlanta, Georgia, on December 17, 1994. He addressed the issue of Old Testament tithing as being one that no longer applies to Christians; instead, free will offerings were the New Covenant way to give. In Big Sandy, Texas, Tkach also announced that working on the Sabbath is permitted for a brief period of time. Both of these doctrines were previously believed to be essential requirements that could affect the outcome of salvation.

Although many regional and local ministers have not accepted the changes and are not teaching them to their congregations, the wider Christian community approves of the ongoing movement within the Worldwide Church of God toward mainstream Christian beliefs. Joseph W. Tkach died of cancer in 1995. He was succeeded by his son, Joe Junior. After Tkach's death, Hank Hanegraaff, president of the Christian Research Institute, a U.S.-based cult-watching organization, likened the transformation of the Worldwide Church of God—"from the status of a cult" to its present position, as to the collapse of the Berlin Wall (*Christian Institute Newsletter*, October 6, 1995).

British Israelitism

The origins of British Israelitism—which provided the source for Armstrong's original preaching and doctrines—can be traced back to John Sadler's book *The Rights of the Kingdom* (1649). Today British Israelitism finds a scant following, but its ideas and beliefs (albeit in varied forms) can be found in publications such as *The Plain Truth*.

British Israelitism has no formal creed, but its central beliefs are based on the biblical account of God's promise to Abraham that Israel would survive as a nation. Thus, continuity must exist between Abraham and the world today. Given that the present state of Israel only came into existence in 1948, that nation cannot claim status as the true nation of Israel and therefore must not be confused with the historic nation of Israel. Arguing from its own interpretation of biblical history—which links the Jewish House of David with the British royal family—British Israelitism believes that the Anglo-Saxon people are the true Israel.

After establishing the Old Testament connection with Britain, the biblical prophecies are applied to the history of the British Empire. America is also included in the theological plan because Genesis 49:22 is said to predict the emigration of the Pilgrim fathers. British Israelites also believed that the Great Pyramid of Egypt proves these truths by its measurements, which are sacred.

British Israelitism flourished around 1900 C.E., with around two million members. Commentators agree that no serious theologian examining the texts that British Israelites use to support their beliefs would accept their rules of biblical exegesis.

UNIT 10:6 THE MORMONS

God is in the still small voice. In all these affidavits, indictments, it is all of the devil—all corruption. Come on! ye prosecutors! ye false swearers! All hell, boil over! Ye burning mountains, roll down your lava! for I will come out on the top at last. I have more to boast of than ever any man had. I am the only man that has ever been able to keep a whole church together since the days of Adam. A large majority of the whole have stood by me. Neither Paul, John, Peter, nor Jesus ever did it. I boast that no man ever did such a work as I. The followers of Jesus ran away from Him; but the Latter-day Saints never ran away from me yet. . . .

Joseph Smith, *History of the Church*

The Mormons or, as they are otherwise known, The Church of Jesus Christ of Latter-day Saints, represent one of the most successful new religious movements of the nineteenth century. Today they fall into two main groups, the Church of Jesus Christ of Latter-day Saints, organized from Salt Lake City, Utah, and the Reorganized Church of Jesus Christ of Latter-day Saints, with its center at Independence, Missouri. A number of smaller "fundamentalist" groups also exist.

Joseph Smith

The Mormons derived from Joseph Smith and the *Book of Mormon*. Joseph Smith (1805–1844) was from a farming family in western New York State. As a young man of fourteen, he prayed for God to show him which of the many types of Christianity was the real and authentic version. Smith claimed that God the Father and Jesus appeared to him in a vision and told him to wait because none of the existing expressions of Christianity were true. In 1822 the angel Moroni appeared to Smith and revealed the location of gold tablets on which were written God's words. In 1827 he was given permission to dig them up, and he started to translate them by using a large pair of eyepieces called the Urim and Thummim. These devices caused him to translate and understand the text, which was written in reformed Egyptian hieroglyphics. He published a translation in 1830.

The Book of Mormon and Other Mormon Texts

Mormonism has its basis in two main events. The first event is the claim of Joseph Smith to have received the golden plates upon which the ancient scriptures were written. The account of Joseph Smith's encounter with Jesus and the discovery of the *Book of Mormon* is found in the Mormon publication *The Pearl of Great Price*, which also contains the text of two Egyptian papyri that Joseph Smith claimed to have translated, plus his translation of certain parts of the Bible.

The second event is Smith's claim to have had an encounter with the living Jesus and subsequently to receive continuing revelations from God. The substance of these continuing revelations is found in the Mormon publication *The Doctrine and Covenants.*

The *Book of Mormon* tells the story of the two lost tribes of Israel: the Jaredites, who came to America after the fall of Lower Babel (c. 2250 B.C.E.), and a group of righteous Jews led by Lehi (c. 600 B.C.E.). Two of Lehi's sons were Nephi and Laman. The Nephites became godly, holy people, but the Lamanites turned evil and God cursed them so that their skin turned dark. Lamanites were the ancestors of the Native Americans. The *Book of Mormon* claims that Christ visited America after his resurrection and revealed himself to the Nephites, to whom he preached the gospel and for whom he founded a church. The Nephites were eventually destroyed by the Lamanites in a great battle near Palmyra, New York, around 428 C.E., the same hill where Joseph Smith found the plates that were written by the prophet Mormon and his son Moroni, the last of the Nephites.

Christian Scholars and the *Book of Mormon*

Christian scholars either reject the authenticity of the *Book of Mormon*, or they tend to raise serious doubts about it. Objections range from the nonexistence of reformed Egyptian hieroglyphics to severe problems with the text. They point to the large number of verses (over twenty-seven thousand words) from the King James version of Bible (1611 C.E.) that are included in the *Book of Mormon* as well as quotations from the seventeenth-century *Westminster Confession of Faith.*

Aaronic Priesthood

In 1829 Joseph Smith and a fellow Mormon, Oliver Cowdery, both claimed to have had an appearance of John the Baptist, who conferred the Aaronic Priesthood on them. Later the apostles Peter, James, and John also appeared to them and conferred the Melchizedek Priesthood on them. The Mormon Church still sees these two priesthoods as fundamental to their beliefs claiming that it is the only true church because its leaders continue to receive revelation from God. The Mormon Church believes it possesses the powers of the priesthood of Aaron and Melchizedek, into which its male members are expected to be initiated.

The doctrine of continual revelation was settled early on by Smith, who declared that although in principle God could speak to any of his followers in the Church, revelations and ongoing commandments could only come through one man: Smith, then his successor Brigham Young, and then through each of the other successive presidents of the Church.

Persecution and Expansion

The Church of Jesus Christ of Latter-day Saints came into being on April 6, 1830, at Fayette, New York. Soon after, the Church moved to Kirtland, Ohio, and then Jackson County, Missouri, because of the fiery opposition that they encountered. They finally settled at Nauvoo on the Mississippi River in Illinois, where they prospered and expanded. In 1840 the Mormons sent missionaries to England, based at Preston, Lancashire, and thousands were converted. During the next few years, some five thousand people emigrated to join the Mormon Church at Nauvoo.

On July 12, 1843, Smith received a revelation allowing for polygamy, which triggered four disillusioned converts to found an anti-Mormon newspaper, the *Nauvoo Expositor*. In the single publication of the paper, on June 7, 1844, Smith was denounced. Smith's brothers retaliated by burning down the newspaper office. As a result, Joseph Smith and his brother Hyrum were placed in the Carthage, Missouri, jail, where on June 27, 1844, a mob brutally murdered them.

After Joseph Smith's assassination, the majority of Mormons accepted the leadership of Brigham Young. A minority rallied around Smith's legal wife and family to form the Reorganized Church. The Reorganized Church today claims rightful leadership as the direct descendants of Joseph Smith.

Young led the Mormons out of Nauvoo in 1847 and began the great trek westward to the Great Salt Lake Valley in Utah. For more than thirty years, Brigham Young ruled the Mormon Church, laying the foundations for its present strength; he is said to have had fifty-six children by his seventeen wives. In Utah the church expanded but was challenged by the U.S. government because of its belief in polygamy. In 1862 and 1882 Congress passed antibigamy laws, and in 1879 the Supreme Court ruled that religious freedom could not be claimed as grounds for the practice of polygamy. The Mormons officially ended the practice of polygamy in 1890, although some Mormons still practice it today.

Religious Beliefs and Doctrines

As a new religious movement, Mormonism represents a creative synthesis that merges frontier revivalism, deep religious experience, and a contemporary belief in ongoing revelation, combined with a respect for Jesus and Christian ethics. This blend of belief attracts many who are either disinterested, disaffected, or unschooled in Christian history and theology.

According to the Articles of Faith of the Mormon Church and to the theology of the *Book of Mormon*, Mormonism is essentially Christian. Because the essence of Mormon theology depends so much on continuing revelations received by Joseph Smith and later Mormon leaders, critics attack its credibility. Article 8 of the Mormon Articles of Faith says, "We believe the Bible to be the word of God, as far as it is translated correctly; we also believe the *Book of Mormon* to be the word of God."

Belief in God

Article 1 of the Mormon Articles of Faith declares, "We believe in God, the Eternal Father, and in His son, Jesus Christ, and in the Holy Ghost." As with other Christian deviations, words such as these can have quite different meanings. For example, Mormonism teaches that God the Father has a body, and many wives who have children: these are spiritual beings without bodies who inhabit children about to be born on earth, turning them into living soul. Human destiny is to evolve to Godhood. This teaching is summed up in the popular Mormon saying, "As man is, God once was: as God is, man may become." The preexisting souls exist on a planet orbiting the star Kolob gain a body on earth, and serve a probationary period by living good or bad lives, thus determining their future heavenly existence.

The Fall

Mormon theology points to Adam eating the forbidden fruit and says that if he had not done this he would never have had children. Therefore, to propagate the race and achieve his heavenly destiny, Adam had to disobey God. On this basis, the Fall of man saved man.

Justification by Faith

The doctrine of justification by faith is rejected in Mormon theology in favor of a doctrine of salvation by works that determine a person's future mode of existence. Likewise, the efficacy of Christ's atonement is not seen in traditional terms as the means of salvation, but rather the assurance that humans will be raised from the dead. The church baptizes by immersion from the age of eight onward. They also believe both in vicarious baptism for those who have died and in marriage for eternity.

The Mormon Church Today

The Morman Church is Millenial, believing that Christ will return to earth and rule. Joseph Smith designated a site in Independence, Missouri, where Christ would establish the New Zion. Joseph Smith and most of the early Mormons were Freemasons. Present-day ritual shows similarity to Masonic symbols and rites. Homosexuality, sex outside of marriage, alcohol, tobacco, tea, coffee, and other stimulants are forbidden. Vegetarianism is encouraged but not mandatory. The church has been plagued with schisms since it began.

As a social organization the Mormon Church makes many contributions for its members in providing welfare programs and education and promoting family life. Mormons participate in "temple work," which involves proxy baptism for deceased ancestors and "celestial marriage." Mormons believe that in addition to temporal marriages, church members may be sealed to their families "for time and eternity" through a process known as celestial marriage.

In 1978 the president of the Church claimed a new revelation that admitted blacks to the priesthood, although women are still excluded from the priesthood. The Church provides strong opposition to the Equal Rights Amendment, believing that the effects would prove disruptive to family life. In recent years Mormons have engaged in serious self-reflection about the translation of the *Book of Mormon* and *The Pearl of Great Price*, and about Joseph Smith, visions, and historical claims.

Mormon critics include Fawn Brodie, who has written a biography of Joseph Smith, *No Man Knows My History*. In this work, she seriously undermines official Mormon histories. The church still continues to thrive, and in 1989 the church reported a worldwide membership of about seven million people.

UNIT 10:7 CHRISTADELPHIANISM

> *There is no hint in the Old Testament that the Son of God was already existent or in any way active at that time.*
>
> *Jesus Christ, the Son of God, was first promised, and came into being only when he was born of the virgin Mary.*
>
> *Jesus worships God: God worships no one.*
>
> Harry Tennant, *The Christadelphians: What They Believe and Preach*

Christadelphianism is a religious movement begun by Dr. John Thomas (1805–1871), who was born in London, England. He was brought up as a Congregationalist. In 1832 he set sail to the United States, but on the way to New York his ship encountered several terrible storms that threatened shipwreck and death. Dr. Thomas vowed to God that if saved from the storm he would devote his life to religion. He arrived safely in America and kept his promise by joining the Campbellites, also known as the Disciples of Christ. They were a Puritan group, akin to both Baptists and Congregationalists but lacking any specific creed. He was baptized and began to study hard. He worked out his own beliefs during this period and left the Campbellites in 1844 to found his own distinct version of Christian belief. Many Campbellites followed him.

Major Writings

In 1834 Dr. Thomas started a magazine called *The Apostolic Advocate*, in which he disseminated his teachings with an emphasis on prophecy and biblical eschatology. In 1839 Thomas moved to Illinois and became editor of a magazine called *The Investigator* in 1842. Five years later, he started another magazine called *The Herald of the Future Age*. By then, he was living in Virginia.

In 1848 he returned to England to speak and found his hearers very responsive. He wrote the book called *Elpis Israel*, which means "Hope of Israel." The work contains an outline and discussion of his beliefs, including the belief that the Latter Days had begun and that before Christ's return, Israel would be restored.

The other major Christadelphian text is *Christendom Astray*, written by Robert Roberts, who led the movement after Thomas's death. Dr. Thomas named the movement "Christadelphian," which in Greek means "Brethren of Christ."

In 1862, Thomas returned to England again to discover that his book *Elpis Israel* had been influential. He lectured extensively to help establish Christadelphianism on a firm footing.Thomas visited England for the last time in 1869 after writing the book *Eureka*. He died on March 5, 1871, in New York and is buried in Brooklyn.

Christadelphian Teaching and Beliefs

Thomas sought to study and discover the true gospel which, in his opinion, had been lost from the earth. Like so many other religious pioneers of the nineteenth century, his religion was a development of his personal philosophy and beliefs.

When studying Christadelphianism misunderstanding the faith is easy because language is used that is identical to mainstream Christianity but which has a wholly different theological meaning behind it. In the interests of accuracy and fair representation, it is important to try and represent Christadelphian views clearly and simply, primarily by comparing their distinctive outlook with mainstream Christian beliefs.

The Bible

Christadelphians are devoted students of the Bible, which they believe to be the infallible and inerrant word of God. They follow a Bible guide called the *Bible Companion*, which takes them through the whole of the Old Testament once a year and the New Testament twice a year. Their beliefs come entirely from the Bible, and they pay no respect or attention to the creeds of the Church Fathers.

Belief in God and the Trinity

Christadelphians disagree with mainstream Christian belief on the nature of Christ, whom they see as "the Son of God, not God the Son." They believe that Christianity is a false religious system (see the tract "Christendom Astray Since the Apostolic Age," available from the Detroit Christadelphian Book Supply), citing the fact that nowhere in the Bible does it teach the doctrine of the Trinity. (We have seen earlier in this book [chapter 6: units 2 and 3] that the doctrine of the Trinity is implicit rather than explicit in the Bible.) Neither do Christadelphians accept that Jesus existed prior to his incarnation.

Christadelphians are not therefore Trinitarian, neither are they Unitarian, because they hold to the belief that Jesus was and still is literally the Son of God as the scriptures describe.

Christadelphians teach that Jesus had to save himself first before he could save others.

> He [Jesus] saved himself in order to save us.
> And it was for that very reason—being a member of a sinful race—that the Lord Jesus himself needed salvation. (Answers, p. 24)

The Christadelphian doctrine of the atonement is not unlike other mainstream Christian churches in that because Jesus was sinless he could be offered as a sacrifice for sin, but they hold that Jesus could not have done this if he himself had been God. The idea of Jesus as God incarnate is to the Christadelphian a pollution of the Christian faith by the church councils of the fourth and fifth centuries.

The Holy Spirit

Christadelphians do not believe in the personhood and deity of the Holy Spirit.

> The Spirit is not a "separate" or "other" person. It is God's own radiant power, ever out flowing from Him, by which His 'everywhereness' is achieved. The Spirit is personal in that it is of God Himself: it is not personal in the sense of being some other person within the Godhead. (Tennant [1986], 115)

Salvation

Christadelphians believe that baptism is necessary for salvation and that it is possible to lose one's salvation. Jesus had to save himself in order to save others.

> Therefore the wonderful work of baptism is essential to salvation. (Tennant [1986], 210)

> Salvation is not a one-for-all, irreversible happening. (Tennant [1986], 212)

Atonement

Forgiveness of sins comes through being baptized.

> The second secret of the cross is that it is the source of the forgiveness of sins. It is not a debt settled by due payment. It is not a substitutionary offering whereby someone is paid a price so that others might then go free. (Tennant [1986], 71)

> A believing, repentant person receives forgiveness of sins by being baptized. (Tennant [1986], 207–8)

> True baptism removes past sins.(Tennant [1986], 208)

Life after Death

There is no existence after death and therefore no hell or eternal punishment. Eternal life is for the saved and resurrected ones (meaning Christadelphians and maybe others who follow the truth) and will take place on this earth after the return of Christ. The unsaved will not be resurrected.

Beliefs about Evil and the Devil

Christadelphians do not believe in the existence of the fallen angel Lucifer as a personal devil. They teach that sinners are responsible for their own sins.

> The terms Satan and Devil are simply expressive of "sin in the flesh" in individual, social, and political manifestations. (Answer, p. 100)

Organization and Ethics

There is no Christadelphian belief in priesthood; rather each local congregation elects members as overseers for a period of usually one, two, or three years. They choose not to fight in times of war; neither do they vote in elections or take part in politics. Christadelphians refused to fight in the American Civil War. In line with traditional Christian values, they affirm what they see as Bible standards of sexuality: heterosexual marriage.

The Millennialist Teaching of Christadelphians

Christadelphians are divided into two camps on the question of whether all or only the faithful will be resurrected on the last day. Christadelphians see the Jews as the Chosen People and the key to the coming millennium, which is very near. They compare current events such as the establishment of the State of Israel in 1948 and the Six-Day War in 1967 with biblical verses. They believe that we are already in the End Times. Predictions were made in 1866 and 1868 about the second coming of Jesus, and again in 1910. Christadelphians recognize the inaccuracy of these predictions, although they sometimes reinterpret the forecast of the dates to explain other important world events. More recently they tend to affirm the view that no one knows the day of the return of Jesus Christ to the earth.

UNIT 10:8 SPIRITUALISM

Of the Lord's Divine mercy it has been granted me now for several years, to be constantly and uninterruptedly in company with spirits and angels, hearing them converse with each other, and conversing with them. Hence, it has been permitted me to hear and see stupendous things in the other life which has never before come to the knowledge of any man, nor entered into his imagination. I have been instructed concerning different kinds of spirits and the state of souls after death; concerning Hell, or the lamentable state of the unfaithful; concerning Heaven, or the most happy state of the faithful, and particularly concerning the doctrines of faith which is throughout Heaven.

Preface to Emanuel Swedenborg's *Arcana Celestia*

The practice of evoking the spirits of the dead are recorded in ancient Near Eastern and Egyptian sources, and spiritualistic practices have a long history in India, where they are regarded as *bhuta* worship, or worship of the dead. A distinction is made here between spiritism and spiritualism.

- *Spiritism* describes the belief that the living can and do communicate with the spirits of the dead.
- *Spiritualism* is a philosophical doctrine proposing (1) the existence of a spiritual order of beings no less real than the material order, and (2) that the human soul is a spiritual substance.

In modern speech the words *spiritism* and *spiritualism* are often used interchangeably.

Modern spiritism generally dates from 1848 from the experiences of the Fox family at Hydesville, and later at Rochester, in New York State. Strange revelations were made through mysterious noises and rappings that the children, Margaret (1833–1893) and Catherine (1839–1892), heard. Eventually the "rapper" began to provide answers in response to their coded questions, and the children came to be regarded as the first "mediums" of modern times. There was widespread interest in their achievements, and many arranged sittings were given, which form the prototype for spiritist meetings today. Arising out of this phenomena came The Society for Psychical Research, formed in 1882, whose activities include detailed ongoing examination of all spiritist claims.

Similar disturbances occurred in the house of a Rev. Dr. Phelps, a Presbyterian minister from Stratford, Connecticut. These manifestations (1850–1851) were often violent and the spirit-answers blasphemous. However, remarkable interest in the subject was promoted by a number of people, including Robert Hare, professor of chemistry at the University of Pennsylvania, and John Worth Edmonds, a judge of the Supreme Court of New York State. Andrew Jackson Davis (1826–1910) wrote *The Principles of Nature* (1847), which he claimed was trance-delivered. The book contained a theory of the universe, closely resembling the Swedenborgian. Swedenborgianism and Mesmerism were popular in the United States in the 1830s and these ideologies prepared the conceptual ground for the spiritist movement. Spiritism also found followers among the clergy in various denominations, especially the Universalists.

Spiritism in Europe

European spiritism also owed its beginnings to Emmanuel Swedenborg's writings on the spirit world, and also received support from Anton Mesmer's experiments in what he called "animal magnetism" (hypnotism). In 1848 Cahagnet published at Paris the first volume of his "*Arcanes de la vie future dévoilées*," containing what purported to be communications from the dead. The excitement aroused in Paris by table-turning and rapping evoked an investigation by Count Agénor de Gasparin, who concluded ("*Des Tables tournantes*," [Paris, 1854]) that the phenomena originated in some physical force of the human body. Baron de Guldenstubbe ("*La Réalité des Esprits*" [Paris, 1857]), disagreed and put forward his belief in the reality of spirit intervention. M. Rivail, known later as Allan Kardec (1804–1869), published the "spiritualistic philosophy" in "*Le Livre des Esprits*" (Paris, 1853), which evolved as a guidebook to the whole subject. The origin of the term *spiritism* has been attributed to Allan Kardec. His cosmology is called Kardecism and remains a vital religious movement in Brazil, where national spiritism congresses have been held twice since the 1940s.

Many Victorians, particularly those disillusioned with traditional religion, were zealous about spiritism. Fashionable and reputable people reported acute phenomena. Early supporters of spiritualistic phenomena included American journalist Horace Greeley, British author Sir Arthur Conan Doyle, and British scientist A. R. Wallace. The celebrated D. D. Home made table-turning and spirit-rapping the talk of the highest circles, including the courts of the French emperor and the Russian czar. Sir William Crookes, a well-known physicist, claimed to have seen the medium, Daniel Dunglas Home, "float out of an upper-story bedroom window, pass over a street seventy feet below, and re-enter the house by a sitting-room window on *the same story*" (W. Irvine and P. Honan, *The Book, the Ring, & the Poet: a Biography of Robert Browning* [New York: McGraw-Hill, 1974]). Spiritism also had its challenges. American magician Harry Houdini offered a substantial reward to any medium whom he could not debunk. In any case, debunking just seemed to raise spiritism's publicity and profile.

The Practice and Phenomena of Spiritism

A person who "channelled" communications between the earthly and spirit worlds was first referred to as a *medium*, although now they are often called *channellers*. The practices of early mediums included table levitations, extrasensory perception, speaking in a spirit's voice during trances, automatic writing, and the manifestation of apparitions and ectoplasmic matter. Mediums attributed these phenomena to the agency of spirits. Support diminished, however, as many nineteenth-century mediums were proven to be fakes. Early spiritism was on the side of reform. Mediums spoke for the abolition of slavery, the rights of women, and prison reform. Spiritism was also democratic as it transcended hierarchical structures and was open to all, including women who were given opportunities for leadership and practice denied them in almost all other religions. Spiritualism achieved popular appeal during the 1850s and 1860s and in the aftermath of World War I, following the tragic loss of life. Belief in spiritualism again became popular during and since the 1980s through New Age beliefs, particularly in the United States. Modern channellers or mediums attempt contact with extraterrestrials or spirits from ancient mythical societies, as well as communication with those recently deceased.

The Roots and Development of Spiritualism in Britain

Spiritualism was brought to Britain by a Mrs. Hayden, who suffered persecution and insult by the press and from the pulpit. Her mediumship found the support of many public figures, including Robert Owen, a socialist and one of the founders of the Co-operative Movement. In 1853 David Richmond established the first Spiritualist Church at Keighley in Yorkshire and two years later followed the *Yorkshire Spiritual Telegraph* (1855), also at Keighley. By the 1870s spiritualist societies and churches had spread throughout the country.

In 1869 the Dialectical Society investigated spiritualism and published the most favorable report on the movement of that time. Two years later Sir William Crookes reported on spiritualism to the Royal Society and published his findings in the *Quarterly Journal of Science*. The British National Association of Spiritualists (renamed in 1884 as the London Spiritualist Alliance, and now known as the College of Psychic Science) was founded in London in 1873, followed by the Society for Psychical Research in 1882. Five years later, Mrs. Emma Hardinge Britten founded the *Two Worlds Spiritualist* weekly newspaper, which is still on sale today. Through her mediumship in 1871, Robert Owen had communicated the basis of the Seven Principles of Spiritualism, which were later to be adopted by the Spiritualists' National Union (1901). The Seven Principles of Spiritualism are as follows:

1. The Fatherhood of God
2. The Brotherhood of Man
3. The Communion of Spirits and the Ministry of Angels
4. The continuous existence of the human soul
5. Personal responsibility
6. Compensation and retribution hereafter for all the good and evil deeds done on earth
7. Eternal progress open to every human soul

The Union has taken a leading part in the foundation of the International Spiritualist Federation, which unites spiritualists of many countries.

Science and Spiritism

Spiritism gained the attention of and divided the scientific world. For people who denied the existence of a soul, that there could be no communications with the dead was a foregone certainty. This view predominated among people who accept the fundamental ideas of materialism. Nevertheless, spiritism has claimed that it alone gives incontestable proof of immortality, as well as the death blow to materialism. This claim, however, rests on the spiritualist hypothesis that the communications come from disembodied spirits; as a concept, immortality is not emboldened by a telepathic hypothesis for spiritism or from the view that disembodied spirit communication is really demonic intervention.

Spiritualism and Spiritistic Beliefs

The spiritistic hypothesis maintains that the communications are received from disembodied spirits and that telepathy is insufficient to account for all the phenomena. Telepathy at most may be the means by which discarnate spirits act upon the minds of living persons.

To explain the phenomena that after careful investigation and exclusion of fraud appear to be authentic, three main alternative explanations or hypotheses emerge.

1. The telepathic hypothesis takes as its starting point the idea of subliminal consciousness, which is subject to disintegration so that parts of consciousness may impress another mind even at a distance. The personality is liberated and invades the soul of another. A medium obtains information by thought-transference, either from the minds of persons present at the séance or from other minds about whom the sitters know nothing. This view tends to support recognized facts of hypnosis.

2. The second hypothesis is one of psychical radiations. This view recognizes that a person has a material body, a soul, and an intermediate principle—the "perispirit"—which is a subtle fluid or astral body. In certain people (mediums) the perispirit can escape from the material organism and thus form a "double." It also accompanies the soul after death and is the means by which communication is established with the perispirit of the mediums.

3. The third view is that manifestations proceed from intelligences other than that of the medium. The question arises whether these intelligences are the spirits of the departed or beings that have never been embodied in human forms. Even committed believers in spirits have been forced to consider the involvement of extraneous or nonhuman intelligences. This conclusion is based on several sorts of evidence:

- The difficulty of establishing spirit-identity, i.e., of establishing whether the spirit is actually the personality it claims to be
- The trivial talk upon which the spirit tends to focus, which undermines the opportunity of serious communication with those in the living world
- The love of the impersonation of celebrities who once lived on earth, although on closer questioning, the spirits reveal their ignorance of those whom they impersonate
- The low moral tone that often marks the tone messages from spirits who claim to enlighten humankind

These inconsistencies have been attributed to the subliminal consciousness, lower-order spirits below the plane of humanity, and demonic intervention.

The Spiritualist Church

By the end of the nineteenth century the mediumistic faith had traveled from home demonstrations and experiential sittings to become an ecclesiastical faith. By the 1890s Spiritualist Churches with ministers, altars, choirs, and other church vestiges had sprung into existence. Today many spiritualists combine their beliefs and practices with Christian belief, although mainstream Christian churches still forbid as an occult practice contacting the dead.

The Christian Church and Spiritism

The fourth-century Council of Nicaea brought to an end the use of mediums and decreed that only divine guidance, through the Holy Spirit, should be sought, only from the priesthood.

In the Middle Ages, religious sanction of persecution was given in 1484 by a papal bull in the publication of the *Malleus Maleficarum* or "Hammer of the Witches." Anyone suspected of using psychic gifts for whatever purpose was in danger of torture, trial, and burning.

The Roman Catholic Church has declared several times on the issue of spirits in the nineteenth and twentieth centuries, including the Congregation of the Inquisition, June 25, 1840, which decreed:

> Where all error, sorcery, and invocation of the demon, implicit or explicit, is excluded, the mere use of physical means which are otherwise lawful, is not morally forbidden, provided it does not aim at unlawful or evil results. But the application of purely physical principles and means to things or effects that are really supernatural, in order to explain these on physical grounds, is nothing else than unlawful and heretical deception.

The Second Plenary Council of Baltimore (1866) declared that some of the manifestations are to be ascribed to Satanic intervention, warning the faithful against supporting spirits or even attending séances. The council emphasized the anti-Christian character of spiritistic teachings concerning religion and characterized them as attempts to revive paganism and magic.

Spiritism has always been controversial to both science and the Christian faith. Despite the ongoing controversy, the movement has continued to grow and flourish, and many people claim to have found faith and comfort through the belief that they are in touch with the whole of reality, not just the living, and especially with their loved ones who have died.

UNIT 10:9 UNITARIANISM

> *We do, then, with all earnestness, though without reproaching our brethren, protest against the irrational and unscriptural doctrine of the Trinity.*
>
> William Ellery Channing

Unitarianism is a religious movement connected with Christianity. Unitarians deny that God exists as a Trinity. A number of religious groups in Transylvania, Poland, Great Britain, and North America have been designated as Unitarian because of this belief. Equally, if not more significant, has been their trust and optimism in the rational and moral abilities of people rather than religious traditions that emphasize original sin and human depravity. Unitarianism has sometimes been called antitrinitarianism. The origins are to be found in the Arian controversy of the early fourth century when Arius, presbyter in the church at Alexandria, denied the orthodox doctrine of the Trinity and asserted that there was a time when God was not the Father and Jesus Christ was not the Son, and that Christ possessed a form of divinity, but he was never of the same substance as the Father. This early form of Unitarianism was condemned by the Council of Nicaea in 325 and by the Council of Constantinople in 381.

Socinianism

Throughout the Middle Ages, Unitarianism reappeared in the writings of Michael Servetus (1511–1553) and was accepted by some radical Anabaptist groups. It received renewed fame in Socinianism of Laelius and Faustus Socinus and in the Racovian Catechism of 1605, which denied, among other things, the doctrine of the Trinity and the deity of Christ. Their belief was that Christ was a man divinely commissioned, who had no existence before he was miraculously and sinlessly conceived by Mary.

Although they rejected the deity of Christ and the doctrine of the Trinity, the

Socinians insisted on the worship of Jesus Christ as a divinely appointed person, believing in his resurrection from the dead and his ascension. However, his divine nature was the result of his perfect obedience. They rejected orthodox belief about the fall of humanity and held to a belief in the full freedom of the will. On this view, the redeeming work of Christ is based on his life and teachings, not in his vicarious death upon the cross.

The Enlightenment brought about an increased confidence in deism. Unitarianism lost its supernatural and religious basis and put more confidence in rationalism, aided by such radicals as Unitarian minister and scientist the Rev. Dr. Joseph Priestley. Congregations such as his formed the basis of the Free Churches.

Unitarianism in America

Unitarianism came to New England as early as 1710; within a relatively short time many Congregational ministers in the Boston area had ceased to regard the doctrine of the Trinity as an essential Christian belief. In 1788 King's Chapel, the first Anglican church in New England, became Unitarian when its rector, with the consent of his congregation, deleted all mention of the Trinity from the liturgy. Another landmark of the Unitarian movement was the occasion of Henry Ware, a strong opponent of Trinitarianism, being appointed to the Hollis chair of divinity at Harvard.

William Ellery Channing's (1780–1842) sermon entitled "Unitarian Christianity" was an influential statement of their beliefs. It was delivered at the ordination of the historian Rev. Jared Sparks, later president of Harvard, in The First Independent Church of Baltimore on May 5, 1819. Here we produce a stirring excerpt:

> We object to the doctrine of the Trinity, that, whilst acknowledging in words, it subverts in effect, the unity of God. According to this doctrine, there are three infinite and equal persons, possessing supreme divinity, called the Father, Son, and Holy Ghost. Each of these persons, as described by theologians, has his own particular consciousness, will, and perceptions. They love each other, converse with each other, and delight in each other's society. They perform different parts in man's redemption, each having his appropriate office, and neither doing the work of the other. . . . [W]hen common Christians hear these persons spoken of as conversing with each other, loving each other, and performing different acts, how can they help regarding them as different beings, different minds? We do, then, with all earnestness, though without reproaching our brethren, protest against the irrational and unscriptural doctrine of the Trinity.

In the nineteenth century, under the influence of transcendentalism, Unitarianism became steadily more radical. Ralph Waldo Emerson and Theodore Parker rejected the remaining supernatural elements that William Ellery Channing had retained, and they made modern Unitarianism more of a humanistic philosophy.

Beliefs

In England and America, Unitarianism is strictly congregational. Each individual congregation is autonomous and manages all its own affairs. It calls and discharges the minister and is the final judge of the religious views expressed in its pulpit. At the heart of Unitarianism is the simple fact that there is no creed and the popular (postmodern) view that no one holds the right to impose their beliefs or views on others. Even so, despite this religious liberalism, generalized agreement exists on a number of doctrines.

- There is one God, not three-in-one. The Father is God.
- Jesus was a man, not coeternal with the Father. They reject the careful formulations of the early church councils. Jesus was divine in the sense that God dwelt in him, so that he was a holy man.
- The Holy Spirit is God's influence in the world.
- Human beings are essentially good rather than sinful. Unitarians are not ignorant of evil in the world, but people themselves choose to live well.
- Jesus' death is not seen as an atonement for sin, but rather as an example of love and sacrifice.
- There is no belief in hell or eternal suffering for nonbelievers.
- The Bible is important to faith but is not in any way inspired or infallible. It has been copied, edited, and altered and should therefore be read in the light of reason.

Many members of the American Unitarian Association, founded in 1825, have come to the conclusion that their movement is not now a part of the Christian church. The Unitarians merged with the Universalists in 1961 to form the Unitarian Universalist Association, which is characterized by an emphasis on seeking truth out of human experience, not out of allegiance to creeds or doctrines. Each congregation is self-governing, and there are more than a thousand congregations, mainly in North America.

In America, Unitarianism was adopted by a large number of intelligent and highly influential writers, thus making it intellectually and socially an acceptable faith. It was known as the "thinking man's religion." Evangelical and conservative Christians tend to view Unitarianians more as wicked and perverse heretics rather than a cult or a sect. Less formidable are those who see it as humanism with a spiritual dimension or a religion that appeals to the skeptical mind.

In his book, the *Unitarian Path* (1994) Andrew Hill says,

> The Unitarian path is a liberal religious movement rooted in the Jewish and Christian traditions but open to insights from world faiths, reason and science; and with a spectrum extending from liberal Christianity through to religious humanism.

Worship

Universalist ritual is diverse. While most congregations root their worship in forms of mainline Protestantism, one might also find a Jewish high holy days service, a Hindu Festival of Divali, a Muslim prayer, or a Wiccan ritual in a Unitarian Universalist church.

The Flaming Chalice

While no single symbol of universal acceptance appears among Unitarians, in recent years the flaming chalice has become the most frequently used symbol. Its origins go back to the martyrdom of Jan Hus in the thirteenth century. The flame in the communion cup symbolized the enduring flame of his faith, burning up from the chalice, together forming the shape of a cross. The flaming chalice has been adapted in many forms by different congregations. Its most common meaning today is the light of knowledge and the search for truth.

Women, Marriage, and Homosexuality

In Britain, the Unitarian Church appointed women ministers in 1904, and the movement retains its strong opposition to racial, sexual, and religious discrimination.

In 1977 a women-and-religion resolution was passed by the Association, to change sexist structures and language, especially with the publication of an inclusive hymnal. Unitarians have affirmed the rights of bisexuals, gays, lesbians, and transgendered persons by including the ordination of homosexual and lesbian clergy, and in 1996 they affirmed same-sex marriage.

The Unitarian Universalist Association (UUA)

The UUA represents the interests of more than one thousand Unitarian Universalist congregations on a continental scale. In 1961 the UUA grew out of the consolidation of two religious denominations: the Universalists, organized in 1793, and the Unitarians, organized in 1825. This consolidation united two denominations with very parallel histories and a mutual tradition of religious liberalism. Each year, delegates of the Unitarian Universalist Association of Congregations (UUA) meet to discuss resolutions, vote on issues and proposed changes, and participate in worship and training at the annual meeting of the Association, called the General Assembly (GA).

In June 1999 some thirty-five hundred Unitarian Universalist clergy and laity congregated in Salt Lake City, Utah, where the UUA heralded a significant development in institutional change. The Department of Ministry statistics had indicated that 51 percent of active ordained ministers in the UUA were women. The UUA thus became the first Protestant denomination in history in which congregations employ more female than male clergy in their leadership. News conferences, parties, and dancing in the aisles in Salt Lake City celebrated this achievement.

UNIT 10:10 THE SWEDENBORGIAN CHURCH

> *Every smallest moment of a person's life involves a series of consequences extending to eternity, each moment being as a new beginning to those which follow; and so with all and each of the moments of his life, both of his understanding and of his will.*
>
> Emanuel Swedenborg, *Arcana Coelestia*

The Swedish scientist, philosopher, and mystic Emanuel Swedenborg (1688–1772) was the son of a Lutheran bishop. He pioneered in both scientific and religious thought and by the age of twenty-one was a doctor of philosophy. He started his career as a natural scientist and official at the Swedish Bureau of Mines, with an emphasis on research and theory. His major scientific work was *Opera philosophica et mineralia* (*Philosophical and Mineralogical Works*, 3 vols., 1734), which showed his unique combination of metaphysics, cosmology, and science. He was an eminent scientist who in many ways anticipated scientific progress by at least a century.

In 1736 he started recording his dreams. In 1745 Swedenborg claimed a direct vision of a world of angels, spirits, heaven, and hell underlying the natural sphere. The vision took place in a London inn where he was having dinner and began with the appearance of a shadowy figure in the corner who told him not to eat so much. Later that night, he was awakened and saw the same figure, who identified himself as the Lord Jesus Christ and told him that he was being chosen to disclose the inner spiritual meaning of the Bible. After this, Swedenborg reported, heaven and hell were opened to him. From that time until the closing days of his life, Swedenborg had constant "waking visions" of the spiritual world, including extended conversations with angels and spirits.

Swedenborg took the spiritual experiences seriously and renewed his study of university Hebrew and Greek. He drafted his own extensive index of Bible passages and began writing a Bible commentary, posthumously published (incomplete) in nine volumes as *The Word Explained*. From 1749 to 1756 he published a multivolume work known as *Arcana Coelestia*, whose full title might be translated "A Disclosure of the Heavenly Depths in Sacred Scripture or the Word of the Lord."

Believing that God had given him special knowledge in the interpretation of the Bible, he wrote several works setting out a system of thought that rejects or reinterprets many traditional Christian beliefs. In 1747 he resigned his job to devote the rest of his life to spiritual writing and investigation. From the outset his work and religious thinking attracted a large following.

Cosmology and Religious Beliefs

Swedenborg's cosmology is neo-Platonic. Creation out of nothing (*ex nihilo*) is therefore rejected, as God is the one and only true substance, the ultimate love and wisdom from which all things proceed. Yet the world is not God (he rejected pantheism).

Swedenborg's fundamental teaching is the "law of correspondences," believing in an exact correlation between the phenomenal plane and the spiritual plane of existence. At this time Cartesian science and Lutheran orthodoxy were moving apart. Unlike other mystics, Swedenborg proposed an approach to spiritual reality and God through material nature; he puts forward a unique synthesis between modern science and religion.

Belief in God

God is love. Swedenborg puts great emphasis on God as Love and the function of love in the life of the believer. He writes in *Heavenly City* (1758):

> The two loves that everything good and true come from (loving the Lord and loving other people) make heaven in us, so they also prevail in heaven. Since they make heaven in us, they make religion in us too. The two loves that everything evil and false come from (selfish love and materialistic love) make hell in us, so they also prevail in hell.
>
> The two loves that everything good and true come from open and develop our inner spiritual self, because that is where they are in us. They are heaven's loves. But when we are controlled by the two loves that everything evil and false come from, these loves close and destroy our inner spiritual self. They make us materialistic and physical-minded in proportion to their control over us. (Emmanuel Swedenborg, *The Heavenly City: A Spiritual Guidebook,* trans. Lee Woofenden [West Chester, Penn.: The Swedenborg Foundation, 1993), 60–61.)

The Trinity

Swedenborg reinterpreted the Christian concept of the Trinity into three principles: God (inexhaustible love), Son (divine wisdom), and Spirit (divine energy).

The Bible

Based on the theory of correspondence, every scripture has a literal meaning and a spiritual meaning. Swedenborg believed his special mission was to reveal the true spiritual meaning of scripture.

Atonement

Christ's saving work is not a sacrifice but a triumph over temptation and evil. It is therefore the prime example of the reconciling power of God, by which all can overcome evil.

Salvation

Salvation is by faith plus works. Though God is the ultimate source of good works, we must choose to cooperate with God's power of love and seek to reform ourselves and live the good life.

Life after Death

The soul is immortal. After death all go to a spirit world and eventually to heaven or hell. To get to heaven a person has to choose Jesus' way of love and courage, forgiveness and self-denial. This choice necessitates doing, practicing, and living the faith, not just believing it. Hell is not a punishment but our own choice, as the Lord is always eager to save us from such a fate.

In addition to these key beliefs Swedenborg believed in the continuance of true marital love in heaven. In 1757 he had a vision of the second coming and last judgment. From this experience he heralded in a new dispensation, i.e., the era of the New Church (from which doctrine the Church of the New Jerusalem was formed).

The Growth of Swedenborgianism

Swedenborg did not found a church or a movement. These institutions followed after people had read his numerous writings. Swedenborg's theology influenced a number of Methodist ministers, one of whom, Robert Hindmarsh, founded the New Jerusalem Church in 1787.

Even John Wesley was affected by Swedenborg's books. Wesley recorded in his diary of February 28, 1770:

> I began with huge prejudice in his favour, knowing him to be a pious man, one of strong understanding, of much learning, and one who thoroughly believed himself. But I could not hold out long. Any one of his visions puts his real character out of doubt. He is one of the most ingenious, lively,

entertaining madmen that ever set pen to paper. But his waking dreams are so wild, so far remote both from Scripture and common sense, that one might as easily swallow the stories of "Tom Thumb" or "Jack the Giant-Killer."

Swedenborg's interest in spirits evoked subsequent research and reflection on psychological research. In particular, Swedenborg influenced Ralph Waldo Emerson, who saw him as a person of special insight.

Published Works

Arcana Coelestia: Or Heavenly Mysteries, 12 vols. (1747–1758)
This study makes up more than a third of the total bulk of Swedenborg's theological writings. The books of Genesis and Exodus are reviewed in phrase-by-phrase commentary.

Heaven and Hell (1757–1758)
This three-part work attracted great attention. The human soul awakes in the world of spirits after death and there prepares for final entrance into either heaven or hell, depending upon the quality of the life that the person lived in the natural world. Each individual determines his own fate by the free choices he makes during his natural life. The last section of the book describes hell as the perfect perversion of heaven and heavenly life.

White Horse (1757–1758)
This work deals largely with the subject of divine revelation and the human need of it.

New Jerusalem and Its Heavenly Doctrine (1757–1758)

Earths in the Universe (1756–1758)
Swedenborg says that all terrestrial bodies were created to support human life of some kind and describes the life of spirits from a number of planets other than Earth.

Last Judgment (1757–1758)
Each individual after death goes through a personal last judgment in the world of spirits. The entire world of spirits, according to Swedenborg, underwent a last judgment in the year 1757.

Doctrine of the Lord (1761–1763)
This important volume explains the workings of the divine trinity. It sets forth the Swedenborgian doctrine of God as a divinely human person, who ministers to the human race as both revealer and redeemer.

Other published works include:

Doctrine of the Sacred Scripture (1761–1763)

Doctrine of Life (1761–1763)

Doctrine of Faith (1761–1763)

Continuation Concerning the Last Judgment

Divine Love and Wisdom. The work may properly be termed the metaphysics of Swedenborg's theological writings.

Divine Providence (1763)

Apocalypse Revealed, 2 vols. (1764–1766)

Conjugial Love (1767–1768)

Summary Exposition (1768–1769)

Intercourse of the Soul and the Body (1769)

True Christian Religion, 2 vols. (1769–1771)

UNIT 10:11 JEHOVAH'S WITNESSES

Millions now living will never die
Judge Joseph Franklin
Rutherford

Jehovah's Witnesses are Millennialists (see unit 9:9) and believe in the literal return of Christ and the inauguration of his kingdom on earth. The group arose late following the Great Disappointment that came after the failure of William Miller's prophecies in 1831 that the world would end with the advent of Christ in 1834. The return of Christ was also expected in 1920, 1925, 1940, 1975, and 1984.

Founder Charles Taze Russell (1852–1916) was raised in a Congregationalist family in Pittsburgh, Pennsylvania. As a young man he reacted against his own upbringing, so that by the age of eighteen he had started his own Bible class in Pittsburgh. This group grew into the organization that is now known as Jehovah's Witnesses. Russell assumed his role as pastor of the group in 1876. In 1879 he started publishing *Zion's Watchtower*, the forerunner of the well-known *Watchtower*.

In 1886 Russell published the first of a series of seven books entitled *Studies in the Scriptures.* The seventh volume was published in 1917, a year after his death. The seventh volume also led to a schism in the organization, with the majority following J. F. Rutherford, the others becoming The Pastoral Bible Institute and the Laymen's Home Missionary Movement, both of which kept to Russell's teachings. The larger group following Rutherford are today's Jehovah's Witnesses. Their magazine, *The Watchtower*, has a circulation of over 64 million copies.

Russell taught that Jesus had initiated a "Millenial Dawn" in 1874, with an invisible return to earth. Russell predicted that the millennium age would start in 1914. The events of the First World War tended to reinforce such beliefs. Russell and Rutherford, however, continued to change the dates in the light of subsequent nonevents. Both men were flagrant in their dismissal of Christians who were not loyal Jehovah's Witnesses. They were called "evil slaves," which included both Catholic and Protestant Christendom. Both mainstream groups were perceived as being under the control of the devil. Being visible in the world they also formed the antichrist.

Russell attracted unfavorable publicity for the movement when in a Canadian court he swore under oath that he was a competent Greek scholar, claiming that all existing Bible translations were unreliable. Under cross-examination, though, he was unable to read the letters of the Greek alphabet. Another controversy was Russell's "Miracle Wheat," which was sold in 1911 by the *Watchtower* for one dollar a pound—some sixty times the normal price—due to the claim that it would exceed normal growth by as much as five times. He tried to sue a newspaper for their accusation that the claim was a fake, but his case was lost as government examiners could find nothing extraordinary in the grain.

Following Russell's death in 1916, Judge Joseph Franklin Rutherford became the leader of the organization. Rutherford (1869–1942) was a prolific writer who influenced the society in its dislike of organized religion and its missionary zeal. In 1920 Rutherford coined the phrase, "Millions now living will never die," which is used in Jehovah's Witnesses' advertising today. At his death, Rutherford left behind an organization that has continued its quick growth. In 1942 Nathan Homer Knorr (1905–1977) succeeded Rutherford, and Knorr's efficient administration enhanced the expansion of the movement.

Scriptures

The Jehovah's Witnesses' interpretation of Christianity and their rejection of orthodoxy influenced them to produce their own translation of the Bible, *The New World Translation of the Christian Greek Scriptures* and *The New World Translation of the Hebrew Scriptures*, in 1950. Although this work claims to be a translation, the Witnesses have yet to prove its reliability. Many biblical scholars regard it as a poor and inaccurate translation and see it as worded to give biblical support to the group's own doctrines. For example, in John 1:1 the Divine Logos (Christ) is reduced in nature and status: "In the beginning . . . and the Word was a god." The normative Greek translation is, "In the beginning was the Word and the Word was with God, and the Word was God."

Beliefs

Jehovah's Witnesses depart from traditional Christian beliefs on major points of doctrine, especially that of the Trinity:

- Jesus is not God, but the son of God, the first of his creations. There was therefore a time when he did not exist; such beliefs are akin to fourth-century Arian heresy.
- Jesus' preexisted form is equated with the angels.
- The Holy Spirit is not a person of the godhead but rather a religious term for the action of God in the world. Probably the best introduction to the theology of the Jehovah's Witnesses is their book *Let God Be True*.

In addition to their rejection of the Christian doctrine of the Trinity, Jehovah's Witnesses (JW) teach a number of distinct doctrines. For example:

> The JW view of the atonement is a ransom paid to the God Jehovah by Jesus Christ which removes the effects of Adam's sin, laying the foundation for a new righteousness and enabling men to save themselves by their good works. The atonement is incomplete and awaits the Millennium Age.
>
> The JW view of the resurrection is that Jesus was resurrected a divine spirit, not a physical one, after offering this ransom to God.
>
> The JW view of life after death is that humans either sleep until the resurrection or, if they are evil, they suffer annihilation.
>
> Regarding the second coming of Christ they believe Jesus returned to earth spiritually in 1914 and is now in the process of overthrowing Satan's worldly organization and establishing a theocratic millennial kingdom. This kingdom will arrive in the near future with the battle of Armageddon. After Armageddon, true believers will be resurrected to a life on earth, while a select group of 144,000 will rule in heaven with Christ.
>
> Jehovah's Witnesses reject professional ministry and, until recently, the idea of church buildings. They are pacifists who have continually refused to take up arms in military conflict. JWs call upon their members to have nothing to do with worldly politics, consequently they do not vote.
>
> Once a year Jehovah's Witnesses observe Memorial that is, Holy Communion—claiming it should be held on the biblical anniversary of Christ's death, the fourteenth day of the Jewish month of Nisan.

Jehovah's Witnesses Today

Jehovah's Witnesses in modern society are known for their refusal to accept blood transfusions. This act is based on Jewish law in the Bible about taking blood into the body through mouth or veins, which violates God's laws (Gen. 9:4; Lev. 17:14; Acts 15:28, 29). Their views on organ transplants and vaccinations have changed several times during the recent past but now seems to have settled as being a matter for the believer's individual conscience.

The movement shares some of the features of a commercial company. The Governing Body provides the powerful lead, beneath are the Religious Servants, and beneath them are the Zone Servants, who are responsible for the local groups known as Companies, which meet in the local Kingdom Hall. Each company is headed by a Service Director who is responsible to the Zone Servant for running his company. He is helped by the Service Committee, which concerns itself especially with home visitations. In 1981 the Jehovah's Witnesses experienced a series of schisms that led to a large number leaving the organization. The leader of the opposition to the Brooklyn, New York, headquarters group was Professor James Penton, whose family had been among Russell's earliest converts. Penton and the people who sided with him sought to reemphasize the doctrine of justification by faith and return the group to its original interest in Bible study. The intention of Penton and other Witnesses who shared his ideas appears to have been to reform the group from within. The Brooklyn leadership rejected their views and expelled anyone who supported them. Although this division was serious, it appears that the majority of Witnesses remained within the official organization, which retained control over all of the group's assets.

Persecution

Along with Gypsies, homosexuals, and other groups, Jehovah's Witnesses were hounded and executed under the Nazi regime. Persecution exists for them still today in various parts of the world. They refuse to fight in times of war, not from strict beliefs that killing is wrong (because God allowed it in the Old Testament) but on the grounds of the invalidity of taking up arms for an earthly power or government. Jehovah's Witnesses have shown great perseverance in the face of opposition and are strongly committed to voluntary work to promote their sincerely held beliefs.

UNIT 10:12 THE FAMILY (THE CHILDREN OF GOD)

A world-famous nonconformist named Jesus, while exhorting His disciples to leave their old lives in order to follow Him, warned them that they would be "as sheep in the midst of wolves." "If you were of the system," He as good as said, "the system would love its own. But you are not of the system, therefore the system hates you."

Dare to be different, He was saying. Venture to vary from the norm which the systematic system addicts have established to conform to their own Establishment behavior, and they will hate you for daring to challenge their authority to tell you what they have decided is right and wrong.

David Brandt Berg, *Dare to Be Different!*

The Family merges traditional evangelical and fundamentalist Christian beliefs with beliefs about universal salvation, contacts with spirits, communal living, and free love among heterosexual adults within the group. They are a major target for countercult and anticult movements who attack its unorthodox theological beliefs and accuse it of mind control and criminal sexual practices. They are also a popular subject for study by scholars interested in new religious movements. Recent studies all indicate that the Family has continued to reform itself and its practices up until the present day.

The roots of the Family (formerly the Children of God) can be traced back to the counterculture "Jesus Movement" of the late 1960s. Young people, often hippies, left their middle-class families to seek a simpler lifestyle in the form of communal life in southern California. Out of this movement came a loosely connected group of evangelical Christian organizations collectively known as The Jesus People.

The founder of the Children of God was David Berg (1919–1994), an evangelist for the Christian and Missionary Alliance in 1964 and later a leader of a Teen Challenge chapter in Huntington Beach, California. From 1964 to 1971 Berg was a regular voice on Christian radio and TV programs alongside Pentecostal evangelist Fred Jordan. In 1969 Berg received a revelation from God that a disastrous earthquake was about to hit California. He led the group out of Huntington Beach on a trek of the American Southwest for eight months, during which time their name was changed to the Children of God and they began to live communally. In these early years, strict controls were maintained: dating, kissing, and holding hands were not allowed and premarital sex was forbidden (there are allegations that Berg was exempt from these rules). In later years, sexual restrictions were lowered among the membership, and free love became the norm. Berg became known under several names and titles such as Father David, Moses David, or Mo. He communicated with the Children of God community via his famous "Mo letters," which often contained comic strip presentations. David Berg became a polygamist by marrying a second wife, Maria.

In the 1970s, the Children of God were known for a recruitment practice called "flirty fishing," basically using sex to attract new recruits. The media delighted in portraying this form of evangelism and called the Children of God women "Hookers for Jesus." In 1979 Berg's annual report stated that his "FFers" (Flirty Fishers) had "witnessed to over a quarter of a million souls, loved over 25,000 of them and won about 19,000 to the Lord."

Scrutiny from outsiders, including government investigations, as well as the scourge of sexually transmitted diseases led the movement to abandon the practice in September 1987. However, the present movement still has a liberal attitude toward heterosexual relations that is not shared by orthodox Christians. The Family retains, however, a stance against homosexuality.

The Children of God was reorganized as the Family of Love in 1977 after some abuses of authority among the leadership came to light. Berg dismissed the whole leadership and formally dissolved the Children of God. People who wanted to remain in the fellowship were invited to form a new group—the Family of Love—

with a new structure. This name was later shortened to the Family. Each commune (called "home") became an autonomous unit and was under far less control. At this time, Berg introduced "sexual sharing," which is free consensual sexual activity among the membership. "The free expression of sexuality, including fornication, adultery, lesbianism (though not male homosexuality), and incest were not just permitted but encouraged." (Richard Kyle, *The Religious Fringe: A History of Alternate Religions in America* [Downers Grove, Ill.: InterVarsity Press, 1993], 361–367)

It is debatable whether Berg's writings are considered authoritative above scripture; accounts of past members vary. The Family believe that Jesus had sexual relations with Mary, and some members believe in "the Gabriel doctrine"—that the angel Gabriel had sexual intercourse with Mary at the time of her conception.

In 1985 David and Maria Berg organized a central office called World Services. The fellowship reverted to a more autocratic model and began restricting sexual activity.

The Family now mostly live in small communities or "communes" around the world. David Berg died in 1994 and his wife, Maria, assumed authority as prophetess and leader of the Family.

Beliefs and Practices

The Family aspires to be close in belief and practice to the early Christian church. Members take seriously Jesus' "challenge" to put the kingdom of God before one's family of origin (Matt. 10:34–37, 12:46–50; Luke 9:59–62, 14:26, 21:16–17), to give possessions away and adopt a simple life of poverty (Matt. 19:21–24, 27–29; Luke 14:33; 18:22–25, 28–30), and to follow a life devoted to propagating the faith. They share their belongings and help the poor.

In common with other evangelical Christian groups, they believe that people can be saved and spend eternity in heaven if they repent of their sins and accept Christ as Lord and Savior. In common with many fundamentalists they believe literally in the biblical account of creation and not in the theory of evolution.

The Family are charismatic Christians, believing in the baptism of the Holy Spirit and the gifts of the Spirit, which include prophecy, speaking in tongues, and healing. They are committed to evangelism in the world, and they believe strongly that these are the last days before Christ will return.

All adults in the Family are expected to be full-time missionaries.

The new converts give all their possessions to the organization.

Among other things, birth control is discouraged, and tobacco, alcohol, and drugs are forbidden.

Differences between the Family and Evangelical Christianity

Two major differences exist between the Family and mainstream evangelical Christianity. The first is to do with the status of the founder David Berg, whom the Family regard as the end-time prophet sent by God. The second concerns the "Law of Love" found in Matthew 22:37–39. Unlike other churches, Christ's law of love is applied to heterosexual relationships between consenting adults, regardless of marital status. The key concept for the Family is that they are motivated by unselfish love:

> Currently, the controversial aspect of The Family's attitude to sex is "sharing"—the practice of having a sexual relationship with another member (other than one's spouse) of the home in which one resides. Again, there are rules governing this practice. All spouses must agree; "sharing" can only be practiced within one home, and not between different homes or with outsiders; one cannot "share" with more than one member in any one month. It also needs the permission of the "Home Mother" and is only done after "much discussion and prayer." (I am not endorsing these policies, I should emphasize, only describing what they are.) (Dr. George Chryssides, message on the NUREL discussion list [www.ucalgary.ca/~nurelweb/links/nurel=i.html], July 17, 1998)

The Family spokesperson for the United Kingdom, Rachel Scott, says that the application of the Law of Love to sexual relationships is misunderstood by outsiders. She says it is

> primarily for the sake of single people within our communities who because of the fact that they cannot have relationships with people outside our communities would otherwise have to remain celibate. We do not believe this would be the loving thing to do. It is not an excuse for excess and it is carried out extremely discreetly with just two people involved. (Rachel Scott, in Barrett [1996])

Accusations and Allegations against the Family

Child abuse allegations have been levied against the Family. The allegations were largely based on the testimony of former Family members claiming to have been sexually abused as children. They refer to a book, *The Story of Davidito*, which was written by David, son of David Berg's wife Maria. The book discusses his witnessing of sexual behavior within the group and the encouragement they gave him to explore his own sexuality, but nothing in the book relates to adult molestation or abuse of children. A psychologist and sociologist from Oakland University studied thirty-two children in two Family homes in California. Subsequently the authors also visited three more Family homes. See *Gary Shepherd & Lawrence Lilliston, "Psychological Assessment of Children in The Family" at: http://www.thefamily.org/dossier/books/book1/chapter5.htm.* They "found no evidence for child abuse among these children. In interviews with adolescents in the group, the authors found no evidence for past sexual abuse despite intensive questioning."

Lord Justice Ward of the High Court in London issued a child custody judgment in 1995 (see Hugh Muir, "Family Values," *The Sunday Telegraph Magazine*, January 5, 1997.) His three-year study of the movement produced 340 pages of judgment, in which he leveled hard criticism of the past eras of Family history but also concluded that it had undergone numerous changes for the good. With reference to its policies regarding children, he said,

> The Family have been black, very black and they are still not white, but the shade of grey grows lighter by the month. . . . I have decided to trust them to continue to bring lightness to their darkness. . . . The Family cannot hide from the world any longer. The Family do not wish to hide from the world any longer. I hope the world will accept them back into the fold.

Despite these reports, ongoing opposition to the Family continues. In 1993 French police raided Family communities and arrested fifty adults and ninety children. After controversial and questionable interrogation, members were charged and tried for a variety of criminal acts and eventually found not guilty by an Aix-en-Provence court in January 1999.

The earlier excesses of the movement that brought suffering and trauma to so many people are now apparently seen as regrettable, and every effort is being made to reform the movement. The Family Web site self-description reads:

> The Family is an international Christian fellowship dedicated to sharing God's Word and love with others. We in The Family seek to comfort, help and minister to those in need, endeavoring to follow the model of Jesus, who said His ministry was to "preach the Gospel to the poor . . . to heal the brokenhearted, to proclaim liberty to the captives and recovery of sight to the blind, to set at liberty those who are oppressed, to proclaim the acceptable year of the Lord" (The Gospel According to Saint Luke, chapter 4, verses 18 and 19). (*www.thefamily.org/ourfounder/tribute/trib_40.htm*)

David Barrett (1996) says:

> The impression given by the Family today is that they are sincere and dedicated Evangelical Christians whose only real difference from any others is that they are honest about sleeping with each other.

Chapter 11
Pagan, Esoteric, and Occult Thought

As Americans continue the ancient quest for the meaning of life, Pagan and Mystical religions are experiencing a resurgence. According to Margot Adler, there are 50,000 to 100,000 self-identified Pagans in the United States. When polled, many people identify themselves with another religion, and so these religious polls are lower. These people are exploring the mystical aspects of "mainstream religions" including Mystic and Druidic Christianity, Jewish Kabbalism and Islamic Sufism. Others are modern-day witches or Wiccans.

Tara Miller, "Pagan Misconceptions," 1997

This chapter covers a number of esoteric and pagan movements that have anywhere from some to a considerable degree of crossover of beliefs and assumptions, as well as many differences, from more mainstream religions. Any simple attempt at categorization is inevitably doomed, in the same way that using the term "Buddhist" or "Hindu" may cover a number of different expressions of a belief system. Some kind of guide, however, is still useful for understanding.

Esoteric Movements

Esoteric movements can be referred to as "occult" movements because they most often practice hidden or secret knowledge within their groups, where only the initiated have access to it. Many of today's Esoteric movements borrow from several older traditions originating in the synthesis of Western (Judeo-Christian) and Eastern (Buddhist or Sufi) thought. Others follow a form of Gnosticism (see units 9:1 and 9:2), where the emphasis is on secret knowledge for the elite few—e.g., the Great White Brotherhood where the aura of white light is believed to surround the Ascended Masters who have guarded the true religious teaching for centuries. In this unit, we look at a representative few movements that have been influential (e.g., Theosophy) or which are becoming so (e.g., The Raelian Religion).

Neo-Pagan or Pagan Movements

"Neo-pagan" is used to describe people who are part of the revival of some of the beliefs and practices of pre-Christian religions. Neo-pagans often drop the prefix and just call themselves pagans.

The pagan and neo-pagan response to religion has been increasing since the middle of the twentieth century. Interest in paganism today in the United Kingdom and the United States has been interpreted as a response to the dissatisfaction many people feel about the way the world is progressing ecologically, spiritually, and materially. Many people are also disillusioned with traditional mainstream religions and the realization that materialism cannot satisfy the inner life of the spirit.

Paganism revives the old gods and goddesses of the pre-Christian polytheistic nature religions and mystery cults (e.g., Celtic, Norse, Greek, Egyptian, and Roman). Pagans are also interested in Sumerian mythologies, tribal religions (e.g., Native American religions and shamanism), science fiction and fantasy, and occultic traditions. Astaroth, Diana, Osiris, and Pan are newly invoked among some adherents. Among the pagan movement are the witches or Wiccans—followers of the "Old Religion" of the great Mother Goddess and her male consort, the Horned God.

The word "pagan" comes from the Latin words *paganus* and *pagana*, meaning "country dweller" or villager. Most neo-pagan traditions share a selection of the following factors:

- A faith that was almost wiped out in the past and has since been reconstructed from ancient sources of information.
- Celebration of main seasonal days each year, associated with the equinoxes; solstices; solar and lunar rites; and fertility, planting and harvest festivals.
- Neo-pagans may be lone practitioners or small groups, which various traditions call covens, garths, circles, groves, hearths, etc. The largest Neo-pagan group is believed to be Wiccans.
- Minimal or no hierarchical structure.

Beliefs

A number of beliefs are common to pagans:

- Duotheistic or polytheistic beliefs that recognize a Goddess and God, and/or believe in many deities.

- A pantheistic worldview, seeing deity as immanent and alive in all things, as opposed to a transcendent view of God.
- Love for, and kinship with, Nature and the realization that all of life is a manifestation of the Divine and therefore sacred. Harming oneself, others, or nature is to be avoided.
- Experience is more important than belief, so the emphasis is on participation and creativity in ritual and a search for the ecstatic.
- The Pagan ethic of "Do what thou wilt, but harm none." Each individual is responsible for discovering his or her own true nature and developing it fully, in harmony with the outer world.
- Humans are meant to have the wisdom and ability to solve their problems without the need for spiritual salvation.
- Decentralization, with hundreds of autonomous or semiautonomous groups. Hierarchical religious organizations, self-appointed messiahs, and gurus are to be avoided.

Recent Religious and Philosophical Roots

From the romantic movement of the nineteenth century came the desire to promote feelings and imagination over the intellect. Thus, the poetry of William Blake is often very influential for pagans.

An important figure in the growth of modern paganism is Alphonse Louis Constant (1810–1875), who called himself Eliphas Levi. He was an ex-Roman Catholic seminarian who described himself as an occult initiate. In his books, Levi claimed he was revealing ancient mysteries and occult laws. His writings drew heavily on various theories of magic and the Kabbalah.

The Foundation of the Order of the Golden Dawn

In Britain, the growth of modern paganism was encouraged by the foundation of the Order of the Golden Dawn in 1888, a famous esoteric group with ongoing influence that grew out of nineteenth-century romanticism. The Order was a secret society similar to the Freemasons and the Rosicrucians because it awarded "degrees" as its members ascended the spiritual ladder. The Order put an emphasis on the study of magical theory and ritual and was successful in influencing the poet W. B. Yeats and the black-magic practitioner Aleister Crowley. Many pagan, ritual magic, and satanistic groups trace their origins to these sources.

Branches of Paganism

The main branches of paganism in the United Kingdom and United States are Shamanism, Goddess Spirituality, Sacred Ecology, and other various magical groups. The two predominant and most public of these are Wicca and Druidry (studied in subsequent units of this book). One recent neo-pagan movement is the Pagan Pathfinders, established in the 1970s in Britain. They use pagan practices combined with practical psychology in order to achieve altered and heightened states of consciousness and to accelerate the rate of personal growth. This practice includes "God-casting," where the group member is assigned to a particular Pagan god or goddess who, when evoked, sends divine power and attributes to the person. Neo-Paganism today often feels at home in the New Age movement.

Neo-Paganism and Fundamentalist Religion

Neo-pagans regard the use of the word "pagan" to describe an idolater or a believer in a false god as the legacy of Christian persecution and misunderstanding of pagan beliefs and practice. As Margot Adler (1986) writes:

> We are not evil. We don't harm or seduce people. We are not dangerous. We are ordinary people like you. We have families, jobs, hopes, and dreams. We are not a cult. This religion is not a joke. We are not what you think we are from looking at TV. We are real. We laugh, we cry. We are serious. We have a sense of humour. You don't have to be afraid of us. We don't want to convert you. And please don't try to convert us. Just give us the same right we give you—to live in peace. We are much more similar to you than you think.

The Occult

I have chosen to use the word "occult," although I am well aware of the negative overtones it carries with many of the world's faiths. The word "occult" comes from the Latin *occultus*, which means "concealed" or "hidden." Occult teachings are currently widely available and so the use of the word is variously applied. Traditionally it referred to knowledge and practice that was beyond the bounds of ordinary knowledge, mysterious, concealed, or hidden from view and available only to those who sought it. Some people still use this meaning.

Three areas of occult can be identified:

1. Forms of Divination (fortune-telling): This area includes soothsaying or augury. The most prevalent form in America is astrology. Others are palmistry, tarot cards, numerology, Ouija, pendulum, and runes.

2. Forms of Psychic Experiences: Experiences that transcend the bounds of the ordinary physical world or the five senses. Examples would be out-of-body experiences, remote viewing, telekinesis, necromancy, trances, and psychic healing.

3. Magick: All types of magick involve use of the will and the imagination. In the esoteric schools, adepts train in visualization techniques and the focus of the will. In unit 11:5 on New Age religion, reference is made by implication to the many thousands of people involved in the New Age movement but who belong to no specific movement. They use a number of means—such as horoscopes, herbal remedies, tarot, and divination—that belong to older and more formal movements.

World Religions and the Occult

A distinction is often made between religion and magic (or magick). The religious objection to magick and the occult rests on the belief that it attempts to manipulate divine forces through human acts. In traditional religions, the prevailing attitude when performing acts such as prayer and sacrifice is one of awe, worship, and thanksgiving.

In the sacred texts of the world, the practices of communing with the dead and communicating with spirits are deeply distrusted and prohibited. Since they may not be compared to ultimate reality, spirits are not privy to the highest truth. Christianity, Judaism, and Islam have a tradition that groups of angels have fallen into error and misunderstood the will of God. Occult practices—such as seeking information from mediums, witches, astrologers, and otherwise penetrating the world of spirits—is condemned in many scriptures because it can lead people astray through communication with spirits from the lower realms.

Based on the higher truth of the revealed or taught word, the belief that the spiritual world is populated by evil spirits, demons, fallen angels, and Satan—as well as intermediate spiritual beings including the jinn, spirits of the dead, and various classes of ghosts—leads to teachings that each person should "test the spirits to see whether they are of God."

> Lord, how can a god or a demon know all the extent of your glory? You alone know what you are, by the light of your innermost nature. (Hinduism. *Bhagavad Gita* 10.14)

Practitioners of magic are mentioned in the Bible: the magicians of Egypt (Exodus 8), King Manasseh (2 Kings 21:1–9), Jezebel (2 Kings 9:22), Simon (Acts 8:9–24), and Bar-Jesus (Acts 13:4–12). Involvement in magical practices was forbidden and punishable by death under the Mosaic Law.

> No one shall be found among you . . . who uses divination, or is a soothsayer, or an augur, or a sorcerer, or one who casts spells, or who consults ghosts or spirits, or who seeks oracles from the dead. For whoever does these things is abhorrent to the LORD. . . . (Deuteronomy 18:10–12 [see also Ex. 22:18; Isa. 47:9–15; and in the New Testament, see Gal. 5:20; Rev. 18:23–24])

> My follower does not study the practice of magic and spells. He does not analyze dreams and signs in sleep and movements in the Zodiac. (Buddhism. Sutta Nipata 927)

> Cursed be occult and miracle-making powers. (Sikhism. Var Sorath 20, M.3, 650)

> Beloved, do not believe every spirit, but test the spirits to see whether they are from God; for many false prophets have gone out into the world. (Christianity. Bible, 1 John 4:1)

UNIT 11:1 THE ROSICRUCIANS

> *. . . the kind of spirituality which is developed by and associated with the emotional nature of the desire body is unreliable in the extreme; this is the variety that is generated in revival meetings where emotionalism is brought up to a high pitch, causing a person to make a great splurge of religious fervor which soon spends itself and leaves him exactly as he was before. . . . They set out to save souls with drums and fifes, with rhythmic revival songs. . . . The vital body is much more set, and it is only when conversion affects this vehicle that it sticks and stays with a man or woman for life. Those who have the true spirituality do not feel saved one day, in the seventh heaven of ecstasy, and the next feel themselves down in the dumps and miserable sinners that can never be forgiven; for their religion is not based upon the emotional nature which feels these things, but is rooted in the vital body which is the vehicle of reason, set and persistent in the path it has once chose. As new forms are propagated through the second ether of the vital body, so the HIGHER SELF, the CHRIST WITHIN, is formed through this same vehicle of generation, the vital body, in its higher aspects embodied in the two upper ethers.*
>
> Max Heindel, *The Web of Destiny*

Rosicrucians do not put forward a definitive body of religious beliefs, but their teachings contain a number of powerful religious and esoteric ideas, including metaphysics, gnosticism, astrology, mysticism, alchemy, psychology, parapsychology, and science, with close links to Freemasonry. The term "Rosicrucian" (Latin = rosy cross) first appeared around 1614 in Germany with three anonymous publications: *The Praiseworthy Order of the Rosy Cross, The Confession of the Rosicrucian Fraternity*, and *The Chymical Marriage of Christian Rosenkreutz.* These books told the life story of Christian Rosenkreutz who was said to have lived to be 106 years old (1378–1484). His tomb was discovered in 1604, but to everyone's amazement, the story goes, his body was uncorrupted.

The three pamphlets were probably written by the Lutheran pastor Johan Valentin Andrea (1586–1654). Together, they focus on initiation into the mysteries of the East (particularly of ancient Egypt). Taken together, the works purport to be a message from advanced spiritual masters concerned for the condition of mankind. Some scholars have seen it as a brotherhood of disappointed Lutherans dissatisfied with the ongoing effects of a hundred years of Reformation history.

The pamphlets of the Order of the Rosy Cross can be seen to have drawn on various literary and alchemist sources such as:

- Hermetic and neo-Platonic scriptures in circulation at the time.
- Neo-Platonist writer Edmund Spenser, who had published *The Faerie Queene* in 1590, which concerns an English knight "Red Cross."

- Alchemistic writings such as the conception, "As above, so below"—pointing to the belief that man mirrors the whole universe.
- Famous alchemist and Swiss physician Paracelsus (1493–1541).

In the *Fama Fraternitas (The Praiseworthy Order of the Rosy Cross)*, all learned men throughout the world are exhorted to join forces towards the establishment of a synthesis of science. It has been said that behind these writings were ideas of an illuminated brotherhood: the children of light, people who had been initiated in the mysteries of the Grand Order. This "Brüderschaft der Theosophen" was said to be founded by Christian Rosencreutz, who had become an initiate during his travels in the Middle East in the fifteenth century. He is said to have founded a brotherhood that has operated in secret to this day.

Soon after the publication of the three pamphlets, other Rosicrucian writings appeared, including one by the Hermetic philosopher and physician Robert Fludd (1574–1637).

The Rosicrucian movement caused quite a stir in European circles and many people applied for initiation, but no records show that the brotherhood survived for very long. By 1623 the German Rosicrucian movement was at the mercy of the Counter-Reformation led by the Jesuits. This era was noted for witch-hunts and the hibernation of occult and esoteric activity. In the eighteenth century several Rosicrucian groups were active in Russia, Poland, and Germany, with a resurgence of interest and growth in the nineteenth century, especially in Britain and America. In 1858 the Fraternitas Rosae Crucis was formed, followed by the Societas Rosicruciana in Anglia in 1865 and the Rosicrucian Fellowship in 1907.

The Growth of Rosicrucianism

The Ancient and Mystical Order Rosae Crucis (AMORC) is the largest and best known of the Rosicrucian groups in America. The organization was formed by Harvey Spencer Lewis (1883–1939), a writer and occultist from New York City who had also founded The New York Institute for Psychical Research in 1904. In 1917 the first national convention approved plans to teach people through correspondence lessons. Through this the movement spread rapidly, and in the 1930s Lewis developed the headquarters complex to include the Rose-Croix University (1934), a planetarium (1936), and the Rosicrucian Research Library (1939). The famous Egyptian Museum has become a popular tourist attraction in San Jose.

AMORC has two publications: *The Rosicrucian Digest* (monthly) and *The Rosicrucian Forum*, for members only. Chapters all over the world put forward the Rosicrucian philosophy of developing humankind's highest potential and psychic powers. The Order's home study course sets out to teach useful techniques to awaken a higher understanding through a process that Rosicrucian students call "self-mastery." AMORC claims that its study process involves ancient truths incorporated into practical, time-tested techniques providing "safe, gradual development of your natural psychic and spiritual abilities."

Rosicrucian Organizations

A variety of Rosicrucian organizations around the world have very differing teachings and beliefs. Whereas some trace their ancestry back to the early times of the movement, others do not. Secrecy is also a factor because of the links between Rosicrucianism and Freemasonry, especially in the higher ranks of the movement. The Lectorium Rosicrucianum or the International School of the Golden Rosycross has centers in Britain and America and over twenty other countries and its magazine *Pentagram* appears in ten different languages.

Beliefs

Some common factors are present over many of the movements—especially the emphasis placed on symbols, including the Pentagras, which is the eternal symbol of the reborn, new human being. The Rosicrucian movement is a blend of mystical and esoteric beliefs and practices including:

- Drawing upon the higher knowledge already within you.
- Accessing your own source of inner wisdom and guidance.
- Developing natural abilities that may have been left dormant throughout your life.
- Initiations conferred in the Temple of a Rosicrucian Lodge drawing on ancient esoteric initiations and mystery-dramas referring to a unique gnosis—that is, knowledge that is revealed to the candidate for initiation.

AMORC rites and ceremonies focus on:

- Causing engagement in introspection, i.e., turning your consciousness within.
- Engendering feelings of aspiration and idealism.
- Exacting a sacred obligation to try and fulfill one's aspirations.

The Rosicrucian Fellowship

Esoteric links can be directly traced between the Theosophical Society and Rosicrucian groups. The Rosicrucian Fellowship was founded by Max Heindel (1865–1919) in 1907. He was an engineer with deep occult interests that led him to the Theosophical Society. His book, *The Rosicrucian Cosmo-Conception*, is a central text of the Fellowship. Heindel's teachings promote the occult worldview of Theosophy. He also drew on the astrological themes of Theosophy, and two of his works *Simplified Scientific Astrology* and *The Message of the Stars* were at the heart of the twentieth-century revival of astrology in America:

> It is a matter of common knowledge among mystics that the evolutionary career of mankind is indissolubly bound up with the divine hierarchies who rule the planets and the signs of the Zodiac, and that passage of the Sun and the planets through the twelve signs of the Zodiac marks man's progress in time and in space. (Max Heindel and Augusta Foss Heindel, *The Message of the Stars*)

The Rosicrucian Fellowship still emphasizes astrology by publishing *Ephemeris*, the annual table of the position of the planets in the astrological signs.

Heindel's ideas have inspired many New Age beliefs. See, for example, his teaching on the newborn Christ from chapter 22 of *Gleanings of a Mystic*

> It has often been said in our literature that the sacrifice of Christ was not an event which, taking place on Golgotha, was accomplished in a few hours once and for all time, but that the mystic births and deaths of the Redeemer are continual cosmic occurrences. We may therefore conclude that this sacrifice is necessary for our physical and spiritual evolution during the present phase of our development. As the annual birth of the Christ Child approaches, it presents a never old, ever new theme for meditation, from which we may profit by pondering it with a prayer that it may create in our hearts a new light to guide us upon the path of regeneration.

Rosicrucian Anthroposophic League

S. R. Parchment, a former member of the Rosicrucian Fellowship, was the founder of the Rosicrucian Anthroposophic League in San Francisco in the 1930s. He has written several books putting forward his own version of Rosicrucian teachings: *Steps to Self Master*, *Operative Masonry*, *The Middle Path*, and *The Just Law of Compensation*. The Anthroposophic League also published a magazine, *Rosicrucian Quarterly*.

The occult basis of the Anthroposophic League can be summarized in the League's directives, as follows:

1. Investigate the occult laws of nature and the superphysical powers of man.
2. Promote the principles that will eventually lead to recognition of the truth of the universal brotherhood of man, without distinction as to sex, creed, race, or color.
3. Acquire, disseminate, and exemplify a knowledge of spiritual truth as given to the world by the Elder Brothers of the White Lodge.
4. Study and teach ancient religion, philosophy, and astrology in the light of modern needs.

5. Encourage the study of science and art in the hope that religion, art, and science—which are a veritable trinity, the equilateral triangle that has always been used as a symbol of the Divine—may again be recognized as portals through which egos must pass in attaining to the mastery of self.
6. Attain to self-conscious immortality, which is the crowning feat of evolution.

Lectorium Rosicrucianum

The Lectorium Rosicrucianum, formed in 1971 by former members of the Rosicrucian Fellowship in Holland under the initiative of J. Van Rijckenborgh, has centers in Britain, America, and over two dozen other countries. Its central teachings are their own particular version of Christian Gnosticism, with the idea of two nature orders contrasting the spiritual world (good) with the material world (evil). The one order is the one we know here on earth, containing both the living and the dead. The other is "the original divine nature-order," which is also known as the kingdom of heaven. The human heart contains a remnant of this Divine Spark, also called Rose of the Heart, which energizes us to search and seek for a state of immortality and oneness with God. Lectorium Rosicrucianism also believes that we are bound by the endless cycles of reincarnation; the way to escape the cycles is through transfiguration—that is, by giving up our lives in order to participate in God's original order. The resurrection of Jesus Christ is an example of such a sacrifice. The American headquarters of the Lectorium are in Bakersfield, California. Rijckenborgh's books include his main work, *Dei Gloria Intacta*.

Other Rosicrucian societies include the Ausar Auset Society, formed around 1980.

UNIT 11:2 GURDJIEFF AND OUSPENSKY

> *There so exist enquiring minds which long for the truth of the heart, seek it, strive to solve the problems set by life, try to penetrate to the essence of things and phenomena and to penetrate into themselves. If a man reasons and thinks soundly, no matter which path he follows in solving these problems, he must inevitably arrive back at himself, and begin with the solution of the problem of what he is himself and what his place is in the world around him. For without this knowledge, he will have no focal point in his search. Socrates' words, "Know thyself," remain for all those who seek true knowledge and being.*
>
> Gurdjieff, *Views from the Real World*

Georgei Ivanovitch Gurdjieff (c. 1874–1949) was the son of a Greek father and an American mother living in Armenia. As a young man he was deeply interested and involved in the world of the supernatural and the esoteric. Some scholars see Gurdjieff's travels as mythical rather than historical. He spent a number of years traveling in the Far East and especially Tibet, where he claimed to have studied under the masters of ancient wisdom. There he learned techniques such as hypnotism and yoga and was influenced by Sufism. He was part of an expedition to the Gobi Desert and also involved in trying to find an ancient brotherhood belonging to Babylon in 2500 B.C.E.. As well as these explorations, he was a very able businessman, setting up commercial ventures such as carpet trading and antiques wherever he traveled and at the same time collecting a group of like-minded people who also sought religious wisdom. He arrived back in Moscow just before the First World War and started passing on the things that he had learned. At this time he came into contact with the Russian mathematician and mystical philosopher Peter Demianovich Ouspensky (1878–1947), who had returned from studying religions in Egypt and India and who had been influenced by Theosophy. He offered a "fourth way." Ouspensky's work was methodical and systematic, and he later wrote his own book clarifying and codifying Gurdjieff's teachings.

Beliefs

Gurdjieff taught that modern "man" is an undeveloped creation with an imbalance and overdependence on the thinking function. Gurdjieff's teachings were centered on restoring the balance, representing a "fourth way" [moving on from the ways of the *fakir* (physical austerity), the monk (development of the emotions), and the yogi (the intellectual reflection)]. Man is not really man, in the sense that he is a unique being whose intelligence and force of action mirror the energies of the source of life itself. Tragically, today man is an automaton and his thoughts, emotions, and actions are barely different from mechanical reactions to external and internal stimuli. Influences such as culture and education serve to engrave in people the illusion of autonomous, conscious selves. The overwhelming truth therefore is that man is asleep. On meeting people there is no authentic "I am" but only an egoism masquerading as the authentic self, and pitifully reflecting the normal human functions of thought, feeling, and will.

The Deceptive "I"

Gurdjieff's basic teaching was that human beings need to be awakened, challenging the mechanical habits that prevent us from being in touch with ourselves. Gurdjieff's goal was in waking man up so that he does not sleepwalk through life. Many factors reinforce this sleep, especially the deceptive sense of "I." An individual has many "I"s, each imagining itself to be the whole, and each separated off from the others. Each of these many I's uses and squanders the energy of consciousness, which as a result is absorbed and degraded. Gurdjieff called this process "identification." Man identifies, or rather squanders, his conscious energy with each passing thought, impulse, and sensation. This energy expresses itself as a form of continuous egoistic emotions, such as anger, self-pity, and fear, which bring pain so that everyone is constantly driven to relieve their condition through the endless and fruitless pursuit of social acclaim, sensory pleasure, or the illusory goal of "happiness."

The Interconnection between Humanity and the Universe

In Gurdjieff's teaching, psychology is inextricably linked with cosmology, metaphysics, and even biology. According to Gurdjieff, the human condition cannot be understood apart from its connection with organic life on earth. The human being is so designed that he or she can transform energies of a specific nature; without this transformation of energy the human nature cannot be properly understood. Man cannot participate consciously in the great universal order of the cosmos but instead is limited to the functions of organic life on earth.

The Ray of Creation and the Food Diagram

How can human beings change their impoverished state and instead draw on the universal conscious energies that they were designed to absorb but which now pass through them untransformed?

"The Food Diagram" and the "Ray of Creation" diagram in the teaching of Gurdjieff illustrate the manner in which different qualities of energy are assimilated and also evolve (according to the law of the octave) in the human organism. An explanation of the diagrams can be found in chapters 5, 7, and 9 of *In Search of the Miraculous*. The Ray of Creation and the Food Diagram are both complex and extraordinary in their ideas, yet they represent only a fraction of the spiritual concepts contained in the book. The many ideas in the book are all interrelated. For example, the Ray of Creation and the Food Diagram are inseparable from Gurdjieff's teaching about the fundamental law of three forces and the law of the sevenfold development of energy (the Law of Octaves). The interrelationship of these laws are shown in the symbol of the enneagram. The outworking of these ideas in individuals cannot be separated from Gurdjieff's teaching about the tripartite division of human nature, the three "centers" of mind, feeling, and body.

Methods of Awakening: The Prieuré at Fontainebleu

Gurdjieff finally settled in France. In 1922 he established his Institute for the Harmonious Development of Man at the Chateau du Prieuré at Fontainebleau near Avon, close to Paris. Activities at the Prieuré have been well detailed in numerous books, but even so the daily activities of the Prieuré still evoke astonishment. By all accounts, Gurdjieff created a community life throbbing with a vital and uncompromising search for truth that involved extremely demanding physical work, intensive emotional encounters, and eclectic spiritual studies, all of which were designed to break unconscious habits and to provide opportunity for unquestioning submission to a teacher; as he said, "One must learn from one who knows."

The practice of the disciplines and exercises was aimed at reaching a higher level of consciousness, but Gurdjieff stressed that the path is long and requires personal death to self-love:

> All religions speak about death during this life on earth. Death must come before rebirth. But what must die? False confidence in one's own knowledge, self-love and egoism. Our egoism must be broken. We must realize that we are very complicated machines, and so this process of breaking is bound to be a long and difficult task. Before real growth becomes possible, our personality must die. (Gurdjieff, *Views from the Real World* [1973])

Breathing, Dancing, and Music

Gurdjieff adopted a new interpretation of Pythagoras's esoteric teaching on the numerical significance of rhythm and the functions of the body. His followers also engaged in mystical dance similar to the Sufi dervishes, advanced breathing exercises, and physical exercises performed to music.

Beliefs about the Self

Gurdjieff taught that each person could transform themselves through a process of self-study leading them to inner growth and change in the inner consciousness. Each person exists on one of seven rungs of an evolutionary ladder:

Instinctive motor man

Emotional man

Intellectual man

Transitional man

Integrated man

Conscious man

The complete man

Ascent up the ladder comes by acquiring wisdom through self-study, self-awareness, self-remembering, and the discovery of the essential unchanging I. His writings are infused with this theme:

> I cannot develop you; I can create conditions in which you can develop yourself.

Gurdjieff and Ouspensky

The break between Ouspensky and Gurdjieff is described graphically in *In Search of the Miraculous* (1949). Ouspensky maintained a spiritual connection with Gurdjieff, but as early as 1918 Ouspensky began to feel that a break with Gurdjieff was inevitable. The break between them has been explained in various ways but never completely understood.

The work of Ouspensky, however, went on in London and then later in New York. Ouspensky's book *Tertium Organum* had been successfully published in England in the early 1920s and had established his reputation as a metaphysical writer.

The Prieuré attracted many artists and literary figures from America and England, many of whom were sent by Ouspensky while he was lecturing in London. Long before psychology was working in these areas, Ouspensky was seriously experimenting with altered states of consciousness and their effect on perception and cognition. His studies helped him to conclude that new categories of thought were needed apart from the classical and positivist forms that had dominated Western thought for over two thousand years. *Tertium Organum* reports the outcome of his experiments and the idea of, "eternal recurrence," that is, the concept that higher forms of knowledge must inevitably connect with the development of the capacity for feeling. In other words, the perception of truth is inseparable from the development of inner moral power. These basic ideas influenced the writings of many modern philosophers and writers both in the West and in Russia. Ouspensky used his own experience as well as traditional conceptual thinking in his work and experiments, thus placing him nearer empiricist methodology.

Gurdjieff's Influence

In 1920s France, Gurdjieff's institute had already achieved fame when he took the dying writer Katherine Mansfield into the community of the Prieuré. She was suffering from tuberculosis. Gurdjieff liked to dabble in medicine and told her to ignore her disease and sleep in the loft above the cowshed. Everyone was surprised at her apparent cure, but a week later she died at age thirty-five. In the late 1920s and early 1930s, several other well-known figures became students, notably Rene Daumal, Margaret Anderson, and Kathryn Hulme. Daumal's writings, especially his unfinished work *Mount Analogue,* are among the most reliable literary expressions of key aspects of Gurdjieff's teaching.

The Gurdjieff Foundation

After Gurdjieff's death in 1949, his work was carried on by his closest pupil, Jeanne de Salzmann, under whose oversight centers of study have been established in Paris, New York, London, and elsewhere. Gurdjieff and Ouspensky movements often included study of the Kabbalah and the study of Tarot. Ouspensky's book on Tarot is still available today. The ongoing influence of Gurdjieff's ideas is incalculable. He is well espoused and sometimes poorly imitated within New Age spirituality. He has influenced several schools of thought, including The School of Economic Science and Rajneeshism. Some of his sayings appear timeless in the sense that they challenge religious believers anywhere to rethink their life and its values:

> Religion is doing; a man does not merely think his religion or feel it, he "lives" his religion as much as he is able, otherwise it is not religion but fantasy or philosophy. Whether he likes it or not he shows his attitude towards religion by his actions and he can show his attitude only by his actions. Therefore if his actions are opposed to those which are demanded by a given religion he cannot assert that he belongs to that religion. (From *In Search of the Miraculous*)
>
> Re-member yourself.
> Live a life of friction. Let yourself be disturbed as much as possible, but observe.
> We waste our lives in associations, chiefly associations of words. Think at night of your words. Our words are aped.
> . . . Knowledge cannot come to people without effort on their part.

UNIT 11:3 THEOSOPHY AND ANTHROPOSOPHY

> *What several rather mystical Scientists taught was that light, heat, magnetism, electricity and gravity, etc., were not the final causes of the visible phenomena, including planetary motion, but themselves the Secondary effects of other causes, for which Science in our day cares very little, but in which Occultism believes, for the Occultists have exhibited proofs of the validity of their claims in every age. And in what age were there no Occultists and no ADEPTS?*
>
> Madame Blavatsky, *Secret Doctrine*

The name "Theosophy" is derived from the Greek: *Theos* (God) and *sophia* (wisdom); hence, Theosophia or Theosophy. Many of the prevailing concepts and ideas of Theosophy are ancient and would have been well known in the classical Greek world. The theosophical writings of Jakob Boehme (1575–1624) have been deeply influential on many Christian movements and groups, such as Quakerism, and individuals such as the modern theologian Paul Tillich and the phenomenologist Martin Heidegger. The modern Theosophical movement cites its origins from the founding of the Theosophical Society in New York City in 1875 by Helena Petrovna Blavatsky (1831–1891), Henry Steel Olcott, and others. Blavatsky was born in Russia into an affluent family. She traveled widely (1848–1858) to the East in search of spiritual understanding of the purpose of human existence. Blavatsky believed in an ancient society of Masters or Adepts possessing understanding of the Divine Wisdom, and she claimed to have been taught by these Masters while in Tibet. After her return she founded the Société Spirite in Cairo. In 1873 she emigrated to New York and in 1874 met Colonel Henry Steel Olcott, with whom she shared an esoteric search. Together with William Q. Judge they founded the Theosophical Society. Olcott was a Civil War veteran who became the first president of the Theosophical Society and extended its influence greatly.

Madame Blavatsky and Spiritualism

Madame Blavatsky practiced a form of spiritualism that combined the old fashioned medium séance with a vocabulary borrowed from Hindu mysticism, the Jewish Kabbalah, and European neo-Platonist hermeticism. Her performances included sensational stunts that brought in the crowds to see the spirits who continued to visit her séances.

Upon moving its headquarters from New York to Adyar in India in 1879, the Theosophical Society linked itself for a short time to the charismatic Hindu reformer and anti-British agitator, Swami Sarasvati Dayanand. The Adyar compound became a rallying point for radical Indian college students involved in the fight against the Raj. Meanwhile, The British Society for Psychical Research sent out Austrian Richard Hodgson to examine the questionable phenomena accompanying Blavatsky's meetings. Hodgson argued that the spirit emanations at regular séances were a collection of bedsheets on strings, and the magic materialization cabinet was a crude trap-door-and-mirror. In 1855 she moved to London, where she wrote her major work, *The Secret Doctrine*.

In 1885 she moved again, to Germany. She died in 1891.

Annie Besant

Another notable figure in the movement was Annie Wood Besant (d. 1933), a radical feminist campaigner and a member of the Fabian Society. At nineteen, Annie married the young Rev. Frank Besant, and within four years they had a daughter and a son. In the process of serving the needy she came to believe that to alleviate poverty and suffering, deeper social changes were needed. When her religious beliefs began to change, she refused to attend Communion, at which point her husband ordered her out of their home. She moved to London and broke away from Christianity to become a freethinker and atheist. In 1874 she joined The Secular Society.

She was soon working for the radical paper, *National Reformer*, whose editor Charles Bradlaugh was also a leader in the secular (nonreligious) movement in England. In partnership, Bradlaugh and Besant wrote a book advocating birth control, only to receive a six-month prison sentence for "obscene libel," which was overturned on appeal. Her London home became the U.K. headquarters of the Theosophical Society, and her intellectual strengths ensured the ongoing growth of the movement after the death of its founders. Annie Besant was well known in the Indian society of her day for her work in education and politics. She founded several schools (one of which became the University of Benares) and became the president of the Indian National Congress. She also committed herself wholeheartedly to the Boy Scouts movement and was involved in Co-Masonry, a branch of Freemasonry that gave equal status and admittance to men and women. Annie joined forces with the Rev. Charles W. Leadbetter, and their partnership steered the direction of the Society towards Esoteric Christianity rather than Buddhism. The Rev. Leadbetter was responsible for discovering the young Jiddu Krishnamurti (1895–1986), who announced himself the Maitreya or fifth Buddha (Gautama was the fourth), the living incarnation of a Master. Both Annie Besant and the Rev. Leadbetter promoted Krishnamurti by founding the organization the Order of the Star in the East (1911), which he was to lead.

Annie Besant's activism included working against unhealthy industrial conditions and low wages for young factory women, leading strikes, and advocating free meals for poor schoolchildren. She was a popular speaker for women's rights, and she continued to work for the legalization of birth control. She also gained a science degree from London University. Her ongoing writing defended free thought and atheism and produced the pamphlet (with Charles Bradlaugh) "Why I Do Not Believe in God," which is still considered one of the best publications defending atheism. The following is a quote from this remarkable and controversial woman.

> Never forget that life can only be nobly inspired and rightly lived if you take it bravely and gallantly, as a splendid adventure in which you are setting out into an unknown country, to meet many a joy, to find many a comrade, to win and lose many a battle.

Beliefs, Philosophy, and Objectives of the Theosophical Society

The movement sees itself as contemporary expression of a tradition going back to the Hellenistic gnostics and neo-Platonists of classical antiquity. Theosophy has three main objectives:

- To form a nucleus of the universal brotherhood of humanity, without distinction of race, creed, sex, caste, or color.
- To encourage the comparative study of religion, philosophy, and science.
- To investigate unexplained laws of nature and the powers latent in humanity.

The Universal Brotherhood

Madame Blavatsky said:

> It is well known that the first rule of the society is to carry out the object of forming the nucleus of a universal brotherhood. The practical working of this rule was explained by those who laid it down, to the following effect:
>
> "He who does not practice altruism; he who is not prepared to share his last morsel with a man weaker or poorer than himself; he who neglects to help his brother man, of whatever race, nation or creed, whenever and wherever he meets suffering, and who turns a deaf ear to the cry of human misery; he who hears an innocent person slandered, whether a brother Theosophist or not, and does not undertake his defence as he would undertake his own—is no Theosophist." (H. P. Blavatsky, in "Let Every Man Prove His Own Work," 1887, CW 8:170–71.)

Theosphy holds that Matter and Spirit are the two main elements of the universe, and everything continues to evolve to a higher plane of spiritual awareness and interconnectedness. In the fundamental unity of all existence, all dichotomies—e.g., matter and spirit, the human and the divine—are seen as transitory aspects of an underlying absolute Oneness.

Through reincarnation, according to Theosophists, a person becomes more aware of unity with the Divine One. After a long cycle of reincarnations one can attain enlightenment, which is attaining unity with all other parts of the universe.

The Earth and humanity are both going through stages. The Earth is in its fourth stage and man is in his fifth. "The human body is comprised of seven qualities: divine, monadic, spiritual, intuitional, mental, astral and physical."

Theosophy is nondogmatic, but many Theosophists believe in reincarnation, karma (or moral justice), the existence of worlds of experience beyond the physical, the presence of life and consciousness in all, the power of thought to affect one's self and surroundings, free will, self-responsibility, altruism, and a concern for the welfare of others.

> If Theosophy, prevailing in the struggle, its all-embracing philosophy strikes deep root into the minds and hearts of men, if its doctrines of Reincarnation and Karma, in other words, of

> Hope and Responsibility, find a home in the lives of the new generations, then, indeed, will dawn the day of joy and gladness for all who now suffer and are outcast. For real Theosophy is Altruism, and we cannot repeat it too often. It is brotherly love, mutual help, unswerving devotion to Truth. If once men do but realize that in these alone can true happiness be found, and never in wealth, possessions or any selfish gratification, then the dark clouds will roll away, and a new humanity will be born upon earth. Then, the Golden Age will be there, indeed. (H. P. Blavatsky, "Our Cycle and the Next," 1889, CW 11:202)

Theosophist Practices and Texts

Theosophy has no developed rituals. Meetings typically consist of talks and discussion or the study of a book. There may be brief meditations or recitals of short texts.

Theosophical writings and texts include *The Secret Doctrine*, *Isis Unveiled*, *The Key to Theosophy*, and *The Voice of the Silence*, all written by Blavatsky and considered to be divinely inspired.

Anthroposophy

Anthroposophy traces its roots back to Austro-Hungarian Rudolf Steiner (1861–1925), who joined the Theosophical Society around 1900 and became leader of the German section of the Society in 1902. For a while he joined various esoteric and occult cults, such as the Rite of Memphis and Misraime, a supposed occult Masonic Order. Most probably he also belonged to the Ordo Templi Orientis, a German occult society, founded in 1906, that studied and perhaps practiced sex magic.

Steiner was eclectic, with interests in agriculture, architecture, the arts, sciences, drama, literature, medicine, philosophy, and religion. His doctoral dissertation centered on Fichte's theory of knowledge. He presented many lectures (over six thousand in twenty-five years) and was the author of many books, including: *The Philosophy of Spiritual Activity* (1894), *Occult Science: An Outline* (1913), and *Investigations in Occultism* (1920). He gravitated towards Goethe's mystical ideas, and much of what Steiner wrote appears to be a reformulation of Hegel's philosophy. He disagreed with Marx, arguing that the spiritual drives history. Steiner lectured extensively in Europe on esoteric subjects, especially clairvoyance. In 1913 he left the Theosophical Society—because of a disagreement with Annie Besant and a shift in his own personal beliefs and practices—to found his own Anthroposophical Society.

Although Steiner had broken away from the Theosophical Society, he did not abandon the eclectic mysticism of the theosophists. He thought of his Anthroposophy as a "spiritual science." Believing that reality is essentially spiritual, he taught people to overcome the material world and to seek comprehension of the spiritual world by the higher, spiritual self. He taught a form of spiritual perception working independently of the body and the bodily senses. This special spiritual sense informed him about the occult.

Steiner's Occult Ideas

Steiner taught that people existed on Earth since the creation of the planet and that humans began as spirit forms and progressed through various stages to reach today's form. He said that humanity is currently living in the Post-Atlantis Period, which began with the gradual sinking of Atlantis in 7227 B.C. The Post-Atlantis Period is divided into seven epochs, the current one being the European-American Epoch, which is to continue until the year 3573. After this time, humans will regain the clairvoyant powers they allegedly possessed prior to the time of the ancient Greeks.

Steiner used a blend of ideas and doctrines derived from Hinduism and Christianity, occult and esoterica. He was especially attracted to two theosophical notions: (1) there is a distinct spiritual consciousness that provides direct access to higher spiritual truths; and (2) spiritual evolution is hindered by being stuck in the material world. His teachings included the following beliefs:

- Human beings used to have wisdom and were like God, but these powers have been lost.
- The world of matter is necessary but evil, for it traps our higher spiritual self.
- Deep within human beings is the lost nature, and through studying and meditating the human spirit can evolve and grow through four different levels: the senses, imagination, inspiration, and intuition.
- This spiritual evolution is a gradual process involving countless reincarnations in its unfolding.

Steiner believed that Christ's life, death, and resurrection were of prime importance. Christ is seen as the archetype of spiritual individuality, and he is entrapped in matter until his second coming, when his spirit will be liberated. This will cause a gradual process of spiritual evolution, which will mean the unfolding of countless reincarnations.

The Anthroposophical Church

The Anthroposophical Church, which was established by Steiner in 1922 and goes by the name of The Christian Community, ordains both men and women priests. The Church engages in rituals that are esoteric.

Steiner is also well-known for his contributions to the field of "child-centered education" and his founding of the Waldorf schools, which teach according to Steiner's principles. The term "Waldorf" schools comes from the school Steiner was asked to open for the children of workers at the Waldorf-Astoria cigarette factory in Stuttgart, Germany, in 1919. The first U.S. Waldorf school opened in New York City in 1928. Today the claim is that there are more than six hundred Waldorf schools in over thirty-two countries with approximately 120,000 students. Steiner's philosophy of education included the view that education is driven not by the needs of children, but by the economic needs of society. He argued that there is a danger in developing the imagination and understanding of young people if schools are dependent upon government. State-funded education will most likely lead to following a curriculum that serves the state, one that is mainly driven by economic and social policies. Steiner schools today have the challenge of harmonizing their practice with the founder's ideals. For example, television viewing tends to be discouraged because of its typical content and because it discourages the growth of the imagination. Waldorf schools also discourage computer use by young children and emphasize wide experience of arts and crafts.

Steiner designed the curriculum of his schools around his spiritual beliefs that we are each comprised of body, spirit, and soul. He believed that children pass through three seven-year stages and that education should be appropriate to the spirit for each stage.

1. At the first stage (birth to age seven) children best learn through imitation.
2. The second stage of growth (ages seven to fourteen) is characterized by imagination and fantasy; children in this stage learn best by acceptance and emulation of authority.
3. In the third stage (ages fourteen to twenty-one), the astral body is drawn into the physical body, causing puberty.

Although these anthroposophical ideas are not part of the standard Waldorf school curriculum, many Steinerian practitioners adhere to them.

One of the distinctive parts of the curriculum involves what Steiner called "eurythmy," an art of movement aiming to make visible what Steiner believed were the inner forms and gestures of language and music. According to the Waldorf FAQ, "it often puzzles parents new to Waldorf education, [but] children respond to its simple rhythms and exercises which help them strengthen and harmonize their body and their life forces."

Steiner made serious attempts to instruct the mentally and physically handicapped, believing that the spirit comprehends knowledge, and that the spirit is the same in all people, regardless of mental or physical differences. There is also the School of Spiritual Science near Basel in Switzerland. Steiner also synthesized and promoted his own spiritual and scientific version of organic farming long before it was fashionable.

Arcane School

The Arcane School is the organization established in 1923 by Alice Bailey to spread her own version of Theosophic beliefs and the teachings of the Great White Brotherhood. Alice Bailey clashed with Annie Besant over her belief that Jiddu Krishnamurti was the expected world savior. Instead, Alice Bailey claimed to have received spiritualist communications promising that Christ was to return in the form of the Buddhist Bodhisattva Maitreya. In recent years Benjamin Creme has claimed that he is the fulfillment of this prophecy. Through books and writings, the Arcane School has influenced the New Age movement.

UNIT 11:4 THE RAELIAN RELIGION

> *We are now today's human beings using tomorrow's technology, with yesterday's religions and yesterday's thinking. Thanks to the Elohim, we will be able to reach new spiritual levels by embracing their own religion, «an atheist one», that of infinity as represented by their symbol. The Guides of the Raelian Movement will become the priests of this new religion, allowing human beings to feel in harmony with the infinitely small and the infinitely great, allowing them to realise we are stardust and energy for ever.*
>
> Rael, *The True Face of God*

The Raelian movement is now called the Raelian religion and claims that the source of their movement is the revelation that came from extraterrestrial beings called the Elohim.

Raelian founder Claude Vorilhon says his mother Marie Vorilhon, a French citizen, was selected by extraterrestrial beings and inseminated by them on December 25, 1945. On December 13, 1973, ex-French automobile journalist Rael (Claude Vorilhon) was contacted by a visitor from another planet who asked him to establish an embassy to welcome these exraterrestrials back to Earth. He explains in his book, *The True Face of God*, that he was taken to the planet Elohim in a flying saucer in 1975 and introduced to such famous prophets as Jesus, Buddha, Joseph Smith, and Confucius. The Elohim are small, human-shaped beings with pale green skin and almond eyes, who informed Vorilhon that he was the final prophet with a mission to bring a message of peace and sensual meditation to humankind before the Elohim would return to Jerusalem in the year 2025.

The Raelian movement is unique among so-called UFO groups in its creation story, which ties it to the sacred books of the monotheistic traditions. The messages dictated to Rael (whose name means, "the messenger of those who come from the sky") explain that life on Earth is not a matter of random evolution or the work of a creator god. We were deliberately created by a race called The Elohim, who are far more advanced than people on earth. In the book of Genesis, in the creation story, the word "Elohim" has been mistranslated as "God" in the singular, but according to Rael the real meaning is "those who came from the sky." The Elohim created humanity in their own image by using DNA. They kept contact with the earth via the prophets, including The Buddha, Moses, Jesus, and Muhammad—who also left written references to the Elohim so that when humanity had advanced scientifically, they would recognize their creators.

> Now that Man has put his foot on the moon, and our scientists are creating life through the synthesis of DNA, we are finally capable of understanding our creators rationally instead of mystifying and dumbly adoring them.

This reason the Elohim have contacted Rael and asked him to communicate their last message to the world is so that he will form an embassy for them that will serve as a meeting place between the Elohim, the people of the world, and their governments. This communication is essential to them, so people will know the Elohim are not invaders and that they respect human choice. Therefore they can wait to be invited by earth to come. According to Rael, *"For us, they are the most important people in the universe. Would you send your guests out to sleep on the street, or do you invite them in to the love and warmth of your own home?"*

Nor do the Elohim wish to favor any government, religion, or ideology other than their own (Raelian Philosophy), so they will arrive at an embassy built by their own in Jerusalem.

Growth of the Movement

Since 1973, the Raelian Movement has grown to include forty thousand members worldwide. It is strongest in France, Canada, and Japan. The movement claims that the Raelians are experiencing strong growth in the United States, Australia, Southeast Asia, Latin America, Africa, Britain, and other European countries (Rael, *The Final Message*, 197). Recent expansion includes members in China and Hawaii.

By 1997, about $7 million had been raised for building the embassy for the Elohim. In 1990, Rael (with the blessing of the Elohim) changed the original symbol of the movement—a swastika inscribed in the Star of David—in an effort to improve prospects of obtaining land in Israel. Since 1991 there have been repeated requests to the Israeli government and the Chief Rabbi in Jerusalem for international neutral territory on which to build the embassy, but to no avail. Rael has suggested that the embassy may have to be built in Palestine or Egypt instead. In the preface to his book, *The True Face of God*, Rael expands on his vision of the embassy:

> Laboratories and universities will be built close to the embassy and there, under the guidance of the Elohim, human scientists

> will be able to improve their knowledge. In this way we will gradually approach the Elohim's scientific level. This will enable us to venture out to other planets to create life ourselves and we will become in our own turn "Elohim" for those we create.

See Rael http://rael.net/ for information on the letter written to Israel requesting land for the embassy.

Raelian Beliefs

Raelians believe . . .

- The Elohim are the creators of humanity.
- In a scientific translation of the Bible.
- An embassy must be built to welcome the Elohim.
- In the concept of Infinity.
- That the world has entered the Age of Apocalypse.
- That God is immaterial and DNA is the source of eternal life.
- In a future political system called geniocracy.
- In a world government based on humanitarianism.

God, the Soul, and Eternal Life

Raelians believe in a concept of God as Infinity, a concept without identity, and without consciousness of our own existence or any other for that matter. At death the soul does not emerge from the body because a soul is in a person only so long as the individual is alive. It is not the soul, but the re-creation of an individual from their DNA that enables eternal life.

Geniocracy

The Raelians support a political system that only allows the most intelligent people to govern. Rael writes in *The True Face of God*: "What kind of people allow humanity to progress? The geniuses. Therefore your world must appreciate its geniuses and allow them to govern the Earth" (p. 85). "We are talking about placing the genius in power, and you may call that 'geniocracy'" (p. 87). Only individuals with an intellect 10 percent above average should be allowed to vote. But Rael says this does not necessarily mean those people who have done the most studying.

One-World Government

The Elohim also told Rael, "You must see to it that all the nations of the Earth unite to form only one government" (*The True Face of God*, 89). This government would impose a system of "humanitarianism," which is a response to the injustice that "unintelligent children should live in luxury thanks to the fortunes amassed by their parents, while geniuses die of hunger and do any menial chore just to eat" (*The True Face of God*, 87).

Is the Raelain Movement a Religion?

The answer is complex. The Raelians describes themselves as atheist:

> "atheist" because it demystifies the old concept of god, and "religion" (in the original sense of the world) because it links us with our creators (from the Latin "religere" meaning "to link").

In Rael's book, *Let's Welcome Our Fathers from Space* (1998), he writes,

> There is no need to kneel down or to lie down with your face in the dirt, . . . but rather to look up at the sky, standing proud . . . living in this day and age when we are able to understand and show love for our creators, who have given us the fantastic potential to create life . . .

Raelian belief also stresses humanity's opportunity to shape its own future. Rael, in *Let's Welcome Our Fathers from Space*, records a message he received from the Elohim. Concerning the Age of Apocalypse that humanity has entered, the message states, "Either humanity will develop an interplanetary consciousness, and the whole of mankind will enter the Golden Age, or the planet will self-destroy. . . . It's your move." Raelians, though, see humanity as able to control its own destiny. However, Rael writes about rewards for those who deserve them.

The Apocalypse

Rael says that the world entered the Age of Apocalypse in 1945 with the use of the atomic bomb at Hiroshima. He goes on to further prove that humanity is living in the Age of Apocalypse by referring to the Bible teaching that the Age of Apocalypse will arrive when the Jews regain their country, which he says has happened because the State of Israel exists. Other biblical inferences are "proved," and as we are able to create life from inert matter and progress in human genetics and DNA continues to expand, so does the final apocalyptic reality hasten to come.

Sacred Texts

Rael believes that traces of the terrestrial masterpiece of creation can be found in practically all religious writings, but writings of the Kabbalah are the closest book to the truth:

> It would take many pages to name all the religions and sects that testify in a more or less obscure way to our work. (*The Final Message*, 80)

Cloning

The Raelian commitment to cloning seems to be linked to Rael's belief that the human race was created in the laboratory from the DNA of aliens, twenty-five thousand years ago. The Raelian sect made headlines in summer 1997, announcing that it would soon clone people. To duplicate oneself would come at a cost of two hundred thousand dollars.

In January 1998, the press reported that the Swiss-based portion of the Raelian Movement offered U.S. physicist Richard Seed financial donations to further his efforts to clone children for people who are unable to have their own naturally. Dr. Brigitte Boiselier of the Raelian Movement reported that already one hundred couples would like to have children cloned. The Raelians' strong support of human cloning is opposed by other members of society for ethical reasons.

On June 9, 1997, the Raelian Movement announced their new project, Valiant Venture, Ltd., offering a service, Clonaid, to give homosexual and infertile couples the opportunity to clone a child from one partner's DNA. ("Religious Cult offers human clone service . . ." The *Herald* [Glasgow], 9 June 1997: 9)

The Raelian Attitude Toward other UFO Groups

Raelians tend to separate themselves from other UFO groups. The Official Homepage states, "We (the Raelians) are not ufologists. We find our evidence on our own planet, within humanity and in scientific progress, which increasingly confirms the messages given to Rael by the Elohim" (www.rael.org).

Sensual Meditation

The Official Homepage writes, "Sensual Meditation is designed to rectify (the inconsistent values conditioned by our present society) by teaching people to start questioning all their values and consequent actions, . . . so as to be able to decondition oneself, uninhibit oneself and appreciate the present in a much deeper way, enjoying every sensation with a maximum of pleasure and love without the paralysis of society's guilt. . . . (Sensual Meditation) is to exercise and develop the senses . . ." (www.rael.org).

The Raelian belief in sensual meditation has been used by the movement's critics to imply that the Raelian movement is only about sex. The *Ottawa Citizen* (March 6, 1995) wrote in "Sex, Extra-Terrestrials Focus of Church," "Among these (messages given to Rael by 'aliens') is a need for people to discover their bodies."

UFO Movements

Although Raelians claim not to be a UFO movement, at least two other groups with extraterrestrial focus are worthy of mention here.

In 1955 George King established the Aetherius Society in London. This society received messages through a "primary terrestrial mental channel" (i.e., telepathy) and sought to prevent Earth from being enslaved by evil space creatures.

In California, 1975, a group called Heaven's Gate was formed under the leadership of Bo and Peep. This group was also called HIM, an acronym for Human Individual Metamorphosis. Followers gave up their personal wealth and journeyed into the woods where they believed they would be carried off into space by UFOs. In 1997 thirty-nine members of a mysterious Heaven's Gate computer cult tragically committed suicide in a pact. Their bodies were found in a rented mansion in an exclusive suburb twenty miles north of San Diego. Clues to their state of mind emerged from video recordings made shortly before they died. In one message, believed to have been received by a former member of the cult, they declared that it was time they "shed their containers" to rendezvous with a spaceship they believed was traveling unseen behind the Hale-Bopp comet, which they apparently saw as a heavenly omen.

UNIT 11:5 NEW AGE RELIGION

> *So we stand on the brink of a new age: the age of an open world and of a self capable of playing its part in that larger sphere. An age of renewal, when work and leisure and learning and love will unite to produce a fresh form for every stage of life, and a higher trajectory for life as a whole.*
>
> Lewis Mumford, *The Transformations of Man*

The influence of the New Age can be seen everywhere. Best-selling books such as *The Celestine Prophecy* and *Seven Spiritual Secrets of Success* are evidence of the pervasive New Age interest in yoga, meditation, and the healing arts. New Age spirituality is not restricted to the world's mystics; there are seminars for businesspeople, and curricula for schools.

The vision of a New Age has several sources, one of which is astrology. In astrological teaching, evolution goes though cycles approximately every twenty-one hundred years, due to the procession of the equinoxes, where the Earth appears to move backwards from one sign of the Zodiac to another. The Age of Pisces has just ended and the Age of Aquarius is upon us, symbolizing spiritual growth and cosmic harmony. Many people have adopted the Age of Aquarius as the metaphor of the New Age which is, for many, a transforming shift across the planet where new values, raised consciousness, and a rediscovering and renaming of what is sacred is taking place.

Influences on New Age Thinking

The New Age movement is a mixture of esoteric and neo-Pagan beliefs and philosophies. Any New Age section at the local bookstore reveals an eclectic blend of literature on astrology, crystals, Reiki, Tarot, divination, spiritualism, Theosophy, Hermetic philosophy, and Esoteric Christianity, to name but a fraction of the subject matter. Its philosophy is rooted in ancient traditions, often based on mystical experiences from different contexts. In this unit we look at some of the past religious and philosophical beliefs that have been reclaimed by New Age spirituality in the present era.

Influences and Sources for New Age Beliefs

Shamanism

Within "primitive" societies there have always been men and women who were seen to possess special knowledge and power. Medicine men, or shamans, maintained contact with the spirit world for the tribe or the clan. Shamanism is the oldest tradition seeking to maintain the connection between Mother Earth and the whole of creation—believing that everything is alive—and interceding between the physical world and the spirit world.

In the past, as communities became more complex, organized contact with the spirit world came under the authority of organized religion. Esoteric tradition was therefore handed down in groups, communes, or societies. At different times and places, mystics, alchemists, and occultists had to avoid accusations of heresy. Even so, the hidden (occult) arts have continued on until this day.

Various New Age thinkers and writers allude to the philosophical and religious roots of the present New Age movement, which has been with Western culture since the 1960s. These influences include:

Hindu Vedas (1800–1200 B.C.E.)
Gnosticism
Astrology
Renaissance philosophy
Spiritualism
Rosicrucianism
Alchemy
Jakob Boehme (1575–1624)
Gurdjieff and Ouspensky
Marilyn Ferguson's Aquarian Conspiracy (1981)
The Findhorn Community
James Lovelock's Gaia hypothesis
Hermetic Philosophy
Greek mystery traditions
Celtic Druidism
Jewish Kabbalah
Freemasonry
Theosophy
Enlightenment Humanism
Arthurian legends
Krishnamurti
William Blake (1757–1827)
Glastonbury

The Hermetic tradition is well represented in New Age religions. The Greek God Hermes was thought to be identical with the ancient Egyptian God of wisdom,

Thoth. Modern scholars have shown that the Egyptian magical and mystical works attributed to Tresmegistus were written in the second and third centuries C.E. These works became known as the Hermetic philosophy. The most important part is the *Corpus Hermeticum*, a compilation of fifteen texts on astrology, alchemy, theosophy, and theurgy.

Gnosticism and the *Nag Hammadi* texts

"Gnosticism" in the academic sense of the word generally describes and includes various esoteric cosmologies and spiritual teachings of the Hellenistic civilization in the centuries immediately after Christ. The famous *Nag Hammadi* codexes (early fourth century C.E.) are a late expression of these teachings, which set out a number of beliefs and myths, including

- A complex unfolding of divine powers (called "Aeons") from the unknowable Godhead.
- A belief that the cosmos was the result of a pre-creation crisis, and therefore it is evil.
- The tragic fall of the Light—the essence of the Spirit or divine soul—into the darkness of matter, where it remains trapped until liberated by saving knowledge (Gnosis).
- Christian Gnosticism, in which Jesus is seen as the divine messenger, the one who brings gnosis to the world. In non-Christian Gnosticism, the messenger may be a biblical figure or Zostrianos (a corruption of "Zoroaster" or Zarathustra) or a mythological or symbolic figure.

Gnosticism and Metaphysical Dualism

"Metaphysical" dualism puts forward a belief in polarity in the universe between two cosmic metaphysical principles: Light and Darkness, or Good and Evil. Ancient Middle Eastern and Persian religions such as Zoroastrianism reflected these gnostic beliefs as did elements of the Essenic beliefs in the Dead Sea Scrolls, and Manichaeism founded in third-century Iran. Elements of gnostic dualism have been incorporated into evangelical or fundamentalist Christianity, which focus on the existence of Satan and his kingdom of darkness and evil in the world in conflict with Jesus and the kingdom of Light, thus creating two opposing and equal forces fighting it out.

Gnosticism: The Esoteric Religion

The term *gnosticism* derives from the Greek *gnosis*, meaning higher or spiritual or divine knowledge. Gnosis tends to be thought of as an aspect of "religion," but it differs from religion in one important respect. Religion, to a lesser or greater degree, rests on knowledge that is revealed and which imposes its own authority from without, e.g. Bible, Torah, Qur'an, Gita. These works are written down, and the knowledge in them is not realized intuitively. Although this does not deny that many religious adherents of the major world faiths engage in a wide range of spiritual experience, they would ultimately see the authority and source of their faith in the external forms of God: their revealed sacred text and/or the historical religious tradition.

For gnostics, the essential knowledge comes from within. A modern gnostic may be a freethinker and autonomous individualist with one's own brand of spirituality, but he or she may also be allied to a religious tradition, for example, Sufi, Kabbalist, Christian, Tantric. Whatever the context, a gnostic will always interpret that tradition in an individual way.

Beliefs

The current eclectic and open-ended nature of the New Age movement means that isolating a set of common beliefs is impossible. But a number of beliefs are generally held in common by many of the groups and individuals within this movement:

- *Monism*. The belief that "all is one." Everything and everyone are interrelated and interdependent. Ultimately there is no real difference between humans, animals, the natural order, or even God. Such perceived differences are only apparent, not real.
- *Pantheism*. The belief that "all is god." All of creation shares in the divine essence. All of life (and even nonlife) possesses a spark of divinity within.
- *Human divinity*. As human beings we are unable to recognize our divinity. The goal is to discover our own divinity.
- *Change in consciousness*. We have forgotten that our true identity is divine and we must therefore effect a change of consciousness to achieve our true human potential.
- *Reincarnation*. In its classic Hindu form, the cycles of birth, death, and reincarnation are necessary to work through bad karma and to finally reach perfection. The doctrine of karma says that one's present condition was determined by one's actions in a past life.

New Age and Monotheistic Faiths

Gnosticism is commonly described or dismissed as a "Christian heresy" by the Christian Church. Until the recent discovery of the *Nag Hammadi* codexes, knowledge of Gnosticism was derived solely from the polemical accounts of the early Christian Fathers, e.g., Justin Martyr, Irenaeus, and Epiphanius. The early

Church rejected the Gnostic search for hidden spiritual knowledge, through astrology or by concentrating on what they called the secret doctrines of Jesus. Such knowledge, rather than faith in Christ or moral conduct, saved them.

Monotheist religions such as Judaism, Islam, and Christianity all adhere to the teachings of their sacred books and therefore are unable to accept many of the religious foundations of New Age beliefs.

- A Christian view of reality does not accept the concept of monism. The Christian Bible teaches that God's creation is not an undivided unity but a diversity of created things and beings. The creation is not unified in itself but held together by Christ in whom "all things hold together" (Col. 1:17).
- New Age beliefs assume notions of God as an impersonal force or cosmic energy field, whereas the Christian Bible teaches that God is both immanent and transcendent, personal to his creation and triune. God is separate from his creation, not merely a part of the creation (pantheism).
- In the Judeo-Christian Bible, humanity is created in God's image (Gen. 1:26) and on this basis has dignity and value (Psalm 8), in contrast to New Age teaching that we are divinity or can aspire to divinity.
- New Age interest and involvement in the occult to achieve changes in consciousness is an area of prohibition for Christianity, Islam, and Judaism. The Judeo-Christian Bible lists such activities as divination and spirit channeling as detestable and forbidden practices (Deut. 18:9–13) linked to idolatry.
- The sacred texts of Judaism, Christianity, and Islam all teach the resurrection of the body, not reincarnation of the soul.

New Age Thinkers and Movements

Jakob Boehme (1575–1624)

Boehme was a Protestant mystic. He was also an occultist and interested in alchemy, astrology, and Jewish Kabbalah. When he was twenty-four years old, he had an experience "like the resurrection of the dead" and subsequently wrote his work *Aurora* describing the experience, but his home town of Gorlitz forbade any further writing. He influenced many later thinkers, including Hegel.

Findhorn and Glastonbury

The Findhorn Community in Great Britain began in 1962 with Peter and Eileen Caddy and Dorothy Maclean, a friend. These three claimed to have spirit guidance. In the Scottish Findhorn Bay Caravan Park, they found that by communing with nature spirits (*devas*), they were able to grow massive vegetables in very poor soil. Within a short time the press published pictures of them with forty-pound cabbages growing in the sand. The heart of the Findhorn community has been to show communication and cooperation with nature, based "on a vision of the life and purposeful intelligence inherent in it." (*The Findhorn Garden*, 2d ed. [Findhorn Press, 1988].)

According to Glastonbury legend, Christianity was brought there in 67 C.E. by Joseph of Arimathaea, who was the wealthy man who provided a tomb in Jerusalem for the body of Jesus (John 19:38–42). He came to England with the disciple Philip and twelve other disciples. He also brought the Holy Grail, which was the cup used by Jesus and his twelve disciples at the Last Supper. The Holy Grail is said to be buried at the foot of Glastonbury Tor. Legends abound about King Arthur and his Queen Guinevere, but Glastonbury is also believed to have been a pre-Christian center of Celtic worship, pointing to goddess religion and earth spirituality. Today it is a New Age center attracting thousands of spiritual travelers each year, especially to its music festival, which was revived in its present form in 1971.

George Adamski

Adamski (1891–1965) was an American occultist and promoter of what has been referred to as pseudo-science. He popularized beliefs about UFOs and flying saucers, claiming to have been contacted by "space brothers." He became famous through his book *Flying Saucers Have Landed* (1953), written with Desmond Leslie. The book relies on Theosophical ideas and sources and promotes the basic ancient astronautics theory found in later writers such as Eric von Daniken and Shirley MacLaine. Adamski's writings were an early influence on the New Age movement.

UNIT 11:6 MAGICK AND THELEMA

> *Magic is the Highest, most Absolute, and most Divine Knowledge of Natural Philosophy, advanced in its works and wonderful operations by a right understanding of the inward and occult virtue of things; so that true Agents being applied to proper Patients, strange and admirable effects will thereby be produced. Whence magicians are profound and diligent searchers into Nature; they, because of their skill, know how to anticipate an effect, which to the vulgar shall seem to be a miracle.*
>
> Aleister Crowley, *The Goetia of the Lemegeton of King Solomon*

Aleister Crowley (1875–1947) was born into a strict Christian Brethren family in England. At an early age he rejected all his parents' beliefs; even his mother could call him "the Great Beast" (666) of Revelation. He is often credited with what has now become the Wiccan Rede, *"Do what thou wilt shall be the whole of the law"* (see biography of Crowley in Leslie Shepart ed., *Encyclopedia of Occultism and Parapsychology* [Detroit: Gale Research, 1984]). But this phrase is said to have originated from François Rabelais, almost four centuries before Crowley. It was never intended to endorse self-gratification and mean "you can do whatever you like." For the would-be esoteric saint, the phrase refers to being at one with the will of God, so that you act always within the will of God.

Aleister Crowley joined the occult order of the Hermetic Order of the Golden Dawn as Frater Perdurabo on November 18, 1898, but he was expelled from the order after repeated disputes with the leader. He then formed his own occult group called Argenteum Astrum or Order of the Silver Star. Crowley's writings were of his travels, which included numerous sexual encounters including group sex, homosexual exploits, sex-magick, bestiality, and the use of drugs. Crowley's version of magic and occult included three main elements:

- The total rejection of Christianity.
- A belief in the supremacy of the self.
- The use of occult and magic to achieve heightened experience and realize goals.

Thelema

Thelema is a Greek word meaning "will" or "intention." One of the earliest mentions of this philosophy is in the writings of Francois Rabelais in 1532. His *Gargantua* and *Pantagruel* speak about the founding of an "Abbey of Thelema" as an institution devoted to the growth of human virtues. The core theme of the philosophy of Pantagruelism is laughter, where life may be both enjoyed and derided, aspiring to the religious goal of indifference or detachment without the need for a debilitating asceticism. Pantagruelism is also known for its extreme affirmation of the life of the body, and a deep and passionate hatred of the Christian Church. The only rule of the Abbey of Thelema was "Do what thou wilt," which is still the basic belief behind Thelemic philosophy today.

Thelema is an eclectic movement that incorporates elements of:

- *Judeo-Christian apocalyptic writings*, especially the Revelation of John in the New Testament and the so-called the Enochian angelic utterances recorded by Edward Kelly and John Dee (the famous Elizabethan humanist scientist), and preserved by Meric Casaubon in his *True and Faithful Relation of What Passed for Many Years Between Dr. John Dee and Some Spirits* (1659).
- *Mediaeval Kabbalah and hermetic thinking and practice.*
- *The modern magickal revival* related to Eliphas Levi, William Butler Yeats, and Samuel Liddell "MacGregor" Mathers (cofounder and last Chief of the Hermetic Order of the Golden Dawn).

In 1904 Crowley was traveling in Egypt with his wife Rose, when they became involved in events that he later claimed inaugurated a new aeon of human evolution. Crowley entered a trance state during which he wrote down the three chapters of 220 verses later called *The Book of the Law* (*Liber AL* and *Liber Legis*). *The Book of the Law* presents a mystical metaphysics that attempts to unify pluralism, dualism, monism, and mystical nihilism in a single, all-embracing cosmic concept. This unified concept presents itself in *The Book of the Law* in complex symbolism. The universe is regarded as the fruit of the coitus of Nuit, the goddess of infinite space, and Hadit, her lord and consort, in which Nuit stands for the continuous and Hadit the discontinuous aspects of creation. Followers hold that *The Book of the Law* is associated with a particular aeon of human spiritual evolution:

- In chapter 1 and the Aeon of Isis, the archetype of female divinity was in ascendancy.
- In chapter 2 and the Aeon of Osiris, the archetype was the slain god and the world's patriarchal religions rose to prominence.
- Chapter 3 heralds the dawning of a new aeon, the Aeon of Horus, the child of Isis and Osiris. In this new aeon the teachings of Thelema are revealed to humanity, for the benefit of the species.

Beliefs

Thelemists have three basic beliefs:

- *Each individual is unique.* "Every man and every woman is a star."
- *The True Will.* Thelemites believe that we each have a True Will, a single overall motivation for our existence. "Do what thou wilt shall be the whole of the Law" and "thou hast no right but to do thy will." The Law of Thelema instructs each person to follow their True Will so that they aspire to fulfillment in life and freedom from the many restrictions of their nature.
- *The notion of absolute freedom for an individual* to follow his or her True Will is central. Magick is of great importance for this journey of self-exploration.

"Love is the law, love under will." Each person unites with his or her true self in love, eventually making the whole universe of conscious beings unite with every other being in love. Thelema accommodates the whole range of individual beliefs from atheism to polytheism focusing on the right of the individual to fulfill themselves. Actions are allowed so long as they do not interfere with the will of others, and only the individual person is qualified to determine what these actions are.

Practices

Crowley founded his own occult order, the Fraternity of the Silver Star, in 1907. In 1909 Crowley worked on putting spiritual wisdom into a coherent practical system based on the Kabbalistic Tree of Life. He undertook to develop his own system of "scientific illuminism" based on his research into comparative mysticism and documented in his many publications. These explore a system of mental self-development that includes invocation, self-control, sex magick, devotional worship, four hours of meditation per day, breathing exercises, guided visualizations, concentration, and other practices to encourage the True or Magickal Will and undo the attachment of the ego to consensual reality. Crowley regarded each aspirant as an individual in their own right, with his or her own unique path to self-realization. For this reason, he refused to codify what was good practice. Aspirants exercised choice in what appealed to them and then reported their progress to their superior. They were required, however, to memorize the Thelemic Holy Books and pass intellectual examinations in different courses of study. A basic underlying pattern of practice emerges from Crowley's writings, to which most Thelemic followers seem to have concurred:

- A daily ritual of "invoking" or sanctification immediately upon awakening in the morning.
- The blessing of one's bath water.
- Adoration of the Sun at sunrise, noon, sunset, and midnight, followed by one hour of meditation.
- A repetition recalling the central imperative of one's life, that is, the Great Work, before eating.
- Eating meals in silence.
- Avoiding mass media.
- Regular use of the Thelemic greetings.
- A formula for the repudiation of the Black Brothers (i.e., Christian clergy) whenever and wherever they are encountered.
- Wearing amulets and talismans.
- Daily Eucharist at sunset.
- Burning one's excrement and nail parings and careful disposal of one's urine.
- Daily ritual of personal empowerment.
- Daily adoration of the phallus.
- Sleeping in a consecrated circle.
- Devotion to the Goddess upon falling asleep.
- Performance of rituals and the celebration of feasts at significant periods of the year.
- The regular practice of "sex magick."

The Gnostic Mass

In 1913 Crowley wrote *The Gnostic Mass* (*Liber XV*), and it has since been adopted as the primary rite of The Gnostic Catholic Church.

Ecclesia Gnostica Catholica (The Gnostic Catholic Church)

Ecclesia Gnostica Catholica (E.G.C.), or the Gnostic Catholic Church, is the ecclesiastical aspect of Ordo Templi Orientis (O.T.O.). The E. G. C. was formed in 1907 by Jean Bricaud, Louis-Sophrone Fugairon, and Gerard Encausse in France. At the center of the E.G.C. is the celebration of the Gnostic Mass as set forth in Crowley's *Liber XV*. Formal membership in E.G.C. comes through baptism, confirmation, and, after training, orders. However, in most locations, no formal affiliation is required to attend the Mass.

While E.G.C. traces its historic origins to the French Gnostic revival at the close of the nineteenth century, which was a movement within Christianity, it has since accepted the Law of Thelema and is no longer to be considered a Christian church. The theology and doctrines of the E.G.C. are based on the principles of the Thelemic religion. The traditional Roman Catholic and Orthodox doctrines and beliefs do not operate within E.G.C.

There are three levels of membership in E.G.C.:

- *The Clergy*—consisting of Father (or Mother) of the Church (also known as the Patriarch or Matriarch), the Primate, the Bishops, the Priests and Priestesses, and the Deacons.
- *The Laity* (lay membership)
- *Bishops in Amity* (advisory membership)

The term "Bishop" does not carry the same meaning within the E.G.C. as it does in Christian churches. Gnostic Bishops assume a mystic name prefaced by the Greek letter "T" or "Tau" upon their consecration.

Lay membership in E.G.C. is conferred by the ceremony of confirmation, which must be preceded by the ceremony of baptism. Lay membership conveys no authority or special privileges within E.G.C. The patriarch may, from time to time, modify or waive the ceremonial requirements for lay membership in E.G.C.

Baptism is open to any person at least eleven years old, but does not in itself confer lay membership. Confirmation is open to any person who has been baptized. Baptism and/or confirmation for any person less than eighteen years of age requires the prior written consent of a parent or guardian.

Aleister Crowley wrote *Liber XV* in 1913 in Moscow, the year after his appointment by Theodor Reuss as the Head of the British Section of O.T.O. According to W. B. Crow in *A History of Magic, Witchcraft and Occultism* (London: Aquarian Press, 1968), Crowley wrote *Liber XV* "under the influence of the Liturgy of St. Basil of the Russian Church." Crowley writes in chapter 73 of his Confessions:

> During this period [the summer of 1913] the full interpretation of the central mystery of freemasonry became clear in

> consciousness, and I expressed it in dramatic form in 'The Ship.' The lyrical climax is in some respects my supreme achievement in invocation; in fact, the chorus beginning: Thou who art I beyond all I am . . . seemed to me worthy to be introduced as the anthem into the Ritual of the Gnostic Catholic Church, which, later in the year, I prepared for the use of the O.T.O., the central ceremony of its public and private celebration, corresponding to the Mass of the Roman Catholic Church.

UNIT 11:7 WICCA

> *Listen to the words of the Great Mother: She, Who was of old also called among mortals, Artemis, Astarte, Athene, Dione, Melusine, Aphrodite, Cerridwen, Dana, Arianrhod, Isis, Bride, and by many other Names:*
>
> *Whenever ye have need of anything, once in the month and better it be when the Moon is Full, then shall ye assemble in some secret place and adore the Spirit of Me, Who am Queen of all the Witches.*
>
> Charge of the Goddess

The word "witchcraft" comes from the Old English word *wiccecræft*, which referred to Pagan and magical practice. Witchcraft is also called Wicca or "The Craft." Today it is the modern revival of ancient Pagan European religion. All witches are Pagans, but all Pagans are not witches. Witchcraft is closely allied to magic, but its power is often considered to be within a person or the power of a supernatural agent. Generally speaking witchcraft is human behavior that uses knowledge of and employs the world of the supernatural to achieve events that are otherwise unattainable. Many people confuse and misreport Wiccan belief. For example, many "Wiccans" deviate from what was originally considered "witchcraft." They meet in covens and consider themselves witches, but they are much more in line with New Age philosophy than "traditional" (occultic) witchcraft practices. They are not Satanists; neither do they worship demons or abuse or sacrifice children, animals, or people. The major Wiccan movements present Wicca as a life-affirming, positive system of spiritual beliefs and ritual practices, although—as with any religion—certain bad practices may occur in its name.

The *Malleus Maleficarum* and the Inquisition

Throughout the ages, witches and other neo-Pagans have complained about the common misunderstanding that they are seen as Satanists, a belief that persists right up to the present day and very largely due to the *Malleus Maleficarum* (*The Witch Hammer*) of 1486, which was written by two Dominicans and which was to become the guide book of the Inquisition. Its appearance incited and sustained some two centuries of witch-hunting hysteria in Europe. People who practiced simple sorcery and folklore, such as village wise women, were increasingly regarded as practitioners of diabolical witchcraft. They came to be seen as in demonic league with Satan.

The *Malleus* was written by Johann Sprenger, dean of the University of Cologne in Germany, and Heinrich (Institoris) Kraemer, professor of theology at the University of Salzburg, Austria. In 1484 Pope Innocent VIII issued the bull *Summis Desiderantes*, expressing his hatred of the spread of witchcraft in Germany, and authorized Sprenger and Kraemer to purge the country. The *Malleus* sought to implement Exodus 22:18: "You shall not permit a female sorcerer to live." The *Malleus* is divided into three parts.

- Part I addresses the depravity of witches, and any disbelief in demonology is seen as heresy. The *Malleus* also allowed any person, whatever their status or reputation, to testify against an accused person.
- Part II is a collection of stories outlining the so-called activities of witches. These included sexual relations with devils (*incubi* and *succubi*). Most of the blame for witchcraft is focused on women. Both of the book's writers were Dominicans and showed a fear and hatred of women that was not uncommon in their day, especially among the religious educated community. "They are more credulous. . . . They have slippery tongues. . . . They are weak. . . . Feebler both in mind and body." The indictments against women become very graphic in the many accounts of men claiming that witches had stolen or taken away their penis:

  > We have already shown that they can take away the male organ, not indeed by actually despoiling the human body of it, in the manner which we have already declared. And of this we shall instance a few examples.
  >
  > In the town of Ratisbon a certain young man who had an intrigue with a girl, wishing to leave her, lost his member; that is to say, some glamour was cast over it so that he could see or touch nothing but his smooth body. In his worry over this he went to a tavern to drink wine; and after he had sat there for a while he got into conversation with another woman who was there, and told her the cause of his sadness, explaining everything, and demonstrating in his body that it was so. The woman was astute, and asked whether he suspected anyone; and when he named such a one, unfolding the whole matter, she said: "If persuasion is not enough, you must use some violence, to induce her to restore to you your health." So in the evening the young man watched the way by which the witch was in the habit

> of going, and finding her, prayed her to restore to him the health of his body. And when she maintained that she was innocent and knew nothing about it, he fell upon her, and winding a towel tightly about her neck, choked her, saying: "Unless you give me back my health, you shall die at my hands." Then she, being unable to cry out, and growing black, said: "Let me go, and I will heal you." The young man then relaxed the pressure of the towel, and the witch touched him with her hand between the thighs, saying: "Now you have what you desire." And the young man, as he afterwards said, plainly felt, before he had verified it by looking or touching, that his member had been restored to him by the mere touch of the witch.

- Part III looks at legal procedures in witch trials. Torture is sanctioned to obtain confessions. Lay and secular authorities can assist the inquisitors to exterminate those whom Satan has enlisted to his diabolical cause.

The *Malleus* went through twenty-eight editions between 1486 and 1600 and was accepted by Roman Catholics and Protestants as authoritative and a reliable source about Satanism.

From about 1450 to 1700, thousands of people, mostly innocent women, were executed because of "proofs" or "confessions" of diabolical witchcraft. During this time people were encouraged to inform against one another, and professional witch finders were paid a fee for each conviction. The most common test was to prick the body. All witches were supposed to have a physical mark that was made by the devil and insensitive to pain. Other "proofs" were sought: additional breasts, the inability to weep, and failure in the water test. Here, a woman was thrown into water; if she sank, she was innocent, but if she stayed afloat, she was guilty.

The Salem Witch Trials

One of the last instances of witch-hunting occurred in Massachusetts in 1692 in the town of Salem in the Massachusetts Bay Colony. A West Indian slave, Tituba, related some voodoo tales to a few young girls with the result that they claimed to be possessed by the devil. They subsequently accused three Salem women, including Tituba, of witchcraft. Tituba and the other accused persons came under duress and pressure resulting in their incrimination of others in false confessions. A wave of public hysteria followed over the threat of witchcraft throughout Massachusetts.

A special course was created to deal with the issue as the number of those accused increased to 150 (even Massachusetts governor William Phips's wife was implicated). Twenty people were executed. This tragic event occurred in a religious community where there were deeply held beliefs about demonic influence. By the time the hysteria had abated, there was little enthusiasm for the persecution of witches in Massachusetts or anywhere else in the surrounding region.

Beliefs and Practices

Most modern witches are followers of a nature-oriented, polytheistic faith. Witches believe that all life is interconnected and in the Creatress. The source of life is the Goddess, who has three aspects of Maiden, Mother, and Crone, thus representing the basic stages of life. Some witches and many neo-Pagans also worship God, who may be seen as the Grain God of the harvest, the Horned God of the hunt, and the Green Man of the forest.

Witchcraft is organized in small autonomous groups called "covens," "groves," "nests," and "circles." Witchcraft shares with neo-Paganism a dislike of large organizations and holy gurus. Wicca is mostly made up of small groups and individuals who have the freedom to disagree with their leaders. Wicca groups meet at various times and at the new and full moons for regular meetings. There are eight major solar festivals:

Samhain or Halloween (October 31)

Yule (December 21)

Oimelc or Candlemas (February 2)

Spring Equinox (March 21)

Beltane (April 30)

Summer Solstice (June 21)

Lammas (August 1)

Autumn (Fall) Equinox (September 21)

The History of Samhain (Halloween)

The observances connected with Halloween are thought to have originated among the ancient Druids, who believed that Saman, the lord of the dead, called forth hosts of evil spirits (*Funk & Wagnalls New Encyclopedia*, vol. 12, 1979). Anne Ross refers to Samhain as a time when "malevolent beings used to come forth from the cave (of Cruachan) and devastate the land." Ward Rutherford explains that "the Celtic festival of the dead, Samain (was) an occasion marked by burning human offerings." (*The Druids and Their Heritage,* p. 24). Samhain seems to have been associated with the blood of human sacrifice. Lewis Spencer writes, "We are informed by Keating that the Irish Druids on the eve of Samhain burned their victims in the holy fire." (*The History and Origins of Druidism*).

Since the late 1970s modern Wicca groups have gathered in an annual Samhain Seminar, with worship, rituals, and guest speakers. "Approximately 40,000 students have taken some part in their course of study" (Adler [1986]).

In their rituals, witches give thanks to the Goddess and the God for the joy and provision of nature and the abundance of harvest. Many Wiccans use or meditate on the Charge of the Goddess. The earliest version of the charge that I have found is from *Aradia: Gospel of the Witches* by Charles Leland (1899). There are many different versions of this text. The charge is traditionally used during the ritual known as "Drawing Down the Moon," where the priestess receives the energy of the Goddess and allows the Goddess to speak through her. Some Wiccans use the charge as invocation, others for group meditation. Here are included some excerpts of this powerful and mystical text:

> Listen to the words of the Great Mother: She, Who was of old also called among mortals, Artemis, Astarte, Athene, Dione, Melusine, Aphrodite, Cerridwen, Dana, Arianrhod, Isis, Bride, and by many other Names:
>
> Whenever ye have need of anything, once in the month and better it be when the Moon is Full, then shall ye assemble in some secret place and adore the Spirit of Me, Who am Queen of all the Witches.
>
> There shall ye assemble, ye who are fain to learn all sorcery yet have not won its deepest secrets; to these will I teach things that are as yet unknown. And ye shall be free from slavery, and as a token that ye be really free, ye shall be naked in your rites and ye shall dance, sing, feast, make music and love all in My praise. For Mine is the ecstasy of the Spirit and Mine also is joy upon Earth, for My love is law unto all beings.
>
> Keep pure your Highest Ideals; strive ever toward them, let naught stop you nor turn you aside, for Mine is the secret door which opens upon the door of youth. And Mine is the Cup of the Wine of Life and the Cauldron of Cerridwen, which is the Holy Grail of Immortality. . . .
>
> Upon Earth I give knowledge of the Spirit Eternal and beyond death I give peace, freedom and reunion with those who have gone before. Nor do I demand sacrifice, for behold, I am the Mother of all living and My love is poured out upon the Earth. . . .
>
> Call unto thy soul, arise and come unto Me, for I am the Soul of Nature, Who gives life to the Universe. From Me all things proceed and unto Me all things must return. And before My face, beloved of Gods and of humans, let thine innermost divine self be enfolded in the rapture of the Infinite. . . .
>
> For behold, I have been with thee from the beginning and I am that which is attained at the end of desire.
>
> Blessed be.

Witchcraft identifies with the symbol of the pentagram, representing the Goddess and the cycle of birth, life, death, and rebirth. The five points represent the elements of earth, air, fire, water, and spirit and their interconnection. The pentagram is also an ancient symbol of protection.

Witchcraft and Paganism in the Modern Era

In the second half of the twentieth century, a self-conscious revival of pre-Christian paganism occurred in the United States and Europe. Wicca, when interpreted as the nature and fertility religion of pre-Christian Europe, has been explored in books such as Leland's *Aradia: The Gospel of the Witches* and Margaret Murray's *The Witch-Cult in Western Europe* (1921). Scholars have been heavily critical regarding the reliability of these texts, but at the times they were written they were a source of great inspiration to spiritual travelers seeking alternative religion.

Margaret Murray

Margaret Murray (1863–1963) was an anthropologist, Egyptologist, and occultist. Her ideas can be found in her two best-known works, *The Witch-Cult in Western Europe* and *The God of the Witches* (1933). Her theory was that witchcraft could be traced back to pre-Christian times, having been kept through the centuries by witches. She argues that witchcraft predates Christianity, as it was once the ancient Pagan religion of Western Europe, but because of Christian persecution witchcraft had to be hidden and clandestine in its practices. Scholars have criticized her ideas on several grounds, especially noting that the history of ancient witchcraft and witchcraft in the Middle Ages is a very complex and confused subject. Although there is little doubt that remnants of Paganistic beliefs and practices persisted throughout the medieval period, these medieval remnants of pre-Christian Paganism do not represent a well-constructed matriarchal Mother Goddess mystery religion, as many contemporary witches think. Nevertheless Margaret Murray's views influenced later writers, such as Gerald Gardner.

Gerald Gardner

Gerald Gardner (1884–1964) popularized and to some extent created witchcraft for the modern world. Gardner had many occult connections. He was a member of Freemasonry and the Rosicrucians, a VII degree initiate of the Ordo Templi Orientis (O.T.O.). He was an acquaintance of Mabel Besant-Scott (daughter of leading Theosophist Annie Besant) and of the well-known Aleister Crowley. Gardner was also a British civil servant who spent time in Ceylon (Sri Lanka), India and Southeast Asia, and the Middle East.

When he retired Gardner became involved with the Corona Fellowship of

Rosicrucians, founded by Mabel Besant-Scott. Here he is thought to have been initiated into witchcraft by Dorothy ("Old Dorothy") Clutterbuck. He revealed some secrets of the coven to which he claimed to belong in a novel called *High Magic's Aid* in 1949, which was written in his magical name of "Scire." In 1951, the witchcraft laws in England were rescinded. Gardner's *Witchcraft Today* was published in 1954, and *The Meaning of Witchcraft* appeared in 1959.

In his writings Gardner founded his own religion and based it upon the Mother Goddess and the belief in reincarnation. Gardner inspired many witches and drew many others into the Old Religion. It is thought that his ideas formed the foundations for modern witchcraft (Wicca) and the contemporary witchcraft movement. Sybil Leek (d. 1983) was greatly influenced by Gardner's version of witchcraft, although she modified his teachings. She popularized them when she moved to the United States in the late 1960s.

Ecologists and feminists have both found kindred spirits in the theology of Wicca, with its focus on life and seasonal cycles, the meaning of nature, and equality of gods and goddesses.

The Wiccan religion has received some acceptance in recent times, including the acceptance of Wiccan chaplains in the U.S. military. In 1985 Wiccans were permitted to register as clergy with the City of New York to perform legal weddings.

UNIT 11:8 DRUIDRY

> *Most Pagans, unless they are hard-core New Agers living permanently in flotation tanks, will have noticed great things happening in the Pagan world over the last few years. Interest in our traditions has never been stronger, and those traditions themselves have been evolving in exciting ways. The magic is growing, and even the formerly enclosed world of Druidry has not been untouched by the huge surge of energy that is revitalising the old/new ways.*
>
> Philip Shallcrass, *Who Are These Bloody Druids?*

There is a resurgence of interest and participation in Druidry today, but we know little for certain about its history and origins. Two of the reasons for this lack of information include the Druids' oral tradition and the colonizing of their culture by the Romans, who have provided the main literary source for their existence. Historians, writers, and poets have engaged in wide and diverse literary exploration and imagination about the Druids and have put forward a vast number of theories about their history. These writings occasionally feature a patriotic tendency (e.g., from England and France) to attribute Christian virtues to the Druids in order to validate their own pre-Christian history. This attribution gave rise to the much-disclaimed view that Druidism was an offshoot of the religion of the pre-Hebrew patriarchs.

The word *Druid* may derive from an Indo-European word *Drus*, meaning "oak," and the Indo-European *wid*, meaning "to know." A Druid was literally one who "understood the oak." Other scholars think that an early Celtic prefix, *dru*, would suggest the meaning of druid as "extremely wise one."

Modern Druids have had to study the religion of the Celts to form a picture of what Druid religion was like, but most of the information available is from biased Roman commentators such as Julius Caesar and Cicero, some archaeological evidence, folklore, and Celtic mythology transcribed by twelfth-century Christian scholars. Although the Celts existed throughout much of Europe, the Druids were known to exist only in the latter Celtic range, which is basically Gaul and the British Isles. Barry Cunliffe in his enlightening book, *The World of the Celts*, says:

> Caesar recognized the druids as the only class of intellectuals in Gaul, but this seems to be an oversimplification. Other writers—Strabo, Diodorus, Athenaeus—supported by the Irish literature, distinguish three distinct categories: the bards, in whose poetry the history and traditions of the tribe were immortalized; the augurers, who oversaw the sacrifices and foretold the future; and the druids proper, versed in law and philosophy—the conservers of the ancient wisdoms.
>
> An occasional overlap in function may have obscured the differences and led Caesar into his somewhat inaccurate generalization.

Druidism experienced a romantic revival of interest in the seventeenth and eighteenth centuries throughout Europe. Britain, for example, saw the founding of Henry Hurle's Ancient Order of Druids. Today, many Druids see their religion as a powerful force for the survival of the planet.

Beliefs

For Druids, the deity is both male and female. The different aspects of deity represent different aspects of life, nature, and the seasons.

The aspects of deity are separate from each other, and Druidism is therefore polytheistic (many gods). The idea that these aspects are part of a larger whole is called pan-polytheism. In Druidism, both polytheism and pan-polytheism are valid views of deity.

Druids are mainly animists, believing that deity exists in all living things and that each human, animal, and plant is a unique expression of the divine. Some Druids extend this belief to "inanimate" objects, such as wells, rivers, and mountains.

Druidism is a nature religion. Many Druids regard the ideal place for worship and ritual as outdoors. The general purpose of rituals is to celebrate the divine and have communion with the gods and each other through meditation, prayer, and invoking the gods, ancestors, and nature spirits.

> Grant, O God/dess, Thy protection;
> And in protection, strength;
> And in strength, understanding:
> And in understanding, knowledge;
> And in knowledge, the knowledge of justice;
> And in the knowledge of justice, the love of it;
> And in that love, the love of all existences;
> And in the love of all existences, the love of God/dess.
> God/dess and all goodness.
>
> Ross Nichols, *The Book of Druidry*

Many Druids honor Awen (literally, "flowing spirit"), invoked during Druid rituals that were originally regarded as a gift given by the goddess Ceridwen, "the Crooked Woman" or "Bent White One." She brewed the cauldron of inspiration (Awen), three drops from which bestowed the gifts of poetic inspiration, prophecy, and shape-shifting.

Ceridwen, who is also a favorite goddess of many witches, was regarded in medieval times as the patroness of the order of Christian bards in Wales. They invoked the Pagan Goddess and the Christian God together in their poetry.

Druid Groups and the Henge of Keltria

Druidry is not only widespread but is equally diverse in its thinking and its beliefs. An accurate summary of Druidry is therefore impossible. But neo-Pagan Druid groups like The Henge of Keltria, based in Minneapolis, have put forward a general summary of their beliefs, which probably reflects what many contemporary Druids believe:

- We believe in Divinity as it is manifest in the Pantheon. There are several valid theistic perceptions of this Pantheon.
- We believe that nature is the embodiment of the Gods and Goddesses.
- We believe that Natural Law reflects the will of the Gods and Goddesses.
- We believe that all life is sacred and should neither be harmed nor taken without deliberation or regard.
- We believe in the immortality of the spirit.
- We believe that our purpose is to gain wisdom through experience.
- We believe that learning is an ongoing process and should be fostered at all ages.
- We believe that morality should be a matter of personal conviction based upon self-respect and respect for others.

- We believe that evil is not a matter of inheritance but of intent; therefore, actions are not in themselves evil. Rather, it is through the intent behind actions that evil can manifest.
- We believe in the relative nature of all things, that nothing is absolute, and that all things, even the Gods and Goddesses, have their dark sides.
- We believe that individuals have the right to pursue knowledge and wisdom through their chosen path.
- We believe in a living religion able to adapt to a changing environment. We recognize that our beliefs may undergo change as our tradition grows.

Druid Festivals and Rituals

Many of today's Druids follow the eightfold festival:

Samhain (October 31) celebrates the last harvest of the year. Samhain literally means "summers end" and is the Celtic new year. The Dagda and the Morrigan are Patron and Matron of this feast. The Dagda represents the fullness of harvest, and the Morrigan, the ending of the year. In the Celtic world, Samhain was the day when barriers between the natural and the supernatural were suspended. The spirits of the dead were free to roam and communicate with the living. Vestiges of this festival survive in the holiday we call Hallowe'en.

Yule or *Winter Solstice* (December 21) is the time of new beginnings. The sun, at its lowest point, begins its renewal as the days will start to get longer. Bridget is the Matron of this rite, and as bringer of light she represents the rebirth of the sun's light.

Imbolc (February 2) As the fire of the sun continues to grow, Bridget continues as Matron for this rite. Angus Og, the God of Young Love, is the Patron.

Spring Equinox (March 21) is when the sun is at the midway point between winter and summer. The mating season starts, Angus Og continues as Patron. Boann, representing fertility and growth, becomes the Matron of the rite.

Beltane (May 1) brings planting of the new crops. Boann continues as Matron. Bilé is Patron. Bilé represents the increasing fire of the sun and fertility.

Summer Solstice (June 21) is the time when the sun is highest in the sky. At this time the sun is at a balance point. Bilé represents the glory of the sun at its highest point. Danu, the all-mother, comes in as Matron. She represents motherhood, pregnancy, and nurturing.

Lughnasadh (August 2) comes when the sun is losing its strength and it is time for the first harvest. Danu continues as Matron. Lugh is Patron, representing the harvest and the sun.

Autumn (Fall) Equinox (September 21) is celebrated when the sun is halfway between summer and winter. Lugh is Patron, representing the declining sun. Morrigan starts her role as Matron now, and continues into Samhain.

Wicca and Druidry

As we have seen, Druidry and Wicca share much in common, but they also differ in emphasis and ethos. Philip Carr-Gomm, as Chosen Chief of the Order of Bards, Ovates and Druids, outlines and summarizes the differences in the following ways:

- Druidry tends to be solar-oriented, while Wicca is lunar-oriented.
- Wiccans tend to work at intuitive and instinctive levels, while Druidry is more philosophical and intellectual—concerning itself, for example, with numerology and geomancy.
- Druids practice "high magic," while Wiccans practice "low magic."
- Druidry is "Apollonian," while Wicca is "Dionysian."

Carr-Gomm writes:

> In common with most generalizations, however, these suggested distinctions mask a far more complex relationship in terms of theory and practice between the two groupings. The similarities are numerous. Both traditions are concerned with opening to the powers of the natural world, and both traditions celebrate the seasonal festivals . . . and both accord great significance to the four elements of earth, air, fire, and water, together with the uniting fifth element—aether, or spirit. An intriguing question is whether these two streams were originally one. We can never know for certain whether in the early days there was just one Old Religion, which at some time forked into these two branches, or whether from the very beginning they were separate but related mysteries. (Philip Carr-Gomm, *The Druid Way*)

Druid Orders

There have been widespread myths that Druids were sun-worshipers performing rituals during daylight hours. Druidry was also regarded as patriarchal, allowing only men into its membership, but there is little resemblance to those times in Druidry today.

The Ancient Druid Order (ADO) is thought to have been founded in 1717 and still holds rites at Stonehenge, Primrose Hill, and Tower Hill. In 1964 W. Ross Nichols led a breakaway group from the ADO. This group is The Order of Bards, Ovates and Druids (OBOD), after the three major subdivisions of the Pagan Celtic Druid caste. The cultural explosion of the 1960s saw great spiritual eclecticism and an increase in witchcraft. Some moved from Wicca into Druidry out of interest in rediscovering Celtic roots. There were new connections between the two traditions, resulting in Druid orders being founded and run by witches.

These orders include The British Druid Order (BDO), the Portsmouth-based Insular Order of Druids (IOD), and the Glastonbury Order of Druids (GOD). These Wiccan-originated groups have also brought goddess energy back into Druidry.

An ecumenical trend in Druidry is the Gorsedd of Bards of Caer Abiri founded in 1993. They are a multifaith group celebrating the eight festivals within the stone circles of Avebury in Wiltshire, England. Gorsedd ceremonies are open to all, as is initiation to the Gorsedd, which always forms a part of each celebration. The Loyal Arthurian Warband is led by the flamboyant King Arthur Pendragon, who campaigns for animal rights and the environment and against nuclear and chemical weapons.

Modern Trends in Druidry

Philip Shallcrass draws attention to the trend in more recent years towards Celtic shamanism, which is a blend of Celtic tradition and various techniques culled from modern tribal cultures leading to the reemergence within Druidry of such concepts as shapeshifters, animal helpers, guides, and totems. Shallcrass also reflects that modern British Druidry is rediscovering the role of the bard as word-magician. Poetry itself was regarded as one of the primary gifts, being more magical than mundane. Poems were sung and such sacred songs lead to the revitalization of the earth and society.

UNIT 11:9 SATANISM

> *There is no God. There is no supreme, all-powerful deity in the heavens that cares about the lives of human beings. There is nobody caught up there who gives a sh—. Man is the only god. Man must be taught to answer to himself and other men for his actions.*
>
> Burton H. Wolfe, *The Devil's Avenger*

The use of the word *Satanism* in this unit of material refers specifically to those who dedicate themselves to the worship of Satan, whatever they mean by that term. We therefore trace historical beliefs, practices, and worship regarding Satan, the one named in the Bible as the chief of evil spirits, and then move on to look at further beliefs that underpin contemporary Satanism.

Many different kinds of Satanism are practiced. The vast majority of Satanists cannot be classified as "reverse Christians" and do not accept Christian theology. Many are atheists who regard "Satan" as a symbol of individuality, autonomy, pride, rebellion, or strength. Others see Satan as a "Dark Force in Nature," or they take a modern version of Ophidian Gnosticism, which venerated the serpent of the Garden of Eden as a bringer of wisdom.

The best-known modern form of Satanism is the Church of Satan, based on *The Satanic Bible* by Anton LaVey. This group uses the term "Satan" to symbolize their rejection of Christianity. They do not believe in the existence of any spiritual being, either Satan or God, but they do believe in the power of the self. Another well-known group known as the Temple of Set is one of the few that actually worships Satan as a deity. Other groups include Ordo Templi Satanas, Church of Satanic Brotherhood, Order of Baal, and the Church of Satanic Liberation.

A general working definition would be that Satanism involves the worship of Satan, whether the term is understood as a supernatural entity, a deity, an evil force, a innate human force, or even the self.

Satan in the Bible

Information about Satan in the Jewish Scriptures can be found in chapter 5. Scholars think that the literature written between the testaments, such as the Apocrypha (influenced by Persian Zoroastrianism), influenced later demonology. The term "the devil" (GK = διάβολος) alternates with "Satan" in the New Testament. What emerges from the pages of the New Testament is belief in an evil, malevolent figure who is the chief of evil spirits. The devil is the supreme Evil One, the Dark Power. He is also "the god of this world" (2 Cor. 4:4), "the prince of the power of the air" (Eph. 2:2), and the opponent of the kingdom of God (Matt. 13:24–30). He seeks to draw humans away from salvation in Christ, but he has no power over Christ (John 14:30). He must always be resisted (1 Pet. 5:8–9). Clearly Christians today who take this view of scripture would fear for a Satanist who believes Satan to be a dark force of nature. The figure of Satan that arises through study of the New Testament is of a personal evil spirit who deceives and destroys. The issue for critical theologians is whether such a personal evil being is a prescientific belief or whether this kind of mythology is necessary to be able to describe evil.

Satan in Western Thought

From New Testament times to the present day there have been theologies, folklore, literature, superstitions, and witchhunts all concerning belief in Satan. How did these beliefs express themselves at various points in Western history?

- St. Augustine (354–430 C.E.) provided the first philosophical grounds for a developed demonology in his allegory of the "city of God" and the "evil city" or "earthly city."
- Gregory the Great (pope from 590–604 C.E.) reconfirmed the biblical demonology of the first Christians but also attempted to sort out difficult theological issues—e.g., if Satan (Lucifer) was created by God, then in what way can God be accountable for Satan's subsequent sin without having to attribute sin or evil to the nature of God?

- In the ninth century, artistic pictures of the devil became more common, especially in connection with the lives of the saints, which included battles with evil.
- In the tenth and eleven centuries, the "mystery plays" used many of the habits and supposed characteristics that were attributed to Satan and his demons. All pagans—that is, unbelievers—were seen to be in a wider sense under the influence of demons, as all unbelief can be traced to the Father of Lies (John 8:44).
- Anselm (Archbishop of Canterbury, 1093–1109) built on St. Augustine's ideas but developed a more thorough theory of evil. He worked on the problem of how God could be sovereign without being the direct cause of either Satan's or mankind's fall into evil.
- Thomas Aquinas (1225–1274) saw hell as a place of deprivation, that is, where God was not, rather than an actual location.
- The Knights Templar was an order of fighting monks who fought in the Crusades during the thirteenth century. Legends associated with them formed the basis for many of the myths later connected with the witches of the Great Witch Hunts. Ever since their disbandment in 1312 secret groups of knights have existed in Europe. The famous occultist Aleister Crowley became the self-appointed "Master of the Templar Order."
- In 1486 two agents of Pope Innocent VIII gave Europe its first text on how to expose and deal with witchcraft. The publication was called the *Malleus Maleficarum* (see unit 11:7), which became the authorization for the Great Witch Hunt of the late Middle Ages and which Geoffrey Parrinder (1963) has called "one of the wickedest and most obscene books ever written."
- Scholars are keen to point out that the Great Witch Hunts of the 1490s onwards have been obscured by numerous stories and confusions about the times, places, and practices of the time. However, between 1550 and 1650 the witch hunts were worse and more intense than at any other time, including tortures, forced confessions, and executions. Some clerics spoke out about witch hunts. The Dutch priest Cornelius Loos Callidus was imprisoned in 1593 for saying that confessions under torture might not be true.
- During the Enlightenment period of the eighteenth and nineteenth centuries antireligious and antimoral movements emerged; for example, the Hell-Fire Clubs in England included elaborate mock rituals, including a "Black Mass" that culminated in riotous drinking and sex. Anti-Christian movements of this sort provide the philosophical and cultural foundations for contemporary satanism.

Satanism in the Modern World

Today many groups who belong to Satanist movements claim to be neo-Pagans. As we have seen (Unit 11 Introduction) the neo-Pagan movement is made up of a large number of small, diverse groups with a common belief that they are inheritors of ancient religious traditions. Some are vigorously anti-Christian, while others claim to be the legitimate heirs of Gnostic Christianity, a revival of Druidism, Greek religions, or ancient Egyptian mystery movements. Others belong to Wicca, claiming it is the ancient witchcraft religion of Europe. Scholars and writers on this subject generally agree that only a few groups claim to be actual Satanists, that is, groups that worship the devil who is named in the Christian traditions.

The Church of Satan in San Francisco

Anton Szandor LaVey (1930–1997) was the High Priest of the Church of Satan. As a young man he was an organ player for a traveling carnival. One of his biographers, Burton Wolfe, quotes LaVey in his introduction to the *Satanic Bible*:

> On Saturday night I would see men lusting after half-naked girls dancing at the carnival, and on Sunday morning when I was playing organ for the tent-show evangelists at the other end of the carnival lot, I would see these same men sitting in the pews with their wives and children, asking God to forgive them and purge them of carnal desires. . . . I knew then that the Christian church thrives on hypocrisy, and that man's carnal nature will out no matter how much it is purged or scourged by any white-light religion.

LaVey visited some of Aleister Crowley's followers (see unit 11:6) but was disappointed with their ideas and practices. LaVey insisted that the church of Satan evolved from people like himself who wished to overturn the sacred rules and icons of society and in its place see individual human freedom. During the 1950s many nonconformists visited his home and attended his informal meetings, which came to be known as his "Magic Circle." During the 1960s LaVey's lectures became more public and formal. When he gave his lecture on The Black Mass he would end it with a ritual intended to purge the participants of the "pain induced by certain societal sacred cows through a lavish ritual of ridicule, parody, and satire." LaVey's aim was to make carnal desires a proper and acceptable object of celebration. Burton Wolfe says, "Satanism is a blatantly selfish, brutal religion."

Public satanists such as LaVey promote beliefs that foster self-indulgence and appeal to many people who have rejected Christianity.

Beliefs

Satanists are not uniform in their beliefs, and they do not hold doctrines that are binding on all Satanists. Even so, LaVey listed nine Satanic statements that form the Satanic "creed":

1. Satan represents indulgence instead of abstinence.
2. Satan represents vital existence instead of spiritual pipe dreams.
3. Satan represents undefiled wisdom instead of hypocritical self-deceit.
4. Satan represents kindness to those who deserve it instead of love wasted on ingrates.
5. Satan represents vengeance instead of turning the other cheek.
6. Satan represents responsibility to the responsible instead of concern for psychic vampires.
7. Satan represents man as just another animal—sometimes better, more often worse than those that walk on all fours—who, because of his "divine spiritual and intellectual development," has become the most vicious animal of all.
8. Satan represents all the so-called sins, as they all lead to physical, mental, or emotional gratification.
9. Satan has been the best friend the church has ever had, as he has kept it in business all these years.

The Church of Satan website www.churchofsatan.com/Pages/Sins.html—states the beliefs of the Church of Satan and the rules of behavior.

Theology

- People have created gods in many forms; pick one that might be useful to you.
- Heaven and hell do not exist.
- Satan is not closely related to the modern (post 1400 AD) concept of the Christian devil. Satanists view Satan as a pre-Christian life principle which represents the carnal, earthly, and mundane aspects of life.
- Satan is not a being, a living entity; he is a force of nature.
- Human life is held in sacred regard.
- "Satan . . . represents love, kindness and respect to those who deserve it."

Rules of Behavior

- Prayer is useless; it distracts people from useful activity.
- Ritual killing (of humans or animals) violates Satanic principles. Blood drawn from a victim is useless. Victims are killed symbolically, not actually.
- Members enjoy indulgence instead of abstinence. They practice with joy all the seven deadly Christian sins (greed, pride, envy, anger, gluttony, lust, and sloth).
- If a man smites you on one cheek, smash him on the other.
- Do onto others as they do onto you.
- Engage in sexual activity freely, in accordance with your needs (which may be best realized either through monogamy, or by having sex with

many others; through heterosexuality, homosexuality, or bisexuality; using sexual fetishes as you wish; by yourself or with one or more consenting adults). The ideal is a monogamous relationship based on compatibility and commitment.
- Suicide is actively discouraged.

LaVey prohibited "harming children; killing non-human animals except for food or in self-defense; telling your troubles or giving opinions unasked; and making sexual advances toward someone who may not appreciate it." He also said, "If a guest in your lair annoys you, treat him cruelly and without mercy," and, "When walking in open territory, bother no one. If someone bothers you, ask him to stop. If he does not stop, destroy him" (from Anton LaVey's "Eleven Rules of the Earth," in Blanche Barton, *The Secret Life of a Satanist: The Authorized Biography of Anton LaVey* [Los Angeles: Feral House, 1990]).

Satanic Festivals and Holidays

The highest of all Satanic holidays is the birthday of the individual Satanist. Of less importance are: Walpurgisnacht (evening of April 30), Halloween (evening of October 31), solstices in June and December, and equinoxes in March and September.

The Temple of Set

The Temple of Set was founded in 1975 by Michael Acquino, who moved on from the international priesthood of the Church of Satan. The Temple of Set was incorporated as a nonprofit church in California in 1975 and qualified for both U.S. federal and state tax-exempt status that same year.

The Temple considers itself to be consecrated by and dedicated to Set, originally an ancient Egyptian deity. Setians employ both conventional and unconventional means of influencing the environment. They use "magic," by which they mean universal forces and psychological influences generally unknown to or unrecognized by society. Setian magic is termed "Black Magic" to distinguish it from "White Magic" (invocation of nonexistent forces/influences for purposes of self-delusion). In their understanding the term "Black Magic" carries no connotation of evil.

The Temple as a California corporation is the property of the International Priesthood of Set, which delegates governing authority to the Council of Nine (board of directors). The council in turn appoints the High Priest of Set, the executive director, and other officers of the Temple.

Satanic Ritual Abuse (SRA)

In the 1980s a satanism scare arose in the United States (and in Ayrshire in the United Kingdom). This scare was based on rumors of a sophisticated network of ritual Satanists engaged in a coordinated campaign of child abduction and abuse, including ritual sacrifice. There were hundreds of SRA reports investigated by the FBI's Behavioral Science Unit, but no corroborative evidence was found. By the mid-1990s still no evidence for a large-scale, organized network of Satanists had been uncovered. Allegations of Satanic crimes were often based on controversial "recovered memories," which are recollections brought to consciousness through psychological therapy.

This unit of the book is not intended to brush over the negative aspects of Satanists or Satanism. Clearly some Satanists do worship Satan as an evil being and practice evil. But perhaps more chilling is the thought of these perpetrators of wicked acts who wear cloaks of decency or wear religious, social labels such as "Christian" or "social worker."

Chapter 12
Belief in Human Potential

The emergent religion of the near future could be a good thing. . . . Instead of worshiping supernatural rulers, it will sanctify the higher manifestations of human nature, in art and love, in intellectual comprehension and aspiring adoration. . . .

Sir Julian Huxley.

The major part of this book has looked at a sample of the different religious, mystical, esoteric, and occult beliefs that have surfaced throughout human history. In this final chapter, the focus is on humanistic and secular equivalents to religion, which are all beliefs in their own right. At the time of writing at the beginning of the twenty-first century, we have witnessed a vast increase in "personal growth" movements. For many, the focus of their spirituality is the self, which arises out of the growth and implementation of beliefs and philosophies about the self as promoted through humanistic psychology from the 1960s onwards.

UNIT 12:1 HUMANISTIC PSYCHOLOGY

The History and Growth of Self-Psychology

Psychologists have recognized three "forces" or "waves" in the development of recent psychology.

In first half of the twentieth century, American psychology was dominated by behaviorism, in which the emphasis was on mechanistic beliefs about human nature. B. F. Skinner (1904–1990) studied at Harvard University. Following in the footsteps of John Broadus Watson (1878–1958), Skinner was the founder of the behaviorist school. Skinner's theory of human behavior is based on the concept of operant conditioning: "When a bit of behavior is followed by a certain kind of consequence, it is more likely to occur again, and a consequence having this effect is called a re-inforcer" (*Beyond Freedom and Dignity* [1972]). Skinner attacks any view of human beings as free to have internal states of knowing, will, and destiny. According to Skinner, a human being is simply a higher animal, and man is a machine: "Man is much more than a dog but like a dog he is within range of scientific analysis" (Ibid).

The second force in the development of modern psychology emerged out of Freudian psychoanalysis and the depth psychologies of Erik Erikson, Erich Fromm, Karen Horney, Carl Jung, Melanie Klein, and others who focused on the dynamic unconscious. They recognized depths in the human psyche that needed to be integrated with those of the conscious mind to produce psychological health. The founders of the depth psychologies believed that human behavior is shaped by what happens in the unconscious mind.

Neither the first nor second wave gave adequate attention to the importance of studying values, motivation, and intentions or meaning as elements in conscious existence. As a result, by the late 1950s a third force was beginning to form. In 1957 and 1958 Abraham Maslow and Clark Moustakas held meetings in Detroit dedicated to a more meaningful, more humanistic vision of psychology. Their discussions centered around such themes as the self, self-actualization, creativity, intrinsic nature, being and becoming, and meaning. In 1961 the American Association for Humanistic Psychology was founded. The first issue of the *Journal of Humanistic Psychology* appeared in the spring of 1961.

In Connecticut in 1964, a meeting of psychologists and humanists established many of the founding themes and principles of humanistic psychology. Psychologists Gordon Allport, J. F. T. Bugental, Charlotte Buhler, Abraham Maslow, Rollo May, and Carl Rogers were present, as well as humanists from other disciplines. This third wave of psychological thought would offer a fuller concept and experience of what it means to be human. Maslow, Rogers, and May became the movement's most respected intellectual leaders in the years to come. From the beliefs and philosophies of humanistic psychology, many self-theories, personal development agencies, and human transcendence movements evolved in the latter part of the twentieth and the first part of the twenty-first centuries.

Humanistic psychology promotes a number of beliefs about the self. Some of these beliefs are as follows:

- Optimistically, human beings have a capacity to be self-determining.
- The basic determinants of human behavior are human intentionality and ethical values.

- Psychological well-being lies in developing human qualities such as choice; the integration of body, mind, and spirit; creativity; increased self-awareness and freedom; and personal responsibility.
- Maslow and Rogers spoke of self-actualization. Their belief in human nature as intrinsically good became a major theme of the "human potential" movement. Rogers introduced person-centered therapy, where the journey toward self-actualization can occur in a therapeutic relationship, where the therapist offers personal congruence, unconditional positive regard, and accurate empathic understanding.
- Rollo May contributed European existentialism and phenomenology to humanistic psychology, emphasizing tragic aspects of the human condition. May wrote about existential questions surrounding the enduring presence of evil and suffering in the world, and the nature of creativity, art, and mythology.
- Humanistic psychologists often stress the courage needed for a person to take responsibility for oneself in the interests of personal growth.

Abraham Maslow

> Human life will never be understood unless its highest aspirations are taken into account. Growth, self-actualization, the striving toward health, the quest for identity and autonomy, the yearning for excellence (and other ways of phrasing the striving "upward") must by now be accepted beyond question as a widespread and perhaps universal human tendency.
>
> And yet there are also other regressive, fearful, self-diminishing tendencies as well, and it is very easy to forget them in our intoxication with "personal growth," especially for inexperienced youngsters. . . . We must appreciate that many people choose the worse rather than the better, that growth is often a painful process. (Abraham Maslow)

Abraham H. Maslow (1908–1970) was born in Brooklyn, New York. He was the son of Russian Jewish immigrants, and he taught psychology at Brooklyn College and Brandeis University.

Early in his career, Maslow was drawn to the study of human motivation and personality. Unlike many psychologists of his day, he refused to study neurosis and human malfunctioning. Instead he was fascinated by what he called "self-actualized" people—that is, extremely healthy, fulfilled, successful individuals. In his book *Toward a Psychology of Being* (1968) he wrote that all human beings have a hierarchy of basic needs, beginning with the "lower" needs of food, drink, sleep, shelter, and clothing; ascending to a sense of belonging, friendship, and self-esteem; and progressing to even higher needs of personal fulfilment, an integrated system of values, and an aesthetic dimension to life.

Maslow's Self-Actualizing Personality

Maslow studied forty-eight different people who he viewed as self-actualizers, including Lincoln, Schweitzer, Einstein, and Jefferson. He identified the following characteristics of self-actualizers, although he acknowledged that not all self-actualized persons show all of these characteristics.

1. An accurate perception of reality. Nondefensive in their perceptions of the world.
2. An acceptance of themselves, others, and nature.
3. Increased spontaneity, simplicity, and naturalness.
4. A sense of mission, call, fate, or vocation.
5. Enjoyment of privacy, reflection, and detachment.
6. Freshness of appreciation. Life not taken for granted.
7. Mystic or peak experiences that include moments of intense ecstasy, similar to a religious or mystical experience, during which the self is transcended.
8. Social interest—similar to the individual psychology of Alfred Adler, who saw psychological health in terms of the individual's capacity to show "community feeling" or social interest.
9. Profound interpersonal relationships, attracting admirers or disciples.
10. Democratic characters with little racial, religious, or social prejudice.
11. Creative in managing their lives.
12. Resistant to cultural conditioning.

Transpersonal Psychology

Abraham Maslow, Anthony Sutich, and Stanislav Grof were responsible for a fourth force of modern psychology, known as *transpersonal psychology*. Together, these individuals established the *Journal of Transpersonal Psychology* (1969) and the Association for Transpersonal Psychology (1972). Transpersonal psychology has been influenced by a number of well-known people, including Aldous Huxley, Teilhard de Chardin, Sri Aurobindo, Carl Gustav Jung, Roberto Assagioli, Charles T. Tart, and William James.

Ken Wilber (b. 1949) is a modern exponent of transpersonal psychology. His books include *The Spectrum of Consciousness* (1977)—which seeks to integrate Western and Eastern psychology—*No Boundary* (1979), *The Atman Project* (1980), and *Up from Eden* (1981). A recent work of Wilber's is the epic *Sex, Ecology, Spirituality* (1995), where he criticizes Western culture and countercultural movements such as the New Age movement. In his view, these movements do not contain the depth and detailed nature of "perennial philosophy," that is, the conception of reality that lies at the heart of all major religions.

Transpersonal psychology is a relatively new development in academic psychology. In 1997 the British Psychological Society approved the formation of an academic Transpersonal Psychology section, as well as one for the related area of

Consciousness and Experiential Psychology. The Transpersonal Psychology Web site lists the topics currently being explored by transpersonal psychologists, including:

- Empathy
- Channeling
- Transpersonal art
- Altered states of consciousness
- Dream consciousness
- Mind-body relationship
- Psychedelic experience
- Mystical experiences
- Spiritual emergencies and crises
- Near-death experiences, death, and dying
- The psychology of meditation
- Practice and experience within Eastern and Western religious and esoteric traditions
- Buddhist psychology
- Ecological consciousness
- Psychology of self and self-realization
- The Higher Self
- Self-transcendence
- Male and female perspectives on the transpersonal
- Paranormal experiences
- Transpersonal approaches in psychotherapy/counseling and in education

Transpersonal psychologists stress that they do not represent a scientific enterprise, a religion, or an ideology. Individuals may or may not have their own religious or spiritual beliefs. Although Buddhist-inspired transpersonal psychologists currently predominate, other traditions are also well-represented, including Christian, Jewish, Sufi, Hindu, Shamanic, Taoist, Tantric, Magical, Gurdjieffian, Theosophical, and agnostic.

Transpersonal psychology also seeks to distance itself from antirationalism and the kind of uncritical adoption of New Age beliefs that characterizes elements of the so-called counterculture. *Transpersonal psychology has very little, if anything, to do with crystals, UFOs, alien abduction, chakras, auras, fairies, psychism, aromatherapy, levitation, fire-walking, or the millennium, except as these phenomena, practices, or experiences may be investigated in terms of their transformational consequences.*

Self-Theory

Humanistic psychology has many other outlets apart from transpersonal psychology. The drive for personal development is not a new concept. In 1936 Dale

Carnegie's *How to Win Friends and Influence People* was published as a result of his training sessions for professional businesspeople. By his death in 1955 the book had sold over 5 million copies and continues to sell to this day. In 1952 Norman Vincent Peale's *The Power of Positive Thinking* taught millions of people to "expect the best and get it." In the 1960s and 1970s personal development movements and self-theory became very popular, appearing in several forms.

Best-selling books such as Eric Berne's *Games People Play* have sold millions of copies and are still in print. Berne's self-theory is called "transactional analysis," and it encourages people to be autonomous, emphasizing spontaneity, direct intimacy, and heightened awareness of reality. Thomas Harris's *I'm O.K.—You're O.K.* is another transactional analysis best-seller, looking at the relationship between the three ego states of Parent, Adult, and Child.

Training seminars such as est (an abbreviation of Erhard Seminar Training) are immersely popular. Founded by the ex-Scientologist, used car salesman, and encyclopedia salesman Werner Erhard in 1971, est is now known as the Forum, run by the Centers network. Landmark Forum was begun in 1985 by people who had purchased the est "technology" from Erhard. (Apparently, however, Erhard is not involved in the current operation.) Est became a multimillion-dollar business, emphasizing the need for people to experience the self. Other seminars came from the Esalen Institute, founded in 1962 by Michael Murphy and Richard Price and based in Big Sur, California. Esalen was a research base at the center of the human potential movement, attracting support from Fritz Perls (Gestalt theory), Carl Rogers (person-centered therapy), and Aldous Huxley. Today Esalen functions as a community providing conferences and seminars that offer

> A center for alternative education, a forum for transformational practices, a restorative retreat, a worldwide community of seekers. . . .
>
> A center designed to foster personal and social transformation, we offer those who join us the chance to explore more deeply the world and themselves.

Criticisms of Self-Theory

Best-selling pop psychologists and self theorists have been criticized in different ways by biologists, scientists, philosophers, and theologians. These criticisms include the accusation that the self-theorists' view of human nature is superficial in its optimism. (Is human nature all that good? Is it valid to assume the goodness of the self?) Some critics say that, on the whole, the human potential movement fails to acknowledge Freud's achievements, which include the acknowledgment of unconscious irrational elements in human nature such as sadism and destructiveness. Another charge made against the self-theorists is that they trivialize life by claiming that suffering is without real meaning. In the human potential movement, suffering is often seen more as a man-made error that can be avoided if the environment can be controlled or the self actualized.

Another criticism is the opinion that psychology has become a secular religion in itself. Paul Vitz (1977) wrote: "Psychology has become a religion, in particular a form of secular humanism based on worship of the self."

Neuro Linguistic Programming

Neuro Linguistic Programming (NLP) is a way of looking at how people think, communicate, and act. The movement also addresses the development of human creativity and learning how to change. NLP practitioners point to the belief that many human problems originate from the models of reality in our minds rather than the world as it really is. Coming to understand one's own inner models of reality gives a person the tools to change thoughts and feelings.

NLP techniques and methods were developed in the mid 1970s by John Grinder, an associate professor of linguistics at the University of California; Richard Bandler, a psychology student at the university; plus the contributions of various other people. Although NLP is not a religious movement, its function in helping people to change and optimize their own behavior is similar to many religious aims found in the alternative religions and movements mentioned in this book.

UNIT 12:2 HUMANISM

It seems to me that the idea of a personal God is an anthropological concept which I cannot take seriously. I also cannot imagine some will or goal outside the human sphere. . . . Science has been charged with undermining morality, but the charge is unjust. A man's ethical behavior should be based effectually on sympathy, education, and social ties and needs; no religious basis is necessary. Man would indeed be in a poor way if he had to be restrained by fear of punishment and hope of reward after death.

Albert Einstein

Humanists trace their roots to the rational philosophy first created in the West in ancient Greece. Many consider Socrates to be the first and greatest of the humanists. Modern secular humanism, however, has a strong affiliation with the Greek philosopher, Epicurus (c. 341–270 B.C.E.), who wrote, "Friendship goes dancing round the world, proclaiming to us all to wake to the praises of a happy life."

Epicurus believed that matter is made of everlasting atoms, so he did not believe in any "uncaused cause" or "prime mover" to explain the formation of the world. He believed that a person's soul (or form) was held together by the body, so the soul must die when the body dies. In this view, death is simply the end of life and nothing can be experienced after it, so fear of death is unreasonable.

Epicurus was more concerned with the art of living, and he defined the good life as one of pleasure and friendship, absence of pain, and peace of mind. Epicurus was not a hedonist. He lived a frugal life and taught that peace of mind requires moderation in all things. He is thought to have written over three hundred books, but only fragments of his writings have survived.

Precursors to Modern Humanism

Renaissance Humanism

From the middle of the fourteenth century, groups of scholars, artists, and writers in Italy and southern Europe were experiencing a reawakening or rebirth of a new age based on a revival of Greek classical culture. In an age where the influence of the pope and the Roman Catholic Church of the West looked secure, these developments were new indeed. Less focus was placed on God and the past and more on the nature and form of humanity and our relationship to the material world. Theologically speaking, St. Thomas Aquinas had ironically opened the way for future discussion on what has been called "nature and grace," because in Aquinas's view the human will is fallen but the intellect is not. In the area of the intellect, humanity is autonomous. One result of this outlook was "natural theology," which can be followed independently of reason and does not rely on God's revelation through the scriptures.

In northern Europe the advance of humanism was distinctly Christian, through the Dutch scholar Desiderius Erasmus (c. 1466–1536). Erasmus was a convinced Christian humanist who believed that the best way to reform the church was to go back to the sources: the Hebrew and Greek Bible and the early Christian fathers. In 1516 he provided the first published edition of the Greek text of the New Testament, with his own translation in Latin. Erasmus wanted the Bible to be made available to everyone, not just to priests and theologians: "I would to God that the ploughman would sing a text of the Scripture at his plough. . . . To be brief, I wish that all communication of the Christian would be of the Scriptures." When humanism is defined (as it used to be) in terms of the dignity of man, Erasmus can be seen as a true humanist, because he believed in human free will to respond to God. He fell out with Martin Luther, who was often seen as antihumanist because he believed that the fallen human will is in bondage and unable to do any good.

The Enlightenment

The seventeenth- and eighteenth-century Enlightenment began with philosophers like Locke, Berkely, and Hume, who were called Empiricists, from the Greek word for "experience." Empiricism was an important philosophical step towards modern humanism. Empiricists stressed the validity of reason over and against revelation as the tool for human knowledge, even though most of the early empiricists were still Christians. The French Enlightenment started with Voltaire and the encyclopedist Diderot. Many empiricists called themselves Deists, which meant they were believers in an unknown supreme being.

The Nineteenth Century

In the mid-1800s, English naturalist Charles Darwin published his *Origin of Species* (1859), putting forward the theory of evolution via a process of "natural selection." This theory contradicted the Christian doctrine that each species had been separately created by God as described in the book of Genesis. The ethical philosophy of utilitarianism developed by John Stuart Mill and others said that moral law is based upon utility—that is, the practical consequences of particular actions are to be assessed in terms of human happiness (see also Epicurus). In the middle of the nineteenth century, the word "humanist" began to be used in print.

The Twentieth-Century: Coming of Age

Humanism flourished in the first half of the twentieth century, especially through the work of Bertrand Russell, who was a philosopher, a mathematician, a politician, and an activist (even in old age he was out on the streets demonstrating against nuclear weapons). From his early years, Russell was an atheist, as he explained in *What I Believe* (1925):

> I believe that when I die I shall rot, and nothing of my ego shall survive. I am not young, and I love life. But I should scorn to shiver with terror at the thought of annihilation. Happiness is none the less true happiness because it must come to an end, nor do thought and love lose their value because they are not everlasting. Many a man has borne himself proudly on the scaffold; surely the same pride should teach us to think truly about man's place in the world.

Through the century, humanism continued to grow to such an extent that numerous different forms of humanism could be recognized. *Humanism* is now a term that is accurately applied to a variety of groups and differing philosophies:

- *Christian humanism* is based on Christian beliefs about the nature of God, seeing human fulfillment by personal effort.
- *Cultural humanism* is founded on the view that knowledge can be attained through rational thought and experimentation. It has its roots in ancient Greece and Rome and represents the scientific method.
- *Literary humanism* addresses pursuit of the humanities (literature, philosophy, history, languages, etc.).

- *Modern humanism* tends to be a generic term that includes both religious and secular humanism.
- *Religious humanism* is usually practiced at a religious venue and includes community meetings and rituals. Unitarian Universalist fellowships and churches are an example of religious humanism.
- *Secular humanism* is a nonreligious philosophy promoting the belief in man/woman as the measure of all things. Its roots lie in the Renaissance and the rationalism of the eighteenth century and the free-thinkers of the nineteenth century.

The rest of this unit looks at secular humanism at the beginning of the twenty-first century.

Beliefs

A *Humanist Manifesto* was prepared in 1933, endorsed by thirty-four leading humanists, including the American educator and philosopher John Dewey. It was published in the 1933 May/June issue of *The New Humanist* (6/3:1–5). It was updated as the *Humanist Manifesto II* in the September/October 1973 issue of *The Humanist* (23/5:4–9). Signatories of the *Humanist Manifesto II* were anxious to stress that they were not formulating a binding credo; their individual views were many and various. The statement instead was an effort at consensus with the vision that new statements should be developed to supersede the document. Behind *Humanist Manifesto II* was the conviction that humanism is able to offer an alternative view of reality that can serve present-day needs and guide humankind toward the future.

Central themes of the *Humanist Manifesto* include:

- Rejection of the concept of a personal God.
- A belief that regards humans as supreme. From this belief naturally follows a number of other beliefs, such as "the preciousness and dignity of the individual person."
- A rejection of a created universe in favor of the theory of evolution and a universe that obeys natural laws.
- A rejection of divinely inspired ethical and moral codes in favor of codes derived by reason from the human condition.
- The belief that full responsibility for the future of the world, its political systems, its ecology, etc., rests with humans. No God in heaven will intervene and save us from a disaster.
- A belief that much historical progress has arisen from the conflict between organized religion and secular society, in which the former's beliefs and practices have been replaced with secular beliefs. Humanists

generally feel that religious groups' "promises of immortal salvation or fear of eternal damnation are both illusory and harmful."

- An acceptance of democracy and rejection of both theocracy and secular dictatorships as political systems that are dangerous to individual freedoms.
- A commitment to freedom of inquiry, expression, and action. Humanists have a history of combating bigotry, hatred, discrimination, intolerance, and censorship.
- A belief in the separation of church and state.
- Liberal beliefs about controversial ethical topics, like abortion, corporal punishment of children, the death penalty, enforced prayer in schools, homosexuality, physician-assisted suicide, etc.
- The belief that "moral values derive their source from human experience." Believing that life after death is nonexistent, they are committed to alleviating pain and misery around the world.
- An absence of beliefs in a personal God, Goddess, or a combination of goddesses and gods; supernatural beings such as angels, demons, Satan, Holy Spirit, etc.; heaven or hell or life after death; the separation of a person into body, soul, and spirit; survival of an individual in any form after death.

To promote humanism in the United States, the American Humanist Association was founded in 1941. This national organization represents both secular and religious naturalistic humanism. Other humanist organizations include the Humanist Institute, the Humanist Society of Friends, the Friends of Religious Humanism, the AHA Feminist Caucus, and the Humanist Chapter Assembly.

Humanism and Religion

The most widely used meaning of the word "religion" addresses the belief that there is a God (or gods) who created the world, who is/are to be worshiped, and who is/are responsible for creating ethics and morality. In this context, humanism is not a religion and would not be perceived as one by most of its followers. Religious humanism is sometimes perceived as a religion, albeit with deity worship and traditional theological belief removed.

Humanism has nonetheless recruited successfully from the liberal religions.

Conflicts over Secular Humanism in the Schools

Conservative Christian groups in the United States often see humanism as the "official religion" of the public educational system. Public (state) schools in the United States are required to base their curriculum on secularism because of the First Amendment of the U.S. Constitution, which mandates that the government shall not be involved in the establishment of a religion.

In most subjects, the presumption of secularism does not present a problem, but in subjects such as human sexuality, geology, science, and anthropology, the secular approach often conflicts with religious traditions and traditional Christian theology. For example, a secular, nonreligious approach to human sexuality would teach that bisexuality and homosexuality are natural sexual variations. Most of the world's religions reject this view and are anxious that such views not be presented as the only version of reality.

In 1987 the U.S. Supreme Court, in *Edwards v. Aguillard*, invalidated a Louisiana "Creationism Act" that forbade the teaching of evolution in the public schools unless accompanied by instruction in the theory of creation science. Writing for the court majority, Justice William Brennan said it was "clear from the legislative history that the purpose" of the act was to narrow the state's science curriculum "to advance the religious viewpoint that a supernatural being created humankind." The ongoing contention between Darwinist creation theory and conservative/fundamentalist Christianity continues in America and shows no signs of abating. Humanism in general remains the subject of vigorous attack from the religious right.

UNIT 12:3 SCIENTOLOGY

> *I have lived no cloistered life and hold in contempt the wise man who has not lived and the scholar who will not share. There have been many wiser men than I, but few have traveled as much road. I have seen life from the top down and the bottom up. I know how it looks both ways. And I know there is wisdom and that there is hope.*
>
> L. Ron Hubbard (www.lronhubbard.org)

Scientology is a religious movement based on the philosophy of American writer and visionary L. Ron Hubbard (1911–1986) whose life and teaching has inspired millions to admire and follow him. Yet Scientology has attracted more adverse publicity than practically any other organization of its kind, partly because of the conflicting claims about Hubbard's life and the practices of the movement, and partly because the Church of Scientology has, in the past, clashed with governments around the world in its attempts to be classed as a tax-exempt religion.

Hubbard started the movement in the 1950s and built it into a multinational organization. The Church of Scientology has put copies of its original publication, *Dianetics*, into numerous bookstores and libraries in America and other countries worldwide. Their public relations campaign for the book claims that it will help you lead a better life, and *Dianetics* centers offer free "personality tests." Scientology is also known for its extensive anti-drug program, which is well-documented in North America and Europe.

The Founder: L. Ron Hubbard

L. Ron Hubbard was born in 1911 and died in 1986. He was a prolific science fiction author in the 1940s. It is now known that Hubbard sent a letter to George Orwell in which he wrote, "The easiest way to make a lot of money, is to found a new religion". L. Ron Hubbard did both, he founded a new religion and he made lots of money, however Hubbard made his money from the royalties on his writings and although a wealthy man, he is known to have lived a relatively modest life. When he died he left all the copyrights on his writings to the church.

The authorized versions of Hubbard's life describe him as an intrepid explorer, notable scholar, and proficient scientist. In his writings and teachings, Hubbard speaks of his possession of two doctorates and a career as a naval commander and a war hero. His critics assert that these claims are either exaggerated or fictional, although his career in the Navy is now well documented. His biographer, Gerry Armstrong, was officially authorized by the Church of Scientology to write a biography, but he later left the movement after asserting discrepancies between the official version of Hubbard's past and his own research findings. He refused to hand back his researched material, and the Church of Scientology took him to court in the mid-1980s to try to acquire it. It was a much-publicized case. Scientologists, however, see L. Ron Hubbard as a man in a million and one of the world's greatest humanitarians.

Beliefs

Dianetics

Hubbard's book *Dianetics: The Modern Science of Mental Health* (1950) outlined a form of therapy (Dianetics) to cure emotional and psychosomatic illnesses and to enhance life.

The Eight Dianetics

A "dynamic" is a drive or impulse to survive at the levels of the self, sex (including procreation as a family), group, survival of humanity, life forms, the physical universe, spiritual beings, and, finally, Infinity or God. Contrary to some of the popular editions of Scientology, the Church has always maintained a belief in a supreme being. In the earliest editions of Scientology, a belief in the supreme being is explicit: "The Eighth Dynamic—is the urge toward existence as Infinity. This is also identified as the Supreme Being" (*Scientology: The Fundamentals of Thought.* Los Angeles: The Church of Scientology of California, 1956).

Followers of Scientology are expected to realize the self as fully as possible on all eight dynamics and therefore develop an understanding of a supreme being, or, as the Scientologists prefer to say, infinity. Scientologists believe that unless one is freed from engrams, one's survival ability on the levels of the eight dynamics will be impaired.

Engrams

Individuals are trained by auditors (therapists) to increase the power of the analytical (conscious) mind and subdue the influence of "engrams" (painful impressions of past traumas), which confuse the "reactive" (unconscious) mind. Hubbard taught that some of the most negative and painful engrams are experienced while a person is still in the womb. In his original book, *Dianetics*, there are graphic accounts of violence in the home, including stories of wives being hit by their husbands during pregnancy. He taught that the fetus could hear the violent words and that those same words that might be heard as an adult in another context could cause feelings of being threatened and under attack.

Stages of Auditing

The stages of auditing are called "grades" or "levels." These stages are shown on the Scientology "Classification, Gradation and Awareness Chart," which depicts metaphorically the span between the lower and higher levels of spiritual existence. For Scientologists the chart is "The Bridge to Total Freedom" or just "The Bridge." The Bridge charts the way from negative "unexistence," through middle-level "communication," "enlightenment," and "ability," and finally to "Clearing," "source," and ultimately "power on all eight dynamics."

Thetans

Scientologists define the spiritual essence of humanity as the "thetan." Auditing frees the thetan from past painful experiences and builds spiritual awareness. The auditor asks the person (called Pre-Clear) about the experiences and leads the Pre-Clear back to the original trauma, which is identified and then its power is dissipated. A device called an E-meter is used to guide individuals during auditing and to help them locate precise areas of spiritual difficulty. When all engrams have been disposed of, the Pre-Clear goes Clear.

The State of Clear

The meaning of "Clear" seems to have changed over time. At one time to "go clear" was the ultimate attainment. In *Dianetics*, Hubbard claims that the person who has reached Clear will have better health and eyesight and even superior intelligence:

> A Clear, for instance, has complete recall of everything which has ever happened to him or anything he has ever studied. He does mental computations, such as those of chess, for example, which a normal would do in half an hour, in ten or fifteen seconds.

Attaining the state of Clear can take a long time. It is not unusual for the person to undertake several hundred hours of auditing at great cost. Scientologists also believe that they should help others attain the state of Clear. When enough people have done so, the central aim of Scientology, espoused by L. Ron Hubbard, will have come to pass: "*A civilization without insanity, without criminals and without war, where the able can prosper and honest beings have rights, and where man is free to rise to greater heights*" (Hubbard, *Scientology: The Fundamentals of Thought*).

OT Levels

Beyond Clear are other levels of Operating Thetan, currently fifteen levels that are secret to other Scientologists who remain lower down on the Bridge. The most powerful level is Level 111, "The Wall of Fire." Scientologists who reach this level are allowed access to Hubbard's handwritten notes of his own personal experience.

The Church of Scientology

Scientology sometimes describes itself as "an applied religious philosophy." Some have used this phrase to argue that Scientology is not a religion. The Church of Scientology was founded in 1954 and claims to have an estimated eight million members in more than seventy countries, with headquarters in Los Angeles. The church claims some one hundred thousand members in Britain. L. Ron Hubbard remains the sole source of Scientology religious doctrine and technology, including the upper OT levels.

Writings

Hubbard's writings and lectures (tapes) are considered to be infallible. He is seen as an exclusive "Source" of the way to spiritual freedom. Scientology's spokeswoman Leisa Goodman writes, *"Mr. Hubbard's writings and lectures on the human spirit comprise the Scripture of Scientology religion. . . . As the sole source of the Scriptures, he has no successor"* (L. Ron Hubbard, *Founder of Dianetics and Scientology*, 1). Furthermore, no one else can alter his teachings. Only Hubbard can revise them (*Scientology Policy Directive* 19, July 7, 1982).

Authority in the Church of Scientology is exercised by Church of Scientology International (CSI) and the Religious Technology Center (RTC). The Sea Organization (Sea Org) was founded by Hubbard as a harsh and intensive training center mainly for young Scientologists who take vows of service "for a billion years." Hubbard spent some ten years sailing around the Mediterranean and elsewhere. Sea Org ships were often refused access to ports because of their lack of expertise as seamen. Toward the end of his lifetime Hubbard suffered declining health and became a recluse. Scientology suffered a corresponding decline in numbers and the Church fragmented. David Miscavige, a young Scientologist and member of the Sea Org, took the overall leadership of the movement, displacing many of the older members who had served Hubbard and the organization for many years.

During the last twenty years of the twentieth century, various countries—including Britain (1980) and Australia (1983)—lifted bans on Scientology. In 1993 the Internal Revenue Service in the United States finally granted religious tax-exemption rights to the movement.

Appendix
World Religions: Some Numbers and Places

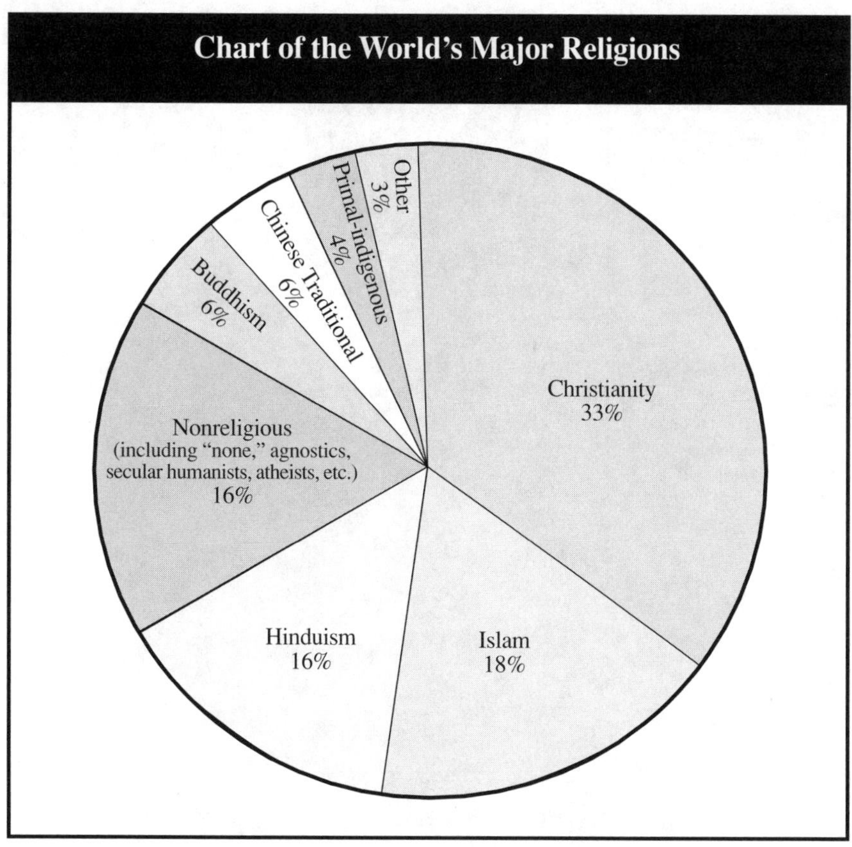

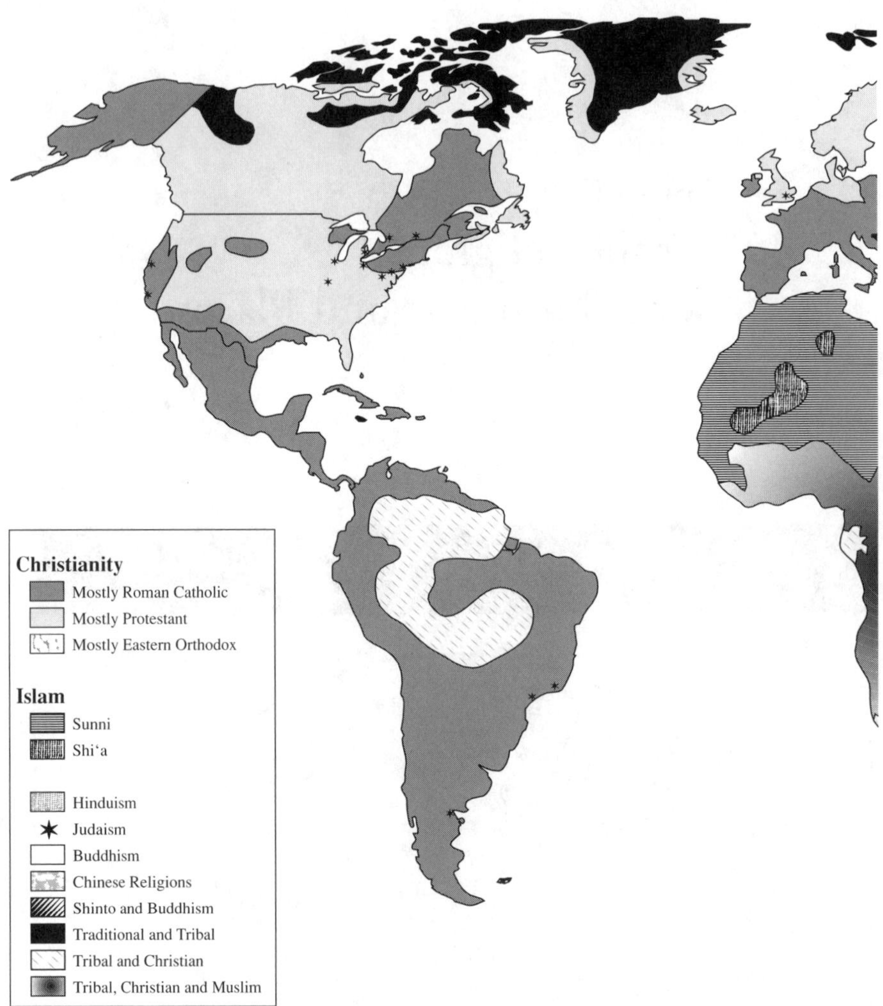

Christianity
Mostly Roman Catholic
Mostly Protestant
Mostly Eastern Orthodox
Islam
Sunni
Shi'a
Hinduism
Judaism
Buddhism
Chinese Religions
Shinto and Buddhism
Traditional and Tribal
Tribal and Christian
Tribal, Christian and Muslim

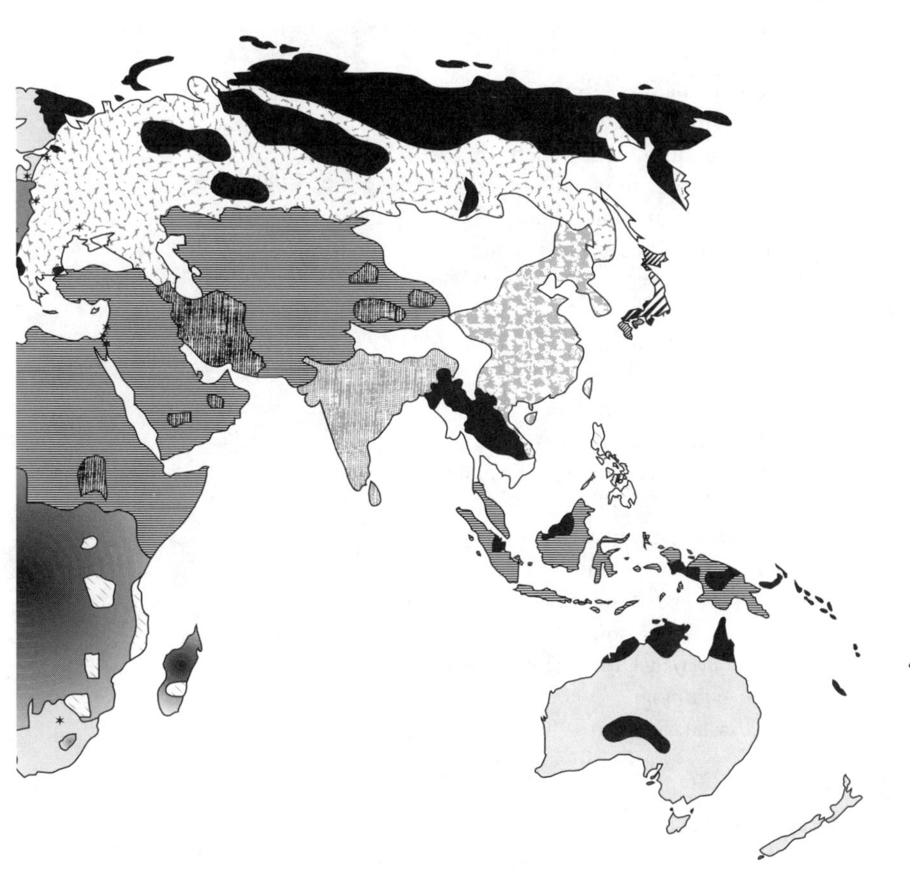

Sizes shown here are approximate estimates and are here mainly for the purpose of ordering the groups, not providing a definitive number.

1. Christianity: 2 billion
2. Islam: 1.3 billion
3. Hinduism: 900 million
4. Secular/Nonreligious/Agnostic/Atheist: 900 million
5. Buddhism: 350 million
6. Chinese traditional religion: 225 million
7. Primal-indigenous: 190 million
8. Yoruba religion: 20 million
9. Juche: 19 million
10. Sikhism: 18 million
11. Judaism: 15 million
12. Spiritism: 14 million
13. Babi & Baha'i faiths: 6 million
14. Jainism: 4 million
15. Shinto: 4 million
16. Cao Dai: 3 million
17. Tenrikyo: 2.4 million
18. Neo-Paganism: 1 million
19. Unitarian-Universalism: 800,000
20. Scientology: 750,000
21. Rastafarianism: 700,000
22. Zoroastrianism: 150,000

The adherent counts presented in the list above are estimates of the number of people who have at least a minimal level of self-identification as adherents of the religion. Levels of participation vary within all groups. These numbers tend toward the high end of reasonable worldwide estimates. Valid arguments can be made for different figures, but if the same criteria are used for all groups, the relative order should be the same. Further details and sources are available below and in the Adherents.com database.

The listing is not a comprehensive list of all religions, only the "major" ones.

Major Branches of Major World Religions Ordered by Number of Adherents

The following table presents all the major branches of major world religions listed above in a single table, ordered by size. Remember that the meaning of a division between branches of a religion differs between religions, and between each branch. Also, remember that some of these estimates may be inaccurate. Be advised against reading too much meaning into this particular table.

Major Branches of Major World Religions
Ordered by Number of Adherents

Branch	Religion	Number of Adherents
Catholic	Christianity	1,030,000,000
Sunni	Islam	940,000,000
Vaishnavites	Hinduism	580,000,000
Orthodox/Eastern Christian	Christianity	240,000,000
Shaivites	Hinduism	220,000,000
Liberal Protestant	Christianity	210,000,000
Conservative Protestant	Christianity	200,000,000
Mahayana	Buddhism	185,000,000
Theravada	Buddhism	124,000,000
Shiite	Islam	120,000,000
African indigenous sect (AICs)	Christianity	110,000,000
Pentecostal	Christianity	105,000,000
Neo-Hindus and reform Hindus	Hinduism	22,000,000
Lamaism (Vajrayana/Tibetan, etc.)	Buddhism	20,000,000
Sikhism	Sikhism	18,000,000
Jehovah's Witnesses	Christianity	14,000,000
Latter-day Saints	Christianity	11,200,000
Ahmadiyya	Islam	10,000,000
Veerashaivas (Lingayats)	Hinduism	10,000,000
Baha'i World Faith	Baha'i Faiths	6,000,000
Conservative	Judaism	4,500,000
Unaffiliated and Secular	Judaism	4,500,000
Svetambara	Jainism	4,000,000
Reform	Judaism	3,750,000
Seicho-No-Ie	New Japanese	3,200,000
Shinto, all branches	Shinto	3,000,000
Tenrikyo	New Japanese	2,800,000
PL Kyodan	New Japanese	2,600,000
Orthodox	Judaism	2,000,000
New Thought (Unity, Christian Science, etc.)	Christianity	1,500,000
Sekai Kyuseikyo	New Japanese	800,000
Sthanakavasis	Jainism	750,000
Zenrinkai	New Japanese	600,000
Druze	Islam	450,000
Tensho Kotai Jingukyo	New Japanese	400,000
Friends (Quakers)	Christianity	300,000
Ennokyo	New Japanese	300,000
Digambaras	Jainism	155,000
Reconstructionist	Judaism	150,000
Parsis	Zoroastrianism	110,000
Gabars	Zoroastrianism	20,000

Remember, this is not a table of all branches of religions, just a summary of major branches of the classical major world religions.

Christianity

Major Traditional Branches of Christianity (mid–1995; source: *Encyclopedia Britannica*)	
Branch	**Number of Adherents**
Roman Catholic	968,000,000
Protestant	395,867,000
Other Christians	275,583,000
Orthodox	217,948,000
Anglicans	70,530,000

Note: Depending on the country, government census records often recognize only one, two, or three divisions of Christians. Religious affiliation in surveys is always defined by self-identification, not by theology or practice. In predominantly non-Christian nations such as India or Iraq, available data may simply identify "Christians," to separate them from the majority populations of Hindus, Muslims, etc. If the data is more detailed (usually because there are larger numbers of Christians), Christians will be divided into "Catholics" and "Protestants" (with Orthodox/Eastern Christians typically classified as Protestant). With more accuracy, Orthodox are added as a third division, leaving all Christians who are not Catholic or Orthodox classified as Protestant. Typically this includes many groups who would prefer not to be grouped with Protestants, such as Jehovah's Witnesses and Latter-day Saints.

(This table does not include all Christians. These numbers are estimates, and are here primarily to assist in ranking branches by size, not to provide a definitive count of membership.)

Catholic: Includes Old Catholic, Aglipayan (Philippines), Uniate.

Orthodox/Eastern Christian: As a "branch," the Orthodox/Eastern churches include Eastern churches not in communion with Constantinople, Chalcedonian and Non-Chalcedonian, Nestorian, Coptic, Ethiopian Orthodox, various Jacobite/Syrian Orthodox, Armenian.

Pentecostal: Examples: Assemblies of God, Church of God in Christ, Universal Church of the Kingdom of God, various Churches of God, etc. Includes officially Pentecostal denominations — those which do not identify primarily with other denominational families, such as Baptist and Methodist. There are denominations and/or congregations which have generic Pentecostal characteristics, or

Major Denominational Families of Christianity	
Branch	**Number of Adherents**
Catholic	1,030,000,000
Orthodox/Eastern Christian	240,000,000
African indigenous sects (AICs)	110,000,000
Pentecostal	105,000,000
Reformed/Presbyterian/Congregational/United	75,000,000
Baptist	70,000,000
Anglican	65,000,000
Lutheran	65,000,000
Methodist	50,000,000
Jehovah's Witnesses	14,000,000
Latter-day Saints	11,200,000
Adventist	11,000,000
Apostolic/New Apostolic	10,000,000
Stone-Campbell ("Restoration Movement")	5,400,000
New Thought (Unity, Christian Science, etc.)	1,500,000
Brethren (incl. Plymouth)	1,500,000
Mennonite	1,250,000
Friends (Quakers)	300,000

are charismatic or evangelical, but are not classified primarily as a Pentecostal denomination.

African indigenous sects: Many African Initiated/Indigenous/Independent/Independent Churches (AICs), such as the Kimbanguist Church (6.5 million).

Latter Day Saints: Mormons. This branch is primarily comprised of the Church of Jesus Christ of Latter-Day Saints (LDS). Note the difference in capitalization and hyphenation between "Latter Day Saints" (a generic term for the entire branch/movement) and "Latter-day Saints" (members of the Church of Jesus Christ of Latter-day Saints, the predominant religious body). Historically this branch also includes the Reorganized Church of Jesus Christ of Latter Day Saints (RLDS) and a small number of even smaller splinter groups. In the year 2000 the RLDS Church changed its name to the "Community of Christ." Theologically, the current form of this religious body may best be classified as Liberal Protestant, although scholars continue to classify it under "Latter Day Saints" in historically based listings.

Adventist: Mostly Seventh-day Adventists, plus some others.

New Thought: The three largest New Thought heirs to Christian Science—Unity Church, Religious Science, and Divine Science—count among them about 780 churches and between 130,000 and 150,000 members in the U.S., according to a 1996 almanac of American religions.

Mennonite: Includes Amish as well as many other "Plain Churches."

Restoration Movement (Stone-Campbell): Primarily includes the "Christian Churches and Churches of Christ," "Church of Christ" (or "Churches of Christ"), and the "Christian Church" (Disciples of Christ)." Stone-Campbell churches should not be confused with Latter Day Saint denominations, which are part of a separate Restoration (usually referred to Latter Day Saints simply as "The Restoration" or "Restoration of the Gospel"). From its organization in 1830 until 1838 the Church of Jesus Christ of Latter-Day Saints was known simply as the "Church of Christ." But despite similarities in names, the Latter Day Saint and Stone/Campbellite movements are not connected.

Note: Division into denominational families offers a more detailed look at the composition of Christianity as a whole, but can be misleading. Among Protestants today, most significant divisions with regard to culture, practice, and doctrine are not between denominational families, but between Liberal and Conservative Protestants. Liberal Protestants number 210,000,000 and Conservative Protestants 200,000,000. Liberal Protestants includes most Anglicans. It is true that African and Asian Anglicans are far more conservative than American Anglicans (Episcopalians) but in those regions as well as in the U.S. Anglicans are now closely allied with more liberal Protestants such as Methodists, Congregationalists, and Lutherans.

Countries Where Christianity Predominates

In the following countries the majority of the population cites one of the branches of Christianity as their preferred religion:

Angola
Anguilla
Antigua and Barbuda
Argentina
Armenia
Aruba
Australia
Austria
Bahamas
Barbados
Belarus
Belgium
Belize
Bermuda
Bolivia
Bosnia and Herzegovina
Brazil
Bulgaria
Burundi
Canada
Cape Verde
Central African Republic
Chile
Colombia
Cook Islands
Costa Rica
Croatia
Cuba
Cyprus
Czech Republic
Denmark
Dominica
Dominican Republic
East Timor
Ecuador
El Salvador
Equatorial Guinea
Estonia
Finland
France
French Guinea
French Polynesia
Gabon
Georgia
Germany
Ghana
Greece
Greenland
Guatemala
Haiti
Honduras
Hungary
Iceland
Ireland
Italy

Jamaica
Kenya
Kiribati
Latvia
Lesotho
Lichtenstein
Lithuania
Luxembourg
Macedonia
Malta
Marshall Islands
Martinique
Mexico
Micronesia, Federated States of
Monaco
Namibia
Nauru
Netherlands
Netherlands Antilles
New Zealand
Nicaragua
Niue
Norfolk Island
Norway
Palau
Panama
Paraguay
Peru
Philippines
Poland
Portugal
Reunion
Romania
Russia
Rwanda
Saints Kitts and Nevis
Saint Lucia
Saint Vincent
Samoa
San Marino
Sao Tome and Principe
Serbia and Montenegro
Seychelles
Slovakia
Slovenia
Solomon Islands
South Africa
Spain
Swaziland
Sweden
Switzerland
Tonga
Trinidad and Tobago
Tuvalu
Uganda
Ukraine
United Kingdom
Uruguay
USA
Vanuatu
Vatican
Venezuela
Wallis and Futuna Islands
Zaire (Democratic Republic of Congo)
Zambia

Roman Catholic Christianity

In the following places (listed alphabetically) at least 85 percent of the population is Roman Catholic (at least nominally):

Andorra
Argentina
Aruba
Austria
Belgium
Bolivia
Cape Verde
Chile
Colombia
Costa Rica
Cuba
Dominican Republic
Ecuador
El Salvador
Equatorial Guinea
France
French Guinea
Gibraltar
Guadeloupe
Guam
Guatemala
Haiti
Honduras
Indonesia: Flores
Ireland
Italy
Lichtenstein
Luxembourg
Malta
Martinique
Mexico
Monaco
Nicaragua
Northern Mariana Islands
Panama
Paraguay
Peru
Philippines
Poland
Portugal
Puerto Rico
Quebec, Canada
Reunion
Saint Lucia
Saint Pierre and Miquelon
San Marino
Seychelles
Slovenia
Spain
Vatican City
Venezuela
Wallis and Futuna Islands

Places in which between 50 percent and 85 percent of the population is Roman Catholic, at least nominally:

Angola
Belize
Brazil
Burundi
Congo
Connecticut
Croatia
Czechoslovakia
Dominica
East Timor
Hungary
Kiribati
Lithuania
Massachusetts
Netherlands Antilles
New Brunswick, Canada
New Caledonia
Rhode Island
Rwanda
Slovakia
Uganda
Uruguay

Protestant Christianity

Countries in which at least 85 percent of the population is Protestant, at least nominally (these lists are not necessarily comprehensive):

- Antigua and Barbuda
- Denmark
- Finland
- Greenland
- Iceland
- Norway
- Sweden
- Tuvalu

Countries in which between 50 percent and 85 percent of the population is Protestant, at least nominally:

Bahamas
Barbados
Bermuda
French Polynesia
Jamaica
Malawi
Namibia
Nauru
New Zealand
Newfoundland
Oceania
Saint Kitts and Nevis
Saint Vincent and the Grenadines
Samoa
Solomon Islands
South Africa
Swaziland
Tahiti
Tonga
United Kingdom
USA
Vanuatu

Orthodox (Eastern) Christianity

Countries in which at least 50 percent and 85 percent of the population is Orthodox:

- Armenia
- Belarus
- Bulgaria
- Cyprus
- Georgia

- Greece
- Macedonia
- Moldova
- Romania
- Russia
- Serbia and Montenegro
- Ukraine

Islam

Major Branches of Islam	
Branch	**Number of Adherents**
Sunni	940,000,000
Shi'ite	120,000,000
Ahmadiyya	10,000,000
Druze	450,000

Note: As with all other religions (including Christianity, Buddhism, Judaism, and Hinduism), not all historical branches of Islam consider each other acceptably orthodox. The numerically largest branch of Islam, Sunnis, believe that adherence to the five pillars of Islam and acceptance of certain key doctrinal positions are requisite for an individual's classification, however, these are primarily based on self-identification and historical considerations.

The Druze, for example, are not considered part of the numerically dominant (i.e. "mainstream") Muslim grouping. But Druze are classified from a secular/historical perspective as a branch of Islam because they are derived from a branch of Shi'ite Islam. Having developed independently for hundreds of years, their cultural and religious self-concept is primarily Druze, without regard to how outside groups perceive or classify them. Nevertheless, they retain some self-concept as Muslims in addition to their clear historical ties.

Countries Where Islam Predominates

The majority of the population are Muslims in the following countries:

Afghanistan
Albania
Algeria
Azerbaijan
Bahrain
Bangladesh
Brunei
Chechnya
Comoros
Dagestan
Djibouti
Egypt

Gambia
Gaza Strip
Guinea
Indonesia
Iran
Iraq
Jordan
Kuwait
Kyrgyzstan
Libya
Malaysia
Mali
Maldives
Mauritania
Mayotte
Morocco
Niger
Pakistan
Qatar
Saudi Arabia
Senegal
Somalia
Sudan
Syria
Tajikistan
Tatarstan
Tunisia
Turkey
Turkmenistan
United Arab Emirates
Uzbekistan
West Bank
Yemen

Shiʿite Islam

The majority (90 percent) of Muslins belong to the Sunni branch of Islam. Historically there has been considerable distance between Sunni and Shiʿites Islam, roughly comparable to the Catholic/Protestant split. But in recent years, leading Sunni councils (such as the Islamic university at Cairo) have increasingly accepted Shiʿites as thoroughly a part of Orthodox Islam, and described Shiʿites as a "fifth" school, on par with traditional Sunni schools such as Shafii or Hanafi Islam.

Nevertheless, although Shiʿites may be thought of theologically as part of the orthodox Islamic "communion," there remain clear cultural, legal, and even doctrinal differences between Shiʿites and Sunni Muslims.

The majority of the population are Shiʿites Muslims in Iran, Azerbaijan, Bahrain, Oman, and Iraq. In virtually all other countries in which one branch of Islam is predominant, the predominant branch is Sunni. There are other branches of Islam that are considered heretical by Sunnis (such as Ahmadiyyans and Druze), but these do not form the majority of the population in any nation.

Hinduism

Major Branches of Hinduism	
Branch	**Number of Adherents**
Vaishnavites	580,000,000
Shaivites	220,000,000
Neo-Hindus and reform Hindus	22,000,000
Veerashaivas (Lingayats)	10,000,000

Note that Lingayats consider their religion separate and distinct from Hinduism, although the Indian government and most general religious texts do not classify them separately.

Countries Where Hinduism Predominates

The world's third largest religion, Hinduism, makes up the majority of the population of three nations:

- Nepal
- India
- Mauritius

It is interesting to note that although the majority of the world's Hindus live in India, the nation as a whole is only about 80 percent Hindu, and is an officially secular state, i.e., there is no state religion.

In Nepal a higher proportion of the population are Hindus than in India, and Nepal is the world's only official Hindu state. Freedom of worship is protected, but the official state religion is Hinduism. (As in many countries, interreligious proselytizing is prohibited.)

In Mauritius, a bare majority of 54 percent of the population are Hindu.

Sikhism

Major Branches of Sikhism	
Branch	**Number of Adherents**
Sikhism	18,000,000

Countries Where Sikhism Predominates

Sikhism does not make up the majority of the population of any nations. It makes up the majority of the population of only one Indian province: Punjab.

It might be said that of the world's largest religions, only Sikhism does not have a state. Sikhism is often called the world's fifth largest organized religion, and with nearly 20 million adherents, is larger than Judaism (about 15 million, many of whom are secular).

For many Sikhs, not having a state of their own is an issue of great importance, and the Punjabi independence movement is hotly debated in the region and in the Sikh community worldwide. Other Sikhs genuinely feel emphasis on achieving their own political state is overly divisive and draws undue attention away from the profound theological and spiritual messages of their religion.

Buddhism

Major Branches of Buddhism	
Branch	**Number of Adherents**
Mahayana	185,000,000
Theravada	124,000,000
Lamaism (Vajrayana/Tibetan/Tantric)	20,000,000

Countries Where Buddhism Predominates

The world's fourth largest organized religion, Buddhism, is the religion of the majority of the population in nine countries:

- Thailand
- Cambodia
- Myanmar
- Tibet
- Bhutan
- Sri Lanka
- Laos
- Vietnam
- Japan

Buddhism is also very important historically and culturally in several other Asian countries, but is no longer cited as the preferred religion by at least 50 percent of the population. In China, Mongolia, and North Korea, Buddhism was forcibly suppressed by Communist regimes. Buddhism remains important in these countries, but is no longer claimed as the religious preference by the majority of the population. Taiwan is heavily Buddhist, but the religion is mixed with Taoism and Confucianism, and exists side by side with other religions to such a degree that Buddhism is probably not a majority religion, strictly speaking. In South Korea, Christianity has recently made enough gains that Buddhism is no longer the religion of the majority of the population.

Currently, many people in traditionally Buddhist countries such as Korea and China are embracing Christianity in greater numbers, while Buddhism is in turn gaining increasing numbers of converts among Westerners in places such as Europe, Australia, and the United States. There are even organizations and books for "JuBus" (Jews who practice Buddhism).

Judaism

Differences in practice and belief between the branches of Judaism are compared in this chart by Gilbert Rosenthal.

Major Branches of Judaism	
Branch	**Number of Adherents**
Conservative	4,500,000
Unaffiliated and Secular	4,500,000
Reform	3,750,000
Orthodox	2,000,000
Reconstructionist	150,000

Countries Where Judaism Predominates

Jews make up the majority (83 percent) in one country: Israel.

A large number of Israel's Jews are secular—nonobservant and either philosophically nonreligious or even agnostic or atheist. Religious Jews are in the minority in Israel.

Interestingly enough, a larger number of Jews live in the United States than in Israel, and a higher proportion of American Jews are religious (i.e., practice Judaism or profess some form of belief in Judaism).

Jainism

Major Branches of Jainism	
Branch	**Number of Adherents**
Svetambara	4,000,000
Sthanakavasis	750,000
Digambaras	155,000

Countries Where Jainism Predominates

There are no countries or provinces in which Jains make up the majority of the population. Jains have no significant, established communities outside of India.

Shintoism

The groups on the following page are officially registered and classified by Japanese government as "Shinto" or "other" (neither Buddhist not Shinto).

Traditionally, comparative religious literature has acknowledged three main

Major Branches of Shintoism and Other Japanese New Religions	
Branch	**Number of Adherents**
Shinto, all branches	3,000,000
Seicho-No-Ie	3,200,000
Tenrikyo	2,800,000
PL Kyodan	2,600,000
Sekai Kyuseikyo	800,000
Zenrikai	600,000
Tensho Kotai Jingukyo	400,000
Ennokyo	300,000

divisions in Shinto: Sect Shinto, State Shinto, and Shrine Shinto. There is no reliable way to determine how many people are in which branches.

Only about 4 million people worldwide (nearly all of them in Japan) claim Shinto as their religion. Most Japanese who consider themselves religious cite Buddhism as their religion, but occasionally participate in Shinto-derived public holidays, celebrations, ceremonies, etc. Individual Shinto organizations and shrines are able to claim at least 80 percent of the Japanese population as "members" due to community-based record-keeping practices that date back hundreds of years. But few Japanese think of themselves as Shintoists.

Most people who do consider Shinto their religion are presumably involved in "Sect Shinto." The largest Shinto-derived sects (such as Tenrikyo, PL Kyodan) do not wish to be considered Shinto any longer and are classified officially as "Other" or "New Religious Movements." These are not included in this 4 million adherents figure.

Note. The table above does not include any officially Buddhist religions, but there are no doubt Buddhist influences found within most or all of these.

Countries Where Shintoism Predominates

Because of historical birth registration laws and customs, Shinto organizations claim over 80 percent of the population of Japan as adherents. (Keep in mind that Buddhist organizations claim 90 percent of the population as adherents.) The majority of Japanese take part in Shinto celebrations, festivals, etc., and may have Shinto shrines in their homes. Although less than 4 percent of Japanese claim Shinto as their religious preference in opinion surveys (most claim Buddhism, and most also say they aren't religious), the religion of Shinto can certainly be said to "have a state." But the religion's influence is more cultural, historical, and traditional—more comparable to the influence of the Anglican Church in England than Islam in Saudi Arabia.

Zoroastrianism

Major Branches of Zoroastrianism	
Branch	**Number of Adherents**
Parsis	110,000
Gabars	20,000

Worldwide there are less than 200,000 Zoroastrians. Many estimates indicate there are only about 100,000 practicing Zoroastrians. As a proud but dwindling group, Zoroastrains are fairly unified and there is little in the way of "denominationalism." But there remains a clear division between the two traditional communities—Iraqi ("Gabars") and Indian ("Parsis"). Although surprisingly similar considering the length of time the two communities were separated from each other, there are differences in dress, custom, ritual, and understanding. The religious calendar is one of the hotly debated areas of difference.

Countries Where Zoroastrianism Predominates

The relatively few Zoroastrians in the world do not make up the majority of the population in any countries, states, or provinces. They do form the majority in a few small Iranian towns, and they are an important segment of the cultural elite in a few major Indian cities.

Zoroastrianism was once the state religion of ancient Persia (present-day Iran), and at one time was one of the largest organized religions in the world.

Chinese Traditional Religion

Chinese Traditional Religion	
Branch	**Number of Adherents**
All branches	220,000,000*

* In older world religion books the estimates of the total number of adherents of Confucianism range up to 350 million. Other books, including older versions of the *Encyclopedia Britannica*, have listed Chinese religionists under "Taoism," with adherent estimates up to about 200 million. But these figures are all based on counts of the same segment of Chinese people throughout the world—people practicing what is, sociologically, more accurately called Chinese traditional religion, and often called Chinese *folk* religion. The word "traditional" is preferable to "folk" because

"folk" might imply only the local, tribal customs and beliefs such as ancestor worship and nature beliefs. But "Chinese traditional religion" is meant to categorize the common religion of the majority Chinese culture: a combination of Confucianism, Buddhism, and Taoism, as well as the traditional non-scriptural/local practices and beliefs. For most religious Chinese who do not explicitly follow a different religion such as Islam or Christianity, these different ancient Chinese philosophies and traditions form a single, seamless composite religious culture and worldview.

Communist laws banning most religion and recent rapid changes introducing increasing openness make accurate estimates difficult to obtain. Recent figures for the number of "Chinese religionists" include 220 and 225 million.

Countries Where Taoism and Confucianism Predominate

No country can really be said to be predominantly Taoist or Confucian in the sense that a majority of people claim one of these systems as their religion. But Taoism and Confucianism (mixed with Buddhism) are major cultural and philosophical influences in many East Asian nations. Religious Taoism is still very significant in Taiwan.

Many writers have noted that the influence of Confucianism is felt more significantly in present-day Japan than Buddhism, Shinto, or any other religion, even though no Japanese people cite it as their "religion." The majority of Chinese people is influenced by combinations of Confucian and Taoist thought, and traditional religious practices and beliefs (ancestor- and nature-oriented), but most do not name themselves exclusively as adherents of these traditions. Other important influences and religions in China which are of non-Chinese origin are Buddhism, Communism, Islam, and Christianity.

Baha'i

Major Contemporary Branches of the Babi and Baha'i Faiths	
Branch	**Number of Adherents**
Baha'i World Faith	6,000,000

Countries Where Baha'i Predominates

There are no nations, provinces or states where Baha'is make up a majority of the population. This is not surprising, as the religion is very young.

There are some villages in Africa which are predominantly Baha'i. (It is not unusual for smaller, close-knit villages in Africa, and sometimes other parts of the world, to adopt a new religion en masse.)

* The author and publisher are grateful to adherents.com Web site for permission to reproduce this material.

Glossary

(Note: Most of the entries relating to Christianity are based on Donald K. McKim, *Westminster Dictionary of Theological Terms* [Louisville, Ky.: Westminster John Knox Press, 1996])

Abba. Aramaic term for "father" used by Jesus in addressing God and connoting intimacy.

absolute. That which exists in and of itself with no dependence. A philosophical description of God.

adept. A term applied to an initiate who has reached the highest degree of attainment in the material world, with complete mastery of the self. Many occult schools teach that adepts are exerting a guiding influence over the development of the human race.

adhan. The Muslim call to prayer.

Adi Granth. Adi means "first." Adi Granth is the first edition of the Guru Granth Sahib, as compiled by Guru Arjun in 1604.

Advaita Vedanta. Nondualistic form of Vedantic philosophy.

Adventism. Belief in the second coming of Jesus Christ. Also a reference to the Seventh-day Adventist denomination.

Africentic (Afrocentric) theology. The construction of Christian theology using the resources and cultural context of Africa, rather than of Europe or North America. It is of particular significance to African-American theologians.

Age of Reason. Historically, a designation used for the eighteenth century in the Western world, when the philosophy of rationalism, stressing the powers of the human mind and reason, was a dominant force.

Agni. A prominent deity in Hinduism and Vedic religion who is able to transform material that is offered in sacrifice into a substance through which the gods (devas) are nourished.

agnosticism. The view that there is insufficient evidence on which to make any decisions about the existence of God.

ahimsa. The Hindu principle of nonviolence and noninjury to living creatures.

Ahura Mazda. In Zoroastrianism, the creator God of all things, the one Eternal Being.

Akhand Path. In Sikhism, an uninterrupted continuous reading of the Guru Granth Sahib by a series of readers which takes about forty-eight hours. It is conducted in such a way that there is no haste and the words are pronounced clearly.

Alexandrian theology. Theology arising from Alexandria in the third to fifth centuries associated with Clement, Origen, Athanasius, and Cyril. Influenced by Platonism, it stressed the allegorical interpretation of scripture and tended to emphasize the divinity of Jesus.

Allah. Arabic word for God deriving from the word "Illah" meaning "the One deserving all worship." The word is in the singular and is not associated with masculine, feminine, or neuter characteristics.

Amida Buddha. In Pure Land Buddhism, the Buddha of infinite light; the personification of compassion revered as the mediator between humanity and ultimate reality; he who presides over the Western Paradise.

amidah. The Jewish standing prayer.

Amritsar. The Sikh city founded by Guru Ram Das in 1577 and in which the Golden Temple (Darbar Sahib) now stands. It is a major religious center and although pilgrimage, strictly speaking, has no place in Sikhism, the city is revered and visited by many Sikhs.

Anabaptism. A term derived from the Greek word for "rebaptizer," and used to refer to the radical wing of the sixteenth-century Reformation, including thinkers such as Menno Simons or Balthasar Hubmaier.

Analects (Lun Yu). Literally meaning "digested conversations," the most reliable of all collections of Confucius's teachings. The principal themes include humanity (*jen*), social custom (*li*), the superior person (*chun-tzu*), filial obedience (*hsiao*), the rectification of names (*cheng ming*), and good government.

analogous term. A term that applies to unlike, but related, things.

***anatta*.** (Hinduism) Not self, egolessness.

angel. (Greek = "messenger") A type of spiritual being, both good (usually) and bad ("demons") who become involved in human affairs; common to Judaism, Christianity, and Islam. A leader among the angels is sometimes called an "archangel" (e.g., Michael, Gabriel).

Anglicanism. The theological movement and churches originating directly or indirectly from the Church of England.

Anglo-Catholicism. Anglicanism with highly developed liturgical practices and strong affinities for Roman Catholicism. It emphasizes the Church of England's historical continuity with medieval Catholicism and interprets Church doctrine in ways that are consistent with Roman Catholic teachings.

***anicca*.** (Hinduism) Impermanence.

Animism. Religious belief and practice relating to spiritual beings that sees natural objects as possessing spiritual life and values.

anthropomorphism. The tendency to ascribe human features (such as hands or arms) or other human characteristics to God.

antinomian. (Greek = "opposing law") A general term for the view of people who are against established rules and laws. In Christian tradition, a name given to those who felt that salvation by grace excused them from obeying temporal law(s).

Antioch, school of. Theological trends developing from Antioch during the early Christian centuries characterized by concern for the literal rather than the allegorical sense of the text of scripture and the perfect humanity of Jesus Christ. Its school of interpretation contrasted with that of Alexandria.

anti-Semitism. Literally means opposed to Semites (which might include Arabic and other semitics), but usually applied specifically to hatred of Jews (anti-Judaism), which may take the form of discrimination or extermination.

Apocalypse (adj. apocalyptic). From the Greek, meaning "revelation." A genre of literature (attested in Jewish, Christian, and Muslim traditions) containing revelation(s), usually about the end-time.

apocalyptic. A type of literature that contains revelations often in symbolic form, e.g., Daniel 7–12 and the book of Revelation. Apocalyptic literature is also marked by the theme of judgment and points toward the future and the end of human history.

Apocrypha. Fifteen Judeo-Hellenistic books that are included in the Greek Septuagint and Roman Catholic Vulgate Old Testament, but excluded from the Jewish Tanakh and Protestant Old Testament. From the Greek, meaning "to hide" or "to uncover."

apophatic way. (Greek = "denial") A way of theological inquiry into the knowledge of God that proceeds by negations or saying what God is not.

apostles. The first twelve disciples or followers of Christ (Matt. 10:2–5; Acts 1:13–14 lists only 11); any Christian sent forth as a messenger for Christ.

Apostolic age. The early period of the Christian church from approximately 30–90 C.E., when the apostles of Jesus were still alive.

arguments for the existence of God. Rational arguments believed by some to be logically valid ways of proving that God exists. Traditionally these arguments have included the causal, cosmological, ontological, moral, and teleological.

Arhat. Literally "the worthy," term in Theravada Buddhism referring to the ideal Buddhist devoted to the achievement of nirvana.

Arianism. An early Christian heresy named after Arius (250–336 C.E.), who taught that Jesus was not in existence for all time, but was created by God.

Armageddon. The place of the final great struggle between the forces of good and evil (Rev. 16:16).

Armenianism. The teaching of James Arminius (1560–1609), which conflicted with Calvinism, particularly on issues of human sinfulness, predestination, and whether or not salvation can be lost. It stressed human response to the gospel, conditional election, unlimited atonement, and resistible grace.

Aryan. Light-skinned migrating people, perhaps from Europe, who settled in India around 1500 B.C.E. and are thought to have instituted Vedic Hinduism.

asanas. Yogic postures and practices.

ascetic. A general term for a person who denies themselves some of the necessities of life, such as food, clothing, and shelter, and employs rigorous spiritual discipline to gain spiritual benefit. (From Greek, to hold oneself under control.)

Ashkenazim. Jews of Central and Eastern European origin.

Athanasianism. Views based on the writings of Athansius (c. 293–373 C.E.), bishop of Alexandria, who vigorously defended the teachings of the Council of Nicaea (325) that Jesus Christ was eternally divine and fully God ("of the same substance," Greek = *homoousios*). He contended against Arianism.

atheism. The belief that there is no ultimate reality.

atman. (Hinduism) The divine soul or life force that emanates from Brahman; the eternal self within.

atonement (Christianity). The belief that the death of Jesus on the cross effects salvation and reconciles the human race to God.

atonement (Judaism). Hebrew: kapparah. Reconciliation with God. In biblical teaching sacrifice was the outward form of atonement. After the destruction of the Temple in 70 C.E. the only means of atonement were prayer, repentance, fasting, charity, and self-restitution.

aum. When sounded, its prolonged tone is associated with the creative sound through which the universe came into being.

avatar (Hinduism). Incarnation of God.

Ba'al Shem. (Hebrew) A phrase meaning "Master of the Divine Name," used by Hasidic Jews and scholars of Kabbalah to refer to someone who possessed knowledge of the Lost Word, the Secret Name of God.

baptism. Initiation into the Christian faith through a worship ceremony in which water is applied by sprinkling, pouring, or immersion while the Trinitarian formula is spoken. Regarded as a sacrament by most churches.

bar/bat mitzvah. A Jewish rite-of-passage of coming of age for boys and girls (in some Jewish traditions) after reaching the age of thirteen. The bar/bat mitzvah marks the completion of religious instruction, after which children become adults who are then responsible for their actions before God.

Beatitudes, the. Teachings of Jesus in the Sermon on the Mount regarding the lives and dispositions of his followers (Matt. 5:3–12; Luke 6:20–22).

being, absolute. A being that can be thought of or that can exist without reference to another.

***Bhagavad-gita*.** Scripture of the avatar Krishna and part of the Hindu epic Mahabharata.

***bhakti*.** Practices of worship or devotion to a Hindu god or goddess.

***bhikkhu*.** A Buddhist monk. A Buddhist nun is a bhikkhuni.

biblical criticism. (from Greek = *krinein*, "to decide") The use of methods and procedures for studying literary and historical documents applied to the Bible.

blasphemy. Expressing through speech or writing that which is mocking or contemptuous toward God. It was met with the death penalty in ancient Judaism (Lev. 24:16) and is warned against in the New Testament (2 Tim. 3:2; 2 Peter 2:2; Rev. 16:9, 11).

Bodhidharma. Buddhist sage reputed to have brought Zen practice from India to China c. 500 C.E..

bodhisattva. Literally "wisdom being"; a Mahayana Buddhist who, out of compassion for all sentient beings, renounces his/her own entry into *nibbana* (nirvana), hence repeatedly being reborn into the world to undertake the infinite task of saving all sentient beings.

Brahma. In Hinduism, the creative force of ultimate reality; also in the neuter form of the noun, Brahman, the divine source and pervading essence of the universe, i.e., ultimate reality itself.

Brahmin. The Indian caste of priests and its family members.

Brahmo Samaj. A reformist Hindu movement founded by Ram Mohan Roy in 1828 as "Brahmo Sabha" and restructured and renamed in 1843 by Debendranath Tagore. It seeks to develop a strong ethical consciousness within Hinduism.

Brunnerian. The theological thought emerging from the writings of Swiss theologian Emil Brunner (1889–1966). He was influenced by Kierkegaard (1813–1855) and identified with neo-orthodoxy. He was open to a "point of contact between God and humans" (against Barth) and emphasized the divine-human encounter.

Buddha. The "Enlightened One" Siddhartha Gautama, called the Buddha, was the first man to discover the "Way of Truth" (dharma) and teach it to humankind. Also (Hinduism) ninth avatar of Vishnu.

Buddhism. Nonorthodox form of Vedic/Aryan teaching founded by the Buddha or enlightened one.

Byzantine rite. Liturgy of Eastern churches (Orthodox and Uniate) deriving from Byzantium (Constantinople). Sometimes called the "Greek Rite," it is rich in liturgical symbolism.

Calif (Caliph). In Sunni Islam, the temporal leader of the *ummah*, the Muslim community.

Calvinism. The developed and systematized teachings of John Calvin (1509–15), which spread throughout Europe and internationally from the sixteenth century to the present day. It is also called the Reformed tradition.

Campbellites. Followers of Alexander Campbell (1788–1866), one of the founders of the Christian Church (Disciples of Christ). They practice a congregational form of church government and believers' baptism, and they celebrate the Lord's Supper each Sunday. They reject all creedal statements.

Cappadocian theologians (fathers). Fourth-century theologians from Cappadocia concerned especially with establishing the doctrines of the Trinity and Christology against Arianism. They were Basil the Great of Caesarea (c. 330–379), Gregory of Nyssa (c. 335–c. 395), and Gregory of Nazianzus (c. 329–390).

caste. The social grouping into which a Hindu is born. Traditionally includes four castes (*varnas*): priests (Brahmins), warriors (*ksatriyas*), artisans (*vaisyas*), and servants (*sudras*).

catechism. A manual of Christian doctrine, usually in the form of question and answer, for the use of religious instruction.

cause, first. A cause whose causality is absolutely independent of any other cause or being, and on which all other causality depends.

Celestial Buddha (*sambhogakaya*). In Mahayana Buddhism's Triple Body (*trikaya*) theory, these are heavenly or godlike Buddhas. The most famous is Amita. When Buddhists show devotion to Celestial Buddhas, they are helped in their search for enlightenment.

chakras. In Tantra (Hinduism), nerve centers of the subtle body through which spiritual energy is channeled.

Chalcedonian definition. The formal declaration at the Council of Chalcedon that Jesus Christ was to be regarded as both human and divine.

Ch'an. (Chinese) A sect of Mahayana Buddhism, better known in the United States by its Japanese name, "Zen." Ch'an is distinctive for the development of a monastic lifestyle and techniques that aid achievement of enlightenment, including *zazen* and the *koan*.

Chandoa. In Sikhism the canopy that is placed over the Guru Granth Sahib.

Channeling. A practice familiar to New Agers where the spirit of a master teacher is contacted in order to receive guidance and knowledge.

Charisma, charismatic. In Christianity, a term associated with the gifts of the Holy Spirit. Since the early twentieth century, the term "charismatic" has referred to styles of theology and worship emphasizing the immediate presence and experience of the Holy Spirit.

charismatic. A modern movement in the Christian Church emphasizing spiritual gifts such as words of knowledge, healing, and speaking in tongues.

Chaur(i). In Sikhism it is Yak hair or a bundle of peacock feathers or manmade fibers fitted in a handle. It is ceremonially waved over the Guru Granth Sahib as a symbol of respect and sovereignty.

Christ. (Greek = Messiah) (Hebrew = Anointed One) Messiah is the Jewish term for an anointed one of God. Christians believe that Jesus was the expected Messiah.

Christology. Christian theology dealing with the identity of Jesus Christ, especially the question of the relation of his human and divine natures.

Chuang-Tzu. Taoist sage who lived about two hundred years after Lao Tzu, the traditional author of the *Tao-Te Ching*; his writings (the Chuang-Tzu) contain linguistic paradoxes and subtle forms of thought that give the basis of philosophical Taoism.

Chun-tzu. In Confucian philosophy, the noble person with *jen* (magnanimity).

circumcision. Removal of the male foreskin as a sign of the covenant in the Hebrew Bible and Christian Old Testament (Gen. 17:9–14). It signifies membership within the Jewish community.

confession. Although referring primarily to the admission of sin, it acquired a technical sense in the sixteenth century: that of a document embodying the principles of faith of a Protestant church. Thus the Augsburg Confession (1530) embodies the ideas of early Lutheranism.

consciousness. The intuitive awareness by which we recognize something as present in the mind.

consubstantiation. A late medieval view of the Lord's Supper. While the "substance" of the bread and wine are not changed into the body and blood of Christ, they coexist or are conjoined in union with each other; bread with body and wine with blood. The term is sometimes used to describe Lutheran views of the Lord's Supper.

Council of Trent. Ecumenical council convened by Pope Paul III in 1545 to reform the Church and oppose the actions of the Protestants by reaffirming core Catholic doctrines.

covenant (*b'rith*). A pact between two parties. In Judaism, the covenant (Hebrew = *brit*) is a major theological concept referring to the eternal bond between God and the people of Israel that calls for the nation's obedience to the divine commandments (*mitzvot*) and instruction (*Torah*). The first covenant is with Noah (covenant of the rainbow, Gen. 6:18; 9:8); the second with Abraham (circumcision, Gen. 17:2); the third with Moses on Sinai (Ten Commandments; Ex. 20:1–17; 20:22–23:33). For Christianity (e.g. Paul), God has made a "new covenant" ("new testament") with the followers of Jesus in the last times, superseding the "old covenant" (thus, "old testament") with Moses at Sinai.

creation *ex nihilo*. The Christian view that God created all things out of "nothing" and is thus the ultimate cause and source of meaning for the whole created order.

creation. The production of a thing from nothing.

creed. A formal summary of the Christian faith, held in common by Christians. The most important are those generally known as the "Apostles' creed" and the "Nicene creed." Also a general term for "belief" declarations, e.g., in Judaism the Shema affirmation, or in Islam the *shahada kalima*.

criterion. The test by which we distinguish true judgments from those that are false.

criticism, biblical. The study and the investigation of biblical writings through many means to understand elements such as their backgrounds, forms, history, authorship, audience, message, language, circumstances, and relation to other biblical writings.

Crusades. A number of military attempts in the eleventh, twelfth, and thirteenth centuries by late-medieval Western kingdoms (France, England, and Germany) and the papal states of Italy to reclaim for Christendom the Holy Lands from Muslim rule. The Crusaders succeeded temporarily by occupying Jerusalem but were driven out by Saladin in 1187 C.E. Subsequent attempts failed, and Crusaders were finally driven from Palestine at the close of the thirteenth century.

cult. (Latin = *cultus*, "devotion," "worship"). The form and practice of worship or the religious rites of a people. Also, a term to designate a "sect." The term is also used to indicate adoration or devotion.

cults. Groups regarded as heretical, often marked by strong social controls.

Daevas. (Zoroastrianism) A pantheon of gods representing the elements, aspects of nature, the shining ones.

Darwinism. The theory propounded by Charles Darwin (1809–1882) that all things now living have emerged through a process of evolution and natural selection from simpler forms of life. The relation of this theory to biblical accounts of God as creator has been a source of controversy.

deconstructionist. Interpretative method that denies the priority or privilege of any single reading of a text (even if the author intends it), indicating that the text is incoherent because its own key terms can be understood only in relation to their opposites. Deconstructionists, e.g. Derrida, seek to uncover the internal conflicts that tend to undermine (or at least to "decenter") the significance of any text.

Deism. A term referring to the beliefs of a group of rationalist English writers, especially during the seventeenth century, whose ideas anticipated the Enlightenment. The term is often used to refer to a view of God that recognizes the divine creatorship, but rejects the notion of a continuing divine involvement with the world.

deist. A person who believes in the existence of a deity, who created the universe, but has not been involved with the world since.

deity. The personification of some force or concept of great magnitude. A being that embodies the essence of an aspect of existence.

demiurge. A philosophical concept found in Platonism to designate the divine agency by which the physical world came into existence. The idea was taken over in Christian gnosticism to distinguish the creator of the physical world (often seen as evil) from the superior/good God who is completely unconnected with matter.

demon. In Christianity, an evil spirit that works contrary to the divine will (Mark 1:34, 39).

demythologization. A theological approach associated with German theologian Ruldolf Bultmann (1884–1976) and his followers, that the New Testament worldview is "mythological." In order for it to be understood within, or applied to, the modern situation, it is necessary that the mythological elements should be eliminated or translated into categories of existential philosophy.

denomination. A sectarian branch of Protestant Christianity whose congregations are united by a single legal and administrative body: for example, Baptists, Methodists, Episcopalians, etc.

Dependent origination (Buddhism). The causal chain that ensures that the wheel of Sansara keeps revolving.

determinism. A philosophical view that all humans and events are prescribed by the law of cause and effect so that human "freedom" is denied as a reality. In its extreme form it may be called "fatalism."

Deva. In Hinduism, a deity.

***Dhammapada*.** A collection of some four hundred short, terse sayings attributed to the Buddha and revealing Buddhist philosophy and psychology.

Dharma. Buddhist term with several different meanings: (1) the teachings of the Buddha, (2) a moment or aspect of the world of flux and impermanence, (3) fate or causal law. In Hinduism, dharma means virtue. In particular, it refers to the duties of a person's caste (*varna* and *jati*) and the idea that it is virtuous always to fulfill those duties willingly and well.

***Dhikr*.** In Islam, the constant repetition of *Shahadah* (profession of faith), especially during salah (prayer). Also a Quranic word commanding remembrance of God. Sufis consider Dhikr a spiritual food, and it is one of their main practices.

dispensationalism. A view of God's activities in history expounded in The Scofield Reference Bible and traced to John Nelson Darby (1800–1882). Each dispensation is a different time period in which humans are tested in responding to God's will. Seven dispensations cover creation to judgment.

divination. The art or practice that seeks to foresee or foretell future events or discover hidden knowledge through augury (e.g., the flight of birds or by examining the entrails of sacrificed animals) or with the aid of supernatural powers, omens, or the occult.

***Diwan*.** Congregational worship where Guru Granth Sahib is present.

Docetism. An early Christological heresy, believing that Jesus Christ was a purely divine being who only had the "appearance" of being human. The view was found among early Gnostics who saw all things material as evil. It was condemned by Ignatius of Antioch (c. 35–c. 107).

doctrine. A general term for a formally defined belief (e.g., the doctrine of the resurrection in Christianity), or for the total system of beliefs ("Christian doctrine").

Doctrine of the Mean (Chung Yung). Philosophical section from the Book of Rites advancing the benefit of attaining a mental state of equilibrium between extreme emotions; it is one of the Four Books (*shu*) of Confucianism.

dogma. In Christianity, an authoritative statement of belief; official doctrine; can also be used as a general term.

Donatism. A separatist movement, centering upon Roman North Africa in the fourth century. Donatus (d. 355) objected to permitting Christians who had "lapsed" in faith during persecution to be reinstated in the church.

***Du'a*.** Term in Islam for various forms of personal prayer and supplication.

dualism. The belief that concepts appear in pairs of opposites, one good and the other bad—e.g., Zoroastrians recognize one all-good deity and one who is all-bad. Some

Christians derive their beliefs from the concept that two equal but opposed supernatural powers influence the world: God and Satan.

Dukkha. In Buddhism, the First Noble Truth stating that suffering—*dukkha*—lies at the heart of human existence.

Durga. The Goddess as the destroyer of demons.

Easter. The yearly Christian festival celebrating the raising of Jesus Christ from the dead three days after his crucifixion. It is preceded by Good Friday. Easter is the first Sunday following the full moon that occurs on or after March 21. The date varies between March 22 and April 25. Theologically it celebrates the victory of Christ over death and evil as well as Christian hope.

Eastern Orthodox Church. Consisting of mainly Greek or Slav Christians including the ancient Eastern Patriarchates. They are in communion with the Patriarchate of Constantinople, which conforms to the creeds of the great ecumenical councils, e.g. Nicaea, Chalcedon.

Ebionites, Ebionism. A Judeo-Christian sect in the second to fourth centuries C.E.; accepted much of Mosaic Torah (circumcision, sabbath, etc.) but rejected sacrifices; accepted Jesus as messiah but not his divinity.

Eid Al-Adha. Feast of the sacrifice. Islamic four-day festival that completes the rites of pilgrimage and commemorates the Prophet Ibrahim's obedience to Allah by being ready to sacrifice his son Ishmael.

Eid Al-Fitr. Islamic three-day festival marking the end of Ramadan.

Eightfold Path. Fourth noble truth of Buddhism, also called the "middle path," which includes proper cultivation of views, aims, speech, conduct, livelihood, effort, mindfulness, and contemplation.

Ein Sof. (Hebrew = "without limit or eternal") In Jewish Kabbalism, a designation for the divine, "the unlimited one." God as *Ein Sof* is completely inconceivable, impersonal, and without attributes.

Elohim. Frequent Hebrew term for God in the Hebrew Bible and Christian Old Testament. The term is plural and was used to designate the one God of Israel. The term intensifies, "God of gods," "The highest God" (Gen. 1:1). It is used in the Psalter (Ps. 42–83). Also a synonym for Yahweh, the self-revealed name of the God of Israel.

empiricism. The doctrine that denies or doubts the validity of all intellectual knowledge and admits only the certainty of sense-knowledge.

Enlightenment (Buddhism). A state beyond suffering when the forces of greed, hatred, and delusion have no more power over a person.

Enlightenment (history). Eighteenth-century intellectual movement that stressed the applicability of reason and science to the improvement of society and humankind in general.

epistemology. The science of the validity, or truth-value, of knowledge.

eschatology. The section of Christian theology dealing with the "last things," especially the ideas of resurrection, hell, and eternal life.

esoteric. (Greek = *esoterikos*, "inner") Referring to the sacred and inner teachings and rituals of a religious group shared only by those initiated into the group.

essence. The act of actuality that perfects and determines a thing in its species; that which makes a thing to be what it is.

essential. Belonging to the essence or nature of a thing.

ethics. The study of human values and moral conduct.

Eucharist. Term used in Christian theology to describe the sharing and giving of the bread and wine at the Last Supper before Christ's death. Performed in memory of Christ's body broken for the world and his blood shed for the sins of the world.

evangelical. The term is generally used to refer to the conservative "wing" of Protestant Christianity. The most conservative evangelicals are called fundamentalists.

Evangelicalism. A form of Protestant Christianity that emphasizes salvation by faith in the atoning death of Christ through personal conversion, and focuses on preaching the Gospels in contrast to the performance of ritual. Evangelicals generally believe in the historical doctrines of the Christian church.

***Fatwa*.** Islamic legal verdict that is given on a religious basis.

feminism. The movement that advocates for the full equality and participation of women in all aspects of society and culture. Among concerns are violence against women, racism, sexism, environmental destruction, and ways of knowing.

fideism. The doctrine that all our knowledge must begin with an act of faith in divine revelation because human reason cannot know with any certainty the fundamental Christian truths.

***Fiqh*.** Islamic law.

Five Pillars of Islam. The required Muslim rituals for serving God: *shahadah*, *salat*, *zakat*, *sawm*, and *hajj*.

Five Ways, the. A standard term for the five "arguments for the existence of God," especially associated with Thomas Aquinas.

Forty Immortals. Forty Sikhs who died in the battle of Muktsar in 1762 and were blessed by Guru Gobind Singh.

Four Noble Truths. Basic truths of human existence revealed by the Buddha: 1—all existence is suffering (*dukkha*); 2—suffering is caused by desire; 3—suffering ceases by extinguishing desire; 4—the way to end desire, and therefore suffering, is the Eightfold Path of Liberation.

free churches. Nonconformist Christian denominations free from the control of the state.

free will. The ability of the will, all conditions for action being present, to decide whether to act or not act and whether to act in this manner or in that manner.

fundamentalism. (1) Originally, a reference to the beliefs of supporters of the early twentieth-century tracts called *The Fundamentals*. (2) More widely a reference to Christians who are seen as "biblical literalists," insisting on strict rather than metaphoric interpretations of scripture. (3) A reference to text literalism in any religion such as Buddhism or Islam.

***feng shui*.** The Chinese art of reading the forces of yin and yang so as to discern the best location for graves, houses, and buildings; practiced by Taoists.

Gaia hypothesis. A contemporary religious movement that professes the earth (Gaia—the Greek Earth Goddess) to be a living, even sentient, organism. This view was first put forward in 1969 by biochemist James Lovelock.

Ganesh. Elephant-faced God (in Hinduism) who destroys all obstacles.

Gathas. In Zoroastrianism, the sacred verses of the gods (Daevas) revealed by Zarathustra.

***ghusl*.** (Islam) The full ritual washing of the body with water to purify the body for prayer.

Globalization. The development of extensive worldwide patterns of economic relationships.

Gnosticism. (From Greek *gnosis* = "knowledge") An amorphous movement during the early church period which featured complex views that focused on the quest for secret knowledge transmitted only to the "enlightened" and marked by the view that matter is evil. Gnostics denied the humanity of Christ.

God (French = *Theos*; Latin = *Deus*). The supreme being who is creator and ruler of the universe.

Goddess. A deity of feminine aspect. Many neo-pagans and witches use the word "Goddess" to refer to the supreme being. For some this is an attempt to redress the separation of flesh and spirit, of humanity and nature, believed to be a result of patriarchal, dualistic, hierarchical Western worldviews.

gospel. (Greek *evangelion* = "good news") The message of the good news of the divine love of God for his creation proclaimed by Jesus and reported in the message of salvation for the world in the New Testament especially the four Gospels of Matthew, Mark, Luke and John.

grace. (Greek *charis*; Latin *gratia* = "favor," "kindness") Unmerited favor. God's grace is extended to sinful humanity in providing salvation and forgiveness through Jesus Christ that is not deserved and withholding the judgment that is deserved (Rom. 3:24; Eph. 1:7; Titus 2:11).

Granthi. One who performs the reading of the Guru Granth Sahib, often acting as custodian of the Gurdwara.

grihasth. In Hinduism, the householder stage of life.

Gurdwara. Name given to a Sikh temple. It means "Gateway to the Guru."

Gurmukh. (Sikhism) Someone who has become God-oriented and God-filled instead of self-filled.

Gurpurb. (Sikhism) The celebration of the anniversary of the birth or death of a guru.

Guru (Sikhism). Three uses for this term: (1) It refers to God and the way in which Akal Purukh (The Being Beyond Time) imbues enlightenment; (2) The word is used of the ten Sikh Gurus; (3) The Guru Granth Sahib refers to the sacred scripture of Sikhism. In its ritual aspect the Guru Granth Sahib is treated as a living Guru.

Guru. Spiritual teacher.

Hadith. The sayings of the Prophet Muhammed and recounted by his companions, household, or followers. A major source of Islamic law. Some *Hadith* are *Hadith Qudsi*, i.e., sacred because they were divinely communicated to the Prophet.

Haggadah. The nonlegal writings of the Jewish Talmud: sermons, theological disputes, etc.

Hajj. A pilgrimage to Mecca in Saudi Arabia that every Muslim is expected to perform at least once, if they are physically and financially able to do so.

Halakah. (Hebrew = "that by which one walks") The body of teaching that grew up in Jewish law that sought to apply the law to all situations and life and to give instruction. It contrasts with "*haggadah*."

Halal (Islam). Lawful as defined by Allah.

Hanuman (Hinduism). The monkey God.

Haram (Islam). Any act or deed that is prohibited by Allah and which will incur his wrath.

Hasidism. A Jewish religious movement founded by Baal Shem Tov in the eighteenth century. It was declared heretical in 1781 by the Talmudists, but Hasidic communities flourish in the United States and Israel. Hasidic Jews regard acts of religious devotion as being more important than scholarly learning.

Hatha Yoga. Yoga of the physical body.

Hebrew. A Jewish person. Also the language of the Jewish nation. In the Table of Nations (Gen. 10:21), the descendants of Eber, son of Shem. In the early church period, the term referred to Hebrew- or Aramaic-speaking Christians (Acts 6:1).

Hellenism (adj. Hellenistic). The civilization that spread from Greece through much of the ancient world from 333 (Alexander the Great) to 63 B.C.E. As a result, many elements of Greek culture (names, language, philosophy, athletics, architecture, etc.) penetrated the Near East and also Europe.

heresy. (Greek *hairesis* = "choice") A view chosen instead of the official teachings of a church. Such a view is thus regarded as wrong and potentially dangerous for faith.

hermeneutics. Principles of interpretation (from the Greek, "to interpret, translate"). The term is often used with reference to the study of Jewish and Christian scriptures.

Hermetic. Alchemy or other occult science. Latin: Hermes Trismegistus. Thrice-greatest Hermes was the founder of Alchemy.

hijab. The veil, headscarf, or modest dress traditionally worn by Muslim women.

Hinayana Buddhism (Mahayana Buddhism). The "lesser vehicle," a name given by

Mahayana Buddhists to earlier forms of Buddhism that they see as either defective or as a preparation in contrast to themselves.

Hinduism. Modern name for the Vedic teaching.

Historical Jesus. A term used, especially during the nineteenth century, referring to the real historical person of Jesus of Nazareth, in contrast to the Christian interpretation of that person, especially as presented in the New Testament and the creeds.

Holocaust. (Greek *holokauston*; Latin *holocaustum*) Consumed by fire. Biblically, "burnt offering" (Heb. 10:6, 8). In ethics, the Holocaust is the name given to the genocide of the Jewish people practiced by the Nazis in twentieth-century Germany during World War II.

Holy Spirit. (Hebrew *Ruah*; Greek *pneuma* = "spirit") The third person of the Trinity. God the Father, God the Son, and God the Holy Spirit constitute the eternal Godhead. The Spirit inspired biblical writers, makes known the saving work of Jesus Christ, and is God as present in and with the church. The Spirit acts to incorporate all things into the life of the triune God.

homoousion. A Greek term meaning "of the same substance," used extensively during the fourth century to show the mainstream Christological belief that Jesus Christ was "of the same substance as God." The term was directed against the Arian view that Christ was "of similar substance" (*homoiousion*) to God.

Humanism. A complex movement, linked with the European Renaissance, that emphasized revival in the cultural achievements of antiquity. These were seen as a major resource for the renewal of European culture and Christianity during the period of the Renaissance.

I Ching. Literally "Book of Changes," a book of written oracles associated with sixty-four hexagrams, or six-line combinations of unbroken (yang) and broken (yin) lines. One of the Five Classics of Confucianism.

Iblis. The Jinn (being created from fire) who defied Allah, refusing to bow to Adam and who became the tempter of all humanity.

icon/ikon. (Greek *eikon* = "image") A representation of someone who is venerated, always on a flat or two-dimensional surface. Icons are used in the decoration of Eastern churches. They point to eternal mysteries of the gospel.

idea. The intellectual image or representation of a thing.

ideas, Platonic. The view of the Greek philosopher Plato (428–348 B.C.) that universals or pure essences exist as "ideas" and that physical realities are only copies or patterned after them.

Imam (Islam). (1) A person who leads the prayer. (2) A Muslim Khalifa. (3) A famous Muslim scholar in Fiqh.

Imbolg, Imbolc, Oimelc. The early Spring Great Pagan Sabbat, celebrated on February 2. It is often known by the name of its Christian equivalent, Candlemas. In Gaelic the name means "in the belly," i.e., the first stirrings in the womb of Mother Earth.

immortality. Endless duration of life.

incarnation (Hinduism and other Eastern religions). The manifestations of a living entity into physical form; specifically, any one of the earthly lives of an immortal human; individuality in the continuing reincarnation process.

incarnation (the). The Christian doctrine which maintains that Jesus was both human and divine.

inerrant. Applied to a sacred text, inerrancy is the belief that the writings are God's revelation to mankind. As originally written, its contents are infallible, totally free of error, and exclusively authoritative.

infallibility without error. For some evangelical or fundamentalist Christians the Bible is infallible. In Roman Catholicism the pope is infallible when speaking "ex cathedra," i.e., in his capacity as bishop of the Western Church.

initiate (Occultism). Someone possessed of a secret or interior knowledge gained through experience.

initiation. A ritual used to signify entrance or progression in a magical or religious organization, frequently induced to produce intense personal experience.

invocation. The summoning (or more properly, invitation) of a nonmaterial entity of a higher order of being than oneself. Often effected through music, chanting, or mantra.

Jainism. Nonorthodox form of Vedic/Aryan teaching that emphasizes nonviolence.

Jehovah's Witnesses. A sect founded by Charles Taze Russell (1852–1916), who announced that they as his followers would be the heirs of the messianic kingdom. The "Russellites" deny the Trinity and the deity of Christ and hold strict moral views.

Jesuits (Society of Jesus). Members of the Society of Jesus founded by Ignatius Loyola (1491–1556) in 1534 and canonically established in 1540. The society focuses on teaching and Roman Catholic higher education. Its unofficial motto is "for the greater glory of God" (*ad majorem Dei gloriam*).

jihad. In Islam, a personal striving for perfection. The Western media often interprets the term as a synonym for "holy war." Collective defense of the Muslim community.

Jinni. A Muslim term for a supernatural being that can take either human or animal form.

jiva. The soul of a person, essentially the same as *atman*.

Jnana Yoga. Yoga of Knowledge.

koan. In the practice of Ch'an, a seemingly nonsensical riddle or statement given by a master to a disciple to meditate upon. Classic examples include, "What was your face before your mother was born?"

Ka'aba (Islam). The cube-shaped stone building in Mecca whose foundations were built by the angels and completed by the prophet Ibrahim (Abraham) and his son, the prophet Ishmael.

Kabbalah. The mystical interpretation of the Jewish scriptures with written sources. *Sefer Yezira* (third century) is thought to be a series of monologues given by the partriarch Abraham. Also, *Zohar*, a mystical commentary on the Torah written by Moses de León in the thirteenth century. Kabbalah appears to have started in eleventh-century France and includes an esoteric method of scriptural interpretation that includes assigning numerical values to Hebrew letters, thus revealing a hidden meaning from each Hebrew word.

kachh (Sikhism). A pair of shorts and part of the required clothing of Sikhs.

Kali (Hinduism). The dark form of the Goddess associated with disease, death, and terror.

Kami (Shintoism). The Kami are forces (encompassing both supernatural gods and nature, e.g., people and things) that pervade everything.

kangha. Comb, one of the five physical symbols that a Khalsa Sikh must wear.

Kantian(ism). Relating to the philosophy of Immanuel Kant (1724–1804) and his followers. Kant synthesized Euopean rationalism and British empiricism, asking what the human mind is able to know. He showed what knowledge is possible and how it is attained. Ethically, he stressed freedom and duty.

kara. Steel bracelet, one of the five physical symbols that a Khalsa Sikh must wear. It is a symbol of restraint and remembrance of God.

karah parshad. A standard dish served at religious ceremonies in the presence of the Guru Granth Sahib and sanctified by prayers. It is a symbol of equality of all members of the Sikh congregation.

karma. Law of cause and effect.

kashrut. Jewish laws relating to keeping a kosher home and way of life.

Kaur. Mandatory last name for a Khalsa Sikh female.

kes. Uncut hair and a symbol of spirituality. One of the five physical symbols that a Khalsa Sikh must have.

Khalsa. ("Pure.") The community of initiated Sikhs founded by Guru Gobind Singh in the great ceremony at Anandpur in 1699.

Kiddush. A Jewish prayer sanctifying Shabbat and festival days, usually said over wine.

kingdom of God. God's sovereign reign and rule in the individual and in the world. The main theme of Jesus' teaching (Matt. 6:33; Mark 1:15). The fullness of the kingdom is in the future tense (Luke 13:29), although it has also come in the person of Jesus himself (Luke 10:9, 17:21).

kirpan. Sword and a symbol of the Sikh fight against injustice and religious oppression.

knowledge (empirical). Information acquired by some sort of observation.

knowledge (objective). Information acquired by reason without any perception, senses, or instruments.

kosher. "Proper." Foods permitted by Jewish religious dietary laws.

Krishna. One of the most popular gods in Hinduism. Eighth avatar of Vishnu.

Kriya Yoga. Yoga of technique.

Kundalini (Tantra Hinduism). The energy of a person conceived of as a snake that is coiled around the base of the spine. When awakened and moving through the chakras, effects bliss and liberation.

Lakshmi (Hinduism). The goddess of prosperity and beauty; consort of Vishnu.

langar. An important Sikh practice of taking food together when visiting a *gurdwara.* A central belief in Sikhism is the rejection of caste distinctions, as proclaimed by Guru Nanak and endorsed by all his successors. *Langar* demonstrates and symbolizes this sense of equality, especially in Hindu society where eating together has often been restricted according to one's caste.

liberation theology. A movement that developed in Latin America in the late 1960s, stressing the role of political action with goals of political liberation from poverty and oppression.

limited atonement. A view of the atonement, especially associated with Calvinist writers, who see Christ's death as only effective for people who have been elected to salvation.

liturgy. The written text of public services, especially of the Eucharist.

Logos. (Greek = "word," "speech"; divine reason). A Greek term found in various connections in Hellenistic thought, including the philosophy of Philo (first-century C.E. Alexandrian Jew), where it is comparable to *hokmah* ("wisdom" or "*sofia*"). In the Christian Gospel of John, *logos* is equated with the divine functions of Jesus Christ (John 1:1–18).

Lotus Sutra. Early Mahayana Buddhist text (composed between 100 B.C.E. and 200 C.E.) emphasizing the means-to-ends ability (*upaya*).

Lutheranism. The beliefs, ideas, and the church arising from the teachings of Martin Luther, particularly as expressed in the Augsburg Confession (1530). A series of internal disagreements within Lutheranism after Luther's death (1546) between hardliners (the so-called "Gnesio-Lutherans" or "Flacianists") and moderates ("Philippists") led to their resolution by the Formula of Concord (1577), which tends to be seen as the authoritative statement of Lutheran theology.

magic, magick. The use of blessings, spells, incantations, etc., to change outcomes. Wiccans and other neo-Pagans limit themselves to "White Magic," avoiding control, domination, or harm to others. Magic(k): "The science and Art of causing Change to occur in conformity with Will" (Aleister Crowley). Crowley added the "k" to distinguish true magic from the debased, escape-from-reality concept of magic, and many occultists have adopted the usage.

Mahabharata. The great war of the Bharatas. A grand Hindu epic tale containing narrative of the Great War (about a fifth of the text) and the rest containing a) long stories about the main characters, the Pandavas and Kauravas; b) ethical discourses and descriptions of large areas of Northern India; and c) a number of independent philosophical and theological discourses.

Mahayana. "Great vehicle." Northern school of Buddhism in contrast to Theravada.

Mahdi (Islam). Literally "the one who is rightly guided." A figure who will appear towards the end of time.

Manicheism. A theory, originating with Manes, which maintained that God is the supreme Principle of Good and matter the supreme Principle of Evil.

mantra. (1) Vedic hymn or sacred text. (2) Powerful formula or word spoken, spiritual or empowered speech.

martyr. (Greek = "witness") A general term for persons who endure persecution, usually leading to death, for the sake of their religious "witness."

Maya. ("deceit," "fraud," "illusion") In Vedanta Hinduism, the universal illusion that veils the minds of human beings.

Mahayana Buddhism. A form of Buddhism that stresses the duty of the enlightened to work compassionately to relieve the suffering of others, and argues that all sentient creatures will ultimately achieve Buddhahood.

merkabah. (Hebrew = "chariot") In mystical Judaism, the "chariot vision" signified a mystical vision of divinity.

messiah. "Anointed one" (Greek = *Christos*). Ancient priests and kings (and sometimes prophets) of Israel were anointed with oil. Also the messiah was the redeemer figure of royal descent of the dynasty of David who would restore the united kingdom of Israel and Judah, bringing in an age of peace and justice. The concept of "messiah" has been taken to mean a time of radical new beginnings, a new heaven and earth, after divine judgment.. The title was applied to Jesus by his followers; Jesus is also "Messiah" in Islam (e.g. Qur'an 3.45).

metanarrative. A term used by postmodern thinkers for the systems of myths that sustain social relationships in a society and form the basis for the society's legitimation. Postmodernists see metanarratives as being in demise because they no longer have credibility since no myths can claim universality.

metaphysics. The science of the ultimate principles and properties of real beings.

method. The proper arrangement of mental processes in the discovery and proof of truth.

mezuzah. Placed on the doorposts of Jewish homes, a scroll that contains a portion of scripture from the Torah. Often put in a decorative case.

Midrash. (Hebrew = "explanation"; from *darash*, "to inquire into") Commentaries on the scriptures produced by Jewish rabbis during the Babylonian exile until approximately 1200 C.E. It contains two parts—*halakah* and *haggadah*.

millenarian. From the Latin for "one thousand." Having to do with the expected millennium, or thousand-year reign of Christ prophesied in the New Testament book of Revelation ("the Apocalypse"), a time in which the world would be brought to perfection. Millenarian movements spring up when predictions say that this perfect time is imminent.

millennialism. The belief that current society will disintegrate and be replaced with a perfect new world.

millennium. In a religious context, an interval of one thousand years after Armageddon when Jesus Christ will rule on earth.

minaret. A tower located beside a mosque used to call Muslims to prayer.

mind control cult. A religious group using manipulation to control its followers. These cults are often small and tightly organized, allowing minimal personal freedom for the members. They also have a single, all-powerful leader.

mind. In epistemology, the conscious knowing subject or the conscious knowing part of the subject.

miracle. A general term for special events that seem inexplicable by normal (rational) means. Miracle reports are frequent in Jewish and Christian scriptures and early traditions, while in Islam, the only "miracle" associated with Muhammad is said to be the reception and transmission of the Qur'an.

***Mishnah*.** An authoritative document forming part of the Talmud which was codified about 200 C.E. The *Mishnah* is the first written document of the Jewish oral tradition.

modalism. A Trinitarian heresy that treats the three persons of the Trinity as different "modes" of the Godhead. A typical modalist approach is to regard God as active as Father in creation, as Son in redemption, and as Spirit in sanctification.

modernity. A term that designates the post-Enlightenment period in Europe and North America, in which people relied on scientific culture and its potential to fill the void that accompanied a decline in religion.

Moksha (Hinduism). Liberation or release from the cycle of death and rebirth.

monarchianism. A Christian heresy teaching that God is a single entity and that Jesus was a pure man, born of a virgin, who was adopted by God.

monism. The doctrine that seeks to deduce all the varied phenomena of both the physical and spiritual worlds from a single principle, which is in a continuous state of evolution.

monotheism. The belief in one God.

mosque. "Masjid" is the name used by Muslims to refer to their house of worship. Mosque is the English term. It literally means "place of prostration."

***Mul* Mantra.** The opening lines of the *Japji* by Guru Nanak and the cornerstone of Sikhism. It is beginning of the Guru Granth Sahib. "God is one. His name is True. He is the Creator. He is without fear. He is inimical to none. His existence is unlimited by time. He is beyond the cycles of birth and death, self-existent and can be realized through the grace of the Guru."

mystic, mysticism (adj. mystical). From Greek for "initiant" into religious "mysteries."

***nam simran*.** In Sikhism, the remembrance of God through meditation, to hold God.

natural theology. Knowledge of God that is attained though God's revelation in nature and which can be understood by human reason.

Ner Tamid (Judaism). The eternal light above the *Aron Hakodesh*.

nirvana. The "goal" of Buddhist practice; the state that results from extinguishing craving and breaking the chain of reincarnation. The exact nature of nirvana is hard to grasp. It is clearer what it is not: Nirvana is not a place like heaven that souls go to after death (although there are various heavens and hells in popular Buddhism). Literally, it means a "blowing out" of the flame of craving. Also liberation, the state of peace.

***niyyah*.** Muslim term for one's intention or attitude that is made prior to devotion.

***nominalism*.** Belief that only particular things exist, as opposed to realism.

Om (also written *Aum*). The mantra of the divine. A mystical syllable often seen as the seed of all mantras.

ontological argument. An attempt to prove the existence of God by a priori reasoning from the content of the concept of God.

ontology. Branch of metaphysics concerned with identifying, in the most general terms, the kinds of things that actually exist.

orthodox. From the Greek for "correct opinion/outlook," as opposed to heterodox or heretical. Historically, the term "orthodox" has come to denote the dominant surviving forms that have proved themselves to be "traditional," "classical," or "mainstream" (e.g., rabbinic Judaism; the Roman Catholic and Greek Orthodox Christian churches; Sunni Islam).

Oxford Movement. A nineteenth-century movement for church renewal within the Church of England (1833–1845). Led by John Keble (1792–1866), E. B. Pusey (1800–1882) and J. H. Newman (1801–1890), the movement aimed at restoring the "catholic" aspects of the church's doctrine and practice.

pagan. Often referring to an animistic, usually polytheistic belief system. Based upon direct perception of the forces of nature, involving the use of idols, talismans, and taboos in order to convey respect for the forces of the universe.

panentheism. Belief that God is all that exists. God is at once the entire universe, and transcends the universe as well.

pantheism. Belief that God is present in all of nature, rather than transcending it.

parousia. A Greek term literally meaning "coming" or "arrival"; used to refer to the second coming of Christ.

patristic. An adjective used to refer to the first centuries in the history of the church, following the writing of the New Testament (the "patristic period"), or scholars writing during this period (the "patristic writers").

Pelagianism. The theological beliefs associated with the British monk Pelagius (c. 354–c. 420), who argued against Augustine of Hippo for belief in a totally free human will to do the good.

Pentecostals. Christians who believe in the Holy Spirit Baptism, a second manifestation or "blessing" of God's power that follows an individual's conversion to Christianity. It is accompanied by glossolalia, or "speaking in tongues."

philosophy. Literally, "love of wisdom." Careful thought about the fundamental nature of the world, the grounds for human knowledge, and the evaluation of human conduct.

pietism. An approach to Christianity that focuses on personal religious experience—often criticized for its inadequate use of the intellect and reason.

piety. A general term for religious devotion.

Plato. Ancient Greek philosopher (fourth century B.C.E.), student of Socrates, and teacher of Aristotle, who identified reality with the nonmaterial world of ideas ("the ideal world"), which played a central role in subsequent philosophy and religion (see neo-Platonism, dualism). Father of "Platonism" and the Platonic Academy as a philosophical institution in Athens.

pluralism (philosophical). Belief that reality ultimately includes many different kinds of things (in contrast to monism). Epistemological pluralism is a common feature in postmodernist thought.

pluralism (religious). A situation in which no single worldview or religion is dominant. It can lead to relative religious tolerance (as in North America) or to intense religious conflict (as in Northern Ireland).

polytheist. One who believes in the existence of more than one deity; usually a belief in both gods and goddesses.

polytheistic. Belief in many gods.

postmillennialism. The eschatological (last times) belief that Jesus Christ will return following the millennium or thousand-year reign mentioned in Revelation 20:1–7.

postmodernism. A general cultural development, especially in North America, that resulted from the general collapse in confidence of a) the universal rational principles of the Enlightenment and b) the idea of "objective truth."

premillennialism. The belief that Jesus Christ will return to earth prior to a period of one thousand years, during which he will reign (Rev. 20:1–50).

protestant. Term for people who "protested" against the corruption and power of the Roman Catholic Church. A general term for the Christians who broke away from Roman papacy at the Reformation.

puja. Hindu worship, especially of an image—often an offering of fruit, cooked food, incense, or flowers. Can be performed in the temple or in the home and includes a minimum of sixteen different acts beginning with the invitation of the diety.

***Puranas*.** An important collection of Hindu texts claiming greater antiquity than the *Vedas*. They deal with the creation of the universe, genealogies of various gods, patriarch myths, rules for living, and descriptions of the end times.

***qiblah*.** The direction in which all Muslims face when praying towards al-Ka'ba in Makkah (Mecca).

Quraish. A great tribe in pre-Islamic Arabia. The prophet Muhammad belonged to this tribe.

rabbi. A teacher of the Jewish law or an ordained Jew who is the spiritual leader of a congregation.

Radical Reformation. A term used frequently to refer to the Anabaptist movement, the wing of the Reformation that went beyond what Luther and Zwingli envisaged.

Raja Yoga (Hinduism). The Royal yoga path involving the process of discriminative knowledge that leads to the liberation of the embodied spirit. It involves theory and physical training, a strong ethical orientation, control of the will, and decision-making. It also focuses on complex states of consciousness that are not presently recognized in Western thought.

Ramadan. The ninth month of the Islamic calendar, which is the month of fasting in which all adult Muslims who are fit and healthy fast from the first light of dawn until sunset each day.

Ramayana (Hinduism). Ancient Sanskrit epic story of Rama.

rationalism. A general term for the perspective which holds that everything is actually or potentially understandable by human reason.

Reformation. Name given to the Protestant Christian movements (and the period itself) in the sixteenth century in which Roman Catholicism was opposed in the interest of "reforming" Christianity to what was considered its earliest known form (found in the New Testament).

Reformed. A term used to refer to a tradition of theology that draws inspiration from the writings of John Calvin (1510–1564) and his successors. The term is generally used in preference to "Calvinist."

reincarnation. The religious belief that the soul of a person can be reborn. Contra to the norm, in Christianity the view was held by Origen (c. 185–254).

relativism. The modern position that affirms that everything is relative to the particularities of the given situation, and that no absolutes exist.

Renaissance. Name usually given to the "rebirth" of classical knowledge that erupted in the fifteenth century and provided background for the Protestant Reformation and associated events in Europe.

repentance. A term used especially in Protestant Christianity to indicate the subjective state of sorrow and concern over sin, on the way to salvation.

resurrection. God's raising of Jesus Christ from the dead. Also the belief of the future rising of all persons prior to the final judgment (1 Cor. 15; Rev. 20:4–15).

revelation. A general term for self-disclosure of the divine (God revealed to humans), which is often considered to be focused in the revealed scriptures. Also, the name of a specific Christian biblical book, the "Apocalypse" (Greek = "uncovered").

***Rig Veda*.** Oldest Hindu scripture, containing 1,017 hymns.

Sabellianism. An early Trinitarian heresy, teaching that God is one nature and person who has three names: Father, Son, and Holy Spirit. The church taught that God is One and that the Godhead consists of three persons.

sacrament. An outward sign established by God to convey an inward or spiritual grace.

Although Roman Catholic theology and church practice recognize seven such sacraments (baptism, confirmation, Eucharist, marriage, ordination, penance, and unction), Protestant theologians generally argue that only two (baptism and Eucharist) were to be found in the New Testament itself.

salah. Prescribed communication and worship of Allah five times daily.

Sama Veda. *Veda* of song.

samsara. The interconnected process of birth and rebirth.

sanctification. The process whereby a Christian believer is made holy, becoming like Jesus Christ.

sannyas. Hindu stage of life of renunciation and liberation.

Sanskrit. Vedic language.

Satanism. A religion based upon Satan, as a form of deity or as a principle. Adherents follow rules of behavior: Give kindness to those who deserve it; indulge in your personal lusts and wants; return vengeance.

schism. A branch of a church, denomination, or religion that is doctrinally, liturgically, or socially distinct and maintains a high tension with the parent/host group. Schisms are often based upon minute points of doctrine or practice and are often viewed by the host group as heretical.

scholasticism. Philosophical study as practiced by Christian thinkers in medieval universities. The scholastics typically relied upon ancient authorities as sources of dogma and engaged in elaborate disputations over their proper interpretation.

séance. A gathering of people who attempt to communicate with the spirits of the dead, usually with the help of a medium.

sect. A small religious group that has split away from an established religion. The early Jewish Christian groups in Jerusalem circa 35 C.E. would have been considered sects of Judaism at the time. A sect may eventually differentiate itself into a new denomination.

secular. A term often associated with the modern period in western European culture and the many forms of life developed that are new and not under any previous authority or sanction of the church. Sometimes the term denotes the absence of religion; on occasion, it denotes (for evangelical Christians, for instance) irreligion.

secularism. The ideology of the secular world without reference to religious thinking.

Septuagint. The Greek translation of the Old Testament, dating from the third century B.C. The abbreviation "LXX" is generally used to refer to this text.

Sermon on the Mount. The standard way of referring to Christ's moral and pastoral teaching in the specific form it takes in chapters 5–7 of Matthew's Gospel.

Shabbat. Jewish day of spiritual refreshing and rest commencing at sunset on Friday and ending at sunset on Saturday.

Shahadah. The Muslim declaration of faith that, "There is no God except Allah, Muhammad is the Messenger of Allah."

Shari'a. Islamic law as ordained by Allah.

Shema. Central Jewish prayer affirming belief in one God.

Shi'a/Shi'ite. Muslim followers who believe in the *Imamah*, sucessorship of Ali after the prophet Muhammad and eleven of his most pious descendants.

Shinto. In Japanese tradition, the "way of the kami (gods)," the indigenous religious traditions of Japan.

Shirk. (Islam) Idol worship that attributes form to Allah as an object, a concept, a ritual, or a myth. Allah has no form and is unlike anything that can be humanly conceived.

Shiva. Form of the Hindu trinity controlling destruction and transcendence.

sin. (Christian) Self-rule in a person's life instead of God's rule.

Singh. "Lion." The common last or middle name of male Sikhs and the compulsory last name.

skepticism. Belief that some or all human knowledge is impossible, since even our best methods for learning about the world sometimes fall short of perfect certainty.

socialization. The process of coming to know, accept, and participate in the social norms of a society.

soteriology. The section of Christian theology dealing with the doctrine of salvation (Greek: *soteria*).

soul. (Greek = *psyche*; Latin = *anima*) The active principle present in living things.

Spiritism. The belief in spirits that affect the world. Also the belief that people can come in contact with these spirits and receive their influence and power.

Spiritualism. The belief that the only realities are spirit; also, a term for those religious movements that seek communication with the spirits of those departed.

structuralism. Method of interpreting social phenomena in the context of a system of signs whose significance lies solely in the interrelationships among them. The linguistics of Saussure and Chomsky as applied to other disciplines by Lévi-Strauss, Piaget, Lacan, Foucault, and Eco.

Sufism. The mystical path of Islam.

Sunni. Muslims who believe in the successorship of Abu Bakr, Umar, Uthman, and Ali (Radhi-Allahu-anhum), after the prophet Muhammad.

***Surah*.** A chapter of the Holy Qur'an, of which there are 114.

Sutra (*sutta*). In Hinduism, verses of the yogi Patanjali (c. 200 B.C.E.), which define yoga disciplines. In Buddhism, the discourses of the Buddha ("a thread on which are strung beads").

sweat lodge. (American Indian Religion) A shelter within which are placed heated rocks splashed with water to create a hot and steamy interior. A place of both physical and spiritual purification, usually visited before undertaking a vision quest.

syncretism. The religious practice of selecting religious symbols, beliefs, or practices from different sources and combining them.

Synoptic Gospels. A term used to refer to the first three gospels (Matthew, Mark, and Luke). The term (Greek "summary") refers to the way in which the three Gospels give similar "summaries" of the life, death, and resurrection of Jesus Christ.

synoptic problem. The scholarly question of how the three Synoptic Gospels relate to each other. The most common recent approach to the issue is the "two source" theory, which claims that Matthew and Luke used Mark as a source, while also drawing upon a second source (usually known as "Q"). There are other ways of viewing the Gospels. For example, the Grisebach hypothesis treats Matthew as having been written first, followed by Luke and then Mark.

***Talmud*.** The "oral" Torah of Judaism, consisting of the *Mishnah*—the code of oral law compiled c. 200 B.C.E.—and the *Gemara*, the commentary of the *Mishnah*. There exists both a Palestinian and a Babylonian *Talmud*.

***Tanakh*.** The Hebrew Bible represented as a "word" created from the first letters of Torah, *Nevi'im*, and *Ketuvim*.

tantra. The term for works or ritual connected to goddess worship.

Tao (Dow). The cosmic way, which is the natural order of the universe. In Confucianism, the wisdom of the past as well as the patterns established in nature.

***Tao Te Ching*.** (Literally, "The Way and its Power") Oldest and central text in Taoism, emphasizing living according to the Tao, the virtuous power (*te*) we attain from the Tao, the return of everything to Tao, and the principles of nonaction, nonmind.

***Taras*.** In Vajrayana Buddhism, female counterparts to Buddhas or bodhisattvas.

***Tefillin*.** Small leather boxes that contain scriptures from the Jewish Torah and which are strapped on the forehead and arm for morning prayers on weekdays.

telos/teleological, Greek term for the end, completion, purpose, or goal of any thing or activity.

theodicy. A term coined by Leibnitz to refer to a theoretical justification of the goodness of God in the face of the presence of evil in the world.

theology. (Greek = "study of deity") A general term for discussions pertaining to God and religious matters. A person who engages formally in theological studies is called a "theologian."

theosophy. (Literally "divine wisdom") A religious movement of the late nineteenth century, founded by Madame Blavatsky, a Russian psychic, and based on Buddhist and Hindu ideas imported into the West. Theosophy promotes a secret, esoteric "wisdom" lying beneath all world religions, which can experienced by consciousness-expanding initiation from unseen, spiritual Masters.

Thomism, via Thomae. The scholastic philosophy associated with Thomas Aquinas.

Torah. The Pentateuch, the first five books of the Hebrew scriptures (Christian Old Testament).

totalitarianism. Authoritarian government that attempts to regulate every aspect of sociocultural life.

Tower of Silence. In Zoroastrianism, a circular building open at the top where corpses are placed, allowing the deceased body to be picked clean by vultures. Bones that remain are bleached clean by the sun and buried in large communal graves with no designation of worldly status.

transcendence. A term used in respect to God's nature, which is above and beyond the world.

transcendental meditation (TM). A type of contemporary Hinduism in the West founded by Maharishi Mahesh Yogi in the 1960s, who claimed great benefits for TM practitioners by simply spending twenty minutes twice a day repeating a secret mantra. TM followers professed to be able to work more efficiently, have more personal happiness and satisfaction, have better athletic prowess and creativity, and have power over drug and alcohol addiction.

transubstantiation. In Roman Catholic practice, the belief that eucharistic elements change at their consecration from bread and wine into the body and blood of Christ with only the accidents (as taste, color, shape, and smell) of the bread and wine remaining.

Trimurrti. The view of God in Bhakti Hinduism consisting of Brahma, Vishnu, and Shiva.

Trinity. The Christian belief that God is a unity composed of three persons: Father, Son, and Holy Spirit. Extensive debate about the nature of God and of Jesus occurred during the early centuries of the Church, culminating in a belief in the Trinity.

Tripitaka. The "three baskets" of Buddhist scriptures: *Vinaya*—rules for monks and nuns; *Sutta*—sermons and teachings of the Buddha; *Abhidhamma*—techniques for disciplining the mind.

Tsumi. In Shinto belief, ritual impurity that is the result of upsetting the balance of nature by offending any of the *kami*.

two natures, doctrine of. A term generally used to refer to the doctrine of the two natures, human and divine, of Jesus Christ. Related terms include "Chalcedonian definition" and "hypostatic union."

Ummah. In Islam, the community of Muslims that is guided by the Qur'an and who are governed by Islamic law (*Shari'ah*).

Unification Church (Moonies). A contemporary religious movement begun in the 1950s based in Korea and founded by Sun Myung Moon, a North Korean whose Confucian parents converted to Christianity. The Rev. Moon proclaims both himself and his wife collectively to be the Messiah, with a mission of the unification of God's love through the institution of marriage and the family.

universalism. A Christian heresy with the belief that everyone would eventually reach heaven after death. In the second and early third centuries, Clement and Origen both promoted universalism.

Upanishads. The last part of the Hindu *Vedas*, containing mystical and philosophical texts.

Vatican II. The second general council (Vatican I was in 1868) of Roman Catholic bishops called in 1962 by Pope John XXII for the purpose of reforming Church practice to make it more accessible to a modern world. The most important changes included the translation of the liturgy into the local languages (rather than Latin) and greater involvement of the laity in local matters of governance and church practice.

Vedas. Ancient scriptures of India.

Vishnu. (Hinduism) The preserving aspect of ultimate reality and embodiment of goodness and mercy.

Voodoo. A popular name commonly referring to the religion of Vodun, which combines elements of African Native spirituality and Roman Catholicism.

Vulgate. The Latin translation of the Bible, largely deriving from Jerome (347–420), upon which medieval theology was largely based. Strictly speaking, "Vulgate" designates Jerome's translation of the Old Testament (except the Psalms), the apocryphal works (except Wisdom, Ecclesiasticus, 1 and 2 Maccabees, and Baruch, which were taken from the Old Latin Version); and all the New Testament. In the Reformation, its inaccuracies were recognized.

Wicca (witchcraft). A neo-Pagan polytheistic religion with roots in pre-Christian, pre-Celtic Europe, focusing on worship of the Goddess and other feminine forms of nature spirituality. Coupled with twentieth-century feminism, Wicca is the most popular form of women's spirituality as an alternative to the more widespread paternalistic and patriarchal religious expressions. Wiccans follow the Wiccan Rede: "Do whatever you wish, as long as you harm nobody, including yourself."

wudu. Muslim ablutions before prayer (*salah*).

Wu-tsin. Nonmind. Taoist belief that we should eliminate knowledge to allow us to live spontaneously.

Wu-wei. Nonaction. Taoist belief that we should avoid all unnatural action and act passively and spontaneously.

Yahweh. The personal name of the God of Israel; written YHWH (without vowels).

Yang. In Taoist philosophy, the bright, active, "masculine" aspect of the Tao.

Yin. In Taoist philosophy, the dark, receptive, "feminine" aspect of the Tao.

Yoga. In Hinduism, one of the major *sadhanas* (practices) for seeking spiritual realization by serious discipline of the body and mind. The four main types are: *bhakti* yoga—intense devotion to a personal aspect of ultimate reality; karma—unselfish acts of goodness as offerings to ultimate reality; *jnana*—intense mental discipline (philosophy) to unite with ultimate reality; raja—physical and psychic discipline using physical postures and breathing techniques that cleanse the body and focus the mind to ultimate reality.

Yogi. In a general sense, anyone who seriously practices yoga (discipline).

Yom Kippur. Jewish Day of Atonement on the tenth day of the month of Tishri (usually late September); a day of fasting, repentance, and reconciliation with God (Leviticus 16).

Zakat. One of the Five Pillars of Islam, the required practice of alms-giving or wealth-sharing; an annual tithe of 2 ½ percent of discretionary wealth to be redistributed to the poor, widows, and orphans, or donated to support a religious institution.

Zarathustra. An Indo-Iranian priest dating to sometime during or before the sixth century B.C.E. who reformed the earlier Iranian polytheism into a complex monotheistic religion referred to in the West as Zoroastrianism.

Zazen. Zen Buddhist practice of sitting and meditating on ordinary conscious experience for long periods of time.

Zen Buddhism. A Chinese (Ch'an) and Japanese Buddhist school emphasizing that all things have Buddha-nature, which can only be grasped when one escapes from the intellectual mind and enters into the field of being/nothingness.

Zion, Zionism. (Mount) Zion is an ancient Hebrew designation for Jerusalem; in biblical times Zion began to symbolize the national homeland (see Ps. 137:1–6). Zionism served as a focus for Jewish national-religious hopes of renewal over the centuries. The goal of Zionism is the political and spiritual renewal of the Jewish people in their ancestral homeland.

Zoroastrianism. A religion of ancient Iran that professes a belief in one Creator God; the existence of an evil force in the world in conflict with a good force; an afterlife in heaven or hell as a reward or punishment for one's moral life; and a dramatic apocalyptic end of the world with a final resurrection of the dead.

Zwinglianism. Used generally to refer to the thought of Huldrych Zwingli, but more often refers to his views on the sacraments, especially on the "real presence" (which, according to Zwingli, was more of a "real absence").

Bibliography

This bibliography represents a selection of the key texts used and referred to in the writing of the book. This listing does not do justice to the hundreds of pamphlets and publications that are also published by religions and religious movements.

Adler, M. *Drawing Down the Moon.* Boston: Beacon Press, 1986.

Al-Adawiyya, Rabi'a. *Doorkeeper of the Heart: Versions of Rabia.* Translated by Charles Upton. Putney, Vt.: Threshold Books, 1988.

Ali Ashraf, Sayed. *Islam.* World Religions Series. Cheltenham: Stanley Thornes Publishers Ltd., 1991.

Arberry, A. J., trans. *Muslim Saints and Mystics.* 1966. Reprint, London: Routledge, Kegan & Paul Ltd., 1979.

Armstrong, G. T. *The Origin and History of the Church of God International.* Church of God International, 1992.

Armstrong, H. W. *The Autobiography of Herbert W. Armstrong.* Vol. 2. Worldwide Church of God, 1987.

Armstrong, Herbert W., and Garner Ted Armstrong. *The Wonderful World Tomorrow: What It Will Be Like.* Belfast: Ambassador College, 1966.

Augustine. *On the Trinity.* Translated by A. W. Haddem. Edinburgh: T. & T. Clarke, 1872.

Aquinas, T. *Summa Theologiae.* Translated by T. McDermott. London: Eyre & Spottiswoode, 1964.

Barbour, I. G. *Issues in Science and Religion.* Englewood, Calif.: Prentice-Hall, 1966.

———. *Sciences and Religion.* London: SCM Press, 1968.

Barker, E. *The Making of a Moonie.* New York: Basil Blackwell, 1984.

Barrett D. V. *Sects, Cults and Alternative Religions.* London: Cassell,1996.

Barrett, Leonard E. *The Rastafarians: The Dreadlocks of Jamaica.* Boston: Beacon Press, 1977.

———. *Rastafarianism: Sounds of Cultural Dissonance.* Boston: Beacon Press, 1988.

Barton, B. *The Secret Life of a Satanist: The Authorized Biography of Anton LaVey.* Los Angeles: Feral House, 1990.

Baudrillard, J. *The Anti-Aesthetic: Essays on Postmodern Culture.* Washington: Bay Press, 1983.

Berger, P. L. *The Heretical Imperative.* Garden City, N.Y.: Anchor Press/Doubleday, 1979.

Bhaktivedanta Swami Prabhupada, A. C. *The Science of Self-Realization.* Bhaktivedanta Book Trust, 1977.

Black, H. "Gender and Cosmology in Chinese Correlative Thinking." In *Gender and Religion: On the Complexity of Symbols*, eds. C. W. Bynum, S. Harrell, and P. Richman. Boston: Beacon Press, 1986.

Blamires, H. *The Christian Mind.* London: SPCK, 1963.

Bowker, J., ed. *The Oxford Dictionary of World Religions.* New York: Oxford University Press, 1997.

Boyne, R. *Foucault and Derrida: The Other Side of Reason.* London: Routledge, 1990.

Broderick, Robert C., ed. *Catholic Encyclopedia.* 1903. Reprint, Nashville: Thomas Nelson, 1990.

Bruce, S. *Religion in Modern Britain.* Oxford: Oxford University Press, 1995.

Buber, M. *I and You.* Translated by W. Kaufmann. 1923. Reprint, New York: Scribner, 1970.

Burckhardt, Titus. *Introduction to Sufism.* San Francisco: Thorsons (An Imprint of HarperCollins Publishers), 1995.

Butterworth, J. *Cults and New Faiths.* Oxford: Lion Publishing, 1981.

Cabot, Laurie. *Power of the Witch.* Arkana, 1989.

Campbell, E. and J. H. Brennan. *Dictionary of Mind, Body, and Spirit: Ideas, People, and Places.* London: Aquarian Press, 1990, 1994.

Camus, A. "The Myth of the Sisyphus." In Martin Esslin, *The Theatre of the Absurd.* Baltimore: Penguin, 1968.

Carr-Gomm, P. *The Elements of the Druid Tradition.* Shaftesbury: Element, 1991.

Cashmore, E. *Rastaman.* London: Allen & Unwin, 1979.

Causton, R. *Nichiren Shoshu Buddhism.* London, Rider, 1988.

Cavendish, R., ed. *Encyclopaedia of the Unexplained.* Arkana, 1989.

Chadwick, H. *The Early Church.* London: Pelican, 1967.

———. "Justin Martyr's Defense of Christianity." *Bulletin of the John Rylands Library* 47 (1965): 275–97.

Channing L. Bete Co. "About Being an Eastern Catholic." South Deerfield, Mass.: Channing L. Bete Co., Inc., 1982.

Chevreau, G. *Catch the Fire: The Toronto Blessing—An Experience of Renewal and Revival.* London: HarperCollins, 1994.

Christian Science Publishing Society. *A Century of Christian Science Healing.* The Christian Science Publishing Society, 1966.

Christie-Murray, D. *A History of Heresy.* Oxford: Oxford University Press, 1976.

Chryssides, A. D. *Exploring New Religions.* New York and London: Casssell, 1999.

Church of Scientology. *What Is Scientology?* Los Angeles: Bridge Publications, 1998.

———. *The Scientology Handbook: Based on the Works of L. Ron Hubbard.* Hollywood, Calif.: Bridge Publications, 1994.

Comstock, W. R. *The Study of Religion and Primitive Religions.* New York: Harper and Row, 1972.

Confucius, *The Analects.* Translated with an introduction by D. C. Lau. Harmondsworth, Middlesex: Penguin, 1979.

Conze, E. *Selected Sayings from the Perfection of Wisdom.* Boulder, Colo.: Buddhist Soc., 1978.

Cooper, R. *The Baha'is of Iran.* London: Minority Rights Group, 1982.

Chryssides, G. D. *Exploring New Religions.* London & New York: Cassell, 1999.

Crim, K., ed. *The Perennial Dictionary of World Religions.* San Francisco: Harper & Row, 1981.

Crowley, A. *The Holy Books of Thelema.* York Beach, Maine: Weiser, 1983.

———. *Magick in Theory and Practice.* Secaucus, N.J.: Castle, 1991.

Crowley, V. *Wicca: The Old Religion in the New Age.* London: Aquarian Press, 1989.

Cuhulain, K. *The Law Enforcement Guide to Wicca.* 3d ed. Victoria, Horned Owl Publishing, 1997.

D'Costa, G. *Theology and Religious Pluralism.* Oxford: Basil Blackwell, 1987.

Davies, B. *An Introduction to the Philosophy of Religion.* 2d ed. Oxford: Oxford University Press, 1993.
Davies, H. *Christian Deviations: The Challenge of the New Spiritual Movements.* 1954. Reprint, London: SCM Press, 1965.
Dawkins, R. *The Blind Watchmaker.* London: Penguin Books, 1988.
———. *Climbing Mount Improbable.* London: Viking, 1996.
Derrida, J. *Of Grammatology*. Baltimore: John Hopkins University Press, 1974.
Dhammapada. Trans. Irving Babbit. New York: New Directions, 1965.
Dole, G. F., trans. *A Thoughtful Soul: Reflections from Swendenborg.* London: Swedenborg Foundation, 1995.
Dorrien, G. *The Remaking of Evangelical Theology.* Louisville, Ky.: Westminster John Knox Press, 1998.
Durkheim, E. *The Elementary Forms of Religious Life*. Translated by J. A. Swain. 1912. Reprint, London: Allen & Unwin, 1915.
Eddy, M. B. *Science and Health, with Key to the Scriptures.* First Church of Christ, Scientist, 1906.
Eliade, Mircea. *The Encyclopedia of Religion.* New York: Collier Macmillan, 1993.
Ellwood, R. S. "UFO Religious Movements." In *America's Alternative Religions*, ed. Timothy Miller. New York: State University of New York Press, 1995.
Encyclopaedia of Mormonism. London: Macmillan, 1992.
Esslemont, J. E. *Baha'u'llah and the New Era.* 1923. Reprint, London: Baha'i Publishing Trust, 1974.
Eusebius. *The History of the Church.* Trans. G. A. Williamson. London: Penguin Classics, 1965.
Evans, R. "Religious Cult Offers Human Clone Service." *The Herald* (Glasgow), 9 June 1997, 9. Available from www.lexis-nexis.com/universe.
Falk, Z. W. "Jewish Law in the Modern and Post-Modern World." Academic paper presented at Harvard Law School.
Family, The. *Position and Policy Statement.* Zurich: World Services, 1992.
Feuerbach, L. "The Essence of Christianity." In *Gesammelte Werke*. Edited by W. Schuffenhauer. Vol. 5. Berlin: Akademie Verlaq, 1973.
Flusser, David. *Jesus.* Jerusalem: Hebrew University, Magnus Press, 1997.
Foucault, M. *Madness and Civilization: A History of Insanity in the Age of Reason.* Translated by R. Howard. London: Vintage Books, 1965.
Gardner G. B. *Witchcraft Today.* London: Rider, 1954.
Gella, L. "Reaction to a Woman Rabbi." In *On Being a Jewish Feminist: A Reader*. Edited by Susan Heschel. New York: Schocker Books, 1983.
Gomes, A. W. *Unmasking the Cults*. OM Publishing, 1995.
Goring, R. *The Wordsworth Dictionary of Beliefs and Religions.* Ware, U.K.: Wordsworth, 1995.
Grapard, A. G. "Japan's Ignored Cultural Revolution." *History of Religions* 23, no. 3 (1984): 240–65.
Guiley, R. E. *Encyclopaedia of Mystical & Paranormal Experience.* London: Harper Collins, 1991.
Guptara, P. *Indian Spirituality*. Nottingham, UK: Grave Books, 1984.
Gurdjieff, G. *Beelzebub's Tales to His Grandson.* 1950. Reprint, Two Rivers Press, 1993.
———. *Meetings with Remarkable Men.* New York: E. P. Dutton & Co., 1963.
———. *Views from the Real World.* New York: E. P. Dutton & Co., 1973.
Hardy, A. *The Spiritual Nature of Man: A Study of Contemporary Religious Experience.* Oxford: Clarendon Press, 1979.
Harris, D. *Awake! To the Watch Tower.* Reachout Trust, 1988.
Hatcher, W. S., and G. D. Martin. *The Bahá'í Faith: The Emerging Global Religion.* San Francisco, Harper & Row, 1986.
Hawkins, C. S. *Goddess Worship, Witchcraft, and Neo-Paganism.* OM Publishing, 1998.

Herbert. J. *Shinto: At the Fountain-Head of Japan.* London: George Allen & Unwin, 1967.
Herman, A. L. *A Brief Introduction to Hinduism.* Westview Press, 1991.
Hesharm, I. *Concise Dictionary of Religion.* Carol Stream, Ill.: Intervarsity Press, 1994.
Hick, J. *Evil and the God of Love.* 1966. Reprint, London: Fontana, 1968.
———. *The Philosophy of Religion.* Englewood Cliffs, N.J.: Prentice-Hall, 1983.
Hinnells, John R., ed. *A New Handbook of Living Religions.* London: Penguin, 1988.
Hoekema, A. A. *Mormonism.* Carlisle: Paternoster Press, 1973.
Holm, J. and J. Bowker, eds. *Women in Religion.* London: Cassell, 1994.
Houdini, H. *Miracle Mongers and Their Methods: A Complete Expose.* Buffalo, N.Y.: Prometheus Books, 1981.
Hounam, P., and A. Hogg. *Secret Cult.* Oxford: Lion Publishing, 1984.
Hubbard, L. Ron. *Dianetics: The Modern Science of Mental Health.* 1950. Reprint, East Grinstead: New Era, 1981.
Hume, D. *Dialogues Concerning Natural Religion.* Indianapolis, Ind.: Hackett, 1980.
Hurtardo, L. W. *One God, One Lord: Early Christian Devotion and Ancient Jewish Monotheism,* 2d ed. Edinburgh: T. & T. Clarke, 2000.
Jackson, R. R. "How Mystical Is Buddhism?" *Asian Philosophy* 6, no. 2 (July 1996): 147–53.
James, W. *The Varieties of Religious Experience.* London: Gifford Lectures, 1902.
Keene, M. L. *The Psychic Mafia.* Loughton: Prometheus, 1997.
Kelly, J. N. D. *Early Christian Creeds.* 3d ed. Harlow: Longman, 1972.
Kramer, H. and J. Sprenger. *Mallews Maleficarium, 1486,* London: Arrow ed., 1971.
Labalme, P. *Beyond Their Sex.* New York: New York University Press, 1980.
Lane, T. *The Lion Concise Book of Christian Thought.* Oxford: Lion Publishing, 1984.
LaVey, A. *The Satanic Bible.* Star Books, 1977.
Leonard, G. *The Encyclopedia of Heresies and Heretics.* London: Robson Books, 1995.
Lewis, C. S. *Miracles: A Preliminary Study.* New York: Macmillan Publishing Co., 1963.
Lewis, J. R. and J. G. Mellon. *Sex, Slander, and Salvation: Investigating the Family/Children of God.* Stanford, Calif.: Center for Academic Publications, 1994.
Linedecker, Clifford L. *Massacre at Waco.* London: True Crime/Virgin, 1993.
Ludlow, D. H., ed. *Encyclopedia of Mormonism.* 5 vols. New York: Collier Macmillan, 1992.
Lyotard, J. F. *The Postmodern Condition.* Manchester: Manchester University Press, 1986.
MacDonald, V. "Swiss Cult Offers Funds to Baby Clone Doctor." The *Ottawa Citizen,* 11 January 1998, A12.
MacIntyre, A. *After Virtue: A Study in Moral Theory.* 2d ed. Norte Dame: University of Notre Dame Press, 1984.
Markham, I. S., ed. *A World Religions Reader.* Oxford: Blackwell Publishers Ltd., 2000.
———. *Plurality and Christian Ethics.* 2d ed. New York: Stevenbridges Press, 1999.
Martin, W. *The Kingdom of the Cults.* 1965. Reprint, Minneapolis: Bethany House, 1985.
Matthews. C. *Elements of the Goddess.* Longmead, Shaftesbury: Element Books, 1989.
Matthews, C., and J. Matthews. *The Western Way.* Vol. 1. Arkana, 1985.
———. *The Western Way.* Vol. 2. Arkana, 1986.
McClory, Robert. *Power and the Papacy.* Triumph Books, 1997.
McGrath, A. E. *An Introduction to Christianity.* Oxford: Blackwell Publishers, 1997.
———. *Christian Theology: An Introduction.* Oxford: Blackwell Publishers, 1994.
Melton, J. G. *Encyclopedia of American Religions.* 5th ed. Detroit: Gale, 1996.
———. *The Encyclopedic Handbook of Cults in America.* New York: Garland Publishing, 1986.
Milgram, S. *Obedience to Authority: An Experimental View.* London, 1974.
Miller, R. *Bare-Faced Messiah: The True Story of L. Ron Hubbard.* London: Michael Joseph, 1987.

Monod, J. *Chance and Necessity: An Essay on the Natural Philosophy of Modern Biology.* Translated by A. Warmhouse. 1970. Reprint, New York: Alfred A. Knopf, 1971.

Moore, J. *Gurdjieff: The Anatomy of a Myth.* Shaftesbury: Element, 1991.

Murray, M. A. *The Witch-Cult in Western Europe: A Study in Anthropology.* Oxford: Clarendon Press, 1921.

Nahar, B. C., and Ghosh, K. C. *Encyclopaedia of Jainism,* 1986.

Neusner, Jacob, ed. "Native Americans and Their Religions," in *World Religions in America: An Introduction.* Louisville, Ky.: Westminster/John Knox Press, 1994.

Newbiggen, L. *Foolishness to the Greeks.* Grand Rapids: Wm. B. Eerdmans Publishing Co., 1986.

Nichols, R. *The Book of Druidry.* London: Aquarian Press, 1990.

Ouspensky, P. D. *In Search of the Miraculous: Fragments of an Unknown Teaching.* 1949. Reprint, New York: Harcourt, Brace, 1974.

Paley, W. *Natural Theology (1802).* Houston, Tex.: St. Thomas Press, 1972.

Palmer, G. E. H., P. Sherrard, and K. Ware, trans. *The Philokalia, The Complete Text.* Vol. 1. London: Faber and Faber Limited, 1979.

———. *The Philokalia, The Complete Text.* Vol. 2. London: Faber and Faber Limited, 1981.

Palmer, S. "The Raelian Movement International." In *New Religions and the New Europe,* ed. Robert Towler. Denmark: Aarhus University Press, 1995.

———. "Women in the Raelian Movement: New Religious Experiments in Gender and Authority." In *The Gods Have Landed,* ed. James R. Lewis. New York: State University of New York Press, 1995.

Palmer, S. *Moon Sisters, Krishna Mothers, Rajneesh Lovers: Women's Roles in New Religions.* New York: Syracuse University Press, 1994.

Parrinder, E. G. *Witchcraft: European and African.* New York: Barnes & Noble, 1963.

Pascal, B. *Pensées.* Translated by A. J. Krailsheimer. 1670. Reprint, London: Penguin Books, 1966.

Passantino, B., and G. Passantino. *Satanism.* Guide to Religious Cults and Movements Series. Grand Rapids: Zondervan Publishing House, 1995.

Pieper, J. *Leisure: The Basis of Culture.* Liberty Fund., Inc., 1999.

Pine, R. *The Zen Teachings of Bodhidharma.* Trans. Red Pine. North Point Press, 1987.

Polkinghorne, J. *Science and Creation.* London: SPCK, 1988.

Popper, K. *The Logic of Scientific Discovery* (Translation of Logik der Forschiring Hutchinson). London: ????, 1959.

Rael. *The Final Message.* London: The Tagman Press, 1998. See also On Cloning and Clonaid (*www.clonaid.com*).

———. *The Message Given to Me by Extraterrestrials: They Took Me to Their Planet.* Japan: AOM Corp., 1986.

Raeper, W., and L. Edwards. *A Brief Guide to Ideas.* Grand Rapids, Mich.: Zondervan, 1997.

Rajneesh, B. S. *Words Like Fire.* San Francisco: Harper and Row, 1976.

Reader, I. *Religion in Contemporary Japan.* London: Macmillan Press, 1991.

Robinson, J. *Honest to God.* London: SCM Press, 1963.

Rogers, A. K. *A Student's History of Philosophy.* 3d ed. New York: Macmillan, 1960.

Rumi, Jalaluddin. *The Essential Rumi.* Trans. Coleman Barks with John Moyne. New York: HarperCollins Publishers, 1995.

———. *Signs of the Unseen: The Discourses of Jalaluddin Rumi.* Trans. W. M. Thackston Jr. Putney, Vt.: Threshold Books, 1994.

Russell, B. *A History of Western Philosophy.* London: Allen & Unwin, 1960.

Seaman, G. "The Sexual Politics of Karmic Retribution." In *The Anthropology of Taiwanese Society,* eds. E. M. Ahernn and H. Gates. Stanford: Stanford University Press, 1983.

Shallcrass, P., ed. *A Druid Directory.* British Druid Order, 1995.
Sheppherd, J. *The Elements of the Bah'ai Faith.* Shaftesbury, U.K.: Element Books, 1992.
Singh, Trilochan et al., trans. "The Japji." In *Selections from the Sacred Writings of the Sikhs.* London: Allen & Unwin, 1960.
Smart, B. *Postmodernity.* London: Routledge, 1993.
Smart, N. *The World's Religions.* Cambridge: Cambridge University Press, 1989.
———. *Worldviews: Crosscultural Explorations of Human Beliefs.* 2d ed. Englewood Cliffs, N.J.: Prentice-Hall, 1995.
Smith, H. *The World's Religions.* New York: HarperCollins, 1991.
Smith, J. Z., ed. *The Harper Collins Dictionary of Religion.* San Francisco: HarperSan-Francisco, 1995.
Smyers, K. A. "Women and Shinto: The Relations between Purity and Pollution." In *Japanese Religions* 12, no. 4 (1983): 7–18.
Sontag, F. *Sun Myung Moon and the Unification Church.* Nashville: Abingdon, 1977.
Spinoza, B. de. *The Ethics.* 1677. Unabridged Elwes trans. 1883. New York: Dover Publications, 1951.
Staines, J. *The Hutchinson Dictionary of Ideas.* Oxford: Helicon Publishing, 1994.
Stein, G., ed. "Spiritualism." In *The Encyclopedia of the Paranormal.* Buffalo, N.Y.: Prometheus Books, 1996.
Steiner, R. *Theosophy.* 1922. Reprint, London: Rudolf Steiner Press, 1970.
Swinburne, R. *The Existence of God.* Oxford: Clarendon Press, 1979.
Tennant, H. *Back to the Bible.* Birmingham: Christadelphian Press, n.d.
———. *The Christadelphians: What They Believe and Preach.* Birmingham, Eng.: *The Christadelphian,* 1986.
Thompson, M. *Teach Yourself Philosophy of Religion.* London: Hodder & Stoughton, 1997.
Underhill, E. *Mysticism, the Nature and Development of Spiritual Consciousness.* 1911. Reprint, Oxford: One World Publications, 1993.
Valiente, D. *ABC of Witchcraft.* Phoenix: Custer, 1973.
Vardy, P. *The Puzzle of Evil.* 1992. Reprint, M. E. Sharpe, 1997.
———. *The Puzzle of God.* London: Flame, Collins Publishing Group, 1990.
———. *What Is Truth?* Sydney, Australia: University of New South Wales Press, Ltd., 1999.
Vita, P. *Psychology as Religion, the Cult of Self Worship.* Grand Rapids: Wms. B. Eerdmans, 1977.
Voltaire. *Epitre a lauteur du livre des Troisimposteurs* (*Ouvres Completes de Voltaire,* Edited by Louis Molan de). Paris: Garnier, 1977–1885. Tome 10.
Wagner, C. P. *The Third Wave of the Holy Spirit: Encountering the Power of Signs and Wonders Today.* Ann Arbor, Mich.: Servant Publications, Vine Books, 1988.
Walker, W. *A History of the Christian Church.* 4th ed. New York: Charles Scribner's Sons, 1986.
Walsh, M. *The Secret World of Opus Dei.* Grafton, 1989.
Walter, M. *The Kingdom of the Cults.* Minneapolis: Bethany House, 1985.
Ware, Bishop K. *The Orthodox Way.* Mowbray, 1979.
Watchtower Bible and Tract Society, *Jehovah's Witnesses—Proclaimers of God's Kingdom.* Brooklyn, New York: Watchtower Bible and Tract Society of New York, 1993.
Watts, A.W. *The Spirit of Zon: A Way of Life, Work, and Art in the Far East.* 1935. Reprint, New York: Grove Press, 1969.
Weber, M. *The Sociology of Religion.* 1922, Reprint, London: Methuen, 1965.
Weller, P., ed. *Religions in the UK: A Multi-Faith Directory.* Derby: University of Derby, 1997.
White, E. G. *The Great Controversy.* Pyramid, 1971.
Whiting, R. *Religions of Man.* 2d ed. Cheltenham: Stanley Thornes (Publishers) Ltd., 1986.

Williams. A. L., trans. *Justin Martyr, The Dialogue with Trypho.* New York: Macmillan, 1931.

Williams, Peter W., and Charles H. Lippy, eds. "Native American Religions." In *Encyclopedia of the American Religious Experience.* Vol. 1. New York: Scribner's Sons, 1987.

Wink, W. *Naming the Powers: The Language and in the New Testament.* Philadelphia: Fortress Press, 1984.

Wolfe, B. H. *The Devil's Avenger.* New York: Pyramid, 1974.

Yates, F. A. *The Rosicrucian Enlightenment.* London: Routledge and Kegan Paul, 1972.

Index